Seventh Edition

The Handy Book
For
Genealogists

Revised And Enlarged

Edited by George B. Everton, Sr.

Published by

The Everton Publishers, Inc.
P.O. Box 368, Logan, Utah 84321

NOAH WEBSTER, L.L.D.

_____

*"He that wishes to be counted among the benefactors of posterity, must
add by his own toil to the acquisitions of his ancestors."*

Rambler

FOREWORD

Seventh Edition
The Handy Book For Genealogists

The first edition of *The Handy Book for Genealogists* was compiled in 1949 by Walter M. Everton. Because of his dedicated efforts and desire to help persons seeking the records of their ancestors, *The Handy Book* has become known as the "genealogist's Bible." Beginning with 10,000 copies for the first edition, it has been updated and improved through seven editions, with over 400,000 copies now in the hands of genealogists worldwide.

Mr. Everton also originated *The How Book for Genealogists,* now in its seventh edition. Thousands of ancestor-record hunters have benefited from the timely suggestions offered in this book, which shows them how to get a good start and how to continue their research. How to record relevant data of generations past, present, and future is also explained, thus helping to make good records better.

The Genealogical Helper came to life through the foresight of Mr. Everton, who saw the need for a medium of exchange where genealogists could help themselves and others in their quest for progenitor data. The *Helper* was dedicated to "helping more people find more genealogy" and it has continued to live up to that goal for more than 35 years. At its birth in 1947 the *Helper* was published quarterly, and each issue had about twelve pages. It has subsequently progressed to a bimonthly publication with a yearly total of about 1200 pages, and plans are underway to publish it monthly. In every issue since its inception, family-tree enthusiasts have advertised their needs for data on their ancestors, and distant relatives and others have answered their calls for help, extending pedigrees many generations.

What greater tribute can we, the descendants of Walter Everton, give than to provide genealogical helps to the fast-growing world of genealogy? Our progenitor would be amazed and delighted if he could see how the popular research tools he originated are helping thousands of family-tree-climbing hobbyists locate records of their forefathers.

Gay P. Kowallis provided much of the updated and new material included in this printing. Special thanks go to her for her dedicated efforts. Thanks also to Valarie N. Chambers and other dedicated members of the staff of the Everton Publishers. Others, not of our staff, also supplied data and offered suggestions, augmenting greatly the usefulness of this edition. We thank them all most sincerely.

George B. Everton, Sr.

DEDICATION

Walter Marion Everton and his wife, Laura Pearl Knowles,
taken on their wedding day.

Walter M. Everton was born in 1876 in Smithfield, Cache, Utah and his wife, Laura Pearl Knowles, was born 1877 in Logan, Cache, Utah. They were married 1899 in Logan, Utah.

Together, this couple was actively engaged in genealogy for many years. They helped many people with their genealogical research pursuits.

In 1943 Mr. Everton retired from his hardware business and devoted the rest of his life to genealogical endeavors for himself and others.

Walter and Pearl served on a mission in California for The Church of Jesus Christ of Latter-day Saints where they helped members of the Mormon Church with their search for their ancestors. Upon returning home from California in 1945 they began making plans to publish "The Genealogical Helper," a quarterly magazine, and two books, "The How Book for Genealogists" and "The Handy Book for Genealogists."

From this humble beginning in one room of their home, the Everton Publishers has grown to its present status, the largest genealogical supply house in the world.

It is with a great deal of pleasure that we dedicate this book to these two pioneer genealogists.

CONTENTS

CONTENTS (continued)

INTRODUCTION

AND INSTRUCTIONS ON THE USE OF THIS BOOK

The Handy Book For Genealogists is a well known, popular reference for American genealogical researchers. Over 400,000 copies of previous editions are in the hands of family tree climbing enthusiasts throughout the country.

This seventh edition begins first with a section on the United States in general. It is then arranged alphabetically by states of the United States. Foreign countries are presented next, also in alphabetical order.

A detailed county map is included for each state and there is also included a complete map of the United States showing counties and how they relate to counties of bordering states.

Again, with this new seventh edition, updated and corrected data was requested from each county official in each county of the United States. A large percentage of these county officials responded to our plea for the latest data concerning their county's records.

The 1980 census returns were consulted for the population figures shown for each county.

The most recent and comprehensive list of archives, libraries, societies, and publications for each state is included in this edition. Updates of these lists will be published yearly in *The Genealogical Helper*. Complete new research has been conducted concerning the compilation of the valuable printed sources and the printed census records and mortality schedules. Mrs. Gay P. Kowallis is to be commended for the fine job that she has done in compiling this information for the seventh edition.

This new edition presents information regarding the following:

1. County and State Histories
2. Vital records - counties, states and some foreign countries.
3. Addresses of genealogical archives, libraries, historical and genealogical societies, and periodicals
4. Printed census records and printed mortality schedules.
5. Valuable printed sources - atlases, gazetteers, maps, place names, state and foreign country guides to genealogical research.
6. Genealogical sources
7. Time period and availability of county records - vital records; land probate, civil court, divorce and miscellaneous records.
8. Check list of *Historical Records Surveys.*
9. Maps
10. Bibliographies

State and County Histories

Moving backward in time to find the records of our family tree is certain to turn up many interesting events. The search for records to identify our progenitors requires careful attention to places where events took place. Many localities have changed names, or may no longer exist. County and state boundaries have changed. Some states were territories before they became states. These changes have an effect on records.

Questionnaires were sent to all county clerks in the United States requesting information about the records in their custody. Most of them returned the questionnaire with information helpful in searching county records. This information, with other county data, is included in this edition.

Examples of helpful information in *The Handy Book for Genealogists* for state and county histories:

Nebraska

Capital - Lincoln. Territory 1854. State 1867. 37th (Nebraska was made a Territory in 1854 and was the 37th state admitted to the Union)

This is followed with a brief sketch of state history.

    1803   - part of the Louisiana Purchase

    1820   - before 1820 it was part of the Missouri Territory

    1823   - First settlement in state - called Bellevue

    1834   - Placed under supervision of Arkansas, Michigan and Missouri

    1850's - German settlements

    1854   - Nebraska territory

    1867   - admitted as 37th state

Most Nebraskans of today are of German, Czech, Swedish or Russian descent.

For additional information check *The Handy Book for Genealogists* under "Valuable Printed Sources" for Nebraska's printed state histories.

Example: Andreas, A. T. History of the State of Nebraska, 1882. Reprint, 2 vols. Evansville Unigraphic, 1975. (This state history contains county histories, sketches of towns and early settlers).

The state's libraries, historical and genealogical societies should also be checked for helpful information.

Example: The Nebraska State Historical Society has published the following 14 valuable reference leaflets:

---

1. Historical Resources for Genealogists
2. Nebraska Territorial Census Enumerations 1854-1857
3. Index to Naturalizations in Nebraska and some Iowa Counties 1906 and Prior
4. Newspaper Indexes
5. *A Selected List of Nebraska History Reference Materials - 1978*
6. *Local Nebraska History 1966-1976*
7. Selected Bibliography of General Genealogical Reference Material - 1978
8. Genealogical Periodicals and Newsletters in the Nebraska State Historical Society Library
9. Genealogical Researchers
10. Genealogical Societies in Nebraska
11. Special Indexes on Microfilm
12. Nebraska Church Records at the Nebraska State Historical Society
13. Records Relating to Veterans
14. *Historical Organizations in Nebraska*

County Histories and County Records

To help researchers use the information in *The Handy Book for Genealogists* the following examples are given:

Suppose you had a progenitor who was one of the first settlers at Key West, Florida. He took his family there in 1822 but died in 1823, leaving his wife and children. One approach is to learn if there is a will, record of real estate, or any other contemporary record about him in the county records. You find that Key West is the county seat of Monroe County, but none of their records help you. You wonder if something might be found in adjoining counties but your search is fruitless in six or eight neighboring counties. Finally you learn about the *Handy Book For Genealogists.* You turn to Florida and find that Monroe County was formed in 1824 from St. Johns County, one year after the death of your forefather. A further check reveals that St. Augustine is the county seat of St. Johns County and it is almost on the other side of the state, over 375 miles from Key West. You go to the records at St. Augustine and there find just what you want.

Next you search for the records of a forebear who lived and died in Ford County, Illinois. He was 75 years old at his death in 1869 - making his birth date about 1794. There is reason to believe he was born at, or near, his place of death and you would like to know everthing possible about him from the county records. You check Ford County, Illinois in *The Handy Book* and find it was formed in 1859 from Clark County. Going back it is found that Clark was formed in 1819 from Crawford County, which was formed from Edwards in 1816. In turn Edwards County was formed in 1814 from Madison and Gallatin Counties, they being formed in 1812. St. Clair, which was formed from the N.W. Territory in 1790, was the parent county of Madison. Randolph, formed from St. Clair and the N.W. Territory in 1795, was the parent county of Gallatin.

You must search the records of six or seven counties to be sure you have all that can be found about a man who supposedly lived all his life within the confines of one county:

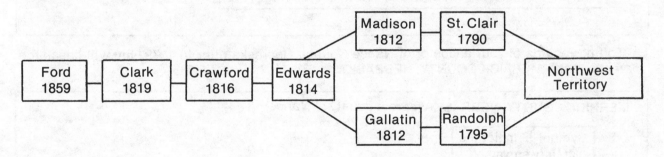

The date each county in the United States was organized, with the name of the former county(ies) is determined by the following:

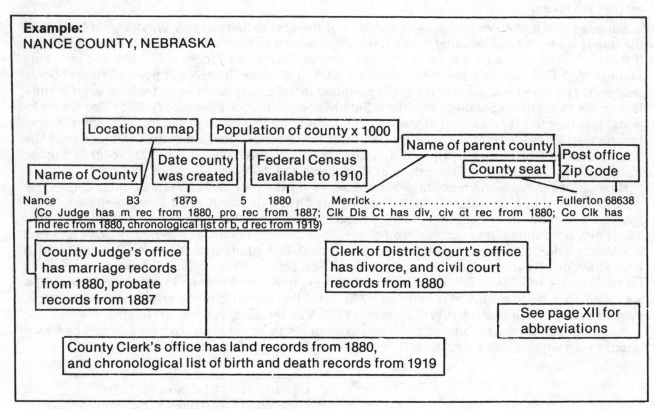

Example:
NANCE COUNTY, NEBRASKA

Location on map

Name of County

Date county was created

Population of county x 1000

Federal Census available to 1910

Name of parent county

County seat

Post office Zip Code

Nance   B3   1879   5   1880   Merrick . . . . Fullerton 68638
(Co Judge has m rec from 1880, pro rec from 1887; Clk Dis Ct has div, civ ct rec from 1880; Co Clk has
Ind rec from 1880, chronological list of b, d rec from 1919)

County Judge's office has marriage records from 1880, probate records from 1887

Clerk of District Court's office has divorce, and civil court records from 1880

See page XII for abbreviations

County Clerk's office has land records from 1880, and chronological list of birth and death records from 1919

To find records of your ancestor of Nance County, Nebraska prior to 1879, you will check the parent county - MERRICK COUNTY, NEBRASKA.

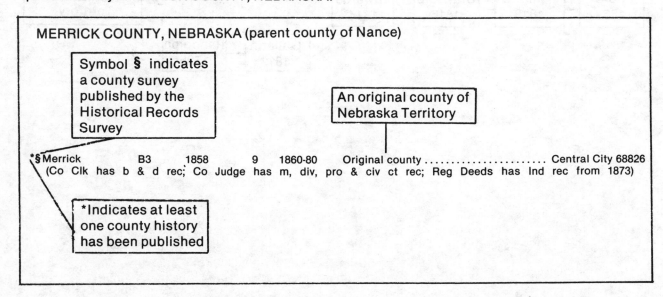

MERRICK COUNTY, NEBRASKA (parent county of Nance)

Symbol § indicates a county survey published by the Historical Records Survey

An original county of Nebraska Territory

*§Merrick   B3   1858   9   1860-80   Original county . . . . Central City 68826
(Co Clk has b & d rec; Co Judge has m, div, pro & civ ct rec; Reg Deeds has Ind rec from 1873)

*Indicates at least one county history has been published

Note: All authorities do not agree on the formation dates of some counties.

Census Records

Since 1790 Federal Census records have been made every ten years. Until 1850 they listed heads of households by full name, with other members in the homes grouped within certain age groups - male and female. All census schedules are useful for genealogical research. Because very few census records are arranged alphabetically by families, census searches can be very time consuming. In the last few years many census records have been printed and indexed. They should be considered as indexes to the original records and not substitutes for them. The indexes are valuable and will save many hours of research time.

Information regarding printed census records and indexes has been compiled from the following sources:

1. Brewer, Mary Marie. *Index to Census Schedules in Printed form 1970-71 Supplement.* Huntsville, Arkansas: Century Enterprises, 1971. (Includes addresses of vendors).

2. Konrad, J. *Directory of Census Information Sources.* Munroe Falls, Ohio: Summit Publications, 1974, 1976, and 1980 editions. (Includes addresses of vendors).

3. Dictionary Card Catalog (DCC) and the International Genealogical Library Catalogue (IGLC) The Genealogical Society of The Church of Jesus Christ of Latter-day Saints, Salt Lake City, Utah.

4. "New on the Book Shelf" section of *The Genealogical Helper,* Logan, Utah: Everton Publishers. (All books reviewed in *The Genealogical Helper* are placed in the Everton Library). The following index will be helpful for locating the book review and call number in the Everton Library:

   Kowallis, Gay P. *New on the Bookshelf Index, 1971-1981.* Logan, Utah: Everton Publishers, 1982.

Printed census schedules appearing as regular features in various publications have not been included in this compilation. The following publications contain indexes to this information:

Mayhew, Catherine M. and Laird C. Towle. *Genealogical Periodical Annual Index: Key to the Genealogical Literature.* Bowie, Maryland: Heritage Books.

NOTE: The "County Histories" column "U.S. Cen Reports Available" includes census records to and including 1880. The 1900 and 1910 census records are also available.

Example:

NEBRASKA COUNTY HISTORIES
(Population figures to nearest thousand - 1980 U.S. Census)

Name	Map Index	Date Created	Pop. By M 1980	U.S. Cen Reports Available	Parent County or Territory From Which Organized	County Seat
				1870-80	NOTE: The 1900 and 1910 census records for all counties of the United States are also available from the National Archives.	
					The 1910 is available only through the Fort Worth Regional office of the National Archives.	

EXAMPLE OF PRINTED CENSUS RECORDS IN THE HANDY BOOK FOR GENEALOGISTS

Printed Census Records and Mortality Schedules

Nebraska Census Records

Indexes (Territory): 1854, 1855, 1856, 1860

State Index: 1870

Federal Census

Printed Census Records (Counties):

Dodge - 1870; 1855, 1856
Douglas - 1870, 1855, 1856

County Census records

State Vital Statistics

The information included in this edition concerning vital records for each state was obtained directly from each state's Bureau of Vital Statistics. Letters were sent to each state asking for an update of the information that was previously printed in the *Handy Book* about that state's vital statistics. Responses were received from all but five of the fifty states of the Union. This overwhelming response is greatly appreciated.

Check List of Historical Records Survey

Surveys of public record archives were conducted in most state during 1936 to 1943 by the Works Progress Administration (WPA). Many of these records are vital to genealogical research. Few WPA publications give full transcripts - they name the records available in the respective archives. Often they give the condition of the records, where stored when the survey was made, dates of commencement and conclusion of the records. The actual records must be examined to gain the information.

A check list of these publications was published by the WPA according to the type of publication. The book was originally published as W.P.A. Technical Series, Research and Records Bibliography No. 7. It was reprinted as follows:

> Child, Sargent B. and Dorothy P. Holmes. *Check List of Historical Records Survey Publications, Bibliography of Research Projects Reports.* Baltimore: Genealogical Publishing Company, 1969. (G.S. film 874,113)

The Sixth Edition of the *Handy Book for Genealogists* contains information regarding the Historical Records Survey. This information will not be given in the Seventh Edition. The only reference to the surveys will be an indication of county archive inventories (§) by county names.

Abbreviations Used In This Edition

The following abbreviations have been used to save space — making it possible for more information to be included.

appr	appraisment	Clk Sup Ct	Clerk of Superior Court
Asr	Assessor	Comm	Commissioners
Aud	Auditor	Com Pleas Ct	Common Pleas Court
b	birth	com	complete
bk	book	Co	County
bur	burial	Co Asr	County Assessor
cem	cemetery	Co Aud	County Auditor
cen	census	Co Clk	County Clerk
Chan	Chancery	Co Health	County Health Department
CH	Courthouse	Co Judge	County Judge
City Clk	City Clerk	Co Ord	County Ordinary
Civ	Civil	Co Rcdr	County Recorder
Clk	Clerk	Co Rgstr	County Registrar
Clk Chan Ct	Clerk of Chancery Court	Ct	Court
Clk Cir Ct	Clerk of Circuit Court	crim	criminal
Clk Cts	Clerk of Courts	d	death
Clk Dis Ct	Clerk of District Court	Dis Ct	District Court
Clk Mag Ct	Clerk of Magistrates Court	div	divorce
Clk of Peace	Clerk of the Peace		

G.S. .... Genealogical Society of The Church of Jesus Christ of Latter-day Saints, Genealogical Department Library, Salt Lake City, Utah.

Hist Soc .... Historical Society	Pro Judge .... Probate Judge
inc .... incomplete	Pub .... Public
J P .... Justice of Peace	Rcdr .... Recorder
lib .... library	Rcdr Deeds .... Recorder of Deeds
lnd .... land	rec .... record
m .... marriage	Reg in Chan .... Register in Chancery
Mag .... Magistrate	Reg of Wills .... Register of Wills
Mil Dis Rec ...... Military Discharge Record	Rgstr .... Registrar
mtg .... mortgage	Supt .... Superintendent
Ord .... Ordinary	Sup .... Superior
Ord Ct .... Ordinary Court	Surr .... Surrogate
Orph Ct .... Orphan's Court	Terr .... Territory
Par Clk .... Parish Clerk	Twn Clk .... Town Clerk
Pro .... Probate	Treas .... Treasurer
	Unorg .... Unorganized
	Vit Stat .... Vital Statistics
	War Ser .... War Service

An asterisk (*) preceding a county name indicates that at least one county history has been published for that county.

An (§) preceding a county name indicates that a Historical Records Survey, a county archive inventory has been made for that county. (See page XII for complete information).

GENERAL UNITED STATES

Valuable Printed Sources

Atlases, Gazetteers, Maps

Adams, James Truslow, ed. *Atlas of American History.* New York: Charles Scribner's Sons. 1943.

Fanning's Illustrated Gazetteer of the United States. New York: Ensign, Bridgman, and Fanning, 1855.

Kirkham, E. Kay. *A Genealogical and Historical Atlas of the United States of America.* Logan, Utah: Everton Publishers, 1976.

Rand-McNally Commercial Atlas and Marketing Guide. New York: Rand-McNally and Co. (annual).

Seltzer, Leon E., ed. *The Columbia-Lippincott Gazetteer of the World.* Morningside Heights, New York: Columbia University Press, 1952.

Place Names

Bullinger's Postal and Shippers Guide for the United States and Canada. Westwood, New Jersey: Bullinger's Guides, 1897- Annual.

United States Directory of Post Offices. Washington D.C. Post Office Department. Annual.

Guides to Genealogical Research

Brown, Mary. *Handy Index To The Holdings of The Genealogical Society Of Utah,* Volume 1, Eastern States. Logan, Utah: The Everton Publishers, 1980.

Greenwood, Val D. *The Researcher's Guide to American Genealogy.* Baltimore: Genealogical Publishing Company, 1973.

Kirkham, E. Kay. *Handy Index To Record-Searching In The Larger Cities of The United Sates.* Logan, Utah: The Everton Publishers, 1974.

Kirkham, E. Kay. *Index To Some of The Family Records of The Southern States.* Logan, Utah: The Everton Publishers, 1979.

There are many helpful guides to genealogical research in the United States. New guides are listed in the "New on the Bookshelf Section" of *The Genealogical Helper.* For text books published from 1971-1981 check the *New on the Book Shelf Index.* Logan, Utah: Everton Publishers, 1982.

Vallentine, John. *Locality Finding Aids For United States Surnames.* Logan, Utah: The Everton Publishers, 1977.

World Conference on Records: Preserving Our Heritage. Lecture Papers. Salt Lake City: The Genealogical Society of the Church of Jesus Christ of Latter-day Saints, 1980.

Directories - Archives, Genealogical and Historical Societies, Libraries, Associations.

American Library Directory. Revised annually. New York: R. R. Bowker Co.

Cunningham, Ronald and Evan Evans. *A Handy Guide to The Genealogical Library and Church Historical Department.* Revised edition. Logan, Utah: The Everton Publishers, 1980.

Directory Historical Societies and Agencies in the United States and Canada. Latest edition. Nashville, Tennessee: American Association for State and Local History.

Encyclopedia of Associations. 3 Vols. Detroit: Gale Research Co., 1980.

Meyer, Mary K. *Directory of Genealogical Societies in the U.S.A. and Canada.* Pasadena, Maryland: author, 1976.

National Historical Publications and Records Commission. *Directory of Archives and Manuscript Repositories in the United States.* Washington D.C.: National Archives and Records Service. 1978.

Directories · Newspapers and Periodicals

80 Ayer Directory of Publications. Bala Cynwyd, Pennsylvania: Ayer Press, Published annually since 1869. Title varies.

Brigham, Clarence Saunders. *History and Bibliography of American Newspapers, 1690-1820.* 2 Vols. Hamden, Connecticut: Shoe String Press, 1962.

Gregory, Winifred, ed. *American Newspapers, 1821-1936; A Union List of Files Available in the United States and Canada.* New York: H. W. Wilson Co., 1937.

Library of Congress. *Newspapers in Microform United States 1948-1972.* Washington: Catalog Publication Division Processing Department, 1973. Supplement, 1976.

Milner, Anita: *Newspaper Indexes: A Location and Subject Guide for Researchers.* 2 Vols.

Metuchen, New Jersey: Scarecrow Press, 1977, 1979.

Parch, Grace D. ed. *Directory of Newspaper Libraries in the U. S. and Canada.* New York: Project of the Newspaper Division Special Libraries Association, 1976.

Indexes and Bibliographies · Published Family Histories and Local Histories

Filby, P. William. *American and British Genealogy and Heraldry,* 2nd edition. Chicago: American Library Association, 1976.

Genealogical Index of the Newberry Library, Chicago, The. 4 Vols. Boston: G.K. Hall, 1960.

Greenlaw Index of the New England Historic Genealogical Society, The. 2 Vols. Boston: G.K. Hall, 1979.

Herbert, Miranda C. and Barbara McNeil. *Biography and Genealogy Master Index.* 8 Vols. Detroit: Gale Research Company, 1980.

Jacobus, Donald Lines. *Index to Genealogical Periodicals.* 3 Vols. 1932. Reprint in 1 vol. Baltimore: Genealogical Publishing Company, 1978.

Kaminkow, Marion J. *Genealogies in the Library of Congress: A Bibliography.* 3 Vols. Baltimore: Magna Carta Book Company, 1972.

_____. *A Complement to Genealogies in the Library of Congress.* 1981.

_____. *United States Local Histories in the Library of Congress, A Bibliography,* 4 Vols. Baltimore, Magna Carta Book Company, 1975.

The New York Public Library Research Libraries. *Dictionary Catalog of the Manuscript Division.* Boston: G. K. Hall and Co. 1967; and *Dictionary Catalog of the Local History and Genealogy Division,* 18 Vols., 1974.

Rider, Fremont. *The American Genealogical-Biographical Index.* 1st series, 48 vols. 1942-1951. 2nd series, 1952-1981. Middletown, Connecticut: Godfrey Memorial Library. *(A Cumulative Key Title Guide,* 1st series only, with Genealogical Society Library Call Numbers, Salt Lake City, Genealogical Society, 1953)

Schreiner-Yantis, Netti. *Genealogical and Local History Books in Print.* Springfield, Virginia: Genealogical Books in Print, 1981.

Sperry, Kip, ed. *Index to Genealogical Periodical Literature, 1960-1977.* Detroit: Gale Research Company, 1979.

Towle, Laird C. ed. and Catherine M. Mayhew, comp. *Genealogical Periodical Annual Index.* Bowie, Maryland: Heritage Books, annually 1962-.

AIDS TO ORIGINAL RECORDS

Census

Dubester, Henry J. *State Censuses, An Annotated Bibliography of Censuses of Population Taken After the Year 1790 by the States and Territories of the United States.* Washington D.C.: Government Printing Office, 1948. Reprint 1975. Knightstown, Indiana: Bookmark.

Parker, J. Carlyle. *City, County, Town and Township Index to the 1850 Federal Census Schedules.* Detroit: Gale Research Company, 1979.

Cemetery and Mortician Records

American Blue Book of Funeral Directors. New York: The American Funeral Director.

Stemmons, Jack and Diane. *Cemetery Record Compendium.* Logan, Utah: The Everton Publishers, 1979.

Church Records

Kirkham, E. Kay. *A Survey of American Church Records,* 4th Edition. Logan, Utah: Everton Publishers, 1978.

Mead, Frank S. *Handbook of Denominations,* 4th ed. New York: Arlington Press, 1965.

Military Records

D.A.R. Patriot Index. 2 Vols. Washington: National Society of Daughters of the American Revolution, 1966, 1979.

Genealogical Society. *Published U.S. Military Sources in the Genealogical Library.* Salt Lake City: U.S. and Canadian Reference Staff, 1980.

_____. *Register of Film Numbers for Revolutionar War Pension and Bounty-Land-Warrant Application Files.* Salt Lake City: Genealogical Society, 1975.

Giller, Sadye, William H. Dumont and Louise M. Dumont (revised by). *Index of Revolutionary War Pension Applications.* Washington D.C. National Genealogical Society, 1966.

Groene, Bertram H. *Tracing Your Civil War Ancestor.* Winston-Salem, North Carolina: John F. Blair, 1973.

Neagles, James C. and Lila L. *Locating Your Revolutionary War Ancestors: A Guide to the Military Records.* Logan, Utah: The Everton Publishers, 1982.

National Archives Records

Babbel, June Andrew, comp. *Lest We Forget: A Guide to Genealogical Research in the Nation's Capital,* 4th revised edition. Annandale, Virginia: Annandale and Oakton Stakes of The Church of Jesus Christ of Latter-day Saints, 1976.

Colket, Meredith B. Jr and Frank E. Bridgers. *Guide to Genealogical Records in the National Archives.* Washington: The National Archives, 1964.

Passenger Lists, Naturalization Records

Filby, P. William, ed. and Mary K. Meyer. *Passenger and Immigration List Index.* 3 Vols. Detroit: Gale Research Company, 1981.

Miller, Olga K. *Migration, Emigration, Immigration.* 2 Vols. Logan: The Everton Publishers, 1975, 1981.

Neagles, James C. and Lila Lee Neagles. *Locating Your Immigrant Ancestor.* Logan: The Everton
    Publishers, 1975.

Vital Records

Deputy, Marilyn. *Vital Records in the United States.* Salt Lake City: Genealogical Society of Utah,
    1981.

Stemmons, John D. and E. Diane Stemmons. *The Vital Record Compendium.* Logan: The Everton
    Publishers, 1979.

Indian Records

Kirkham, E. Kay. *Our Native Americans, Their Records of Genealogical Value.* Logan, Utah: The
    Everton Publishers, 1980.

ALABAMA

CAPITAL, MONTGOMERY - TERRITORY 1817 - STATE 1819 - (22nd)

The first permanent white settlers to establish homes in Alabama arrived there in 1702, although some historians say 1699. About 174 years earlier the Spanish explorers, De Narvaes and Cabeza de Vaca, passed through this area on their exploration trips. The first white settlers to move into the territory were Spanish and French. Mobile was established in 1702 as the first community. England won control of the region in 1763.

To evade participation in the Revolutionary War many British sympathizers living in Georgia moved westward into the Alabama section in 1775. They were followed in 1783 by other planters from Georgia, Virginia and the Carolinas. A group of Scotch-Irish who had tried farming in Tennessee in 1809 settled in the northern part of Alabama, in the rich Tennessee Valley district. In the early 1800's former Carolinians and Virginians came into the central part of the territory. Other groups from the same section came to the western part of Alabama along the Tombigbee and the Black Warrior Rivers. But it was not until the end of the War of 1812 that Alabama saw a real influx of settlers. The conclusion of that war was the beginning of a gigantic southward and westward movement which resulted in statehood for four territories between 1816 and 1819. Alabama was the last of the four to gain statehood.

In 1798 the territory now comprising Alabama was made part of the Territory of Mississippi. On 3 March 1817, St. Stephens became the capital of the newly created territory. In November 1818 Cahaba, a community existing only in the blueprint stage, without buildings or a population, was made the capital.

The influx of people into the southwestern section was so great that two years and four months after Alabama had become a territory a political convention prepared a state constitution. This gathering was held on 5 July 1819 in the temporary state capital, Huntsville, the seat of Madison County, located between the Tennessee River and the southern boundary of the State of Tennessee. Representatives were present from the then existing twenty-two counties of Alabama namely Autauga, Baldwin, Blount, Cabela which in 1820 became Bibb, Clarke, Conecuh, Cotaco which in 1821 became Morgan, Dallas, Franklin, Lauderdale, Lawrence, Limestone, Madison, Marengo, Marion, Montgomery, Monroe, St. Clair, Shelby, Tuscaloosa, and Washington.

The Bureau of Vital Statistics, Department of Public Health, Montgomery, Alabama 36130 has birth and death records since 1908 and incomplete records prior to 1908. Similar records prior to 1908 are kept in the office of some county clerks. Marriage records are in counties where the Probate Courts also have old records of deeds and wills. Some Alabama counties have courthouses in cities or towns in addition to the county seats. The records in those places must be searched as well as those at the county seat. Undoubtedly the Alabama Department of Archives and History, Montgomery, Alabama, may be able to furnish some information or give directions to other sources.

Genealogical Archives, Libraries, Societies, and Publications

Alabama Archives and History Dept., World War Memorial Building, Montgomery, AL 36104.

Alabama Genealogical Society, P.O. Box 35, Epes, AL 35460.

Auburn University Library, Auburn, AL 36830.

Birmingham Genealogical Society, Inc., P.O. Box 2432, Birmingham, AL 35201.

Birmingham Public Library, 2020 7th Ave. N., Birmingham, AL 35203.

Coosa County Historical Society, Route 2, Box 128, Rockford, AL 35136.

Cullman County Public Library, 200 Clarke St., NE, Cullman, AL 35055.

Huntsville Public Library, Box 443, 108 Fountain, Huntsville, AL 35804.

Liles Memorial Library, Box 308, 108 E. 10th St., Anniston, AL 36201.

Mobile Public Library, 701 Government Street, Mobile, AL 36602.

Mobile Genealogical Society, Inc., P.O. Box 6224, Mobile, AL 36606.

Natchez Trace Genealogical Society, P.O. Box 1645, Florence, AL 35631.

Tennessee Valley Genealogical Society, P.O. Box 1512, Huntsville, AL 35807.

University of Alabama Library, University, AL 35486.

Alabama Genealogical Quarterly, P.O. Box 577, Mobile, AL 36601.

Deep South Genealogical Quarterly, Mobile Genealogical Society, Inc., P.O. Box 6224, Mobile, AL 36606.

Natchez Trace Newsletter, Natchez Trace Genealogical Society, P.O. Box 1645, Florence, AL 35631.

Pea River Trails, Pea River Historical and Genealogical Society, P.O. Box 628, Enterprise, AL 36331.

Pioneer Trails, Birmingham Genealogical Society, P.O. Box 2432, Birmingham, AL 35201.

Trails, North Alabama Genealogical Society, 1206 Plaza St., SE, Decatur, AL 35603.

Valley Leaves, Tennessee Valley Genealogical Society, Inc., P.O. Box 1512, Huntsville, AL 35807.

Printed Census Records and Mortality Schedules

State Indexes - 1820, 1830, 1840 and 1850; 1797.

Other printed census records follow:

Autauga - 1830
Baldwin - 1810, 1820, 1830, 1860; 1816
Barbour - 1840, 1850, 1860; 1833
Bibb - 1830, 1850.
Blount - 1830, 1840, 1850, 1860
Butler - 1830, 1860
Choctaw - 1850
Clarke - 1830, 1850; 1816
Conecuh - 1820, 1830, 1870
Covington - 1830, 1850
Cullman - 1880
Dale - 1830, 1850
Dallas - 1820, 1830
Fayette - 1830
Franklin - 1820, 1830
Greene - 1830
Henry - 1830, 1840, 1850
Jackson - 1830, 1860
Jefferson - 1830, 1840, 1850, 1870
Lauderdale - 1830, 1880
Lawrence - 1820, 1830, 1840, 1850
Limestone - 1830, 1840
Lowndes - 1830, 1850

Madison - 1830, 1850; 1809, 1816
Marengo - 1830
Marion - 1830
Marshall - 1850
Mobile - 1830, 1840, 1850, 1860, 1870; 1706, 1816
Monroe - 1830; 1816
Montgomery - 1830
Morgan - 1830
Perry - 1830, 1850, 1890
Pickens - 1830
Pike - 1830·
Randolph - 1840, 1850, 1860
Russell - 1840
St. Clair - 1820, 1830, 1850
Shelby - 1820, 1830, 1850
Sumter - 1850; 1866
Talladega - 1840, 1850
Tallapoosa - 1840
Tuscaloosa - 1830
Walker - 1830, 1850
Washington - 1810, 1830, 1850, 1860; 1808, 1816
Wilcox - 1820, 1830, 1860
Winston - 1850

Mobile Spanish Census - 1786, 1787, 1789, 1805

Valuable Printed Sources

Atlases, Maps, Gazetteers

Birmingham Public Library. *A List of Nineteenth Century Maps of the State of Alabama,* Oxmoor University Press, 1973.

Birmingham Public Library. *A List of 16th, 17th, and 18th Century Material in the Rucker Agee Map Collection.* Birmingham, 1978.

The Society of Pioneers of Montgomery. *Yesterday's Faces of Alabama: A Collection of Maps, 1822-1909.* Montgomery: Brown Printing Company, 1978.

Place Names

Harris, W. Stuart, *Dead Towns of Alabama.* University, Alabama: University of Alabama Press, 1977.

Read, William A. *Indian Place-Names in Alabama*. Baton Rouge: LSU Press, 1937.

Guides To Genealogical Research

Stryker-Rodda, Kenn, ed. *Genealogical Research, Vol. 2*, "Alabama" by Jean Stephenson (Chapter X, pages 162 - 182).

Webb, Mary Frances. "Alabama, Its Devlopment and Records" (talk given before the National Genealogical Society, 17 February 1968, printed in *National Genealogical Society Quarterly*, Volume 57, March 1969).

Wright, Norman Edgar. *North American Genealogical Sources - Southern States* Provo, Utah: B.Y.U. Press, 1968.

State Histories

Brewer Willis. *Alabama, Her History, Resources, War Record, and Public Men From 1540 to 1872*. Montgomery: Barrett and Brown, 1872. Reprint 1975.

McMillan, Malcolm C. *The Land Called Alabama*. Austin: Steck-Vaughn Company, 1968.

Owen, Thomas M. *History of Alabama and Dictionary of Alabama Biography*. Chicago: S. J. Clarke Publishing Company, 1921. Reprinted by Reprint Company, Publishers, Spartanburg, South Carolina, 1978.

Saunders, James Edmonds. *Early Settlers of Alabama*, printed 1899. Reprinted by Genealogical Publishing Company, Baltimore, Maryland 1969 and 1977.

Summersell, Charles Grayson. *Alabama History for Schools*. Fifth Edition. Montgomery: Viewpoint Publications, Inc., 1975.

Genealogical Sources

Alabama Department of Archives and History, 624 Washington Avenue, Montgomery, Alabama, 36104.

Alabama Society, DAR *Index to Alabama Wills, 1808-1870*. Baltimore, Maryland: Genealogical Publishing Company, reprinted 1977.

DAR Genealogical Collection*

Gandrud, Pauline Jones. *Marriage, Death and Legal Notices From Early Alabama Newspapers, 1818-1880*. Easley, South Carolina: Southern Historical Press, 1981.

Jones and Gandrud. *Alabama Records*, 235 volumes*

Julich, Louise, *Roster of Revolutionary Soldiers and Patriots in Alabama*. Montgomery: Parchment Press, 1979.

Many cemetery and Bible records for various counties in Alabama have been published. (Check *New on the Book Shelf Index*, Card Catalogue of Genealogical Society and Periodical Indexes)

Owen, Thomas M. *Revolutionary Soldiers in Alabama*. Baltimore, Maryland: Genealogical Publishing Company, reprinted 1967.

---

*Microfilm - Genealogical Society of The Church of Jesus Christ of Latter-day Saints, Salt Lake City, Utah.

ALABAMA COUNTY HISTORIES
(Population figures to nearest thousand 1980 U.S. Census)

Name	Map Index	Date Created	Pop. By M 1980	U.S. Cen Reports Available	Parent County or Territory From Which Organized	County Seat
* Autauga	D3	1818	32	1830-80	Montgomery .... Prattville 36067	
(Judge of Pro has m, pro, adpt, and land deed rec)						
Baine (abolished 1867, changed to Etowah 1868)						

Name	Map Index	Date Created	Pop. By M 1980	U.S. Cen Reports Available	Parent County or Territory From Which Organized	County Seat
Baker (see Chilton)						
* Baldwin	F1	1809	78	1820-80	Washington, part of Fla	Bay Minette 36507
* Barbour	D4	1832	25	1840-80	Creek Cession 1832	Clayton 36016

(Judge of Probate has m, Ind rec from 1832 to present; plat bk 1, early Ind owners; Co Comm has div rec from 1860; civil court rec from 1912).

Name	Map Index	Date Created	Pop. By M 1980	U.S. Cen Reports Available	Parent County or Territory From Which Organized	County Seat
Benton (See Calhoun)						
* Bibb	C2	1818	16	1830-80	Monroe, Montgomery	Centerville 35042

(changed from Cahawba 1820) (Co Clk has m pro, Ind rec 1818 to present; Reg in Chan has div rec; Clk Cir Ct has civ ct rec)

Name	Map Index	Date Created	Pop. By M 1980	U.S. Cen Reports Available	Parent County or Territory From Which Organized	County Seat
* Blount	B3	1818	36	1830-80	Cherokee Cession, Montgomery	Oneonta 35121

(Clk Cir Ct has div, pro & civ ct rec; Co Clk has m, civ ct, Ind rec from 1818 to present; pro rec 1837 to present Judge of Pro)

Name	Map Index	Date Created	Pop. By M 1980	U.S. Cen Reports Available	Parent County or Territory From Which Organized	County Seat
* Bullock	D4	1866	11	1870-80	Barbour, Macon, Montgomery, Pike	Union Springs 36089

(Cir Ct. Clk has div & civ ct rec)

Name	Map Index	Date Created	Pop. By M 1980	U.S. Cen Reports Available	Parent County or Territory From Which Organized	County Seat
* Butler	E3	1819	21	1830-80	Conecuh, Monroe	Greenville 36037

(Courthouse burned April 1853 - Pro Judge has b and d rec 1894 to 1919; m pro Ind rec 1853 to present)

Name	Map Index	Date Created	Pop. By M 1980	U.S. Cen Reports Available	Parent County or Territory From Which Organized	County Seat
Cahawba (see Bibb)						
* Calhoun	B3	1832	120	1860-80	Creek Cession of 1832	Anniston 36201

(Name changed from Benton Jan 29, 1858) (Pro Judge has m rec 1834 to 1979; Ind rec 1865 to 1979; Reg in Chan has div; Clk Cir Ct has civ ct rec)

Name	Map Index	Date Created	Pop. By M 1980	U.S. Cen Reports Available	Parent County or Territory From Which Organized	County Seat
* Chambers	C4	1832	39	1840-80	Creek Cession of 1832	La Fayette 36862
* Cherokee	B4	1836	19	1840-80	Cherokee Cession 1835	Centre 35960

(Rec burned in 1882)

Name	Map Index	Date Created	Pop. By M 1980	U.S. Cen Reports Available	Parent County or Territory From Which Organized	County Seat
* Chilton	C2	1868	30	1880	Autauga, Bibb, Perry, Shelby	Clanton 35045

(Cir Clk has pro, div rec; civ ct rec from 1868 to present; State Bur of Vit Stat has b, d, bur rec; Pro Judge has m, Ind rec)

Name	Map Index	Date Created	Pop. By M 1980	U.S. Cen Reports Available	Parent County or Territory From Which Organized	County Seat
Choctaw	D1	1847	17	1850-80	Sumter, Washington	Butler 36904

(Co Clk has m, pro & Ind rec from 1873; Clk Cir Ct has div rec)

Name	Map Index	Date Created	Pop. By M 1980	U.S. Cen Reports Available	Parent County or Territory From Which Organized	County Seat
* Clarke	E1	1812	28	1830-80	Washington	Grove Hill 36451

(Pro Judge has m & pro rec from 1814, Ind from 1820; Clk Cir Ct has div & civ ct rec, Health Clinic has b and d rec)

Name	Map Index	Date Created	Pop. By M 1980	U.S. Cen Reports Available	Parent County or Territory From Which Organized	County Seat
§ Clay	C3	1866	14	1870-80	Randolph, Talladega	Ashland 36251
Cleburne	B4	1866	13	1870-80	Calhoun, Randolph, Talladega	Heflin 36264
* Coffee	E3	1841	38	1850-80	Dale	Elba 36323 & Enterprise 36330

(Pro Judge has m rec 1877 to present; Ind rec early 1800's to present; Bur of Vit Stat has b, d rec; Cir Clk, Elba, has div, civ ct rec)

Name	Map Index	Date Created	Pop. By M 1980	U.S. Cen Reports Available	Parent County or Territory From Which Organized	County Seat
*§ Colbert	A1	1867	54	1870-80	Franklin	Tuscumbia 35674

(Abolished same year created, re-established 1869; Pro Judge has m, pro, Ind rec; Clk has div Rec; Co Health Dept has b, d bur rec)

Name	Map Index	Date Created	Pop. By M 1980	U.S. Cen Reports Available	Parent County or Territory From Which Organized	County Seat
*° Conecuh	E2	1818	16	1820-80	Monroe	Evergreen 36401

(Pro Judge has m, pro Judge has m, pro & Ind rec)

Name	Map Index	Date Created	Pop. By M 1980	U.S. Cen Reports Available	Parent County or Territory From Which Organized	County Seat
* Coosa	C3	1832	11	1840-80	Creek Cession of 1832	Rockford 35136

(Pro Judge has b 1934-1941; m pro, Ind rec 1832 to present; Clk Cir Ct has civ ct rec from 1900)

Name	Map Index	Date Created	Pop. By M 1980	U.S. Cen Reports Available	Parent County or Territory From Which Organized	County Seat
Cotaco (see Morgan)						
Covington	E3	1821	36	1830-80	Henry	Andalusia 36420

(Pro Judge has pro & Ind rec; Reg in Chan has div; Clk Cir Ct has civ ct rec) (Rec burned 1895)

Name	Map Index	Date Created	Pop. By M 1980	U.S. Cen Reports Available	Parent County or Territory From Which Organized	County Seat
* Crenshaw	E3	1866	14	1870-80	Butler, Coffee, Covington, Lowndes, Pike	Luverne 36049

(Pro Judge has m, pro & Ind rec from 1866; Clk Cir Ct has div & civ ct rec)

Name	Map Index	Date Created	Pop. By M 1980	U.S. Cen Reports Available	Parent County or Territory From Which Organized	County Seat
§ Cullman	B2	1877	62	1880	Blount, Morgan, Winston	Cullman 35055

(Pro Judge has m, div, pro, civ ct, Ind rec 1877 to present; final rec, wills 1877 to present; old newspapers, scattered volumes from 1880, not indexed)

Name	Map Index	Date Created	Pop. By M 1980	U.S. Cen Reports Available	Parent County or Territory From Which Organized	County Seat
* Dale	E4	1824	48	1830-80	Covington, Henry	Ozark 36360

(Pro Judge has m rec from 1885, pro rec from 1885; Co Clk has civ ct & div rec from 1885; Co Health dept has bur rec)

Name	Map Index	Date Created	Pop. By M 1980	U.S. Cen Reports Available	Parent County or Territory From Which Organized	County Seat
* Dallas	D2	1818	53	1820-80	Montgomery	Selma 36701

(Pro Judge has m from 1818, div from 1917, pro from 1821 & Ind rec from 1820) (State of Ala has b, d and bur rec)

Name	Map Index	Date Created	Pop. By M 1980	U.S. Cen Reports Available	Parent County or Territory From Which Organized	County Seat
DeKalb	A3	1836	53	1840-80	Cherokee Cession of 1835	Fort Payne 35967

(Pro Judge has m, div, pro, Ind rec; Health Dept has b, d, bur rec; Cir Clk has civ ct rec)

Name	Map Index	Date Created	Pop. By M 1980	U.S. Cen Reports Available	Parent County or Territory From Which Organized	County Seat
* Elmore	C3	1866	44	1870-80	Autauga, Coosa, Montgomery, Tallapoosa	Wetumpka 36092
Escambia	E2	1868	38	1870-80	Baldwin, Conecuh	Brewton 36426

Name	Map Index	Date Created	Pop. By M 1970	U.S. Cen Reports Available	Parent County or Territory From Which Organized	County Seat
* Etowah	B3	1868	103	1870-80	Blount, Calhoun, Cherokee, DeKalb, Marshall, St. Clair	Gadsden 35902
(Pro Judge has m, div, pro & Ind rec from 1867)						
* Fayette	B1	1824	19	1830-80	Marion, Pickens, Tuscaloosa	Fayette 35555
* Franklin	A1	1818	28	1830-80	Cherokee & Chickasaw Cession of 1816	Russellville 35653

(Rec burned 1890) (Pro Clk has cem and Bible rec; Co Clk has civ & crim ct rec from 1923; Pro Judge has m & pro rec from 1896)

Name	Map Index	Date Created	Pop. By M 1970	U.S. Cen Reports Available	Parent County or Territory From Which Organized	County Seat
Geneva	E3	1868	24	1870-80	Dale, Henry, Coffee	Geneva 36340
*§ Greene	C1	1819	11	1830-80	Marengo, Tuscaloosa	Eutaw 35462
§ Hale	C2	1867	15	1870-80	Greene, Marengo, Perry, Tuscaloosa	Greensboro 36744

(Pro Judge has m, div, pro, civ ct, deeds, and mtg rec from 1868)

Hancock (see Winston)

Name	Map Index	Date Created	Pop. By M 1970	U.S. Cen Reports Available	Parent County or Territory From Which Organized	County Seat
* Henry	E4	1819	15	1830-80	Conecuh	Abbeville 36310
Houston	E4	1903	75		Dale, Geneva, Henry	Dothan 36301

(Health Dept has b, d, bur rec; Pro Office has m, pro, Ind rec 1903 to present; Cir Clk has civ Ct, crim rec 1903 to present; Reg in Chancery has div rec 1903 to present)

Name	Map Index	Date Created	Pop. By M 1970	U.S. Cen Reports Available	Parent County or Territory From Which Organized	County Seat
* Jackson	A3	1819	51	1830-80	Cherokee Cession of 1816	Scottsboro 35768

(Pro Judge has m, pro & Ind rec; Clk Cir Ct has civ ct rec from 1920)

Name	Map Index	Date Created	Pop. By M 1970	U.S. Cen Reports Available	Parent County or Territory From Which Organized	County Seat
* Jefferson	B2	1819	650	1830-80	Blount	Birmingham 35203

Jones (see Lamar)

Name	Map Index	Date Created	Pop. By M 1970	U.S. Cen Reports Available	Parent County or Territory From Which Organized	County Seat
* Lamar	B1	1867	16	1880	Marion, Fayette, Pickens	Vernon 35592

(Jones co formed Feb 4, 1867, abol Nov 3 1867 & ret to parent cos. Sanford Co org Oct 8 1868 from orig Jones, name changed to Lamar 1877. Co Clk has pro rec from 1886 and will rec from 1880)

Name	Map Index	Date Created	Pop. By M 1970	U.S. Cen Reports Available	Parent County or Territory From Which Organized	County Seat
§ Lauderdale	A1	1818	80	1830-80	Cherokee & Chickasaw Cession in 1816	Florence 35630
(Pro Judge has m & pro rec)						
* Lawrence	A2	1818	30	1830-80	Cherokee & Chickasaw Cession 1816	Moulton 35650

(Pro Judge has m, div, pro & Ind rec from 1810; Clk Cir Ct has civ ct rec)

Name	Map Index	Date Created	Pop. By M 1970	U.S. Cen Reports Available	Parent County or Territory From Which Organized	County Seat
* Lee	C4	1866	77	1870-80	Chambers, Macon, Russell, Tallapoosa	Opelika 36801
* Limestone	A2	1818	46	1820-80	Cherokee & Chickasaw Cession 1816	Athens 35611

(Bur vit Stat has b, d rec; Pro Judge has m from 1832; pro, Ind rec from 1818, Wills and min from 1830; Cir Clk has div rec 1896-1979; civ ct rec 1916-1979)

Name	Map Index	Date Created	Pop. By M 1970	U.S. Cen Reports Available	Parent County or Territory From Which Organized	County Seat
*§ Lowndes	D3	1830	13	1830-80	Butler, Dallas, Montgomery	Hayneville 36040
* Macon	D4	1832	27	1840-80	Creek Cession of 1832	Tuskegee 36083

(Pro Judge has m, pro & Ind rec from 1835; Clk Cir Ct has civ ct rec from 1868)

Name	Map Index	Date Created	Pop. By M 1970	U.S. Cen Reports Available	Parent County or Territory From Which Organized	County Seat
*§ Madison	A3	1808	197	1830-80	Cherokee & Chickasaw Cession 1806-7	Huntsville 35801

(Pro Judge has m, pro & Ind rec from 1809; Cir Ct Clk has div & civ ct rec)

Name	Map Index	Date Created	Pop. By M 1970	U.S. Cen Reports Available	Parent County or Territory From Which Organized	County Seat
*§ Marengo	D1	1818	25	1830-80	Choctaw Cession of 1816	Linden 36748
(Pro Judge has m, pro & Ind rec; Reg in Chan has div; Clk Cir Ct has civ ct rec)						
* Marion	B1	1818	30	1830-80	Tuscaloosa	Hamilton 35570
(Rec burned 1883)						
* Marshall	A3	1836	66	1840-80	Blount, Cherokee Cession 1835, Jackson	Guntersville 35976
* Mobile	F1	1812	362	1830-80	West Florida	Mobile 36602

(Pro Judge ct has m rec from 1813, pro rec from 1809 and will books 1 to 44)

Name	Map Index	Date Created	Pop. By M 1970	U.S. Cen Reports Available	Parent County or Territory From Which Organized	County Seat
Monroe	E2	1815	23	1830-80	Creek Cession 1814, Washington	Monroeville 36460

(Pro Judge has m, pro & Ind rec from 1832) (1816 census of Monroe Co pub by Monroe Journal, Monroeville, Ala)

Name	Map Index	Date Created	Pop. By M 1970	U.S. Cen Reports Available	Parent County or Territory From Which Organized	County Seat
* Montgomery	D3	1816	198	1830-80	Monroe	Montgomery 36104

(Clk of Bd of Revenue has m & pro rec from 1817, div rec from 1852, deeds & mtg from 1817, civ ct rec from 1917) (State bur Vit Stat has b, d rec; State Court has div, civ ct rec)

Name	Map Index	Date Created	Pop. By M 1970	U.S. Cen Reports Available	Parent County or Territory From Which Organized	County Seat
* Morgan	A2	1818	90	1830-80	Cherokee Turkeytown Cession	Decatur 35601

(Name changed from Cotaco 1821. Pro Judge has m and pro rec from 1818)

Name	Map Index	Date Created	Pop. By M 1970	U.S. Cen Reports Available	Parent County or Territory From Which Organized	County Seat
* Perry	C2	1819	15	1830-80	Montgomery	Marion 36756
(Co Clk has m, pro, Ind rec)						
* Pickens	C1	1820	21	1830-80	Tuscaloosa	Carrollton 35447
(Pro Judge has m, pro & Ind rec from 1876; Clk Cir Ct has div & civ ct rec)						
* Pike	E3	1821	28	1830-80	Henry, Montgomery	Troy 36081

(Pro Judge has m, pro & Ind rec from 1830)

COUNTY MAP FOR THE STATE OF ALABAMA

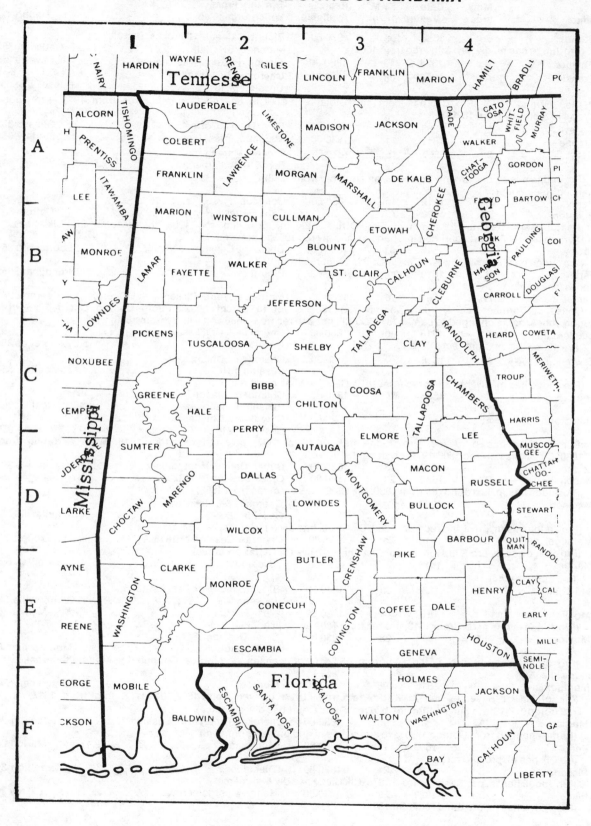

Name	Map Index	Date Created	Pop. By M 1980	U.S. Cen Reports Available	Parent County or Territory From Which Organized	County Seat
Randolph	C4	1832	20	1840-80	Creek Cession 1832	Wedowee 36278
(Courthouse burned 1897 records destroyed)						
* Russell	D4	1832	48	1840-80	Creek Cession 1832	Phenix City 36867
(Co Health Dept has b, d rec; Cir Ct has div, civ ct rec; Judge of Pro has m, pro, Ind rec 1833 to present) (Some rec at Seale)						
Sanford (see Lamar)						
* St. Clair	B3	1818	41	1820-80	Shelby	Ashville 35953 & Pell City 35125
(Pro Judge at Ashville has m, pro, Ind & Estate rec from 1800; Clk Cir Ct has div & civ ct rec)						
* Shelby	C2	1818	66	1820-80	Montgomery	Columbiana 35051
(Pro Judge has m, pro & Ind rec from 1824)						
§ Sumter	C1	1832	17	1840-80	Choctaw Cession of 1830	Livingston 35470
(Pro Judge has scattered b rec from 1888 to 1918; m & pro rec from 1833, Ind rec, historical, voters maps)						
*§ Talladega	C3	1832	74	1840-80	Creek Cession of 1832	Talladega 35160
* Tallapoosa	C4	1832	39	1840-80	Creek Cession of 1832	Dadeville 36853
(Pro Judge b rec from 1881 to 1919; m rec from 1835; d rec from 1881 to 1919; pro rec from 1835; approx 25% of total co b were put on rec; approx 10% of total co d were put on rec; div & civ ct rec kept by Cir Clk; 90 acres were swapped between Tallapoosa & Coosa Cos in 1963)						
Tuscaloosa	C2	1818	137	1830-80	Cherokee & Choctaw Cession 1816	Tuscaloosa 35401
(Pro Judge has m & pro rec from 1823)						
*Walker	B2	1823	68	1830-80	Marion, Tuscaloosa	Jasper 35501
(Rec burned 1877) (Pro Judge has m & pro rec)						
Washington	E1	1800	17	1830-80	Mississippi Terr., Baldwin	Chatom 36518
§ Wilcox	D2	1819	15	1820-80	Monroe, Dallas	Camden 36726
(Pro Judge has m, pro & Ind rec from 1819)						
*§ Winston	B2	1850	22	1860-80	Walker	Double Springs 35553
(Name changed from Hancock 1858) (Pro Judge has m, pro & Ind rec from 1891; Clk Cir Ct has div & civ ct rec)						

* - At least one county history has been published about this county.

§ - Inventory of county archives was made by the Historical Records Survey. (see introduction)

ALASKA

CAPITAL, JUNEAU - TERRITORY 1912 - STATE 1959 - (49TH)

The first permanent white settlement was established at Kodiak Island in 1784 by the Russians and soon British and American traders began to enter the area. After Russia's defeat in the Crimean War, Alaska was purchased by the United States on 30 March 1867. American settlement was sparce until 1880 when gold was discovered near Juneau. New discoveries of gold in Canada's Yukon Territory (1896), at Nome (1899), and at Fairbanks (1902) added to the influx of settlers.

In 1906 Juneau succeeded Sitka as the seat of government, in 1912 Alaska gained territorial status, and in 1959 statehood.

Judicial Districts created between 1897 and 1901, all of which have courthouses are:

First Judicial Dist .... Juneau

Second Judicial Dist. .... Nome

Third Judicial Dist. .... Anchorage

Fourth Judicial Dist. .... Fairbanks

Bureau of Vital Statistics, Department of Health and Social Services, Pouch H-02G, Juneau, Alaska 99811.

Genealogical Archives, Libraries, Societies, and Publications

Alaska Division of State Libraries, Pouch G, State Capitol, Juneau, AK 99801.

Alaska Historical Library and Museum, Juneau, AK 99801.

Kenai Totem Tracers, c/o Kenai Community Library, Box 157, Kenai, AK 99611.

University of Alaska Library, College, AK 99701.

Valuable Printed Sources

Gazetteers

Polk. *Alaska-Yukon Gazetteer.* 1903, 1905-1906, 1909-1910, 1911-1912, 1915-1916, 1917-1918, 1923-1924. Three rolls of microfilm. Juneau: Microfilms, Alaska State Library (Pouch G. Juneau, AK 99811)

Polk. *Alaska-Yukon Gazetteer.* 1902, 1907-1908. (Available for purchase from Public Archives of Canada, Central Microfilm Unit, 79 Bentley Ave., Ottawa, Ontario K2E 6T7)

Ferguson. *Dawson City, Yukon Territory and Alaska Directory and Gazetteer, 1901.* (Available for purchase on microfilm from Elmer E. Rasmuson Library, University of Alaska, Fairbanks, 99701).

Place Names

Orth, Donald J. *Dictionary of Alaska Place Name.* Washington D.C. Government Printing Office. 1902.

Genealogical Sources

Index to Bapt., Marriages, and Deaths in the Archives of the Russian Orthodox Greek Catholic Church in Alaska 1900-1936 compiled by Elizabeth Dorosh and John Dorosh, Manuscript Division, Reference Department, Library of Congress. Washington: 1964.*

Bibliographies

1878 - *Census of Unalaska and Aleutian Villages, Alaska 1878.* Original documents at University of Alaska Archives. Includes the Aleutian Islands and the mainland Aleut Indian Villages of Belkovsky, Micholayevsk and Protossoff (Morzovoy). (G.S. Film 908,376)

Alaska Historical Library, Pouch G, Juneau, AK 99811 (907) 465-2925 provided the following information:

The Alaska Historical Library is not staffed to do genealogical research. However, materials can be used by walk-in patrons and some are available through interlibrary loan channels - check with your local library.

Library genealogical sources are:

Dawson City, Yukon Territory and Alaska Directory & Gazetteer, 1901 (microfilm #54, 1 roll).

*Directory and Gazetteer of Seward Peninsula, 1904 (hardcopy, 1 volume).

Founding of Juneau, The (hardcopy, 1 volume; pioneers and prominent persons, 1880-1895)

*Juneau-Douglas City Directory, 1914-15 (hardcopy, 1 volume)

1900 Census Schedule (microfilm #'s AR29-1 through AR29-21, 21 rolls; by enumeration districts and Soundex index system)

*Nome and Seward Peninsula (hardcopy, 1 volume; pioneers and prominent persons, 1905)

Polk. *Alaska-Yukon Gazetteer and Business Directory, 1903-18, 1923-24, 1932-35* (hardcopy and microfilm #82, 5 rolls)

*Tewkesbury. Who's Who in Alaska and Alaska Business Directory, 1947 (hardcopy, 1 volume)

Who's Who in Alaskan Politics (hardcopy, 1 volume; prominent persons, 1884-1974)

---

*Microfilm - Genealogical Society of The Church of Jesus Christ of Latter-day Saints, Salt Lake, City, Utah.

Alaska's early newspapers, most of which are on microfilm and listed in *A Guide To Alaska's Newspapers,* are another source of information on people. Though **few** of them are indexed, there is a guide to the *Alaskan* which was published in Sitka, Alaska from 1885-1907.

Additional sources are early Alaskan periodicals, most of which are hardcopy and, except for limited issues, have no indexes. Our holdings are:

* *Alaska Life, 1938-49*
  Alaska Monthly Magazine, 1906-07 (microfilm #84)
* *Alaska Sportsman (Alaska Magazine),* 1935-present
* *Alaska-Yukon Magazine,* 1906-12
* *Alaska's Magazine,* 1905-06
* *The Magazine Alaska,* 1938-39
  The Pathfinder, 1919-26 (microfilm #75)

For further information contact the Alaska Historical Library, Pouch G, Juneau, AK 99811. (907) 465-2925.

Helm, June. *The Indians of the Subarctic: A Critical Bibliography, 1976* Bloomington: Indiana University Press.

Jackson, Ronald Vern and Gary Ronald Teeples. *Alaskan Records 1870-1907* Salt Lake City, Utah: Accelerated Indexing Systems, Inc.

Lada-Mocarski, Valerian. *Bibliography of Books on Alaska Published Before 1868.* New Haven: Yale University Press, 1969.

Other Sources of Genealogical Information In Alaska Are:

- Dept. of Health & Social Services, Bureau of Vital Statistics, Pouch H-02G, Juneau, AK 99811.

- Christy's Genealogical Service, P.O. Box 10061, Fairbanks, AK 99701.

- Alaskan Records Research, 9119 Nagoon Lane, Juneau, AK 99801

Histories

Bancroft, Hubert Howe. *History of Alaska.* San Francisco: A. L. Bancroft and Company Publishers, 1885.

Sherwood, Morgan B. *Alaska and Its History.* Seattle: University of Washington Press, 1967.

---

*non-circulating material

ALASKA ELECTION DISTRICTS
(Population figures to nearest thousand 1980 U.S. Census)

Election Districts	Map Index	Pop. By M 1980	Election Districts	Map Index	Pop. By M 1980
Aleutian Islands, 14	E2	8	Kuskokwim, 17	C2	2
Anchorage, 10	C3	126	Matanuska-Susitna		7
Angoen		5	Nome, 23	B2	6
Barrow, 21	A2	3	Outer Ketchikan		2
Bethel, 16	D2	8	Prince of Wales, 1	D4	2
Bristol Bay, 15	D2	3	Seward, 11	D3	2
Cordova-McCarthy, 7	C3	2	Sitka, 4	D4	6
Fairbanks, 19	C3	46	Skagway-Yukutat		2
Haines		2	Southeast Fairbanks		4
Juneau, 5	D4	14	Upper Yukon, 20	B2	2
Kenai-Cook Inlet, 12	D3	14	Valdez-Chitina Whittier, 8	C3	3
Ketchikan, 2	D5	10	Wade Hampton, 24	C2	4
Kobuk, 22	B2	4	Wrangell-Petersburg, 3	D4	5
Kodiak, 13	D3	9	Yukon-Koyukuk, 18	B3	5

COUNTY MAP FOR THE STATE OF ALASKA

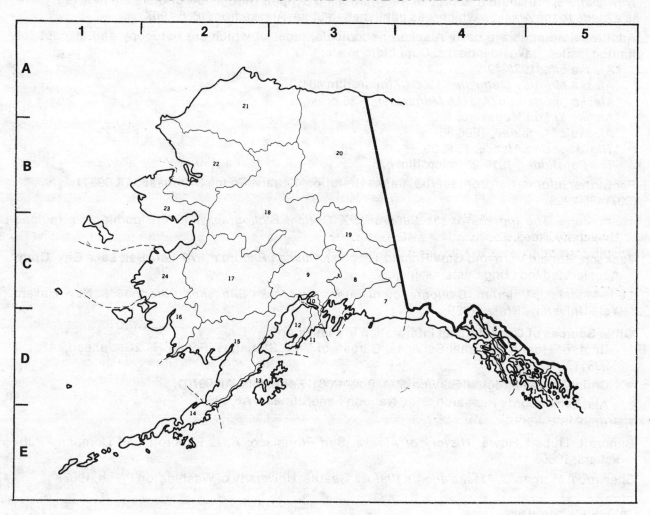

ARIZONA

CAPITAL, PHOENIX - TERRITORY 1863 - STATE 1912 - (48th)

The first white people to come to Arizona were attracted there by the tale of the fabulous "Seven Cities of Cibola" which they had heard time and again in Mexico City. As early as 1539 the first European explorers came into the region but it was about one hundred fifty years later before Catholic missions were started among the Indians. Tucson became a village about the time the American colonies along the Atlantic coast were fighting their mother country in the Revolutionary War. As a section of New Mexico, Arizona came under the ownership and guidance of Mexico in 1821.

At the close of the Mexican War in 1848, a new dispute arose relative to the ownership of a tract of land at the international border. To alleviate any further difficulties the United States minister to Mexico, James Gadsden, negotiated a deal very unpopular in Mexico, by which the United States paid ten million dollars for slightly less than 50,000 square miles of land, lying south of the Gila River and extending east from the California border to the Rio Grande River.

In the beginning the new territory attracted very few settlers. In 1870, seven years after Arizona became an organized territory, the entire state held less than ten thousand residents. In the forty-year period that followed the Arizona population increased twenty fold, and the following half century more than trebled the 1910 population.

The foreign-born population of Arizona comes in the following order: Mexico, Canada, England and Wales, Germany, Russia, Italy, Poland, Austria, Sweden, Greece, Ireland, Scotland, Yugoslavia, and Czechoslovakia.

Since 1850 many Mormon families from Utah have settled in Arizona. In fact, in several large agricultural districts, the Mormon population predominates.

The Territorial Board of Health established the Bureau of Vital Statistics on March 18, 1909. Birth and Death records are available since that date along with similar records originating in the county seats since 1887. Mailing address: Vital Records Section, Department of Health Services, P.O. Box 3887, Phoenix, Arizona 85030.

Marriage records are on file with the Clerk of the Superior Court of county in which the license was issued.

Divorce actions are maintained by the Clerk of the Superior Court in county seat where the action was granted.

Citizenship or naturalization papers are filed in the district court of the county where examination was conducted. Also in the office of the clerk of the United States district courts in Tucson, Tombstone, Phoenix, Prescott, and Solomonville.

All real estate records are on file in the office of the recorder of the county in which the land is located.

Genealogical Archives, Libraries, Societies, and Publications

Arizona and the West Library, 318 University of Arizona, Tucson, AZ 85721.

Arizona Pioneer's Historical Society, 949 East Second St., Tucson, AZ 85719.

Arizona State Library, State Capitol, 3rd Floor, 1700 W. Washington, Phoenix, AZ 85007.

Arizona State Genealogical Society, Box 6027, Tucson, AZ 85733.

Mohave County Genealogical Society, P.O. Box 928, Kingman, AZ 86402.

Prescott Historical Society, W. Gurley St., Prescott, AZ 86301.

Sun City Genealogical Society, P.O. Box 1494, Sun City, AZ 85372.

Tucson Public Library, 200 South 6th Ave., Tucson, AZ 85701.

Copper State Bulletin, Arizona State Genealogical Society, P.O. Box 6027, Tucson, AZ 85716.

Printed Census Records and Mortality Schedules

State Indexes - 1860 (Territory of New Mexico); 1864, 1866, 1867, 1870, 1880 (Territory of Arizona).

Mortality Schedules (Printed) - 1850, 1860, 1870, 1880

Printed census records (Counties)
Mohave - 1870   Yavapai - 1900; 1869
1870 Phoenix Territory Census

Valuable Printed Sources

Atlas

Walker, Henry Pickering and Don Bufkin. *Historical Atlas of Arizona.* Norman, Oklahoma: University of Oklahoma Press, 1979.

Place Names

Barnes, William Croft. *Arizona Place Names* (revised and enlarged by Byrd H. Granger). Tucson: University of Arizona Press, 1960.

Theobald, John and Lillian. *Arizona Territory Post Offices and Postmasters.* Phoenix: Arizona Historical Foundation, 1961.

Guides To Genealogical Research

Temple, Thomas Workman III. *Sources for Tracing Spanish-American Pedigrees in Southwestern United States.* Salt Lake City: Genealogical Society of The Church of Jesus Christ of Latter-day Saints, 1969

Histories

Bancroft, Hubert Howe. *History of Arizona and New Mexico 1530-1888.* Albuquerue: (Facsimile of 1889 edition) Horn and Wallace, 1962

Peplow, Edward Hadduck, Jr. *History of Arizona,* Three Volumes. New York: Lewis Historical Publishing Company, 1958.

Wagoner, Jay J. *Arizona Territory 1863-1912.* Tucson: University of Arizona Press, 1970.

Genealogical Sources

Arizona Death Records: An Index Compiled from Mortuary, Cemetery and Church Records, Vols. I, II. Tucson: Arizona State Genealogical Society, 1976.

Carl Hayden Biographical Files 1825-1927*

Bibliographies (Newspapers, Periodicals)

Lutrell, Estelle. *Newspapers and Periodical of Arizona 1859-1911.* Tuscon: University of Arizona Bulletin #15, 1950.

Newspapers of Arizona Libraries: A Union List of Newspapers Published in Arizona. Compiled by the Department of Library and Archives of the State of Arizona. Tuscon: Pioneers Historical Society, 1965.*

---

*Microfilm - Genealogical Society of The Church of Jesus Christ of Latter-day Saints, Salt Lake City, Utah.

ARIZONA COUNTY HISTORIES
(Population figures to nearest thousand - 1980 U.S. Census)

Name	Map Index	Date Created	Pop. By M 1980	U.S. Cen Reports Available	Parent County or Territory From Which Organized	County Seat
Apache	B4	1879	52	1880	Yavapai	St. Johns 85936
(Clk Sup Ct has m, div, pro, ct rec 1879 to present; Co Rcdr has Ind rec 1879 to 1979)						
Cochise	F4	1881	86		Pima	Bisbee 85603
(Clk Sup Ct has m, div, pro civ ct rec; Co Recdr has Ind rec)						
* Coconino	B3	1891	75		Yavapai	Flagstaff 86001
(Clk Sup Ct has m, div, civ ct and Ind rec)						
Gila	D3	1881	37		Maricopa, Pinal	Globe 85501
(Dept of Health, Phoenix has b, d rec; Co Clk has m, div, pro, civ ct rec 1881 to present; Co Rcdr has Ind rec; Col Clk has immigration and naturalization rec)						
* Graham	D4	1881	23		Apache, Pima	Safford 85546
(Clk Sup Ct has m rec 1881-1979; div, pro, civ ct rec 1882-1979; Bur Vit Statistics, Phoenix has b, d, bur rec; Co Rcdr has Ind rec)						
Greenlee	D4	1909	11		Graham	Clifton 85533
(Clk Sup Ct has m, div, pro & civ ct rec from 1911; Co Rcdr has Ind rec)						
§ Maricopa	D2	1871	1,512	1880	Yavapai, Yuma	Phoenix 85003
(Clk Sup Ct has m from 1877, div from 1930, pro & civ ct rec from 1871, criminal from 1879; Co Rcdr has Ind rec)						
Mohave	B1	1864	56	1870-80	Original County	Kingman 86401
(Clk Sup Ct has m rec 1888 to present; div, pro, civ ct 1850-1979; Bur Vit Statistics, Phoenix has b, d rec; Co Rcdr has Ind rec)						
Navajo	B4	1895	67		Apache	Holbrook 86025
(Clk Sup Ct has m, div, pro, civ ct rec; Co Rcdr has Ind rec; Bur Vit Statistics, Phoenix has b, d, bur rec)						

Name	Map Index	Date Created	Pop. By M 1980	U.S. Cen Reports Available	Parent County or Territory From Which Organized	County Seat
Pah Ute (disolved 1895 returned to Mohave)						
§ Pima	E3	1864	532	1870-80	Original county	Tucson 85701

(Clk Sup Ct has m, div, pro & civ ct rec from ca 1863)

| Pinal | D3 | 1875 | 88 | 1880 | Pima | Florence 85232 |

(Clk Sup Ct has m, pro, civ ct rec from 1875; div rec from 1883; Bur Vit Statistics, Phoenix has b, d rec; Co Rcdr has Ind rec)

| § Santa Cruz | F3 | 1899 | 19 | | Pima | Nogales 85621 |

(Clk Sup Ct has m, div, pro & civ ct rec from 1900)

| Yavapai | C2 | 1864 | 68 | 1870 | Original county | Prescott 86301 |

(Clk Sup Ct has m, div, pro & civ ct rec; Co Rcdr has Ind rec)

| Yuma | D1 | 1864 | 90 | 1870 | Original county | Yuma 85364 |

(Clk Sup Ct has m, div, pro & civ ct rec from 1863)

* - At least one county history has been published about this county.

§ - Inventory of county archives was made by the Historical Records Survey. (see introduction)

COUNTY MAP FOR THE STATE OF ARIZONA

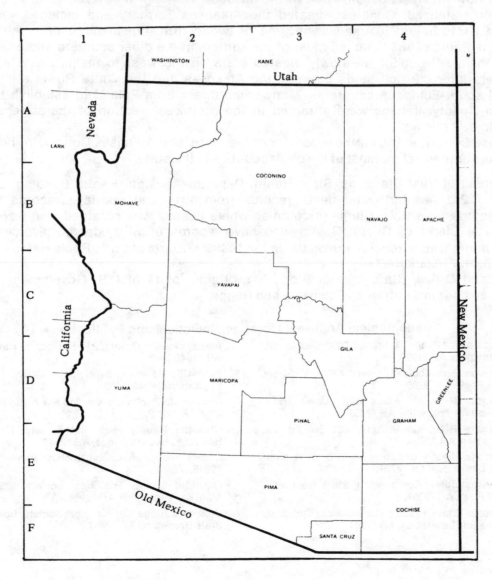

ARKANSAS

CAPITAL, LITTLE ROCK · TERRITORY 1819 · STATE 1836 · (25TH)

The Indians had free reign in Arkansas until after the United States completed negotiations with the French for the Louisiana Purchase in 1803. Off and on during the previous 262 years several French explorers came to the region with their parties in search of whatever loot they could find. They came today and were gone tomorrow.

With the land in the ownership of the United States it was immediately thrown open for settlement at attractive low prices. The new opportunities beckoned thousands of earlier settlers of the mideast and southeast sections. The first comers were mainly of English, Irish and Scottish stock. Many moved into the new section from nearby Kentucky and Tennessee.

What is now Arkansas became part of the Missouri Territory in 1812. In 1819, when Missouri applied for statehood, Congress created the Arkansas Territory and included what is now Oklahoma. On 15 June 1836 Arkansas became the twenty-fifth state in the Union.

When the Panic of 1837 drained most of the settlers in the older southern and eastern states many of them set out for the newly created state on the west to make a new start in life. Thirty years later the rich lands between the Arkansas and the White Rivers attracted large groups of south European emigrants. Many came direct from Poland to establish themselves in Pulaski County. Italians were attracted to the northwest section of the state where they engaged in fruit raising.

Lawrence County, in the northeast corner of the state, and Arkansas County, in the southeast corner, were settled before most of the other counties in the state.

The Bureau of Vital Statistics, State Health Department, State Health Building, Little Rock, Arkansas 72201 has birth and death records from 1914 and marriage records from 1917, divorce records from 1921. Clerks of counties where license was obtained also have marriage records. The Clerks of Circuit Courts also have records of wills, deeds, divorces, and war service. Naturalization records are on file in the District Courts at Little Rock, Helena, Batesville, Fort Smith, and Texarkana.

State Land Office, State Capitol Bldg., has original plats of U.S. Government surveys of Arkansas and original entries by Township and Range.

Genealogical Archives, Libraries, Societies, and Publications

Arkadelphia Public Library, 609 Caddo St., Arkadelphia, AR 71923.

Arkansas Genealogical Society, 4200 "A" Street, Little Rock, AR 72205.

Arkansas Historical Association, University of Arkansas, Fayetteville, AR 72701.

Arkansas Historical Society, 422 So. 6th St., Van Buren, AR 72956.

Arkansas History Commission, 300 West Markham, Little Rock, AR 72201.

Arkansas Library Commission, 506½ Center St., Little Rock, AR 72201.

Arkansas State History Commission, Old State House Rd., Little Rock, AR 72201.

Ashley County Library, 211 E. Lincoln, Hamburg, AR 71646.

Batesville Genealogical Society, 460 W. Morrow St., Batesville, AR 72501.

Bentonville Public Library, 315 SW A St., Bentonville, AR 72712.

Cleburne County Historical Society, Route 2, Box 326K, Heber Springs, AR 72543.

Carroll County Historical Society, Berryville, AR 72616.

Crawford County Historical Society, 929 East Main St., Van Buren, AR 72956.

Crowley's Ridge Genealogical Society, Box 2091, State University, AR 72467.

Crowley Ridge Regional Library, 315 W. Oak, Jonesboro, AR 72401.

Dallas County Arkansas Genealogical and Historical Society, c/o Dallas County Library, Fordyce, AR 71742.

Faulkner County Historical Society, Conway, AR 72032.

Fayette Public Library, 217 E. Dickson St., Fayetteville, AR 72701.

Ft. Smith Public Library, 61 S. 8th St., Ft. Smith, AR 72901.

Garland-Montgomery Regional Library, 200 Woodbine St., Hot Springs, AR 71901.

Grand Prairie Historical Society, P.O. Box 122, Gillett, AR 72055.

Independence County Historical Society, Box 1412, Batesville, AR 72501.

Johnson County Historical Society, P.O. Box 505, Clarksville, AR 72830.

Little Rock Public Library, 700 Louisiana St., Little Rock, AR 72201.

Melting Pot Genealogical Society, P.O. Box 2186, Hot Springs National Park, AR 71901.

Mississippi County Historical and Genealogical Society, 505 S.W. Pkwy., Blytheville, AR 72315.

North Arkansas Genealogical Society, Mountain Home, AR 72653.

Northwest Arkansas Genealogical Society, P.O. Box K, Rogers, AR 72756.

Pine Bluff and Jefferson Counties Public Library, 219 West Fifth Ave., Pine Bluff, AR 71601.

Pope County Genealogical Assn., Rt. 5, Box 249-A, Russellville, AR 72801.

Pulaski County Historical Society, P.O. Box 653, Little Rock, AR 72203.

Southern Arkansas Genealogical Society, 976 Lyons Lane, S.W. Camden, AR 71701.

So-We-Ar Genealogical Society, P.O. Box 0, Magnolia, AR 71753.

Van Buren County Library, Clinton, AR 72031.

Arkansas Family Historian, The, Arkansas Genealogical Society, 4200 A St., Little Rock, AR 72205.

Arkansas Genealogical Register, The, Northeast Arkansas Genealogical Association, 314 Vine St., Newport, AR 73112.

Backtracker, The, published by the Northwest Arkansas Genealogical Society, P.O. Box K, Rogers, AR 73756.

Bits Of Bark From The Family Tree, Batesville Genealogical Society, 460 Morrow St., Batesville, AR 72501.

Cleburne County Historical Quarterly, Cleburne County Historical Society, Route 2, Box 326K, Heber Springs, AR 72543.

Johnson County Historical Society Journal, Johnson County Historical Society, P.O. Box 505, Clarksville, AR 72830.

Pulaski County Historical Review, published by Pulaski County Historical Society, P.O. Box 653, Little Rock, AR 72203.

Printed Census Records and Mortality Schedules

State Indexes - 1830, 1840, 1850, 1860, 1870

Other printed census records follow: Counties

Arkansas - 1830, 1840, 1850, 1860, 1870; 1823-1829
Ashley - 1850, 1870
Benton - 1840, 1850, 1860, 1870
Bradley - 1850, 1870
Calhoun - 1870
Carroll - 1840, 1850, 1860, 1870; 1834
Chicot - 1830, 1840, 1850
Clark - 1830, 1840, 1850, 1860, 1870
Columbia - 1860
Conway - 1830, 1840, 1850, 1860, 1870
Crawford - 1830, 1840, 1850
Crittenden - 1830, 1840, 1850
Dallas - 1850
Desha - 1840, 1850, 1860
Drew - 1850
Franklin - 1840, 1850, 1860, 1870
Fulton - 1850
Grant - 1870
Greene - 1840, 1850, 1860, 1870
Hempstead - 1830, 1840, 1850, 1860
Hot Springs - 1830, 1840, 1850
Independence - 1830, 1840, 1850
Izard - 1830, 1840, 1850
Jackson - 1830, 1840, 1850, 1870
Jefferson - 1830, 1840, 1850, 1860
Johnson - 1840, 1850

Lafayette - 1830, 1840, 1850
Lawrence - 1830, 1840, 1850
Madison - 1840, 1850, 1860, 1870, 1880
Marion - 1840, 1850, 1870
Miller - 1830, 1880
Mississippi 1840, 1850, 1860
Monroe - 1830, 1840, 1850
Montgomery - 1850
Newton - 1850, 1860, 1870, 1880, 1890, 1900
Ouachita - 1850
Perry - 1850, 1870
Phillips - 1830, 1840, 1850
Pike - 1840, 1850
Poinsett - 1840, 1850
Polk - 1850
Pope - 1830, 1840, 1850, 1860, 1870, 1880, 1900
Prairie - 1850
Pulaski - 1830, 1840, 1850
Randolph - 1840, 1850
St. Francis - 1830, 1840, 1850
Saline - 1840, 1850, 1870
Scott - 1840, 1850, 1870
Searcy - 1840, 1850, 1870
Sebastian - 1860, 1870
Sevier - 1830, 1840, 1850, 1860
Sharp - 1870, 1880
Union - 1830, 1840, 1850
Van Buren - 1840, 1850, 1860, 1870
Washington - 1830, 1840, 1850, 1860, 1870

White - 1840, 1850, 1860, 1870
Woodruff - 1870, 1880
Yell - 1850, 1860, 1870

Mortality Schedules -
(Printed) 1850, 1860, 1870, 1880
Arkansas Territory Census 1823-1829
(Sheriff's Census)

Valuable Printed Sources

Maps

Map Book 1936 Reprint of all the Counties in Arkansas. Little Rock: Arkansas Genealogical Society.

Place Names

List of Post Offices in Arkansas as Shown in Early Newspaper Files 1817-1874. Historical Records Survey, WPA Project #5261-3. Arkansas Historical Commission.

Guides To Genealogical Reseach

Dillard, Tom W. and Valerie Thwing. *Researching Arkansas History A Beginners Guide.* Little Rock: Rose Publishing Company, 1979.

Morgan, James Logan. *A Survey of the County Records of Arkansas.* Newport: Arkansas Records Association, 1972.

Histories

Hallum, John. *Biographical and Pictorial History of Arkansas.* Albany, New York: Weed, Parsons and Company Printers, 1887.

Thomas, David Y. *Arkansas and Its People, A History 1541-1930.* 4 Vols. New York: The American Historical Society, 1931.

Genealogical Sources

Christensen, Katheren. *Arkansas Military Bounty Grants (War 1812).* Hot Springs: Arkansas Ancestors, 1972.

Core, Dorothy Jones. *Abstract of Catholic Register of Arkansas (1764-1858).* Gillett: Grand Prairie Historical Society, 1976.

D.A.R. Collections. Family Histories, Bibles, cemetery, marriage records, church and miscellaneous records.

Index to Sources for Arkansas Cemetery Inscriptions compiled and published as a Bi-Centennial Project by The Prudence Hall Chapter, D.A.R. Little Rock, 1976.

ARKANSAS COUNTY HISTORIES

(Population figures to nearest thousand - 1980 U.S. Census)

Name	Map Index	Date Created	Pop. By M 1980	U.S. Cen Reports Available	Parent County or Territory From Which Organized	County Seat
* Arkansas	C3	1813	24	1830-80	Original county	Stuttgart 72160 & De Witt 72042
(Co Clk has pro rec from 1809, m rec from 1838; Clk Cir Ct has div & civ ct rec from 1803, War ser discharge from 1917)						
* Ashley	D3	1848	27	1850-80	Chicot, Union, Drew	Hamburg 71646
(Co Clk has m rec 1848-1979; pro, Ind rec. Cir Clk has Div rec)						
*§ Baxter	A2	1873	27	1880	Fulton, Izard, Marion & Searcy	Mountain Home 72653
*§ Benton	A1	1836	78	1840-80	Washington	Bentonville 72712
(Co Clk has m from 1861, pro from 1859; Clk Cir Ct has div, civ ct & Ind rec)						
* Boone	A2	1869	26	1870-80	Carrol, Madison	Harrison 72601
(Co Clk has m & pro from 1869; Clk Cir Ct has div, civ ct & Ind rec)						

Name	Map Index	Date Created	Pop. By M 1980	U.S. Cen Reports Available	Parent County or Territory From Which Organized	County Seat
Bradley	D3	1840	14	1850-80	Union	Warren 71671

(Co Clk has m rec 1846 to present; pro rec 1850 to present; State Dept of Health, Little Rock has b, d rec; Cir Clk has div rec)

| Calhoun | D2 | 1850 | 6 | 1860-80 | Dallas, Ouachita | Hampton 71744 |

(Co Clk has m rec 1851 to present; Div, pro, civ ct, 1880 to present; Ind rec 1851 to present)

| *§ Carroll | A1 | 1833 | 16 | 1840-80 | Izard | Berryville 72616 & Eureka Springs 72632 |

Co Clk has m & pro rec from 1870; Clk Cir Ct has div from 1870 & Ind rec)

| Chicot | D3 | 1823 | 18 | 1830-80 | Arkansas | Lake Village 71653 |

(Co Clk has m & pro rec from 1839; Clk Cir Ct has civ ct rec from 1824)

| Clark | C2 | 1818 | 23 | 1830-80 | Arkansas | Arkadelphia 71923 |

(Co Clk has m from 1821, pro from 1800; Clk Cir Ct has div, civ ct & Ind rec)

| * Clay | A4 | 1873 | 19 | 1880 | Randolph, Green | Corning 72422 & Pigott 72454 |

(Co Clk has m, pro rec Nov 1893 to present; Bur Vit Statistics, Little Rock has b and d rec; Clk Cir Ct has div and civ ct rec)

| § Cleburne | B3 | 1883 | 17 | | White, Van Buren, Independence | Heber Springs 72543 |

(Co Clk has m, pro, div, civ ct, Ind rec 1883 to present; Bur Vit Statistics, Little Rock has b and d rec)

| § Cleveland | C2 | 1873 | 8 | 1880 | Dallas, Bradley, Jefferson, Lincoln | Rison 71655 |

(Changed from Dorsey 5 March 1885) (Co Clk has m rec 1880 to 1979; div, pro, civ ct rec; Bur Vit Statistics, Little Rock has b, d rec)

| * Columbia | D2 | 1852 | 27 | 1860-80 | Lafayette, Hempstead, Ouachita | Magnolia 71753 |

(Co Clk has m, Ind rec 1853 to present; div, civ ct rec 1860 to present; pro rec; Co Library has cem rec; Bur Vit Statistics, Little Rock has b, d rec)

| * Conway | B2 | 1825 | 19 | 1830-80 | Pulaski | Morrilton 72110 |

(Co Clk has m, pro rec; Cir Clk has div, civ ct, Ind rec; Bur Vit Statistics, Little Rock has b, d, bur rec)

| * Craighead | A4 | 1859 | 65 | 1860-80 | Mississippi, Greene, Poinsett | Jonesboro 72401 & Lake City 72437 |

(Co Clk has m rec from 1878; pro rec; Clk Cir Ct has div, civ ct and Ind rec)

| * Crawford | B1 | 1820 | 37 | 1830-80 | Pulaski | Van Buren 72956 |

(Co Clk has m, div, pro, civ ct & crim ct rec 1883 for eastern dist of co only)

| Crittenden | B4 | 1825 | 49 | 1830-80 | Phillips | Marion 72364 |

(Co Clk has m & pro rec; Clk Cir Ct has civ ct rec; Chancery Clk has div rec)

| *§ Cross | B4 | 1826 | 20 | 1870-80 | Crittenden, Poinsett, St. Francis | Wynne 72396 |

(Co Clk has m rec 1863 to present; pro rec 1865 to present; Cir Clk has civ ct, Ind rec 1865 to present; Chancery Cir Clk has div rec 1866 to present; Bur Vit Statistics, Little Rock has b, d rec from 1914; Kernodle Funeral Home, Whynne Ark has bur rec from 1936; Co Clk has wills, bonds 1863 to present; Tax, county ct rec 1865 to present)

| * Dallas | C2 | 1845 | 11 | 1850-80 | Clark, Bradley | Fordyce 71742 |

(Co Clk has m rec 1855-1979; Ind rec 1845-1979; div, pro, civ ct to 1979; Bur Vit Statistics, Little Rock has b, d, rec)

| Desha | C3 | 1838 | 20 | 1840-80 | Arkansas, Chicot | Arkansas City 71630 |

(Co Clk has m rec 1865 to present; pro rec; Cir Clk has div, civ ct, Ind rec; Bur Vit Statistics, Little Rock has b, d rec)

Dorsey (see Cleveland)

| Drew | D3 | 1846 | 18 | 1850-80 | Arkansas, Bradley | Monticello 71665 |

(Co Clk has m, pro rec; Cir Clk has div, civ ct, Ind rec; Bur Vit Statistics, Little Rock has b, d rec)

| *§ Faulkner | B2 | 1873 | 46 | 1880 | Pulaski, Conway | Conway 72032 |

(Co Clk has m, pro, co ct rec from 1873)

| Franklin | B1 | 1837 | 15 | 1840-80 | Crawford | Charleston 72933 and Ozark 72949 |

(Co Clk has m rec 1850-1979; pro rec 1838-1979; Ind rec 1899-1979)

| Fulton | A3 | 1842 | 10 | 1850-80 | Izard | Salem 72576 |
| Garland | C2 | 1873 | 71 | 1880 | Montgomery, Hot Springs, Saline | Hot Springs N. P. 71901 |

(Co Clk has m, pro rec; Cir Clk has div, civ ct, Ind rec; Bur Vit Statistics, Little Rock has b, d rec)

| Grant | C2 | 1869 | 13 | 1870-80 | Jefferson, Hot Springs, Saline | Sheridan 72150 |

(Co Clk has m, div, pro, civ ct & Ind rec from 1877)

| * Greene | A4 | 1833 | 31 | 1840-80 | Lawrence | Paragould 72450 |

(Co Clk has m, pro rec; Cir Clk has div, civ ct, Ind rec; Bur Vit Statistics, Little Rock has b, d rec)

| Hempstead | D1 | 1818 | 24 | 1830-80 | Arkansas | Hope 71801 |

(Co Clk has m, pro rec 1823 to present; Ind rec 1900 to present)

Name	Map Index	Date Created	Pop. By M 1980	U.S. Cen Reports Available	Parent County or Territory From Which Organized	County Seat
§ Hot Springs	C2	1829	27	1830-80	Clark	Malvern 72104

(Co Clk has m rec 1835-1979; div, pro rec 1850-1979; Bur Vit Statistics, Little Rock has b, d rec Clk Cir Ct has civ ct rec)

| Howard | C1 | 1873 | 14 | 1880 | Pike, Hempstead, Polk, Sevier | Nashville 71852 |

(Co Clk has m, pro, Ind rec 1873-1979; Cir Clk has div, civ ct Ind rec 1873-1979)

| * Independence | A3 | 1820 | 30 | 1830-80 | Lawrence, Arkansas | Batesville 72501 |

(Co Clk has m rec from 1826 & pro rec from 1839; Clk Cir Ct has div, and civ ct rec)

| *§ Izard | A3 | 1825 | 11 | 1830-80 | Independence, Fulton | Melbourne 72556 |

(Line between Izard & Sharp changed 9 Mar 1877) (Co Clk has m, div, pro, civ ct, Ind rec 1889 to present)

| *§ Jackson | B3 | 1829 | 22 | 1830-80 | Woodruff | Newport 72112 |

(Co Clk has m rec 1843-1979; pro rec 1845-1979; Clk Cir Ct has div, civ ct rec from 1845)

| * Jefferson | C3 | 1829 | 91 | 1830-80 | Arkansas, Pulaski | Pine Bluff 71601 |

(Co Clk has m, rec 1830-1979; pro rec 1845-1979; Dir Clk has div, civ ct, Ind rec)

| * Johnson | B2 | 1833 | 17 | 1840-80 | Pope | Clarksville 72830 |

(Co Clk has m rec 1855 to present; pro rec 1844 to present; Cir Clk has div, civ ct, Ind rec; extension office has bur rec; Bur Vit Statistics, Little Rock has b, d rec)

| Lafayette | D1 | 1827 | 10 | 1830-80 | Hempstead | Lewisville 71845 |

(Co Clk has m rec 1848 to 1980; pro rec; Cir Clk has div rec)

| * Lawrence | A3 | 1815 | 18 | 1830-80 | New Madrid, Mo | Walnut Ridge 72476 |

(Co Clk has m & pro rec)

| * Lee | C4 | 1873 | 16 | 1880 | Phillips, Monroe, Crittenden, St. Francis | Marianna 72360 |

(Co Clerk has m, pro rec 1883 to present)

| Lincoln | C3 | 1871 | 13 | 1880 | Arkansas, Bradley, Desha, Drew, Jefferson | Star City 71667 |

(Co Clk has m, pro, & Ind rec from 1871, tax rec)

| Little River | D1 | 1867 | 14 | 1870-80 | Hempstead | Ashdown 71822 |

(Co Clk has m & pro rec from 1898; Clk Cir Ct has div & Ind rec)

| *Logan | B1 | 1871 | 20 | 1880 | Pope, Franklin, Johnson, Scott, Yell | Booneville 72927 & Paris (1) 72885 |

(Co Clk at Paris has m, pro rec; Co Clk at Booneville has m, pro rec 1901-1979; Cir Clk div, civ ct, Ind rec; Bur Vit Statistics, Little Rock has b, d rec)

| * Lonoke | B3 | 1873 | 35 | 1880 | Pulaski, Prairie | Lonoke 72086 |

(Co Clk has m, pro & Ind rec)

| Lovely | | 1827 | | Abolished 1828 | | |

| § Madison | A1 | 1836 | 11 | 1840-80 | Washington | Huntsville 72740 |

(Co Clk has m & pro rec from 1901)

| * Marion | A2 | 1836 | 11 | 1840-80 | Izard | Yellville 72687 |

(Co Clk has m, div, pro, civ ct, Ind rec 1888 to present; Abstractors have Ind rec; Bur Vit Statistics, Little Rock have b, d, rec)

| * Miller | D1 | 1820 | 38 | 1880 | Lafayette Abolished 1836 & ret to Arkansas Re-established 1874 | Texarkana 75501 |

(Co Clk has m, pro, Ind rec 1875 to present; Cir Clk has div, civ ct rec)

| * Mississippi | A4 | 1833 | 60 | 1840-80 | Crittenden | Blytheville 72315 & Osceola 72370 |

(Co Clk has m from 1850, pro from 1865; Clk Cir Ct has div, civ ct rec from 1866, Ind rec from 1865)

| § Monroe | C3 | 1829 | 14 | 1830-80 | Phillips, Arkansas | Clarendon 72029 |

(Co Clk has m rec 1851 to present; pro rec 1839 to present; Cir Clk has div rec 1839 to present; civ ct rec 1830 to present; Ind rec 1829 to present; Bur Vit Statistics, Little Rock has b, d rec; local mortuary has some bur rec)

| § Montgomery | C1 | 1842 | 8 | 1850-80 | Hot Springs | Mount Ida 71957 |

(Co Clk has m from 1854, div, pro, civ ct & Ind rec)

| * Nevada | D2 | 1871 | 11 | 1880 | Hempstead, Columbia, Ouachita | Prescott 71857 |

(Co Clk has m, pro, Ind rec 1871-1979 rec of headstones all cemeteries; Cir Clk has div, civ ct rec 1871-1979; Bur Vit Statistics, Little Rock has b, d rec)

| * Newton | A2 | 1842 | 8 | 1850-80 | Carroll | Jasper 72641 |

(Co Clk has m, Ind rec 1866-1979; div rec 1820-1979; pro, civ ct rec 1880-1979)

| * Ouachita | D2 | 1842 | 31 | 1850-80 | Union | Camden 71701 |

(Co Clk has m pro rec Dec 1875 to present; Cir Clk has div, civ ct, Ind rec; Bur Vit Statistics, Little Rock has b, d rec)

| Perry | B2 | 1840 | 7 | 1850-80 | Conway | Perryville 72126 |

(Co Clk has m, div, pro, civ ct & Ind rec from 1882)

| Phillips | C4 | 1820 | 35 | 1830-80 | Arkansas, Hempstead | Helena 72342 |

(Co Clk has m rec 1831 to present; pro rec 1850 to present; Cir Clk has div, civ ct, Ind rec 1820 to present)

COUNTY MAP FOR THE STATE OF ARKANSAS

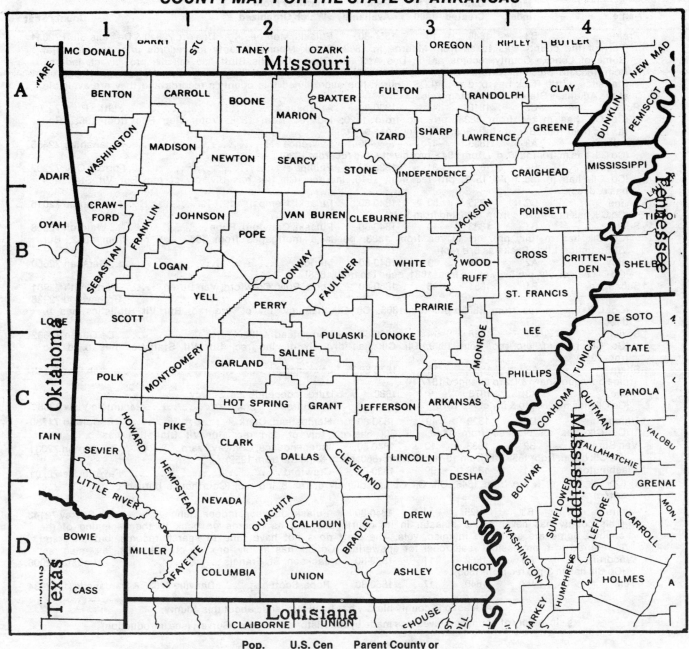

Name	Map Index	Date Created	Pop. By M 1980	U.S. Cen Reports Available	Parent County or Territory From Which Organized	County Seat
* Pike	C1	1833	10	1840-80	Clark, Hempstead	Murfreesboro 71958

(Co Clk has m, div, pro, civ ct, Ind, wills, discharge rec 1895 to present; Bur Vit Statistics, Little Rock has b, d, rec)

| Poinsett | B4 | 1838 | 27 | 1840-80 | Greene, St Francis | Harrisburg 72432 |

(Co Clk has m from 1878, pro rec; Clk Cir Ct has div, civ ct & Ind rec)

| *§ Polk | C1 | 1844 | 17 | 1850-80 | Sevier | Mena 71953 |

(Co Clk has m rec 1883 to present; Pro rec 1912 to present; co ct rec from 1873; Clk Cir Ct has div rec from 1907; crim ct rec from 1873, and Ind rec from 1882)

| * Pope | B2 | 1829 | 38 | 1830-80 | Crawford | Russellville 72801 |

(Co Clk has m & pro rec from 1830)

Name	Map Index	Date Created	Pop. By M 1980	U.S. Cen Reports Available	Parent County or Territory From Which Organized	County Seat
Prairie	B3	1846	10	1850-80	Pulaski, Monroe	Des Arc 72040 & De Valls Bluff 72041

(Part of the county was taken from Monroe in 1869; Check Monroe County for records prior to this date) (Some of Lonoke County records are in Des Arc) (Co Clk in DeValls Bluff has m, div, pro, civ ct, Ind rec from 1885 to present; Naturalization rec 1907-1912; Discharge records beginning with World War I) (Bur Vit Statisitcs, Little Rock has b, d rec.) (LDS Church has microfilmed this county's records and they are available at the Arkansas State History Commission)

Pulaski	C3	1818	341	1830-80	Arkansas	Little Rock 72201

(Co Clk has m rec from 1838; pro rec from 1820; Ind rec from 1838; Voter Reg Rec from 1965; Poll tax rec from 1892; Bur vit statistics, Little Rock has b, d rec)

* Randolph	A3	1835	17	1840-80	Lawrence	Pocahontas 72455

(Co Clk has m from 1836, div from 1841, pro, civ ct & Ind rec from 1836)

* St. Francis	B4	1827	31	1830-80	Phillips	Forrest City 72207

(Co Clk has m rec from 1875; pro rec from 1910, Ind rec; Cir Clk has div, civ ct rec; Bur Vit Statistics has b, d rec)

*§ Saline	C2	1835	53	1840-80	Pulaski, Hempstead	Benton 72015

(Co Clk has m & pro rec from 1836, Ind from 1871)

*§ Scott	B1	1833	10	1840-80	Pulaski, Crawford, Pope	Waldron 72958

(Co Clk has m, div, pro, civ ct rec from 1883; deeds & mortgages from 1882; tax rec from 1832; Bur Vit Statistics, Little Rock has b, d rec)

§ Searcy	A2	1838	9	1840-80	Marion	Marshall 72650

(Co Clk has m, div, pro & civ ct rec from 1881, deed rec from 1866)

* Sebastian	B1	1851	95	1860-80	Scott, Polk, Crawford, Van Buren	Fort Smith 72901
						Greenwood 72936

(Co Clk has m rec from 1865; pro rec 1866; Cir Clk has div, civ ct, Ind rec; Bur Vit Statistics has b, d rec)

* Sevier	C1	1828	14	1830-80	Hempstead, Miller	De Queen 71832

(Co Clk has m, pro rec from 1829; Cir Clk has div, civ ct, Ind rec; Bur Vit Statistics has b, d rec from 1914)

Sharp	A3	1868	15	1870-80	Lawrence	Ash Flat 72513

(line between Sharp & Izard changed 1877)

Stone	A3	1873	9	1880	Izard, Independence, Searcy, Van Buren	Mountain View 72560

(Co Clk has m, div, pro & civ ct rec 1873)

* Union	D2	1829	49	1830-80	Hempstead, Clark	El Dorado 71730

(Co Clk has m, pro rec from 1846; Cir Clk has div, civ ct, Ind rec; Bur Vit Statistics has b, d rec)

Van Buren	B2	1833	13	1840-80	Independence, Conway, Izard	Clinton 72031

(Co Clk has m from 1859, div from 1874, pro from 1860, civ ct & Ind rec from 1959)

* Washington	A1	1828	99	1830-80	Crawford	Fayetteville 72701

(Co Clk has m, & pro from 1845; Clk Cir Ct has div, civ ct rec & Ind rec) (Courthouse burned during CW, rec saved)

* White	B3	1835	51	1840-80	Pulaski, Jackson, Independence	Searcy 72143

(This county has never had a disaster in its courthouse and its records go back to the beginning of the county. Some are scattered in misc. vols. The staff does not have time to search records, but all crspd is referred to a professinal researcher for answering) (Co Clk has m, div, pro, civ ct, Ind, wills, tax, misc rec)

Woodruff	B3	1862	11	1870-80	Jackson, St. Francis	Augusta 72006

(Co Clk has m & pro rec from 1865)

* Yell	B2	1840	17	1850-80	Pope, Scott	Danville 72833 & Dardanelle (1) 72834

* - At least one county history has been published about this county.

§ - Inventory of county archives was made by the Historical Records Survey. (see introduction)

CALIFORNIA

CAPITAL, SACRAMENTO - STATE 1850 - (31ST)

Various expeditions from Mexico, Spain, Russia and England visited California from 1540 to 1792. The first permanent settlement was made in 1769 by Spaniards on San Diego Bay. Spanish and Mexican settlers began to develop the area along the coast. An American sailing vessel first reached the coast in 1796. In 1839 a Swiss, John Augustus Sutter, established the "Kingdom of New Helvetia" in the Sacramento River Valley. Americans began to arrive overland in significant numbers in 1841. Spain controlled until 1822 when Mexico came into possession and held power until 1846. In 1848 it ceded California to the United States. The fever that struck all sections of the United States and every country of Europe with the finding of gold at Sutter's Mill brought people to California from all parts of the world. The gold rush increased the population from 15,000 to 250,000. In 1957 the population was more than eleven million. About one tenth of the population is foreign born.

The foreign born residents of California, listed in point of numbers, originated in the following countries: Mexico, Canada, Italy, England and Wales, Russia, Germany, Sweden, Ireland, Scotland, Poland, Austria, France, Denmark, Norway, Switzerland, Portugal, Greece, Yugoslavia, Hungary, Netherlands, Spain, Finland, Czechoslovakia, Rumania, Lithuania, and Belgium.

Records of births, deaths, and marriages since 1905 are on file in the Office of the State Registrar, 410 N Street, Sacramento, CA 95814.

Records prior to July 1, 1905 are available in the Offices of the County Recorders and in many of the Health Departments of the larger cities.

The Bureau of Records and Statistics, address as above, and all County Clerks have records of marriage licenses issued in the respective counties.

Divorce records are available in the office of the Clerk of the Superior Court in the county in which the proceedings were conducted.

Many of the County Recorders have early birth and marriage records. County Clerks have divorce, probate, civil court and other records of interest to genealogists.

Naturalization records are kept in the county offices of the Superior Courts, and also in the United States Circuit Courts in Los Angeles and San Francisco.

Deeds for real estate and lands are filed in the office of the County Recorder in the county in which the land concerned is located.

A communication from the Chief of the Bureau of Records and Statistics and the Chief of the Vital Records Section of the Department of Public Health says, "In the case of a request for a search for an unknown event, we require a fee (make inquiry as to amount), paid in advance. An example of this kind of a record search is when a person was last known to be alive on a given date, and we are asked to search for a death record of the person from that date forward.

"There are certain items of information which we require in order to make a search of our records. These items vary with the type of record sought and the time period involved.

"As we now have over ten million records on file, duplication of names is common. It is therefore desirable that secondary identifying data be furnished."

Genealogical Archives, Libraries, Societies, and Publications

Amador County Genealogical Society, P.O. Box 1115, Sutter Creek, CA 95685.

Antelope Valley Genealogical Society, P.O. Box 1049, Lancaster, CA 93534.

Bancroft Library, University of California, Berkeley, CA 94720.

California Central Coast Genealogical Society, P.O. Box 832, Morro Bay, CA 93442.

California Genealogical Society, 2099 Pacific Ave., San Francisco, CA 94115.

California Historical Society, 2090 Jackson St., San Francisco, CA 94109.

California State Archives, Rm. 200, 1020 "O" St., Sacramento, CA 95814.

California State Library, Capitol Mall, Sacramento, CA 95814.

California State Library (Sutro Branch), 2945 Golden Gate Ave., San Francisco, CA 94118.

Contra Costa County Genealogical Society, P.O. Box 910, Concord, CA 94522.

East Bay Genealogical Society, 918 Willow Street, Alameda, CA 94501.

El Dorado Research Society, P.O. Box 56, El Dorado, CA 95623.

Fresno California Genealogical Society, P.O. Box 2042, Fresno, CA 93718.

Genealogical Association of Sacramento, P.O. Box 28301, Sacramento, CA 95828.

Genealogical Society of Riverside, P.O. Box 2664, Riverside, CA 92506.

Genealogical Society of Santa Cruz County, P.O. Box 72, Santa Cruz, CA 95060.

Genealogical Society of Siskiyou County, P.O. Box 225, Yreka, CA 96097.

Genealogy Collection, San Francisco Public Library, Civic Center, San Francisco, CA 94102.

Hayward Area Genealogical Society, P.O. Box 754, Hayward, CA 94543.

Hi Desert Genealogical Society, P.O. Box 616, Victorville, CA 92392.

Historical Society of Southern California, 200 E. Ave. 43, Los Angeles, CA 90031.

Humboldt County Genealogical Society, P.O. Box 868, Arcata, CA 95527.

Huntington Beach Library, 7111 Talbert, Huntington Beach, CA 92648.

Huntington Library, The. San Marino, CA 91108.

Imperial County Genealogical Society, P.O. Box 2643, El Centro, CA 92244.

Kern County Genealogical Society, P.O. Box 2214, Bakersfield, CA 93303.

Lake County Genealogical Society, P.O. Box 1323, Lakeport, CA 95453.

Long Beach Public Library, Ocean at Pacific Ave., Long Beach, CA 90802.

Los Angeles Public Library, 630 West Fifth, Los Angeles, CA 90071.

Los Banos, California Genealogical Society, P.O. Box 1106, Los Banos, CA 93635.

Marin County Genealogical Society, P.O. Box 1511, Novato, CA 94947.

Mendocino Coast Genealogical Society, P.O. Box 762, Fort Bragg, CA 95437.

Mojave Desert Genealogical Society, The, P.O. Box 1320, Barstow, CA 92311.

Montrose Library, Montrose, CA 91020.

Napa Valley Genealogical and Biographical Society, P.O. Box 385, Napa, CA 94550.

North San Diego County Genealogical Society, Inc., P.O. Box 581, Carlsbad, CA 92008.

Oakland Public Library, 14th and Oak St., Oakland, CA 94612.

Orange County Genealogical Society, P.O. Box 1587, Orange, CA 92668.

Paradise Genealogical Society, P.O. Box 335, Paradise, CA 95969.

Pasadena Public Library, 285 East Walnut St., Pasadena, CA 91101.

Plumas County Historical Society, P.O. Box 695, Quincy, CA 95971.

Pomona Public Library, 625 South Garey Ave., P.O. Box 2271, Pomona, CA 91766.

Pomona Valley Genealogical Society, P.O. Box 286, Pomona, CA 91766.

Questing Heirs Genealogical Society, P.O. Box 15102, Long Beach, CA 90813.

Redwood Genealogical Society, Box 645, Fortuna, CA 95540.

Riverside Public Library, Box 468, 3581 7th St., Riverside, CA 92502.

Sacramento Genealogical Society, 5240 Tyosa Street, Fair Oaks, CA 95628.

San Bernardino Valley Genealogical Society, P.O. Box 2505, San Bernardino, CA 92406.

San Diego Genealogical Society, 3030 Kellogg Street, San Diego, CA 92106.

San Diego Public Library, 820 "E" St., San Diego, CA 92101.

San Joaquin Genealogical Society, P.O. Box 4817, Stockton, CA 95104.

San Mateo County Historical Association, San Mateo Junior College, San Mateo, CA 94402.

Santa Barbara County Genealogical Society, P.O. Box 1174, Goleta, CA 93017.

Santa Clara County Historical and Genealogical Society, 2635 Homestead Road, Santa Clara, CA 95051.

Santa Clara County Free Library, 1095 N. 7th St., San Jose, CA 95112.

Santa Maria Valley Genealogical Society, P.O. Box 1215, Santa Maria, CA 93453.

Santa Rosa-Sonoma County Library, Third and E Sts., Santa Rosa, CA 95404.

Genealogical Archives, Libraries, Societies, and Publications

Sequoia Genealogical Society, Inc., P.O. Box 3473, Visalia, CA 90807.

Shasta Historical Society, P.O. Box 277, Redding, CA 96001.

Shasta Genealogical Society, Box 793, Anderson, CA 96007.

Shields Library, University of California, Davis, CA 95616.

Siskiyou County Public Library, 719 4th St., Yreka, CA 96097.

Society of California Pioneers, 456 McAllister St., San Francisco, CA 94102.

Society of Mayflower Desc. in the State of California, 681 Market St., Room 670, San Francisco, CA 94105.

Sonoma County Genealogical Society, P.O. Box 2273, Santa Rosa, CA 95405.

South Bay Genealogical Society, 1121 8th Street, Manhattan Beach, CA 90206.

South Bay Cities Genealogical Society, P.O. Box 5341, Torrance, CA 90510.

South County Branch, California Central Coast Genealogical Society, 421 Cornwall, Arroyo Grande, CA 93420.

Southern California Genealogical Society, 103 South Golden Mall, Burbank, CA 91502.

Spanishtown Historical Society, Box 62, Half Moon Bay, CA 94019.

Sutter-Yuba Genealogical Society, P.O. Box 1274, Yuba City, CA 95991.

Tulare Public Library, 113 N. F St., Tulare, CA 93274.

Tuolumne County Genealogical Society, The Golden Roots of the Mother Lode, P.O. Box 3956, Sonora, CA 95370.

Ukiah Tree Tracers Genealogical Society, P.O. Box 72, Ukiah, CA 95482.

Whittier College Library, Whittier, CA 90602.

Yorba Linda Genealogical Society, c/o The Yorba Linda District Library, 18262 Lemon Drive, Yorba Linda, CA 92686.

Ancestors West, published by the Santa Barbara Genealogical Society, P.O. Box 1174, Goleta, CA 93017.

Ash Tree Echo, Fresno Genealogical Society, P.O. Box 2042, Fresno, CA 93718.

Bulletin of California Central Coast Genealogical Society, P.O. Box 832, Morro Bay, CA 93442.

Kern-Gen, Kern County Genealogical Society, P.O. Box 2214, Bakersfield, CA 93303.

Kinships, quarterly publication of the South Bay Cities Genealogical Society, P.O. Box 5341, Torrance, CA 90510.

Lifeliner, Genealogical Society of Riverside, P.O. Box 2664, Riverside, CA 92506.

Marin Kin Tracer, The, publication of the Marin County Genealogical Society, P.O. Box 1511, Novato, CA 94947.

Mojave Nugget, The, the Mojave Desert Genealogical Society, P.O. Box 1320, Barstow, CA 92311.

Searcher, The, quarterly publication of the Southern California Genealogical Society, 103 South Golden Mall, Burbank, CA 91502.

Under Construction, newsletter of the Mendocino Coast Genealogical Society, P.O. Box 762, Fort Bragg, CA 95437.

Ventura County Genealogical Society Quarterly, P.O. Box D N, Ventura, CA 93001.

Printed Census Records and Mortality Schedules

State indexes - 1850

Other printed census records -
  Counties:

Humboldt - 1860
Kern - 1870
Los Angeles - 1830, 1850, 1860
Mariposa - 1852
San Diego - 1850, 1860, 1870, 1880
San Luis Obispo - 1870, 1880
Shasta - 1850

Europeans in 1850, 1852, 1860, 1870, 1880 Census of Los Angeles.

1880 Census of Riverside Precinct, San Bernardino County.

1860 Census of the Portion of Tulare County that became Kern County in 1866.

1860 Hungarians in San Francisco

Valuable Printed Sources

Atlas

Beck, Warren A. and Ynez D. Haase. *Historical Atlas of California.* Norman, Oklahoma: University of Oklahoma Press, 1974.

Place Names

Gudde, Erwin Gustav. *California Place Names: The Origin and Etymology of Current Geographical Names.* Revised edition. Berkeley: University of California Press, 1969. (3rd Edition, revised and enlarged, includes maps and reference list of obsolete names.)

Hanna, Phil Townsend. *The Dictionary of California Land Names.* Los Angeles: Automobile Club of Southern California, 1951. (Revised and enlarged).

Sanchez, Nellie. *Spanish and Indian Place Names of California Their Meaning and Romance.* San Francisco: A. M. Robertson, 1930.

Guides To Genealogical Research

Barton, Noel R. "Genealogical Research in the Records of the California Spanish Mission," *Genealogical Journal,* Vol. 4, number 1 (Mar. 1975), pages 13-33. Salt Lake City: Utah Genealogical Association, 1975.

Lo Buglio, Rudecinda. *"Survey of Prestatehood Records: A New Look at Spanish and Mexican-California Genealogical Records",* Spanish-American Genealogist, Numbers 35-38 (1980): 625-81. (Also in World Conference on Records Lecture Paper, Vol. 9, Number 714. Salt Lake City: G.S., 1980).

Parker, J. Carlyle. *Sources of Californiana: From Padron to Voter Registration.* Salt Lake City: Genealogical Society of The Church of Jesus Christ of Latter-day Saints, 1969. (World conference on Records Series I No. 34; film 897,217-31).

Schwartz, Mary and Luana Gilstrap. *A Guide to Reference Aids for Genealogists:* 3rd edition. Culver City, California: Genealogy Publishing Service, 1981.

Temple, Thomas Workman II. *Sources for Tracing Spanish-American Pedigrees in the Southwestern United States: Part II, California and Arizona.* Salt Lake City: The Genealogical Sosociety of The Church of Jesus Christ of Latter-day Saints, 1969. (World Conference on Records Series F No. 14B; film 897,215-35).

Genealogical Sources

Bancroft, Hubert Howe. *Register of Pioneer Inhabitants of California, 1542 to 1848, and Index to Information Concerning them in Bancroft's History of California, Volumes I to V.* Los Angeles: Dawson's Book Shop, 1964, and Baltimore: Regional Publishing Company, 1964.

California Adjutant Geneal's Office. *Records of California Men in the War of the Rebellion, 1861-1867.* Revised and compiled by Brig. Gen. Richard H. Orton. Sacramento: State Office of Printing, 1890.

California Voter Registration Records. Prior to 1900 some of these records have been indexed on a county basis. Available at California State Library, Sacramento, California.*

D.A.R., California. Genealogical Records Committee. *Vital Records from Cemeteries in California. 1934-.*

Northrop, Marie E. *Spanish-Mexican Families of Early California: 1769-1850.* New Orleans, Louisiana: Polyanthos Inc., 1976.

Parker, J. Carlyle. *A Personal Name Index to Orton's "Records of California Men in the War of the Rebellion, 1861-1867."* Detroit: Gale Research Company, 1978.

Parker, J. Carlyle. *An Index to the Biographies in 19th Century California Histories.* Detroit, Michigan: Gale Research Company, 1979.

Parker, Nathan C. *Personal Name Index to the 1856 City Directories of California.* Detroit, Michigan: Gale Research Company, 1980.

Rasmussen, Louis J. *California Wagon Lists.* 2 Vols. Colma, California: San Francisco Historic Records, 1976-. *Railway Passenger Lists of Overland Trains to San Francisco and the West.* 2 Vols. Colma: San Francisco Historic Record. 1966.

Rasmussen, Louis J. *San Francisco Ship Passenger Lists.* Baltimore: Genealogical Publishing Company, 1978.

Society of California Archivists. *Directory of Archival and Manuscript Repositories in California.* Redlands: Printed Beacon Printery, 1975.

Spinazze, Libera Martina. *Index to the Argonauts of California by Charles Warren Haskins.* New Orleans: Polyanthos, 1975.

Vital Records of the San Francisco Daily Bulletin, 1855-1906, 20 Vols. *

Histories

Canghey, John W. *California: A Remarkable State: Life History,* 3rd edition. Englewood Cliffs, New Jersey: Prentice-Hall, 1970.

Bibliographies

Dillon, Richard H., ed. "Local Indexes in California Libraries," *New Notes of California Libraries,* Vol. 49, pages 501-542, Oct. 1954.

Rocq, Margaret Miller. *California Local History: A Bibliography and Union List of Library Holdings.* 2nd edition, revised and enlarged. Stanford: Stanford University Press, 1970.

---

*Microfilm - Genealogical Society of The Church of Jesus Christ of Latter-day Saints, Salt Lake City, Utah.

CALIFORNIA COUNTY HISTORIES
(Population figures to nearest thousand - 1980 U.S. Census)

Name	Map Index	Date Created	Pop. By M 1980	U.S. Cen Reports Available	Parent County or Territory From Which Organized	County Seat
*§ Alameda	C2	1853	1,101	1860-80	Contra Costa & Santa Clara	Oakland 94612
(Co Clk has b from 1919 (some prior to 1919) m, div, civ ct from 1853)						
Alpine	C2	1864	1,000	1870-80	Eldorado, Amador, Calaveras	Markleeville 96120
(Co Clk has b, m, d, div, pro, civ ct & Ind rec from 1900)						
* Amador	C2	1854	19	1860-80	Calaveras	Jackson 95642
(Co Clk has b, d rec from 1872; m, div, pro, civ ct, Ind rec from 1854)						
Branciforte (changed to Santa Cruz 1850)						
* Butte	B2	1850	144	1850-80	Original county	Oroville 95965
(Co Rcdr has b, m, d & Ind rec; Co Clk has div, pro & civ rec from 1850)						
Calaveras	C2	1850	20	1850-80	Original county	San Andreas 95249
(Co Clk has b from 1860, m, d & div from 1882, pro & civ ct rec from 1866, Ind rec from 1852, mining claims from 1850)						
* Colusa	C2	1850	13	1850-80	Original county	Colusa 95932
(Colusa County was created in 1850 but attached to Butte County for administration until it was organized in January, 1851. Co Clk has b rec from 1873; m rec from 1853; d rec from 1889; pro, civ ct, Ind and assessment rolls from 1851; Great Registers from 1866; mil rolls from 1879. Note: There is a fee of $2.00 per hour when staff is requested to search records)						
* Contra Costa	C2	1850	651	1860-80	Original county	Martinez 94553
(Co Clk has b, m, d, div, pro, civ ct, Ind rec from 1850)						
* Del Norte	A1	1857	18	1860-80	Klamath	Crescent City 95531
(Co Clk has div, pro & civ ct rec from 1848; Co Rcdr has b, m, d & Ind rec)						
* El Dorado	C2	1850	86	1850-80	Original county	Placerville 95667
(Co Clk has civ ct and pro rec; Co Rcdr has d, m, b rec)						
*§ Fresno	D2	1856	507	1860-80	Merced, Mariposa	Fresno 93721
(Co Clk has b, m, d rec 1855-1979)						
Glenn	B2	1891	21		Colusa	Willows 95988
(Co Clk has m, div, pro, civ ct rec from 1891)						
* Humboldt	B1	1853	108	1860-80	Trinity	Eureka 95501
(Co Clk has m, div, pro, civ ct rec; Co Rcdr has d and Ind rec)						
* Imperial	G4	1907	92		San Diego	El Centro 92243
(Co Clk has m, div, pro & civ ct rec from 1907; Co Rcdr has b, m & d rec from 1907)						
* Inyo	E3	1866	18	1870-80	Tulare	Independence 93526
(Co Clk has b, d rec from 1904; m, Ind rec from 1866; mining rec from 1872)						

COUNTY MAP FOR THE STATE OF CALIFORNIA

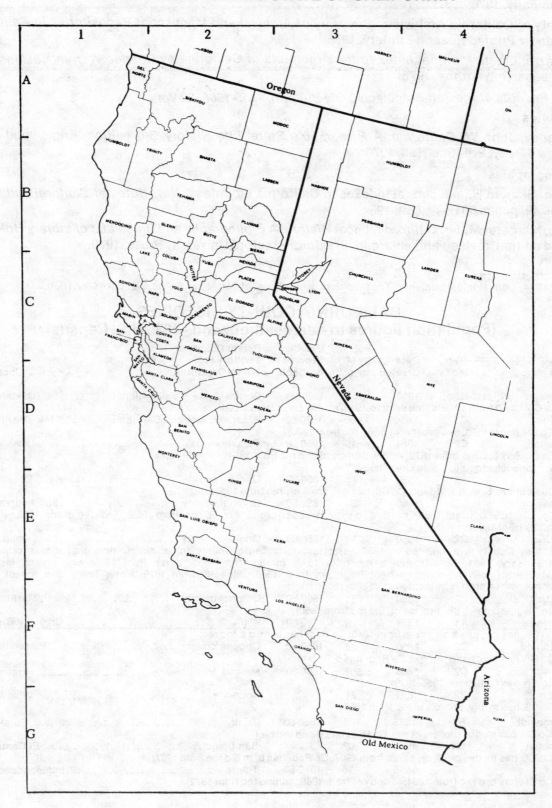

Name	Map Index	Date Created	Pop. By M 1980	U.S. Cen Reports Available	Parent County or Territory From Which Organized	County Seat
*§ Kern	E3	1866	402	1870-80	Tulare, Los Angeles	Bakersfield 93301

(Co Clk has div, pro & civ ct rec from 1866; Co Rcdr has b, m & d rec; An exchange of territory with San Bernardino Co in 1963; Co Clk has registration voting rec from 1866)

| * Kings | E2 | 1893 | 74 | | Tulare, Fresno | Hanford 93230 |

(Co Clk has b, m, d, div, pro, civ ct, naturalization rec from 1893. Each cem district has bur rec)

| * Lake | C1 | 1861 | 37 | 1870-80 | Napa | Lakeport 95453 |

(Co Clk has b, m, d, Ind rec from 1867; Co Clk has mining rec, misc rec; Clk Sup Ct has div, pro, civ ct rec)

| * Lassen | B2 | 1864 | 22 | 1870-80 | Plumas, Shasta | Susanville 96130 |

(Co Clk has div, pro & civ ct rec from 1864; Co Rcdr has b, m, d & Ind rec)

| *§ Los Angeles | F3 | 1850 | 7,445 | 1850-80 | Original county | Los Angeles 90012 |

(Co Clk has div rec from 1880, pro & civ ct rec from 1850 & criminal rec; Co Rcdr has b, m, d & Ind rec)

| * Madera | D2 | 1893 | 63 | | Mariposa, Fresno | Madera 93637 |

(Co Clk has b, m, d, div, pro, civ ct, Ind rec from 1893, some voting rec)

| *§ Marin | C1 | 1850 | 217 | 1850-80 | Original county | San Rafael 94903 |

(Co Rcdr has b, d rec from 1863; m rec from 1856; Ind rec from 1852; Co Clk has div, civ ct rec from 1900; pro rec from 1880)

| * Mariposa | D2 | 1850 | 11 | 1850-80 | Original county | Mariposa 95338 |

(Co Clk has div, pro & civ ct rec; Co Rcdr has b, m, d & bur rec; the dates on all these rec are indefinite)

| * Mendocino | B1 | 1850 | 67 | 1850-80 | Original county | Ukiah 95482 |

(Co Clk has div rec from 1858, pro from 1872, civ ct rec from 1858; Co Rcdr has b, m, d & Ind rec) (Some old rec in Sonoma Co)

| * Merced | D2 | 1855 | 134 | 1860-80 | Mariposa | Merced 95341 |

(Co Clk has div, pro & civ ct rec from 1855; Co Rcdr has b, m, d & bur rec)

| Modoc | A3 | 1874 | 9 | 1880 | Siskiyou | Alturas 96101 |

(Co Clk has div, pro, civ ct, voter registration rec from 1874; Co Rcdr has b, m, d rec)

| *§ Mono | D3 | 1861 | 9 | 1870-80 | Calaveras, Fresno | Bridgeport 93517 |

(Co Clk has b, m rec from 1861; d, bur, div, pro, civ ct, Ind rec from 1900)

| * Monterey | D2 | 1850 | 283 | 1850-80 | Original county | Salinas 93901 |

| *§ Napa | C2 | 1850 | 97 | 1850-80 | Original county | Napa 94558 |

(Co Clk has div, pro & civ ct rec from 1850; Co Rcdr has b, m, d & Ind rec)

| * Nevada | C2 | 1851 | 52 | 1860-80 | Yuba | Nevada City 95959 |

(Co Clk has b rec from 1873, m from 1856, d from 1873, div, pro, civ ct from 1880, Ind rec from 1856)

| * Orange | F3 | 1889 | 1,926 | | Los Angeles | Santa Ana 92701 |

(Co Rcdr has b, m, d & Ind rec; Co Clk has div, pro & civ ct rec from 1889)

| * Placer | C2 | 1851 | 117 | 1860-80 | Yuba, Sutter | Auburn 95603 |

(Co Clk has b, m, d rec from 1873; pro rec from 1851; civ ct rec from 1880; Ind rec from 1951)

| * Plumas | B2 | 1854 | 17 | 1860-80 | Butte | Quincy 95971 |

(Co Clk has div, pro & civ ct rec from 1860)

| * Riverside | F4 | 1893 | 660 | | San Diego, San Bernardino | Riverside 92501 |

(Co Clk has div, pro & civ ct rec from 1893; Co Rcdr has b, m, d & Ind rec from 1893)

| * Sacramento | C2 | 1850 | 780 | 1850-80 | Original county | Sacramento 95814 |

(Co Clk has div, pro & civ ct rec from 1880; Co Rcdr has b, m, d & Ind rec)

| *§ San Benito | D2 | 1874 | 25 | 1880 | Monterey | Hollister 95023 |

(Co Clk has b, m, d, div, pro civ ct, Ind rec from 1900)

| *§ San Bernardino | F4 | 1853 | 878 | 1860-80 | Los Angeles | San Bernardino 92401 |

(Co Clk has m lic rec from 1887, div and pro from 1856, civ and crim rec from 1853, insanity and inebriate rec from 1887, guardianship rec from 1856, Ind rec from 1854; Co Rcdr has b, d rec from 1853, m rec from 1857)

| *§ San Diego | G3 | 1850 | 1,857 | 1850-80 | Original county | San Diego 92101 |

(Co Clk has div, pro & civ ct rec from 1855)

| *§ San Francisco | C1 | 1850 | 674 | 1860-80 | Original county | San Francisco 94101 |

(Co Clk has div, pro & civ ct rec from 1906; Health Officer has b, & bur rec; Co Rcdr has m rec)

| * San Joaquin | C2 | 1850 | 347 | 1850-80 | Original county | Stockton 95202 |

(Co Clk has div, pro & civ ct rec from 1851; Co Rcdr has b, m, d, Ind & Clk of Board of Supervisors)

| *§ San Luis Obispo | E2 | 1850 | 155 | 1850-80 | Original county | San Luis Obispo 93401 & Templeton 93465 |

(Co Rcdr has b, m, d & Ind rec; Co Clk has div, pro & civ ct rec from 1854)

| *§ San Mateo | D1 | 1856 | 583 | 1860-80 | San Francisco | Redwood City 94063 |

(Co Rcdr has b, m, d rec from 1866, div, civ ct, Ind from 1880, pro from 1856)

| *§ Santa Barbara | E2 | 1850 | 298 | 1850-80 | Original county | Santa Barbara 93104 |

(Co Clk has b rec from 1873, m rec from 1850, d rec from 1878, div, pro, civ ct rec from 1850)

Name	Map Index	Date Created	Pop. By M 1980	U.S. Cen Reports Available	Parent County or Territory From Which Organized	County Seat
*§ Santa Clara	D2	1850	1,290	1860-80	Original county	San Jose 95110

(Co Clk has pro rec from 1850; Co Rcdr has b, d rec from 1873, m rec from 1850 and deeds from 1846. Note: b and d rec are scattered ones where were recorded voluntarily. On July 1, 1905 it became obligatory to record these records)

* Santa Cruz	D1	1850	187	1850-80	Original county (formerly Branciforte)	Santa Cruz 95060

(Co Clk has b & d from 1873, m from 1852, bur from 1905, div, pro, civ ct, Ind from 1850, naturalizations & voters registration rec from 1866)

Shasta	B2	1850	115	1850-80	Original county	Redding 96001

(Co Clk has div, pro & civ ct rec from 1880; Co Rcdr has b, m & d rec)

Sierra	C2	1852	3	1860-80	Yuba	Downieville 95936

(Co Clk has b, m, d, div, pro & civ ct rec from 1852, also register of voters from 1852)

* Siskiyou	A2	1852	40	1860-80	Shasta, Klamath	Yreka 96097

(Co Rcdr has b, m, d, bur, rec; Co Clk has div, pro, civ ct rec from 1853; Co Clk has election rec, board of supervisor's minutes from 1860)

* Solano	C2	1850	228	1850-80	Original county	Fairfield 94533

(Co Rcdr has b, m, d, Ind rec; bur rec are maintained by cem district; Co Clk has div, pro, civ ct rec from 1850)

* Sonoma	C1	1850	292	1850-80	Original county	Santa Rosa 95402

(Co Rcdr has b, m, d, bur, Ind rec; Co Clk has div, pro, civ ct rec from 1850)

* Stanislaus	D2	1854	266	1860-80	Tuolumne	Modesto 95350

(Co Clk has div, pro & civ ct rec from 1854; Co Rcdr has b, m & d rec)

* Sutter	C2	1850	52	1850-80	Original county	Yuba City 95991

(Co Clk has div, pro & civ ct rec from 1850)

Tehama	C2	1856	39	1860-80	Colusa, Butte, Shasta	Red Bluff 96080

(Co Clk has b & d rec from 1889, m from 1856, div, pro, civ ct & Ind rec from 1856)

* Trinity	B1	1850	12	1860-80	Original county	Weaverville 96093

(Co Clk has b, m, d, bur, div, pro, civ ct, Ind, misc mining, newspaper rec from 1860)

* Tulare	E2	1852	245	1860-80	Mariposa	Visalia 93277

(Co Clk has div, pro & civ ct rec; Co Rcdr has b, m, d & bur rec; Co Asr has Ind rec)

* Tuolumne	C2	1850	34	1850-80	Original county	Sonora 95370

(Co Clk Rcdr has b from 1858, m from 1850, d from 1859, bur from 1916, div, pro, civ ct & Ind from 1850, old newspapers from 1862 to 1948)

*§ Ventura	F2	1872	529	1880	Santa Barbara	Ventura 93001 (San Buena Ventura)

(Co Clk Rcdr has b, m, d, div, pro & civ ct from 1873; Ind rec from 1871)

* Yolo	C2	1850	113	1850-80	Original county	Woodland 95695

(Co Clk has b, m, d & Ind rec, div, pro & civ ct rec from 1850)

* Yuba	C2	1850	50	1850-80	Original county	Marysville 95902

(Co Clk has m from 1865, div, pro & civ ct rec from 1850, voting rec 1866)

* - At least one county history has been published about this county.

§ - Inventory of county archives was made by the Historical Records Survey. (see introduction)

COLORADO

CAPITAL, DENVER - TERRITORY 1861 - STATE 1876 - (38TH)

Dr. LeRoy R. Hafen, for many years executive director of the State Historical Society of Colorado and the author of several works on Colorado, says, "Colorado was named for the great river that rises in the snowbanks of her western slope. The musical Spanish word meaning 'red' was bestowed on the river by Spanish explorers a century before it was applied to Colorado Territory."

The Colorado area, first claimed by France and Spain in the 18th century, was acquired in part by the Louisiana Purchase (1803) and explored by U.S. Army officers Zebulon Pike (1806), Stephen Long (1819-20), and John Fremont (1842-43). Additional lands came from Mexico in 1848 as a result of the Mexican War, and from Texas in 1850.

Early Spanish explorers who came to Mexico heard the natives tell exciting tales of cities of gold and silver to the north. To find the precious metals many of these fortune hunters pressed northward, some of them coming into sections of the present New Mexico, Arizona, Utah, and Colorado. Some of these adventurers were the first white men to see the Grand Canyon of the Colorado, the Rio Grande Valley, and other sections of the Rocky Mountain Territory. Escalante, the Catholic priest who tried to find a shortcut from Santa Fe to the Pacific coast, came through there on his unsuccessful trip in the summer of 1776.

About fifty years later these sections swarmed with competing trappers and fur traders working for the various large fur companies of the eastern United States and Canada.

The real settlers of Colorado didn't come until 1858, thus making the state the last to be occupied by permanent settlers. Many of the first comers were attracted there by the discovery of gold and other metals. Not too successful in their fortune hunt, they turned to the land and the ranges for their livelihood.

The territory of Jefferson was voted by the residents in 1859 but was never recognized by congress. Thus some of the counties have organization dates and records prior to 28 February 1861 when the Territory of Colorado was recognized.

The 1860 Census showed a population of about 33,000 men, and 1,500 women. This was taken when Colorado was still a part of Kansas.

The first territorial assembly created the first seventeen counties in September 1861. They were Arapahoe, Boulder, Clear Creek, Costilla, Douglas, El Paso, Fremont, Gilpin, Guadalupe (later named Conejos), Huerfano, Jefferson, Lake, Larimer, Park, Pueblo, Summit and Weld.

A few birth records before January 1907 may be obtained from the respective county registrars, after January 1907 from the State Bureau of Vital Statistics, Denver, Colorado 80202.

A few death records before January 1900 may be obtained at the office of the county registrars, after January 1900 at the Bureau of Vital Statistics.

Marriage records are kept by the county clerks. Marriages were not recorded generally until after 1881, but some counties have marriage records as early as 1860.

Probate matters and wills are on file in the office of the county clerk.

All land titles, deeds, mortgages, leases, etc. are kept by the county recorder.

Genealogical Archives, Libraries, Societies, and Publications

Boulder Genealogical Society, P.O. Box 3246, Boulder, CO 80303.

Boulder Public Library, 1000 Canyon Blvd., Boulder, CO 80302.

Charles Leaming Tutt Library, Colorado College, Colorado Springs, CO 80903.

Colorado Historical Society, Colorado Heritage Center, 1300 Broadway, Denver, CO 80203.

Colorado Genealogical Society, P.O. Box 9671, Denver, CO 80209.

Colorado Springs Public Library, 21 W. Kiowa St., Colorado Springs, CO 80902.

Colorado State Archives and Public Records, 1313 Sherman, Denver, CO 80203.

Columbine Genealogical and Historical Society, Inc., P.O. Box 2074, Littleton, CO 80161.

Denver Public Library, 1357 Broadway, Denver, CO 80203.

Foothills Genealogical Society of Colorado, Inc., P.O. Box 15382, Lakewood, CO 80215.

Greeley Public Library, City Complex Bldg., 919 7th St., Greeley, CO 80631.

Historical Society Library, 14th and Sherman, Denver, CO 80203.

Larimer County Genealogical Society, 600 S. Shields Street, Fort Collins, CO 80521.

Mesa County Genealogical Society, Box 1506, Grand Junction, CO 81502.

Montrose Public Library, City Hall, Montrose, CO 81401.

Norlin Library, University of Colorado, Boulder, CO 80304.

North Fork Genealogy Society, P.O. Box 101, Paonia, CO 81428.

Penrose Public Library, 20 North Cascade, Colorado Springs, CO 80902.

Pueblo Regional Library, 100 Abriendo Ave., Pueblo, CO 81005.

Southeastern Colorado Genealogical Society, Inc., P.O. Box 4086, Pueblo, CO 81003.

Tutt Library, Colorado College, Colorado Springs, CO 80903.

Weld County Genealogical Society, P.O. Box 278, Greeley, CO 80631.

Weld County Library, 2227 23rd Ave., Greeley, CO 80631.

Genealogical Society of Weld County, Colorado Newsletter, P.O. Box 278, Greeley, CO 80631.

Genealogical Archives, Libraries, Societies, and Publications

Colorado Genealogists, The, publication of the Colorado Genealogical Society, P.O. Box 9654, Denver, CO 80209.

Foothills, quarterly publication of the Foothills Genealogical Society of Colorado, Inc., P.O. Box 15382, Lakewood, CO 80215.

Pinion Whispers, P.O. Box 4086, Pueblo, CO 81003

Printed Census Records and Mortality Schedules

State census indexes - 1850, 1860, 1870, 1880

Printed MORTALITY SCHEDULES: 1870, 1880

Valuable Printed Sources

Place Names

Crofutt, George A. *Grip Sack Guide of Colorado,* description of every city, town, village, station, postoffice and mining camp in the state. Golden, Colorado: Cubar Associates, 1885, reprinted 1966.

Dawson, J. Frank. *Place Names in Colorado.* Lakewood, Colorado: Jefferson Records, n.d.

Biographies

Byers, William Newton. *Encyclopedia of Biography of Colorado: History of Colorado.* Chicago: Century Publishing and Engraving Company, 1901.

Colorado Families: A Territorial Heritage. Denver, Colorado: Colorado Genealogical Society, 1981.

Guides

Griffin, Walter R. and Jay L. Rasmussen. *A Comprehensive Guide to the Location of Published and Unpublished Newspaper Indexes in Colorado Repositories,* 1972.

Oehlerts, D. E. *Guide to Colorado Newspapers 1859-1963.* *

Major Resource Centers

Western Historical Collection, Norlin Library, University of Colorado, Boulder, Colorado.

Special Collections

Charles L. Tutt Library, Colorado College, Colorado Springs, Colorado.

---

*Microfilm - Genealogical Society of The Church of Jesus Christ of Latter-day Saints, Salt Lake City, Utah.

COLORADO COUNTY HISTORIES
(Population figures to nearest thousand - 1980 U. S. Census)

Name	Map Index	Date Created	Pop. By M 1980	U.S. Cen Reports Available	Parent County or Territory From Which Organized	County Seat
Adams	B2	1901	245		Arapahoe	Brighton 80601
(Co Clk has m rec from 1902, bur rec from 1940, Ind rec; Bur Vit Statistics has b, d rec; Hall of Justice has div, civ ct rec)						
§ Alamosa	D4	1913	12		Costilla, Conejos	Alamosa 81101
(Co Clk has m & Ind from 1913; Clk Dis Ct has div, pro & civ ct rec)						
*§ Arapahoe	C2	1861	294	1870-80	Original county	Littleton 80120
(First formed in 1855 as Territorial County. For Arapahoe 1860 U.S. Cen figures see Kansas 1860. Co Clk has m, Ind rec from 1902, bur rec from 1941, Co Court has div, pro, civ ct rec; Bur Vit Statistics has b, d rec)						
Archuleta	E4	1885	4		Conejos	Pagosa Springs 81147
(Co Clk has m & d from 1886, Ind from 1885; Clk Dis Ct has div, pro, civ ct rec & adoptions)						
Baca	A4	1889	5		Las Animas	Springfield 81073
(Co Clk has m, Ind rec from 1889; Clk Dist Ct has div, pro, civ ct rec from 1910; Registrar of Vit Statistics as b, d rec from 1910)						
*§ Bent	B4	1874	6	1880	Greenwood	Las Animas 81054
(Co Clk has m rec from 1888, Ind rec, voters reg, plat maps from 1888; Local Rgstr has b, d rec from 1910)						

COUNTY MAP FOR THE STATE OF COLORADO

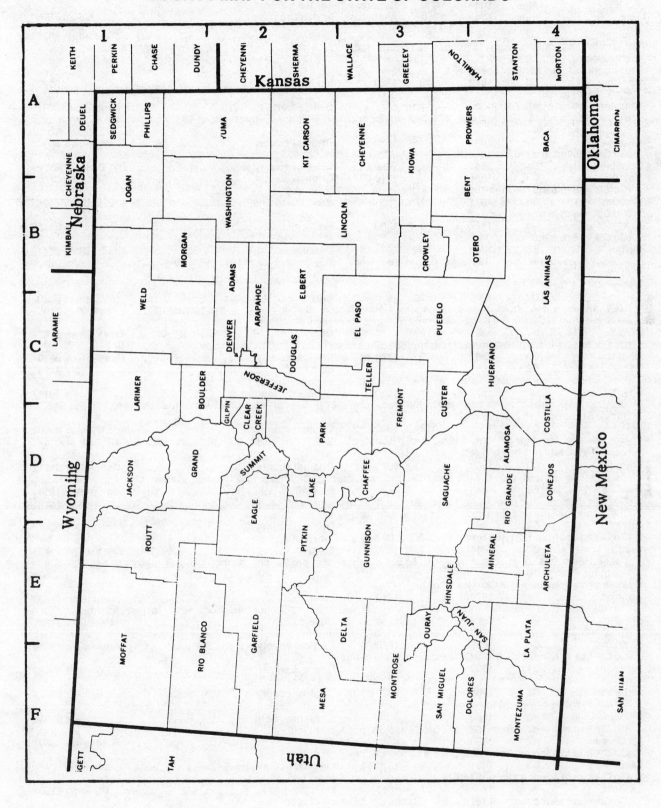

Name	Map Index	Date Created	Pop. By M 1980	U.S. Cen Reports Available	Parent County or Territory From Which Organized	County Seat
* Boulder	C2	1861	187	1870-80	Original county	Boulder 80301

(Co Clk has m rec from 1866, Ind rec from 1864; Co Health Dept has b, d rec; Civ Ct has div, pro, civ ct rec)

Carbonate (original name of Lake Co)

| Chaffee | D3 | 1879 | 13 | 1880 | Lake | Salida 81201 |

(Co Clk has m rec)

| Cheyenne | A3 | 1889 | 2 | | Bent, Elbert | Cheyenne Wells 80810 |

(Rgstr has b, d & bur rec; Co Clk has m from 1889 & Ind rec from 1888; Dis Ct has div & pro rec; Co Judge has civ ct rec)

| * Clear Creek | D2 | 1861 | 7 | 1870-80 | Original county | Georgetown 80444 |

(Co Clk has m & Ind rec from 1862)

| § Conejos | D4 | 1861 | 8 | 1880 | Original county | Conejos 81129 |
| § Costilla | C4 | 1861 | 3 | 1870-80 | Original county | San Luis 81152 |

(Co Clk has m & Ind rec from 1853; Clk Dis Ct has div, pro & civ ct rec)

| Crowley | B3 | 1911 | 3 | | Bent, Otero | Ordway 81063 |

(Co Clk has m rec)

| * Custer | C3 | 1877 | 2 | 1880 | Fremont | Westcliffe 81252 |

(Co Clk has m & bur rec)

| Delta | E3 | 1883 | 20 | | Gunnison | Delta 81416 |

(Co Clk has b rec from 1920, m, d, Ind rec from 1883, school cen 1891-1964; Dist Ct has div, pro, civ ct rec)

Denver, City & Co of

| | C2 | 1901 | 489 | | Arapahoe | Denver 80202 |

(Has annexed terr from Arapahoe, Adams & Jefferson Co on several occasions) (Co Clk has m from 1905, Ind from 1858; Clk Dis Ct has div from 1967, pro, civ ct rec from 1858)

| Dolores | F4 | 1881 | 2 | | Ouray | Dove Creek 81324 |

(Co Clk has b rec from 1882, m, Ind rec from 1881, d rec from 1895)

| Douglas | C2 | 1861 | 25 | 1870-80 | Original county | Castle Rock 80104 |
| Eagle | D2 | 1883 | 13 | | Summit | Eagle 81631 |

(Co Clk has b & m from 1883, d & Ind rec; Clk Dis Ct has div, pro & civ ct rec)

| Elbert | B2 | 1874 | 7 | 1880 | Douglas, Greenwood | Kiowa 80117 |

(Co Clk has m rec from Nov 1893, Ind rec from 1874; Clk of combined Cts has div, pro, civ ct rec; Bur Vit Statistics has b, d, bur rec)

| El Paso | C3 | 1861 | 310 | 1880 | Original county | Colorado Springs 80902 |

(Co Clk has m, Ind rec from 1861, ser discharges 1919; District ct has div, pro rec; Co Ct has civ ct rec; Bur Vit Statistics has b, d rec)

| § Fremont | C3 | 1859 | 29 | 1870-80 | Original county | Canon City 81212 |

(Co Clk has m, Ind rec; Dis Ct has div, pro, civ ct rec; City clks in Florence, Canon City have bur rec)

| § Garfield | E2 | 1883 | 22 | | Summit | Glenwood Springs 81601 |

(Co Clk has m, Ind rec from 1892; Dis Ct has div, pro, civ ct rec; Registrar has b, d rec from 1892; City clerks for Rifle and Glenwood Springs have bur rec)

| * Gilpin | C2 | 1861 | 2 | 1880 | Original county | Central City 80427 |

(Co Clk has m from 1881, Ind from 1861; Clk Dis Ct has div & pro rec)

| Grand | D2 | 1874 | 7 | 1880 | Summit | Hot Sulphur Spr. 80451 |

(Local Rgstr has b, d & bur rec; Co & Dis Ct has div, pro & civ ct rec; Co Asr has Ind rec; Co Clk has m rec from 1874)

Guadalupe (original name of Conejose Co)

| Gunnison | E3 | 1877 | 11 | 1880 | Lake | Gunnison 81230 |

(Co Clk has b, d rec from 1910, m, div, pro, Ind rec from 1877, bur rec from 1890, civ ct rec from 1900)

| § Hinsdale | E4 | 1874 | 1 | 1880 | Conejos | Lake City 81235 |

(Co Clk has b rec from 1900, m rec from 1880, d, bur, div & Ind rec; Clk Dis Ct has pro & civ ct rec)

| Huerfano | C4 | 1861 | 6 | 1870-80 | Original county | Walsenburg 81089 |

(Co Clk has m & Ind rec; Clk Dis Ct has div, pro & civ ct rec)

| * Jackson | D1 | 1909 | | | Grand, Larimer | Walden 80480 |

(Co Clk has m from 1909, bur & Ind rec; Clk Dis Ct has div, pro & civ ct rec)

| Jefferson | C2 | 1861 | 372 | 1870-80 | Original county | Golden 80401 |

(Co Clk has m rec from 1861, Ind rec from 1863)

| Kiowa | A3 | 1889 | 2 | | Cheyenne, Bent | Eads 81036 |

(Co Clk has m & Ind rec from 1889; Clk Dis Ct has div, pro & civ ct rec)

| Kit Carson | A2 | 1889 | 8 | | Elbert | Burlington 80807 |

(Co Clk has m & Ind rec from 1889; Clk Dis Ct has div, pro & civ ct rec)

| * Lake | D2 | 1861 | 9 | 1870-80 | Original county | Leadville 80461 |

(Co Clk has m & Ind rec from 1874; Clk Dis Ct has div, pro & civ ct rec)

| La Plata | E4 | 1874 | 27 | | Conejos, Lake | Durango 81301 |

(Co Clk has m & Ind rec from 1874; Clk Dis Ct has div, pro & civ ct rec)

Name	Map Index	Date Created	Pop. By M 1980	U.S. Cen Reports Available	Parent County or Territory From Which Organized	County Seat
*§ Larimer	C1	1861	148	1870-80	Original county	Fort Collins 80521

(Co Clk has m rec from 1865, Ind rec from 1862; Co Health Dept has b and d rec)

| * Las Animas | B4 | 1866 | 15 | 1880 | Huerfano | Trinidad 81082 |

(Co Clk has m rec from 1887; Ind rec from 1883, mil discharge rec from 1918; Co Pub Health Dept has b, d rec; Clk Dis Ct has div, pro, civ ct rec; individual cemeteries have bur rec, co clk has bur permits)

| Lincoln | B3 | 1889 | 5 | | Elbert | Hugo 80821 |

(Co Clk has m & Ind rec from 1889; Clk Dis Ct has div, pro & civ ct rec)

| *§ Logan | B1 | 1887 | 20 | | Weld | Sterling 80751 |

(Co Clk has m, Ind, homestead, mil discharges, voter reg rec from 1887; Co Health Dept has b, d rec; Dis Ct has div, pro, civ ct rec)

| * Mesa | F3 | 1883 | 81 | | Gunnison | Grand Junction 81501 |

(Co Clk has m, Ind rec from 1883; Co Health Dept has b, d rec; Dis Ct has div, pro, civ ct rec; City of Grand Junction or Co Health Dept has bur rec)

| Mineral | E4 | 1892 | 1 | | Hinsdale | Creede 81130 |

(Co Clk has m & Ind rec from 1893; Clk Dis Ct has div, pro & civ ct rec)

| Moffatt | E1 | 1911 | 13 | | Routt | Craig 81625 |

(Co Clk has m rec from 1911; Clk Dis Ct has div, pro & civ ct rec)

| * Montezuma | F4 | 1889 | 16 | | La Plata | Cortez 81321 |
| Montrose | F3 | 1883 | 24 | | Gunnison | Montrose 81401 |

(Co Clk has b, m, d, Ind rec from 1883)

| § Morgan | B1 | 1889 | 22 | | Weld | Fort Morgan 80701 |

(Co Clk has m, Ind rec from 1889; Co Health Dept has b, d rec from 1910; Clk Dis Ct has div, pro rec from 1889; Co Ct has civ ct rec from 1889)

| Otero | B4 | 1889 | 22 | | Bent | La Junta 81050 |

(Co Clk has m from 1892, Ind rec from 1889; Clk Co Ct has div & pro rec; Clk Dis Ct has civ ct rec)

| Ouray | E3 | 1877 | 2 | 1880 | Hinsdale, San Juan | Ouray 81427 |

(Co Clk has m, div, pro, civ ct rec from 1877, Discharge, unpatented mines, patented mines, transcripts from San Juan Co from 1918)

| Park | D2 | 1861 | 5 | 1870-80 | Original county | Fairplay 80440 |

(Co Clk has m from 1893 & Ind rec; Clk Dis Ct has div, pro & civ ct rec)

| § Phillips | A1 | 1889 | 5 | | Logan | Holyoke 80734 |

(Co Clk has m, d, bur, Ind rec from 1889; Clk Dis Ct has div, pro, civ ct rec)

| Pitkin | D2 | 1881 | 10 | | Gunnison | Aspen 81611 |
| § Prowers | A4 | 1889 | 13 | | Bent | Lamar 81052 |

(Co Clk has m & Ind rec; Clk Dis Ct has div, pro & civ ct rec)

| * Pueblo | C3 | 1861 | 126 | 1880 | Original county | Pueblo 81003 |

(Co Clk has m rec from 1880; Clk Dis Ct div, pro & civ ct rec)

| Rio Blanco | E2 | 1889 | 6 | | Summit | Meeker 81641 |

(Co Clk has b rec from 1900, m rec from 1889, d rec from 1900, also early day agriculture & stock rec, bounty books brand rec registered as Summit Co, Garfield Co & finally Rio Blanco; Co Clk also has rec of bur for rural cem only; Clk Dis Ct has div, pro & civ ct rec from 1889)

| Rio Grande | D4 | 1874 | 10 | 1880 | Conejos, Costilla | Del Norte 81132 |
| Routt | E1 | 1877 | 13 | 1880 | Grand | Steamboat Springs 80477 |

(Co Clk has m rec from 1893, Ind rec from 1885; Co Health Dept has b, d rec; Clk Dis Ct has div, pro, civ ct rec)

| Saguache | D3 | 1866 | 4 | 1880 | Rio Grande | Saguache 81149 |

(Co Clk has m rec from 1900, Ind rec from 1861)

| San Juan | E4 | 1876 | 1 | 1880 | La Plata | Silverton 81433 |

(Twn Clk has b, d & bur rec; Co Clk has m & Ind rec from 1876; Clk Dis Ct has div, pro & civ ct rec)

| § San Miguel | F3 | 1883 | 3 | | Ouray | Telluride 81435 |

(Co Clk has m & Ind rec from 1883; Clk Dis Ct has div, pro & civ ct rec from 1883; some b, d & bur rec were destroyed in a recent fire so files are incomplete; Co Clk has various chattles, papers, agreements, inventories, clippings & misc, maps, some indexed)

| Sedgwick | A1 | 1889 | 3 | | Logan | Julesburg 80737 |

(Co Clk has m & Ind rec from 1889; Clk Dis Ct has div, pro & civ ct rec)

| Summit | D2 | 1861 | 9 | 1870-80 | Original county | Breckenridge 80424 |

(Co Clk has m & Ind rec)

| Teller | C3 | 1899 | 8 | | El Paso | Cripple Creek 80813 |

(Co Clk has m, Ind rec from 1899; Ethel Pedrie, Victor, Colo has b, d rec; Clk Dis Ct has div, pro, civ ct rec)

Uncompahgre (changed to Ouray 1883)

| *§ Washington | B2 | 1887 | 5 | | Weld, Arapahoe | Akron 80720 |

(Co Clk has m & Ind rec from 1887; Clk Dis Ct has div, pro & civ ct rec)

| * Weld | B1 | 1861 | 123 | 1870-80 | Original county | Greeley 80631 |

(Co Clk has m & Ind rec; Clk Dis Ct has div, pro & civ ct rec)

Name	Map Index	Date Created	Pop. By M 1980	U.S. Cen Reports Available	Parent County or Territory From Which Organized	County Seat
§ Yuma	A2	1889	10		Washington, Arapahoe	Wray 80758

(Co Clk has m rec from 1889, Ind rec from 1897)

* - At least one county history has been published about this county.

§ - Inventory of county archives was made by the Historical Records Survey. (see introduction)

CONNECTICUT

CAPITAL, HARTFORD - NINTH COLONY - STATE 1788 - (5TH)

The settlement of Connecticut began in 1633 by former Massachusetts colonists. Some of them left Massachusetts on order of narrow religious leaders, and others because they had become weary of the intolerant attitude displayed by those leaders. The green Connecticut valley had beckoned them with abundant evidences of opportunities for material prosperity. Most of the settlers in the Massachusetts towns of Newtown, Watertown and Dorchester, all near Boston, moved their families and all of their belongings to the central part of Connecticut, where along the Connecticut River they established three new communities which later came to be called Windsor, Hartford and Wethersfield. It was an attack on these three communities that later caused the Pequot Indian War.

As early as 1614 a Dutch seafarer, Adriaen Block, sailed up the broad river, which he named the Varsche River. The first knowledge of the fertile section of Connecticut, the early settlers of Massachusetts learned from the Indians who gave them a highly painted word picture of the section. It was this that brought about the settlement of the three communities mentioned above. Late in 1635 about fifty persons left what is now Cambridge, then called Newtown, and established themselves at Suckiaug, now Hartford. New migrations continued throughout the next few years. While the Dutch remained at the trading posts or forts, the English spread all over the territory.

From 1635 to 1644 another English colony flourished at Saybrook, near the mouth of the Connecticut, but then faded away. In 1643, New Haven was extended as a colony to include Milford (1639), Guilford (1639), and Stamford (1641).

During the ten-year period from 1640 to 1650, there was a heavy influx of settlers into Connecticut. The new settlers came almost entirely directly from England. The following forty years saw a tremendous migration away from the newly settled district. The movement was generally westward where fertile fields beckoned those anxious to secure their independence. In many instances the entire population of some of the towns participated in the migration and established themselves again among their old neighbors in a new environment.

In 1772 about thirty English families under the leadership of the Reverend Richard Mosely left Litchfield, Connecticut, for the Kingsborough Patent, now in Fulton County, New York. (Then in Tryon County).

Connecticut acquired its present borders in 1799 after giving up its present longstanding claims to other territories, including the Ohio region and part of Pennsylvania.

The 1790 Census of Connecticut shows a population of 232,236. All residents, with the exception of three and eight-tenths percent or 223,437, had come from England proper. Scotland was represented with two and eight-tenths percent, or 6,425. Ireland with seven-tenths percent, or 1,589. France, two-tenths percent, or 512. Holland, one-tenth percent, or 258. There were also five Hebrew, four German, and six from other countries.

During the early days of the American colonies, Connecticut had more home industries than any other colony. All kinds of household gadgets were invented and manufactured in the homes. These early necessities were carried all over the eastern section of the present United States, even down to New Orleans, by the so called "Yankee Pedlars." With the heavy migration in the latter part of the eighteenth century away from the state, Connecticut sent lavish invitations to Europe for more families to settle there.

About that time a severe potato crop failure in Ireland brought four million people to the verge of starvation. It didn't take many inducements for them to accept suggestions or invitations to make their homes in Connecticut. Thousands of them came in the late 1850's although many had come for ten years previously. It is estimated that more than 70,000 Irish came during that period who, with their descendants, now number more than 200,000.

Since 1880 it is estimated that more than 80,000 Germans have sought residence in various sections of the state. Unlike many other nationalities the Germans seldom live in solid nationality groups but are more intermingled with the already existing population.

Canada has always contributed freely to the population of Connecticut. The English-Canadians have generally come to Hartford or some of the other larger cities in the state, while the French-Canadians have been satisfied to cross over the border separating them from the United States and settle down in some of the northeastern industrial cities where upwards of seventy thousand of them have been employed in the textile industry.

During the past eighty years a heavy influx of Scandinavians has been registered in Connecticut. The earlier migration was much heavier than the later. It is estimated that upwards of fifty-five thousand persons have come from those nations to the Nutmeg State, about eight percent from Norway, eleven percent from Denmark, and eighty-one percent from Sweden. The majority of them have engaged in the mechanical arts, while some have engaged in gardening and farming.

The Italians have been coming to Connecticut in quite a solid stream over the past eighty years. The greatest influx was during the first sixteen years of the twentieth century. The first and second generation of Italians number approximately more than 300,000 in Connecticut today. While good-sized colonies of them live in many of the cities, most of them are centered around Hartford.

With about an equal distribution in agricultural and industrial pursuits there are about 150,000 former residents of Poland in Connecticut. They have concentrated especially around Bridgeport and New Britain. The factories and industrial plants of Waterbury have employed most of the 40,000 Lithuanians who have come here over the years, while about an equal number from Czechoslovakia have centered around the Bridgeport plants. About 30,000 Magyars (Hungarians) are also established in the state, about nine thousand foreign born living there in 1950.

Unlike most states the town clerk, rather than the county clerk, is the custodian of marriage licenses and records, birth and death records, and land records. Long before the counties were organized, the town clerks were recording these statistics. Record of wills, inventories and administrations of estates are in the probate districts. These are not always identical with the town. Superior and common pleas court records are kept by court clerks.

The church records are still in the respective churches. If information is desired from them, it would be best to write the town clerk and ask him to help you decide where to seek the data desired.

Connecticut State Department of Health Services, Vital Records Section, 79 Elm Street, Hartford, Connecticut 06115, has birth, death and marriage records since 1 July 1897. Earlier similar records are on file in the city or town offices of the respective communities.

Information on divorces may be obtained for a fee in the office of the clerk of the Superior Court in the county where the proceedings were heard.

Naturalization records are on file in the office of the United States Circuit court Hartford, or in the county offices of the Superior Courts.

The Lutheran and the Episcopal churches have available besides the vital statistics, the christening, baptism, confirmation, entrance and departure dates and burials.

The district courts of the counties are the custodians of wills, inventories and administrations of estates. Sometimes a town constitutes a district. Sometimes several smaller towns are grouped into one probate district. There are 118 districts and 169 towns.

Almost every city or town in the state has printed histories containing a great deal of genealogy especially concerning the early inhabitants. Many family genealogies have also been printed.

A wealth of information on early-day families of Connecticut may be found in almost every library. Many books have been published giving the names of the participants in all of wars. Numerous family histories have been printed and are available at most of the libraries, and most of the towns and cities have valuable histories of their founding, growth and progress. Many of the family histories in the libraries are in manuscript form. Many of them have been indexed to facilitate research activities. Information regarding these indexes may be obtained from the libraries if self-addressed, stamped envelopes accompany the request. No research is done by library staff members, but information regarding professional researchers may be given by the libraries.

The various counties of Connecticut are at present divided into the following townships:

Fairfield: Bethel, Bridgeport, Brookfield, Danbury, Darien, Easton, Fairfield, Greenwich, Monroe, New Canaan, Fairfield, Newtown, Norwalk, Redding, Ridgefield, Sheldon, Sherman, Stamford, Stratford, Trumbull, Weston, Westport, Wilton.

Hartford: Avon, Berlin, Bloomfield, Bristol, Burlington, Canton, East Granby, East Hartford, East Windsor, Enfield, Farmington, Glastonbury, Granby, Hartford, Hartland, Manchester, Marlborough, New Britain, Newington, Plainville, Rock Hill, Simsbury, Southington, South Windsor, Suffield, West Hartford, Wethersfield, Windsor, Windsor Locks.

Litchfield: Barkhamsted, Bethlehem, Bridgewater, Canaan, Colebrook, Cornwall, Goshen, Harwinton, Kent, Litchfield, Morris, New Hartford, New Milford, Norfolk, North Canaan, Plymouth, Roxbury, Salisbury, Sharon, Thomaston, Torrington, Warren, Washington, Watertown, Winchester, Woodbury.

Middlesex: Chester, Clinton, Cromwell, Deep River, Durham, East Haddam, East Hampton, Essex, Haddam, Killingworth, Middlefield, Middletown, Old Saybrook, Portland, Westbrook.

New Haven: Ansonia, Beacon Falls, Bethany, Branford, Cheshire, Derby, East Haven, Guilford, Hamden, Madison, Meriden, Middlebury, Milford, Naugatuck, New Haven, North Branford, North Haven, Orange, Oxford, Prospect, Seymour, Southbury, Wallingford, Waterbury, West Haven, Woodbridge, Wolcott.

New London: Bozrah, Colchester, East Lyme, Franklin, Griswold, Groton, Lebanon, Ledyard, Lisbon, Lyme, Montville, New London, North Stonington, Norwich, Old Lyme, Preston, Salem, Sprague, Stonington, Voluntown, Waterford.

Tolland: Andover, Bolton, Columbia, Coventry, Ellington, Hebron, Mansfield, Somers, Stafford, Tolland, Union, Vernon, Willington.

Windham: Ashford, Brooklyn, Canterbury, Chaplin, Eastford, Hampton, Killingly, Plainfield, Pomfret, Putnam, Scotland, Sterling, Thompson, Windham, Woodstock.

Connecticut Towns organized before 1800:

Fairfield County -- Brookfield 1788; Danbury 1684; Fairfield 1639; Greenwich 1640; Huntington 1788; New Fairfield 1740; Newton 1700; Norwalk 1649; Redding 1757; Ridgefield 1709; Stamford 1648; Stratford 1639; Trumbull 1798; Weston 1717.

Hartford County -- Berlin 1785; Bristol 1747; Canton 1740; East Windsor 1680; Enfield 1681; Farmington 1640; Glastonbury 1690; Granby 1786; Hartford 1635; Hartland 1753; Simsbury 1670; Southington 1779; Suffield 1674; Wethersfield 1635; Windsor 1633.

Litchfield County -- Barkhamsted 1746; Bethlehem 1787; Canaan 1739; Colebrook 1779; Cornwall 1740; Goshen 1739; Harwinton 1731; Kent 1739; Litchfield 1719; New Hartford 1739; New Milford 1712; Norfolk 1744; Plymouth 1795; Roxbury 1796; Salisbury 1730; Sharon 1732-3; Torrington 1740; Washington 1779; Warren 1786; Watertown 1780; Winchester 1771; Woodbury 1674.

Middlesex County -- Chatham 1767; Durham 1698; E. Haddam 1685; Haddam 1662; Killingsworth 1667; Middletown 1653; Saybrook 1635.

New Haven County -- Branford 1644; Cheshire 1723; Derby, S. 1675; Guilford 1639; Hamden 1786; Meriden 1796; Millford 1639; New Haven 1638; North Haven 1786; Oxford 1798; Seymour 1672; Southbury 1672; Wallingsford 1669; Waterbury 1686; Wolcott 1796; Woodbridge 1786.

New London County -- Bozrah 1786; Colchester 1703; Franklin 1786; Groton 1705; Lebanon 1700; Lisbon 1786; Lyme 1664; Montville 1786; New London 1646; Norwich 1660; Preston 1687; Stonington 1649.

Tolland County -- Bolton 1716; Coventry 1709; Ellington 1786; Hebron 1704; Mansfield 1713; Somers 1734; Stafford 1718; Tolland 1700; Union 1727; Vernon 1716; Willington 1720.

Windham County -- Ashford 1710; Brooklyn 1786; Canterbury 1690; Hampton 1786; Killingly 1700; Plainfield 1699; Pomfret 1686; Sterling 1794; Thompson 1715; Voluntown 1696; Windham 1689; Woodstock 1749.

Genealogical Archives, Libraries, Societies, and Publications

Aspincok Historical Society of Putnam, Inc., P.O. Box 465, Putnam, CT 06260.

Abington Social Library, Abington Four Corners, Route 97, Abington, CT 06230.

Beardsley and Memorial Library, The, Munro Place, Winsted, CT 06098.

Bridgeport Public Library, 925 Broad St., Bridgeport, CT 06603.

Bristol Public Library, 5 High Street, Bristol, CT 06010.

Connecticut College Library, Mohegan Avenue, New London, CT 06320.

Connecticut Historical Commission, 59 South Prospect Street, Hartford, CT 06106.

Connecticut Historical Society, 1 Elizabeth St., Hartford, CT 06105.

Connecticut League of Historical Societies, P.O. Box 906, Darien, CT 06820.

Connecticut State Library, 231 Capitol Ave., Hartford, CT 06115.

Cyrenius H. Booth Library, 25 Main St., Newton, CT 06470.

Danbury Public Library, 170 Main Street, P.O. Box 1160, Danbury, CT 06810.

Darien Historical Society, Leroy Ave., Darien, CT 06820.

East Hartford Public Library, 840 Main Street, East Hartford, CT 06108.

Essex Historical Society, 6 New City St., Essex, CT 06426.

Fairfield Historical Society, 636 Old Post Rd., Fairfield, CT 06430.

Fairfield Public Library, 1080 Old Post Road, Fairfield, CT 06430.

Farmington Museum, 37 High Street, Farmington, CT 06032.

Ferguson Library, 96 Broad Street, Stamford, CT 06901.

Godfrey Memorial Library, 134 Newfield St., Middletown, CT 06457.

Greenwich Library, 101 West Putnam Avenue, Greenwich, CT 06830.

Groton Public Library, Ft. Hill Rd., Groton, CT 06340.

Guilford Keeping Society, 171 Boston Street, Guilford, CT 06437.

Hartford Public Library, 500 Main Street, Hartford, CT 06103.

Kent Memorial Library, 50 North Main Street, Hartford, CT 06103.

Kent Memorial Library, 50 North Street, Suffield, CT 06078.

Litchfield Historical Society, Litchfield, CT 06759.

Middlesex County Historical Society, 151 Main Street, Middletown, CT 06457.

Mystic Seaport, G.W. Blunt White Library, Greenmanville Avenue, Old Mystic, CT 06372.

New Britain Public Library, 20 High Street, P.O. Box 1291, New Britain, CT 06050.

New Canaan Historical Society, 13 Oenoke Ridge, New Canaan, CT 06480.

New Haven Colony Historical Society, 114 Whitney Ave., New Haven, CT 06510.

New Haven Public Library, 133 Elm Street, New Haven, CT 06510.

New London County Historical Society, 11 Blinman Street, New London, CT 06320.

Noah Webster Memorial Library, 205 Main St., West Hartford, CT 06107.

Otis Library, 261 Main Street, Norwich, CT 06360.

Pequot Library, 720 Pequot Avenue, Southport, CT 06490.

Phoebe Griffin Noyes Library, Lyme St., Lyme, CT 06371.

Public Library, 63 Huntington St., New London, CT 06320.

Seymour Public Library, 46 Church Street, Seymour, CT 06483.

Silas Bronson Library, Public Library of the City of Waterbury, Connecticut, 267 Grand St., Waterbury, CT 06702.

Society of Mayflower Descendants, in Connecticut, 36 Arundel Avenue, Hartford, CT 06107.

Southington Public Library, 255 Main Street, Southington, CT 06489.

Stamford Genealogical Society, Inc., The, Box 249, Stamford, CT 06904.

Trinity College, Watkinson Library, 300 Summit Street, Hartford, CT 06106.

Trumbull Historical Society, Trumbull Town Hall, Trumbull, CT 06611.

Wadsworth Atheneum, 600 Main Street, Hartford, CT 06103.

Western Connecticut State College, 181 White Street, Danbury, CT 06810.

West Hartford Public Library, 20 South Main Street, West Hartford, CT 06107.

Wethersfield Historical Society, 150 Main Street, Wethersfield, CT 06109.

Wilton Historical Society, 150 Danbury Rd., Wilton, CT 06897.

Yale University Libraries, Box 1603A, Yale Station, New Haven, CT 06520.

Connecticut Ancestry, Stamford Genealogical Society, Inc., P.O. Box 249, Stamford, CT 06901.

Connecticut Nutmegger, The, Connecticut Society of Genealogists, Inc., P.O. Box 305, West Hartford, CT 06107.

Printed Census Records and Mortality Schedules

State indexes - 1790, 1800, 1810, 1820, 1830, 1840, and 1850

Other printed census records (counties):

Fairfield - 1800	New Haven - 1800
Hartford - 1800	New London - 1800
Litchfield - 1800	Tolland - 1800
Middlesex - 1800	Windham - 1800

1670 - Reconstructed listing taken from household, estate, tax, landowners, church and freemans lists. Colony of Connecticut.

Mortality Schedules (Printed): State - 1850, 1860, 1870

Valuable Printed Sources

Atlas

Town and City Atlas of the State of Connecticut. Boston: D.H. Hurd and Company, 1893.

Place Names

Gannett, Henry. *A Geographic Dictionary of Connecticut and Rhode Island,* 2 Vols. in 1. 1894. Reprint. Baltimore: Genealogical Publishing Company, 1978.

Hughes, Arthur H. and Morse S. Allen. *Connecticut Place Names.* Hartford: Connecticut Historical society, 1976.

Pease, John C. and John M. Niles. *A Gazetteer of the States of Connecticut and Rhode Island.* Hartford: William S. Marsh, 1819.

Guides To Genealogical Research

Kemp, Thomas J. *Connecticut Researcher's Handbook.* Detroit: Gale Research Co., 1891.

Sperry, Kip. *Connecticut Sources for Family Historians and Genealogists.* Logan, Utah: Everton Publishers, 1980.

State Histories

Cutter, William Richard. *Genealogical and Family History of the State of Connecticut.* 4 Vols. New York: Lewis Historical Publishing Co., 1911.

Roth, David M. *Connecticut: A Bicentennial History.* W. W. Norton & Co., 1979.

Van Dusen, Albert E. *Connecticut.* New York: Random House, 1961.

Genealogical Sources

Bailey, Frederic W. *Early Connecticut Marriages.* 7 Vols. in 1. 1896-1906. Reprint. Baltimore: Genealogical Publishing Co., 1976.

Barbour collection - Vital Records copied from town, church and other original sources located at the Connecticut State Library in Hartford.*

Claus, Robert, comp. *Guide to Archives in the Connecticut State Library.* 2nd ed. Hartford: Connecticut State Library, 1978.

Connecticut State Library. *List of Church Records in the Connecticut State Library.* Hartford: Connecticut State Library, 1976.

Connecticut. *The Public Records of the Colony of Connecticut (1636-1776)* 15 Vols. Hartford, 1850-90. Reprinted.

D.A.R. Collection contains bible, cemetery, church, death, deeds, family, marriage, probate, town, and Will records. Records available at the National Society, Daughters of the American Revolution Library in Washington, D.C.*

Hale Collection - Notices of deaths and marriages compiled from newspaper notices, 1600's-1934. Also includes cemetery inscriptions. Connecticut State Library.*

Manwaring, Charles William. *A Digest of the Early Connecticut Probate Records.* 3 Vols. Hartford, 1904-6.

---

*Microfilm - Genealogical Society of The Church of Jesus Christ of Latter-day Saints, Salt Lake City, Utah.

CONNECTICUT COUNTY HISTORIES
(Population figures to nearest thousand - 1980 U.S. Census)

Cities, not counties, in the State of Connecticut have their own Bureau of Vital Statistics under the local Health Departments.

Name	Map Index	Date Created	Pop. By M 1980	U.S. Cen Reports Available	Parent County or Territory From Which Organized	County Seat
* Fairfield	C2	1666	801	1790-80	Original county	Bridgeport 06602

(Twn Clk Bridgeport has b, m & d rec from 1700, pro & Ind rec)

* Hartford	A3	1666	806	1790-80	Original county	Hartford 06103

(City Clk has b, m, d rec from 1847, bur rec from 1847) (1919-1958 missing, Ind rec from 1871, city directories from 1876)

* Litchfield	A2	1751	157	1790-80	Hartford, Fairfield	Litchfield 06759 & Winsted 06098

(Twn Clk, Litchfield has b, m & d rec from 1720, bur from 1887, Ind from 1720; Clk Sup Ct has div; Pro Judge has pro rec) (Twn Clk of Winchester has b, m & d from 1771, Ind from 1744; Clk Sup Ct has div rec; Pro Judge has pro rec; Clk Cir Ct has civ ct rec)

* Middlesex	C3	1785	129	1790-80	Hartford, New London, New Haven	Middletown 06458

(Twn Clk, Middletown has b, m, d & Ind rec; Clk Sup Ct has div & civ ct rec from 1800; Pro Judge has pro rec)

* New Haven	C3	1666	757	1790-80	Original county	New Haven 06510

(Twn Clks have b, m, d, Ind rec; Co Clk has div, civ ct rec; Pro Ct has pro rec)

* New London	C4	1666	238	1790-80	Original county	New London 06320 & Norwich 06360

(Twn Clks have b, m, d rec from 1659, bur rec from 1893; Deeds and town meeting rec from 1659; Pro Judge has pro rec; Clk Sup Ct has div rec)

* Tolland	A3	1785	115	1790-80	Windham	Rockville 06066

(Twn Clk, Rockville has b, m, d & Ind rec; Pro Judge has pro rec; Clk Sup Ct has civ ct rec)

* Windham	A4	1726	92	1790-80	Hartford, New London	Putnam 06260 & Willimantic 06226

(Twn Clk, Willimantic has b, m & d rec from 1692, bur rec from 1900; Pro Judge has pro rec; Clk Sup Ct has div rec)

* - At least one county history has been published about this county.

COUNTY MAP FOR THE STATE OF CONNECTICUT

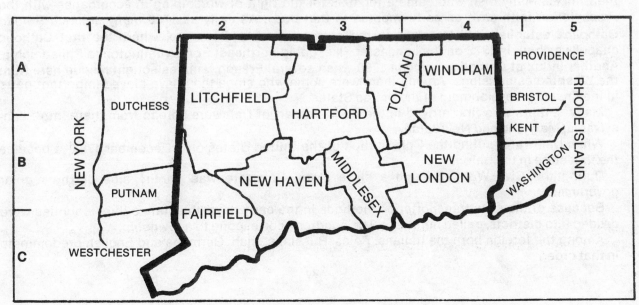

DELAWARE

CAPITAL, DOVER - FIRST STATE - STATE 1787 - (1ST)

Late in August 1609, Henry Hudson, a British sea captain and adventurer in the service of the Dutch West India Company, visited the Delaware section enroute to the Hudson River in search of a northwest passage.

During a six-year period between 1614 and 1620 a group of sailors under the captaincy of Cornelius Hendricksen, a Dutch navigator, visited the section. As a result of information brought back to Holland by these sailors the Dutch West India Company was organized in 1621. In 1629 this company adopted a charter to grant land in the new world to feudal lords. The following year the company bought land adjoining the Delaware River, and in 1631 David Pietersen de Vries established a camp on Lewes Beach.

Hearing how other European monarchs fostered expeditions and settlements in the new world, the Swedish rulers encouraged the New Sweden Company to outfit an expedition of two boats, "The Kalmar Nyckel" and "Grip." They arrived at Jamestown, Virginia, in March 1638, remained there ten days and then continued to Delaware. They established settlements in the rich section south of the present Wilmington, in the extreme north of the colony. They were attacked by the Dutch at different times from 1651 to 1655 when the Swedes were routed from Fort Christina, named after the then twenty-one year-old Queen Kristina, daughter of Gustaf Adolf, who lost his life on the battlefield at Lutzen, Germany in 1632.

The first Finnish colonists came to Delaware in 1656 aboard a Swedish ship.

The British forces took possession of the Delaware Colony and Amsterdam (New York) in 1664. Two years later a large influx of English people from Virginia, Maryland, New Jersey, New York, and Europe made their homes among the Swedes and the Dutch in Delaware. From then on conditions among the colonists greatly improved and more unity was established.

Most of the colonists came to the New World for religious as well as material or financial purposes. Churches were among the first buildings erected as each new community was established. The Swedes brought with them the religious desires of their groups. The Dutch settlers their flocks. Many Irish who came after 1698 for the right of worshipping in accordance with the their flocks. Many Irish who came after 1698 for the right of worshiping in accordance with the Presbyterian faith gave an early impetus to that body. As early as 1730 many staunch Roman Catholics established themselves in the northern part of Delaware, where the first Catholic chapel was built in 1772 on the Lancaster Pike, going northeast from Wilmington to Philadelphia. Another influx of Catholics came in 1790 when several French families sought rescue here from the West Indies uprisings. Among them were some who since then have played important parts in the financial development of the United States.

Many settlers who first arrived in the northern part of Delaware spread from there into Pennsylvania, Maryland and New Jersey.

When Delaware ratified the Constitution of the United States on 7 December 1787, it became the first state in the Union.

During the Civil War, although a slave state, Delaware was on the side of the regular government.

Because of the slow transportation methods in the early days, the state's three counties were divided into districts, called hundreds. The hundreds correspond to a township.

Among the foreign born the Italians, Poles, Russians, Irish, Germans and English predominate in that order.

The early colonial records of Delaware are scattered, some are in the archives of the state of New York. After 1681 they were stored in the Archives of Pennsylvania. As the counties exercised full powers as governments, not all of the colonial records went to Pennsylvania, some are to be found in the Delaware Archives in Dover. Land records after 1785 will be found in the county courthouses and wills also after 1800.

Vital statistics since 1913 are in the custody of the Bureau of Vital Statistics, Jesse S. Cooper Memorial Building, Dover, Delaware 19901. All vital events are filed by year of occurrence, so it is necessary to have a date before a search can be made.

Doc. 20-06 / 79 / 07 /13 from the Delaware Division of Historical and Cultural Affairs in Dover, Delaware includes the following information:

"The Hall of Records is the repository for all the noncurrent records of the State of Delaware, its counties, and large municipalities. Among the State's holdings are documents from the Swedish colonial period, 1638-55; the Dutch settlement, 1655-64; the Duke of York regime, 1664-82; and the Penn Proprietorship, 1682-1776. Most of the records, however, date from statehood in 1776.

"The State records that can be consulted at the Hall of Records include: Executive Papers (RG 1301), 1776-1850, 1930-1976; Governor's Register (RG 1302), 1674-1976; reports and accounts of executive agencies; military files from the Revolution; Legislative Papers (RG 1111), 1776-1976; enrolled bills (RG 1111), 1776-; Minutes of the Assembly (RG 1110), 1739-1742; Judicial Papers (RG 1200), 1676-1976; papers and dockets of colonial courts, 1676-1776; Court of Chancery (RG 1225, 2835, 3835, 4835) 1776-1970; Orphans Court (RG 1226, 2835, 3835, 4835), 1776-1873; Court of General and Quarter Sessions (RG 2805, 3805, 4805) 1776-1831; Common Pleas (RG 2815, 3815, 4815), 1726-1860, 1917-1952; Oyer and Terminer (RG 2825, 3825, 4825), 1776-1868; Supreme Court (RG 1220, 2815, 3815, 4815) Writs and Executions, 1798-1831; Superior Court (RG 1217, 2810, 3810, 4810), 1832-1976.

"The county papers include: Levy Court minutes (RG 2200, 3200, 4200), 1775-1957; records of elected and appointed county officials, 1640-1950; land warrants, surveys, and deeds (RG 2555, 3555, 4555), 1640-1870; probate records (RG 2545, 3545, 4545) (wills, administrations, settlements, and inventories), 1676-1916; Vital Statistics files (births, baptisms, marriage, deaths), 1713-1913 (N.B.: certificates were not filed **by law** in Delaware before 1913).

"Municipal holdings include the records of the Borough and City of Wilmington (RG 5100), 1769-1971; Dover (RG 6100), 1770-1931; Lewes (RG 7140), 1807-1909; and Frederica (RG 6050), 1866-1920. These files consist of minutes, accounts, reports, and correspondence.

"Although the official records of the State contain many genealogical references, the Archives has also collected useful materials from other sources. Federal census schedules, 1800-1880 and 1900, are available on microfilm. Items of private origin include: Reverend Joseph Brown Turner Genealogical Collection of notes on over one thousand Delmarva families; Walter G. Tatnall Collection of Delaware tombstone records; Millard F. Hudson Collection of Sussex County tombstone inscriptions; and manuscript and transcribed church records.

"Manuscript collections contain correspondence and papers of George Read, Caesar Rodney, John M. Clayton, and others. The largest holdings of manuscript are the Ridgely Papers, the John Dickinson Collection, and the Private Accounts Collection. The latter includes business records of storekeepers, farmers, craftsmen, and professional men dating from the eighteenth century.

"The Archives maintains a library of Delawareana. The Delawareana collection includes State publications, books, genealogies, pamphlets, maps, newspaper clippings, microfilm, photographs, motion pictures, slides, and sound recordings. The files of the Bureau of Archaeology and Historic Preservation are also open to the public.

"The research facilities at the Hall of Records are open Monday through Friday from 8:30 a.m. to 12 noon and 1:00 p.m. to 4:15 p.m. Photostatic copies of records are available for research purposes at established rates. For further information telephone (302) 678-5314 or call the Governor's toll free number (800) 292-9570 and that office will refer your inquiry to us.

"An area has been created strictly for the viewing of microfilm and microfiche. Much of our holdings are now on microfilm, including Census records, County Deeds, County Wills, Kent County Probates, etc. This area is basically a self-service area, but staff is available for assistance when needed. In addition to governmental records on film, we also have a large general reference collection available. All film checklists are available in the work area."

Genealogical Archives, Libraries, Societies, and Publications

Delaware Genealogical Society, 505 Market Street Mall, Wilmington, DE 19801.

Division of Historical and Cultural Affairs, Department of State, Hall of Records, Dover, DE 19901.

Historical Society of Delaware, Old Town Hall, Wilmington, DE 19801.

Lower Del-Mar-Va Genealogical Society, Wicomico County Library, Salisbury, MD 21801.

The Public Archives Commission, Hall of Records, Dover, DE 19901.

University Library, University of Delaware, Newark, DE 19711.

Wilmington Institute Free Library, Tenth and Market Sts., Wilmington, DE 19801.

Delaware Genealogical Society Journal, published bimonthly by the Delaware Genealogical Society, 505 Market Street Mall, Wilmington, DE 19801.

Printed Census Records and Mortality Schedules

State indexes - 1665-1697, 1790, 1800, 1810, 1820, 1830, 1840, 1850

Other printed census records (counties):

Kent - 1800   New Castle - 1800

Mortality Schedules (Printed): State - 1860, 1870, 1880

Valuable Printed Sources

Atlases, Maps, Gazetteers

Beer, D. G. *Atlas of the State of Delaware.* Philadelphia, 1868, reprinted, Sussex Prints, 1978.

Gannett, Henry. *A Gazetteer of Maryland and Delaware.* Reprinted, Baltimore: Genealogical Publishing Company, 1976.

Place Names

Heck, L. W. *Delaware Place Names.* Prepared by Geological Survey. Washington, D.C. Government Printing Office, 1966.

Histories

Conrad, Henry C. *History of the State of Delaware.* 3 Vols. Wilmington, 1908.

Ferris, Benjamin. *A History of the Original Settlements on the Delaware.* Wilmington: Wilson and Heald, 1846.

Johnson, Amandus. *The Swedish Settlements on the Delaware.* 2 Vols. 1638-1664. Reprinted, Baltimore: Genealogical Publishing Company, 1969.

Scarf, J. Thomas. *History of Delaware.* Philadelphia, 1888.

Waterston, Elizabeth. *Churches in Delaware During the Revolution with a Brief Account of their Settlement and Growth.* Wilmington: Historical Society of Delaware, 1925.

Important Genealogical Sources - Printed

Gehring, Charles T. *New York Historical Manuscripts: Dutch Volumes XX-XXI Delaware Papers 1664-1682.* Baltimore: Genealogical Publishing Company, 1977.

Weiss, Frederick Lewis. *The Colonial Clergy of Maryland, Delaware and Georgia.* Reprinted, Baltimore: Genealogical Publishing Company, 1978.

Microfilm

Vital Records, Bureau of Vital Statistics. *Index Cards of Delaware Marriages, Baptisms, Births, and Deaths 1680-1913.* Filmed at State Archives Hall of Records, Dover, Delaware. 18 rolls*

Vital Records Births 1861-1913; deaths 1855-1910. Filmed at State Archives Hall of Records, Dover, Delaware. 87 rolls.*

Microfiche

Turner, Joseph Brown Collection. (The collection includes both the family folders and the index cards, which cross-reference genealogical publications not found in the collection, as well as the files themselves). Hall of Records, Dover, Delaware.* (Available on 647 microfiche from Bureau of Archives and Records, Hall of Records, Dover, Delaware 19901)

Bibliographies

Bibliography of Delaware 1960-1974. Newark: University of Delaware, 1976.

Reed H. Clay and Marion B. *A Bibliography of Delaware through 1960.* Newark: University of Delaware Press, 1966.

---

*On Microfilm at the Genealogical Society of The Church of Jesus Christ of Latter-day Saints, Salt Lake City, Utah.

DELAWARE COUNTY HISTORIES
(Population figures to nearest thousand - 1980 U. S. Census)

Name	Map Index	Date Created	Pop. By M 1980	U.S. Cen Reports Available	Parent County or Territory From Which Organized	County Seat
Deale (changed to Sussex Co, 1683)						
* Kent	B2	1682	99	1800-80	St. Jones, Name changed to Kent in 1682	Dover 19901
(Clk of Peace has m rec; Clk Sup Ct has div & civ ct rec; Rcdr Deeds has lnd rec from 1680)						
* New Castle	A2	1673	399	1800-80	Original county	Wilmington 19801
(Clk of Peace has m rec from 1911; Prothonotary has div & civ ct rec; Reg of Wills has pro rec; Rcdr Deeds has lnd rec)						
St. Jones (changed to Kent Co, 1682)						
* Sussex	C2	1682	97	1800-80	Early 17th Century Horrekill District (see Deale)	Georgetown 19947

* - At least one county history has been published about this county.

COUNTY MAP FOR THE STATE OF DELAWARE

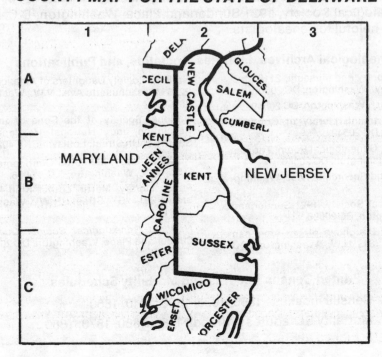

DISTRICT OF COLUMBIA

TERRITORY OF WASHINGTON, D. C.
ORGANIZED 1790, SEAT OF GOVERNMENT 1800

The capital of the United States covers about seventy square miles on the northeast side of the Potomac River, about 38 miles southwest of Baltimore.

The Bureau of Vital Statistics, Health Department, D.C., 300 Indiana Ave., N.W., Washington, D.C. 20001, is the custodian of births from 1871 to the present, and deaths from 1855 to the present, except 1861 and 1862. Custodian of marriages is the clerk, U.S. District Court for the District of Columbia, Fourth and E Streets, N.W., Washington, D.C. 20001. Custodian of wills is the Register of Wills, Fifth and E Streets, N.W. 20001. In charge of all real estate records and land titles is the Recorder of Deeds, Sixth and D. Streets, N.W. 20004. Census records may be obtained from the U.S. Bureau of the Census, Washington, D.C. 20025. Taxpayer lists are at the office of the Tax Collector, District of Columbia, District Bldg., Washington, D.C. 20004. All cemetery records are kept at the individual cemeteries.

"In 1800," says a historian, "Washington, the new capital, had been recently occupied. It was hardly a village, except on paper, and contained only the Capitol, the White House, two departmental buildings, a few boarding houses. The public buildings were still uncompleted. Mrs. Adams (the wife of President John Adams) found the audience room of the White House convenient for drying clothes, and the representatives met in a temporary building erected in the middle of the unfinished Capitol."

The National Society, Daughters of the American Revolution, (DAR) 1776 D. St. N.W. Washington, D.C. 20004 maintain a library of over 40,000 vols., many manuscripts and genealogical records.

The Genealogical Department of the Library of Congress and the National Archives, both Washington, D.C. 20025, are two of the richest sources of genealogical material in the U.S.

The National Genealogical Society, 1921 Sunderland Place, Washington, D.C. 20036, also has considerable material helpful to genealogists.

Genealogical Archives, Libraries, Societies, and Publications

Anderson House Library and Museum, 2118 Massachusetts Ave., N.W., Washington, DC 20008.

Congressional Library, Washington, DC 20540.

Genealogical Department, Library of Congress Annex, Washington, DC 20540.

Library of Congress, Genealogical Room, Thomas Jefferson Annex, Washington, DC 20540.

National Archives and Records Service, Washington, DC 20408.

National Genealogical Society, 1921 Sunderland Place, N.W., Washington, DC 20036.

National Society of Daughters of the American Revolution, 1776 D. St., N.W., Washington, DC 20006.

National Society Daughters of American Colonists, 2205 Massachusetts Ave., N.W., Washington, D.C. 20008.

National Society of the Sons of the American Revolution, Inc., National Headquarters, 1000 South Fourth Street, Louisville, KY 40203.

NSDAR Library, Memorial Continental Hall, 1776 D St., N.W., Washington, D.C. 20006.

Public Library, Martin Luther King Memorial Library, 901 "G" Street, N.W., Washington, DC 20001.

National Genealogical Society Quarterly, 1921 Sunderland Place, Washington, DC 20036.

Printed Census Records and Mortality Schedules

Census indexes - 1800, 1820, 1830, 1840, 1850

Mortality Schedules (Printed): 1850, 1860, 1870, 1880

Valuable Printed Sources

Place Names

Brown, Mary Ross. *An Illustrated Genealogy of the Counties of Maryland and District of Columbia as a Guide to Locating Records.* Baltimore: French Bray Printing (1967)

Guides To Genealogical Research

Colket, Meredith and Frank E. Bridgers. *Guide to Genealogical Records in The National Archives.* Washington D.C. General Services Administration The National Archives and Records Service (1964)

Histories

Crew, H. W. History of Washington, D.C., Dayton, Ohio: United Brethren Publishing House, (1892)

Proctor, John Clogett. *Washington, Past and Present.* New York City: Lewis Historical Publishing Company (1930)

Important Genealogical Sources

Library of Congress - Washington, D.C.

National Archives and Records Services - Washington, D.C.

National Genealogical Society Library, Washington, D.C.

The National Society of Daughters of the American Revolution Library - Washington, D.C.

Bibliographies

National Genealogical Society Library Booklist available to members on registration for National Genealogical Society Library Loan Service.

Babbel, June Andrew, comp. Lest We Forget: *A Guide to Genealogical Research in the Nation's Capitol.* 4th rev. ed. Annandale, Virginia: Annandale and Oakton Stakes of The Church of Jesus Christ of Latter-day Saints, 1976.

National Genealogical Society, 1921 Sunderland Place, N.W. Washington, D.C. 20036 has considerable material helpful to genealogists. The Library maintains collections of published and unpublished works relevant to genealogy, local history, and heraldry. Publications include *The National Genealogical Society Quarterly,* the quarterly *Newsletter* (sent to members of the society and subscribers of the quarterly), and a non-periodical series of Special Publication.

FLORIDA

CAPITAL, TALLAHASSEE - TERRITORY 1822 - STATE 1845 - (27TH)

Maps existing in Spain for nearly five centuries indicate that the contours of the American continent were already known there. Ponce de Leon, the intrepid Spanish explorer, reached the Florida coast as early as 1513. Landing there on Easter Sunday, he called the new land Florida, from the Spanish name for Easter, Pascua Florida. Attempts to locate Spanish settlers in the new region a few years later failed when the colony was routed by the Indians.

Efforts by the French Huguenots to establish colonies on the south bank of the St. John's River in 1564 had an encouraging beginning but ended in disaster in a couple of years.

In the 1763 peace treaty of Paris, which ended the Seven Years' War, in which the British and the Prussians fought France, Spain and Austria, all her North American possessions east of the Mississippi were ceded by France to Britain. In the same treaty Spain traded

Florida to Britain for Havana.

That same year a proclamation by the King of England established among other American provinces, East and West Florida. The two sections were divided by the Chattahoochee and the Apalachicola Rivers.

Twenty years later, the Florida sections were returned to Spain in the treaty ending the Revolutionary War in 1783.

West Florida was taken by the United States in 1810 and 1812, and, after many efforts, finally succeeded in 1819 in getting Florida by promising to pay indemnities to her citizens who had been damaged by Spain. The section embracing West Florida was added to Louisiana, Mississippi, and Alabama.

In 1821 about eight thousand whites lived in Florida, most of them Spaniards, although there was a goodly number of Anglo-Saxons. As early as 1740 many British, Scottish and Irish populated the Cumberland and the Shenandoah valleys and spread through every southern state east of the Mississippi. The early population in the deep south was predominantly of Irish ancestry. They were the "Okies" of the early days. They built Jacksonville in 1822, Quincy in 1825, Monticello in 1828, Marianna and Apalachicola in 1829, and St. Joseph in 1836. Many wealthy people established their homes in Florida, but their bad treatment of the Indians caused the Seminole wars during 1835-42.

A considerable number of Greeks from southern Greece and the Dodecanese Islands moved into Florida as early as 1820. As expert sponge divers, they established themselves as energetic and successful citizens. Religiously they are affiliated with the Orthodox Greek Catholic Church.

The first railroad in the state was built in 1831 and extended from Tallahassee to St. Marks. The middle section of Florida was settled about 1820 by former settlers from Virginia, North Carolina, and South Carolina. Most of the people who came to East Florida from 1845 to 1860 had lived in Georgia, Alabama, and North and South Carolina.

Florida became a territory of the United States on 30 March 1822, from which time her county records begin. She became a state on 3 March 1845, the twenty-seventh state to join the Union.

During the 1840's the population of Florida increased about fifty-six percent. The census of 1860 shows the white population to have increased to 78,000. At that time there were in the state seventy-seven plantations embracing more than one thousand acres each. The 1860 census also showed that about half the population was native born while twenty-two percent had come from Georgia, eleven percent from South Carolina and five percent from North Carolina.

In 1912 a large group of Lutheran Slovaks moved from Cleveland, Ohio, on to a large tract of land they had purchased in Seminole County where they established a communal agricultural and poultry business.

Office of Vital Statistics, Post Office Box 210, Jacksonville, FL 32231, is custodian of the following records: Incomplete records of births from 1865 to 1917, and births from 1917 to date; incomplete records of deaths from 1877 to 1917, and deaths from 1917, to date. Marriages from June 1927 to date; divorce records also available there.

Some birth and death records are in the city or county health departments from 1893 to 1913 in Jacksonville; from 1897 to 1916 in Pensacola; prior to 1917 in St. Petersburg.

The office of the County Judge of the bride's home county has marriage records prior to June 1927. These offices also have the records of wills of their constituents.

Divorce records before 1927 are filed in the office of the clerk of the Circuit Court where divorce was granted. Similar records before or after 1927 are in the mentioned office of the Bureau of Vital Statistics.

Mortality schedules for Florida, 1850, 1860, 1870, 1880, are on microfilm at the Florida State University Library, Tallahassee, Florida. The library has copies available for inter-library loan.

Genealogical Archives, Libraries, Societies, and Publications

Alachua County Genealogical Society, P.O. Box 12078, Gainesville, FL 32604.

Brevard Genealogical Society, P.O. Box 1123, Cocoa, FL 32922.

Broward County Genealogical Society, Inc., Room 310D, 351 Bldg., N.W. 40th Ave., Plantation, FL 33314.

Central Florida Genealogical and Historical Society, P.O. Box 177, Orlando, FL 32810.

Charlotte County Genealogical Society, P.O. Box 2682, Port Charlotte, FL 33952.

Cocoa Public Library, 430 Delannoy Ave., Cocoa, FL 32922.

Collier County Public Library, Central Ave., Naples, FL 33940.

DeLand Public Library, 212 West Rich Ave., DeLand, FL 32720.

Florida Genealogical Society, Inc., P.O. Box 18624, Tampa, FL 33609.

Florida Historical Society, P.O. Box 3645, University Station, Gainesville, FL 32601.

Florida State Genealogical Society, P.O. Box 10249, Tallahassee, FL 32302.

Gainesville Public Library, 222 E. University Ave., Gainesville, FL 32601.

Genealogy Society of Bay County Florida, P.O. Box 662, Panama City, FL 32401.

Genealogical Society of Greater Miami, 1702 Ponce de Leon Blvd., Coral Gables, FL 33134.

Genealogical Society of South Brevard County, Florida, P.O. Box 786, Melbourne, FL 32901.

Hillsborough County Historical Commission Museum Historical and Genealogical Library, County Courthouse, Tampa, FL 33602.

Jacksonville Genealogical Society, 4589 Amherst Street, Jacksonville, FL 32205.

Jacksonville, Public Library, 122 N. Ocean St., Jacksonville, FL 32202.

Manasota Genealogical Society, Inc., P.O. Box 9433, Bradenton, FL 33506.

Miami-Dade Public Library, 1 Biscayne Blvd., No., Miami, FL 33132.

Okaloosa County, Florida Genealogical Society, P.O. Drawer 1175, Fort Walton Beach, FL 32548.

Orlando Public Library, 10 N. Rosalind Ave., Orlando, FL 38201.

Palm Beach County Genealogical Society, P.O. Box 1745, West Palm Beach, FL 33402.

P.K. Yonge Library of Florida History, University of Florida, Gainesville, FL 32601.

Polk County Historical and Genealogical Library, P.O. Box 1719, Bartow, FL 33830.

Selby Public Library, 1001 Boulevard of the Arts, Sarasota, FL 33577.

Southern Genealogist's Exchange Society, Inc., P.O. Box 2801, Jacksonville, FL 32203.

State Library of Florida, R.A. Gray Building, Tallahassee, FL 32301.

Tampa Public Library, 900 N. Ashley St., Tampa, FL 33602.

Treasure Coast Genealogical Society, P.O. Box 3804, Fort Pierce, FL 33450.

Volusia County Genealogical and Historical Society, Inc., P.O. Box 2039, Daytona Beach, FL 32015.

Volusia County Public Library, City Island, Daytona Beach, FL 32014.

Florida Genealogist, published quarterly by the Florida State Genealogical Society, P.O. Box 10249, Tallahassee, FL 32302.

Journal, Florida Genealogical Society, P.O. Box 18624, Tampa, FL 33609.

Printed Census Records and Mortality Schedules

State census indexes - 1830, 1840, 1850

Other printed census records (counties) -

Alachua - 1830, 1840, 1850, 1860, 1870
Benton - 1850
Calhoun - 1850
Columbia - 1850
Dade - 1850
Duval - 1850
Escambia - 1850
Franklin - 1850
Gadsden - 1850
Hamilton - 1850
Hillsborough - 1830, 1840, 1850, 1860, 1870
Holmes - 1850
Jackson - 1850
Jefferson - 1850
Leon - 1850

Levy - 1850; 1868
Madison - 1850
Marion - 1850
Monroe - 1830, 1840, 1850, 1860, 1870
Mosquito - 1830
Nassau - 1850; 1895
Orange - 1850
Putnam - 1850
St. Johns- 1850
St. Lucas - 1850
Santa Rosa - 1850
Wakulla - 1850
Walton - 1850
Washington - 1850

Caker, William S. and G. Douglas Inglis. *Spanish Censuses of Pensacola, 1784-1820: A Genealogical Guide to Spanish Pensacola.* Pensacola, Florida: Perdido Bay Press 1981.

Valuable Printed Sources

Atlas

Ladd, Edward Johnson. *Atlas and Outline History of Southeastern United States.* Fort Payne, Alabama, 1973.

Place Names

Morris, Allen Covington. *Florida Place Names.* Coral Gables, Florida: University of Miami Press, 1974.

Histories

Cutler, H. G. *History of Florida, Past and Present,* Three Volumes. Chicago: Lewis Publishing Company, 1923.

Dovell, J. E. *Florida Historic - Dramatic - Contemporary,* Four Volumes. New York: Lewis Historical Publishing Company, 1952.

Genealogical Sources D.A.R. Collection*

St. Augustine Historical Society Collection. Biographical Card Index and Genealogical File, Chronological document files contains letters, wills, and other miscellaneous documents dating from 1566-1778*

Soldiers of the Seminole Indian: Civil and Spanish-American Wars. Live Oak, Florida: Prepared and published under the supervision of the Board of State Institutions, Democrat Book and Job Print.

Bibliographies

Parks, Karl E. II. *A Check List of Genealogical Materials in the Mease Memorial Genealogical Section of The Dunedin Public Library.* Tarpon Springs, Florida: author, 1981.

---

*On microfilm at the Genealogical Society Library of The Church of Jesus Christ of Latter-day Saints, Salt Lake City, Utah.

FLORIDA COUNTY HISTORIES
(Population figures to nearest thousand - 1980 U.S. Census)

Name	Map Index	Date Created	Pop. By M 1980	U.S. Cen Reports Available	Parent County or Territory From Which Organized	County Seat
* Alachua	B4	1824	147	1830-80	Duval, St. John	Gainesville 32601

(Co Clk has m rec from 1837 (m rec missing are 1856-1857, 1860-1863, 1867-1868) Pro rec from 1840; Ind rec from 1848, civ ct rec, mortgages from 1882, plats from 1884, co minute bk from 1873; Bur Vit Statistics, Jacksonville has b rec)

| Baker | B4 | 1861 | 15 | 1870-80 | New River | Macclenny 32063 |

(Co Judge has m & pro rec; Clk Cir Ct has div & civ ct rec from 1880)

| Bay | A2 | 1913 | 97 | | Calhoun, Washington | Panama City 32401 |

(Health Dept has b, d rec; Clk Cir Ct has m, pro, div, civ ct, Ind rec from 1913)

| Benton | | 1843 | | 1850 | Alachua (Now Hernando) | |
| Bradford | B4 | 1861 | 20 | 1870-80 | "New River" up to 1861 | Starke 32091 |

(Co Clk has m rec from 1875, pro, civ ct rec from 1892, Ind rec from 1876; Bur Vit Statistics, Jacksonville, has b, d rec)

| * Brevard | C5 | 1855 | 270 | 1860-80 | Mosquito, "St. Lucie" up to 1855 | Titusville 32780 |

(Clk Cir Ct has m, div, pro, civ ct, Ind rec from 1885; Bur Vit Statistics, Jacksonville has b, d rec)
(All records prior to 1885 were destroyed by fire)

| Broward | E5 | 1915 | 999 | | Dade, Palm Beach | Ft. Lauderdale 33301 |

(Clk Cir Ct has m, pro rec from 1915; div, civ ct, Ind rec from 1915, crim ct rec from 1915)

| Calhoun | A2 | 1838 | 9 | 1840-80 | Franklin, Washington, Jackson | Blountstown 32424 |

(Co Judge has m & pro rec; Co Clk has div, civ ct & Ind rec)

| § Charlotte | D4 | 1921 | 56 | | DeSoto | Punta Gorda 33950 |

(Clk Cir Ct has m, div, pro, civ ct, Ind rec from 1921)

| Citrus | D4 | 1887 | 53 | | Hernando | Inverness 32650 |

(Clk Cir Ct has m, div, pro, civ ct rec from 1887, Ind rec from 1878, Health Dept, Inverness, has b, d rec)

COUNTY MAP FOR THE STATE OF FLORIDA

Name	Map Index	Date Created	Pop. By M 1980	U.S. Cen Reports Available	Parent County or Territory From Which Organized	County Seat
§ Clay	B4	1858	67	1860-80	Duval . . . . Green Cove Springs 32043	
(Co Judge has m & pro rec; Clk Cir Ct has div, civ ct & Ind rec)						
*§ Collier	E4	1923	85		Lee, Monroe . . . . Naples 33940	
(Co Judge has m & pro rec; Clk Cir Ct has div, civ ct & Ind rec from 1923)						
* Columbia	B4	1832	35	1840-80	Alachua . . . . Lake City 32055	
(Clk Cir Ct has b rec from 1943, m, Ind rec from 1875, Div, civ ct rec 1892, pro rec from 1895, delayed birth certificates issued by the County Judge's Office)						
* Dade	E5	1836	1,573	1840-80	Monroe, St. Lucie (1855) . . . . Miami 33101	
(Co Judge has m & pro rec; Clk Cir Ct has div & Ind rec from 1890)						
DeSoto	D4	1887	19		Manatee . . . . Arcadia 33821	
(Co Judge has pro rec from 1887; Clk Cir Ct has div, civ ct & Ind rec from 1887)						
Dixie	B3	1921	8		Lafayette . . . . Cross City 32628	
(Clk Cir Ct has div, pro, civ ct & Ind rec)						
*§ Duval	B4	1822	571	1830-80	St. John . . . . Jacksonville 32202	
(Clk Cir Ct has div, cir ct rec, deeds & mtg from 1921, service rec bk from 1920; Co Judge has m & pro rec)						
* Escambia	A1	1822	229	1830-80	One of two original counties . . . . Pensacola 32502	
(Clk Co Ct has m, pro, civ ct, crim rec from 1821; Clk Cir Ct has civ and felony rec from 1822; Co Health Dept has b, d rec; Comptroller has Ind rec from 1821)						
§ Flagler	B5	1917	11		St. John, Volusia . . . . Bunnell 32010	
(Co Judge has m & pro rec from 1917; Clk Cir Ct has div, civ ct & Ind rec from 1917)						
Franklin	B2	1832	8	1840-80	Jackson . . . . Apalachicola 32320	
(Co Judge has m & pro rec; Clk Cir Ct has div, civ ct & Ind rec)						
Gadsden	A3	1823	40	1830-80	Jackson . . . . Quincy 32351	
(Co Judge has m & pro rec; Clk Cir Ct has div, civ ct & Ind rec)						
* Gilchrist	B4	1925	6		Alachua . . . . Trenton 32693	
(Clk Cir Ct, has m rec, div, pro, civ ct rec from 1926)						
Glades	D4	1921	6		DeSoto . . . . Moore Haven 33471	
(Co Judge has m & pro rec; Clk Cir Ct has div, civ ct & Ind rec from 1921)						
Gulf	B2	1925	10		Calhoun . . . . Port St. Joe 32456	
(Clk Cir Ct has m, pr, div, civ ct, Ind, service discharges from 1925)						
Hamilton	A4	1827	9	1830-80	Duval . . . . Jasper 32052	
(Co Judge has m & pro rec; Clk Cir Ct has div, civ ct rec from 1881, Ind rec from 1837)						
*§ Hardee	D4	1921	17		DeSoto . . . . Wauchula 33873	
(Clk Cir Ct has m, div, pro, civ ct, Ind rec from 1921; Co Health Dept has b, d rec)						
§ Hendry	D4	1923	19		Lee . . . . LaBelle 33935	
(Co Judge has m & pro rec; Clk Cir Ct has div, civ ct & Ind rec from 1923)						
* Hernando	C4	1850	44	1870-80	Alachua (formerly Benton) . . . . Brooksville 33512	
(Clk Co Ct has m rec; Clk Cir Ct has div, pro, civ ct, Ind rec from 1877)						
Highlands	D4	1921	47		DeSoto . . . . Sebring 33870	
(Clk Cir Ct has m, div, pro, civ ct, Ind rec from 1921)						
* Hillsborough	C4	1834	641	1840-80	Alachua, Monroe . . . . Tampa 33601	
(Co Judge has m & pro rec; Clk Cir Ct has div & Ind rec)						
Holmes	A2	1848	15	1850-80	Walton, Washington, Calhoun . . . . Bonifay 32452	
(Clk Cir Ct has m, pro, div, civ ct and Ind rec)						
Indian River	C5	1925	57		St. Lucie . . . . Vero Beach 32960	
(Clk Cir Ct has m, div, pro, civ ct, Ind rec from 1925; County Health Dept has b, d rec)						
* Jackson	A2	1822	39	1830-80	Escambia . . . . Marianna 32446	
(Co Judge has m & pro rec; Clk Cir Ct has div, civ ct & Ind rec from 1850)						
Jefferson	A3	1827	10	1830-80	Leon . . . . Monticello 32344	
(Clk Cir Ct has m rec from 1840, div rec from 1900, pro rec from 1850, Civ Ct rec from 1850, Ind rec from 1827; State Dept of Health, Jacksonville has b, d rec)						
* Lafayette	B3	1856	4	1860-80	Madison . . . . Mayo 32066	
(Co Judge has m & pro rec; Clk Cir Ct has div from 1902, civ ct rec from 1907 & Ind rec from 1893)						
* Lake	C4	1887	104		Orange, Sumter . . . . Tavares 32778	
(Clk Cir Ct, has d, civ ct, div, Ind, crim rec from 1887, m rec from 1887, pro rec from 1893, adoption rec)						
Lee	D4	1887	204		Monroe . . . . Ft. Myers 33902	
(Clk Cir Ct has m, div, pro, civ ct, Ind rec; Bur Vit Statistics, Jacksonville has b, d rec)						
*§ Leon	A3	1824	146	1830-80	Gadsden . . . . Tallahassee 32302	
(Clk Cir Ct has m, div, pro, civ ct, Ind rec from 1825; Leon Co Health Dept has b, d, bur rec)						
Levy	B4	1845	19	1850-80	Alachua, Marion . . . . Bronson 32621	
(Clk Cir Ct has m, div, pro, civ ct, Ind rec from 1850)						
Liberty	B2	1855	4	1860-80	Franklin, Gadsden . . . . Bristol 32321	
(Co Judge has m & pro rec; Clk Cir Ct has div, civ ct & Ind rec)						

Name	Map Index	Date Created	Pop. By M 1980	U.S. Cen Reports Available	Parent County or Territory From Which Organized	County Seat
Madison	A3	1827	15	1830-80	Jefferson	Madison 32340

(Clk Cir Ct has m, pro, civ ct rec from 1838, Ind rec from 1831, div rec)

* Manatee	D4	1855	146	1860-80	Hillsboro	Bradenton 33505

(Clk Cir Ct has m, div, pro, civ ct, Ind rec from 1857; State Division of Heath, Jacksonville, has b, d, bur rec)

* Marion	B4	1844	119	1850-80	Alachua, Hillsborough, Mosquito	Ocala 32670
Martin	D5	1925	63		Palm Beach, St. Lucie	Stuart 33494

(Clk Cir Ct has m, div, pro, civ ct, Ind rec from 1925; Martin Co Health Dept has b, d, bur rec)

Monroe	E5	1823	62	1830-80	St. Johns	Key West 33040

(Clk Cir Ct has m, div, pro, civ ct, Ind rec from 1853; State Bur Vit Statistics has b, d rec)

Mosquito	C3	1824		1830-40	(changed to Orange, 1845)	
Nassau	A4	1824	33	1830-80	Duval	Fernandina Beach 32034
New River		1858		1860	(changed to Bradford, 1861)	
§ Okaloosa	A1	1915	110		Santa Rosa, Walton	Crestview 32536

(Co Judge has m & pro rec; Clk Cir Ct has div, civ ct & Ind rec from 1915)

Okeechobee	D5	1917	20		Osceola, Palm Beach, St. Lucie	Okeechobee 33472

(Clk Cir Ct has m, div, pro, civ ct rec from 1917, Ind rec from 1880's, early Ind rec of those portions of Osceola and St. Lucie counties which were taken to form Okeechobee County. County Dept of Health has b, d rec)

* Orange	C5	1824	468	1850-80	(changed from Mosquito, 1845), Sumter (1871)	Orlando 32802

(Clk Cir Ct has m rec from 1890, civ, pro, civ ct rec from 1869; Fla Dept of Vit Statistics has b, m rec)

* Osceola	C5	1887	49		Brevard, Orange	Kissimmee 32741

(Co Judge has m & pro rec; Clk Cir Ct has div, civ ct & Ind rec)

Palm Beach	D5	1909	552		Dade	West Palm Beach 33401

(Co Judge has m & pro rec; Clk Cir Ct has div, civ ct & Ind rec)

* Pasco	C4	1887	189		Hernando	Dade City 33525

(Clk Cir Ct, has div, civ ct, Ind rec from 1887, m, pro rec)

*§ Pinellas	C4	1911	721		Hillsboro	Clearwater 33516

(Clk Cir Ct has m, div, pro, civ ct, Ind rec from 1911; Bur Vit Statistics, Jacksonville, has b, d rec)

* Polk	C4	1861	322	1870-80	Brevard, Hillsborough (Boundaries changed 1871)	Bartow 33830

(Clk Cir Ct has m, div, pro, civ ct, Ind rec from 1861)

* Putnam	B4	1849	49	1850-80	Alachua, Marion, Orange, St. Johns	Palatka 32077

(Clk Cir Ct has m, div, pro, civ ct, Ind rec from 1849, cem rec survey 19th, 20th centuries; Bur Vit Statistics, Jacksonville, has b, d rec various cem associations have bur rec)

St. Johns	B5	1822	50	1830-80	One of two original cos	St. Augustine 32084

(Co Judge has m & pro rec; Clk Cir Ct has div from 1900, civ ct & Ind rec from 1821)

St. Lucas	C4	1844			(changed to Brevard, 1855)	
* St. Lucie	D5	1905	87	1850	Brevard	Fort Pierce 33450

(Clk Cir Ct has m, pro, div, civ ct, Ind rec from 1905; Co Health Dept had d rec (if recorded) and bur rec; Bur Vit Statistics, Jacksonville, has b rec)

Santa Rosa	A1	1842	56	1850-80	Escambia	Milton 32570

(Clk Cir Ct has m, div, civ ct from 1869) (courthouse burned in 1869)

*§ Sarasota	D4	1921	202		Manatee	Sarasota 33578

(Co Judge has m & pro rec from 1921; Clk Cir Ct has div, civ ct & Ind rec from 1921)

Seminole	C5	1913	178		Orange	Sanford 32771

(Co Judge has m & pro rec; Clk Cir Ct has div, civ ct, Ind rec & mtg from 1915)

Sumter	C4	1853	23	1860-80	Marion	Bushnell 33513

(Clk Cir Ct has m, Ind rec from 1853, pro rec from 1856, div rec from 1900, civ ct rec from 1913; Clk Cir Ct has delayed b rec 1943-1972)

Suwannee	B4	1858	22	1860-80	Columbia	Live Oak 32060

(Clk Cir Ct has div & civ ct rec from 1858, also some b & m rec from 1858)

Taylor	B3	1856	16	1860-80	Madison	Perry 32347

(Co Judge has m & pro rec; Clk Cir Ct has div & Ind rec)

Union	B4	1921	10		Bradford	Lake Butler 32054

(Clk Cir Ct has div & civ ct rec)

* Volusia	B5	1854	249	1860-80	St. Lucas	DeLand 32720

(Clk Cir Ct has m, div, civ ct, pro, Ind rec)

§ Wakulla	B3	1843	11	1850-80	Leon	Crawfordville 32327

(Clk Cir Ct has m, div, pro, civ ct, Ind rec from late 1800's; Bur Vit Statistics, Jacksonville, has b, d rec)

Name	Map Index	Date Created	Pop. By M 1980	U.S. Cen Reports Available	Parent County or Territory From Which Organized	County Seat
* Walton	A2	1824	21	1830-80	Jackson	De Funiak Springs 32433

(Clk Cir Ct has m rec from 1885, pro rec from 1882, div, civ ct, Ind rec; County Health Dept has b, d rec; Clk Cir Ct has newspaper rec from 1905)

Name	Map Index	Date Created	Pop. By M 1980	U.S. Cen Reports Available	Parent County or Territory From Which Organized	County Seat
Washington	A2	1825	14	1830-80	Jackson, Walton	Chipley 32428

(Co Judge has m & pro rec; Clk Cir Ct has div, civ ct & Ind rec from 1890)

* - At least one county history has been published about this county.

§ - Inventory of county archives was made by the Historical Records Survey. (see introduction)

GEORGIA

CAPITAL, ATLANTA - STATE 1788 - (4TH)

For one hundred sixty years or more England and the Spanish were playing a gigantic game of chess with the dominance of Georgia as the prize. This continued from 1540 to early in 1700. When South Carolina became a royal province in 1732, the land between the Savannah and the St. Mary's Rivers was set aside for a new British colony.

It was the practice in England at that time to imprison individuals unable to pay their debts. This practice irked a humanitarian army officer and member of Parliament, James Oglethorpe, who conceived the idea of rehabilitating these poor people by taking them to the New World, giving them a tract of land and assisting and guiding them in establishing their homes. He induced King George II to grant to him and twenty other men the English territory south of the Savannah.

With thirty-five families he arrived there in 1733 and established a community at the mouth of the Savannah, which he named after the river. Halfway between the mouth of that river and the southern border of South Carolina they established Augusta in 1734. In the meantime persecuted Protestants in Europe had been invited to come to the colony. At first Roman Catholics were refused entrance in the new country.

By 1738 Swiss, German, Italian, Scottish Highlanders, Salzburger, and Moravian settlers had arrived in Georgia. In 1739 another community called Frederica was established on the south banks of the Altamaha. Two years later Georgia was divided into two counties - north of the Altamaha was called Savannah, and south of that river Frederica.

Many of the Moravians had come from North Carolina to Spring Place and New Echota. Unsuccessful in their desire to convert the Indians to their faith, the Moravians later moved from Georgia to Pennsylvania, where they increased rapidly in Bethlehem and Nazareth.

Many of the Presbyterians who came to Georgia as Scottish Highlanders settled in Darien, which they renamed New Inverness. In 1752 a group of Massachusetts Puritans came to Midway.

Georgia became a royal province in 1732. The colony claimed all of the land between North Carolina and Florida, and the Atlantic and the Mississippi River.

After the Revolution, conflict between Georgia and the federal government over states' rights led to passage of the 11th Amendment (1798). Further confusion arose when the legislature fraudulently sold state lands to speculators; and, although Georgia set its present boundaries in 1802, Indian claims to much of its territory persisted for years.

The first counties in Georgia were formed in 1777. These counties covered only a fraction of the land claimed by the province. They covered the section between the Savannah River and the Oconee and the Altamaha Rivers, and a strip about thirty-five miles wide extending from the Altamaha to the Florida border. In 1790 there were eleven counties as follows, from north to south: Franklin, Wilkes, Greene, Richmond, Burke, Washington, Effingham, Chatham, Liberty, Glynn, and Camden. These counties included the area now occupied by the present counties as follows:

Franklin: the south three-fourths of Stephens, Franklin, Banks, Jackson, all of Oconee but the southern most tip, all of Clarke but the southern fourth, all of Madison but the southeast tip, and Hart.

Wilkes: the southern tip of Clarke, Oglethorpe, the southeastern tip of Madison, Wilkes, Elbert, Lincoln, Columbia, McDuffie, Glascock, Warren, all but the west fourth of Taliaferro, and small piece of east corner of Greene.

Greene: small south corner of Oconee, small west corner of Oglethorpe, all of Greene but small north triangle, west fourth of Taliaferro, all of Hancock but south fourth, triangular small northeast corner of Baldwin.

Richmond: Triangular northeast fourth of Jefferson and Richmond.

Burke: all of Jefferson but southwest triangular quarter of northeast triangular quarter, Burke, all of Jenkins but southwest third, and northern triangular half of Screven.

Washington: south fourth of Hancock, triangular small southeast corner of Baldwin, Washington, southwest quarter of Jefferson, Johnson, east third of Laurens, east triangular half of Montgomery, Emanual, southeast quarter of Jenkins, Bulloch, Bryan, and west half of Tattnall, and Toombs.

Effingham: the southern half of Screven, and Effingham.

Chatham: Chatham, and southern half of Bryan.

Liberty: eastern half of Tattnall, Liberty Long, and McIntosh.

Glynn: eastern half of Wayne, Glynn, and northeastern third of Brantley.

Camden: southeastern third of Brantley, eastern half of Charlton, and Camden.

Today Georgia has 159 counties. Only nineteen states have a larger area.

In 1798 the Territory of Mississippi was created from the western half of Georgia. Later that territory was formed into the states of Alabama and Mississippi.

Many settlers in Virginia and the Carolinas were attracted to Georgia by the early land lotteries. Families who had lived in the territory for at least one year were permitted to draw for acreages as large as 400 acres. Such lotteries, the participant lists of which are now in the office of the Secretary of State, were held in 1803, 1806, 1819, 1827, and 1832.

Georgia Department of Human Resources, Vital Records Service, Room 217-H, 47 Trinity Avenue, S.W., Atlanta, Georgia 30334 has records on file for births from 1919 to present, deaths from 1919 to present, marriages from 1952 to present and divorces from 1952 to present.

Certified copies of births are issued at county and state offices to a. the person named on the certificate, b. either parent, c. legal representative. Index is closed to public.

Death certificates are issued at state and county offices. Index is closed to public.

Certified copies of marriages are issued in the county where marriage was performed. Index is open to the public and copies of the license may be purchased.

Certified copies of divorce records are issued in the county where decree was granted. Index is open to the public. Copy of decree issued by clerk of superior court.

Atlanta and Savannah and other cities may have vital records recorded before 1919.

The county clerk or the clerk of the Ordinary Court have records of marriages performed in that county.

Records of divorce actions are kept by Superior Court Clerk in county where granted. They also have Civil Court Records.

Naturalization records are filed in the office of the Superior Court in the county where hearing was held. Similar records are also found in the office of the clerk of the federal district courts in Atlanta and Savannah.

The deeds to lands are recorded in the office of the Court of Ordinary where land is located. Abstracts of land grants are furnished for a fee in the office of the clerk of the Secretary of State.

Wills are recorded in the office of the clerk of the Court of Ordinary in county where testator resided.

Genealogical Archives, Libraries, Societies, and Publications

Athens Regional Library, 120 W. Dougherty St., Athens, GA 30601.

Atlanta Historical Society, 3099 Andrews Drive, N.W., Atlanta, GA 30305.

Augusta Genealogical Society, P.O. Box 3743, Augusta, GA 30904.

Bradley Memorial Library, Bradley Dr., Columbus, GA 31906.

Brunswick Regional Library, 208 Gloucester St., Brunswick, GA 31521.

Carnegie Library, 607 Broad St., Rome, GA 30161.

Central Georgia Genealogical Society, P.O. Box 2024, Warner Robins, GA 31093.

Chattahoochee Valley Historical Society, 1213 Fifth Avenue, West Point, GA 31833.

Chestatee Regional Library, 127 North Main, Gainesville, GA 30501.

Cobb County Public Library System genealogical collection, housed in the Georgia Room, Marietta Library, 30 Atlanta Street, Marietta, GA 30060.

Colquitt-Thomas Regional Library, P.O. Box 1110, Moultrie, GA 31768.

Decatur-DeKalb Library, 215 Sycamore St., Decatur, GA 30030.

Genealogical Center Library, 15 Dunwoody Park Road, #130, Atlanta, GA 30338.

Georgia Department of Archives and History, 330 Capitol Ave., Atlanta, GA 30334.

Georgia Genealogical Society, P.O. Box 38066, Atlanta, GA 30334.

Georgia Historical Society Library, 501 Whittaker St., Savannah, GA 31401.

Georgia State Library, 301 State Judicial Bldg., Capitol Hill Station, Atlanta, GA 30334.

Georgia State University Archives, 104 Decatur St., S.E., Atlanta, GA 30303.

Gwinnett Historical Society, Inc., P.O. Box 261, Lawrenceville, GA 30246.

Lake Blackshear Regional Library, 307 E. Lamar St., Americus, GA 31709.

Lake Lanier Regional Library, Pike St., Lawrenceville, GA 30245.

Middle Georgia Regional Library, 911 1st St., Macon, GA 31201.

Murrell Memorial Library, Box 606, 207 5th Ave., N.E. Eastman, GA 31203.

Northeast Cobb County, Georgia Genealogical Society, P.O. Box 1413, Marietta, GA 30060.

Northwest Georgia Historical and Genealogical Society, P.O. Box 2484, Rome, GA 30161.

Oconee County Library, Watkinsville, GA 30677.

Okefenokee Regional Library, Box 1669, 401 Lee Ave., Waycross, GA 31501.

Piedmont Regional Library, Winder, GA 30680.

Pine Mountain Regional Library, Box 508, 218 Perry St., Manchester, GA 31816.

Satilla Regional Library, 617 E. Ward St., Douglas, GA 31533.

Savannah Public and Chatham, Effingham Liberty Regional Library, 2002 Bull St., Savannah, GA 31401.

Southwest Georgia Regional Library, Shotwell at Monroe, Bainbridge, GA 31717.

Statesboro Regional Library, 124 S. Main St., Statesboro, GA 30458.

Washington Memorial Library, 1190 Washington Ave., Macon, GA 31201.

Whitfield-Murray Historical Society, Crown Garden and Archives, 715 Chattanooga Avenue, Dalton, GA 30720.

Ancestoring II, publication of the Augusta Genealogical society, P.O. Box 3743, Augusta, GA 30904.

Ancestors Unlimited, P.O. Box 490336, College Park, GA 30349.

Central Georgia Genealogical Society Quarterly, P.O. Box 2024, Warner Robins, GA 31093.

Genealogical Gazette, published quarterly. Library Productions Corporation, 15 Dunwoody Park, Suite 130, Atlanta, GA 30338.

Georgia Genealogical Magazine, The, P.O. Box 738, Easley, SC 29640.

Georgia Genealogical Society Quarterly, The, P.O. Box 38066, Atlanta, GA 38066.

Georgia Pioneers, Genealogical Magazine, P.O. Box 1028, Albany, GA 31702.

Northwest Georgia Historical and Genealogical Society Quarterly. P.O. Box 2484, Rome, GA 30161.

Printed Census Records and Mortality Schedules

State indexes - 1790, 1820, 1830, 1840, 1850

County printed census records:

Appling - 1820, 1830, 1860
Baker - 1850
Baldwin - 1820, 1830
Berrien - 1860
Bibb - 1850
Bleckley - 1830, 1840, 1850, 1860
Brooks - 1860
Bryan - 1850
Bulloch - 1860, 1870; 1865
Burke - 1850

Butts - 1850
Camden - 1850
Campbell - 1850
Chatham - 1850, 1860; 1845
Cherokee - 1850; 1834
Clayton - 1860, 1870
Clinch - 1860, 1870
Coffee - 1860, 1870
Colquitt - 1860
Columbia - 1850

Dade - 1840, 1850, 1860, 1870, 1880
Decatur - 1850
DeKalb - 1850
Dooly - 1850
Early - 1850
Echols - 1860, 1870
Effingham - 1850
Elbert - 1820, 1830, 1840, 1850, 1860
Emanuel - 1850
Fayette - 1850

Floyd - 1850, 1860
Franklin - 1850
Gilmer - 1840, 1850
Glynn - 1850
Gordon - 1850
Greene - 1850
Heard - 1850, 1860, 1870
Howard - 1850
Henry - 1850
Houston - 1850
Irwin - 1850, 1860
Jefferson - 1850
Laurens - 1850
Lee - 1850
Liberty - 1850

Lincoln - 1800, 1850
Lowndes - 1850
Lumpkin - 1850
Macon - 1850
Madison - 1850
Marion - 1850
McIntosh - 1850
Monroe - 1850
Muscogee - 1850
Oglethorpe - 1800
Pierce - 1860
Pike - 1850
Pulaski - 1830, 1840, 1850, 1860
Putnam - 1850
Randolph - 1850

Richmond - 1850
Screven - 1820, 1830, 1850
Sumter - 1850
Talbot - 1850
Tattnall - 1820, 1850
Telfair - 1820, 1850
Thomas - 1850
Troup - 1850
Upson - 1850
Walker - 1850
Ware - 1850, 1860
Washington - 1820, 1830, 1840, 1850
Wayne - 1850
Wilkes - 1850

Mortality Schedules (printed): 1850, 1860, 1870

Other Printed Census Records:

Townsend, Brigid S. *Indexes to Seven State Census Reports For Counties in Georgia 1838-1845* Atlanta, Georgia: R. J. Taylor, Jr. Foundation, 1975.

Valuable Printed Sources

Atlases and Gazetteers

Bonner, James C. *Atlas for Georgia History.* Milledgeville, Georgia: George College (1969). Reprint from *Georgia Historical Quarterly,* Sept. 1967.

Sherwood, Adiel. *A Gazetteer of the State of Georgia.* Athens, Georgia: The University of Georgia Press (1939)

Place Names

Hemperley, Marion R. *Cities, Towns and Communities of Georgia Between 1847-1962, 8500 Places and the County in Which Located.* Easley, South Carolina: Southern Historical Press, 1980.

Krakow, Kenneth K. *Georgia Place Names.* Macon: Winship Press, 1975.

Guides To Genealogical Research

Davis, Robert Scott, Jr. *Research in Georgia - With A Special Emphasis Upon The Georgia Department of Archives and History.* Easley: Southern Historical Press, 1981.

Ellis, Gayle. *Retracing Our Ancestors Steps Through Georgia,* 1976.

Thomas, Kenneth H. Jr. *Ken Thomas on Genealogy,* WH Wolfe Associates, 1981.

Histories

Candler, Allen D. and General Clement A. Evans. *Cyclopedia of Georgia,* Three Volumes. Atlanta, Georgia: State Historical Association, 1906.

McCall, Hugh. *The History of Georgia.* Atlanta: Cherokee Publishing Company, Reprint of 1909 edition, 1969.

Genealogical Sources

D.A.R. Collection*

Warren, Mary Bondurant. *Marriages and Deaths, 1763-1830, Abstracted from Extant Georgia Newspapers* Two Volumes. Danielsville, Georgia: Heritage Papers.

An Index to Georgia Colonial Conveyances and Confiscated Lands Records 1750-1804. Atlanta, Georgia: R. J. Taylor Jr. Foundation, 1981.

Lucas, Silas Emmett, Jr. *Index to the Headright and Bounty Grants in Georgia From 1756-1909.* Easley, South Carolina: Southern Historical Press, 1970 Reprinted 1981.

Maddox, Joseph T. *Early Georgia Marriages,* Volumes 1-4 Irwinton, Georgia: Privately published, 1975-1978.

Brooke, Ted O. *Georgia Wills 1733-1860.* Marietta, Georgia: Pilgrim Press, 1976.

Hollingsworth, Leon S. *Genealogical Card File* (During the course of his long genealogical career, Mr. Hollingsworth accumulated an extensive card file of references to persons and families from Georgia, the Carolinas, Virginia and Alabama. The cards contain references to persons mentioned in genealogical records. The notations include a brief abstract of the information and a citation to the original record). Atlanta, Georgia: R. J. Taylor, Jr. Foundation, 1979 (microfilm).

Bibliographies

Simpson, John Eddins, comp. *Georgia History: A Bibliography.* Metuchen, New Jersey: The Scarecrow Press, 1976 (Includes individual biographies and Family Histories).

GEORGIA COUNTY HISTORIES
(Population figures to nearest thousand - 1980 U.S. Census)

Name	Map Index	Date Created	Pop. By M 1980	U.S. Cen Reports Available	Parent County or Territory From Which Organized	County Seat
Appling	D3	1818	15	1820-80	Creek Indian Lands	Baxley 31513

(Rec begin 1879; some 1859; Pro Ct has b, m, d & bur rec; Clk Sup Ct has div, pro & civ ct rec)

| Atkinson | E3 | 1917 | 6 | | Coffee, Clinch | Pearson 31642 |

(Clk Sup Ct has div, pro & civ ct rec from 1919; Pro Ct has b & d rec from 1929, m rec from 1919)

| Bacon | D3 | 1914 | 9 | | Appling, Pearce, Ware | Alma 31510 |

(Clk Sup Ct has div, civ ct rec & deeds from 1915; Pro Ct has b, m, d & pro rec from 1915)

| Baker | E1 | 1825 | 4 | 1830-80 | Early | Newton 31770 |
| * Baldwin | C2 | 1803 | 34 | 1820-80 | Creek Indian Lands | Milledgeville 31061 |

(Pro Ct. has b, m, d & bur rec; Co Clk has div, civ ct & Ind rec from 1861)

| Banks | A2 | 1858 | 7 | 1860-80 | Franklin, Habersham | Homer 30547 |

(Pro Ct. has b & m rec; Clk Sup Ct has div, civ ct & Ind rec from 1859)

| Barrow | B2 | 1914 | 21 | | Jackson, Walton, Guinett | Winder 30680 |

(Pro Ct. has b, m, d & bur rec; Clk Sup Ct. has div, civ ct & Ind rec from 1915)

| * Bartow | A1 | 1861 | 41 | 1870-80 | Changed from Cass 1861 | Cartersville 30120 |

(Pro Ct. has b, m & Pro rec; Clk Sup Ct has div rec from 1862, civ ct rec from 1869, Ind rec from 1837, also service discharges)

| Ben Hill | D2 | 1906 | 15 | | Irwin, Wilcox | Fitzgerald 31750 |

(Co Clk has div, civ ct, Ind rec from 1907; Pro Judge has b, m, d, bur rec.)

| Berrien | E2 | 1856 | 13 | 1860-80 | Lowndes, Coffee, Irwin | Nashville 31639 |

(Clk Sup Ct has div & civ ct rec from 1856; Pro Ct. has b & d rec from 1919, m & pro rec from 1856)

| Bibb | C2 | 1822 | 149 | 1830-80 | Jones, Monroe, Twiggs, Houston | Macon 31201 |

(Macon-Bibb Co Health Dept has b, d, bur rec; Pro Ct has m, pro rec; Co Clk has div, civ ct, Ind rec from 1823)

| * Bleckley | C2 | 1912 | 11 | | Pulaski | Cochran 31014 |

(Clk Sup Ct has div, pro & civ ct rec)

| Brantley | E3 | 1920 | 9 | | Charlton, Pierce, Wayne | Nahunta 31553 |

(Clk Sup Ct has b, div, pro & civ ct rec from 1921)

| * Brooks | E2 | 1858 | 15 | 1860-80 | Lowndes, Thomas | Quitman 31643 |
| * Bryan | D4 | 1793 | 8 | 1820-80 | Effingham, Liberty | Pembroke 31321 |

(Pro Judge has m, pro, b and some d rec; Co Clk has div rec from 1920, civ ct, Ind, crim rec from 1793)

| Bulloch | C4 | 1796 | 35 | 1820-80 | Franklin | Statesboro 30458 |

(Pro Ct. has b & m rec; Clk Sup Ct has div, civ ct rec from 1891, Ind rec from 1876)

| * Burke | C3 | 1777 | 19 | 1820-80 | St. George Parish | Waynesboro 30830 |

(Courthouse burned in January, 1856, all records prior to that date destroyed. Pro Ct. has b, d rec from 1927, m, pro rec from 1856. b and d rec not open to public. Full time Clk available and interested in assisting with available rec.)

| * Butts | B2 | 1825 | 13 | 1830-80 | Henry, Monroe | Jackson 30233 |

(Pro Ct. has b, m, d, pro rec; Clk Sup Ct has div, civ ct, Ind rec from 1825; History of Butts Co 1825-1976, copy available Clerk's office or county library.)

| Calhoun | D1 | 1854 | 6 | 1860-80 | Baker & Early | Morgan 31766 |

(Co Clk has b, m, d, div, pro, civ ct, Ind rec from 1854.)

COUNTY MAP FOR THE STATE OF GEORGIA

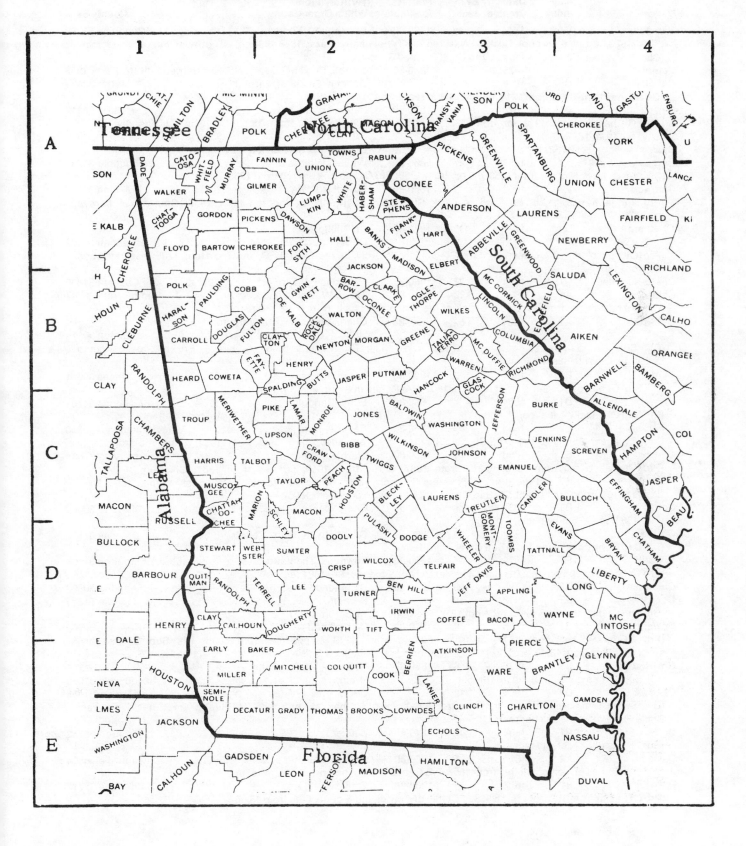

Name	Map Index	Date Created	Pop. By M 1980	U.S. Cen Reports Available	Parent County or Territory From Which Organized	County Seat
* Camden	E4	1777	13	1820-80	St. Mary, St. Thomas	Woodbine 31569

(Fire 1870, only one book lost - Will rec "B" between years 1828-1860 - all others intact & legible); (Clk Sup Ct has div, civ ct & Ind rec; Pro Ct has b, m, d & pro rec)

| Campbell | B1 | 1828 | | 1830-80 | Carroll, Coweta | Merged Fulton 1926 & 1932 |
| Candler | C3 | 1914 | 7 | | Bulloch, Emanuel, Tattnall | Metter 30439 |

(Co Clk has b, m, d rec from 1915; div, civ ct, Ind rec from 1914)

| * Carroll | B1 | 1826 | 56 | 1830-80 | Indian Lands | Carrollton 30117 |

(Pro Ct has b from 1919, m from 1827, d from 1919 & pro rec from 1827; Clk Sup Ct has div, civ ct & Ind rec from 1827)

| Cass | | 1832 | | 1840-60 | Changed to Bartow 1861 | |
| * Catoosa | A1 | 1853 | 37 | 1860-80 | Walker, Whitfield | Ringgold 30736 |

(Clk Sup Ct has civ ct rec from 1833; div rec from 1853; Pro Ct has m & pro rec from 1853)

| * Charlton | E3 | 1854 | 7 | 1860-80 | Camden, Ware | Folkston 31537 |

(Pro Judge has b, m, d, bur, pro rec; Clk Sup Ct has div, civ ct, Ind rec from 1877; Courthouse burned in 1877)

| *§ Chatham | D4 | 1777 | 197 | 1820-80 | St. Phillip, Christ Church Parish | Savannah 31402 |

(Pro Ct has b, m, d, pro rec; Clk Sup Ct has div rec, civ ct rec from 1783, Ind rec from 1785; naturalization rec from 1801)

| * Chattahoochee | C1 | 1854 | 22 | 1860-80 | Muscogee, Marion | Cusseta 31805 |
| Chattooga | A1 | 1838 | 22 | 1840-80 | Floyd, Walker | Summerville 30747 |

(Clk Cts has div rec from early 1900's & civ ct rec; Ord office has b, m, d, bur & pro rec)

| * Cherokee | A2 | 1831 | 52 | 1840-80 | Cherokee Lands, Habersham, Hall | Canton 30114 |

(Clk Sup Ct has div. civ ct rec & deeds from 1833; Pro Ct has b, m, d, bur & Pro rec; deeds comp except bk Q; Wills bks A & B lost)

| * Clarke | B2 | 1801 | 72 | 1820-80 | Jackson, Green | Athens 30601 |

(Clk Sup Ct has div, deeds & civ ct rec from 1801; Pro Ct has m & pro rec from 1801)

| Clay | D1 | 1854 | 4 | 1860-80 | Early, Randolph | Ft. Gaines 31751 |

(Clk Sup Ct has div & Ind rec)

| Clayton | B2 | 1858 | 150 | 1860-80 | Fayette, Henry | Jonesboro 30236 |

(Pro Ct has b, m, d & pro rec; Clk Sup Ct has div from 1946, civ ct rec from 1964 & Ind rec from 1859)

| *§ Clinch | E3 | 1850 | 7 | 1850-80 | Ware, Lowndes | Homerville 31634 |

(Pro Ct has b rec from 1919, m rec from 1867, d rec from 1919, pro rec from 1867; Clk Sup Ct has div, civ ct rec from 1867, Ind rec from 1868, voters list from 1890; all rec burned 1867. Previously burned 1856. Most deeds re-recorded since 1868. Clk Sup Ct has old co newspapers from 1895)

| * Cobb | B1 | 1832 | 295 | 1840-80 | Cherokee | Marietta 30060 |

(Fire 1864; rec lost previously)

| * Coffee | D3 | 1854 | 26 | 1860-80 | Clinch, Irwin, Ware, Telfair | Douglas 31533 |

(Clk Sup Ct has div, civ ct, Ind & Sup Ct rec from 1854)

| * Colquitt | E2 | 1856 | 35 | 1860-80 | Lowndes, Thomas | Moultrie 31768 |

(Pro Ct has b, m, d & pro rec; Clk Sup Ct has div, civ ct & Ind rec; fire 1881 rec lost)

| * Columbia | B3 | 1790 | 39 | 1820-80 | Richmond | Appling 30802 |
| § Cook | E2 | 1918 | 13 | | Berrien | Adel 31620 |

(Clk Sup Ct has div, pro & civ ct rec from 1919; Pro Ct has b, m, d from 1918)

| * Coweta | B1 | 1826 | 39 | 1830-80 | Indian Lands | Newman 30263 |

(Pro Ct has b rec from 1919, m from 1828, d from 1919 & pro rec from 1828; Clk Sup Ct has div, civ ct & Ind rec from 1828)

| * Crawford | C2 | 1822 | 8 | 1830-80 | Houston, Marion, Talbot, Macon | Knoxville 31050 |

(Clk Sup Ct has div & civ ct rec from 1850)

| * Crisp | D2 | 1905 | 19 | | Dooly | Cordele 31015 |

(Clk Sup Ct has div, civ ct, Ind rec from 1905; Pro Ct has m, pro rec; Co Health Dept has b, m rec; Dekle Funeral Home has bur rec)

| Dade | A1 | 1837 | 12 | 1840-80 | Walker | Trenton 30752 |

(Co Clk has div, civ ct, Ind rec)

| Dawson | A2 | 1857 | 5 | 1860-80 | Lumpkin, Gilmer | Dawsonville 30534 |

(Clk Sup Ct has div, civ ct, Ind rec from 1857; Pro Ct has b, m, d, bur, pro rec from 1858)

| * Decatur | E1 | 1823 | 25 | 1830-80 | Early | Bainbridge 31717 |

(Pro Ct has m from 1823, pro rec; Clk Sup Ct has div, civ ct, Ind & crim ct rec from 1823)

Name	Map Index	Date Created	Pop. By M 1980	U.S. Cen Reports Available	Parent County or Territory From Which Organized	County Seat
* DeKalb	B2	1822	476	1830-80	Fayette, Gwinett, Newton, Henry	Decatur 30030

(Clk Sup Ct has div, civ ct & Ind rec from 1842; Pro Ct has m & pro rec from 1842; Couthouse burned 1842 & 1916)

* Dodge	D3	1870	17	1880	Montgomery, Pulaski, Telfair	Eastman 31023

(Pro Ct has b, m, d & pro rec; Clk Sup Ct has div, pro, civ ct & Ind rec)

Dooly	D2	1821	11	1830-80	Indian Lands	Vienna 31092

(Clk Sup Ct has div & civ ct rec from 1846, deed rec from 1850; Pro Ct has b, m, d, bur & pro rec; fire dest early rec few m left 1848)

*§ Dougherty	D2	1852	101	1860-80	Baker	Albany 31702

(Clk Sup Ct has div & civ ct rec from 1856)

Douglas	B1	1870	54	1880	Carroll, Campbell	Douglasville 30134

(Pro Rec has b, m, d & pro rec; Clk Sup Ct has div, civ ct & Ind rec from 1870)

Early	E1	1818	13	1820-80	Creek Indian Lands	Blakely 31723

(Many rec lost; first m bk 1854)

§ Echols	E3	1858	2	1860-80	Clinch, Lowndes	Statenville 31648

(Most rec burned 1897) (Clk Sup Ct has div, civ ct & Ind rec)

Effingham	C4	1777	18	1820-80	St. Mathews, St. Phillips	Springfield 31329

(Pro Ct has b & d rec from 1927, m & pro rec from 1790; Clk Sup Ct. has div & civ ct rec from 1777; some rec lost CW and fire 1890)

* Elbert	B3	1790	19	1820-80	Wilkes	Elberton 30635

(Pro Ct has b, m, d, bur, pro rec; Clk Sup Ct has div, civ ct, Ind rec from 1790)

Emanuel	C3	1812	21	1820-80	Montgomery, Bulloch	Swainsboro 30401

(Pro Ct has b, m, d & pro rec; Clk Sup Ct has div, civ ct rec, Ind rec from 1812)

Evans	D4	1914	8		Bulloch, Tattnall	Claxton 30417

(Pro Ct has b, m, d, bur, pro rec; Clk Sup Ct has div rec, civ ct, Ind rec from 1915)

Fannin	A2	1854	15	1860-80	Gilmer, Union	Blue Ridge 30513

(Pro Ct has b, m, d rec; Clk Sup Ct has div, civ ct, Ind rec from 1854)

Fayette	B2	1821	29	1830-80	Indian Lands, Henry	Fayetteville 30214

(Pro Ct has b, m, d & pro rec; Clk Sup Ct has div, civ ct & Ind rec)

* Floyd	A1	1832	80	1840-80	Cherokee, Chattooga, Palding	Rome 30161

(Pro Ct has m & pro rec; Clk Sup Ct has div, civ ct & Ind rec from 1883)

Forsyth	A2	1832	28	1840-80	Cherokee, Lumpkin	Cumming 30130
* Franklin	A2	1784	15	1830-80	Cherokee Lands	Carnesville 30521

(Clk Sup Ct has div & civ ct rec from 1900, Ind rec from 1860) (some rec prior to 1850 in Ga. Archives)

* Fulton	B1	1853	586	1860-80	DeKalb, Campbell	Atlanta 30303

(Pro Ct has m & pro rec; Clk Sup Ct has div, civ ct & Ind rec from 1854)

* Gilmer	A2	1832	11	1840-80	Cherokee	Ellijay 30540

(Pro Ct has b, m, d & bur rec; Clk Sup Ct has div from 1927, pro & civ ct from 1900 & Ind rec from 1833)

* Glascock	B3	1857	2	1860-80	Warren, Jefferson	Gibson 30810

(Pro Ct has b, m, d rec; Clk Sup Ct has div, civ ct, Ind, fine, forfeits)

Glynn	E4	1777	54	1820-80	St. David, St. Patrick	Brunswick 31520

(Pro Ct has m rec from 1845, administrators, guardianship & pro rec from 1792; Clk Sup Ct has div & civ ct rec from 1792; deeds 1824-1829 burned, all rec to 1818 damaged)

* Gordon	A1	1850	30	1850-80	Cass, Floyd	Calhoun 30701

(Clk Sup Ct has div & civ ct rec from 1864; Pro Ct has b, m, d, bur & pro rec; rec destroyed 1864)

Grady	E2	1905	20		Decatur, Thomas	Cairo 31728

(Clk Sup Ct has div, civ ct, Ind rec from 1906)

* Greene	B3	1786	11	1820-80	Washington, Oglethorpe, Wilkes	Greensboro 30642

(Pro Ct has m, d, pro rec; Co Health Dept has b rec from 1927; Clk Sup Ct has div rec from 1790, civ ct, Ind rec from 1785)

* Gwinnett	B2	1818	166	1820-80	Cherokee Lands, Jackson	Lawrenceville 30245

(Clk Sup Ct has div, civ ct & Ind rec; Courthouse burned 1871, few rec saved)

* Habersham	A2	1818	26	1820-80	Cherokee Lands, Franklin	Clarkesville 30523

(Pro Ct has b, m, d & pro rec; Clk Sup Ct has div, civ ct & Ind rec from 1819)

* Hall	A2	1818	73	1820-80	Cherokee Lands, Jackson, Franklin	Gainesville 30501

(Clk Sup Ct has div & civ ct rec from 1819; Pro Ct has m & pro rec; tornado leveled courthouse 1936, many rec lost, deeds saved)

Name	Map Index	Date Created	Pop. By M 1980	U.S. Cen Reports Available	Parent County or Territory From Which Organized	County Seat
* Hancock	B3	1793	9	1820-80	Greene, Washington	Sparta 31087

(Pro Ct has b, d rec from 1927, m rec from 1805; Clk Sup Ct has div, civ ct rec from 1919, Ind rec from 1794)

| Haralson | B1 | 1856 | 18 | 1860-80 | Carroll, Polk | Buchanan 30113 |

(Pro Ct has b, m, d, bur, pro rec; Clk Sup Ct has div, civ ct, Ind rec)

| * Harris | C1 | 1827 | 15 | 1830-80 | Muscogee, Troup | Hamilton 31811 |

(Pro Ct has m rec; Clk Sup Ct has div, civ ct & Ind rec from 1828)

| * Hart | A3 | 1853 | 19 | 1860-80 | Elbert, Franklin | Hartwell 30643 |

(Pro Ct has b, m, d, bur, pro rec; Clk Sup Ct has div, civ ct, Ind, plats, crim, mort rec from 1856)

| Heard | B1 | 1830 | 7 | 1840-80 | Carroll, Coweta, Troup | Franklin 30217 |

(Pro Ct has b & d rec from 1927 and m & pro rec from 1894; fire 1894)

| Henry | B2 | 1821 | 35 | 1830-80 | Indian Lands, Walton | McDonough 30253 |

(Clk Sup Ct has div, civ ct & Ind rec from 1821)

| Houston | C2 | 1821 | 77 | 1830-80 | Indian Lands | Perry 31069 |

(Pro Ct has b, m & d rec; Clk Sup Ct has div, civ ct & Ind rec from 1822)

| * Irwin | D2 | 1818 | 9 | 1820-80 | Indian Lands, Coffee, Telfair | Ocilla 31774 |

(Pro Ct has b & m rec; Clk Sup Ct has div, civ ct & Ind rec from 1900)

| * Jackson | B2 | 1796 | 25 | 1820-80 | Franklin | Jefferson 30549 |

(Clk Sup Ct has b & d rec from 1927, m, div & pro rec from 1800, civ ct & Ind rec from 1796)

| Jasper | B2 | 1812 | 7 | 1820-80 | Baldwin (changed from Randolph 1812) | Monticello 31064 |

(Clk Sup Ct has div rec, civ ct, Ind & Sup Ct minutes from 1808) (Jasper Co was formed as Randolph Co in 1808 & name changed to Jasper 1812, rec go back to 1808)

| Jeff Davis | D2 | 1905 | 11 | | Appling, Coffee | Hazelhurst 31539 |

(Clk Sup Ct has div, civ ct & Ind rec from 1905)

| *§ Jefferson | C3 | 1796 | 18 | 1820-80 | Burke, Warren | Louisville 30434 |

(Rec not complete; deeds 1797-1802; 1865)

| Jenkins | C3 | 1905 | 9 | | Bullock, Burke, Emanuel, Screven | Millen 30442 |

(Pro Ct has m & pro rec; Clk Sup Ct has div, civ ct & Ind rec from 1905)

| Johnson | C3 | 1858 | 9 | 1860-80 | Emanuel, Laurens, Washington | Wrightsville 31096 |

(Clk Sup Ct has div, civ ct, Ind rec from 1858)

* Jones	C2	1807	16	1820-80	Baldwin, Bibb, Putnam	Gray 31032
Kinchafoonee		1853			Stewart, changed to Webster 1856	
* Lamar	C2	1920	12		Monroe, Pike	Barnesville 30204

(Clk Sup Ct has div, civ ct, Ind rec from 1921)

| Lanier | E3 | 1919 | 6 | | Berrien, Lowndes, Clinch | Lakeland 31635 |

(Clk Sup Ct has div & civ ct rec from 1921; Pro Ct has b, m, d & pro rec from 1921)

| * Laurens | C3 | 1807 | 37 | 1820-80 | Montgomery, Washington, Wilkinson | Dublin 31021 |

(Pro Ct has m rec; Clk Sup Ct has div, civ ct & Ind rec from 1807)

| § Lee | D2 | 1826 | 12 | 1830-80 | Indian Lands | Leesburg 31763 |

(Clk Sup Ct has m, div & civ ct rec) (all rec lost in courthouse fire 1858)

| Liberty | D4 | 1777 | 37 | 1820-80 | St. Andrew, St. James, St. Johns | Hinesville 31313 |

(Early rec lost; first m rec 1819)

| * Lincoln | B3 | 1796 | 7 | 1820-80 | Wilkes | Lincolnton 30817 |

(Pro Ct has b rec from 1920, m rec from 1810. d rec from 1930; pro rec from 1796; Clk Sup Ct has div, civ ct rec from 1796, Ind rec from 1790)

| Long | D4 | 1920 | 5 | | Liberty | Ludowici 31316 |

(Pro Ct has b, m, d, bur & pro rec; Clk Sup Ct has div, civ ct, Ind, adoptions & Sup Ct crim rec from 1920)

| * Lowndes | E2 | 1825 | 67 | 1830-80 | Irwin | Valdosta 31601 |

(Pro Ct has m & pro rec; Clk Sup Ct has div, civ ct & Ind rec from 1858)

| * Lumpkin | A2 | 1832 | 11 | 1840-80 | Cherokee, Habersham, Hall | Dahlonega 30533 |

(Pro Ct has b, m, d, bur rec; Clk Sup Ct has div, civ ct, Ind rec from 1833)

| * Macon | C2 | 1837 | 14 | 1840-80 | Houston, Marion | Oglethorpe 31068 |

(Courthouse burned 1857, all rec lost; Clk Sup Ct has div, civ ct, Ind rec)

| Madison | B3 | 1811 | 18 | 1820-80 | Clarke, Elbert, Franklin, Jackson, Oglethorpe | Danielsville 30633 |

(Pro Ct has b, m, d, bur, pro rec; Clk Sup Ct has div, civ ct rec, Ind rec from 1812)

Name	Map Index	Date Created	Pop. By M 1980	U.S. Cen Reports Available	Parent County or Territory From Which Organized	County Seat
* Marion	C1	1827	5	1830-80	Lee, Muscogee, Stewart	Buena Vista 31803

(Clk Sup Ct has div, civ ct & Ind rec; Courthouse fire 1845; all rec lost)

| * McDuffie | B3 | 1870 | 18 | 1880 | Columbia, Warren .... | Thomson 30824 |

(Pro Ct has b, m, d & pro rec from 1872; Clk Sup Ct has div rec from 1872, civ ct rec, Ind rec from 1870)

| McIntosh | D4 | 1793 | 8 | 1820-80 | Liberty .... | Darien 31305 |

(Clk Sup Ct has div, civ ct, pro & Ind rec; many rec lost during CW; Courthouse fire 1931)

| Meriwether | C1 | 1827 | 21 | 1830-80 | Troup .... | Greenville 30222 |

(Pro Ct has b rec from 1927, m rec from 1828, d rec from 1929, pro rec from 1838; Clk Sup Ct has div rec, civ ct, Ind rec from 1827, Vet discharge rec)

| Miller | E1 | 1856 | 7 | 1860-80 | Baker, Early .... | Colquitt 31737 |

(Courthouse fire 1873; all rec lost)

| Milton | B1 | 1857 | | 1860-80 | Cobb, Cherokee, Forsyth Merged Fulton 1911 .... |

| * Mitchell | E2 | 1857 | 21 | 1860-80 | Baker .... | Camilla 31730 |

(Clk Sup Ct has div rec from 1857 & civ ct rec from 1947; minutes kept of civ ct rec from 1947 to present not before; Courthouse fire 1869; Sup Ct rec and some others saved; address correspondence to Clk Sup Ct together with money order in advance & stamped, addressed envelope, or no attention will be given)

| * Monroe | C2 | 1821 | 14 | 1830-80 | Indian Lands .... | Forsyth 31029 |

(Pro Ct has m, pro rec from 1824; Clk Sup Ct has div, civ ct, Ind rec from 1821)

| Montgomery | D3 | 1793 | 7 | 1820-80 | Washington, Laurens, Tattnall, Telfair .... | Mr. Vernon 30445 |

(Pro Ct has b, d rec from 1918, m rec from 1807, pro rec from 1793; Clk Sup Ct has div rec, civ ct rec from 1800, Ind rec from 1793)

| Morgan | B2 | 1807 | 11 | 1820-80 | Baldwin, Jasper .... | Madison 30650 |

(Co Health Dept has b rec; Pro Ct has m, d, bur, pro rec; Clk Sup Ct has div, civ ct, Ind rec from 1807)

| Murray | A1 | 1832 | 20 | 1840-80 | Cherokee .... | Chatsworth 30705 |

(Pro Ct has b & d rec from 1924, m rec from 1842, pro rec from 1890; Clk Sup Ct has civ ct rec from 1834)

| § Muscogee | C1 | 1826 | 169 | 1830-80 | Creek Lands, Harris, Lee, Marion .... | Columbus 31902 |

(Clk Sup Ct has div, civ ct & Ind rec from 1838)

| Newton | B2 | 1821 | 34 | 1830-80 | Henry, Jasper, Morgan, Walton .... | Covington 30209 |

(Clk Sup Ct has div, civ ct & Ind rec from 1822, service rec from 1917)

| Oconee | B2 | 1875 | 12 | 1880 | Clarke .... | Watkinsville 30677 |

(Pro Ct has b, m & d rec; Clk Sup Ct has div, civ ct & Ind rec from 1875)

| Oglethorpe | B3 | 1793 | 9 | 1800-80 | Clarke, Wilkes .... | Lexington 30648 |

(Pro Ct has b, m, d & pro rec; Clk Sup Ct has div, civ ct & Ind rec from 1794) (Courthouse fire 1941)

| * Paulding | B1 | 1832 | 26 | 1840-80 | Cherokee Lands, Carroll, Cobb .... | Dallas 30132 |

(Clk Sup Ct has div, civ ct rec from 1876, Ind rec from 1848)

| Peach | C2 | 1924 | 19 | | Houston, Macon .... | Fort Valley 31030 |

(Pro Ct has b, m, d, pro rec from 1925; Clk Sup Ct has div, civ ct, Ind rec from 1925)

| * Pickens | A2 | 1853 | 12 | 1860-80 | Cherokee, Gilmer .... | Jasper 30143 |

(Pro Ct has b, m, d, bur, pro rec from 1924; Clk Sup Ct has div, civ ct, Ind rec from 1854)

| Pierce | E3 | 1857 | 12 | 1860-80 | Appling, Ware .... | Blackshear 31516 |

(Pro Ct has b rec from 1926, m rec from 1875, d rec from 1924; Clk Sup Ct has div & civ ct rec from 1875; Courthouse fire 1874)

| *Pike | C2 | 1822 | 9 | 1830-80 | Monroe .... | Zebulon 30295 |

(Clk Sup Ct has civ ct & Ind rec from 1823)

| Polk | B1 | 1851 | 32 | 1860-80 | Paulding .... | Cedartown 30125 |

(Pro Ct has b, m & d rec; Clk Sup Ct has div, civ ct & Ind rec from 1852)

| * Pulaski | D2 | 1808 | 9 | 1820-80 | Laurens, Wilkinson .... | Hawkinsville 31036 |

(Clk Sup Ct has div, civ ct rec from 1850, Ind rec from 1810; Pro Ct has m, pro rec from 1810, b rec from 1935, d rec from 1920)

| Putnam | B2 | 1807 | 10 | 1820-80 | Baldwin .... | Eatonton 31024 |

(Clk Sup Ct has div & civ ct rec from 1807; Pro Ct has b, m, d, bur & pro rec)

| Quitman | D1 | 1858 | 2 | 1860-80 | Randolph, Stewart .... | Georgetown 31754 |

(Courthouse burned; Clk Sup Ct has b rec from 1927, m rec from 1919, d rec, div, civ ct rec from 1923, Ind rec from 1879)

| * Rabun | A2 | 1819 | 10 | 1830-80 | Cherokee Lands, Habersham .... | Clayton 30525 |

(Pro Ct has m & pro rec; Clk Sup Ct has div, civ ct & Ind rec)

Name	Map Index	Date Created	Pop. By M 1980	U.S. Cen Reports Available	Parent County or Territory From Which Organized	County Seat
Randolph		1807			(changed to Jasper 1812)	
Randolph	D1	1828	10	1830-80	Baker, Lee	Cuthbert 31740
					(Pro Ct has m & pro rec from 1835; Clk Sup Ct has div, civ ct & Ind rec from 1835)	
§ Richmond	B3	1777	177	1820-80	St. Paul Parish	Augusta 30902
Rockdale	B2	1870	37	1880	Henry, Newton	Conyers 30207
* Schley	D2	1857	3	1860-80	Marion, Sumter	Ellaville 31806
					(Pro Ct has b, d, bur rec from 1927, m rec from 1858, pro rec; Clk Sup Ct has div, civ ct, Ind rec from 1857)	
* Screven	C4	1793	14	1820-80	Burke, Effingham	Sylvania 30467
					(Pro Ct has b, d rec from 1927, m, pro rec from 1817; Clk Sup Ct has div, civ ct rec from 1816, Ind rec from 1790)	
Seminole	E1	1920	9		Decatur, Early	Donalsonville 31745
					(Pro Ct has b, m, d & pro rec; Clk Sup Ct has div, civ ct & Ind rec from 1921)	
Spalding	B2	1851	48	1860-80	Fayette, Henry, Pike	Griffin 30223
					(Clk Sup Ct has div, civ ct & Ind rec from 1852)	
Stephens	A2	1905	20		Franklin, Habersham	Toccoa 30577
					(Co Health Dept has b, d rec; Pro Ct has m, pro rec; Clk Sup Ct has div, Civ Ct, Ind rec from 1906)	
* Stewart	D1	1830	6	1840-80	Randolph	Lumpkin 31815
					(Pro Ct has b, d, bur rec from 1927, m rec from 1828, pro rec; Clk Sup Ct has div, civ ct, Ind rec from 1830)	
Sumter	D2	1831	29	1840-80	Lee	Americus 31709
					(Co Health Dept has b, d, bur rec; Pro Ct has m, pro rec; Clk Sup Ct has div, civ ct, Ind rec from 1831)	
Talbot	C1	1827	6	1830-80	Crawford, Harris, Marion, Macon, Muscogee	Talbotton 31827
					(Pro Ct has b, m, d & pro rec; Clk Sup Ct has div, ct & Ind rec)	
* Taliaferro	B3	1825	2	1830-80	Green, Hancock, Oglethorpe, Warren, Wilkes	Crawfordville 30631
					(Pro Ct has b rec from 1927, m & pro rec from 1826, d rec from 1920, Ind grants from 1750, church rec from 1802; Clk Sup Ct has div & civ ct rec 1826)	
Tattnall	D3	1801	18	1820-80	Montgomery, Liberty	Reidsville 30453
					(Pro Ct has b, m & d rec; Clk Sup Ct has div rec from 1880, civ ct & Ind rec)	
Taylor	C2	1852	8	1860-80	Marion, Talbot	Butler 31006
					(Pro Ct has b, m, d, bur, pro rec; Clk Sup Ct has div, civ ct, Ind rec from 1852)	
*Telfair	D3	1807	11	1820-80	Wilkinson, Appling	Mac Rae 31055
Terrell	D2	1856	12	1860-80	Lee, Randolph	Dawson 31742
					(Clk Sup Ct has div, civ ct & Ind rec from 1856)	
* Thomas	E2	1825	38	1830-80	Grady, Decatur, Irwin	Thomasville 31792
					(Co Health Dept has b, d rec; Pro Ct has m, pro rec; Clk Sup Ct has div, civ ct rec from 1919, Ind rec from 1826)	
* Tift	D2	1905	33		Berrien, Irwin, Worth	Tifton 31794
					(Pro Ct has m rec; Clk Sup Ct has div, pro, civ ct & Ind rec from 1905)	
Toombs	D3	1905	22		Emanuel, Tattnall, Montgomery	Lyons 30436
					(Pro Ct has b, m, d, bur & pro rec from 1905; Clk Sup Ct has div, civ ct & Ind rec from 1905)	
Towns	A2	1856	6	1860-80	Rabun, Union	Hiawassee 30546
					(Pro Ct has b, m, d, bur, pro rec; Clk Sup Ct has div, civ ct, Ind rec from 1856)	
Treutlen	C3	1917	6		Emanuel, Montgomery	Soperton 30457
					(Pro Ct has b, m & d rec; Clk Sup Ct has div, pro, civ ct & Ind rec from 1919)	
* Troup	C1	1826	50	1830-80	Indian Lands	LaGrange 30240
					(Pro Ct has b rec from 1918, m, d & pro rec; Clk Sup Ct has div & Ind rec from 1827, civ ct rec)	
* Turner	D2	1905	10		Dooly, Irwin, Wilcox, Worth	Ashburn 31714
					(Clk Sup Ct has div & civ ct rec from 1906; Pro Ct has b, m, d, bur & pro rec)	
Twiggs	C2	1809	9	1830-80	Wilkinson	Jeffersonville 31044
* Union	A2	1832	9	1840-80	Cherokee Lands, Lumpkin	Blairsville 30512
					(Pro Ct has b, m, d & pro rec; Clk Sup Ct has div, civ ct & Ind rec)	
* Upson	C2	1824	26	1830-80	Crawford, Pike	Thomaston 30286
					(Pro Ct has m rec from 1825, pro rec from 1920; Clk Sup Ct has div, civ ct, Ind rec, inferior ct rec from 1825, newspaper files from 1870)	
* Walker	A1	1833	57	1840-80	Murray	LaFayette 30728
					(Clk Sup Ct has div, civ ct & Ind rec from 1883; Courthouse fire 1883)	
Walton	B2	1818	31	1820-80	Cherokee Lands	Monroe 30655
					(Co Health Dept has b, d, bur rec; Pro Ct has m, pro rec; Clk Sup Ct has div, civ ct, Ind rec from 1819)	
* Ware	E3	1824	36	1830-80	Appling	Waycross 31501
					(rec burned 1854)	

Name	Map Index	Date Created	Pop. By M 1980	U.S. Cen Reports Available	Parent County or Territory From Which Organized	County Seat
* Warren	B3	1793	6	1820-80	Columbia, Richmond, Wilkes	Warrenton 30828

(Pro Ct has b, m, d & pro rec; Clk Sup Ct has div, civ ct & Ind rec)

* Washington	C3	1784	19	1820-80	Indian Lands	Sandersville 31082

(Pro Ct has b & m rec; Clk Sup Ct has div, civ ct & Ind rec from 1865)

* Wayne	D4	1803	20	1820-80	Indian Lands, Appling, Glynn, Camden	Jesup 31545

(Pro Ct has b, m, d & pro rec; Clk Sup Ct has div, civ ct & Ind rec)

Webster	D1	1856	2	1860-80	Changed from Kinchafoonee 1856	Preston 31824

(Clk Sup Ct has div & civ ct rec from 1903; Pro Ct has b, m, d & bur rec)

Wheeler	D3	1912	5		Montgomery	Alamo 30411

(Co Health Dept has b, d rec from 1927; Pro Ct has m, pro rec from 1913; Clk Sup Ct has div, civ ct, Ind rec from 1913)

White	A2	1857	10	1860-80	Habersham	Cleveland 30528

(Pro Ct has b, m, d, pro rec; Clk Sup Ct has div, civ ct, Ind rec from 1858, discharges and mtg rec)

* Whitfield	A1	1851	66	1860-80	Murray, Walker	Dalton 30720

(Pro Ct has b & d rec from 1927, m & pro rec from 1852; Clk Sup Ct has div, civ ct & Ind rec from ca 1852)

* Wilcox	D2	1857	8	1860-80	Dooly, Irwin, Pulaski	Abbeville 31001

(Pro Ct has b, m, d & pro rec; Clk Sup Ct has div & civ ct rec from 1919, Ind from 1868)

* Wilkes	B3	1777	11	1820-80	Original territory	Washington 30673

(Pro Ct has b, m, d, pro rec from 1792; Clk Sup Ct has div, civ ct rec from 1778, Ind rec from 1777, crim ct, juvenile ct, financing statements, discharge rec, medical and atty. registers)

* Wilkinson	C2	1803	10	1820-80	Creek Cession	Irwinton 31042

(Courthouse burned in 1852 & 1924, however property rec were not burned in 1924; Clk Sup Ct has some div rec & property rec from 1852)

* Worth	D2	1852	18	1860-80	Dooly, Irwin	Sylvester 31791

(Clk Sup Ct has div, civ ct & Ind rec)

* - At least one county history has been published about this county.

§ - Inventory of county archives was made by the Historical Records Survey. (see introduction)

HAWAII

CAPITAL, HONOLULU - TERRITORY 1900 - STATE 1959 - (50TH)

Hawaii, 2,100 miles west-southwest of San Francisco, is a 390-mile chain of islets and eight main islands - Hawaii, Kahoolawe, Maui, Lanai, Molokai, Oahu, Kauai, and Niihau. It was discovered in 1778 by Captain James Cook, who named it the Sandwich Islands. It was ruled by native monarchs until 1893, thereafter as a republic until 1898, when it ceded itself to the United States.

Certified copies of birth, death, marriage and divorce records are available through the office of Research and Statistics, State Department of Health, P.O. Box 3378, Honolulu, Hawaii 96801.

Genealogical Archives, Libraries, Societies, and Publications

D.A.R. Memorial Library, 1914 Makiki Hts. Dr., Honolulu, HI 96822.

Hawaiian Historical Society 560 Kawaiahao St., Honolulu, HI 96813.

Library of Hawaii, King and Punchbowl Sts., Honolulu, HI 96813.

HAWAII COUNTIES
(Population figures to nearest thousand - 1980 U. S. Census)

County	Map Index	Pop. By M 1980	County Seat	County	Map Index	Pop. By M 1980	County Seat
Hawaii	G6	92	Hilo	Kauai	A1	39	Lihue
Honolulu	C3	762	Honolulu	Maui	E5	71	Wailuku
Kalawao	D4	1	Kalaupapa				

COUNTY MAP FOR THE STATE OF HAWAII

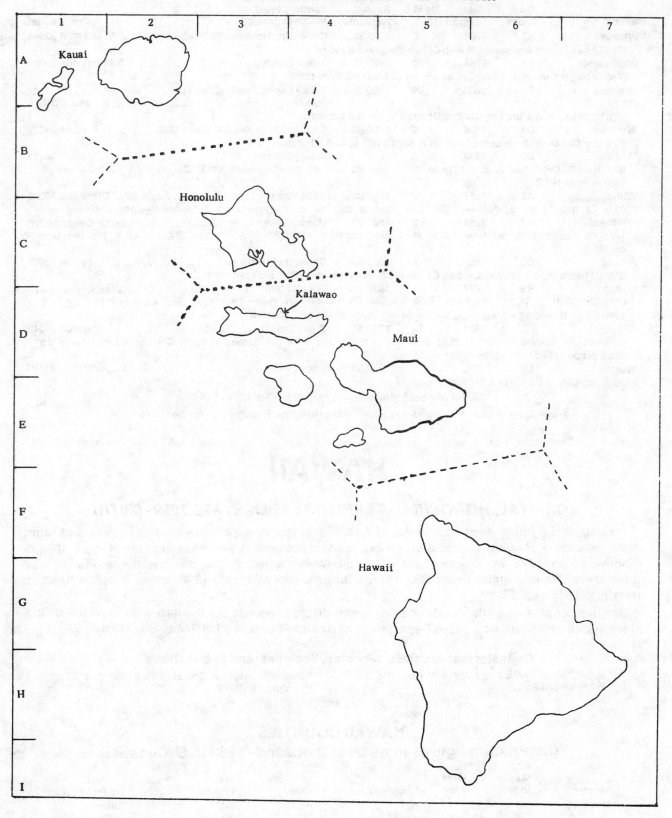

Valuable Printed Sources

Atlas

Armstrong, R. Warrick, ed. *Atlas of Hawaii.* Honolulu: Dept. of Geography, University Press of Hawaii, 1973.

Place Names

Pukui, Mary Kawena, Samuel H. Elbert, Esther T. Mookini. *Place Names of Hawaii.* Honolulu: The University Press of Hawaii, 1974.

Histories

Daws, Gavan. *Shoal of Time.* New York, Macmillan, 1968.

Kuykendal, Ralph S. *The Hawaiian Kingdom, 1778-1893.* Honolulu: University Press of Hawaii, 1938-1967. Three Volumes.

Genealogical Sources

Index to Births, Marriages and Deaths in Hawaiian Newspapers prior to 1950. *

Bradley, Harold Whitman. *The American Frontier in Hawaii - The Pioneers 1789-1843.* Gloucester, Massachusetts: Peter Smith, 1968.

Bibliographies

Alcantara, Ruben R. *The Filipinos in Hawaii: An Annotated Bibliography.* Honolulu: Social Science Research Institute, University of Hawaii, 1972.

Dickson, Diane, compiler. *World Catalogue of Theses on the Pacific Islands.* Honolulu: University of Hawaii Press, 1970.

Gardner, Arthur L. *The Koreans in Hawaii: An Annotated Bibliography.* Honolulu: Social Science Research Institute, University of Hawaii, 1970.

Matsuda, Mitsugu. *The Japanese in Hawaii: An Annotated Bibliography.* Honolulu: University of Hawaii, 1975.

Murdock, Clare G. - *Basic Hawaiiana,* An annotated bibliography of the basic Hawaiiana printed materials. State of Hawaii, Department of Education, Hawaii State Library, 1969.

Young, Nancy Foon. *The Chinese in Hawaii: An Annotated Bibliography.* Social Science Research Institute. Honolulu: University of Hawaii, 1973.

---

*On microfilm in the Genealogical Society Library of The Church of Jesus Christ of Latter-day Saints, Salt Lake City, Utah.

IDAHO

CAPITAL, BOISE - TERRITORY 1863 - STATE 1890 - (43RD)

Idaho was the last state to be carved from the Oregon Territory. When Idaho became a territory on 3 March 1863, it included all of Montana and nearly all of Wyoming. Montana became a territory in 1864 and Wyoming in 1868. The six original counties of Idaho were formed between 1861 and 1865. Idaho was admitted as a state 3 July 1890, the forty-third state in the Union.

The southern part of the state, which borders Utah was the first section to be settled starting about 1860. Mormon emigrants from northern Europe were the first to establish permanent settlements in the region.

A mining boom in 1860 attracted people from the east and midwest to the mountainous Idaho valleys. The later construction of large irrigation systems and districts around the long Snake River section about 1910 brought many western and midwestern farm families to take advantage of the farming opportunities in the new state.

Catholic and Protestant churches are represented in most Idaho communities, but more than half of its church membership belongs to the Church of Jesus Christ of Latter-day Saints.

The Bureau of Vital Statistics, Statehouse, Boise, Idaho 83720, has information on births and deaths from 1 July 1911; marriages and divorces since 1947.

The county recorder has records of marriages solemnized in his county. No marriage licenses were required before 11 March 1895.

The county clerk has records of births in that county between January 1907 and July 1911. Wills and probate matters are also filed in the clerk's office.

All records pertaining to land transactions are in custody of the county recorder in the respective county courthouses.

Genealogical Archives, Libraries, Societies, and Publications

Boise State University Library, Boise, ID 83725.

College of Idaho Library, Caldwell, ID 83605.

College of St. Gertrude Library, Cottonwood, ID 83522.

College of Southern Idaho Library, Twin Falls, ID 83301.

Family Scanner Chapter, IGS, P.O. Box 581, Caldwell, ID 83605.

Idaho County Chapter, IGS, Grangeville Centennial Library, 215 W. North, Grangeville, ID 83530.

Idaho Genealogical Society, 325 State St., Boise, ID 83702.

Idaho Historical Society, 325 State St., Boise, ID 83702.

Idaho State University Library, Pocatello, ID 83209.

Latah County Genealogical Society, 611 East 3rd, Moscow, ID 83843.

Lewis-Clark State College Library, Lewiston, ID 83501.

Lewiston-Nez Perce County Library, 533 Thain Rd., Lewiston, ID 83501.

McCall City Library, McCall, ID 83638.

North Idaho College Library, Coeur d' Alene, ID 83814.

North Idaho Genealogical Society, c/o Hayden Lake Area Free Library, Hayden Lake, ID 83835.

North Idaho Genealogical Society, c/o 1623 Birch Avenue, Coeur d' Alene, ID 83814.

Northwest Nazarene College Library, Nampa, ID 83651.

Post Falls Genealogical Library, P.O. Box 512, W. 9900 - 16th, Post Falls, ID 83854.

Ricks College Library, Rexburg, ID 83440.

Shoshone County Genealogical Society Chapter, IGS, P.O. Box 183, Kellogg, ID 83837.

Treasure Valley Chapter, IGS, 325 W. State Street, Boise, ID 83702.

Twin Rivers Chapter, IGS, c/o Lewiston Public Library, Pioneer Park, Lewiston, ID 83501.

University of Idaho Library, Moscow, ID 83843.

Idaho Genealogical Society Quarterly, The, 325 State St., Boise, ID 83702.

Printed Census Records and Mortality Schedules

Indexes (Territory) - 1850, 1860, 1870, 1880

Printed Mortality Schedules - 1870, 1880

County Printed Census Records -

Ada - 1870
Alturas - 1870
Boise - 1870

County printed mortality schedules -

Ada - 1880	Idaho - 1880
Alturas - 1880	Kootenai - 1880
Bear Lake - 1880	Lemhi - 1880
Boise - 1880	Nez Perce - 1880
Camas - 1880	Oneida - 1880

Valuable Printed Sources

Atlases and Gazetteers:

Idaho Department of Highways. *Gazetteer of Cities, Villages, Unicorporated Communities and Landmark Sites in The State of Idaho,* 3rd edition (1966).

Maps of Early Idaho. Corvallis, Oregon: Western Guide Publishers, 1972.

Place Names:

Federal Writers' Project. *The Idaho Encyclopedia.* Caldwell, Idaho: Caxton Printers, 1938.

Kramer, Fritz L. "Idaho Town Names." In 23rd *Biennial Report of The Idaho State Historical Department,* 1951-52, pp. 14-114.

Histories:

Beal, Merrill D. and Merle W. Wells. *History of Idaho.* 3 vols. New York: Lewis Historical Publishing Co., 1959.

Defenbach, Byron. *Idaho, The Place and Its People.* 3 vols. Chicago: The American Historical Society, 1933.

Idaho, An Illustrated History. Boise: Idaho State Historical Society, 1976.

An Illustrated History of The State of Idaho. Chicago: Lewis Publishing Co., 1899.

Genealogical Sources

Idaho State Historical Society / Idaho Genealogical Society Library, 325 W. State St., Boise, ID 83702, (208) 334-2305

Ricks College Library, Rexburg, ID 83440, (208) 356-2351

Bibliographies:

Etulain, Richard W. and Merwin Swanson. *Idaho History: A Bibliography.* Revised edition. Pocatello: Idaho State University Press, 1979.

Nelson, Milo G. and Charles A. Webbert, editors. *Idaho Local History: A Bibliography With A Checklist of Library Holdings.* Moscow: University Press of Idaho, 1976.

IDAHO COUNTY HISTORIES
(Population figures to nearest thousand - 1980 U. S. Census)

Name	Map Index	Date Created	Pop. By M 1980	U.S. Cen Reports Available	Parent County or Territory From Which Organized	County Seat
Ada	E1	1864	173	1870-80	Boise	Boise 83702
(Co Clk has m, div & civ ct rec from 1864)						
Adams	D1	1911	3		Washington	Council 83612
(Co Clk has m, div, pro, civ ct & Ind rec from 1911)						
* Alturas		1863		1870-80	Original county; discontinued	
(transferred to Lincoln?)						
* Bannock	F4	1893	65		Oneida, Bear Lake	Pocatello 83201
(Co Clk has b & d rec from 1902, m rec from 1893, div, pro & civ ct rec)						
Bear Lake	F4	1875	7	1880	Oneida	Paris 83261
(Co Clk has b rec 1907-1911, d rec 1907-1915, m, Ind rec from 1875, div rec from 1884)						
* Benewah	B1	1915	8		Kootenai	St. Maries 83861
(Co Clk has m, bur, div, pro, civ ct, Ind rec from 1915)						
§ Bingham	E3	1885	36		Oneida	Blackfoot 83221
(Co Clk has b, d rec 1907-1911, m Ind rec from 1885, div, civ ct rec from 1900, pro rec from 1892, homestead rec from 1889, Commissioners minutes from 1855; special school census taken 1898 to 1933)						
* Blaine	E2	1895	10		Alturas	Hailey 83333
(Co Clk has b & d rec from 1907 to 1911, m, div, pro, civ ct Ind rec from 1885)						
Boise	E2	1864	3	1870-80	Original county	Idaho City 83631
(Co Clk has m rec from 1868, div from 1904, pro from 1865, civ ct from 1867 & Ind rec 1865)						
Bonner	A1	1907	24		Kootenai	Sandpoint 83864
(Co Clk has b & d rec from 1907 to 1911, m div & civ ct rec from 1907, pro from 1890, Ind rec from 1889)						
* Bonneville	E4	1911	66	Bingham	Bingham	Idaho Falls 83401
(Co Clk has m, div, pro, civ ct & Ind rec from 1911)						
§ Boundary	A1	1915	7		Bonner	Bonners Ferry 83805
(Co Clk has m, div, pro, civ ct, Ind, mining rec, some b, d rec from 1915; State Bur Vit Statistics has b, d, rec)						
Butte	E3	1917	3		Bingham, Blaine, Jefferson	Arco 83213
(Co Clk has m, bur, div, pro, school rec from 1917, civ ct rec from 1895, Ind rec from 1890)						
Camas	E2	1917	1		Blaine	Fairfield 83327
(Co Clk has m, div & civ ct rec from 1917, bur rec incomplete; Bur of Vit Stat has b & d rec from 1941; Pro Ct has pro rec from 1890)						

Name	Map Index	Date Created	Pop. By M 1980	U.S. Cen Reports Available	Parent County or Territory From Which Organized	County Seat
Canyon	E1	1892	84		Owyhee, Ada	Caldwell 83605

(Bur Vit Statistics, Boise has b, d rec; Co Clk has some b, d rec 1907-1911, m rec from 1895, Ind rec from 1892; Dist Ct has div rec from 1892, Magistrate Ct has pro, civ ct rec from 1892)

* Caribou	E4	1919	9		Bannock, Oneida	Soda Springs 83276

(Co Clk has m rec from 1919, div, pro, civ ct & Ind rec)

Cassia	F3	1879	19	1880	Oneida	Burley 83318

(Co Clk has b, d rec 1908-1911, m, div, civ ct, Ind rec from 1879)

§ Clark	D3	1919	1		Fremont	Dubois 83423

(State Bur Vit Statistics, Boise has b, d rec; Co Clk has m, div, civ ct, Ind rec from 1919)

Clearwater	C2	1911	10		Nez Perce	Orofino 83544

(Co Clk has m, div, pro, civ ct & Ind rec from 1911)

Custer	D2	1881	3		Alturas	Challis 83226

(Co Clk has m, div, civ ct & deeds rec from 1872; Bur of Vit Stat has b & d rec; Cem Dis (Challis & Big Lost River) has bur rec; Pro Ct has pro rec)

* Elmore	E2	1889	22		Alturus, Ada	Mountain Home 83647

(Co Clk has b rec 1907-1911, m div, pro, civ ct, Ind rec from 1889)

* Franklin	F4	1913	9		Oneida	Preston 83263

(Bur Vit Statistics, Boise has b, d rec; Co Clk has m rec from 1913)

Fremont	D4	1893	11		Bingham, Lemhi	St. Anthony 83445

(Co Clk has m, div, pro, civ ct & Ind rec)

Gem	E1	1915	12		Boise, Canyon	Emmett 83617

(Co Clk has m, div, civ ct rec, Ind rec from 1915; Magistrate has pro rec from 1915)

Gooding	E2	1913	12		Lincoln	Gooding 83330

(Bur Vit Statistics, Boise has b, d rec; Local cem dist has bur rec; Co Clk has m, div, pro, civ ct, Ind rec from 1913)

* Idaho	C2	1864	15	1870-80	Original county	Grangeville 83530

(Co Clk has b & d rec from 1907 to 1911, m & Ind rec from 1862, div & civ ct rec from 1888)

* Jefferson	E3	1913	15		Fremont	Rigby 83442

(Co Clk has m, div, pro, civ ct, Ind rec from 1914)

Jerome	F2	1919	15		Gooding, Lincoln	Jerome 83338

(Co Clk has m, div, pro, civ ct, Ind rec from 1919)

Kootenai	B1	1864	60	1880	Nez Perce	Coeur d'Alene 83814

(created in 1864, but not organized or officered until 1881. Co Clk has b & d rec from 1907 to 1912, m, div, pro & civ ct rec from 1881)

Latah	B1	1888	29		Nez Perce	Moscow 83843

(created & organized by U.S. congressional enactment, said to be the only Co in the U.S. so created. Co Clk has b & d rec from 1907 to 1911, m, div & civ ct rec from 1888)

§ Lemhi	D3	1869	7	1870-80	Idaho	Salmon 83467

(Co Clk has m, div, civ ct & Ind rec)

Lewis	C1	1911	4		Nez Perce	Nezperce 83543

(Bur Vit Statistics, Boise has b, d rec; cem districts have bur rec; Co Clk has m, div, pro, civ ct, Ind rec from 1911)

Lincoln	E2	1895	3		Alturas	Shoshone 83352

(Bur Vit Statistics, Boise has b, d rec; Bergen Funeral Home has bur rec; Co Clk has some b, d rec 1895-1913, m, div, pro, civ ct, Ind rec from 1895, some school rec)

Madison	E4	1913	20		Fremont	Rexburg 83440

(Bur Vit Statistics, Boise has b, d rec; Co Clk has m, div, pro, civ ct, Ind rec from 1914)

§ Minidoka	E3	1913	20		Lincoln	Rupert 83350

(Co Clk has m, div, pro, civ ct & Ind rec from 1913)

*§ Nez Perce	C1	1861	33		Original county	Lewiston 83501

(Co Clk has b, d rec 1907-1911, m, div, pro, civ ct, Ind rec from 1863)

Oneida	F3	1865	3		Original county	Malad City 83252

(Co Clk has b rec from 1907 to 1911, m rec from 1866, div, pro, civ ct & Ind rec)

* Owyhee	F1	1863	8	1870-80	Original county	Murphy 83650

(Co Clk has b & d rec from 1907 to 1913, m rec from 1895, div & civ ct rec from 1864, naturalization rec 1893-1911)

Payette	E1	1917	16		Canyon	Payette 83661

(Co Clk has m, div, pro & civ ct rec from 1917, Ind rec from 1865)

COUNTY MAP FOR THE STATE OF IDAHO

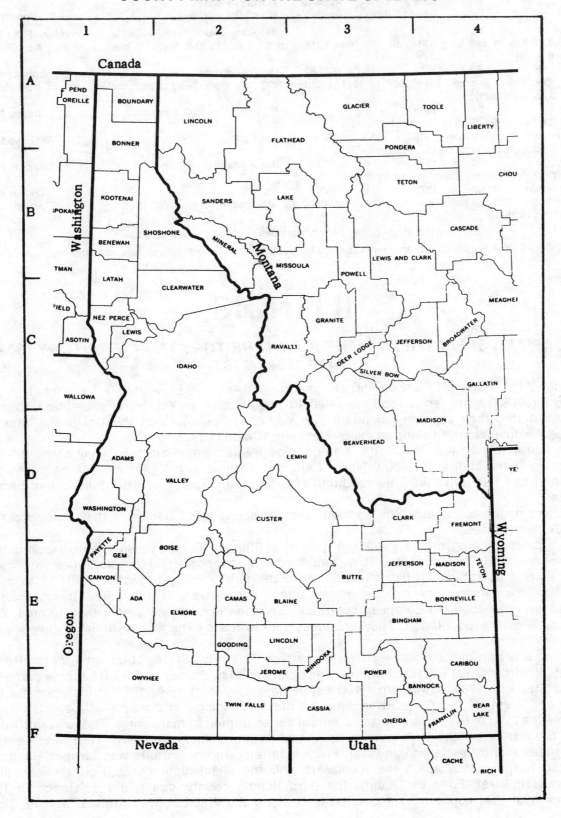

Name	Map Index	Date Created	Pop. By M 1980	U.S. Cen Reports Available	Parent County or Territory From Which Organized	County Seat
§ Power	E3	1913	7		Bingham, Blaine, Oneida	American Falls 83211

(Co Clk has m rec from 1914, div rec from 1916; Pro Ct has pro rec; Mag Ct has civ ct rec; Asr Office has Ind rec)

* Shoshone	B2	1864	19	1870-80	Original county	Wallace 83873

(Co Clk has b & d rec from 1907 to 1911, m from 1875, div from 1887, pro from 1885, civ ct from 1884 & Ind rec from 1871)

*§ Teton	E4	1915	3		Madison, Fremont, Bingham	Driggs 83422

(Co Clk has m, div, civ ct rec from 1916, Ind rec)

Twin Falls	F2	1907	53		Cassia	Twin Falls 83301

(Co Clk has m, div, pro, ct & Ind rec from 1907)

Valley	D2	1917	6		Boise, Idaho	Cascade 83611

(Co Clk has m, div, pro, civ ct, Ind rec from 1917)

Washington	D1	1879	9	1880	Boise	Weiser 83672

(Bur Vit Statistics, Boise has b, d rec after 1911; Co Clk has b, d rec 1907-1911, m, div, pro, civ ct, Ind rec from 1879)

* - At least one county history has been published about this county.

§ - Inventory of county archives was made by the Historical Records Survey. (see introduction)

ILLINOIS

CAPITAL, SPRINGFIELD - AMERICAN TERRITORY 1787 - TERRITORY 1809 STATE 1818 - (21ST)

Illinois, the transportation center of the United States, was visited by French explorers in the late 1600's. Its fertile land appealed to members of various early expeditions passing through during their exploring or hunting or war activities. Many of them returned later and farmed the deep, rich soil along its many rivers and streams.

The southern part was the first to be occupied by permanent settlers. They came from the earlier southern states, including North Carolina, Virginia and Kentucky. Others came from Maryland and Pennsylvania. This condition existed until some years after Illinois had become a state.

Settlers began to arrive in the northern section about 1825. Generally they came from the New England states.

With the beginning of the industrial growth of Illinois, European emigrants flocked there by the thousands every month. They furnished the manpower for the factories and industrial plants that sprung up like mushrooms in the Lake Michigan section. This is a reason why more than forty percent of the state's population centers in that area. They came from Ireland, and the southern European countries. Germans flocked there until they formed about one-fourth of the population. They are closely crowded by the Poles, Italians, Swedes and Russians.

Illinois was part of the Northwest Territory which the United States obtained after the Revolutionary War from Great Britain to whom it had been ceded by France in 1763. It became part of the United States in 1783. It was organized as an American territory in 1787. It included the land north and west of the Ohio River, east of the Mississippi, and south of Canada. Illinois became the third of five territories and eventual states formed from that area. That was in 1818.

St. Clair became the first county organized in the Illinois Territory. That was in 1790. It extended along the Kaskaskia River. Five years later another county was formed, Randolph, situated farther south along the Kaskaskia and the Mississippi rivers. Farther east, along the Wabash River, Edwards County, the third Illinois county, came into existence in 1814. And north of that county, Clark County, also along the Wabash, was formed in 1819. Those four counties were the forerunners of 98 others to be formed in Illinois. The last two of her present 102 counties were formed in 1859, Ford and Douglas.

A communication from the Department of Public Health at Springfield says, "Illinois has no provisions for giving genealogical service from the official birth and death records. Our law authorizes the State Department of Public Health, the County Clerks, and the Local Registrars to issue a certified copy of a specified record at a statutory fee. The law forbids us to issue any information from the records except by certified copy as described to legally authorized (related) persons.

"Marriage records are in sole custody of the county clerks. Births and deaths from 1877 to 1916 were registered (if at all) by the county clerks. In a few counties there are some records existing prior to 1877, also in some cities.

"After 1916 all original birth and death certificates have been deposited with this department. A copy of each is deposited with the county clerk of the county where the event occurred.

"Such genealogical research as is done in the state offices is done in the Illinois State Archives from its miscellaneous historical records. For further information about the services from the Archives communicate with The State Archivist, Archives Building, Springfield, Illinois 62706.

"The best source of the kind of information you request is to be found in a publication by the Historical Records Survey Project of the W.P.A. in May, 1941, entitled, "Guide to Public Vital Statistics Records in Illinois," (137 pp. mimeographed)."

Counties with a population of more than 70,000 have probate courts, in other counties probate matters and wills are handled by the county clerk. Matters pertaining to real estate are in the offices of the county recorder of deeds.

The War Veterans Graves Registration Files contain names of about 350,000 veterans buried in the State of Illinois. It is in alphabetical order, by veterans names, broken down by wars. Also a cemetery listing set up by counties on which veterans' burials are listed and cemeteries in alphabetical order by county. The files carry only those veterans buried within the state. The records are within ninety percent, possibly more, for veterans buried in Illinois. Each card gives name of veteran, serial, claim, rank, organization, enlistment, discharge, date and place of birth, date and place of death, cemetery where buried, name of town, county, grave description, next of kin and address. A separate index file is carried on peace time soldiers, whose names are not listed on the cemetery listings; also those with service unknown but thought to have had military service. Address: 221 West Jefferson Street, Springfield, IL 62705.

Genealogical Archives, Libraries, Societies, and Publications

Blackhawk Genealogical Society, P.O. Box 912, Rock Island, IL 61201.

Bloomington-Normal Genealogical Society, P.O. Box 488, Normal, IL 61761.

Bryan-Bennett Library, 402 S. Broadway, Salem, IL 62881.

Carnegie Public Library, 6th and Van Buren Sts., Charleston, IL 61920.

Carroll County Genealogical Society, P.O. Box 347, Savanna, IL 61074.

Champaign County Genealogical Society, Urbana Free Library - Archives Room, 201 S. Race, Urbana, IL 61801.

Chicago Genealogical Society, P.O. Box 1160, Chicago, IL 60690.

Chicago Historical Society, North Ave. and Clark St., Chicago, IL 60614.

Clark County Genealogical Society and Library, P.O. Box 153, Marshall, IL 62441.

Clinton County Historical Society, P.O. Box 82, Aviston, IL 62216.

Coles County Illinois Genealogical Society, P.O. Box 225, Charleston, IL 61920.

Crawford County Genealogical Society, P.O. Box 110, Robinson, IL 62454.

Cumberland and Coles County of Illinois Genealogical Society, Rt. 1, Box 141, Toledo, IL 62468.

Danville Public Library, 307 N. Vermilion St., Danville, IL 61834.

Decatur Genealogical Society, P.O. Box 2205, Decatur, IL 62526.

Des Plaines Historical Society, P.O. Box 225, Des Plaines, IL 60017.

DeWitt County Genealogical Society, Box 329, Clinton, IL 61727.

Douglas County Illinois Genealogical Society, Box 50, Camargo, IL 61919.

Dunton Genealogical Society, 500 North Dunton, Arlington Heights, IL 60004.

Du Page County (Illinois) Genealogical Society, P.O. Box 133, Lomard, IL 60148.

Edwards County Historical Society, P.O. Box 205, Albion, IL 62806.

Effingham County Genealogical Society, P.O. Box 1166, Effingham, IL 62401.

Elgin Genealogical Society, 1035 Hill Avenue, Elgin, IL 60120.

Elmhurst Genealogical Group, P.O. Box 84, Elmhurst, IL 60126.

Evans Public Library, 215 S. 5th St., Vandalia, IL 62471.

Fayette County Genealogical Society, Box 177, Vandalia, IL 62471.

Fort La Motte Genealogical and Historical Society, c/o LaMotte Township Library, Palestine, IL 62451.

Frankfort Area Genealogy Society, 2000 East St. Louis, West Frankfort, IL 62896.

Fulton County Historical and Genealogical Society, 45 N. Park Drive, Canton, IL 61520.

Gail Borden Public Library, 200 North Grove Avenue, Elgin, IL 60120.

Galena Public Library, Galena, IL 61036.

Galesburg Public Library, Galesburg, IL 61401.

Genealogical Guild of La Salle County, P.O. Box 278, Utica, IL 61373.

Genealogical Committee of the Stephenson County Historical Society, 110 Coates Pl., Freeport, IL 61032.

Genealogical Society of DeKalb County, Illinois, P.O. Box 295, Sycamore, IL 60178.

Genealogical Society of Southern Illinois, c/o John A. Logan College, Carterville, IL 62918.

Glenview Public Library, 1930 Glenview Rd., Glenview, IL 60025.

Great River Genealogical Society, c/o Quincy Public Library, Quincy, IL 62302.

Greene County Historical and Genealogical Society, P.O. Box 137, Carrollton, IL 62016.

Henry Historical and Genealogical Society, 610 North St., Henry, IL 61537.

Illiana Genealogical Historical Society, P.O. Box 207, Danville, IL 61834.

Illinois Mennonite Historical and Genealogical Society, 918 S. University, Normal, IL 61761.

Illinois State Archives, Archives Bldg., Springfield, IL 62706.

Illinois State Genealogical Society, P.O. Box 2225, Springfield, IL 62705.

Illinois State Historical Library, Old State Capitol, Springfield, IL 62706.

Iroquois County Genealogical Society, Old Courthouse Museum, 103 West Cherry St., Watseka, IL 60970.

Jackson County Historical Society, Box 7, Murphysboro, IL 62966.

Jacksonville Area Genealogical and Historical Society, P.O. Box 21, Jacksonville, IL 62651.

John Mosser Public Library, 106 W. Meek St., Abingdon, IL 61410.

Kane County Genealogical Society, P.O. Box 504, Geneva, IL 60134.

Kankakee Valley Genealogical Society, 304 S. Indiana Ave., Kankakee, IL 60901.

Knox County Genealogical Society (Illinois), P.O. Box 13, Galesburg, IL 61401.

LaGrange Public Library, 10 W. Cossitt, LaGrange, IL 60525.

Lake County, Illinois Genealogical Society, Cook Memorial Library, 413 N. Milwaukee Ave., Libertyville, IL 60048.

Lexington Genealogical and Historical Society, 318 W. Main St., Lexington, IL 61753.

Logan County Genealogical Society, P.O. Box 283, Lincoln, IL 62656.

Madison County Genealogical Society, P.O. Box 89, Troy, IL 62294.

Marion County Genealogical and Historical Society, P.O. Box 342, Salem, IL 62881.

Marissa Historical and Genealogical Society, P.O. Box 27, Marissa, IL 62257.

Mascoutah Historical Society, Mascoutah, IL 62258.

Mattoon Public Library, Charleston Ave., and 17th St., Mattoon, IL 61938.

McDonough County Genealogical Society, P.O. Box 202, Macomb, IL 61455.

McHenry County, Illinois Genealogical Society, June Stuart, McHenry Library, 1011 Green Street, McHenry, IL 60050.

Mercer County Historical Society, Genealogical Division, Aledo, IL 61231.

Montgomery County Genealogical Society, P.O. Box 212, Litchfield, IL 62056.

Moultrie County Historical and Genealogical Society, P.O. Box MM, Sullivan, IL 61951.

Mt. Vernon Genealogical Society, c/o Mt. Vernon Public Library, 101 S. 7th, Mt. Vernon, IL 62864.

Newberry Library, 60 West Walton St., Chicago, IL 60610.

North Central Illinois Genealogical Society, P.O. Box 1071, Rockford, IL 61105.

North Suburban Genealogical Society, Winnetka Public Library, 768 Oak Street, Winnetka, IL 60093.

Northwest Suburban Council of Genealogists, P.O. Box AC, Mt. Prospect, IL 60056.

Odell Historical and Genealogical Society, P.O. Box 82, Odell, IL 60460.

Ogle County Illinois Genealogical Society, P.O. Box 183, Oregon, IL 61061.

Peoria Genealogical Society, P.O. Box 1489, Peoria, IL 61602.

Peoria Public Library, 111 No. Monroe St., Peoria, IL 61602.

Piatt County Historical and Genealogical Society, R.R. 1, Box 30, White Heath, IL 61884.

Polish Genealogical Society, 984 Milwaukee Ave., Chicago, IL 60622.

Poplar Creek Genealogical Society, P.O. Box 248, Streamwood, IL 60103.

Richland County, Illinois Genealogical Society, Box 202, Olney, IL 62450.

Rock Island Public Library, Rock Island, IL 61201.

Rockford Public Library, 215 N. Wyman St., Rockford, IL 61101.

Sangamon County Genealogical Society, P.O. Box 1829, Springfield, IL 62705.

Schuyler-Brown Historical and Genealogical Society, P.O. Box 96, Rushville, IL 62681.

Schuyler County Historical Museum and Genealogical Center, Madison and Congress (or) Box 96, Rushville, IL 62681.

Shawnee Library System, Rural Route 2, Box 136A, Carterville, IL 62918.

Shelby County Historical and Genealogical Society, P.O. Box 287, Shelbyville, IL 62565.

Southern Illinois Genealogical Society, Miss Alice L. Grant, 607 North Logan Street, Marion, IL 62959.

South Suburban Genealogical and Historical Society, P.O. Box 96, South Holland, IL 60473.

Staunton Area Genealogical Society, Box 95, Staunton, IL 62088.

St. Clair County, Illinois Genealogical Society, P.O. Box 431, Belleville, IL 62221.

Swedish Pioneer Historical Society, 5125 No. Spaulding Ave., Chicago, IL 60625.

Tazewell County Genealogical Society, P.O. Box 312, Pekin, IL 61554.

Thornton Township Historical Society, Genealogical Section, 154 East 154th St., Harvey, IL 60426.

Tri-County Genealogical Society, P.O. Box 355, Augusta, IL 62311.

Union County Genealogical / Historical Research Committee, 101 East Spring St., Anna, IL 62906.

University of Illinois Library, Urbana, IL 61801.

Urbana Free Library, 201 So. Race St., Urbana, IL 61801.

Warren County Genealogical Society, P.O. Box 240, Monmouth, IL 61462.

Warren County Library, 60 West Side Square, Monmouth, IL 61462.

Waverly Genealogical and Historical Society, c/o Mrs. Louise M. Dennis, Waverly, IL 62692.

Whiteside County Genealogists, Box 145, Sterling, IL 61081.

Winnetka Public Library, 768 Oak St., Winnetka, IL 60093.

Withers Public Library, 202 East Washington, Bloomington, IL 61701.

Zion Genealogical Society, sponsored by the Zion Benton Public Library, 2600 Emmaus Avenue, Zion, IL 60099.

Central Illinois Genealogical Quarterly, Decatur Genealogical Society, P.O. Box 2205, Decatur, IL 62526.

Chicago Genealogist, Chicago Genealogical Society, P.O. Box 1160, Chicago, IL 60690.

Clinton County Historical Society Quarterly, publication of the Clinton County, Illinois Historical Society, P.O. Box 82, Aviston, IL 62216.

Illinois State Genealogical Society Quarterly, P.O. Box 2225, Springfield, IL 62705.

Newsletter, Genealogical Society of Southern Illinois, c/o John A. Logan College, Carterville, IL 62818.

Saga Of Southern Illinois, The, quarterly publication of the Genealogy Society of Southern Illinois, Box 104, Carterville, IL 62918.

South Suburban Genealogical and Historical Society, P.O. Box 96, South Holland, IL 60473.

Where The Trails Cross, South Suburban Genealogical and Historical Society, P.O. Box 96, South Holland, IL 60473.

Yellowjacket, The, Great River Genealogical Society, c/o Quincy Public Library, Quincy, IL 62301.

Printed Census Records and Mortality Schedules

The name index to Illinois records compiled by the Illinois State Archives, Springfield, Illinois (microfilmed 1975 by Genealogical Society of the Church of Jesus Christ of Latter-day Saints) includes the following state and federal census records: 1810, 1818, 1820, 1825, 1830, 1835, 1840, 1845, 1850, 1855.

State Indexes - 1810, 1820, 1830, 1840, 1850.

County printed census records:

Adams - 1830, 1840	Champaign - 1840, 1850	Crawford - 1860
Alexander - 1830, 1850, 1860	Christian - 1850, 1860, 1880	Cumberland - 1850, 1860
Bond - 1830, 1850, 1860	Clark - 1830	DeKalb - 1840, 1850; 1855
Boone - 1850	Clay - 1830, 1850, 1860	DeWitt - 1850, 1860
Bureau - 1850	Clinton - 1830, 1850	DuPage - 1840, 1850
Calhoun - 1830, 1850, 1860	Coles - 1850, 1860	Edgar - 1830, 1840, 1850
Carroll - 1850, 1860	Chicago City - 1840, 1850	Edwards - 1830, 1850; 1825
Cass - 1850, 1860; 1855	Cook - 1850, 1860, 1870	Effingham - 1840, 1850

Fayette - 1840, 1850
Franklin - 1830, 1840, 1850, 1860
Fulton - 1830, 1840, 1850
Gallatin - 1830, 1850
Greene - 1830
Grundy - 1850
Hamilton - 1830, 1840, 1850, 1860
Hancock - 1830, 1850
Hardin - 1850
Henderson - 1850
Henry - 1830, 1850
Jackson - 1830, 1850
Jasper - 1850, 1860
Jefferson - 1830, 1840, 1850
Jersey - 1850
Jo Daviess - 1830, 1850, 1860
Johnson - 1830, 1850
Kane - 1850
Knox - 1830
Lake - 1860
LaSalle - 1850
Lawrence - 1830, 1850
Lee - 1850

Logan - 1840, 1850
Macon - 1830, 1850
Macoupin - 1830, 1850
Madison - 1830, 1850
Marion - 1830, 1850
Marshall - 1850
Mason - 1850
Massac - 1850; 1855
McDonough - 1830
McHenry - 1850
McLean - 1850
Menard - 1850
Mercer - 1830, 1850
Monroe - 1830, 1850
Montgomery - 1830, 1840, 1850; 1825, 1855
Morgan - 1830
Moultrie - 1850, 1860, 1870
Ogle - 1850
Peoria - 1830, 1850
Perry - 1830, 1850
Piatt - 1850
Pike - 1830, 1850
Pope - 1830, 1850

Pulaski - 1850
Putnam - 1830, 1850
Randolph - 1830, 1850; 1825
Richland - 1850, 1860, 1880
Saint Clair - 1830, 1840, 1850
Saline - 1850
Sangamon - 1830, 1850
Schuyler - 1830, 1850
Shelby - 1830, 1840, 1850, 1860
Stark - 1850
Stephenson - 1850
Tazewell - 1830; 1845
Union - 1820, 1830, 1840, 1850, 1860, 1870, 1880; 1835
Vermilion - 1830, 1850
Wabash - 1830, 1850, 1860
Warren - 1830, 1850
Washington - 1830, 1850
Wayne - 1830, 1850
White - 1830, 1850
Whiteside - 1850; 1865
Will - 1850
Williamson - 1850, 1860, 1870
Winnebago - 1850

Mortality Schedules:

State - 1850

Clay - 1860, 1870, 1880
Crawford - 1860, 1870, 1880
Edwards - 1860, 1870, 1880
Effingham - 1860, 1870, 1880

Jackson - 1850
Jasper - 1860, 1870, 1880
Lawrence - 1860, 1870, 1880
Richland - 1860, 1870, 1880

Sangamon - 1850
Schuyler - 1850, 1860, 1870, 1880
Wabash - 1860, 1870, 1880
Wayne - 1860, 1870, 1880

Valuable Printed Sources

Atlases and Gazetteers

Atlas of the State of Illinois 1876, reprinted 1972. Knightstown, Indiana: Mayhill Publications.

Illinois Land Atlas Index 1876. Published by the North Central Kansas Genealogical Society, Cawker City, Kansas.

Peck, J. M. *A Gazetteer of Illinois.* Philadelphia: Grigg and Elliot, 1837.

Illinois Guide and Gazetteer. Prepared by Illinois Sesquicentennial Commission Chicago: Rand McNally, 1969.

Place Names

Adams, James N. *Illinois Place Names,* Springfield, Illinois: *Illinois State Historical Society (1968).*

Guides to Genealogical Research

McCay, Betty L. *Sources for Genealogical Searching in Illinois.* (1970)

Volkel, Lowell M. and Marjorie Smith. *How to Research A Family with Illinois Roots.* Thomson, Illinois: Heritage House (1977)

Wolf, Joseph C. *A Reference Guide for Genealogical and Historical Research in Illinois.* Detroit, Michigan: Detroit Society for Genealogical Research (1963)

Histories

Bateman, Newton, ed. *Historical Encyclopedia of Illinois.* Chicago: Munsell Publishing Company, 1902-1925.

Smith, George W. *History of Illinois and Her People.* Chicago: American Historical Society, 1927.

Genealogical Sources

Name Index to Early Illinois Records. Springfield, Illinois: Illinois State Archives. Microfilm 248 reels.*

D.A.R. Collection*

The Genealogical Index of the Newberry Library, Chicago. Boston: G.K. Hall and Company, 1960. Four Volumes: Vol. 1, A-Fetherelf; (928,135); Vol. 2 Fethers - Libby (Pet); Vol. 3, Libby (Pink) - Saltonstall (N.H.) (928,136) and Vol. 4, Saltonstall - Zyn (928,137)*

Bibliographies and Directories

Bowers, Doris R. *Directory of Illinois Genealogical Societies.* Springfield: Illinois State Genealogical Society (1980)

Byrd, Cecil K. *A Bibliography of Illinois Imprints.* Chicago: University of Chicago Press (1966)

Irons, Victoria and Patricia C. Brennan. *Descriptive Inventory of the Archives of the State of Illinois.* Springfield: Illinois State Archives (1978)

Newspapers in Illinois State Historical Library. Springfield: Illinois State Historical Library (1979)

---

*Microfilm - Genealogical Society of The Church of Jesus Christ of Latter-day Saints, Salt Lake City, Utah.

ILLINOIS COUNTY HISTORIES
(Population figures to nearest thousand - 1980 U.S. Census)

Name	Map Index	Date Created	Pop. By M 1980	U.S. Cen Reports Available	Parent County or Territory From Which Organized	County Seat
*§ Adams	C1	1825	71	1830-80	Pike	Quincy 62301
(Co Clk has b & d rec from 1878, m rec from 1825; Clk Cir Ct has div, pro & civ ct rec)							
* Alexander	E3	1819	12	1820-80	Johnson	Cairo 62914
(Co Clk has b, d rec from 1878, m Ind rec from 1819; Clk Cir Ct has div, pro, civ ct rec)							
* Bond	D2	1817	16	1820-80	Madison	Greenville 62246
(Co Clk has b, d rec from 1877, m rec from 1817, Ind rec from 1870 discharge rec; Clk Cir Ct has div, pro, civ ct rec)							
* Boone	A3	1837	29	1840-80	Winnebago	Belvidere 61008
(Co Clk has b, m, d rec from 1877, Ind rec from 1843; Clk Cir Ct has div, pro, civ ct rec)							
*§ Brown	C2	1839	5	1840-80	Schuyler	Mt. Sterling 62353
* Bureau	B2	1837	39	1840-80	Putnam	Princeton 61356
(Co Clk has m, d rec from 1880, m rec from 1838, Ind rec from 1837, bur permits from 1971)							
* Calhoun	C1	1825	6	1830-80	Pike	Hardin 62047
(Co Clk has b & d rec from 1877, m & Ind rec from 1825)							
*§ Carroll	A2	1839	19	1840-80	Jo Daviess	Mt. Carroll 61053
(Co Clk has b & d rec from 1877, m rec from 1839 & Ind rec)							
* Cass	C2	1837	15	1840-80	Morgan	Virginia 62691
(Co Clk has b rec 1860, m rec 1837, d rec 1878; Cir Clk has div, pro & civ ct rec)							
*§ Champaign	C3	1833	167	1840-80	Vermillion	Urbana 61801
(Co Clk has b & d rec from 1916, m & pro rec from 1833; scattered b rec 1878, com from 1916, d from 1835 incom)							
* Christian	C3	1839	36	1840-80	Sangamon, Shelby	Taylorville 62568
(formerly Dane) (Co Clk has b & d rec from 1878, m & Ind from 1839; Clk Cir Ct has div, pro & civ ct rec from 1875)							
*§ Clark	C4	1819	17	1820-80	Crawford	Marshall 62441
(Co Clk has b, d rec from 1877, m rec from 1819, Ind rec from 1818; Local Register has bur rec; Clk Cir Ct has div, pro, civ ct rec)							
* Clay	D3	1824	15	1830-80	Wayne, Lawrence, Fayette	Louisville 62858
(Co Clk has b & d rec from 1878, m rec from 1825; also deeds from 1825 & veteran discharges & entry bks; Cir Clk has div, pro & civ ct rec)							
* Clinton	D2	1824	32	1830-80	Washington, Bond, Fayette, Crawford	Carlyle 62231
(Co Clk has b, d rec from 1877, m rec from 1825, Ind rec from 1818; Clk Cir Ct has div, pro, civ ct rec)							
* Coles	C3	1830	52	1840-80	Clark, Edgar	Charleston 61920
(Co Clk has b, d rec from 1878, m, Ind rec from 1830; Bur Vit Statistics Springfield has b, m, d rec from 1916)							
* Cook	A4	1831	5,223	1840-80	Putnam	Chicago 60606
(Co Clk has b, m, d & bur rec from 1871)							

COUNTY MAP FOR THE STATE OF ILLINOIS

Name	Map Index	Date Created	Pop. By M 1980	U.S. Cen Reports Available	Parent County or Territory From Which Organized	County Seat
* Crawford	D4	1816	21	1820-80	Edwards	Robinson 62454

(Co Clk has b & d rec from 1878, m rec from 1817, bur rec from 1915; Cir Clk has div, pro & civ ct rec)

| *§ Cumberland | C3 | 1843 | 11 | 1850-80 | Coles .... | Toledo 62468 |

(Co Clk has b, m, d, bur & Ind rec from 1885; Clk Cir Ct has div, pro & civ ct rec from 1885)

| Dane | | 1839 | | | Name changed in 1840 to Christian County | |
| * DeKalb | A3 | 1837 | 74 | 1840-80 | Kane .... | Sycamore 60178 |

(Co Clk has b, d rec 1878-1916 not complete, from 1916 complete, m, Ind rec from 1837, naturalization rec from 1850, poll bk recs from 1858-1872, War Patent rec 1845-1856; Clk Cir Ct has div, civ ct rec from 1850, pro rec from 1859. DeKalb Co Gen Soc has person who will research this county's records for a small fee)

| *§ DeWitt | A3 | 1839 | 18 | 1840-80 | Macon, McLean .... | Clinton 61727 |

(Co Clk has b, d & bur rec from 1877, m & Ind rec from 1839; Clk Cir Ct has div, pro & civ ct rec from 1839)

| *§ Douglas | C3 | 1859 | 20 | 1860-80 | Coles .... | Tuscola 61953 |

(Co Clk has b, m, d & Ind rec from 1859; Clk Cir Ct has div, pro & civ ct rec)

* DuPage	A3	1839	654	1840-80	Cook	Wheaton 60187
* Edgar	C4	1823	22	1830-80	Clark	Paris 61944
* Edwards	D3	1814	8	1820-80	Madison, Gallatin	Albion 62806

(Co Clk has b, d rec from 1877, m, Ind rec from 1815, Clk Cir Ct has div, pro, civ ct rec)

| *§ Effingham | D3 | 1831 | 31 | 1840-80 | Fayette, Crawford .... | Effingham 62401 |

(Co Clk has b, d rec from 1878 (very incomplete prior to 1916), m rec from 1834; Ind rec from 1833; Clk Cir Ct has div, pro, civ ct rec)

| *§ Fayette | D3 | 1821 | 22 | 1830-80 | Bond, Wayne, Clark, Jefferson .... | Vandalia 62471 |

(Co Clk has b, d rec from 1877, m, Ind rec from 1821; Clk Cir Ct has div, pro, civ ct rec)

| * Ford | B3 | 1859 | 15 | 1860-80 | Clark .... | Paxton 60957 |

(Co Clk has b & d rec from 1878, m & Ind rec from 1859; Clk Cir Ct has div, pro & civ ct rec)

| *§ Franklin | E3 | 1818 | 43 | 1820-80 | White, Gallatin .... | Benton 62812 |

(Co Clk has b & d rec from 1877, m rec from 1836, pro & civ ct rec from 1838)

| * Fulton | B2 | 1823 | 44 | 1830-80 | Pike .... | Lewistown 61542 |

(Co Clk has m & d rec from 1877, m rec from 1842 & Ind rec from 1823; Clk Cir Ct has div, pro & civ ct rec)

| * Gallatin | E3 | 1812 | 8 | 1820-80 | Randolph .... | Shawneetown 62984 |

(Co Clk has b, d rec from 1878, m rec from 1830, Ind rec from 1800; Clk Cir Ct has pro rec from 1860)

| * Greene | C2 | 1821 | 17 | 1830-80 | Madison .... | Carrollton 62016 |

(Co Clk has b & d rec from 1877, m rec from 1821)

| * Grundy | B3 | 1841 | 30 | 1850-80 | LaSalle .... | Morris 60450 |

(Co Clk has b rec from 1877, d rec from 1878, m, Ind rec from 1841, Bur rec from 1976; Clk Cir Ct has div, pro, civ ct rec from 1841)

| * Hamilton | D3 | 1821 | 8 | 1830-80 | White .... | McLeansboro 62859 |

(Co Clk has b, m, d, bur, div & pro rec from 1821)

| * Hancock | B1 | 1825 | 24 | 1830-80 | Pike, Unorg. Terr .... | Carthage 62321 |
| * Hardin | E3 | 1839 | 5 | 1840-80 | Pope .... | Elizabethtown 62931 |

(Co Clk has b, d, m, Ind rec from 1844, bur rec; Clk Cir Ct has div, civ ct rec from 1880, pro rec)

| * Henderson | B1 | 1841 | 9 | 1850-80 | Warren .... | Oquawka 61469 |

(Co Clk has b, m, d rec from 1878, Ind rec from 1841; Clk Cir Ct has div, pro, civ ct rec from 1841)

| * Henry | B2 | 1825 | 58 | 1830-80 | Fulton .... | Cambridge 61238 |

(Co Clk has b, d rec from 1877, m rec from 1837, bur rec from 1839, Ind rec)

| * Iroquois | B3 | 1833 | 33 | 1840-80 | Vermillion .... | Watseka 60970 |

(Co Clk has b, d rec from 1877, m rec from 1866, bur rec from 1973 Ind rec from 1835; Clk Cir Ct has div, pro, civ ct rec from 1855)

| *§ Jackson | E2 | 1816 | 61 | 1820-80 | Randolph, Johnson .... | Murphysboro 62966 |
| * Jasper | D3 | 1831 | 11 | 1840-80 | Clay, Crawford .... | Newton 62448 |

(Co Clk has b & d rec from 1877, m & Ind rec from 1835; Clk Cir Ct has div, pro & civ ct rec)

| * Jefferson | D3 | 1819 | 36 | 1820-80 | Edwards, White .... | Mt. Vernon 62864 |

(Co Clk has b, m & d rec)

| * Jersey | D2 | 1839 | 21 | 1840-80 | Greene .... | Jerseyville 62052 |

(Co Clk has b & d rec from 1878, m & Ind rec from 1839, div rec from 1840, pro rec from 1850 & civ ct rec from 1845)

| *§ Jo Daviess | A2 | 1827 | 23 | 1830-80 | Henry, Mercer, Putnam .... | Galena 61036 |

(Co Clk has b rec from 1877, a few before this date, m rec from 1830, d rec from 1877; d rec state place of bur; Cir Clk has pro rec from 1830, div & civ ct rec)

Name	Map Index	Date Created	Pop. By M 1980	U.S. Cen Reports Available	Parent County or Territory From Which Organized	County Seat
* Johnson	E3	1812	10	1820-80	Randolph	Vienna 62995

(Co Clk has b, d rec from 1878, m rec from 1834, Ind rec from 1815; Clk Cir Ct has div, pro, civ ct rec)

| * Kane | A4 | 1836 | 274 | 1840-80 | LaSalle | Geneva 60134 |

(Co Clk has b, d rec from 1878, m rec from 1836; Clk Cir Ct has div, pro, civ ct rec)

| * Kankakee | B3 | 1853 | 103 | 1860-80 | Iroquois, Will | Kankakee 60901 |

(Co Clk has b, d rec from 1878, m rec from 1853, div, pro, civ ct, Ind rec)

| * Kendall | A3 | 1841 | 37 | 1850-80 | LaSalle, Kane | Yorkville 60560 |

(Co Clk has b & d rec from 1878, m & Ind rec from 1841)

| *§ Knox | B2 | 1825 | 62 | 1830-80 | Fulton | Galesburg 61401 |

(Co Clk has b & d rec from 1878, m rec from 1830)

| * Lake | A3 | 1839 | 436 | 1840-80 | McHenry | Waukegan 60085 |

(Co Clk has b rec from 1871, m rec from 1839 & d rec from 1877; Clk Cir Ct has div, pro, civ ct rec; Rcdr Deeds has Ind rec)

| * LaSalle | B3 | 1831 | 109 | 1840-80 | Putnam, Vermillion | Ottawa 61350 |

(Co Clk has b & d rec from 1877, m from 1832; Clk Cir Ct has div & civ ct rec; Pro Office has pro rec)

| * Lawrence | D4 | 1821 | 18 | 1830-80 | Crawford, Edwards | Lawrenceville 62439 |

(Co Clk has b rec from 1877, d rec from 1878, m, Ind rec from 1821; City Clks have bur rec; Clk Cir Ct has div, pro, civ ct rec)

| * Lee | A3 | 1839 | 36 | 1840-80 | Ogle | Dixon 61021 |

(Co Clk has b, d rec from 1916, m, Ind rec; Clk Cir Ct has pro, div, civ ct rec)

| *§ Livingston | B3 | 1837 | 41 | 1840-80 | LaSalle, McLean | Pontiac 61764 |

(Co Clk has b rec from 1878, a few from 1856-1877, d rec from 1878, m rec from 1866, Ind rec from 1836, records are not complete prior to 1916; Clk Cir Ct has div, pro, civ ct rec)

| *§ Logan | C2 | 1839 | 32 | 1840-80 | Sangamon | Lincoln 62656 |

(Co Clk has b, d rec from 1879, m rec from 1859, Ind rec from 1849; Clk Cir Ct has div, pro, civ ct rec; City Clk has bur rec)

| *§ Macon | C3 | 1829 | 131 | 1830-80 | Shelby | Decatur 62521 |

(Co Clk has b rec from 1850, m rec from 1829, d rec from 1877, bur rec from 1 Jan 1964; Clk Cir Ct has div, pro, civ ct rec)

| *§ Macoupin | C2 | 1829 | 49 | 1830-80 | Madison, Greene | Carlinville 62626 |

(Co Clk has b & d rec from 1877, m & Ind rec from 1829; Clk Cir Ct has div, pro & civ ct rec)

| * Madison | D2 | 1812 | 246 | 1820-80 | St. Clair | Edwardsville 62025 |

(Co Clk has b rec from 1860, m rec from 1913 & d rec from 1878; Clk Cir Ct has div, pro & civ ct rec)

| * Marion | D3 | 1823 | 43 | 1830-80 | Fayette, Jefferson | Salem 62881 |

(Co Clk has b rec from 1878, m rec from 1821, d rec from 1877 & Ind rec from 1823; Clk Cir Ct has div & civ ct rec from 1858, pro rec from 1840)

| * Marshall | B2 | 1839 | 14 | 1840-80 | Putnam | Lacon 61540 |

(Co Clk has a few b, d rec from 1877, m rec from 1840, Ind rec; Clk Cir Ct has div, pro, civ ct rec)

| * Mason | C2 | 1841 | 19 | 1850-80 | Tazewell | Havana 62644 |

(Co Clk has b, d rec from 1877, m, Ind rec from 1841; City Clk has bur rec; Clk Cir Ct has div, pro, civ ct rec)

| * Massac | E3 | 1843 | 15 | 1850-80 | Pope, Johnson | Metropolis 62960 |

(Co Clk has b rec from 1864, m rec from 1854, d rec from 1878, bur rec from 1977, Ind rec from 1843)

| * McDonough | B2 | 1826 | 37 | 1830-80 | Schuyler | Macomb 61455 |

(Co Clk has b, d rec from 1877, m rec from 1830, Ind rec from 1812; City Clk has bur rec; Clk Cir Ct has div, pro, civ ct rec)

| * McHenry | A3 | 1836 | 148 | 1840-80 | Cook | Woodstock 60098 |

(Co Clk has b & d rec from 1877, m rec from 1837, div & civ ct rec from 1836 & pro rec from 1840; Rcdr Deeds has mil ser rec, deeds & Ind rec from 1841)

| * McLean | B3 | 1830 | 119 | 1840-80 | Tazewell, Unorg., Terr. | Bloomington 61701 |

(Co Clk has b rec from 1860, m from 1830 & d rec from 1878; Clk Cir Ct has div, pro & civ ct rec; Co Rcdr has Ind rec)

| *§ Menard | C2 | 1839 | 12 | 1840-80 | Sangamon | Petersburg 62675 |

(Co Clk has b & d rec from 1877, m & Ind rec from 1839; Clk Cir Ct has div, pro & civ ct rec)

| * Mercer | B2 | 1825 | 19 | 1830-80 | Unorg. Terr., Pike | Aledo 61231 |

(Co Clk has b & d rec from 1877, m & Ind rec from 1835 & bur rec from 1916; Clk Cir Ct has div, pro & civ ct rec)

Name	Map Index	Date Created	Pop. By M 1980	U.S. Cen Reports Available	Parent County or Territory From Which Organized	County Seat
* Monroe	D2	1816	20	1820-80	Randolph, St. Clair	Waterloo 62298

(Co Clk has b, d rec from 1865, m, Ind rec from 1816, pro rec 1845, civ ct rec 1843)

| *§ Montgomery | C2 | 1821 | 32 | 1830-80 | Bond, Madison | Hillsboro 62049 |

Co Clk has b, d rec from Dec. 1877, m, Ind rec from 1821; Clk Cir Ct has div, pro, civ ct rec)

| *§ Morgan | C2 | 1823 | 37 | 1830-80 | Sangamon | Jacksonville 62650 |

(Co Clk has b, d, bur rec from 1878, m rec from 1827, div rec from 1831, pro rec from 1836, civ ct rec from 1828)

| *§ Moultrie | C3 | 1843 | 15 | 1850-80 | Shelby, Macon | Sullivan 61951 |

(Co Clk has b rec from 1859, m, Ind rec from 1840, d rec from 1877, bur rec from 1961; Clk Cir Ct has div, pro, civ ct rec)

| *§ Ogle | A3 | 1836 | 46 | 1840-80 | Jo Daviess | Oregon 61601 |

(Co Clk has b rec from 1860, d rec from 1878, m & Ind rec from 1837; Clk Cir Ct has div, pro & civ ct rec)

| *§ Peoria | B2 | 1825 | 200 | 1830-80 | Fulton | Peoria 61602 |

(Co Clk has b, m & civ ct rec from 1878, m rec from 1825)

| * Perry | E2 | 1827 | 22 | 1830-80 | Randolph, Jackson | Pinckneyville 62274 |

(Co Clk has incom b rec from 1879, com from 1916 to present, m rec incom from 1827, com from 1916 to present, d rec from 1879, com from 1916 to present; Cir Clk has div, pro & civ ct rec from 1827)

| *§ Piatt | C3 | 1841 | 17 | 1850-80 | DeWitt, Macon | Monticello 61856 |

(Co Clk has b, d rec from 1877, m rec from 1841, Ind rec from 1852; Clk Cir Ct has div, pro, civ ct rec from 1841)

| *§ Pike | C1 | 1821 | 19 | 1850-80 | Madison, Bond, Clark | Pittsfield 62363 |

(Co Clk has b, d rec from 1877, m rec from 1827, Ind rec from 1821)

| * Pope | E3 | 1816 | 4 | 1820-80 | Gallatin, Johnson | Golconda 62938 |

Co Clk has b rec from 1875, d rec from 1878, b pro, Ind rec from 1816; Clk Cir Ct has div, civ ct rec)

| * Pulaski | E3 | 1843 | 9 | 1850-80 | Johnson | Mound City 62963 |

(Co Clk has b rec from 1866, m rec from 1861, d rec from 1882, bur rec from 1950, tax rec from 1851; Cir Clk has div, pro & civ ct rec)

| * Putnam | B3 | 1825 | 6 | 1830-80 | Fulton | Hennepin 61327 |

(Co Clk has b & d rec from 1878, m, pro & civ ct rec from 1831)

| * Randolph | E2 | 1795 | 35 | 1820-80 | NW Territory, St. Clair | Chester 62233 |

(Co Clk has b & d rec 1877, m pro & civ ct rec from 1809)

| * Richland | D3 | 1841 | 18 | 1850-80 | Clay, Lawrence | Olney 62450 |

(Co Clk has b & d rec from 1878, m rec from 1841; Clk Cir Ct has div, pro & civ ct rec)

| *§ Rock Island | B2 | 1831 | 166 | 1840-80 | Jo Daviess | Rock Island 61201 |

(Co Clk has b, d rec from 1877, m rec from 1833, tax collector rec from 1870, Supervisor's rec from July 1833; Co Rcdr has Ind rec; Clk Cir Ct has div, pro, civ ct rec; Local registrar has bur rec)

| *§ St. Clair | D2 | 1790 | 264 | 1820-80 | NW Territory | Belleville 62220 |

(Co Clk has b, m, d & bur rec)

| *§ Saline | E3 | 1847 | 28 | 1850-80 | Gallatin | Harrisburg 62946 |

(Co Clk has b, d rec from 1878, m rec from 1848, Ind rec from 1821, City Clk has bur rec; Clk Cir Ct has div, pro, civ ct rec)

| *§ Sangamon | C2 | 1821 | 174 | 1830-80 | NW Territory | Springfield 62701 |

(Co Clk has b & d rec from 1877, m rec from 1821)

| * Schuyler | C2 | 1825 | 8 | 1830-80 | Pike, Fulton | Rushville 62681 |

(Co Clk has b, d rec from 1877, m rec from 1825; Clk Cir Ct has div, pro, civ ct rec. Schuyler Co Jail Museum gen lib has m rec from 1825, b, d rec, obits 1856-1900, tax, school, mil rec, cen rec from 1790, cem rec, hist for Schuyler and surrounding cos, fam rec and published genealogies)

| *§ Scott | C2 | 1839 | 6 | 1840-80 | Morgan | Winchester 62694 |

(Co Clk has b rec from 1860, d rec from 1877, m, Ind rec from 1839; Clk Cir Ct has div, pro, civ ct rec)

| *§ Shelby | C3 | 1827 | 24 | 1830-80 | Fayette | Shelbyville 62565 |

(Co Clk has b rec from 1849, m rec from 1827, d rec from 1878 & Ind rec from 1833)

| * Stark | B2 | 1839 | 7 | 1840-80 | Knox, Putnam | Toulon 61483 |

(Co Clk has b rec from 1855, m rec from 1839 & d rec from 1878; Clk Cir Ct has div, pro & civ ct rec)

| *§ Stephenson | A2 | 1837 | 49 | 1840-80 | Jo Daviess, Winnebago | Freeport 61032 |

(Co Clk has m & d rec from 1878, m rec from 1837, pro & civ ct rec from 1894)

| * Tazewell | B2 | 1827 | 131 | 1830-80 | Sangamon | Pekin 61554 |

(Co Clk has b & d rec from 1878, m rec from 1827; Cir Clk has bur, div, pro & civ ct rec)

Name	Map Index	Date Created	Pop. By M 1980	U.S. Cen Reports Available	Parent County or Territory From Which Organized	County Seat
* Union	E3	1818	18	1820-80	Johnson	Jonesboro 62952

(Co Clk has b rec from 1862, d rec from 1877, m, Ind rec from 1818)

| *§ Vermilion | C4 | 1826 | 95 | 1830-80 | Unorg. Terr., Edgar | Danville 61832 |

(Co Clk has b rec from 1858, m rec from 1826, d rec from 1877 & bur rec from 1900)

| * Wabash | D4 | 1824 | 14 | 1830-80 | Edwards | Mt. Carmel 62863 |

(Co Clk has b & d rec from 1878; Clk Cir Ct has div, pro & civ ct rec)

| * Warren | B2 | 1825 | 22 | 1830-80 | Pike | Monmouth 61462 |

(Co Clk has b, d rec from 1875, m rec from 1830; Clk Cir Ct has pro, civ Ct rec from 1825)

| * Washington | D2 | 1818 | 15 | 1820-80 | St. Clair | Nashville 62263 |

(Co Clk has b, d, bur rec from 1877, m rec from 1832, Ind rec from 1818; Clk Cir Ct has div, pro, civ ct rec)

| * Wayne | D3 | 1819 | 18 | 1820-80 | Edwards | Fairfield 62837 |

(Co Clk has b, m, d, bur rec from 1886; Ind rec; Clk Cir Ct has pro, div, civ ct rec)

| * White | D3 | 1815 | 18 | 1820-80 | Gallatin | Carmi 62821 |

(Co Clk has b, d rec from 1870, m, Ind rec from 1816, pro rec from 1850)

| * Whiteside | A2 | 1836 | 66 | 1840-80 | Jo Daviess, Henry | Morrison 61270 |

(Co Clk has b, d rec from 1878, m rec from 1839, CW rec 1869-70, Tax Assessments from 1840; Clk Cir Ct has div, pro, civ ct rec)

| * Will | B3 | 1836 | 323 | 1840-80 | Cook, DuPage | Joliet 60431 |

(Co Clk has b, d rec from 1877, m rec from 1836; Clk Cir Ct has div, pro, civ ct rec; Co Rcdr has Ind rec)

| * Williamson | E3 | 1839 | 56 | 1840-80 | Franklin | Marion 62959 |

(Co Clk has b rec from 1858, m rec from 1878, d rec from 1840, Ind rec from 1823; City Clk has bur rec; Clk Cir Ct has div, pro, civ ct rec)

| * Winnebago | A3 | 1836 | 250 | 1840-80 | Jo Daviess | Rockford 61101 |

(Co Clk has b & d rec from 1877 & m rec from 1837)

| * Woodford | B3 | 1841 | 33 | 1850-80 | Tazewell, McLean | Eureka 61530 |

(Co Clk has b, d rec from 1871, m rec from 1841; Co Rcdr has Ind rec from 1832; Clk Cir Ct has div, pro, civ ct rec)

* - At least one county history has been published about this county.

§ - Inventory of county archives was made by the Historical Records Survey. (see introduction)

INDIANA

CAPITAL, INDIANAPOLIS - TERRITORY 1800 - STATE 1816 - (19TH)

When the French explorers first came into the Indiana region about 1679, the entire territory was more or less a wilderness inhabited by a few Indians. During the most of the 1700's, the only white men there were some fur traders.

The first permanent community was developed around Vincennes, which was fortified about 1732. In 1763 the area fell to Britain, but Indian uprisings made settlement extremely difficult. Americans captured Vincennes in 1779 and acquired the whole region as part of the Northwest Territory in 1787. Indiana Territory was organized in 1800 and statehood came in 1816.

The first counties to be settled were Knox, Harrison, Switzerland and Clark, in the extreme south end. Settlers in those counties came from Virginia, Kentucky and the Carolinas, although a group of Swiss emigrants established themselves in the southeast part of the state. The Wabash and the Ohio Rivers section drew many of the first settlers. Many Germans and Irish came there about 1830. About twenty years later New Englanders established themselves in the northern counties. The central part of the state was the last to be settled. Less than seventy years after the settlement of the state, the population had reached more than a million and a half. Abhorring slavery Quakers left Tennessee and the Carolinas and established themselves in Wayne and Randolph counties along the Ohio border midway north and south in Indiana.

With the development of the industrial area of the Calumet section, adjacent to the South Chicago area in the northwest part of the state many central Europeans flocked there to man the rapidly increasing factories.

Indiana State Board of Health, 1330 West Michigan Street, Indianapolis, Indiana 46206 has original birth records from October 1907, death records begin in 1900. Prior to these dates, records were filed with the local health office in the county where the event occurred. Most local health offices in Indiana have records beginning with the year 1882.

Marriages occurring prior to 1958 are NOT recorded with this office. Please direct requests to the clerk of the court in the county where the marriage license was issued.

Records of wills and all probate matters are in the custody of the clerk of the Circuit Court or County Clerk in most County Seats.

Real estate records, land titles, etc., are in the office of the county recorder in the various counties.

Genealogical Archives, Libraries, Societies, and Publications

Allen County Indiana Genealogical Society, P.O. Box 7003, Fort Wayne, IN 46807.

American Legion National Headquarters Library, 700 N. Pennsylvania St., Indianapolis, IN 46204.

Anderson Public Library, 32 W. 10th, Anderson, IN 46016.

Bloomfield Carnegie Public Library, S. Franklin St., Bloomfield, IN 47424.

Eckhart Public Library, 603 S. Jackson St., Auburn, IN 46706.

Emline Fairbanks Memorial Library, 222 No. 7th, Terre Haute, IN 47807.

Frankfort Community Public Library, 208 W. Clinton St., Frankfort, IN 46401.

Goshen College Historical Library, Goshen, IN 46526.

Greene County Historical Society, 255 E. Mechanic Street, Bloomfield, IN 47424.

Howard County Genealogical Society, c/o Kokomo Public Library, 220 N. Union, Kokomo, IN 46901.

Huntington Public Library, 44 East Park Drive, Huntington, IN 46750.

Indiana Historical Society, 315 W. Ohio Street, Indianapolis, IN 46202.

Indiana Historical Society Library, William Henry Smith Memorial Library, 140 N. Senate Ave., Indianapolis, IN 46204.

Indiana State Library, 140 N. Senate Ave., Indianapolis, IN 46204.

Kosciusko County Historical Society, P.O. Box 1071, Warsaw, IN 46580.

Lewis Historical Collections Library, Vincennes University, Vincennes, IN 47591.

Logansport Public Library, 616 E. Broadway, Logansport, IN 46947.

Madison County Historical Society, Inc., P.O. Box 523, Anderson, IN 46015.

Madison-Jefferson County Public Library, Madison, 420 W. Main St., Madison, IN 47250.

Marion Public Library, 600 S. Washington St., Marion, IN 46952.

Marshall County Historical Center, 317 W. Monroe St., Plymouth, IN 46563.

Miami County Genealogical Society, Ray Bakehorn, R.R. 3, Kokomo, IN 46901.

Michigan City Public Library, 100 East Fourth Street, Michigan City, IN 46360.

Middletown Public Library, Box 36, 554 Locust St., Middletown, IN 47356.

Monroe County Library, c/o Bobbie Taylor, Public Library, 303 E. Kirkwood Ave., Bloomington, IN 47401.

New Albany Public Library, New Albany, IN 47150.

Noble County Genealogy Society, c/o Noble County Library, Albion, IN 46701.

Noblesville Public Library, 16 S. 10th St., Noblesville, IN 46060.

Northern Indiana Historical Society, 112 So. Lafayette Blvd., South Bend, IN 44601.

Northwest Indiana Genealogical Society, Westville, IN 46391.

Paoli Public Library, NE Court, Paoli, IN 47454.

Pike County Historical Society, Petersburg, IN 47567.

Plymouth Public Library, 201 N. Center St., Plymouth, IN 46563.

Public Library of Fort Wayne and Allen County, 900 Webster, Fort Wayne, IN 46802.

Pulaski County Genealogical Society, c/o Mrs. Orval Burgess, R.R. 1, Winamac, IN 46996.

Pulaski County Public Library, 121 S. Riverside Dr., Winamac, IN 46996.

Rockville Public Library, 106 N. Market St., Rockville, IN 47872.

South Bend Public Library, 122 W. Wayne, South Bend, IN 46601.

Southern Indiana Genealogical Society, P.O. Box 665, New Albany, IN 47150.

Sullivan County Historical Society, P.O. Box 326, Sullivan, IN 47882.

Tippecanoe County Area Genealogical Society, 909 South Street, Lafayette, IN 47901.

Tri-State Genealogical Society, c/o Williard Library, 21 First Avenue, Evansville, IN 47710.

Valparaiso Public Library, 107 Jefferson St., Valparaiso, IN 46383.

Vigo County Historical Society, 1411 So. 6th St., Terre Haute, IN 47802.

Vigo County Public Library, One Library Square, Terre Haute, IN 47807.

Wabash Valley Genealogical Society, P.O. Box 85, Terre Haute, IN 47808.

Warsaw Public Library, 315 E. Center St., Warsaw, IN 46580.

White County Genealogical Society, P.O. Box 149, Monticello, IN 47960.

Willard Library of Evansville, 21 1st Ave., Evansville, IN 47710.

Worthington Public Library, Worthington, IN 47471.

Allen County Lines, published by the Allen County Genealogical Society of Indiana. Published quarterly, P.O. Box 7003, Fort Wayne, IN 46807.

Hoosier Genealogist, The, Genealogical Section of the Indiana Historical Society, 140 North Senate Ave., Indianapolis, IN 46204.

Southern Indiana Genealogical Society Quarterly, published by the Southern Indiana Genealogical Society, P.O. Box 665, New Albany, IN 47150.

Tri-State Packet, The, published by the Tri-State Genealogical Society, c/o Williard Library, 21 First Avenue, Evansville, IN 47710.

Printed Census Records and Mortality Schedules

State Indexes - 1820, 1830, 1840, 1850

Printed Census Records (Counties):

Adams - 1850	Jay - 1870	Posey - 1820
Allen - 1850	Jefferson - 1870	Pulaski - 1860
Benton - 1900	Jennings - 1860	Scott - 1860, 1870, 1900
Brown - 1900	Lawrence - 1850	Switzerland - 1900
Cass - 1830, 1840, 1850	Madison - 1830	Tipton - 1850
Clay - 1850	Monroe - 1820, 1830, 1840, 1850	Vanderburgh - 1820
Clinton, 1850	Montgomery - 1830, 1840	Warrick - 1830, 1850
Crawford - 1900	Morgan - 1850	Washington - 1850, 1860
Fayette - 1900	Ohio - 1900	Wayne - 1850
Franklin - 1840	Porter - 1840, 1850	

Indiana Territory - 1807

Mortality Schedules - 1850

Valuable Printed Sources

Atlases and Gazetteers

Chamberlain, E. *The Indiana Gazetteer or Topographical Dictionary of the State of Indiana.* Indianapolis: E. Chamberlain (1849)

New Topographical Atlas and Gazetteer of Indiana 1871. New York: George H. Adams and Company. Reproduction by Unigraphic Inc., Evansville, Indiana (1975)

Maps

Indiana Historical Society. *Maps of Indiana Counties in 1876.* Reprinted from Illustrated Atlas of State of Indiana published 1876 by Baskin Forster and Company. (1968)

Place Names

Baker, Ronald L. and Marvin Carmony. *Indiana Place Names.* Bloomington and London: Indiana University Press (1975)

Pence, George and Nellie C. Armstrong. *Indiana Boundaries, Territory, State and County.* (Indiana Historical Collections, volume XIX), reprinted by the Indiana Historical Bureau, 1967.

Guides to Genealogical Research

Indiana Source Book, Genealogical Material from "The Hoosier Genealogist" Indianapolis, Indiana: Indiana Historical Society.

Miller, Carolynne L. (Wendel). *Aids for Genealogical Searching in Indiana.* Detroit, Michigan: The Detroit Society for Genealogical Research (1970), 1978.

McCay, Betty L. *Sources for Genealogical Searching in Indiana.* Indianapolis (1969).

Newhard, Malinda E. E. *A Guide to Genealogical Records in Indiana.* Harlan, Indiana: Published privately (1979).

Histories

Barnhart, John Donald and Donald F. Carmony. *Indiana From Frontier to Industrial Commonwealth.* Indianapolis: Reprinted by Indiana Historical Bureau, 1979 (ca 1954). 2 Vols.

Dunn, Jacob Piatt. Indiana and Indianans. Chicago and New York, American Historical Society, 1919. 6 volumes.

Esarey, Logan. *A History of Indiana.* Indianapolis: Reprinted by Hoosier Heritage Press, 1970 (ca 1915-1918).

Haymond, William S. An illustrated history of the state of Indiana. ... Indianapolis, S. L. Marrow & Co., 1879

Bibliographies

Waters, Margaret R. *Revolutionary Soldiers Buried in Indiana.* Reprinted 1970 Baltimore: Genealogical Publishing Company.

Cammack, Eleanor. *Indiana Methodism: A Bibliography of Printed and Archival Holding in Archive of DePauw University.* (Greencastle: DePauw University) (1964)

A Roster of Revolutionary Ancestors of the Indiana Daughters of the American Revolution. Evansville, IN, Unigraphic, 1976. 2 Vols.

Thompson, Donald E. *Preliminary Checklist of Archives and Manuscripts in Indiana Repositories.* Indianapolis: Indiana Historical Society, 1980.

INDIANA COUNTY HISTORIES
(Population figures to nearest thousand - 1980 U.S. Census)

Name	Map Index	Date Created	Pop. By M 1980	U.S. Cen Reports Available	Parent County or Territory From Which Organized	County Seat
* Adams	B3	1835	29	1840-80	Allen, Randolph	Decatur 46733
(Co Clk has m, div, pro & civ ct rec)						
*§ Allen	A3	1824	292	1830-80	Unorg. Terr., Randolph	Fort Wayne 46802
(Co Clk has m rec from 1824, div, pro, civ ct rec from 1823, bur rec of soldiers from Spanish-American War; Rcrd Office has Ind rec; Co Board of health has b, d rec)						
* Bartholomew	C3	1821	65	1832-80	Unorg. Terr., Jackson, Delaware	Columbus 47201
(Co Health Office has b, d rec; Co Clk has m rec from 1821, ct rec, pro, wills from 1821, Co Rcdr has Ind rec; Co Clk has cem rec recorded by the DAR, and some naturalization rec)						
* Benton	B2	1840	10	1850-80	Jasper	Fowler 47944
(Co Health has b & d rec from 1880; Clk Cir Ct has m & div rec from 1840, pro & civ ct rec; Co Rcdr has Ind rec; Hist Soc has historical rec)						
*§ Blackford	B3	1838	16	1840-80	Jay	Hartford City 47348
(Co Clk has m, div, pro & civ ct rec from 1839; City & Co Health Officers have b rec; Co Coroner has d & bur rec)						
*§ Boone	B2	1830	36	1830-80	Hendricks, Marion	Lebanon 46052
(Co Clk has m, civ ct rec from 1831, div rec from 1830, pro rec from 1833; Co Health Dept has b, d rec; Co Rcdr has Ind rec)						
* Brown	C2	1836	12	1840-80	Monroe, Bartholomew, Jackson	Nashville 47448
(Co Health has b & d rec; Co Clk has m rec from 1836, div, pro & civ ct rec)						
* Carroll	B2	1828	19	1830-80	Unorg. Terr	Delphi 46923
(Co Clk has m, div, pro & civ ct rec from 1828; Co Health Officer has b, d & bur rec)						
* Cass	B7	1829	41	1830-80	Carroll	Logansport 46947
(Co Health has b & d rec; Co Clk has m & pro rec from 1892, div & civ ct rec from 1894; Co Aud has Ind rec)						
* Clark	D3	1801	89	1820-80	Knox	Jeffersonville 47130

Name	Map Index	Date Created	Pop. By M 1980	U.S. Cen Reports Available	Parent County or Territory From Which Organized	County Seat
*§ Clay	C2	1825	25	1830-80	Owen, Putnam, Vigo, Sullivan	Brazil 47834

(Co Health Dept has b, d rec; Co Clk has m, div, pro, civ ct rec from 1851; Co Rcdr has Ind from 1825, some bur rec)

| * Clinton | B2 | 1830 | 31 | 1830-80 | Tippecanoe | Frankfort 46041 |

(Co Health has b & d rec; Co Clk has m & will rec from 1830, div, pro & civ ct rec from 1888; Co Rcdr has Ind rec)

| Crawford | D2 | 1818 | 10 | 1820-80 | Orange, Harrison, Perry | English 47118 |

(Co Clk has b, m, d, bur, div, pro & civ ct rec)

| * Daviess | C2 | 1817 | 28 | 1830-80 | Knox | Washington 47501 |

(Co Clk has m, div, pro & civ ct rec from 1817)

| * Dearborn | C3 | 1803 | 34 | 1820-80 | Clark | Lawrenceburg 47025 |

(Clk Cir Ct has m rec, lic 1826, application 1905, div, pro & civ ct rec; Health Officer has b & d rec)

| * Decatur | C3 | 1822 | 24 | 1830-80 | Unorg. Terr | Greensburg 47240 |

(Co Clk has m rec from 1822, div, pro & civ ct rec)

| * DeKalb | A3 | 1835 | 33 | 1840-80 | Allen, Lagrange | Auburn 46706 |

(Co Health has b & d rec; Co Clk has m & civ ct rec from 1837, pro rec from 1855, school rec from 1903 to 1932; Co Rcdr has Ind rec)

| *§ Delaware | B3 | 1827 | 127 | 1820-80 | Randolph | Muncie 47305 |

(Co Clk has m, div, pro & civ ct rec from 1827)

| * Dubois | D2 | 1818 | 34 | 1820-80 | Pike | Jasper 47546 |

(Co Clk has m, div, pro, civ ct rec from 1839)

| * Elkhart | A3 | 1830 | 137 | 1830-80 | Allen, Cass | Goshen 46526 |

(Co Health has b & d rec; Co Clk has m rec from 1831, div & civ ct rec from 1853, pro rec from 1852; Co Aud has Ind rec)

| * Fayette | C3 | 1819 | 28 | 1820-80 | Wayne, Franklin | Connersville 47331 |
| Floyd | D3 | 1819 | 61 | 1820-80 | Harrison, Clarke | New Albany 47150 |

(Co Health has b & d rec; Co Clk has m rec from 1813, div & civ ct rec from 1863, pro rec from 1819)

| Fountain | B2 | 1826 | 19 | 1830-80 | Montgomery, Parke | Covington 47932 |

(Co Health Dept has b, d rec from 1885; Co Clk has m, pro, civ ct rec from 1830, div rec; Co Rcdr has Ind rec from 1828)

| * Franklin | C3 | 1811 | 20 | 1820-80 | Clark, Dearborn, Jefferson | Brookville 47012 |

(Co Health Dept has b, d rec from 1882; Co Clk has m, div, pro, civ ct rec from 1811, declaration of intent 1826-1925, rec of apprentices 1831-54; Pub Lib has cem rec; Co Rcdr has Ind rec from 1803, soldier's discharge rec from 1866)

| *§ Fulton | A2 | 1835 | 19 | 1840-80 | Allen, Cass, St. Joseph | Rochester 46975 |

(Co Clk has m, div, pro & civ ct rec from 1836; Co Health has b & d rec; Co Rcdr has Ind rec)

| * Gibson | D1 | 1813 | 33 | 1820-80 | Knox | Princeton 47570 |

(Co Health has b & d rec; Co Clk has m rec from 1813, div, pro & civ ct rec from 1820)

| * Grant | B3 | 1831 | 81 | 1840-80 | Delaware, Madison, Cass | Marion 41952 |

(Co Health has b & d rec; Co Clk has m, div, pro & civ ct rec from 1831; Co Aud has Ind rec)

| *§ Greene | C2 | 1821 | 30 | 1830-80 | Daviess, Sullivan | Bloomfield 47424 |

(Co Health has b rec from 1885, d rec from 1893; Co Clk has m rec from 1821, div, pro & civ ct rec from 1820; Co Aud has Ind rec from 1824)

| * Hamilton | B2 | 1823 | 81 | 1830-80 | Unorg. Terr., Marion | Noblesville 46060 |

(Co Health has b & d rec; Co Clk has m, div, pro & civ ct rec from 1843)

| * Hancock | B3 | 1828 | 44 | 1830-80 | Madison | Greenfield 46140 |

(Co Health Dept has b rec from July 1941, d rec; Co Clk has m, div, pro, wills, civ ct rec from 1828; Co Rcdr has Ind rec)

| * Harrison | D2 | 1808 | 27 | 1820-80 | Knox, Clark | Corydon 47112 |

(Co Health Dept has b, d rec from 1882; Co Clk has m, pro, civ ct rec from 1809, div rec from 1815, Ind rec from 1807)

| * Hendricks | C2 | 1824 | 69 | 1830-80 | Unorg. Terr., Putnam | Danville 46122 |

(Co Health has b rec from 1882 to 1920, d rec from 1882; Co Clk has m, div, pro & civ ct rec from 1823; Co Aud has Ind rec)

| * Henry | B3 | 1822 | 53 | 1830-80 | Unorg. Terr | New Castle 47362 |

(Co Health Dept has b, d rec; Co Clk has m, div, civ ct rec from 1823, pro rec; Co Auditor has Ind rec from 1823)

| *§ Howard | B2 | 1844 | 87 | 1850-80 | Carroll, Cass, Miami, Grant, Hamilton (Originally Richardville Co) | Kokomo 46901 |

(Co Clk has m, div, pro & civ ct rec)

COUNTY MAP FOR THE STATE OF INDIANA

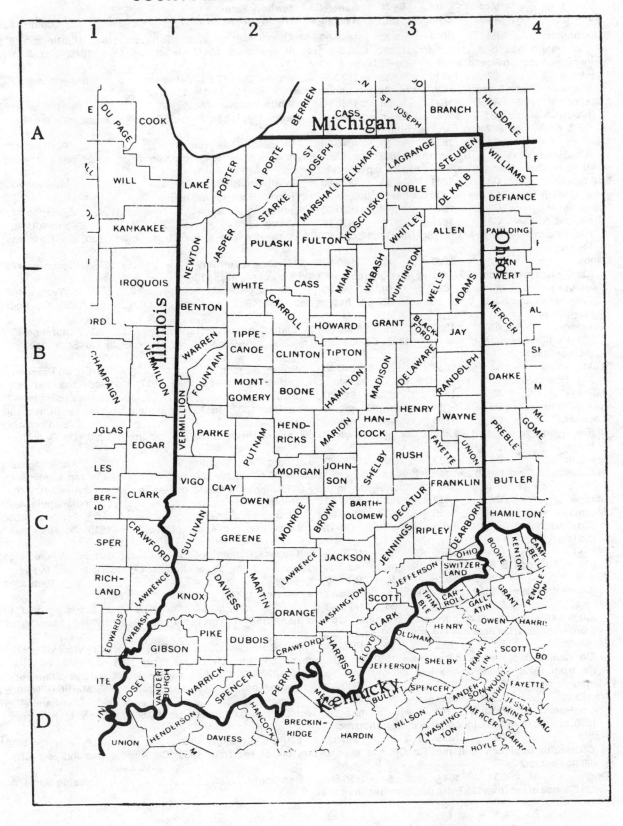

Name	Map Index	Date Created	Pop. By M 1980	U.S. Cen Reports Available	Parent County or Territory From Which Organized	County Seat
* Huntington	B3	1832	35	1840-80	Allen, Grant	Huntington 46750

(Co Health has b & d rec from 1882; Co Clk has m rec from 1847, civ ct rec from 1840, pro & div rec from 1850; Co Rcdr has Ind rec from 1834)

* Jackson	C2	1816	36	1820-80	Washington, Clark, Jefferson	Brownstown 47220

(Co Health has b & d rec; Co Clk has m, div, pro & civ ct rec from 1816; Co Aud has Ind rec)

* Jasper	A2	1835	26	1840-80	White, Warren	Rensselaer 47978

(Courthouse burned in 1862, all rec destroyed. Co Health Dept has b rec; Co Clk has m, div rec from 1865, d rec from 1882, pro, civ ct rec from 1864)

*§ Jay	B3	1835	23	1840-80	Randolph, Delaware	Portland 47371

(Co Health has b & d rec from 1882; Co Clk has m rec from 1843, div rec from 1882, pro rec from 1836, civ ct rec from 1837; Co Aud has Ind rec from 1836)

* Jefferson	C3	1881	30	1820-80	Dearborn, Clark	Madison 47250

(Co Health has b, d & bur rec; Co Clk has m, div, pro & civ ct rec; Co Rcdr has Ind rec)

* Jennings	C3	1817	23	1820-80	Jefferson, Jackson	Vernon 47282
* Johnson	C2	1823	77	1830-80	Unorg. Terr.	Franklin 46131

(Co Health has b, d & bur rec from 1883; Co Clk has m, div, pro & civ ct rec from 1830; Co Rcdr has Ind rec)

* Knox	C2	1790	42	1820-80	Northwest Territory	Vincennes 47591

(Co Clk has m rec from 1807, div rec, also pro rec from 1806 & civ ct rec from 1796)

* Kosciusko	A3	1835	59	1840-80	Elkhart, Cass	Warsaw 46580

(Co Health Dept has b, d, bur rec; Co Clk has m rec from 1853, div, pro, civ ct rec from 1850; Co Rcdr has Ind rec)

* Lagrange	A3	1832	25	1840-80	Elkhart, Allen	Lagrange 46761

(Co Health has b & d rec from 1882; Co Clk has m, div, pro & civ ct rec from 1832; Co Rcdr has Ind rec from 1832)

* Lake	A2	1836	520	1840-80	Porter, Newton	Crown Point 46307

(Co Health has b & d rec; Clk Cir Ct has m, div, pro & civ ct rec from 1837; Co Rcdr has Ind rec)

*§ LaPorte	A2	1832	107	1840-80	St. Joseph	LaPorte 46350

(Co Clk has m rec from 1892, div rec from 1837, pro, civ ct rec from 1832; Co Commissioners have Ind rec from 1829)

* Lawrence	C2	1818	43	1820-80	Orange	Bedford 47421

(Co Health has b & d rec; Co Clk has m, div & civ ct rec from 1818, pro rec from 1820; Co Rcdr has Ind rec)

* Madison	B3	1823	139	1830-80	Unorg. Terr., Marion	Anderson 46011

(Co Health Dept has b rec from 1891, d rec from 1895; local cem have bur rec; Co Clk has m rec from 1884, div, pro, civ ct rec from 1880; Co Auditor has Ind rec from 1867; Co Board of Health has school rec 1904-32)

*§ Marion	C2	1822	762	1830-80	Unorg. Terr.	Indianapolis 46206
*§ Marshall	A2	1835	40	1840-80	St. Joseph, Elkhart	Plymouth 46563

(Co Health has b, d & bur rec from 1882; Co Clk has m, div, pro & civ ct rec from 1836; Co Rcdr has Ind rec)

* Martin	C2	1820	11	1820-80	Daviess, Dubois	Shoals 47581

(Co Health has b & d rec; Co Clk has m rec from 1820, div & civ ct rec from 1842; Co Rcdr has Ind rec)

* Miami	B2	1832	40	1840-80	Cass	Peru 46970

(Co Health has b, d & bur rec; Co Clk has m, div, pro & civ ct rec from 1843)

*§ Monroe	C2	1818	98	1820-80	Orange	Bloomington 47401

(Co Health has b, d & bur rec from 1882; Co Clk has m & civ ct rec from 1818, div rec from 1870 & pro from 1831; Co Rcdr has Ind rec)

* Montgomery	B2	1823	35	1830-80	Parke, Putnam	Crawfordsville 47933

(Co Health Dept has b, d rec from 1882; Co Clk has m, div, pro, civ ct rec from 1823, Co Rcdr has Ind rec from 1823; Crawfordsville Pub Lib has cem rec from 1823; Co Clk has partial list of naturalization rec)

*§ Morgan	C2	1822	52	1830-80	Unorg. Terr.	Martinsville 46151
* Newton	A2	1859	15	1860-80	Jasper	Kentland 47951

(Co Health Dept has b, d rec; Town Hall has bur rec; Co Clk has m rec from 1850, div, civ ct rec from 1878, pro rec from 1861, incomplete immigration rec)

* Noble	A3	1835	35	1840-80	Elkhart, Lagrange, Allen	Albion 46701

(Co Health Dept has b, d rec; Co Clk has m, div, pro, civ ct rec from 1859; Co Auditor has Ind rec; City Clk has bur rec)

* Ohio	C3	1844	5	1850-80	Dearborn	Rising Sun 47040

(Co Clk has m rec from 1882, div, pro, civ ct rec from 1844)

Name	Map Index	Date Created	Pop. By M 1980	U.S. Cen Reports Available	Parent County or Territory From Which Organized	County Seat
* Orange	D2	1816	20	1820-80	Washington, Knox, Gibson	Paoli 47454

(Co Health has b rec from 1882, d & bur rec; Co Clk has m, div, pro & civ ct rec from 1816; Co Rcdr has Ind rec from 1816)

| * Owen | C2 | 1819 | 16 | 1820-80 | Daviess, Sullivan | Spencer 47460 |

(Co Health Dept has b, d rec from 1882; Co Clk has m, civ ct rec from 1819, div rec from 1832, pro rec from 1833; Co Rcdr has Ind rec from 1819)

| * Parke | C2 | 1821 | 16 | 1830-80 | Unorg. Terr., Vigo | Rockville 47872 |

(Co Health Dept has b, d rec; Co Clk has m, div, pro, civ ct rec from 1833, early naturalization rec, not indexed, hard to find; Co Rcdr has Ind rec)

| * Perry | D2 | 1814 | 19 | 1820-80 | Warrick, Gibson | Cannelton 47520 |

(Co Health Dept has b, d rec from 1890; Co Clk has m, div, pro, civ ct rec from 1813; Co Rcdr has Ind rec from 1813)

| * Pike | D2 | 1817 | 13 | 1820-80 | Gibson, Perry | Petersburg 47567 |

(Co Health Dept has b, d rec; Co Clk has m, div, pro, civ ct rec from 1817; Co Rcdr has Ind rec)

| * Porter | A2 | 1835 | 119 | 1840-80 | St. Joseph | Valparaiso 46383 |

(Co Health Dept has b, d rec; Co Clk has m, div, pro, civ ct rec from 1836; Co Auditor has Ind rec)

| *§ Posey | D1 | 1814 | 26 | 1820-80 | Warrick, Knox, Gibson | Mount Vernon 47620 |

(Co Health Dept has b, d rec from 1882; Co Clk has m, div, pro, civ ct rec from 1815; Co Rcdr has Ind rec)

| Pulaski | A2 | 1835 | 13 | 1840-80 | Cass, St. Joseph | Winamac 46996 |

(Co Clk has m, div, pro, civ ct rec from 1839; Co Rcdr has b, d rec from 1882, Ind rec)

| * Putnam | C2 | 1822 | 29 | 1820-80 | Unorg. Terr., Vigo, Owen | Greencastle 46135 |

(Co Health Dept has b, d rec; Co Clk has m rec from 1822, div, pro rec from 1825, civ ct rec from 1828; Co Rcdr has Ind rec)

| * Randolph | B3 | 1818 | 30 | 1820-80 | Wayne | Winchester 47394 |

(Co Health has b & d rec; Co Clk has m, div, pro & civ ct rec; Co Rcdr has Ind rec from 1818 & newspapers from 1876)

Richardville (see Howard)

| * Ripley | C3 | 1816 | 24 | 1820-80 | Dearborn, Jefferson | Versailles 47042 |

(Co Health Dept has b, d rec; Co Clk has m, div, pro, civ ct rec from 1818; Co Rcdr has Ind rec)

| * Rush | C3 | 1822 | 20 | 1830-80 | Unorg. Terr. | Rushville 46173 |

(Co Health has b, d & bur rec from 1882; Co Clk has m, div, pro, civ ct rec from 1822; Co Rcdr has Ind rec)

| *§ Saint Joseph | A2 | 1830 | 238 | 1830-80 | Cass | South Bend 46601 |

(Co Health has b, d & bur rec; Co Clk has m, div, pro & civ ct rec; Co Asr has Ind rec)

| * Scott | C3 | 1820 | 20 | 1820-80 | Clark, Jefferson, Jennings | Scottsburg 47170 |

(Co Health Dept has b, d rec; Co Clk has m, div, pro, civ ct rec from 1820; Co Rcdr has Ind rec)

| *§ Shelby | C3 | 1822 | 40 | 1830-80 | Unorg. Terr. | Shelbyville 46176 |

(Co Health has b, d & bur rec; Co Clk has m, div, pro & civ ct rec; Co Aud has Ind rec)

| * Spencer | D2 | 1818 | 19 | 1820-80 | Warrick, Perry | Rockport 47635 |

Co Health Dept has b rec from 1882, d rec from 1830; Cem trustees have bur rec; Co Clk has m rec from 1818, div, civ ct rec from 1833, pro rec from 1848; Co Rcdr has Ind rec)

| * Starke | A2 | 1835 | 22 | 1840-80 | St. Joseph | Knox 46534 |

(Co Clk has m rec from 1850, div, pro, civ ct rec from 1851)

| * Steuben | A3 | 1835 | 24 | 1840-80 | LaGrange | Angola 46703 |

(Co Health Dept has b, d rec; Co Clk has m, div, pro, civ ct rec from 1837, Ind rec from middle 1800's)

| * Sullivan | C2 | 1817 | 21 | 1820-80 | Knox | Sullivan 47882 |

(Co Clk has m, div, pro & civ ct rec from 1850)

| * Swtizerland | C3 | 1814 | 7 | 1820-80 | Dearborn, Jefferson | Vevay 47043 |

(Co Health has b, d & bur rec; Co Clk has m, div & civ ct rec from 1814, pro rec from 1831; Co Rcdr has Ind rec)

| *§ Tippecanoe | B2 | 1826 | 121 | 1830-80 | Unorg. Terr., Parke | Lafayette 47901 |

(Clk Cir Ct has m rec from 1830, d rec, also div rec from 1850, pro & civ ct rec from 1832 & naturalization rec)

| *§ Tipton | B2 | 1844 | 17 | 1850-80 | Hamilton, Cass, Miami | Tipton 46072 |

(Co Clk has m rec from 1844, div, pro & civ ct rec from 1850)

| * Union | C3 | 1821 | 7 | 1830-80 | Wayne, Franklin, Fayette | Liberty 47353 |

(Clk Cir Ct has m, div, pro & civ ct rec from 1821; Co Health has b rec from 1882, d rec from 1907)

Name	Map Index	Date Created	Pop. By M 1980	U.S. Cen Reports Available	Parent County or Territory From Which Organized	County Seat
*§ Vanderburgh	D1	1818	167	1820-80	Gibson, Posey, Warrick	Evansville 47708

(Co Health Dept has b, d, bur rec; Co Clk has m, civ ct rec from 1835, div, pro rec from 1850; Co Assessor has Ind rec)

| * Vermillion | B2 | 1824 | 18 | 1830-80 | Parke | Newport 47966 |

(Co Health Dept has b, d rec from 1882; Co Clk has m, div, pro, civ ct rec from 1824; Co Rcdr has Ind rec)

| * Vigo | C2 | 1818 | 112 | 1820-80 | Sullivan | Terre Haute 47801 |

(Co Clk has m, pro & civ ct rec from 1818, div rec from 1825)

| * Wabash | B3 | 1832 | 37 | 1840-80 | Cass, Grant | Wabash 46992 |

(Co Clk has m rec from 1943, div, pro & civ ct rec from 1850; Health Dept has b, d & bur rec)

| * Warren | B2 | 1827 | 9 | 1830-80 | Fountain | Williamsport 47993 |

(Co Health Dept has b, d rec from 1882; Co Clk m, div, civ ct rec from 1828, pro rec from 1829; Co Rcdr has Ind rec; Co Cem Assn has bur rec)

| *§ Warrick | D2 | 1813 | 40 | 1820-80 | Knox | Boonville 47601 |

(Co Health has b, d & bur rec; Co Clk has m rec from 1819, div & civ ct rec from 1813; Com Pleas Ct has pro rec from 1813; Co Rcdr has Ind rec)

| * Washington | D2 | 1814 | 22 | 1820-80 | Clark, Harrison, Jefferson | Salem 47167 |

(Co Health has b & d rec from 1882; Co Clk has m, div, pro & civ ct rec from 1814, wills from 1813, newspapers from 1891; Co Rcdr has Ind rec; Co Hist Soc has many family rec)

| * Wayne | B3 | 1811 | 76 | 1820-80 | Clark, Dearborn | Richmond 47374 |

(Co Clk has m rec from 1810, div & civ ct rec from 1873, pro rec from 1818; City-Co Health Officer has b, d & bur rec)

| *§ Wells | B3 | 1835 | 25 | 1840-80 | Allen, Delaware, Randolph | Bluffton 46714 |

(Co Health Dept has b, d rec; Co Clk has m, div, civ ct rec from 1837, pro rec from 1838; Co Rcrd has Ind rec)

| * White | B2 | 1834 | 24 | 1840-80 | Carroll | Monticello 47960 |

(Co Clk has m, div, pro & civ ct rec from 1834)

| * Whitley | A3 | 1835 | 26 | 1840-80 | Elkhart, Allen | Columbia City 46725 |

(Co Health Dept has b, d rec from 1882; Co Clk has m rec from 1836, div, civ ct rec from 1853, pro rec; Co Rcdr has Ind rec)

* - At least one county history has been published about this county.

§ - Inventory of county archives was made by the Historical Records Survey. (see introduction)

IOWA

CAPITAL, DES MOINES - TERRITORY 1838 - STATE 1846 - (29TH)

Outside of a few explorers and priests passing by on the Mississippi River and some fur traders trapping along the rivers, no white man came to Iowa until about 1788, when Dubuque became the first permanent settlement.

Before Iowa became a territory in its own name in 1838, it had been part of the Missouri Territory, 1812-1821; unorganized territory, 1824-1834; the Michigan Territory, 1834-1836, and the Wisconsin Territory, 1836-1838.

Five years prior to becoming a territory, Iowa had an influx of white settlers, after a treaty with some of the numerous Indian tribes inhabiting the country made it possible for settlements to be established. The first settlers came from the eastern and the southern states. Most of them were originally from the British Isles.

Among the thousands of immigrants who flocked to Iowa immediately prior to and after it had gained statehood were Scandinavians to the central and the western sections of the state, Hollanders to the south central section, Germans along the Mississippi River, Scottish and Welch to the mining towns of the southern counties, and many Czechs to the east central section.

Iowa City, Johnson County, was the capital of Iowa until 1857 when it was moved about 110 miles west to Des Moines, Polk County.

The Division of Vital Records, Iowa State Department of Health, Lucas State Office Building, Des Moines, Iowa 50319 has no birth, marriage or death records before July 1, 1880. Marriage records before that date may be obtained from the county in which the event occurred. Additional information may be obtained from the Census Division of the Iowa Historical Building, East 12th and Grand Avenue, Des Moines, Iowa 50319.

Statewide indexes (which cover all of Iowa) are by year and begin as follows: births, July 1, 1880; marriages, July 1, 1916; deaths, January, 1891. Example: any death prior to 1891 cannot be searched without the date and place of death. The parentage is not listed on any death record until July, 1904.

Iowa's mandatory registration law was enacted in July, 1921. Prior to 1921, less than 50% of the vital events were registered and the percentage decreases the further back in time the event occurred.

Genealogical Archives, Libraries, Societies, and Publications

Benton County Historical Society, Box 217, Van Horne, IA 52346.

Central Community Historical Society, RR 2, Box 98, DeWitt, IA 52742.

Cherokee County Historical Society, P.O. Box 247, Cleghorn, IA 51014.

Des Moines County Genealogical Society, P.O. Box 493, Burlington, IA 52601.

Ericson Public Library, 702 Greene St., Boone, IA 50036.

Gibson Memorial Library, 310 North Maple, Creston, IA 50801.

Glenwood Public Library, Glenwood, IA 51534.

Gutherie County Genealogical Society, Chapter of the Iowa State Genealogical Society, P.O. Box 96, Jamaica, IA 50128.

Harrison County Genealogical Society, c/o Judy White, Box 158, Modale, IA 51556.

Iowa County Historical Society, c/o Pauline Lillie, Ladora, IA 52251.

Iowa Genealogical Society, P.O. Box 3815, Des Moines, IA 50322.

Iowa Historical and Genealogical Library, Iowa Dept. of History and Archives, East 12th St. and Grand Ave., Des Moines, IA 50319.

Iowa State Dept. of History and Archives Historical Bldg., East 12th and Grand Ave., Des Moines, IA 50319.

Jasper County Genealogical Society, P.O. Box 163, Newton, IA 50208.

Jefferson County Genealogical Society, c/o Verda Baird, Route 1, Fairfield, IA 52556.

Johnson County Historical Society, P.O. Box 5081, Coralville, IA 51141.

Lee County Genealogical Society of Iowa, P.O. Box 303, Keokuk, IA 52632.

LeMars Public Library, 46 First St., S.W., Le-Mars, IA 51031.

Linn County Heritage Society, P.O. Box 175, Cedar Rapids, IA 52406.

Marion County Genealogical Society, 702 East South Street, Knoxville, IA 50138.

Marshalltown Public Library, 36 N. Center St., Marshalltown, IA 50158.

Mills County Genealogical Society, c/o Beverly Boileau, Henderson, IA 51541.

Museum of History and Science, Park Avenue at South St., Waterloo, IA 50701.

North Central Iowa Genealogical Society, P.O. Box 237, Mason City, IA 50401.

Northeast Iowa Genealogical Society, c/o Grout Museum of History and Science, 503 South Street, Waterloo, IA 50701.

Northwest Iowa Genealogical Society, c/o Le-Mars Public Library, 46 First St., S.W., LeMars, IA 51031.

Public Library, S. Market and Second St., Oskaloosa, IA 52577.

Public Library, Sixth & Jackson Sts., Sioux City, IA 51101.

Ringgold County Genealogical Society, 405 W. Monroe, Mount Ayr, IA 50854.

Sac County Genealogical Society, P.O. Box 234, Lytton, IA 50561.

Scott County Iowa Genealogical Society, P.O. Box 3132, Davenport, IA 52808.

State Historical Society of Iowa Library, University of Iowa, Box 871, Iowa City, IA 52240.

Taylor County Genealogical Society, R. 3, Bedford, IA 50833.

Urbandale Public Library, 7305 Aurora Ave., Urbandale, IA 50322.

Wayne County Genealogical Society, 304 North Franklin, Corydon, IA 50060.

Webster County Genealogical Society, P.O. Box 1584, Fort Dodge, IA 50501.

Wright County Genealogical Searchers, P.O. Box 225, Clarion, IA 50525.

Hawkeye Heritage, Iowa Genealogical Society, P.O. Box 3815, Des Moines, IA 50322.

Cedar Tree, The, publication of the Northeast Iowa Genealogical Society, c/o Grout Museum of History and Science, 503 South Street, Waterloo, IA 50701.

Northwest Iowa Root Diggers, publication of the Northwest Iowa Genealogical Society, LeMars Public Library, 46 First Street, S.W., LeMars, IA 51031.

Ringgold Roots, published quarterly by the Ringgold County Genealogical Society, 405 W. Monroe, Mount Ayr, IA 50854.

Printed Census Records and Mortality Schedules

Indexes (Territory) 1836, 1838, 1841-1849, 1840

State Census Index - 1840, 1850

Printed Census Records (Counties):

Allamakee - 1850	Fremont - 1870	Muscatine - 1850; 1851
Appanoose - 1850	Henry - 1840; 1854	Page - 1850
Benton - 1850; 1849, 1861	Iowa - 1850	Polk - 1850; 1846
Black Hawk - 1850	Jackson - 1840; 1849	Pottawattamie - 1850
Boone - 1850; 1849	Jasper - 1850	Poweshiek - 1850; 1849
Buchanan - 1850	Jefferson - 1840, 1850	Scott - 1850; 1847, 1849
Cedar - 1860; 1851	Jones - 1850	Tama - 1850
Clarke - 1850	Keokuk - 1844	Taylor - 1850, 1860, 1870, 1880; 1854, 1856
Clinton - 1850; 1847, 1849	Kossuth - 1856	Union - 1860
Dallas - 1850, 1870, 1880; 1854, 1856	Linn - 1850	Van Buren - 1838, 1847, 1849
Davis - 1847	Louisa - 1850; 1846, 1847, 1849	Wapello - 1846, 1847
Decatur - 1850	Lucas - 1850	Warren - 1849, 1853
Delaware - 1840, 1850	Madison - 1849	Washington - 1849
Des Moines - 1836	Marion - 1847	Wayne - 1850
Dubuque - 1850; 1836	Marshall - 1850	Winneshiek - 1850
Fayette - 1850		

Mortality Schedules:

State index - 1850

Counties: Lucas - 1850
              Pottawattamie - 1850

Valuable Printed Sources

Atlases and Gazetteers

Hair, James T. *Iowa State Gazetteer.* Chicago: Bailey and Hair (1865)

Illustrated Historical Atlas of the State of Iowa. Chicago: Lakeside Press (1875) Andreas Atlas Company.

Place Names

Iowa Postal History Society, comp. *Alphabetical Listings of Iowa Postoffices 1833-1970.* n.d.

Mott, David C. *Abandoned Towns, Villages and Postoffices of Iowa* Reprint from the Annals of Iowa Vols. XVII and XVIII 1930-1932. Council Bluffs, Iowa (1973)

Guides to Genealogical Research

Cheever, L. O. *Newspaper Collection of the State Historical Society of Iowa.* Iowa City: State Historical Society (1969)

Cox, E. Evelyn. *Ancestree Climbing in the Midwest.* Published privately.

Morford, Charles. *Biographical Index to the County Histories of Iowa.* Baltimore: Gateway Press, Inc. (1979)

Histories

Petersen, William J. *Iowa History Reference Guide.* Iowa City, State Historical Society of Iowa (1952)

Genealogical Sources

Daughters of the American Revolution collection contains cemetery records, church records, family records and early vital records.*

Iowa Department of History and Archives collection includes historical and genealogical materials.

State Historical Society of Iowa collection includes newspapers published in Iowa from the early 1840's.

Bibliographies

A *Bibliography of Iowa Newspapers, 1836-1976.* Iowa City: State Historical Society of Iowa (1979)

_____

*On microfilm at the Genealogical Society Library of The Church of Jesus Christ of Latter-day Saints, Salt Lake City, Utah.

IOWA COUNTY HISTORIES
(Population figures to nearest thousand - 1980 U. S. Census)

Name	Map Index	Date Created	Pop. By M 1980	U.S. Cen Reports Available	Parent County or Territory From Which Organized	County Seat
* Adair	C2	1851	10	1860-80	Cass	Greenfield 50849

(Clk Dis Ct has b rec from 1880, m, div & civ ct rec from 1852)

* Adams	C2	1851	6	1860-80	Taylor	Corning 50841

(Clk Dis Ct has b & d rec from 1880, m rec from 1853, div rec 1910, pro & civ ct rec from 1860; Co Rcdr has Ind rec)

* Allamakee	A4	1847	15	1850-80	Clayton	Waukon 52172

(Co Clk has b rec from 1880 except 1905-09, 1935-1941, m, pro rec from 1850, d, div rec from 1880, civ ct rec; Co Auditor has old newspapers from 1899)

* Appanoose	C3	1843	16	1850-80	Davis	Centerville 52544

(Clk Dis Ct has b, d rec from 1880 to 1935 and from 1941 to present, m, rp rec from 1846, div, civ ct rec from 1848; Co Rcdr has Ind rec)

* Audubon	B2	1851	9	1860-80	Cass, Black Hawk	Audubon 50025

(Clk Dis Ct has b, d & bur rec from 1880, m rec from 1856, div from 1867 & civ ct rec)

* Benton	B3	1837	24	1850-80	Indian Land Purchase	Vinton 52349

(Clk Dis Ct has b, d, bur rec from 1880, m rec from 1852, div rec from 1900, pro rec from 1874, civ ct rec)

* Black Hawk	B3	1843	138	1850-80	Delaware	Waterloo 50703

(Clk Dis Ct has m rec from 1854, div & pro rec from 1880, b & d rec from 1880 to 1935)

* Boone	B2	1846	26	1850-80	Polk	Boone 50036

(Clk Dis Ct has b & d rec from 1880, m & pro rec from 1850, div rec from 1900, civ ct rec from 1851; Co Rcdr has Ind rec)

* Bremer	A3	1851	25	1860-80	Winnebago, Indian Reserve	Waverly 50677
* Buchanan	B3	1837	23	1850-80	Delaware	Independence 50644

(Clk Dis Ct has b, d rec from 1880, m rec from 1848, div, pro, civ ct rec from 1845)

Buncombe (changed to Lyon, 1862)

* Buena Vista	A1	1851	21	1860-80	Sac, Clay	Storm Lake 50588

(Clk Dis Ct has b, m, d, bur, div, pro & civ ct rec from 1880)

* Butler	A3	1851	18	1860-80	Buchanan, Black Hawk	Allison 50602

(Clk Dis Ct has b, d, div, pro, civ ct rec from 1880, m rec from 1854, old cir ct rec from 1870)

* Calhoun	B2	1855	14	1860-80	Formerly Fox County	Rockwell City 50579

(Clk Dis Ct has b, d, pro rec from 1880; m rec from 1863; bur rec from 1900; div rec from 1906 & civ ct rec from 1872)

*§ Carroll	B2	1851	23	1860-80	Guthrie	Carroll 51401

(Clk Dis Ct has b & d rec from 1880, m rec from 1854 & div, pro & civ ct rec; Co Rcdr has Ind rec)

* Cass	C1	1851	17	1860-80	Pottawattamie	Atlantic 50022

(Clk Dis Ct has b & d rec from 1880, m rec from 1877, div rec from 1906, pro rec from 1870, dis ct rec from 1865)

* Cedar	B4	1837	19	1840-80	Wisconsin Territory	Tipton 52772

(Clk Dis Ct has b, d, bur rec from 1880, m, pro, civ ct rec from 1839, div rec from 1850; Co Rcdr has Ind rec)

* Cerro Gordo	A3	1851	48	1860-80	Floyd	Mason City 50401
*§ Cherokee	A1	1851	16	1860-80	Crawford	Cherokee 51012
* Chickasaw	A3	1851	15	1860-80	Fayette	New Hampton 50659

(Clk Dis Ct has b, d, div & civ ct rec from 1880, m rec from 1853, pro rec from 1856; Co Rcdr has Ind rec)

* Clarke	C2	1846	9	1850-80	Lucas	Osceola 50213

(Clk Dis Ct has b & d rec from 1880, m rec from 1850, pro rec from 1865, div rec from 1905 & civ ct rec; Co Rcdr has Ind rec)

COUNTY MAP FOR THE STATE OF IOWA

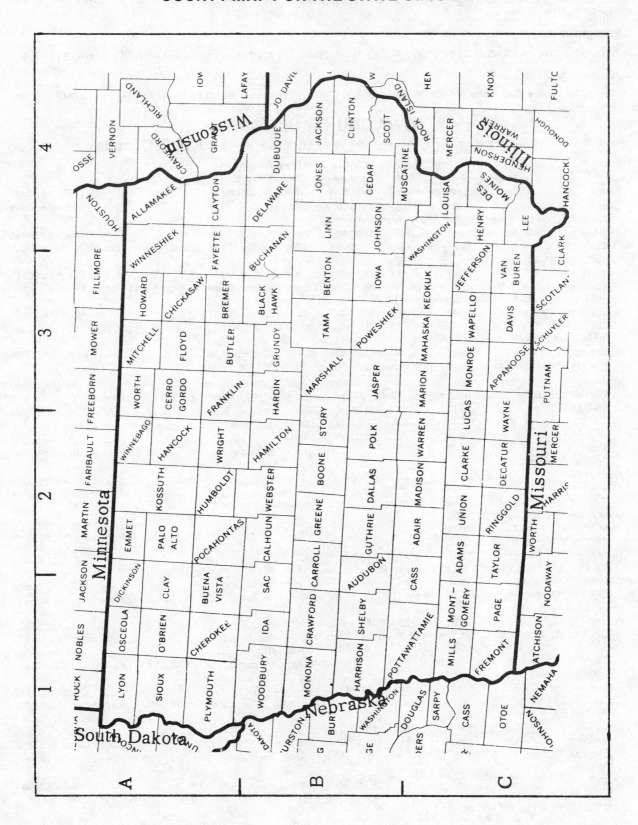

Name	Map Index	Date Created	Pop. By M 1980	U.S. Cen Reports Available	Parent County or Territory From Which Organized	County Seat
* Clay	A1	1851	19	1850-80	Indian Lands	Spencer 51301

(Clk Dis Ct has b & d rec from 1880, m rec from 1864, div rec from 1906, pro rec from 1871 & civ ct rec from 1869; Co Aud has Ind rec)

* Clayton	A4	1837	21	1840-80	Dubuque	Elkader 52043

(Clk Dis Ct has b rec from 1880, m rec from 1848, d rec from 1880 to 1921 and from 1941 to present, div rec from 1880, pro, civ ct rec from 1840, Naturalization rec from 1858; Co Rcdr has Ind rec from 1839)

* Clinton	B4	1837	57	1840-80	Dubuque	Clinton 52732
* Crawford	B1	1851	19	1860-80	Shelby	Denison 51442

(Clk Dis Ct has b & d rec from 1880, m rec from 1855, div rec from 1906, pro rec from 1869, civ ct rec from 1866 & Ind rec from 1859)

*§ Dallas	B2	1846	30	1850-80	Polk	Adel 50003

(Clk Dis Ct has b & d rec from 1880, m rec from 1850, div rec from 1881, pro rec from 1863 & civ ct rec from 1860; Co Rcdr has Ind rec)

* Davis	C3	1843	9	1850-80	Van Buren	Bloomfield 52537

(Clk Dis Ct has b & d rec from 1880, m rec from 1844, div, pro & civ ct rec from 1830)

* Decatur	C2	1846	10	1850-80	Appanoose	Leon 50144

(Courthouse burned in 1874; Co Clk has b, d, div, pro, civ ct rec from 1880; m rec from 1874; Co Rcdr has Ind rec)

* Delaware	B4	1837	19	1840-80	Dubuque	Manchester 52057

(Clk Dis Ct has b, d rec from 1880, m, div, civ ct rec from 1851, pro rec from 1849; Co Rcdr has Ind rec)

* Des Moines	C4	1834	45	1840-80	Wisconsin Territory	Burlington 52601

(Clk Dis Ct has b rec from 1880, m, div, pro, civ ct rec from 1835, d rec from 1880 to 1921 and then from 1941, naturalization rec from 1840)

* Dickinson	A1	1851	16	1860-80	Kossuth	Spirit Lake 51360

(Clk Dis Ct has b, m, d, bur, div, pro, civ ct rec from 1880; Co Rcdr has Ind rec)

*§ Dubuque	B4	1834	94	1840-80	Michigan Territory	Dubuque 52001

(Clk Dis Ct has b & d rec from 1880, m rec from 1840, div from 1900, pro from 1835 & civ ct rec from 1836; Co Rcdr has Ind rec from 1836)

* Emmet	A2	1851	13	1860-80	Kossuth, Dickinson	Estherville 51334

(Clk Dis Ct has b rec from 1883, m & d rec from 1890, div from 1915, pro rec from 1885)

* Fayette	A3	1837	25	1850-80	Clayton	West Union 52175

(Clk Dis Ct has b & d rec from 1880, m rec from 1851, div from 1897, pro from 1869, civ ct from 1852 & Ind rec from 1855)

* Floyd	A3	1851	20	1860-80	Chickasaw	Charles City 50616

(Clk Dis Ct has b & d rec from 1880, m & div rec from 1860, pro & civ ct rec from 1854)

Fox (see Calhoun)

* Franklin	A3	1851	13	1860-80	Chickasaw	Hampton 50441

(Clk Cir Ct has b, d rec from 1880, m rec from 1855, pro rec from 1864, div, civ ct rec from 1869; Co Rcdr has Ind rec)

* Fremont	C1	1847	9	1850-80	Pottawattamie	Sidney 51652

(Clk Dis Ct has b, d rec from 1880, except 1935-41, limited m rec from 1848, div, pro, civ ct rec; Co Rcdr has Ind rec)

* Greene	B2	1851	12	1860-80	Dallas	Jefferson 50129

(Clk Dis Ct has b, d, div & civ ct rec from 1880, m & pro rec from 1854; Co Rcdr has Ind rec)

* Grundy	B3	1851	14	1860-80	Black Hawk	Grundy Center 50638

(Clk Dis Ct has b, div, civ ct rec from 1880, m rec from 1856, d rec from 1881, pro rec from 1870; Co Rcdr has Ind rec)

* Guthrie	B2	1851	12	1860-80	Jackson	Guthrie Center 50115

(Clk Dis Ct has b, d rec from 1880, m rec from 1852, div rec from 1883, pro rec from 1881, civ ct rec from 1916)

* Hamilton	B2	1856	18	1860-80	Webster	Webster City 50595

(Clk Dis Ct has b, m, d, div, pro, civ ct rec from 1880)

* Hancock	A2	1851	14	1860-80	Wright	Garner 50438

(Clk Dis Ct has b, m, d, bur, div rec from 1880, pro, civ ct rec from 1856)

* Hardin	B3	1851	22	1860-80	Black Hawk	Eldora 50627

(Clk Dis Ct has b, d rec from 1880, m rec from 1864, div rec from 1889, Pro, civ ct, Ind rec from 1853)

* Harrison	B1	1851	16	1860-80	Pottawattamie	Logan 51546

(Clk Dis Ct has b & d rec from 1880, m & div rec from 1853, pro rec from 1869, civ ct rec from 1850)

	Map Index	Date Created	Pop. By M 1980	U.S. Cen Reports Available	Parent County or Territory From Which Organized	County Seat
Name						
* Henry	C4	1836	19	1840-80	Wisconsin Territory................	Mount Pleasant 52641

(Clk Dis Ct has b, d, bur rec from 1880, m, div, pro, civ ct from 1836, naturalization rec from 1841, adoption rec from 1836; Co Rcdr has Ind rec from 1836)

| * Howard | A3 | 1851 | 11 | 1860-80 | Chickasaw, Floyd.......................... | Cresco 52136 |

(Clk Dis Ct has b, m, d, div, pro & civ ct rec from 1880)

| * Humboldt | A2 | 1851 | 12 | 1860-80 | Webster............................... | Dakota City 50529 |

(Clk Dis Ct has b rec from 1880, m rec from 1858, d rec from 1895, div rec from 1890, pro rec from 1873 & civ ct rec from 1892)

| *§ Ida | B1 | 1851 | 9 | 1860-80 | Cherokee................................ | Ida Grove 51445 |

(Clk Dis Ct has b, m, d, div, pro, civ ct rec from 1880)

| * Iowa | B3 | 1843 | 15 | 1850-80 | Washington............................ | Marengo 52301 |

(Clk Dis Ct has b, m & d rec from 1860, div, pro & civ ct rec)

| * Jackson | B4 | 1837 | 22 | 1840-80 | Wisconsin Territory.................... | Maquoketa 52060 |

(Clk Dis Ct has b & d rec from 1880, m rec from 1850, div rec from 1906, pro rec from 1869 & civ ct rec from 1858)

| *§ Jasper | B3 | 1846 | 36 | 1850-80 | Mahaska................................ | Newton 50208 |

(Clk Dis Ct has b, d rec from 1880, m rec from 1849, pro rec from 1882, civ ct rec from 1857, div rec)

| * Jefferson | C3 | 1839 | 16 | 1840-80 | Indian Land Purchase..................... | Fairfield 52556 |

(Clk Dis Ct has b, d, div & civ ct rec 1880, m rec 1839 & pro rec 1850)

| * Johnson | B4 | 1837 | 82 | 1840-80 | Des Moines............................ | Iowa City 52240 |

(Clk Dis Ct has b & d rec from 1880, m rec from 1839, pro rec from 1840, div & civ ct rec; Co Aud has Ind rec)

| * Jones | B4 | 1837 | 20 | 1840-80 | Wisconsin Territory...................... | Anamosa 52205 |

(Clk Dis Ct has b & d rec from 1880, m rec from 1840, div rec from 1895, also pro & civ ct rec; Co Rcdr has Ind rec)

| * Keokuk | C3 | 1837 | 13 | 1850-80 | Washington............................ | Sigourney 52591 |

(Clk Dis Ct has b, d rec from 1880, m, div, pro, civ ct rec from 1845; Co Rcdr has Ind rec)

Kishkekosh (changed to Monroe, 1846)

| * Kossuth | A2 | 1851 | 22 | 1860-80 | Webster................................ | Algona 50511 |

(Clk Dis Ct has b rec from 1880 to 1935 and from 1941 to present, m rec from 1857, d bur rec from 1880, pro rec from 1877, div, civ ct rec)

| * Lee | C4 | 1836 | 43 | 1840-80 | Des Moines........... | Ft. Madison 52627 & Keokuk 52632 |

(Clk Dis Ct, Keokuk, has b rec from 1880; Clk Dis Ct, Ft. Madison, has b, d rec 1880 to 1921, 1941 to present, pro rec from 1838; Clk Dis Ct, Keokuk, has m, pro rec from 1873, d rec from 1867, div rec from 1906, civ ct rec from 1898; Co Rcdr has Ind rec)

| * Linn | B4 | 1837 | 170 | 1840-80 | Wisconsin Territory.................. | Cedar Rapids 52401 |

(Clk Dis Ct has b rec 1880-1934, 1941 to present; d rec 1880-1919, 1941 to present, m rec from 1840, div, pro, civ ct rec from 1860)

| * Louisa | C4 | 1836 | 12 | 1840-80 | Des Moines............................ | Wapello 52653 |

(Clk Dis Ct has b, d rec from 1880, m rec from 1842, div, pro, civ ct rec)

| * Lucas | C2 | 1846 | 10 | 1850-80 | Monroe.................................. | Chariton 50049 |

(Clk Dis Ct has b & d rec from 1880, m rec from 1849, div rec from 1900, pro rec from 1850 & civ ct rec from 1900)

| * Lyon | A1 | 1851 | 13 | 1870-80 | Woodbury............................ | Rock Rapids 51246 |

(Clk Dis Ct has b, m, d, div, pro, civ ct, Ind rec from 1880)

| * Madison | C2 | 1846 | 13 | 1850-80 | Polk.................................... | Winterset 50273 |

(Clk Dis Ct has b, d rec from 1880, m rec from 1855, bur rec from 1849, div, civ ct rec from 1861, pro rec from 1852; Co Rcdr has Ind rec)

| * Mahaska | C3 | 1843 | 23 | 1850-80 | Fox, Sac Indian Purchase............... | Oskaloosa 52577 |

(Clk Dis Ct has b & d rec from 1880, m, div, pro & civ ct rec from 1844)

| * Marion | C3 | 1845 | 29 | 1850-80 | Washington............................ | Knoxville 50138 |

(Clk Dis Ct has b, d rec from 1880, m rec from 1846, div, pro rec from 1845)

| * Marshall | B3 | 1846 | 42 | 1850-80 | Jasper............................ | Marshalltown 50158 |

(Clk Dis Ct has b & d rec from 1880, m, pro, civ ct rec from 1850, div rec from 1906 & crim rec)

| * Mills | C1 | 1851 | 13 | 1860-80 | Pottawattamie.......................... | Glenwood 51534 |

(Clk Dis Ct has incom b rec 1880, d & div rec 1880, pro & civ ct rec 1851)

| * Mitchell | A3 | 1851 | 12 | 1860-80 | Chickasaw................................ | Osage 50461 |

(Clk Dis Ct has m rec from 1860, b, d, div, pro & civ ct rec from 1880; Co Rcdr has Ind rec)

Name	Map Index	Date Created	Pop. By M 1980	U.S. Cen Reports Available	Parent County or Territory From Which Organized	County Seat
* Monona	B1	1851	12	1860-80	Harrison	Onawa 51040

(Clk Dis Ct has b rec from 1880, m rec from 1857, d rec from 1880, bur rec from 1950, div rec from 1856, pro rec from 1858 & civ ct rec from 1856)

| * Monroe | C3 | 1843 | 9 | 1850-80 | Wapello (formerly Kishkekosh) | Albia 52531 |

(Clk Dis Ct has b & d rec from 1880, m, div, pro & civ ct rec from 1845; Co Rcdr has Ind rec)

| *§ Montgomery | C1 | 1851 | 13 | 1860-80 | Polk | Red Oak 51566 |

(Clk Dis Ct has b & d rec from 1880, m rec from 1856, div rec from 1873, pro rec from 1860 & civ ct rec from 1873; Co Rcdr has Ind rec)

| * Muscatine | A4 | 1836 | 40 | 1840-80 | Des Moines | Muscatine 52761 |

(Clk Dis Ct has b & d rec from 1880, m rec from 1837, div & civ ct rec from 1861 & pro rec from 1866)

| * O'Brien | A1 | 1851 | 17 | 1860-80 | Cherokee | Primghar 51245 |

(Clk Dis Ct has b, m, div, pro & civ ct rec from 1880, some d & bur rec)

| * Osceola | A1 | 1851 | 8 | 1870-80 | Woodbury | Sibley 51249 |

(Clk Dis Ct has b, m, d, div, pro, civ ct rec from 1880)

| * Page | C1 | 1847 | 19 | 1850-80 | Pottawattamie | Clarinda 51632 |
| * Palo Alto | A2 | 1858 | 13 | 1860-80 | Kossuth | Emmetsburg 50536 |

(Clk Dis Ct has b rec from 1880 to 1904, m rec from 1880, some d rec from 1880, div pro & civ ct rec)

| * Plymouth | A1 | 1851 | 25 | 1860-80 | Woodbury | Le Mars 51031 |

(Clk Dis Ct has b, d, div & pro rec from 1880, m rec from 1869, civ ct rec from 1869; Co Rcdr has Ind rec)

| * Pocahontas | A2 | 1851 | 11 | 1860-80 | Humboldt, Greene | Pocahontas 50574 |

(Clk Dis Ct has b & d rec from 1880, m rec from 1881, div & civ ct rec from 1860, pro rec from 1872; Co Rcdr has Ind rec)

| *§ Polk | B2 | 1846 | 303 | 1850-80 | Indian Lands | Des Moines 50309 |

(Clk Ct has b & d rec from 1941, m rec from 1870, div rec from 1870, pro rec from 1855 & civ ct rec from 1850)

| * Pottawattamie | C1 | 1848 | 86 | 1850-80 | Indian Lands | Council Bluffs 51501 |

(Clk Ct has b rec from 1880 to 1921 & 1941 to present, b rec between 1921 & 1941 are in Des Moines; m rec from 1846, d rec from 1941, div rec from 1907 & pro rec from 1898)

| * Poweshiek | B3 | 1843 | 19 | 1850-80 | Mesquakie Indian Lands | Montezuma 50171 |

(Clk Dis Ct has b, d, div & civ ct rec from 1880, m pro rec from 1860)

| * Ringgold | C2 | 1847 | 6 | 1860-80 | Taylor | Mount Ayr 50854 |

(Clk Dis Ct has b, m, d, div, pro, civ ct rec from 1880)

| * Risley | | 1851 | | | Changed to Webster 1853 | |
| * §Sac | B1 | 1851 | 14 | 1680-80 | Greene | Sac City 50583 |

(Clk Dis Ct has b, m, d, bur, div, pro, civ ct rec from 1888; Co Rcdr has Ind rec from 1856; Courthouse burned 1888, some charred rec recovered)

| * Scott | B4 | 1837 | 160 | 1840-80 | Wisconsin Territory | Davenport 52801 |

(Clk Dis Ct has b, d & bur rec from 1880, m rec from 1837, div & pro rec from 1838 & civ ct rec from 1851)

| * Shelby | B1 | 1853 | 15 | 1860-80 | Cass | Harlan 51537 |

(Clk Ct has b, m, d, div, pro & civ ct rec from 1880, pro rec are limited from 1853, newspapers are available at Public Library)

| * Sioux | A1 | 1851 | 31 | 1860-80 | Plymouth | Orange City 51041 |

(Clk Dis Ct has b, d rec from 1880, m, pro, civ ct rec from 1870, div rec from 1908)

Slaughter (changed to Washington, 1839)

| * Story | B2 | 1846 | 72 | 1860-80 | Jasper, Polk, Boone | Nevada 50201 |

(Clk Dis Ct has b & d rec from 1880, m, div, pro, civ ct crim rec from 1854)

| * Tama | B3 | 1843 | 20 | 1850-80 | Boone, Benton | Toledo 52342 |

(Clk Dis Ct has b & d rec from 1880, m rec from 1853, div rec from 1908, pro rec from 1895 & civ ct rec from 1859)

| *§ Taylor | C2 | 1847 | 8 | 1850-80 | Page | Bedford 50833 |

(Clk Dis Ct has b, d & bur rec from 1880, m rec from 1854, div rec from 1858, pro rec from 1863, civ ct rec from 1858; Co Rcdr has Ind rec)

| * Union | C2 | 1851 | 14 | 1860-80 | Clarke | Creston 50801 |

(Clk Dis Ct has b, d, div, pro & civ ct rec from 1880, m rec from 1856; Co Asr has Ind rec)

| * Van Buren | C3 | 1836 | 9 | 1840-80 | Des Moines | Keosauqua 52565 |

(Clk Dis Ct has b & d rec from 1880, m, div, pro & civ ct rec from 1837)

Wahkaw (changed to Woodbury, 1853)

Name	Map Index	Date Created	Pop. By M 1980	U.S. Cen Reports Available	Parent County or Territory Which Organized	County Seat
* Wapello	C3	1843	40	1850-80	Indian Lands	Ottumwa 52501
* Warren	C2	1846	35	1850-80	Polk	Indianola 50125

(Clk Dis Ct has b, d, bur rec from 1880, m rec from 1850, div, pro & civ ct rec)

Name	Map Index	Date Created	Pop. By M 1980	U.S. Cen Reports Available	Parent County or Territory Which Organized	County Seat
* Washington	C4	1837	20	1840-80	Wisconsin Territory (formerly Slaughter)	Washington 52353

(Clk Dis Ct has b & d rec from 1880, m rec from 1844, div, pro & civ ct rec from 1836)

Name	Map Index	Date Created	Pop. By M 1980	U.S. Cen Reports Available	Parent County or Territory Which Organized	County Seat
* Wayne	C2	1846	8	1850-80	Appanoose	Corydon 50060

(Clk Dis Ct has b & d rec from 1880, m rec from 1851, div rec from 1906, pro rec from 1891, civ ct rec from 1875 & cir ct rec from 1860)

Name	Map Index	Date Created	Pop. By M 1980	U.S. Cen Reports Available	Parent County or Territory Which Organized	County Seat
* Webster	B2	1851	46	1860-80	*Yell, *Risley	Fort Dodge 50501

*Now known as Hamilton

(Clk Dis Ct has b rec from 1876, m rec from 1853, d rec from 1860, div rec from 1870, pro rec from 1855 & civ ct rec 1860; Co Aud has Ind rec)

Name	Map Index	Date Created	Pop. By M 1980	U.S. Cen Reports Available	Parent County or Territory Which Organized	County Seat
* Winnebago	A2	1857	13	1860-80	Kossuth	Forest City 50436

(Clk Ct has b & d rec from 1880, m, div, pro & civ ct rec from 1865; Co Regstr has bur rec)

Name	Map Index	Date Created	Pop. By M 1980	U.S. Cen Reports Available	Parent County or Territory Which Organized	County Seat
* Winneshiek	A3	1847	22	1850-80	Indian Lands	Decorah 52101

(Clk Dis Ct has b & d rec from 1880, m rec from 1851, div rec from 1855, pro rec from 1853 & civ ct rec from 1855)

Name	Map Index	Date Created	Pop. By M 1980	U.S. Cen Reports Available	Parent County or Territory Which Organized	County Seat
*§ Woodbury	B1	1851	101	1860-80	Indian Lands (formerly Wahkaw)	Sioux City 51101

(Clk Dis Ct has b, d rec from 1880, some m rec from 1854, m rec from 1880, div rec from 1857, pro rec from 1868, civ ct rec from 1850, adoption rec from 1920, mental rec from 1871)

Name	Map Index	Date Created	Pop. By M 1980	U.S. Cen Reports Available	Parent County or Territory Which Organized	County Seat
* Worth	A3	1851	9	1860-80	Mitchell	Northwood 50459

(Clk Dis Ct has b rec from 1880 incom, m rec from 1858, d rec from 1880 to 1919, div rec from 1879, pro & civ ct rec from 1857)

Name	Map Index	Date Created	Pop. By M 1980	U.S. Cen Reports Available	Parent County or Territory Which Organized	County Seat
* Wright	A2	1851	16	1860-80	Webster	Clarion 50525

* - At least one county history has been published about this county.

§ - Inventory of county archives was made by the Historical Records Survey. (see introduction)

KANSAS

CAPITAL, TOPEKA - TERRITORY 1854 - STATE 1861 - (34TH)

Kansas was part of the Louisiana Purchase when it became annexed to the United States in 1803. It was included in the Missouri Territory until 1821. For 33 years it was known as an unorganized territory, inhabited mainly by Indians. For many years there was constant trouble between the Indians and the settlers, until the Indians were gradually pushed into the Oklahoma area.

Fort Leavenworth became the first community in the area in 1827. To thousands enroute to the valleys of Utah, the gold fields of California or the beckoning Oregon country, it was a welcome stopover, outfitting place.

Kansas became a state in 1861, the thirty-fourth. The population then was about 110,000 consisting mostly of Southerners and New Englanders with a sprinkling from Missouri, Illinois, Indiana, Ohio and Kentucky. Many Civil War veterans took up homesteads in Kansas following the war. Among the foreign-born settlers many came from Germany, Russia, Sweden, and England. Many Mexicans also settled in the state.

Birth and death records since July 1, 1911, marriages since May 1, 1913, and divorces since July 1, 1951 are obtainable at the Kansas Department of Health and Environment, Bureau of Vital Statistics, Topeka, Kansas 66620. Records are indexed alphabetically by the year.

The Probate Judge of each county has records of marriages in his county before 1913.

Records of divorces granted before 1951 are on file in the office of the clerk of the District Court handling the matter. Divorces granted after July 1951 are filed in the office of the above mentioned Bureau of Vital Statistics.

The Naturalization files are kept in the Topeka office of the United States Circuit Court and the district court in each of the counties in the state.

Probate matter and wills are handled by the Probate Judges who also have Civil Court records in most counties.

Real estate property is listed with the county recorder and county assessor in the county where land is located.

Among available autobiographies or biographies of important Kansans are the following: Earl Browder, Walter P. Chrysler, John Steuart Curry, Charles Curtis, Amelia Earhart, Dwight D. Eisenhower, Dorothy Canfield Fisher, Frederick Funston, John James Ingalls, Hugh S. Johnson, Martin (Elmer) Johnson and Osa Helen Leighty Johnson, Edgar Lee Masters, Carry Amelia Moore Nation, Fred Andrew Stone, and William Allen White.

Genealogical Archives, Libraries, Societies, and Publications

Arkansas City Public Library, 213 W. 5th Ave., Arkansas City, KS 67705.

Bethel Historical Library, Bethel College, No., Newton, KS 67114.

Chanute Genealogy Society, 1000 South Allen Street, Chanute, KS 66720.

Cowley County Genealogical Society, P.O. Box 102, Arkansas City, KS 67005.

Crawford County Genealogical Society, c/o Pittsburg Public Library, 211 West 4th St., Pittsburg, KS 66762.

Douglas County Genealogical Society, P.O. Box 3664, Lawrence, KS 66044.

East Central Kansas Genealogical Society, P.O. Box 78, Iola, KS 66749.

Finney County Genealogical Society, P.O. Box 592, Garden City, KS 67846.

Flint Hills Genealogical Society, c/o Emporia Public Library, 118 East 6th, Emporia, KS 66801.

Fort Hayes Kansas Genealogical Society, Hays, KS 67601, c/o Fort Hays Kansas College Library.

Grant County Library, 215 E. Grant St., Ulysses, KS 67880.

Garden City Public Library, 210 N. 7th, Garden City, KS 67846.

Heritage Genealogical Society, The, W. A. Rankin Memorial Library, Neodesha, KS 66757.

Jefferson County Genealogical Society, Box 174, Oskaloosa, KS 66066.

Johnson County Genealogical Society, Inc., P.O. Box 8057, Shawnee Mission, KS 66208.

Johnson County Library, 8700 West 63rd St., Shawnee Mission, KS 66202.

Kansas Genealogical Society, P.O. Box 103, Dodge, City, KS 67801.

Kansas State Historical Society Library, 120 W. 10th, Topeka, KS 66612.

Kansas State Historical Society, Memorial Bldg., Topeka, KS 66603.

Leavenworth County Genealogical Society, Inc., P.O. Box 362, Leavenworth, KS 66048.

Linn County Historical Society, Box 137, Pleasanton, KS 66075.

Midwest Historical and Genealogical Society, Inc., Box #1121, Wichita, KS 67201.

Montgomery County Genealogical Society, Box 444, Coffeyville, KS 67337.

North Central Kansas Genealogical Society, Box 251, Cawker City, KS 67430.

Osborne County Genealogical and Historical Society, c/o Osborne Public Library, Osborne, KS 67473.

Phillips County, Kansas Genealogical Society, Box 114, Phillipsburg, KS 67661.

Public Library, Independence, KS 67301.

Public Library, Sixth and Minnesota Sts., Kansas City, KS 66101.

Reno County Genealogical Society, P.O. Box 5, Hutchinson, KS 67501.

Riley County Genealogical Society, 2005 Claflin Road, Manhattan, KS 66502.

Sherman County Historical and Genealogical Society, P.O. Box 684, Goodland, KS 67735.

Smoky Valley Genealogical Society and Library, Inc., 615 South 11th, Salina, KS 67401.

Thomas County Genealogical Society, c/o Historical Society, Colby, KS 67701.

Topeka Genealogical Society, The, P.O. Box 4048, Topeka, KS 66604.

Topeka Public Library, 1515 West 10th, Topeka, KS 66604.

Wheatland Genealogical Society, 1616 N. Irving, Independence, KS 67301.

Wichita City Library, 220 So. Main St., Wichita, KS 67202.

Heritage Genealogical Society Quarterly, The, W. A. Rankin Memorial Library, Neodesha, KS 66756.

Kansas Kin, publication of the Riley County Genealogical Society, 2005 Claflin Road, Manhattan, KS 66502.

Kansas Review, published by the Kansas Council of Genealogical Societies, 2827 Ashland St., St. Joseph, MO 64506.

Topeka Genealogical Society Quarterly, P.O. Box 4048, Topeka, KS 66604.

Treesearcher, The, Kansas Genealogical Society, P.O. Box 103, Dodge City, KS 67801.

Printed Census Records and Mortality Schedules

Indexes (Territory): 1855, 1860, 1865

State Index-1860, 1880; 1895

Printed Census Records (Counties):

Bourbon - 1865	Marshall - 1860	Osage - 1860, 1880
Godfrey - 1860	McGhee - 1860	Saline - 1870; 1865, 1875
Linn - 1860	Morris - 1860	Shawnee - 1860
Lykins - 1860	Nemaha - 1860	Wilson - 1860, 1880
Madison - 1860		

Mortality Schedules:

State indexes - 1860, 1870, 1880

Valuable Printed Sources

Atlas

Socolofsky, Homer E. and Huber Self. *Historical Atlas of Kansas.* Norman, Oklahoma: University of Oklahoma Press, 1972.

Maps

Baughman, Robert W. *Kansas in Maps.* Topeka, Kansas State Historical Society.

Place Names

Baughman, Robert W. *Kansas Post Offices May 29 1828 - Aug. 3, 1961.* Topeka: Kansas State Historical Society, 1961.

Rydjord, John. *Kansas Place Names.* Norman, Oklahoma: University of Oklahoma Press, 1972.

Histories

Andreas, A. T. *History of Kansas,* 1883. Reprinted with index. Atchison County Historical Society, 1976.

Bright, John D. *Kansas, The First Century,* 4 Vols. New York: Lewis Historical Publishing Company, 1957.

Cyclopedia of State History, 3 Vols. Chicago: Standard Publishing Company, 1912.

Genealogical Sources

D.A.R. collection contains cemetery records, church records, family records and early vital records.

Kansas State Historical Society holds one of the largest newspaper collections in the United States.

Kansas Genealogical Society and D.A.R. Library, Dodge City, Kansas combined facilities have early census records and important collections of early records.

Riley County Genealogical Society, Manhattan, Kansas has a good collection of early records.

Bibliographies and Indexes

Magazine of Bibliographies Featuring Kansas: The Formative Years, Vol. 1 No. 2 Dec. 1972. Fort Worth, Texas.

Barry, Louise, comp. *Comprehensive Index 1875-1930 to Collections, Biennial Reports and Publications of The Kansas State Historical Society.* Topeka; Kansas State Historical Society, 1959.

KANSAS COUNTY HISTORIES
(Population figures to nearest thousand - 1980 U. S. Census)

Name	Map Index	Date Created	Pop. By M 1980	U.S. Cen Reports Available	Parent County or Territory From Which Organized	County Seat
* Allen	A3	1855	16	1860-80	Original county	Iola 66749

(City Clk has b, d & bur rec; Pro Judge has m & pro rec; Clk Dis Ct has div & civ ct rec; Reg Deeds has Ind rec)

* Anderson	A3	1855	9	1860-80	Original county	Garnett 66032

(State Dept Vit Statistics has b, d rec from 1900; Clk Dis Ct has m, div, pro, civ ct rec from 1857; Co Appraiser has Ind rec from 1900; individual twps have bur rec)

Arapahoe (Disorganized)				1860-80	(1870 census missing) (Inc. some of Colo)	
* Atchison	A2	1855	18	1860-80	Original county	Atchison 66002

(Co Clk has b rec from 1891-1906, d rec from 1891-1911; City Clk has b, d rec from 1911; Clk Dis Ct has div rec; Magistrate Ct has pro rec; Reg of Deeds has Ind rec)

Barber	D4	1867	7	1880	Harper	Medicine Lodge 67104
* Barton	D2	1867	31	1870-80	Ellsworth	Great Bend 67530
Billings (see Norton)						
* Bourbon	A3	1855	16	1860-80	Original county	Fort Scott 66701

(Clk Ct has div rec from 1870; Pro Judge has m, pro rec from 1870, civ ct rec from 1963; Bur Vit Statistics, Topeka has b, d rec from 1911)

Breckenridge (see Lyon)				1860		
* Brown	A1	1855	12	1860-80	Original county	Hiawatha 66434

(Clk Dis Ct has div, pro, civ ct rec from 1800's, m rec; Reg of Deeds has Ind rec from 1857)

* Butler	B3	1855	45	1860-80	Original county	El Dorado 67042

(Co Clk has b & d rec from 1890 to 1909 incom)

Calhoun		1855			Name changed to Jackson after Civil War	
Chase	B3	1859	3	1860-80	Butler	Cottonwood Falls 66845

(Co Clk has b rec from 1886 to 1911, d rec from 1886 to 1910)

Chautauqua	B4	1875	5	1880	Howard	Sedan 67361

(Pro Judge has m & pro rec; City Clk has d & bur rec; Clk Dis Ct has div & civ ct rec; Reg Deeds has Ind rec)

* Cherokee	A4	1855	22	1870-80	Unorg. Terr.	Columbus 66725
* Cheyenne	F1	1875	4	1880	Kirwin Land District	Saint Francis 67756

(City Clk has b & d rec; Pro Judge has m & pro rec; Clk Dis Ct has div & civ ct rec; Reg Deeds has Ind rec)

* Clark	E4	1885	3	1880	Ford	Ashland 67831

(Co Clk has b rec from 1904-1910, City Clk has b, bur rec from 1910; Pro Judge has m, pro rec; Clk Dis Ct has div, civ ct rec; Reg Deeds has Ind rec)

* Clay	C2	1857	10	1860-80	Original county	Clay Center 67432

(Co Clk has b, m, d rec 1885-1911; Clk Dis Ct has div, pro, civ ct rec; Reg Deeds has Ind rec)

* Cloud	C2	1860	13	1870-80	Formerly Shirley County	Concordia 66901

(Co Clk has b, m & d rec from 1885 to 1910; Clk Dis Ct has div rec; Pro Judge has pro & civ ct rec; Reg Deeds has Ind rec)

* Coffey	B3	1855	9	1860-80	Original county	Burlington 66839

(Pro Judge has m & pro rec from 1857; Clk Dis Ct has div & civ ct rec from 1859; Reg Deeds has Ind rec)

Comanche	D4	1867	3	1880	Kiowa	Coldwater 67029

(Co Clk has b, d rec from 1891-1911; Magistrate Judge has m rec from 1891-1912, pro, civ ct rec; Clk Dis Ct has div rec; Reg Deeds has Ind rec)

* Cowley	B4	1867	37	1870-80	Formerly Hunter	Winfield 67156

(Clk Dis Ct has div rec from 1870, civ ct rec; Pro Judge has m rec & pro rec from 1870)

* Crawford	A3	1867	38	1870-80	Bourbon	Girard 66743

(Co Clk has b rec from 1887 to 1911; Board of Health has b rec from 1911 to present; Co Clk has d rec from 1887 to 1908; Pro Ct has m & pro rec; Clk Dis Ct has div & civ ct rec)

Davis		1871		1860-80	Riley - see Geary, Junction City	
Decatur	E1	1875	5	1880	Norton	Oberlin 67749

(Pro Judge has m, div & mil rec from 1880, pro rec from 1900, civ ct rec from 1937 & Ind rec; b & d rec from 1885 & bur rec from 1913 are sent to Topeka, Kans by the City Clk)

Dickinson	C2	1855	20	1860-80	Original county	Abilene 67410

(Co Clk has incom b rec from 1892, m rec & d rec from 1892)

Name	Map Index	Date Created	Pop. By M 1980	U.S. Cen Reports Available	Parent County or Territory From Which Organized	County Seat
* Doniphan	A1	1855	9	1860-80	Original county	Troy 66087

(Pro Judge has m & pro rec from 1856; Clk Dis Ct has div & civ ct rec from 1856; Reg Deeds has Ind rec from 1856)

| Dorn | | | | 1860 | See Nesho | |
| * Douglas | A2 | 1855 | 67 | 1860-80 | Original county | Lawrence 66044 |

(Co Clk has Ind rec)

| Edwards | D3 | 1874 | 4 | 1880 | Kiowa | Kinsley 67547 |

(Pro Judge has m, div, pro & civ ct rec from 1874; Reg Deeds has Ind rec from 1874)

| Elk | B3 | 1875 | 4 | 1880 | Howard | Howard 67349 |

(Courthouse burned 1906, all rec destroyed)

| * Ellis | D2 | 1867 | 26 | 1870-80 | Unorg. Terr. | Hays 67601 |

(Co Clk has b, m, d, div, immi, naturalization rec from 1868, pro rec from 1867, civ ct rec from 1951, Ind rec from 1871, co school rec from 1896; individual cem have bur rec)

| * Ellsworth | C2 | 1867 | 7 | 1870-80 | Saline | Ellsworth 67439 |

(Pro Judge has m & pro rec; City Clk has d & bur rec; Clk Dis Ct has div rec; Co Ct has civ ct rec; Reg Deeds has Ind rec)

| * Finney | F3 | 1883 | 24 | | Arapahoe, Foote, Sequoyah | Garden City 67846 |

(Pro Judge has m, pro rec from 1885; Clk Dis Ct has div, civ ct rec from 1885; formerly Sequoyah Co, Sequoyah Co has rec in Ford Co; Garfield Co is now part of Finney Co and Finney Co has the rec of Garfield Co)

| Foote | | | | 1880 | See Gray | |
| Ford | E3 | 1873 | 24 | 1880 | Unorg. Terr. | Dodge City 67801 |

(City Clk has b, d & bur rec; Pro Judge has m, pro & civ ct rec; Clk Dis Ct has div rec; Co Clk has Ind rec)

*§ Franklin	A2	1855	22	1860-80	Original county	Ottawa 66067
Garfield (annexed to Finney, 1893)						
* Geary	B2	1855	30		Davis Co 1875 to 1888, Riley	Junction City 66441

(Pro Ct has m, pro rec from 1860; Clk Dis Ct has div rec from 1860; Co Ct has civ ct rec from 1937; City Ct records b, d rec and then sends data to Bur Vit Statistics, Topeka; Reg Deeds has Ind rec from 1858)

Godfrey				1860	Changed to Seward 1861	
§ Gove	E2	1868	4	1880	Unorg. Terr.	Gove 67736
*§ Graham	E2	1867	4	1880	Rooks	Hill City 67642

(Pro Judge has m & pro rec; Clk Dis Ct has div & civ ct rec; Reg Deeds has Ind rec)

| * Grant | F3 | 1873 | 7 | 1880 | Finney, Kearney | Ulysses 67880 |

(Pro Judge has m, pro & civ ct rec; Clk Dis Ct has div rec; Reg Deeds has Ind rec)

| *§ Gray | E3 | 1887 | 5 | | Finney, Ford | Cimarron 67835 |

(Pro Judge has m rec from 1887, pro rec from 1885; Clk Dis Ct has div rec from 1887; Reg Deeds has Ind rec from 1887) (Gray Co has been named Foote, Buffalo & Sequoia before it became Gray Co. Co Clk has tax rolls census of 1889 to present, also dis school rec of pupils with various information; Reg Deeds has deeds from 1886, mtg rec are available from 1887)

| * Greeley | F2 | 1873 | 2 | 1880 | Hamilton | Tribune 67879 |

(City Clk has b rec; Pro Judge has m & pro rec; Co Ct has civ ct rec; Reg Deeds has Ind rec)

| § Greenwood | B3 | 1855 | 9 | 1860-80 | Original county | Eureka 67045 |

(Pro Judge has m & pro rec; Clk Dis Ct has div rec; Reg Deeds has Ind rec)

| Hamilton | F3 | 1873 | 3 | 1880 | Unorg. Terr. | Syracuse 67878 |

(Pro Judge has m & pro rec from 1886; City Clk has d & bur rec; Clk Dis Ct has div rec; Co Clk has Ind rec from 1884)

| Harper | C4 | 1867 | 8 | 1880 | Kingman | Anthony 67003 |

(Pro Judge has m & pro rec; Clk Dis Ct has div & civ ct rec; Reg Deeds has Ind rec)

| Harvey | C3 | 1872 | 30 | 1880 | McPherson, Sedgwick, Marion | Newton 67114 |
| Haskell | F3 | 1887 | 4 | | Finney | Sublette 67877 |

(Dept of Legal Stat has b & d rec; Pro Judge has m & pro rec; Dis Ct has div rec)

| Hodgeman | E3 | 1879 | 2 | 1880 | Indian Lands (Est. 1868) | Jetmore 67854 |

(City Clk has b, d & bur rec from 1911; Pro Judge has m & pro rec from 1887; Clk Dis Ct has div & civ ct rec from 1880)

| Howard | | 1875 | | | Taken to form Elk & Chautauqua | |
| Hunter | | | | 1860 | See Cowley | |

COUNTY MAP FOR THE STATE OF KANSAS

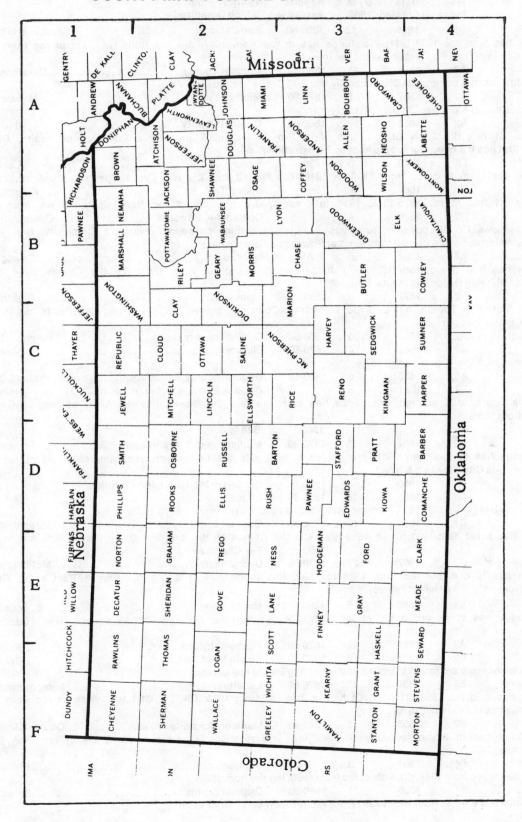

Name	Map Index	Date Created	Pop. By M 1980	U.S. Cen Reports Available	Parent County or Territory From Which Organized	County Seat
* Jackson	B2	1855	12	1860-80	See Calhoun	Holton 66436

(Co Clk has b, d rec 1903-1911; Pro Judge has m rec from 1867, pro rec from 1857, civ ct rec from 1900; Clk Dis Ct has div rec; Reg Deeds has Ind rec from 1858)

* Jefferson	A2	1855	15	1860-80	Original county	Oskaloosa 66066

(Pro Judge has m & pro rec; Clk Dis Ct has div rec; Reg Deeds has Ind rec)

Jewell	C1	1867	5	1870-80	Mitchell	Mankato 66956

(Pro Judge has m & pro rec; Clk Dis Ct has civ ct rec)

*§ Johnson	A2	1855	268	1860-80	Original County	Olathe 66061

(Clk Dis Ct has div & civ ct rec from 1861; Pro Ct has m & pro rec; State Dept of Health, Divison of Vital Stat has b & d rec; bur rec are kept by Registration Dis)

Kearny	F3	1873	3	1880	Finney	Lakin 67838

(Co Clk has b, m & d rec from 1900 to 1910; Clk Dis Ct has div rec; Pro Judge has pro & civ ct rec)

Kingman	C3	1886	9	1880	Unorg. Terr.	Kingman 67068

(Clk Dis Ct has m rec 1875-1915, 1917 to present, div, pro, civ ct rec from 1878, Ind rec from 1890)

Kiowa	D3	1886	4		Comanche, Edwards	Greensburg 67054

(In 1875 Kiowa Co disappeared from map & terr was divided between Edwards & Comanche Cos. Kiowa reappeared in 1886 being formed from parts of Edwards & Comanche)

* Labette	A4	1867	26	1870-80	Neosho	Oswego 67356

(Co Clk has b & d rec from 1885; Pro Judge has m & pro rec from 1867; Clk Dis Ct has div & civ ct rec from 1867; Reg Deeds has Ind rec from 1867)

Lane	E2	1877	2	1880	Finney	Dighton 67839

(Bur Vit Statistics, Topeka, has b, d rec; Magistrate Court has m, div, pro, civ ct rec; Reg Deeds has Ind rec; City of Dighton has bur rec)

* Leavenworth	A2	1855	55	1860-80	Original county	Leavenworth 66048
* Lincoln	C2	1867	4	1870-80	Ellsworth	Lincoln 67455

(Co Clk has m, d, pro & div rec from 1870)

* Linn	A3	1855	8	1860-80	Original county	Mound City 66056
* Logan	F2	1881	3		Wallace (changed from St. John 1887)	Oakley 67748

(City Clk has b, d & bur rec; Pro Judge has m & pro rec; Clk Dis Ct has div & civ ct rec; Co Clk has Ind rec from 1885)

Lykins				1860	See Miami	
* Lyon	B2	1857	35	1870-80	Madison (see Breckenridge)	Emporia 66801

(Pro Judge has m rec from 1861, pro rec from 1859; Clk Dis Ct has div rec from 1860, civ ct rec from 1858; Emporia City Clk has b & d rec)

Madison		1860		1860	Divided to Morris & Lyon Counties	
Marion	C3	1855	14	1860-80	Chase	Marion 66861

(Co Clk has b rec from 1885 to 1911, m rec from 1892 to 1899 & d rec from 1893 to 1903)

* Marshall	B1	1855	13	1860-80	Original county	Marysville 66508

Co Clk has b rec 1885-1911, d rec 1889-1911; Clk Dis Ct has m, div, pro, civ ct rec; Reg Deeds has Ind rec)

McGhee				1860	See Cherokee	
* McPherson	C3	1867	27	1870-80	Unorg. Terr.	McPherson 67460

(Co Clk has b, d & bur rec from 1888 to 1892; Pro Judge has m & pro rec from 1870; Clk Dis Ct has div rec from 1873; Co Ct has civ ct rec)

* Meade	E4	1885	5	1880	Unorg. Terr.	Meade 67864

(Pro Judge has b, m, pro & civ ct rec; City Clk has bur rec; Clk Dis Ct has div rec; Reg Deeds has Ind rec)

Miami	A2	1855	22	1870-80	Formerly Lykins	Paola 66071
Mitchell	C2	1867	8	1870-80	Kirwin Land District	Beloit 67420

(Pro Judge has m & pro rec; Clk Dis Ct has div rec; Reg Deeds has Ind rec)

*§ Montgomery	B4	1867	42	1870-80	Labette	Independence 67301

(Co Clk has b, d rec 1886-1911; Pro Ct has m, pro rec from 1870; Clk Dis Ct has div, civ ct rec from 1870; Reg Deeds has Ind rec from 1870)

§ Morris	B2	1855	6	1860-80	Madison (formerly Wise)	Council Grove 66846

(Pro Judge has m & pro rec; City Clk has bur & d rec; Clk Dis Ct has div & civ ct rec; Reg Deeds has Ind rec)

Morton	F4	1881	3		Stanton	Elkhart 67950

(Co Clk has m rec from 1887, div & civ ct rec from 1900, Ind rec from 1887)

* Nemaha	B1	1855	11	1860-80	Original county	Seneca 66538

(Co Clk has b, d & m rec from 1885 to 1911, pro rec 1857, civ ct rec from 1859)

Name	Map Index	Date Created	Pop. By M 1980	U.S. Cen Reports Available	Parent County or Territory From Which Organized	County Seat
* Neosho	A3	1855	19	1870-80	Original county	Erie 66733

(originally Dorn - name changed 1861)

| Ness | E2 | 1867 | 5 | 1880 | Hodgeman | Ness City 67560 |

(Pro Judge has m, pro rec, Clk Ct has div rec; City Clk has civ ct rec; Reg Deeds has Ind rec; State Bur Vit Statistics has b, d rec)

| * Norton | E1 | 1867 | 7 | 1880 | Unorg. Terr. (changed to Billings 1873, back to Norton 1874) | Norton 67654 |

(Pro Judge has m, div, pro & civ ct rec; Reg Deeds has Ind rec)

| § Osage | B2 | 1855 | 15 | 1860-80 | Formerly Weller | Lyndon 66451 |

(Co Clk has b rec from 1886 to 1921, m rec from 1885 to 1911, d rec from 1885 to 1909; Clk Dis Ct has div rec from 1863; Co Ct has civ ct rec from 1929; Reg Deeds has Ind rec from 1858)

| Osborne | D2 | 1867 | 6 | 1870-80 | Mitchell | Osborne 67473 |

(Pro Judge has m, pro, civ ct rec, div rec from 1872; Reg Deeds has Ind rec)

| Otoe | | | | 1860 | | |
| Ottawa | C2 | 1860 | 6 | 1870-80 | Saline | Minneapolis 67467 |

(Co Clk has m, div & pro rec; City Officers have b rec from 1911, d rec)

| * Pawnee | D3 | 1867 | 8 | 1880 | Rush, Stafford | Larned 67550 |

(Pro Judge has m & pro rec; City Clk has bur rec; Clk Dis Ct has div rec; Reg Deeds has Ind rec)

| *§Phillips | D1 | 1867 | 7 | 1880 | Kirwin Land District | Phillipsburg 67661 |

(Pro Judge has m & pro rec; City Clk has d & bur rec; Clk Dis Ct has div & civ ct rec; Co Clk has Ind rec)

| * Pottawatomie | B2 | 1857 | 15 | 1860-80 | Riley, Calhoun | Westmoreland 66549 |

(Co Clk has b, m, d rec 1885-1910; Unified Ct System has div, pro, civ ct rec, Reg Deeds has Ind rec)

| Pratt | D3 | 1867 | 10 | 1880 | Stafford | Pratt 67124 |

(Co Clk has b rec from 1887 to 1900)

| Rawlins | F1 | 1873 | 4 | 1880 | Kirwin Land District | Atwood 67730 |
| * Reno | C3 | 1867 | 65 | 1880 | Sedgwick, McPherson | Hutchinson 67501 |

(Co Clk has b rec from 1890 to 1910; Clk Dis Ct has div rec; Pro Judge has pro rec)

| * Republic | C1 | 1860 | 8 | 1870-80 | Washington, Cloud | Belleville 66935 |
| * Rice | C3 | 1867 | 12 | 1870-80 | Reno | Lyons 67554 |

(Co Clk has Ind rec from 1871)

| Richardson (changed to Wabaunsee, 1859) | | | | | | |
| * Riley | B2 | 1855 | 63 | 1860-80 | Unorg. Terr., Wabaunsee | Manhattan 66502 |

(Co Clk has b, d rec 1885-1886, 1892-1909; City Clk has b, d rec from 1910; Pro Ct has pro rec; Reg Deeds has Ind rec; City cems have bur rec)

| Rooks | D2 | 1867 | 7 | 1880 | Kirwin Land District | Stockton 67669 |

(Clk Dist Ct has m, div, pro, civ ct rec; Reg Deeds has Ind rec)

| Rush | D2 | 1867 | 5 | 1880 | Unorg. Terr. | La Crosse 67548 |

(City Clk has b, d & bur rec; Pro Judge has m from 1876, pro & civ ct rec; Clk Dis Ct has div; Reg Deeds has Ind rec)

| Russell | D2 | 1867 | 9 | 1870-80 | Ellsworth | Russell 67665 |

(Co Clk has m, pro & civ ct rec from 1876, also div rec)

| St. John (see Logan) | | | | | | |
| * Saline | C2 | 1860 | 49 | 1870-80 | Original county | Salina 67401 |

(Pro Judge has m & pro rec; Reg Deeds has Ind rec)

| Scott | F2 | 1873 | 6 | 1880 | Finney | Scott City 67871 |

(City Clk has b & d rec; Pro Judge has m & pro rec; Co Clk has bur rec; Clk Ct has div & civ ct rec)

| * Sedgwick | C3 | 1867 | 366 | 1870-80 | Butler | Wichita 67203 |

(Pro Judge has m & pro rec; Clk Dis Ct has div & civ ct rec; Co Clk has Ind rec)

| Sequoyah | | | | 1880 | See Gray & Finney | |
| § Seward | F4 | 1855 | 17 | 1880 | Indian Lands | Liberal 67901 |

(City Clk has b, d & bur rec; Pro Judge has m & pro rec; Clk Dis Ct has div & civ ct rec; Reg Deeds has Ind rec; Co Clk has newspapers from 1873)

| *§ Shawnee | B2 | 1855 | 154 | 1860-80 | Original county | Topeka 66603 |

(Co Clk has b, d rec 1894-1911; Bur Vit Statistics has b, d rec after 1911; Clk Dis Ct has m, div, pro, civ ct rec; Reg Deeds has Ind rec)

| Sheridan | E2 | 1873 | 4 | 1880 | Unorg. Terr. | Hoxie 67740 |

(Co Clk has inc b rec 1887 to 1910, d rec 1887 to 1910, m, div, pro, civ ct rec from 188?)

Name	Map Index	Date Created	Pop. By M 1980	U.S. Cen Reports Available	Parent County or Territory From Which Organized	County Seat
Sherman	F2	1873	8	1880	Kirwin Land District	Goodland 67735

(Co Clk has newspaper files from 1898, school & census rec; City Clk has b & d rec; Pro Judge has m & pro rec from 1886; Clk Dis Ct has div & civ ct rec from 1887; City Clk has Ind rec from 1888)

Shirley (see Cloud)						
Smith	D1	1867	6	1870-80	Unorg. Terr.	Smith Center 66967

(Pro Judge has m & pro rec from 1875; Clk Dis Ct has div & civ ct rec from 1875; Co Clk has Ind rec from 1872)

Stafford	D3	1867	6	1880	Unorg. Terr.	Saint John 67576
Stanton	F3	1873	2	1880	Reorganized	Johnson 67855

(City Clk has b & bur rec; Pro Judge has m & pro rec; Clk Dis Ct has div & civ ct rec)

Stevens	F4	1873	5	1880	Indian Lands	Hugoton 67951
* Sumner	C4	1867	25	1870-80	Cowley	Wellington 67152

(Pro Judge has m & pro rec; Clk Dis Ct has div rec; Co Clk has Ind rec)

* Thomas	F2	1873	8	1880	Kirwin Land District	Colby 67701

(Pro Judge has m, pro & civ ct rec; City Clk has d rec; Clk Dis Ct has div rec; Reg Deeds has Ind rec)

* Trego	E2	1867	4	1880	Ellis	Wakeeney 67672

(Pro Judge has m & pro rec; Clk Dis Ct has div & civ ct rec)

* Wabaunsee	B2	1855	7	1860-80	Riley, Morris (formerly Richardson)	Alma 66401

(Co Clk has b, m, d rec 1892-1910; Dis Ct has div, pro, civ ct rec)

Wallace	F2	1868	2	1870-80	Indian Lands (see Logan)	Sharon Springs 67758

(Co Clk has b, m, d rec 1895-1911; Clk Dis Ct has div rec; Pro Judge has pro, civ ct rec; Reg Deeds has Ind rec)

* Washington	C1	1855	9	1860-80	Original county	Washington 66968

(Co Clk has b rec from 1898 to 1911; Pro Judge has m, pro & civ ct rec; Clk Dis Ct has div rec; Reg Deeds has Ind rec)

Weller (see Osage)						
* Wichita	F2	1873	3	1880	Indian Lands	Leoti 67861

(Pro Judge has m & pro rec from 1887, civ ct rec; City Clk has d & bur rec from 1887; Clk Dis Ct has div rec from 1887; Reg Deeds has Ind rec from 1885)

* Wilson	B3	1855	12	1860-80	Original county	Fredonia 66736

(Pro Judge has m, pro & civ ct rec; Clk Dis Ct has div rec; Reg Deeds has Ind rec)

Wise (see Morris)						
* Woodson	B3	1855	5	1860-80	Original county	Yates Center 66783

(Co Clk has b rec from 1885 to 1911, m rec from 1860, div rec from 1863, pro rec from 1863, civ ct rec from 1934 & Ind rec from 1861)

* Wyandotte	A2	1859	171	1860-80	Original county	Kansas City 66101

(City Clk has b & d rec; Pro Judge has m & pro rec; Clk Dis Ct has div rec; Reg Deeds has Ind rec)

* - At least one county history has been published about this county.

§ - Inventory of county archives was made by the Historical Records Survey. (see introduction)

KENTUCKY

CAPITAL, FRANKFORT - STATE 1792 - (15TH)

The settling of Kentucky from the mid 1700's to the early part of the 1800's included some of the most hazardous and bloody events of America's history. Several thousand of those early settlers lost their lives in skirmishes with Indians. They were determined to protect their hunting grounds from the encroachments of the white man.

Long before any white man had explored the entire Kentucky area, it was claimed by Virginia as part of her Augusta County. It was included in the Virginia County of 1584.

Daniel Boone, born in Pennsylvania of English parents, moved his family in September 1773 into the Kentucky area from Rowan County, North Carolina, on the Yadkin River. However, he had previously explored that section some seven years earlier. Boone was not the first to investigate the possibilities of Kentucky. The eastern section of the area was explored by Dr. Thomas Walker as early as 1750. Twenty-five years later the Transylvania Company was organized under the leadership of Col. Richard Henderson of North Carolina. From Indian tribes he purchased almost half of what is now the state of Kentucky, all of the land between the Kentucky River, in the central part of the state, and the Cumberland River, in the extreme western part.

The first permanent settlement in Kentucky was at Harrodsburg in 1774. Boonesboro was founded in the following year by Daniel Boone.

Previous to these explorations all of Kentucky had been made part of Fincastle County, Virginia. During Boone's activities in the section, Kentucky was designated as Kentucky County, Virginia. This designation was made in December 1776. In 1780 it was divided into three counties, Fayette, Jefferson, and Lincoln. By 1790 those three counties were subdivided into nine counties, Mason, Bourbon, Woodford, Fayette, Madison, Jefferson, Mercer, Nelson, and Lincoln.

By 1900 those nine 1790 counties had been subdivided into the following present counties:

MASON: The east six-seventh of Pike, Floyd, Martin, Johnson; the east half of each of Magoffin and Morgan; Lawrence, Elliott, Rowan, Carter, Boyd, Greenup, Lewis, Fleming, Mason, Robertson, Bracken, Campbell, and the east third of Pendleton.

BOURBON: East four-fifths of Harlan, Letcher, west one-seventh of Pike, Knott, Perry, east of Leslie, Breathitt, west half of each of Magoffin and Morgan, Wolfe, north half of each of Lee and Estill, Bath, Powell, Manifee, Montgomery, east half of Clark, Bourbon, Nicholas, east three-fourths of Harrison, and triangular shaped south one-fifth of Pendleton.

WOODFORD: Woodford, Scott, east half of Franklin, Owen, Grant, Boone, Gallatin and east half of Carroll.

FAYETTE: Fayette, Jessamine and west half of Clark.

MADISON: Madison, east half of Garrard, south half of Estill, Jackson, north-east third of Rockcastle, Owsley, south half Lee, Clay, west half of Leslie, and west one-fifth of Harlan.

JEFFERSON: North half of each of Spencer and Bullit, Jefferson, Shelby, Oldham, Henry, northwest corner of Anderson, Trimble, and west half of Carroll.

MERCER: Triangular south third Franklin, east half of Anderson, Mercer, north two-thirds of Boyle, and northwest third of Garrard.

NELSON: Washington, Marion, Taylor, north half of each of Green, Hart, Edmonson, Butler, and McLean; Ohio, Davies, Hancock, Breckinridge, Meade, Hardin, south half of each of Bullitt and Spencer; Nelson, Larue, and Grayson.

LINCOLN: Henderson, Webster, Hopkins, south half of McLean; Muhlenberg; south half of Butler; Warren, south half of each of Edmonson, Hart and Green, Adair, Casey, Lincoln, west of Garrard, southwest two-thirds of Rockcastle; Laurel, south one-third of Boyle, Knox, Bell, Whitley, Pulaski, Wayne, Russell, Clinton, Cumberland, Metcalf, Monroe, Barren, Allen, Simpson, Logan, Todd, Christian, Trigg, Caldwell, Lyon, Marshall, Calloway, Graves, Fulton, Hickman, Carlisle, Ballard, McCracken, Livingston, Crittenden and Union.

The extreme western tip of Kentucky, surrounded on three sides by water - the Mississippi on the west, the Ohio and the Tennessee Rivers on the north, and the Kentucky Reservoir on the east - is sometimes referred to as the Jackson Purchase Region from the fact that it was purchased in 1818 from the Chickasaw Indians during the presidency of Andrew Jackson. It includes the following eight counties, sometimes included in the old Lincoln County: Calloway, Marshall, McCracken, Graves, Fulton, Hickman, Carlisle, and Ballard.

The descriptions of the Kentucky counties carved out of the nine counties existing in 1790 given in earlier paragraphs follow the Kentucky map printed in "A Century of Population Growth - 1790-1900" by the Bureau of Census, Washington, D.C. 20025. In several instances these descriptions do not harmonize with those on a map arranged by Bayless Hardin of Kentucky State Historical Society and published in Heineman and Brumbaugh's "First Census of Kentucky, 1790" (Kentucky Taxpayers of the Time.)

On 1 June 1792, Kentucky became the fifteenth state admitted into the Union.

It took courageous men and women to make their homes in a country as full of danger and excitement as existed in Kentucky in its early days. They came mostly, to begin with, from Maryland, North Carolina, Pennsylvania, Tennessee, and Virginia. Originally they were of German, English, Irish and Scottish descent. As new territories, new states were carved from the large American expanse, many of them were settled by the descendants of the original Kentuckians. With the increased European migration many people have also come to Kentucky from Russia, Italy, Poland and Austria.

Kentucky began registering births and deaths on January 1, 1911. The Vital Statistics Branch has no records of births and deaths occurring prior to the above date except:

1. City of Louisville, local birth records from 1898 to 1911 and death records from 1866 to 1911.
2. City of Lexington, local birth records from 1906 to 1911 and death records from 1898 to 1911.
3. City of Covington, local birth records from 1896 to 1911 and death records from 1880 to 1911.
4. City of Newport, local birth records from 1890 to 1911 and death records from 1884 to 1911.

Marriage and divorce records have been collected since June 1, 1958.

For a search of these records write to the Office of Vital Statistics, 275 East Main Street, Frankfort, Kentucky 40621.

Records of births and deaths from some counties as early as 1851 are in the library of the Kentucky Historical Society, Frankfort, Kentucky 40601.

County Clerk of county where transaction was completed may have wills, probate, marriage and divorce records.

Naturalization records are filed in the district courts in Bowling Green, Catlettsburg, Covington, Frankfort, London, Louisville, Owensboro, and Paducah. They may also be obtained in the office of the Clerk of the Circuit Court in the various county seats in the state.

Genealogical Archives, Libraries, Societies, and Publications

Ashland Public Library, 1740 Central Ave., Ashland, KY 41101.

Breckinridge County Public Library, Hardinsburg, KY 40143.

Cowley County Genealogical Society, P.O. Box 102, Arkansas City, KS 67005.

Eastern Kentucky Genealogical Society, Box 1544, Ashland, KY 41101.

Filson Club Library, 118 W. Breckinridge St., Louisville, KY 40203.

George Coon Public Library, Box 230, 114 S. Harrison St., Princeton, KY 42445.

Harlan County Genealogical Society of Kentucky, 800 Sheridan Circle, Olathe, KS 66061.

Harrodsburg Historical Society, Genealogical Committee, Box 316, Harrodsburg, KY 40330.

Henderson Public Library, 101 South Main St., Henderson, KY 42420.

John Fox Memorial Library, D.A. Shrine, Duncan Tavern St., Paris, KY 40361.

Kentucky Genealogical Society, P.O. Box 153 Frankfort, KY 40601.

Kentucky Historical Society Library, 200 Broadway, Frankfort, KY 40601.

Kentucky State Library and Archives, State Government Reference Service, 851 East Main Street, Frankfort, KY 40601.

KYOWVA Genealogical Society, P.O. Box 1254, Huntington, WV 25715.

Laurel County Public Library, 116 E. 4th St., London, KY 40741.

Lexington Public Library, 2nd and Market Sts., Lexington, KY 40507.

Louisville Free Public Library, 4th and York Sts., Louisville, KY 40203.

Margaret I. King Library, University of Kentucky, Lexington, KY 40506.

Morganfield Public Library, Morganfield, KY 42437.

National Society of the Sons of the American Revolution, National Headquarters, 1000 South Fourth Street, Louisville, KY 40203.

Owensboro-Daviess County Public Library Kentucky Room: Local History and Genealogy, 450 Griffith Ave., Owensboro, KY 42301.

Pikeville Public Library, 210 Pike Ave., Pikeville, KY 41501.

Public Library, 109 S. Main St., Winchester, KY 40391.

Pulaski County Historical Society, Public Library Building, Somerset, KY 42501.

Simpson County Historical Society, P.O. Box 162, Franklin, KY 42134.

Southern Historical Association, The, c/o University of Kentucky, Lexington, KY 40506.

Southern Kentucky Genealogical Society, 1425 Audubon Drive, Bowling Green, KY 42101.

Wayne County Public Library, 159 South Main Street, Monticello, KY 42633.

West-Central Kentucky Family Research Association, P.O. Box 1465, Owensboro, KY 42301.

Western Kentucky University, Kentucky Library, Bowling Green, KY 42101.

Bluegrass Roots, Kentucky Genealogical Society, P.O. Box 153, Frankfort, KY 40601.

Kentucky Ancestors, Kentucky Historical Society, P.O. Box H, Frankfort, KY 40601.

Kentucky Pioneer Genealogy and Records, published by Cook-McDowell Publications, 3318 Wimberg Ave., Evansville, IN 47712.

KYOWVA Genealogical Society Newsletter, published by the KYOWVA Genealogical Society, P.O. Box 1254, Huntington, WV 25715.

South Central Kentucky Historical and Genealogical Society Quarterly, P.O. Box 80, Glasgow, KY 42141.

Printed Census Records and Mortality Schedules

State Indexes - 1790, 1800, 1810, 1820, 1830, 1840, 1850, 1880

The 1790 and 1800 schedules are missing, however, reconstructed lists have been made from the taxpayer lists and published in the following books:

Heinemann, Charles B. *First Census of Kentucky 1790.* Baltimore, Maryland: Genealogical Publishing Company, 1965. Originally published 1940.

Clift, G. Glenn. *Second Census of Kentucky 1800.* Baltimore, Maryland: Genealogical Publishing Company, 1970. Originally published, 1954.

Printed Census Records (Counties):

Adair - Cumberland: 1810, 1820
Adair - Campbell: 1830
Estill - Hopkins: 1810
Jefferson - Mecklenburg: 1810
Nelson - Woodford: 1810
Daviess - Hopkins: 1820
Jefferson - Nichols: 1820
Ohio - Woodford: 1820
Casey - Gallatin: 1830
Garrard - Hopkins: 1830
Jefferson - Meade: 1830
Mercer - Rensal: 1830
Scott - Woodford: 1830

Adair - 1810, 1850, 1890
Allen - 1850
Anderson - 1850
Ballard - 1850
Barren - 1810
Bath - 1850
Bell - 1890
Boone - 1810, 1850
Bourbon - 1810, 1850
Boyle - 1850, 1890
Bracken - 1810, 1850
Breathitt - 1850, 1890
Breckinridge - 1810, 1850
Bullitt - 1810, 1850
Butler - 1810, 1850, 1870
Caldwell - 1810, 1830, 1850
Calloway - 1830, 1840, 1850
Campbell - 1810, 1820, 1830, 1840, 1850
Carroll - 1850
Carter - 1850
Casey - 1810, 1850
Christian - 1810, 1850
Clark - 1810, 1850
Clay - 1810, 1820, 1850, 1890
Clinton - 1850, 1890
Crittenden - 1850
Cumberland - 1800, 1810, 1820, 1830, 1840, 1850, 1860, 1870, 1880, 1890

Daviess - 1850
Edmonson - 1850
Estill - 1810, 1820, 1850, 1890
Fayette - 1810, 1850
Fleming - 1810, 1850
Floyd - 1810, 1820, 1840, 1850, 1860, 1870
Franklin - 1850
Fulton - 1850
Gallatin - 1810, 1850
Garrard - 1810, 1850, 1890
Graves - 1830, 1840, 1850
Grayson - 1810, 1850
Green - 1810, 1850, 1860
Greenup - 1810, 1850
Hancock - 1840, 1850
Hardin - 1810, 1850
Harlan - 1830, 1850
Harrison - 1810, 1890
Henderson - 1810, 1850
Henry - 1810, 1850
Hickman - 1830, 1840, 1850, 1870
Hopkins - 1810, 1820, 1830, 1840, 1850, 1860, 1870, 1880
Jackson - 1890
Jefferson - 1810
Jessamine - 1810
Johnson - 1850
Kenton - 1840, 1850
Knott - 1880, 1890
Knox - 1810, 1820, 1850, 1890
Larue - 1850
Laurel - 1830, 1840, 1850, 1890
Lawrence - 1850
Lee - 1890
Leslie - 1890
Letcher - 1850, 1880, 1890
Lewis - 1810, 1850
Lincoln - 1810, 1850, 1890
Livingston - 1810
Logan - 1810
Lyon - 1860
Madison - 1810, 1820, 1830, 1840, 1850, 1890

Magoffin - 1860, 1870, 1880
Marshall - 1850
Mason - 1810, 1820, 1850
McCracken - 1830, 1840, 1850
McLean - 1860
Meade - 1850
Mercer - 1800, 1810, 1820, 1850; 1789
Metcalfe - 1870
Monroe - 1820, 1830, 1850
Montgomery - 1810, 1850, 1870
Morgan - 1830, 1850
Muhlenberg - 1810, 1850, 1860
Nelson - 1810, 1850, 1860, 1870
Nicholas - 1810, 1850
Ohio - 1810, 1850, 1860, 1880
Oldham - 1850
Owen - 1850
Owsley - 1850, 1890
Pendleton - 1810, 1850
Perry - 1850, 1890
Pike - 1810, 1850
Pulaski - 1810, 1850, 1890
Rockcastle - 1820, 1830, 1850, 1880, 1890
Rockwith - 1810, 1850, 1860
Rowan - 1850
Russell - 1850, 1890
Scott - 1810, 1850
Shelby - 1810, 1850
Simpson - 1820, 1830, 1850
Spencer - 1850
Taylor - 1850
Todd - 1850
Trigg - 1850
Trimble - 1850
Union - 1850
Warren - 1810, 1850
Washington - 1810, 1850
Wayne - 1810, 1820, 1830, 1840, 1850, 1860, 1870, 1880, 1890
Webster - 1860
Whitley - 1820, 1890
Woodford - 1810

Mortality Schedules:

State - 1860, 1870, 1880

Counties:

Clinton - 1860, 1870, 1880	Metcalfe - 1860, 1870, 1880
Cumberland - 1860, 1870, 1880	Monroe - 1860, 1870, 1880

Valuable Printed Sources

Maps

Sames, James W. III. *Index of Kentucky and Virginia Maps 1562-1900.* Frankfort: Kentucky Historical Society (1976)

Place Names

Field, Thomas P. *A Guide to Kentucky Place Names.* Lexington: University of Kentucky (1961)

Murphy, Thelma M. *Kentucky Post Offices 1794-1819.* Indianapolis, Indiana (1975)

Guides to Genealogical Research

Hathaway: Beverly W. *Inventory of County Records of Kentucky.* West Jordan, Utah: Allstates Research Company (1974).

Hathaway, Beverly W. *Kentucky Genealogical Research Sources.* West Jordan, Utah: Allstates Research Company (1974).

McCay, Betty L. *Sources for Genealogical Searching in Kentucky.* Indianapolis (1969)

Histories

Coleman, J. Winston, Jr. *A Bibliography of Kentucky History.* Lexington: University of Kentucky Press, 1949.

Collins, Richard H. *History of Kentucky,* Two Volumes. Frankfort: Kentucky Historical Society, 1966.

Genealogical Sources

Ardery, Julie H. S. *Ardery Collection 1750-1967* Lexington, Kentucky.*

Barton E. E. *Collection of Northern Kentucky Families.* Lexington and Bowling Green.*

D.A.R. Collection*

Microfilm Department of Kentucky Historical Society. Microfilm catalog (1975) Excerpted Manuscripts and Pertinent Genealogical Source Material

Bibliographies

Kentucky Historical Society. Index to Tax Lists (1973).

The Archives Branch Division of Archives and Records Management Department of Library and Archives Commonwealth of Kentucky has compiled and published nine descriptive inventories (finding aids) for most historically significant record groups which are useful to the family researcher.

---

*Microfilm - Genealogical Society of The Church of Jesus Christ of Latter-day Saints, Salt Lake City, Utah.

KENTUCKY COUNTY HISTORIES
(Population figures to nearest thousand - 1980 U. S. Census)

Name	Map Index	Date Created	Pop. By M 1980	U.S. Cen Reports Available	Parent County or Territory From Which Organized	County Seat
* Adair	C3	1802	15	1810-80	Green	Columbia 42728
(Co Clk has m & Ind rec from 1802)						

Name	Map Index	Date Created	Pop. By M 1980	U.S. Cen Reports Available	Parent County or Territory From Which Organized	County Seat
Allen	D3	1815	14	1820-80	Barren, Warren	Scottsville 42164

(Co Clk has m & pro rec from 1902; Cir Ct Clk has div rec from 1902)

*§ Anderson — C2 — 1827 — 13 — 1830-80 — Franklin, Mercer, Washington — Lawrenceburg 40342

(Co Clk has m & pro rec from 1857, deeds from 1827, school rec; Cir Clk has civ ct rec from 1857)

Ballard — F3 — 1842 — 9 — 1850-80 — Hickman, McCracken — Wickliffe 42087

(Co Clk.has m, Ind rec from 1880; Clk Cir Ct has div, pro rec; Courthouse burned 1880)

* Barren — D3 — 1799 — 34 — 1810-80 — Green, Warren — Glasgow 42141

(Co Clk has m, pro, civ ct, Ind rec from 1799; Clk Cir Ct has div rec)

Bath — B2 — 1811 — 10 — 1820-80 — Montgomery — Owingsville 40360

(Co Clk has m, pro & Ind rec from 1811)

* Bell — B3 — 1867 — 34 — 1880 — Knox, Harlan — Pineville 40977

(Co clk has m & Ind rec)

* Boone — C1 — 1799 — 46 — 1810-80 — Campbell — Burlington 41005

(Co Clk has m & pro rec from 1799)

* Bourbon — B2 — 1786 — 19 — 1810-80 — Fayette — Paris 40361

(Co Clk has m & pro rec from 1786; Clk Cir Ct has civ ct rec from 1786 & div rec)

Boyd — A1 — 1860 — 55 — 1860-80 — Carter, Lawrence, Greenup — Catlettsburg 41129

(Co Clk has b & d rec from 1911 to 1949, m & Ind rec from 1860, pro rec from 1880; Clk Cir Ct has div rec; Co Judge has civ ct rec)

* Boyle — C2 — 1842 — 25 — 1850-80 — Mercer, Lincoln — Danville 40422

(Co Clk has m, Ind rec, wills from 1842; State has b, d rec; Clk Cir Ct has div, pro, civ ct rec)

* Bracken — B1 — 1797 — 8 — 1810-80 — Campbell, Mason — Brooksville 41004

(Co Clk has m, pro & Ind rec from 1797)

Breathitt — B2 — 1839 — 17 — 1840-80 — Clay, Estill, Perry — Jackson 41339

(Co Clk has m, pro & Ind rec from 1875; Clk Cir Ct has div & civ ct rec)

*§ Breckinridge — D2 — 1800 — 17 — 1810-80 — Hardin — Hardinsburg 40143

(Co Clk has m rec from 1852, wills & Ind rec from 1800; Clk Cir Ct has div & civ ct rec)

* Bullitt — C2 — 1797 — 43 — 1810-80 — Jefferson, Nelson — Shepherdsville 40165

(Co Clk has m rec from 1796, pro, Ind rec; State Dept Health, Frankfort has b, d, bur rec; Clk Cir Ct has div, civ ct rec)

* Butler — D3 — 1810 — 11 — 1810-80 — Logan, Ohio — Morgantown 42261

(Co Clk has m, pro & Ind rec; Clk Cir Ct has div & civ ct rec)

* Caldwell — E3 — 1809 — 13 — 1810-80 — Livingston — Princeton 42445

(Co Clk has m, pro, Ind rec, wills, court orders, guardians, inventories, and settlements from 1809; Clk Cir Ct has div, civ ct rec)

Calloway — E3 — 1821 — 30 — 1830-80 — Hickman — Murray 42071

(Co Clk has m, Ind, service discharge, ministers bonds, election rec; Clk Cir Ct has div rec)

* Campbell — B1 — 1795 — 83 — 1810-80 — Harrison, Mason, Scott — Alexandria 41001 & Newport 41071

(Co Clk has m, pro & Ind rec from 1785)

§ Carlisle — F3 — 1886 — 5 — — Ballard — Bardwell 42023

(Co Clk has m, pro & Ind rec)

Carroll — C1 — 1838 — 9 — 1840-80 — Gallatin, Henry, Trimble — Carrollton 41008

(Co Clk has m, pro rec, Ind rec & inventories from 1838; Clk Cir Ct has div & civ ct rec)

Carter — A1 — 1838 — 25 — 1840-80 — Greenup, Lawrence — Grayson 41143

(Co Clk has b & d rec from 1911 to 1954, m rec from 1838; Cir Ct Clk has div, pro & civ ct rec)

* Casey — C2 — 1807 — 15 — 1810-80 — Lincoln — Liberty 42539

(Co Health Dept has b, d rec; Co Clk has m, pro, Ind rec from 1806; Clk Cir Ct has pro rec from 1978, Clk Cir Ct has div, civ ct rec)

* Christian — E3 — 1797 — 66 — 1810-80 — Logan — Hopkinsville 42240

(Co Clk has m, pro, Ind rec, wills from 1797; Clk Cir Ct has pro rec from 1978, div, civ ct rec; Bur Vit Statistics, Frankfort has b, d rec)

* Clark — B2 — 1793 — 28 — 1810-80 — Bourbon, Fayette — Winchester 40391

(Clk Ct has m & pro rec from 1793, deeds, will, settlements & mtgs from 1793; Clk Cir Ct has div & civ ct rec)

Clay — B3 — 1807 — 23 — 1810-80 — Madison, Floyd, Knox — Manchester 40962

(Co Clk has m, Ind rec from 1807, pro rec, wills; Clk Cir Ct has div rec; Bur Vit Statistics, Frankfort, has b, d rec)

COUNTY MAP FOR THE STATE OF KENTUCKY

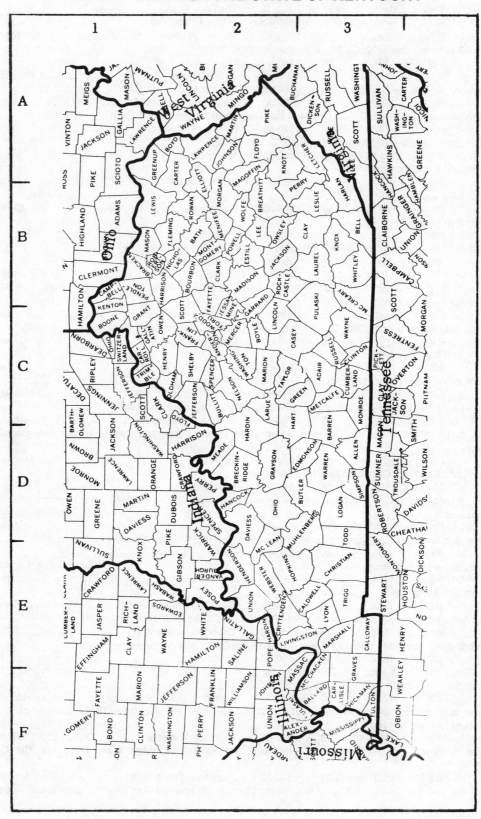

Name	Map Index	Date Created	Pop. By M 1980	U.S. Cen Reports Available	Parent County or Territory From Which Organized	County Seat
* Clinton	C3	1836	9	1840-80	Wayne, Cumberland	Albany 42602

(Co Clk has m, deeds, mtgs, wills from 1865)

| Crittenden | E2 | 1842 | 9 | 1850-80 | Livingston | Marion 42064 |

(Co Clk has m, pro & Ind rec from 1842; Clk Cir ct has div & civ ct rec)

| Cumberland | C3 | 1799 | 7 | 1810-80 | Green | Burkesville 42717 |

(Co Clk has m rec from 1882 to 1927 & some 1927 to 1971, pro rec from 1800, Ind rec from 1798; Clk Cir Ct has div & civ ct rec)

| * Daviess | D2 | 1815 | 86 | 1820-80 | Ohio | Owensboro 42301 |

(Co Clk has m & Ind rec from 1815, pro rec; Clk Cir Ct has div & civ ct rec)

| Edmonson | D3 | 1825 | 10 | 1830-80 | Grayson, Hart, Warren | Brownsville 42210 |

(Co Clk has m rec from 1840)

| Elliott | A2 | 1869 | 7 | 1870-80 | Carter, Lawrence, Morgan | Sandy Hook 41171 |

(Co Clk has b rec from 1882, m rec from 1934, pro rec from 1957, Ind rec from 1869; Clk Cir Ct has div rec from 1957 & civ ct rec)

| Estill | B2 | 1808 | 15 | 1810-80 | Clark, Madison | Irvine 40336 |

(Co Clk has m, pro & Ind rec)

| *§ Fayette | B2 | 1780 | 203 | 1810-80 | Kentucky Co Virginia | Lexington 40507 |

(Co Clk has m rec from 1795, pro rec & Ind rec from 1794; Clk Cir Ct has div & civ ct rec)

| * Fleming | B1 | 1798 | 12 | 1810-80 | Mason | Flemingsburg 41041 |

(Co Clk has m, pro & Ind rec from 1798)

| * Floyd | A2 | 1800 | 49 | 1810-80 | Fleming, Mason, Montgomery | Prestonsburg 41653 |

(Co Clk has m & Ind rec from 1800)

| * Franklin | C2 | 1795 | 42 | 1810-80 | Woodford, Mercer, Shelby | Frankfort 40601 |

(Co Clk has m rec from 1700, Ind rec; Bur Vital Statistics, Frankfort, has b rec)

| Fulton | F3 | 1845 | 9 | 1850-80 | Hickman | Hickman 42050 |

(Co Clk has m, pro & Ind rec from 1845; Clk Cir Ct has div & civ ct rec)

| Gallatin | C1 | 1799 | 5 | 1810-80 | Franklin, Shelby | Warsaw 41095 |

(Co Clk has m, pro & Ind rec from 1799; Clk Cir Ct has div & civ ct rec)

| * Garrard | B2 | 1797 | 11 | 1810-80 | Madison, Lincoln, Mercer | Lancaster 40444 |
| * Grant | C1 | 1820 | 13 | 1820-80 | Pendleton | Williamstown 41097 |

(Co Clk has m, pro & Ind rec from 1820)

| Graves | F3 | 1824 | 34 | 1830-80 | Hickman | Mayfield 42066 |

(Bur Vit Statistics, Frankfort has b, d rec; Co Clk has m, pro, civ ct, Ind rec from 1888; Clk Cir Ct has div rec)

| * Grayson | D2 | 1810 | 20 | 1810-80 | Hardin, Ohio | Leitchfield 42754 |

(Co Clk has m, pro & Ind rec from 1896)

| * Green | C2 | 1793 | 11 | 1810-80 | Lincoln, Nelson | Greensburg 42743 |

(Co Clk has m, Ind rec, wills from 1793, pro rec to 1978; Clk Cir Ct has div, civ ct rec; Co Health office has b, d rec)

| * Greenup | A1 | 1804 | 39 | 1810-80 | Mason | Greenup 41144 |

(Co Clk has m rec 1803, pro rec 1837, b & d rec from 1911 to 1949; Clk Cir Ct has div & civ ct rec 1803)

| Hancock | D2 | 1829 | 8 | 1830-80 | Daviess, Ohio, Breckinridge | Hawesville 42348 |

(Co Clk has m, pro & Ind rec from 1829; Clk Cir Ct has div & civ ct rec)

| * Hardin | D2 | 1793 | 89 | 1810-80 | Nelson | Elizabetown 42701 |

(Co Clk has m & Ind rec; will not make rec searches)

| * Harlan | B3 | 1819 | 42 | 1820-80 | Knox | Harlan 40831 |

(Co Clk has m & Ind rec from 1820; Clk Cir Ct has div & civ ct rec)

| * Harrison | B1 | 1794 | 15 | 1810-80 | Bourbon, Scott | Cynthiana 41031 |

(Co Clk has m, pro & Ind rec from 1794)

| * Hart | D2 | 1819 | 15 | 1820-80 | Hardin, Barren, possibly Green | Munfordville 42765 |
| * Henderson | E2 | 1799 | 41 | 1810-80 | Christian | Henderson 42420 |

(Co Clk has b & d rec from 1911 to 1949, m pro & Ind rec from 1811; Clk Cir Ct has div & civ ct rec)

| * Henry | C1 | 1799 | 13 | 1810-80 | Shelby | New Castle 40050 |

(Co Clk has m rec from 1798, Ind rec from 1800; Clk Cir Ct has div, pro & civ ct rec)

| * Hickman | F3 | 1821 | 6 | 1830-80 | Caldwell, Livingston | Clinton 42031 |
| Hopkins | W2 | 1807 | 46 | 1810-80 | Henderson | Madisonville 42431 |

(Co Clk has m, pro, civ ct rec & Ind rec)

| Jackson | B2 | 1858 | 12 | 1860-80 | Rockcastle, Owsley, Madison, Clay, Estill, Laurel | McKee 40447 |

(Co Clk has b, m, d & Ind rec)

Name	Map Index	Date Created	Pop. By M 1980	U.S. Cen Reports Available	Parent County or Territory From Which Organized	County Seat
* Jefferson	C2	1780	681	1810-80	Kentucky Co Virginia	Louisville 40202

(Co Clk has m & pro rec from 1781; Clk Cir Ct has div rec from 1850; Archivist has civ ct rec from 1780)

*§ Jessamine	C2	1799	25	1810-80	Fayette	Nicholasville 40356

(Co Clk has m, pro, deeds & mtges from 1799; Cir Ct Clk has div rec)

* Johnson	A2	1843	24	1850-80 1870	Floyd, Morgan, Lawrence	Paintsville 41240
Josh Bell						
* Kenton	B1	1840	136	1840-80	Campbell	Independence 41051

(Bur Vit Statistics, Frankfort, has b, d rec; Co Clk has m rec from 1874, Pro rec from 1860 to 1977, Ind rec from 1860; Clk Cir Ct has div, civ ct rec)

Knott	A2	1884	18		Perry, Breathitt, Floyd, Letcher	Hindman 41822

(Co Clk has m, civ ct rec & Ind rec from 1886)

§ Knox	B3	1800	30	1810-80	Lincoln	Barbourville 40906

(Co Clk has m & Ind rec)

Larue	C2	1843	12	1850-80	Hardin	Hodgenville 42748

(Co Clk has m, Ind rec from 1843, pro rec from 1843 to 1979; Clk Cir Ct has div rec, pro rec from 1979)

§ Laurel	B3	1826	38	1830-80	Whitley, Clay, Knox, Rockcastle	London 40741
Lawrence	A2	1822	14	1830-80	Floyd, Greenup	Louisa 41230

(Co Clk has m, pro & Ind rec from 1825; Clk Cir Ct has div rec)

Lee	B2	1870	8	1870-80	Owsley, Breathitt, Wolfe, Estill	Beattyville 41311

(Co Clk has m, pro, Ind rec from 1870; Clk Cir Ct has div, civ ct rec; Bur Vit Statistics has b, d rec)

Leslie	B3	1878	15	1880	Clay, Harlan, Perry	Hyden 41749

(Co Clk has m, pro & Ind rec; Clk Cir Ct has div & civ ct rec)

* Letcher	A3	1842	30	1850-80	Perry, Harlan	Whitesburg 41858

(Co Clk has m & Ind rec from 1842 & pro rec)

* Lewis	B1	1807	15	1810-80	Mason	Vanceburg 41179

(Co Clk has m rec from 1813, pro rec from 1806, Ind rec from 1816 & civ ct rec)

Lincoln	C2	1780	19	1810-80	Kentucky Co., Virginia	Stanford 40484

(Co Clk has m, div, pro, civ ct rec from 1792)

* Livingston	E3	1798	9	1810-80	Christian	Smithland 42081

(Co Clk has m rec from 1799, pro & Ind rec from 1800; Clk Cir Ct has div & ct rec; rec through 1865 have been microfilmed)

* Logan	D3	1792	24	1810-80	Lincoln	Russellville 42276

(Co Clk has m, pro, Ind & order bks rec from 1792, survey bks from 1792 to 1860)

Lyon	E3	1854	7	1860-80	Caldwell	Eddyville 42038

(Co Clk has b rec from 1912 to 1932, m & Ind rec from 1854; Clk Cir Ct has div rec)

* Madison	B2	1786	53	1810-80	Lincoln	Richmond 40475

(Co Clk has m & Ind rec from 1787, pro rec from 1850; Clk Cir Ct has div & civ ct rec)

Magoffin	A2	1860	13	1860-80	Floyd, Johnson, Morgan	Salyersville 41465

(Co Clk has m rec from 1860)

Marion	C2	1834	18	1840-80	Washington	Lebanon 40033

(Co Health Dept has b, d, bur rec; Co Clk has m, pro, Ind rec from 1863; Clk Cir Ct has civ ct rec)

* Marshall	E3	1842	26	1850-80	Callaway	Benton 42025

(Co Clk has m & Ind rec from 1848)

Martin	A2	1870	14	1880	Lawrence, Floyd, Pike, Johnson	Inez 41224

(Co Clk has b rec from 1903 to 1949, m rec from 1883, d rec from 1911 to 1949; Cir Clk has div, pro & civ ct rec)

* Mason	B1	1789	18	1810-80	Bourbon	Maysville 41056

(Co Clk has m, pro & Ind rec from 1789; Clk Cir Ct has div rec from 1929 & civ ct rec from 1792)

McCracken	F3	1825	61	1830-80	Hickman	Paducah 42001

(Co Clk has m, pro & Ind rec from 1825)

§ McCreary	B3	1912	16		Wayne, Pulaski, Whitley	Whitley City 42653

(Co Clk has m rec from 1912, 1923 to 1927 burned, also Ind rec)

McLean	D2	1854	10	1860-80	Muhlenberg, Daviess, Ohio	Calhoun 42327

(Co Clk has m, pro, Ind rec from 1854, m bonds bef 1907 were burned, but Co Clk has the index for these rec)

§ Meade	D2	1824	23	1830-80	Hardin, Breckinridge	Brandenburg 40108

(Bur Vit Statistics, Frankfort, has b, d bur rec from 1911; Co Clk has m, div, Ind rec from 1824; Clk Cir Ct has div, pro rec from 1825)

Name	Map Index	Date Created	Pop. By M 1980	U.S. Cen Reports Available	Parent County or Territory From Which Organized	County Seat
Menifee	B2	1869	5	1870-80	Powell, Wolfe, Bath, Morgan, Montgomery	Frenchburg 40322

(Co Clk has m rec from 1869; Clk Cir Ct has div rec from 1869)

* Mercer	C2	1786	19	1810-80	Lincoln	Harrodsburg 40330

(Co Clk has m, pro, Ind rec from 1786; Clk Cir Ct has div rec; Co Judge has civ ct rec)

* Metcalfe	C3	1860	9	1860-80	Monroe, Adair, Barren, Cumberland, Green	Edmonton 42129

(Co Clk has m & Ind rec)

* Monroe	C3	1820	12	1820-80	Barren, Cumberland	Tompkinsville 42167

(Co Clk has m, pro & Ind rec from 1863; Clk Cir Ct has div & civ ct rec)

* Montgomery	B2	1797	20	1810-80	Clark	Mount Sterling 40353

(Co Health Dept has b, d rec; Co Clk has m rec from 1864, pro rec from 1797; Clk Cir Ct has div, civ ct rec)

Morgan	B2	1823	12	1830-80	Floyd, Bath	West Liberty 41472

(Co Clk has b rec from 1911 to 1949, m, pro & Ind rec)

* Muhlenberg	D3	1799	32	1810-80	Christian, Logan	Greenville 42345
* Nelson	C2	1785	27	1810-80	Jefferson	Bardstown 40004

(Co Clk has m & pro rec from 1784)

* Nicholas	B1	1800	7	1810-80	Bourbon, Mason	Carlisle 40311

(Co Clk has m, pro & Ind rec from 1800; Clk Cir Ct has div & civ ct rec)

* Ohio	D2	1799	22	1810-80	Hardin	Hartford 42347

(Bur Vit Statistics, Frankfort, has b rec; Co Health Dept has d rec from 1911; Co Clk has m, Ind rec from 1798, pro rec from 1798 to 1977, Veteran's discharge rec from 1861; Clk Cir Ct has div rec, pro rec from 1978)

Oldham	C1	1824	27	1830-80	Henry, Shelby, Jefferson	LaGrange 40031

(Co Clk has m, pro & Ind rec from 1824; Clk Cir Ct has div & civ ct rec)

Owen	C1	1819	9	1820-80	Scott, Franklin, Gallatin, Pendleton	Owenton 40359

(Co Clk has b & d rec from 1911 to 1949, m, pro & Ind rec from 1819; Cir Clk has div rec)

Owsley	B2	1843	6	1850-80	Clay, Estill, Breathitt	Booneville 41314

(Co Clk has m, pro & Ind rec from 1929; Clk Cir Ct has div & civ ct rec; Co Judge has pro rec)

* Pendleton	B1	1799	11	1810-80	Bracken, Campbell	Falmouth 41040

(Co Clk has m rec from 1799, pro rec from 1800 & Ind rec; Clk Cir Ct has div & civ ct rec)

* Perry	B2	1821	34	1830-80	Clay, Floyd	Hazard 41701

(Bur Vit Statistics, Frankfort has b, d rec; Co Clk has m, Ind rec from 1821, Clk Cir Ct has div rec; Clk Dis Ct has pro, civ ct, wills)

Pike	A2	1822	81	1830-80	Floyd	Pikeville 41501

(Co Clk has b & d rec from 1911 to 1949, m & Ind rec from 1824, pro rec from 1822 & school rec from 1895 to 1934)

Powell	B2	1852	11	1860-80	Clark, Estill, Montgomery	Stanton 40380

(Co Clk has m & Ind rec from 1865; Clk Cir Ct has div, pro & civ ct rec)

* Pulaski	C3	1799	46	1810-80	Green, Lincoln	Somerset 42501

(Co Clk has m, pro & Ind rec from 1799; Clk Cir Ct has div & civ ct rec)

Robertson	B1	1867	2	1870-80	Nicholas, Bracken, Mason, Fleming, Harrison	Mt. Olivet 41064

(Co Clk has m, Ind, wills from 1867, school census rec from 1895; Clk Cir Ct has div, pro & civ ct rec from 1867)

Rockcastle	B2	1810	14	1810-80	Pulaski, Lincoln, Madison	Mount Vernon 40456

(Co Clk has m rec from 1873; Clk Cir Ct has div rec from 1873, pro & civ ct rec)

Rowan	B2	1856	19	1860-80	Fleming, Morgan	Morehead 40351

(Co Clk has m, pro & Ind rec from 1890; Clk Cir Ct has div rec; Co Judge has civ ct rec)

Russell	C3	1826	13	1830-80	Cumberland, Adair, Wayne, Pulaski	Jamestown 42629

(Co Clk has m, pro, civ ct & Ind rec from 1826; Clk Cir Ct has div rec)

* Scott	C2	1792	22	1810-80	Woodford	Georgetown 40324

(Co Clk has m, pro & Ind rec; Clk Cir Ct has div & civ ct rec)

* Shelby	C2	1792	24	1810-80	Jefferson	Shelbyville 40065

(Co Clk has b rec from 1911 to 1948, also m & pro rec)

Simpson	D3	1819	15	1820-80	Allen, Logan, Warren	Franklin 42134

(Co Clk has m rec from 1892)

Spencer	C2	1824	6	1830-80	Shelby, Bullitt, Nelson	Taylorsville 40071

(Co Clk has m rec from 1852, pro & Ind rec from 1824; Clk Cir Ct has div & civ ct rec)

Name	Map Index	Date Created	Pop. By M 1980	U.S. Cen Reports Available	Parent County or Territory From Which Organized	County Seat
* Taylor	C2	1848	21	1850-80	Green .... Campbellsville 42718
* Todd	D3	1820	12	1820-80	Christian, Logan .... Elkton 42220

(Co Clk has m, div, pro, civ ct, Ind rec, wills, inventory & appr rec)

| Trigg | E3 | 1820 | 9 | 1820-80 | Christian, Caldwell .... Cadiz 42211 |

(Co Health Dept has b, d rec; Co Clk has m, Ind rec from 1820, pro rec 1820-1977; Clk Cir Ct has div, civ ct rec)

| Trimble | C1 | 1837 | 6 | 1840-80 | Henry, Oldham, Gallatin .... Bedford 40006 |

(Co Clk has b rec from 1911 to 1950, m rec from 1865, Ind rec from 1800)

| * Union | E2 | 1811 | 18 | 1820-80 | Henderson .... Morganfield 42437 |

(Co Clk has m, pro & Ind rec from 1811)

| * Warren | D3 | 1797 | 70 | 1810-80 | Logan .... Bowling Green 42101 |

(Co Clk has m & pro rec from 1800, Ind rec from 1797)

| * Washington | C2 | 1792 | 11 | 1810-80 | Nelson .... Springfield 40069 |

(Co Clk has m, Ind rec from 1793, pro rec 1792 to 1978, school census rec 1898-1917)

| * Wayne | C3 | 1801 | 17 | 1810-80 | Pulaski, Cumberland .... Monticello 42633 |

(Co Clk has m, Ind rec from 1800, pro rec 1800 to 1978)

| Webster | E2 | 1860 | 15 | 1860-80 | Hopkins, Union, Henderson .... Dixon 42409 |

(Bur Vit Statistics, Frankfort, has b, d rec; Co Clk has m, Ind rec from 1860, pro rec from 1860 to 1977; Clk Cir Ct has div, civ ct rec, pro reg after 1978)

| Whitley | B3 | 1818 | 33 | 1820-80 | Knox .... Williamsburg 40769 |

(Co Clk has b rec from 1915 to 1949, m & pro rec from 1865 & Ind rec from 1818)

| * Wolfe | B2 | 1860 | 7 | 1870-80 | Owsley, Breathitt, Powell, Morgan .... Campton 41301 |

(Bur Vit Statistics, Frankfort, has b, d rec; Co Clk has m rec from 1913, Ind rec from 1860; Clk Cir Ct has div, pro, civ ct rec)

| * Woodford | C2 | 1789 | 18 | 1810-80 | Fayette .... Versailles 40383 |

(Co Clk has m, pro & Ind rec from 1789)

* - At least one county history has been published about this county.

§ - Inventory of county archives was made by the Historical Records Survey. (see introduction)

LOUISIANA

CAPITAL, BATON ROUGE - TERRITORY 1805 - STATE 1812 - (18TH)

Ownership of the Louisiana sector for the first 250 or 300 years of its discovery zigzagged between France, Spain, and England until it was sold to the United States as part of the Louisiana Purchase in 1803. Some of the quaint customs of the early French settlers have been perpetuated over the years and give the state an atmosphere of antiquity.

Every school boy and girl remembers with nostalgic feelings Longfellow's "Evangeline," the poetic story of the transfer of large groups of French settlers from Nova Scotia to Louisiana. Many descendants of these Acadians still live in Louisiana where they are known as Cajuns.

Rather than to fight against the mother country during the Revolutionary War, many loyal Britons moved their families from the Atlantic states to Louisiana where they have perpetuated themselves.

On 1 October 1804 Louisiana was divided into two parts by Congressional action. The upper portion was given the name "District of Louisiana" and the lower portion "Territory of Orleans." Immediately after the formation of the Territory of Orleans, large numbers of Americans from south of the Ohio moved into the new acquisition. In 1805 Louisiana was divided into 12 counties and in 1807 the Orleans Territory was partitioned into 19 parishes.

There is nothing different between a Louisiana parish and a county in any other state except the name. Otherwise everything is the same. Some of the early church parish records are now held by the parish or court clerks.

For information regarding wills, deeds, divorces, civil court records and marriages write the clerk of the respective parishes.

The State Registrar, Division of Vital Records, Department of Health and Human Resources, P.O. Box 60630, New Orleans, LA 70160, has records of birth and death for the state of Louisiana since 1914. This is generally true except for the parish of Orleans where records for births, deaths, and marriages are available as far back as 1790. (Please note that marriage records are available only if the license was purchased in Orleans parish). Additionally, some birth and death records for Caddo Parish are available since 1899.

Genealogical Archives, Libraries, Societies, and Publications

Alexandria Historical and Genealogical Library, 503 Washington, Alexandria, LA 71301.

Ark-La-Tex Genealogical Association, P.O. Box 4462, Shreveport, LA 71161.

Baton Rouge Genealogical and Historical Society, P.O. Box 80565 SE Station, Baton Rouge, LA 70898.

Centroplex Library, 120 St. Louis St., Baton Rouge, LA 70821.

Genealogical Research Society of New Orleans, P.O. Box 51791, New Orleans, LA 70150.

Hill Memorial Library, Louisiana State University, Baton Rouge, LA 70803.

Howard Tilton Library, The Map and Genealogy Room, Tulane University, New Orleans, LA 70118.

Louisiana Genealogical and Historical Society, P.O. Box 3454, Baton Rouge, LA 70821.

Lincoln Parish Library, Box 637, 509 W. Alabama, Ruston, LA 71270.

Louisiana State Library, State Capitol Ground, Baton Rouge, LA 70804.

Northeast Louisiana Genealogical Society, P.O. Box 2743, Monroe, LA 71201.

Ouachita Parish Public Library, 1800 Stubbs Ave., Monroe, LA 71201.

Rapides Parish Library, 411 Washington St., Alexandria, LA 71301.

Shreve Memorial Library, 400 Edwards St., Shreveport, LA 71101.

Southwest Louisiana Genealogical Society, P.O. Box 5652 Drew Station, Lake Charles, LA 70606.

St. Bernard Genealogical Society, P.O. Box 271, Chalmette, LA 70044.

Tangipahoa Parish Library, Amite, LA 70422.

Ark-La-Tex Newsletter, Genealogical Association, P.O. Box 71, Shreveport, LA 71161.

Le Reconteur, quarterly publication of Le Comite des Archives de la Louisiane, P.O. Box 44370, Capitol Station, Baton Rouge, LA 70804.

L'Heritage, P.O. Box 271, Chalmette, LA 70044.

The Louisiana Genealogical Register, P.O. Box 3454, Baton Rouge, LA 70821.

Printed Census Records and Mortality Schedules

State Indexes: 1810, 1820, 1830, 1840, 1850

Printed Census Records (Counties):

Ascension - 1810, 1820
Assumption - 1810, 1820
Attakaps - 1810
Avoyelles - 1810, 1820
Baton Rouge - 1810; 1774
Caddo - 1830, 1840
Caldwell - 1830, 1840
Catahoula - 1820, 1830, 1840
Claiborne - 1830, 1840
Concordia - 1820
East Baton Rouge - 1810, 1820, 1830
East Feliciana - 1820, 1830

Iberville - 1810, 1820
Lafourche - 1810
Livingston - 1840, 1850, 1860, 1870
Natchitoches - 1810, 1820, 1830, 1840
Opelousas - 1810
Orleans - 1810
Ouachita - 1830, 1840
Plaquemines - 1810, 1850
Pointe Coupee - 1810, 1820; 1745
Rapides - 1810, 1820, 1850
Sabina - 1850

St. Bernard - 1810, 1820
St. Charles - 1810, 1820; 1770
St. Helena - 1820, 1830, 1850
St. James - 1810, 1820; 1766-1777, 1807
St. John the Baptist - 1810, 1820; 1770
St. Landry - 1810, 1820; 1796, 1813
St. Tammany - 1820
Union - 1830, 1840, 1850, 1860
Washington - 1820, 1830, 1850
West Baton Rouge - 1810, 1820
West Feliciana - 1830, 1850

Other printed census records:

Maduell, Charles R. Jr. (comp.) *The Census Tables for the French Colony of Louisiana from 1699 through 1732.* Baltimore, Maryland: Genealogical Publishing Company, 1973.

State Census - 1770-1789

Mortality Schedules:

State Indexes - 1850, 1860, 1870

County:

Morehouse - 1850

Valuable Printed Sources

Place Names

Gibson, Dennis A. *Index to Louisiana Place Names Mentioned in the "War of the Rebellion: A Compilation of the Official Records of the Union and Confederate Armies."* Fayette: University of Southwestern Louisiana, 1975.

Guides to Genealogical Research

Herbert, Donald J. *A Guide to Church Records in Louisiana (1720-1975).* Eunice, Louisiana: Published privately, 1975.

Resources in Louisiana Libraries. Baton Rouge: Louisiana State Library, 1971.

Histories

Fortier, Alcee. *A History of Louisiana,* Four Volumes. New York: Manzi, Joyant and Company.

Gayarre, Charles. History of Louisiana. New Orleans: Pelican Publishers.

Genealogical Sources

Conrad, Glenn R. *First Families of Louisiana,* Volumes One and Two. Baton, Rouge: Claitor's Publishing Division, 1970.

Hebert, Rev. Donald J. *South Louisiana Records - Lafourche-Terrebonne,* Six Volumes. Cecilia, Louisiana: Published privately, 1978.

Hebert, Rev. Donald J. *Southwest Louisiana Records.* Eunice, Louisiana: Published privately, 1976. 25 Volumes.

LOUISIANA PARISH HISTORIES
(Population figures to nearest thousand - 1980 U. S. Census)

Name	Map Index	Date Created	Pop. By M 1980	U.S. Cen Reports Available	Parent Parish or Territory From Which Organized	Parish Seat
Acadia	C2	1886	57		St. Landry	Crowley 70526
(Par Clk has m, div, pro & civ ct rec from 1886)						
§ Allen	C2	1912	21		Calcasieu	Oberlin 70655
(Par Clk has m, div, pro & civ ct rec from 1913; Dept of Health has b & d rec)						
* Ascension	C3	1807	52	1810-80	St. James	Donaldsonville 70346
(Par Clk has m rec from 1763, div, pro & civ ct rec from 1800 & Ind rec from 1770)						
*§ Assumption	C3	1807	22	1810-80	Original Parish	Napoleonville 70390
(Par Clk has m & div rec from 1800, pro, civ ct & Ind rec from 1788)						
* Attakapas				1810	Original Parish - discontinued	
* Avoyelles	C2	1807	41	1810-80	Original Parish - reorg. 1873	Marksville 71351
(Par Clk has m, Ind rec from 1808, div, pro, civ ct rec from 1856)						
*§ Beauregard	C1	1913	30		Calcasieu	DeRidder 70634
(Par Clk has m, div, pro, civ ct & Ind rec from 1913)						
Baton Rouge				1810		
Bienville	B2	1848	16	1850-80	Claiborne	Arcadia 71001
(Par Clk has m, div, pro & civ ct rec from 1848)						
§ Bossier	A1	1843	81	1850-80	Claiborne	Benton 71006
(Par Clk has m, div, pro & civ ct rec from 1843; Bureau of Vital Stat has b rec)						
Caddo	A1	1838	252	1840-80	Natchitoches	Shreveport 71101
(Par Clk has m, div, pro, civ ct, mtg & conveyance rec from 1835)						
*§ Calcasieu	C1	1840	167	1840-80	St. Landry	Lake Charles 70601
(Par Clk has m, div, pro, civ ct & Ind rec from 1910)						
Caldwell	B2	1838	11	1840-80	Catahoula, Ouachita	Columbia 71418
(Par Clk has m, div, pro, civ ct, conveyance, mtg & leases from 1838)						

PARISH MAP FOR THE STATE OF LOUISIANA

Name	Map Index	Date Created	Pop. By M 1980	U.S. Cen Reports Available	Parent Parish or Territory From Which Organized	Parish Seat
* Cameron	C1	1870	9	1870-80	Calcasieu, Vermillion	Cameron 70631

(Dept Health, New Orleans, has b, d rec; Par Clk has m, Ind rec from 1870, div, pro, civ ct rec; area churches and funeral homes have bur rec)

| Carroll | | | | 1840-70 | See East & West Carroll | |
| Catahoula | B2 | 1808 | 12 | 1810-80 | | Harrisonburg 71340 |

(Par Clk has m, pro, Ind rec from early 1800's, div, civ ct rec from early 1900's)

Name	Map Index	Date Created	Pop. By M 1980	U.S. Cen Reports Available	Parent Parish or Territory From Which Organized	Parish Seat
* Claiborne	A2	1828	17	1830-80	Natchitoches	Homer 71040

(Bur Vit Statistics, New Orleans, has b, d rec; Par Clk has m, div, pro, civ ct, Ind rec from 1850; Courthouse burned 1849)

Name	Map Index	Date Created	Pop. By M 1980	U.S. Cen Reports Available	Parent Parish or Territory From Which Organized	Parish Seat
Concordia	B2	1805	23	1810-80	Avoyelles	Vidalia 71373

(Par Clk has m rec from 1840, div, pro, civ ct & Ind rec from 1850)

| De Soto | B1 | 1843 | 26 | 1850-80 | Natchitoches, Caddo .... | Mansfield 71052 |

(Par Clk has m rec from 1843, div, pro, civ ct, Ind rec)

| East Baton * Rouge | C3 | 1810 | 368 | 1820-80 | Original parish .... | Baton Rouge 70801 |

(Par Clk has m rec from 1840, div, pro, civ ct, Ind rec from 1782)

| East Carroll | A3 | 1877 | 12 | 1880 | Carroll .... | Lake Providence 71254 |
| * East Feliciana | C3 | 1824 | 19 | 1830-80 | Seceded from Feliciana .... | Clinton 70722 |

(Par Clk has m, div, pro, civ ct, Ind, slave sales, contracts, mtgs, sheriffs sales & donations rec from 1824)

| * Evangeline | C2 | 1911 | 33 | | St. Landry .... | Ville Platte 70586 |

(Par Clk has m, div, pro, civ ct, Ind rec from 1911)

| Feliciana | | | | 1820 | | |
| Franklin | B2 | 1843 | 24 | 1850-80 | Catahoula, Ouachita, Madison .... | Winnsboro 71295 |

(Par Clk has m, div, pro, civ ct & Ind rec from 1843)

| § Grant | B2 | 1869 | 17 | 1870-80 | Rapides, Winn .... | Colfax 71417 |

(Par Clk has m, div, pro, civ ct & Ind rec from 1880)

| Iberia | C2 | 1868 | 64 | 1870-80 | St. Martin, St. Mary .... | New Iberia 70560 |

(Par Clk has m, div, pro, civ ct & Ind rec from 1868)

| * Iberville | C2 | 1807 | 32 | 1810-80 | Assumption, Ascension .... | Plaquemine 70764 |

(Par Clk has m & Ind rec from 1770, div, pro, civ ct rec from 1807)

| Jackson | B2 | 1845 | 17 | 1850-80 | Claiborne, Ouachita, Union .... | Jonesboro 71251 |
| § Jefferson | D4 | 1825 | 452 | 1830-80 | Orleans .... | Gretna 70072 |

(Par Clk has m, div, pro, civ ct & Ind rec from 1825, mtg rec from 1892, conveyance rec from 1827)

| * Jefferson Davis | C2 | 1913 | 32 | | Calcasieu .... | Jennings 70546 |

(Par Clk has m, div, pro, civ ct, Ind rec from 1913, a few transcribed rec from Calasieu Parish; Courthouse burned 1910)

| *§ Lafayette | C2 | 1823 | 149 | 1830-80 | St. Martin .... | Lafayette 70501 |

(Par Clk has m, div, pro, civ ct & Ind rec from 1823)

| § Lafourche | D3 | 1807 | 82 | 1810-80 | .... | Thibodaux 70301 |

(Par Clk has b, m, div, pro, civ ct & Ind rec from 1808)

| * LaSalle | B2 | 1910 | 17 | | Catahoula .... | Jena 71342 |

(Par Clk has m, div, pro, civ ct & Ind rec from 1910)

| * Lincoln | A2 | 1873 | 40 | 1880 | Bienville, Jackson, Union, Claiborne .... | Ruston 71270 |

(Par Clk has m, div, pro & civ ct rec from 1873)

| Livingston | C3 | 1832 | 58 | 1840-80 | Baton Rouge, Ascension .... | Livingston 70754 |

(Par Clk has m, div, pro, civ ct & Ind rec from 1875)

| Madison | B3 | 1838 | 15 | 1840-80 | Concordia .... | Tallulah 71282 |

(Par Clk has m rec 1866, div rec 1839, pro rec 1850, civ ct rec 1882, deeds 1839 & mtg 1865)

| *§ Morehouse | A2 | 1844 | 35 | 1850-80 | Ouachita .... | Bastrop 71220 |

(Par Clk has m, div, pro & civ ct rec from 1870, Ind rec & mtg rec from 1844, cem abstract from 1867 to 1957)

| *§ Natchitoches | B2 | 1807 | 39 | 1810-80 | Original Parish .... | Natchitoches 71457 |

(Clk Ct has m rec from 1780, also div, pro & civ ct rec)

| Opelousas | | | | 1810 | | |
| *§ Orleans | C4 | 1807 | 558 | 1810-80 | Original Parish .... | New Orleans 70112 |

(Clk Civ Dis Ct has div, pro & civ ct rec from 1805; Reg of Conveyances has Ind rec from 1832; Pub Lib has voter registration rec from 1895 to 1941, city directories from 1805, precinct bks from 1895 to 1952)

| § Ouachita | A2 | 1807 | 138 | 1810-80 | Original Parish .... | Monroe 71201 |

(Par Clk has m, div, pro, civ ct rec from 1805)

| § Plaquemines | D4 | 1807 | 26 | 1810-80 | Orleans .... | Pointe a la Hache 70082 |

(Par Clk has m rec from 1896, div, pro, civ ct & Ind rec from 1807)

Name	Map Index	Date Created	Pop. By M 1980	U.S. Cen Reports Available	Parent Parish or Territory From Which Organized	Parish Seat
Pointe Coupee	C2	1807	24	1810-80	Feliciana, Avoyelles	New Roads 70760

(Clk Ct has m rec from 1735, div rec from 1800, pro, civ ct, conveyances & mtg from 1780; Board of Health has b, d & bur rec)

* Rapides	B2	1807	135	1810-80	Original Parish	Alexandria 71301

(Par Clk has m, div, pro, civ ct & Ind rec from 1864)

Red River	B1	1871	10		Caddo, Bossier, Bienville, Natchitoches, DeSoto	Coushatta 71019

(Clk Ct has m & pro rec from 1871, div & civ ct rec from 1904)

Richland	A2	1868	22	1870-80	Ouachita, Carroll, Franklin, Morehouse	Rayville 71269

(Par Clk has m, div, pro, civ ct, Ind rec from 1869)

*§ Sabine	B1	1843	25	1850-80	Natchitoches	Many 71449

(Par Clk has m, div, pro, civ ct & Ind rec from 1843)

§ St. Bernard	C4	1807	64	1810-80	Original Parish	Chalmette 70043
§ St. Charles	C3	1807	37	1810-80	Original Parish	Hahnville 70057
St. Helena	C3	1810	10	1820-80	Livingston	Greensburg 70441

(Par Clk has rec from 1804, Co employees do not have time to chk rec)

* St. James	C3	1807	21	1810-80	Original Parish	Convent 70723

(Par Clk has m rec from 1846, div, pro & civ ct rec from 1809)

* St. John the Baptist	C3	1807	32	1810-80	Original Parish	Edgard 70049

(Par Clk has m, div, pro, civ ct & Ind rec)

* St. Landry	C2	1807	84	1820-80	Avoyelles, Rapides	Opelousas 70570

(Par Clk has m rec from 1808, div rec from 1813, pro rec from 1809 & civ ct rec from 1813; Bureau of Vital Stat has b, d & bur rec)

* St. Martin	C2,3	1807	40	1810-80	Original Parish	St. Martinville 70582
St. Mary	D3	1811	65	1820-80	Assumption	Franklin 70538

(Par Clk has m, div, pro, civ ct & Ind rec from 1800)

* St. Tammany	C4	1810	110	1820-80	St. Helena, Orleans	Covington 70433

(Par Clk has m, div, pro, civ ct rec from 1812, Ind rec from 1810, mark & brand bks from 1816, early road dis listing persons working on pub road from 1816, tax rec from 1880, rec discharge papers WWI WWII & others)

* Tangipahoa	C3	1869	80	1870-80	Livingston, St. Tammany, St. Helena, Washington	Amite 70422

(Par Clk has m, div, pro & civ ct rec, also conveyance, will, donation rec from 1869)

Tensas	B3	1843	8	1850-80	Concordia	St. Joseph 71366

(Par Clk has m, div, pro & civ ct rec from 1843)

*§ Terrebonne	D3	1822	95	1830-80	La Fourche	Houma 70360
* Union	A2	1839	21	1840-80	Ouachita	Farmerville 71241

(Par Clk has m, div & pro rec from 1839 & civ ct rec)

Vermilion	D2	1844	48	1850-80	Lafayette	Abbeville 70510

(Par Clk has m, div, pro, civ ct & Ind rec from 1885)

Vernon	B1	1871	53	1880	Natchitoches, Rapides, Sabine	Leesville 71446

(Par Clk Ct has m rec from 1890, div, pro & civ ct rec from 1871)

*§ Washington	C4	1819	44	1820-80	St. Tammany	Franklinton 70438

(Par Clk Ct has m, div, pro, civ ct & Ind rec from 1897)

* Webster	A1	1871	43	1880	Claiborne, Bienville, Bossier	Minden 71055

(Par Clk has m, div, pro, civ ct & Ind rec from 1871)

West Baton Rouge	C3	1807	19	1820-80	Baton Rouge	Port Allen 70767
West Carroll	A3	1877	13	1880	Carroll	Oak Grove 71263
* West Feliciana	C3	1824	14	1830-80	Feliciana	Saint Francisville 70775

(Par Clk has m rec from 1879, div, pro & civ ct rec from 1900, Ind rec from 1811)

§ Winn	B2	1851	17	1860-80	Natchitoches, Catahoula, Rapides	Winnfield 71483

(Par Clk has m, div, pro, civ ct & Ind rec from 1886)

* - At least one Parish history has been published about this Parish

§ - Inventory of county archives was made by the Historical Records Survey. (see introduction)

MAINE

CAPITAL, AUGUSTA - STATE 1820 - (23RD)

English and French explorers visited the present Maine region many times from 1598 to 1605. It was not until 1623 that the first permanent settlement was established. A community came into existence that year on the Saco River, in the extreme southwestern section. The settlers came into the district as English subjects and they brought with them the laws of England. They came with permission granted them by the English rulers to create for themselves property ownership in American lands.

One hundred Englishmen aboard two vessels left Plymouth on 31 May 1607. At the mouth of the Kennebec, then known as the Sagadahoc, they established a settlement which was disbanded the next year when the remaining settlers returned to England. Some historians maintain that not all of the settlers returned to England. Some, they say, appeared in the present Pemaquid, Lincoln County, in 1608.

The appetite of many a hardworking, low paid, stay-at-home Englishman was whetted by the description of the new land by one of the returning explorers when he wrote, "Here are no hard landlords to rack us with high rents, or extorted fines to consume us. Here, every man may be master and owner of his own labor and land, or the greatest part, in a small time."

Various small groups brought over from England had settled along the coast of Maine where they engaged in fishing, but the first large contingent to come were the English Pilgrims or Puritans who arrived via Holland and Plymouth off Cape Cod in Massachusetts on 10 November 1620 (o/s). Most of these so called dissenters came originally from Scrooby, Nottinghamshire.

In 1622 two members of the Plymouth Company in England, Sir Ferdinando Gorges and Captain John Mason, were granted all of the land between the Kennebec and the Merrimac Rivers. It was about that time that Dover and Portsmouth in New Hampshire were established. Later the grant was divided, Mason taking the part that is now New Hampshire, and Gorges, the eastern section called Maine.

Late in the 1600's many communities existed along the coast of Maine and the many rivers in that section. Among them were Kittery, York, Kennebunk, Saco, Arundel (Kennebunkport), and several others which in that early period had a population of several thousand. Dissatisfaction among the early settlers toward the aristocratic regime of Gorges and his sons led to Maine's annexation to Massachusetts. After the death of King Charles in 1685, and the brief ascension of James II, Massachusetts suddenly lost all of its former legal standings, and landholders had to resecure their holdings at high fees. The new land titles were recorded in Boston, but Maine also established a special land office in York.

In those early days the population east of the Kennebec River was slim, indeed, most of the settlers gathered on the ocean shore or along the rivers between the Kennebec and the Piscataqua. Among the settlements of those early 1700's were Biddeford, opposite Saco on the southwest bank of the Saco River; Portland, then known as Falmouth Neck; Berwick, on the east side of the Piscataqua, which is the border between Maine and New Hampshire; Sanford and Alred, north of Berwick and west of Biddeford; and a long line of smaller communities extending north along the western state border, such as Hollis (Little Falls), Newfield (Hubbardstown), Waterborough (Massabesic), Limington (Ossipee), Baldwin (Flintstown), Bridgton (Bridgetown), Fryeburg (Pequawkett), and Stow.

As a county of Maine, Yorkshire from 1716 until 1760, covered the entire state. In the latter year it was divided into three counties, Lincoln, Cumberland and York. At that time the population was about 17,000 of which 10,000 lived in the cities mentioned in the sixth paragraph above. Above Oxford County, the entire section was a wilderness into which few, if any, settlers had dared to enter. For more than a hundred years transportation was one of the greatest handicaps of the settlements. Travel was mainly along the river courses. The extremely few roads then existing were in such terrible condition that the limited number of cart roads were a dread to travelers.

In 1775 both York and Biddeford were county seats or shire towns of Yorkshire, which at that time had a population of about 15,000 or about half the population of the state. Fryeburg, on the New Hampshire borderline about 65 miles north of Kittery, was made a deed registration office for the section north of the Ossipee River in 1799.

Like York County so Cumberland County had a string of fair sized communities along the coast in those early days, including Scarboro, Cape Elizabeth, Falmouth (Portland), and Yarmouth. These Cumberland County coast towns had a population of a little less than ten thousand. Among the inland plantations, running almost parallel with the coast from twelve to fifteen miles, were Gorham, Windham, New Gloucester, Gray (New Boston), Raymond, Turner (Sylvester Canada), and Harrison (Otisfield). Very few, if any, settlements existed then in the eastern part of the present Oxford County, not even a road or a trail.

From the east boundary of Cumberland extending to the Canadian line, the rest of Maine formed the large county of Lincoln. Only two towns were established along the ocean in all of that territory, Topsham in the west part of the present Sagadahoc County, and Belfast in the present Waldo County. About a dozen other small communities existed along the Kennebec River for a distance of about seventy miles from its mouth. Between the northernmost Norridgewock in the present Somerset County and the coast, some of the other towns then existing were Waterville, Winslow, Sidney, Hallowell, Gardiner (Pittston), Richmond, and Bowdoinham. Pownalborough (Dresden) was the early county seat of Lincoln County.

From 1650 to 1819, Maine was under the jurisdiction of Massachusetts. After many attempts Maine finally succeeded in breaking away in 1819. A year later she was admitted into the union as the twenty-third state.

Although the early settlers were mainly from England, many Scotch-Irish and Huguenots came during the first century. Some German families came to Waldoboro, straight west from Rockland on the southeastern Atlantic shore line, from 1740 to 1800. During the nineteenth century many artisans came from England, Scotland and the Scandinavian countries to work in factories and ship yards. About 1870 many Swedes settled in the northeast corner of the state as indicated by such Swedish place names as New Sweden, Stockholm, Jemtland, and Linneus. The large lumber camps in the northwest section of the state later beckoned many Finns.

Very early in their history, Maine towns began to keep records of births, marriages, and deaths. Notwithstanding the many repeated governmental changes during the first two hundred years the vital statistics of the territory were disturbed but little. Many of the records have been printed and are now in genealogical libraries in most of the states. Unpublished information may be searched in the various city offices in the state. The large majority of the early communities still existing have printed their town histories. Most of those histories contain genealogical information about the early settlers.

Division of Vital Statistics, Department of Human Services State House, Station 11, Augusta, Maine 04333, has records of birth, marriage, death, and divorce dating from 1892 to present dates. Adoption decrees are on file at the Probate or Superior Court where adoption was granted. These are closed records after August 8, 1953, and copies cannot be obtained without a judge of the Probate or Superior Court giving an order to release the document. Records before 1892 (about one-half million) are at the Main State Archives Building, State House, Augusta, Maine 04333.

The city clerks of nearly five hundred towns and cities are in possession of the original records of vital statistics long before 1892. Authorities have reported that "the completeness of the early records varies all the way from absent to quite complete. Portland's records, for instance, are very complete and date from 1712."

In the sixteen offices of clerks of court are the records of land titles as well as the divorce records. The sixteen registrars of probate have the settlements of estates and the adoption records. They also have the 1880 census enumerations for their respective counties, but six of the sixteen, it is reported, have strangely mislaid them. The courts are located in the county seats of each county.

War service records, including grave registrations, is under the office of the Adjutant General in Augusta.

Maine Towns Organized Before 1800

ANDROSCOGGIN COUNTY -- Durham, 1772; E. Livermore 1780; Greene, 1780; Leeds, 1780; Lewiston, 1768; Lisbon 1788; Livermore, 1779; Minot, 1769; Turner, 1772; Webster 1774.

CUMBERLAND COUNTY -- Bridgeton, 1768; Brunswick 1628; Cape Elizabeth, 1630; Casco, 1729; Cumberland, 1640 Deering 1637; Falmouth, 1632; Freeport, 1658; Gorham, 1732 Gray, 1756; Harpswell, 1659; New Gloucester, 1735; Portland 1632; Scarborough, 1631; Standish, 1763; Windham, 1735; Yarmouth, 1636.

FRANKLIN COUNTY -- Avon, 1790; Chesterville, 1782 Farmington, 1794; Freeman, 1797; Industry, 1793-4; Jay, 1795 New Sharon, 1794; Philips, 1790; Wilton, 1792.

HANCOCK COUNTY -- Blue Hill, 1762; Brookline S., 1688 Bucksport, 1764; Carline, O. 1626; Demariscotta, S. 1630 Deer Isle, O. 1789; Eastbrook, S. 1800; Eden, 1763; Ellsworth S. 1763; Gouldsborough, S. 1700; Hancock, S. 1764-5; Penobscot S. 1765; Fremont, S. 1613.

KENNEBEC COUNTY -- Augusta, 1761-2; Harrington, 1797 Belgrade, 1774; Bingham, 1784; China, 1774; Clinton, 1775 Fayette, 1779; Hallowell, 1771; Litchfield, 1795; Manchester 1774; Monmouth, 1777; Pittston bef. 1676; Vassalboro, 1760 Wayne, 1773; Waterville, 1760; Windsor, 1790; Winslow, 1771 Winthrop, 1771.

KNOX COUNTY -- Camden, 1770; Cushing, 1789; Friendship, 1750; Hope 1782; Rockland, 1767; St. George, 1635 Thomaston, 1770; Union, 1786; Vinal Haven, 1765; Warren 1736.

LINCOLN COUNTY -- Boothbay, 1630; Bremen, 1735; Dresden, 1649; Edgecomb, 1744; Jefferson, bef. Rev. New Castle, 1630; Pownalsborough, 1760; Waldoborough, 1733-40; Wiscasset, 1730.

OXFORD COUNTY -- Andover, 1789, Bethel, 1774; Brownsfield, 1770; Buckfield, 1776; Canton, 1790; Denmark, 1788-9; Dixfield, 1793; Fryeburg, 1763; Hanover, 1774; Hartford, aft-Rev. Hebron, 1778; Hiram, 1774; Lovell, 1777; Norway, 1786; Oxford, Dur. Rev. Oxford, 1780; Rumford, 1782; Waterford, 1775.

PENOBSCOT COUNTY -- Bangor, 1769; Carmel, 1695 Charlestown, 1795; Corinth, 1796; Eddington, 1785; Hampden, 1767; Orono, 1770; Orrington, 1770.

SAGADAHOC COUNTY -- Arrowsic, 1679; Bath, 1660; Bowdoin, previous Rev. Bowdoinham, 1762; Georgetown, 1716; Richmond, 1650; Sagadahoc, 1623; Topsham, 1658; Woolwich 1638.

SOMERSET COUNTY -- Anson, 1798; Athens, 1782; Cannaan, 1770; Concord, aft. Rev.; Cornville, 1794; Embden, 1779 Fairfield, 1774; Harmony, 1796; Norridgewock, aft Rev.; Skowhegan, 1792; Palmyra, 1779; Pittsfield, 1794; Waterville, 1760.

WALDO COUNTY -- Belfast, 1769; Frankfort, 1770; Freedom, 1794; Isleborough, 1769; Jackson, 1708; Monroe, 1760; Montville, 1778-9; Troy, 1778.

WASHINGTON COUNTY -- Calais, bef. 1758; Cutler, 1785; Dennyville, 1786; Eastport, 1780-2; Edmonds, 1775; Harrington, 1762; Lunec, 1776; Machias, 1762-3; Pembroke, 1774.

YORK COUNTY -- Acton, 1776; Alfred, 1764; Berwick, 1624; Biddeford, 1617-18; Buxton, 1772; Cornish, 1794; Dayton, 1664; Eliot, 1632; Hollis, 1753; Kennebunk, 1643; Kennebunkport, 1653; Kittery, 1623; Lebanon, 1746; Limerick, 1775; Lyman, 1778; N. Berwick, 1630; Parsonfield, 1772; Saco, 1653; Sanford, 1745; S. Berwick, 1624; Waterborough, 1768; Wells, 1640; York, 1663.

Genealogical Archives, Libraries, Societies, and Publications

Auburn Public Library, Court & Spring Sts., Auburn, ME 04210.

Bangor Public Library, 145 Harlow St., Bangor, ME 04401.

Camden Historical Society, 80 Mechanic St., Camden, ME 04843.

Cherryfield - Narraguagus Historical Society, P.O. Box 96, Cherryfield, ME 04622.

Kennebunk Free Library, 112 Main Street, Kennebunk, ME 04043.

Maine Genealogical Society, P.O. Box 221, Farmington, ME 04938.

Maine Historical Society, 485 Congress St., Portland, ME 04111.

Maine State Library, State House, Augusta, ME 04330.

Downeast Ancestry, P.O. Box 398, Machias, ME 04654.

Printed Census Records and Mortality Schedules

State indexes: 1790, 1800, 1810, 1820, 1830, 1840, 1850, 1860

Printed Census Records (Counties):

Cumberland-Early Settlers
Hancock-1800; 1785
Penobscot-1800, 1830

Valuable Printed Sources

Gazetteer

Varney, George Jones. *A Gazetteer of the State of Maine.* Boston: B. B. Russell (1881)

Maps

Eckstorm, Fannie Hardy. *Maine Maps of Historical Interest.* The Maine Bulletin Vol. XLII, Aug. 1939, pages ix-xxxv.

Place Names

Chadbourne, Ava Harriet. *Maine Place Names and the Peopling of Its Towns.* Portland, Maine: The Bond Wheelwright Co. (1955)

Rutherford, Phillip R. *The Dictionary of Maine Place Names.* Freeport, Maine: The Bond Wheelwright Co. (1970)

Guides To Genealogical Research

Frost, John E. *Maine Genealogy, A Bibliographical Guide.* Portland, Maine: The Maine Historical Society (1977)

New England Library Association. *Genealogist's Handbook for New England Research.* Lynnfield, Massachusetts: Bibliography Committee, 1980.

Public Record Repositories in Maine. Augusta: Maine State Archives (1976)

Wright, Norman Edgar. *Genealogy in America Vol. 1, Massachusetts, Connecticut, and Maine.* Salt Lake City, Utah: Deseret Book Company (1968)

Histories

Hatch, Louis Clint. *Maine A History.* Five Volumes. New York: The American Historical Society, 1919.

Sprague, John Francis. *Sprague's Journal of Maine History,* 14 Vols. Privately published, 1913-1926.

Genealogical Sources

Daughters of the American Revolution collection of cemetery, church, Bible, family, town, vital and other records. The records are located at the D.A.R. Library in Washington, D.C.*

Flagg, Charles Alcott. *An Alphabetical Index of Revolutionary Pensioners Living in Maine.* Baltimore: Genealogical Publishing Company, 1967.

Little, George Thomas. *Genealogical and Family History of the State of Maine,* 4 Vols. New York: Lewis Historical Publishing Company, 1909.

Noyes, Sybil, Charles Thornton Libby and Walter Goodwin Davis. *Genealogical Dictionary of Maine and New Hampshire.* Originally published in five parts in Portland, Maine (1928-1938) Reprint. Baltimore: Genealogical Publishing Company, 1973.

Province and Court Records of Maine, 5 Vols.

Sargent, William M. *Maine Wills 1670-1760.* Portland, Maine: Brown Thurston and Company, 1887.

Watson, S. M. ed. *The Maine Historical and Genealogical Recorder 1884-1898* 9 Vols. Portland, Maine, S.M. Watson.

Bibliographies

Haskel, John D. Jr. ed. *Maine, A Bibliography of Its History.* Boston: G.K. Hall & Co.

Williamson, Joseph. *A Bibliography of the State of Maine from the Earliest Period to 1891.* Portland: The Thurston Print (1896).

COUNTY MAP FOR THE STATE OF MAINE

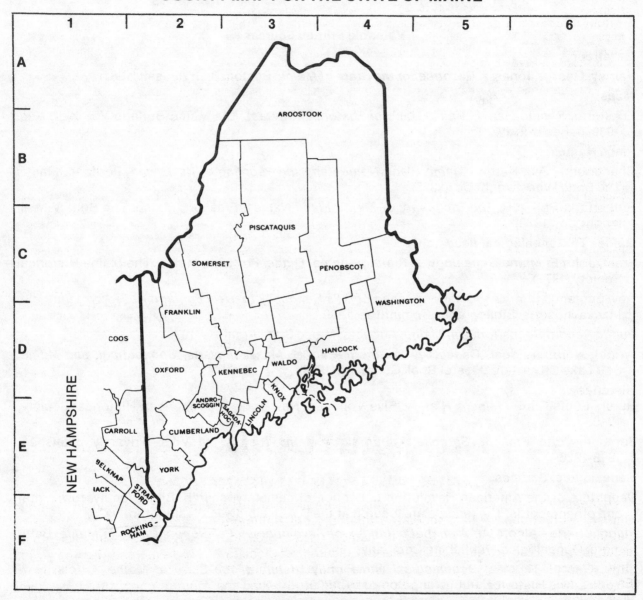

MAINE COUNTY HISTORIES
(Population figures to nearest thousand - 1980 U. S. Census)

Name	Map Index	Date Created	Pop. By M 1980	U.S. Cen Reports Available	Parent County or Territory From Which Organized	County Seat
* Androscoggin	E2	1854	100	1860-80	Cumberland, Oxford, Kennebec	Auburn 04210
(Clk Sup Ct has div, civ ct rec from 1854; City Clk has m, b, d, bur rec; Reg of Pro has pro rec)						
* Aroostook	B3	1839	91	1840-80	Washington	Houlton 04730
(Co Clk has div & civ ct rec from 1839; Twn Clks keep b, m, d & bur rec; Pro Ct has pro rec)						

Name	Map Index	Date Created	Pop. By M 1980	U.S. Cen Reports Available	Parent County or Territory From Which Organized	County Seat
* Cumberland	E2	1760	216	1800-80	York	Portland 04111

(Co Clk has div & civ ct rec; City or Twn Clks have b, m, d & bur rec; Pro Ct has pro rec)

* Franklin	D2	1838	28	1840-80	Cumberland	Farmington 04938

(Twn Clk, Farmington has b rec, m, d & bur rec; Clk Sup Ct has div rec from 1852 & civ ct rec; Reg Deeds has Ind rec; Pro Judge has pro rec)

* Hancock	D4	1789	42	1800-80	Lincoln	Ellsworth 04605

(Town Clks have b, m, d rec; Clk Cts has div, pro, civ ct, Ind rec)

* Kennebec	D3	1799	110	1800-80	Lincoln	Augusta 04330
* Knox	E3	1860	33	1860-80	Lincoln, Waldo	Rockland 04841

(Clk Cts has div, pro, civ ct & Ind rec)

* Lincoln	E3	1760	26	1800-80	York	Wiscasset 04578

(Clk Cts has m, pro, Ind rec from 1860, civ ct rec from 1861; Clk Sup Ct has pro rec from 1760)

* Oxford	D2	1805	49	1810-80	York, Cumberland	So. Paris 04281

(Twn Clks have b, m, d rec; Clk Cts has m rec from 1877 to 1897, div rec from 1930, pro, Ind rec from 1805, civ ct rec from 1930)

* Penobscot	C3	1816	137	1820-80	Hancock	Bangor 04401

(Clk Cts has div rec from 1900 & civ ct rec from 1821)

* Piscataquis	C3	1838	18	1840-80	Penobscot, Somerset	Dover-Foxcroft 04426

(Clk Cts has div, pro, civ ct, Ind rec from 1838; Town Clks have b, m, d, bur rec)

* Sagadahoc	E3	1854	29	1860-80	Lincoln	Bath 04530

(Clk Cts has pro, Ind rec from 1854, div, civ ct rec)

* Somerset	C2	1809	45	1810-80	Kennebec	Skowhegan 04976

(Clk Cts has scattered m rec from 1800, div & civ ct rec from 1827, pro & property rec from 1809)

* Waldo	D3	1827	28	1830-80	Hancock, Lincoln, Kennebec	Belfast 04915

(Co Clk has m rec from 1828 to 1887 not indexed, also has div & Sup Ct rec from 1828; Twn or City Clks have b, m, d & bur rec; Pro Ct has pro rec)

Washington	D4	1789	35	1800-80	Lincoln	Machias 04654

(Twn Clks have b, m, d, bur rec; Clk Cts has div, civ ct rec from 1931, pro rec from 1785, Ind rec from 1783, naturalizations from 1854; Div, civ ct rec prior to 1931 are in the custody of Maine State Archives, Augusta, Maine)

* York(shire)	F2	1652	139	1800-80	Original county reorg. 1658	Alfred 04002

(Civ ct, Ind, pro rec 1636 to 1929 at State Historical Bldg., Augusta, Maine; Clk Cts has pro, civ ct, Ind rec; part of 1800 census missing)

* - At least one county history has been published about this county.

MARYLAND

CAPITAL, ANNAPOLIS - STATE 1788 - (7TH)

Depressed by the constant persecution in England of the members of the Roman Catholic Church, with which he had become affiliated, Lord Baltimore (George Calvert), a member of Parliament and Secretary of State of James I from 1609 to 1625, sponsored movements to establish colonies in America for the persecuted religionists in his homeland. Failing in his first attempt to build a colony in Newfoundland about 1620, he persuaded the King of England to grant him land for a colony farther south along the Atlantic coast. After the grant was made, but before the charter had been signed, Lord Baltimore died. King Charles I then transferred the grant to Lord Baltimore's son, Cecilius Calvert, the second Lord Baltimore.

The grant included all of the land between the fortieth parallel and the southern bank of the Potomac River. The first contingent of emigrants to be shipped to the new colony in 1634 consisted of about twenty Catholic gentlemen and two hundred Protestant laborers. They established a settlement about nine miles up the St. George's River, which empties into the north side of the Potomac River, near its mouth.

Already occupying Kent Island in the Chesapeake Bay, just opposite the present site of

Annapolis, were William Claiborne, a Virginia planter, and a large group of settlers he had brought there from Virginia several years ahead of the Calvert colonists. Continuous warfare ensued between the two factions, as Claiborne refused to adhere to orders from the British King granting the territory to Lord Baltimore. It was not until Claiborne's death in 1677 that hostilities ceased.

The Maryland colony enjoyed a rapid growth. This was due, in a measure, to the pronouncement of its founder that religious toleration and protection would be extended to all Christians of whatever shade of religious belief who would come there to establish their homes. The Act Concerning Religion, passed by the colony in 1649, declared that "no person professing to believe in Jesus Christ shall henceforth be troubled or molested on account of religion."

This attracted a large group of Puritans who had become disgusted with the activities of the Church of England controlling Virginia. They left Virginia and came into Maryland. They settled and built up what is now Anne Arundel County. This influx increased the population of Maryland to about thirty thousand people.

In 1660 another migration brought many settlers to the so called Eastern Shore, the land east of Chesapeake Bay. This movement was so great it necessitated the organization of Talbot County. About five years later with the migration continuing steadily, Somerset County was formed south of Talbot.

During the first century of the settlement of Maryland, the settlers clung to the land along the many water courses, the rivers and the bays. No one ventured far away from the streams which provided about the only mode of transportation in those days. It was not until about 1740 that the Appalachian section of Maryland was claimed by settlers. English, Scotch, and Scotch-Irish emigrants came up from St. Mary's Charles and Prince George's Counties at that time. Joining with them shortly afterward were large groups of Germans who had come down from Pennsylvania. The population increased so rapidly that in 1748 Frederick County was organized in the northwest section of Maryland.

To Baltimore in 1755 came many Acadians driven from Nova Scotia. Less than forty years later another group of French people, upwards of a thousand, sought refuge in Baltimore from the race riots in Santo Domingo in 1793. From 1817 to 1847 thousands of Irish immigrants came to Baltimore as canal diggers. Later they established themselves as farmers and miners in the Appalachian section. Thousands of people who fled Germany after the 1848 Revolution in that country were given shelter in Baltimore.

The rapid increase in the Maryland population is indicated by the fact that eleven of her twenty-three counties were formed before 1700, and eight of the remaining before 1800.

Concerning vital records of Maryland, the Division of Vital Records and Statistics, Department of Health, 201 West Preston St., Baltimore, Maryland 21201, says "This office is primarily issuing copies of births, deaths and marriages. Our birth and death records cover the years 1898 to the present time. Our marriage records begin 1 June 1951. Marriage records prior to that date may be obtained from the clerk of the Circuit Court in the county of marriages. Deeds may, in some cases, be found at the Clerk of Court's office in each county. Land grants are only in custody of Land Office, Annapolis, Maryland 21401. Wills are in the Register of Wills' Office in each county."

Genealogical Archives, Libraries, Societies, and Publications

Allegany County Historical Society, 218 Washington St., Cumberland, MD 21502.

Anne Arundel Genealogical Society, P.O. Box 221, Pasadena, MD 21122.

Baltimore County Historical Society, Agriculture Bldg., 9811 Van Buren Lane, Cockreysville, MD 21030.

Calvert County Historical Society, Prince Frederick, MD 20678.

Cantonsville Historical Society, 1824 Frederick Road, Cantonsville, MD 21228.

Cecil County Historical Society, Box 11, Charlestown, MD 21914.

Dorchester County Historical Society, Meredith House, 904 LaGrange St., Cambridge, MD 21613.

Dorchester County Public Library, 305 Gay St., Cambridge, MD 21613.

Dundalk Patapsco Neck Historical Society, P.O. Box 9235, Dundalk, MD 21222.

Emmitsburg Historical Society, Emmitsburg, MD 21727.

Enoch Pratt Free Library, 400 Cathedral St., Baltimore, MD 21201.

Essex and Middle River, Heritage Society of, 113 Riverside Road, Essex, MD 21221.

Frederick County, Historical Society of, 24 E. Center St., Frederick, MD 21701.

Garrett County Historical Society, The Courthouse, Oakland, MD 21550.

Hall of Records Commission, College Ave. & St. John Sts., Annapolis, MD 21401.

Harford County Historical Society of, 324 Kenmore Ave., (The Hayes House), Bel Air, MD 21014.

Howard County Historical Society, 53 Court Ave., Ellicott City, MD 21043.

Jewish Historical Society of Maryland, Inc., 5800 Park Heights Ave., Baltimore, MD 21215.

Kent County, Historical Society of, Church Alley, Chestertown, MD 21620.

Lower Del-Mar-Va Genealogical Society, Wicomico County Library, Salisbury, MD 21801.

Maryland Genealogical Society, 201 W. Monument St., Baltimore, MD 21201.

Maryland Historical Society, 201 West Monument St., Baltimore, MD 21201.

Maryland State Library, Court of Appeals Bldg., 361 Rose Blvd., Annapolis, MD 21401.

Montgomery County Historical Society, 103 W. Montgomery Ave., (Beall-Dawson House), Rockville, MD 20850.

Old Bohemia Historical Society, Warwick, MD 21912.

Prince George's County Genealogical Society, Box 819, Bowie, MD 20715.

Prince George's County Historical Society, Montpelier Mansion, Laurel, MD 20810.

Queene Anne's County Historical Society, Wright's Chance, Commerce Street, Centreville, MD 21617.

St. Mary's County Historical Society, Leonardtown, MD 20650.

Somerset County Historical Society, Treackle Mansion, Princess Anne, MD 21853.

Talbot County, Historical Society of, 29 S. Washington St., Easton, MD 21601.

Washington County Historical Society, The Miller House, 135 W. Washington St., Hagerstown, MD 21740.

Maryland and Delaware Genealogist, The, Box 352, St. Michaels, MD 21663.

Maryland Genealogical Society Bulletin, Maryland Genealogical Society, 201 West Monument St., Baltimore, MD 21201.

Printed Census Records and Mortality Schedules

State Indexes-1790, 1800, 1810, 1820, 1830, 1840, 1850

Printed Census Records (Counties):

Allegany-1800	Dorchester-1800	Queen Mary's-1778
Anne Arundel-1800	Frederick-1800, 1850	Somerset-1800, 1850
Baltimore City-1800	Harford-1800	St. Mary's-1800, 1850
Calvert-1800	Kent-1800	Talbot-1800
Caroline-1800, 1820, 1860	Montgomery-1800, 1810; 1778	Washington-1800
Cecil-1800	Prince Georges-1800, 1850	Worcester-1800
Charles-1800	Queen Annes-1800	

Other Printed Census Records
State-1633-1680, 1776, 1778

Valuable Printed Sources

Atlases and Gazetteers

Atlases are available for Anne Arundel, Baltimore City and County, Cecil, Frederick, Montgomery, Prince George's, Washington, and all Eastern Shore counties. Various dates.

Brown, Mary Ross. *An Illustrated Genealogy of the Counties of Maryland and District of Columbia and a Guide to Locating Records.* Silver Spring, Maryland: the author.)

Gannett, Henry. *A Gazetteer of Maryland and Delaware.* Baltimore: Genealogical Publishing Company, 1976, reprinted.

Gazetteer of Maryland. Baltimore: Maryland State Planning, Commission, 1941.

Guides To Genealogical Research

McCay, Betty L. Sources for Genealogical Searching in Maryland. Indianapolis: Privately published, 1972.

Meyer, Mary K., *Research in Maryland: A Guide.* Baltimore: Maryland Historical Society, 1982.

Passano, Eleanor Phillips. *An Index of the Source Records of Maryland: Genealogical, Biographical, Historical.* Reprint. Baltimore: Genealogical Co., 1967.

Histories

Scarf, J. Thomas. *History of Maryland from the Earliest Period to the Present Day.* 3 Vols. 1879. Reprint. Hatboro, Pennsylvania: Tradition Press, 1967.

Genealogical Sources

A Guide to the Index Holdings at the Hall of Records, Bulletin No. 17. Annapolis: Hall of Records, 1972.

A Name Index to the Baltimore City Tax Records, 1798-1808, of the Baltimore City Archives. Baltimore: City Archives, 1981.

Archives of Maryland, 70 Vols. Baltimore: Maryland Historical Society.

Barnes, Robert. *Maryland Marriages, 1634-1777.* Baltimore: Genealogical Publishing Company, 1975.

Brumbaugh, Gaius Marcus and Margaret Roberts Hodges. *Revolutionary Records of Maryland* (Contains militia lists and Oaths of Allegiance). Reprint. Baltimore: Genealogical Publishing Company, 1967.

Brumbaugh, Gaius Marcus. *Maryland Records, Colonial, Revolutionary, County and Church from Original Sources.* Reprint. Baltimore: Genealogical Publishing Company, 1967.

Cotton, Jane Baldwin. *The Maryland Calendar of Wills,* 8 Vols. Baltimore: Genealogical Publishing Company, 1968.   *Vol VIII*

Hartsook, Elisabeth and Gust Skordas. *Land Office and Prerogative Court Records of Colonial Maryland.* Publication No. 4, Hall of Records Commission. Reprint. Baltimore: Genealogical Publishing Company, 1968.

Magruder, James M. Jr. *Index of Maryland Colonial Wills.* Baltimore: Genealogical Publishing Company, 1967.

Magruder, James M. *Magruder's Maryland Colonial Abstracts: Wills, Accounts, and Inventories 1772-1777.* Reprint (Five volumes in one). Baltimore: Genealogical Publishing Company, 1968.

Muster Rolls and Other Records of Service of Maryland Troops in the American Revolution. (Volume 18, Maryland Archives, 1900). Reprint. Baltimore: Genealogical Publishing Company, 1972.

Pedley, Avril J. M. *The Manuscript Collections of The Maryland Historical Society.* Baltimore: Maryland Historical Society, 1968.

Skordas, Gust. *Early Settlers of Maryland.* Baltimore: Genealogical Publishing Co., 1968, (An index to names of immigrants compiled from records of Land Patents 1633-1680 in the Hall of Records, Annapolis, Maryland.

Sullivan, Larry E. et. al. *Guide to the Research Collections of The Maryland Historical Society.* Baltimore: Maryland Historical Society, 1981.

Bibliographies

Pritchett, Morgan H. and Susan R. Woodcock. *The Eastern Shore of Maryland, an Annotated Bibliography.* Queenstown, Maryland:

COUNTY MAP FOR THE STATE OF MARYLAND

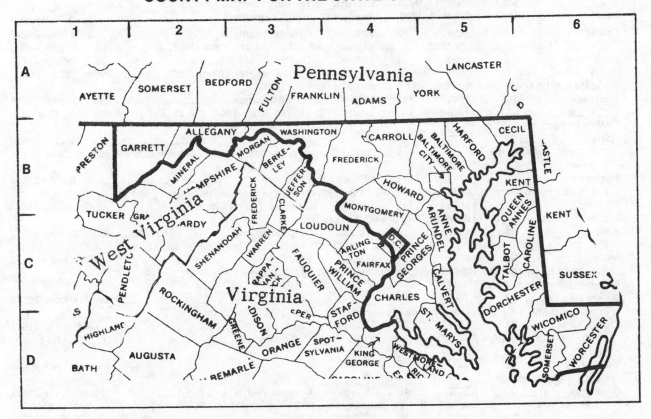

MARYLAND COUNTY HISTORIES
(Population figures to nearest thousand - 1980 U. S. Census)

Name	Map Index	Date Created	Pop. By M 1980	U.S. Cen Reports Available	Parent County or Territory From Which Organized	County Seat
*§ Allegany	B2	1789	80	1800-80	Washington	Cumberland 21502

(Clk Cir Ct has m, div, civ ct, Ind rec from 1791, naturalization rec from 1821 to 1973; Reg of Wills has pro rec; Co Health Dept and Div of Vit Recs, Baltimore, have b, d rec)

| *§ Anne Arundel | C5 | 1650 | 370 | 1790-80 | Original county | Annapolis 21404 |

(Clk Cir Ct has m rec from 1905, div & civ ct rec from 1870, Ind rec from 1851; Reg of Wills has pro rec; Hall of Rec has m rec from 1770 to 1904 also earlier rec of civ ct & Ind rec)

| * Baltimore | B5 | 1659 | 651 | 1790-80 | Original county | Towson 21204 |

(Clk Cir Ct has m, div, civ ct & Ind rec from 1851; Reg of Wills has pro rec)

| Baltimore City | B5 | 1729 | 785 | 1800-80 | Baltimore | Baltimore 21202 |

(City Health has b, d & bur rec; Com Pleas Ct has m rec; Clk Cir Ct has div rec, trust estates, adoptions & change of name from 1853; Reg of Wills has pro rec)

| * Calvert | C5 | 1654 | 34 | 1800-80 | Original county (formerly Patuxent) | Prince Frederick 20678 |

(Clk Cir Ct has m, div, civ ct & Ind rec from 1882; Reg of Wills has pro rec from 1882; Courthouse burned 1882, most rec destroyed; earlier rec available State Hall of Rec)

| * Caroline | C6 | 1773 | 23 | 1790-80 | Dorchester, Queen Annes | Denton 21629 |

(Clk Cir Ct has m, div, civ ct & Ind rec from 1774; Reg of Wills has d & pro rec)

| *§ Carroll | B4 | 1837 | 96 | 1840-80 | Baltimore, Frederick | Westminster 21157 |

(Clk Cir Ct has m rec 1837-1900 not indexed, from 1900 indexed, div, civ ct, Ind rec from 1837)

| * Cecil | B6 | 1674 | 60 | 1790-80 | Kent | Elkton 21921 |

(Clk Ct has m rec from 1777, div & civ ct rec; Health Dept, Courthouse has b rec from 1898, d rec from 1898 & bur rec; actual wills 1674 to 1850 are at Hall of Rec; Clk Ct has indices only 1674 to present)

Name	Map Index	Date Created	Pop. By M 1980	U.S. Cen Reports Available	Parent County or Territory From Which Organized	County Seat
* Charles	C4	1658	72	1790-80	Original county	La Plata 20646

(Clk Cir Ct has m rec from 1865, div, civ ct rec from 1796, Ind rec from 1658; Reg of Wills has pro rec)

* Dorchester	C5	1668	31	1790-80	Original county	Cambridge 21613

(Clk Cir Ct has m rec from 1780, div rec from 1821, civ ct rec from 1860, Ind rec from 1669, plat rec from 1912, equity dock rec from 1821 & corporation rec from 1858)

* Frederick	B4	1748	114	1790-80	Prince Georges	Frederick 21701

(Clk Cir Ct has b, d rec 1865-1870, m rec from 1778, div rec from 1807, civ ct, Ind rec from 1847; Reg of Wills has pro rec)

*§ Garrett	B2	1872	27	1880	Allegany	Oakland 21550

(Clk Cir Ct has m, div, civ ct, Ind rec from 1872; Reg of Wills has pro rec; Maryland State Health Dept has b, d rec)

* Harford	B5	1773	144	1790-80	Baltimore	Bel Air 21014

(Co Health has b & d rec; Clk Ct has m & Ind rec from 1773, div & civ ct rec from 1803)

*§ Howard	B4	1851	118	1860-80	Baltimore, Anne Arundel	Ellicott City 21043

(Clk Cir Ct has m, div, civ ct & Ind rec; Reg of wills has pro rec)

* Kent	B6	1642	17	1790-80	Original county	Chestertown 21620

(Clk Cir Ct has m rec from 1796, div rec from 1867, civ ct rec from early 1800's & Ind rec from 1656)

*§ Montgomery	B4	1776	574	1790-80	Frederick	Rockville 20850

(Clk Cir Ct has m rec from 1799, div, civ ct & Ind rec from 1776) (1830 census missing)

Patuxent (changed to Calvert, 1658)

* Prince George's	C4	1695	658	1790-80	Charles, Calvert	Upper Marlboro 20870

(many rec with Clk Cir Ct before 1785 - deeds complete - no fires) (1830 census missing)

* Queen Anne's	B5	1706	26	1790-80	Talbot	Centreville 21617

(1830 census missing) (Clk Cir Ct has m rec from 1817, div rec from 1824, also civ ct rec; Reg of Wills has pro rec)

* Saint Mary's	D5	1637	60	1790-80	Original county	Leonardtown 20650

(1830 census missing)

* Somerset	D6	1666	19	1800-80	Original county	Princess Anne 21853

(1830 census missing) (Clk Cir Ct has m, div, civ ct & Ind rec from 1666; Reg of Wills has pro rec)

* Talbot	C5	1662	25	1790-80	Kent	Easton 21601

(Clk Cir Ct has m rec from 1792, div rec from 1908, civ ct rec from 1818 & Ind rec from 1662; Reg of Wills has pro rec)

*§ Washington	B3	1776	113	1790-80	Frederick	Hagerstown 21740

(Clk Cir Ct has m rec from 1799, div, pro, civ ct & Ind rec; other rec may be found at Washington Co Free Library, Hagerstown, Md)

*§ Wicomico	D6	1867	65	1870-80	Somerset, Worcester	Salisbury 21801

(Clk Cir Ct has m, div, civ ct & Ind rec from 1867, crim rec, equity ct rec, naturalization & juvenile ct rec)

* Worcester	D6	1742	30	1790-80	Somerset	Snow Hill 21863

(Clk Cir Ct has m rec from 1866, div rec from 1900, civ ct rec from 1916; Reg of Wills has pro rec)

* - At least one county history has been published about this county.

§ - Inventory of county archives was made by the Historical Records Survey. (see introduction)

MASSACHUSETTS

CAPITAL BOSTON - STATE 1788 - (6TH)

It was on 10 November 1620, according to the calendar then in vogue, 21 November, according to our calendar that Massachusetts came into existence with the landing of the Pilgrims on Plymouth Rock. Through the initiative of the Massachusetts Bay Company another colony was formed at Salem in 1628, and two years later more than a thousand colonists arrived founding the towns of Boston, Charleston, Roxbury, Dorchester, Watertown, and New-town, which later became Cambridge. Within ten years, more than 20,000 immigrants, almost entirely British, had landed in Massachusetts. For the first 200 years or more by far the larger number of immigrants were from England.

Disasters and political troubles of various kinds in Europe from 1850 on brought a large influx from Ireland, Germany and France. A few years later Italians, Russians, Poles, and Portuguese came into the state to work in its rapidly growing factories, mills and fisheries.

Families from Dorchester, England settled in Massachusetts and then migrated to South Carolina. Three separate settlements between Charleston and Georgetown were settled by New England families.

The people of few states have been of greater assistance to the genealogical researcher than have those of Massachusetts. From its earliest days, records of all vital statistics were kept and preserved. It is said that it is easier to trace genealogy in Massachusetts than in any other state. The reason is because more records are available. Every town not only kept records from its earliest days, but has printed those records for the convenience of the researcher.

Births, marriages and deaths are recorded first at the town and city clerk's offices. Since 1841, it has been mandated that a copy of each record be sent to the State Registrar of Vital Records, Room 103, McCormack Building, 1 Ashburton Place, Boston, MA 02108. Therefore, after that date, either the town or the centralized state records may be consulted. Similar records for Boston are available since 1630 in the office of the City Registrar, Registry Division, City Hall, Boston, Mass. At the local level, prices and policies vary from town to town. At the State Vital Records Department, state-wide indexes to births, marriages and deaths greatly facilitate the search for records. The town records of deaths may show other information not on the state copy, such as name of cemetery.

Divorce records from 1887 are with the Clerk of the Superior Court or from 1972 with the Register of Probate in the county where divorce was granted.

The record of wills, deeds and land transactions are in the county offices.

The city or county assessors have all records of taxpayers.

The office of the Adjutant General controls all war service records after the Revolutionary War.

The cities and towns of no other state have so many published community histories and vital statistics as has Massachusetts. If your ancestors were there before 1850 it would be well to check with the libraries and town clerks to ascertain what information may be had from the printed records.

The present Massachusetts counties are divided into the following townships:

BARNSTABLE -- Barnstable, Bourne, Brewster, Chatham, Dennis, Eastham, Falmouth, Harwich, Mashpee, Orleans, Provincetown, Sandwich, Truro, Wellfleet, and Yarmouth.

BERKSHIRE -- Adams, Alford, Becket, Cheshire, Clarksburg, Dalton, Edgemont, Florida, Great Barrington, Hancock, Hinsdale, Lanesborough, Lee, Lenox, Monterey, Mount Washington, New Ashford, New Marlborough, North Adams, Otis, Peru, Pittsfield, Richmond, Sandisfield, Savoy, Sheffield, Stockbridge, Tyringham, Washington, West Stockbridge, Williamstown, and Windsor.

BRISTOL -- Acushnet, Attleboro, Berkley, Dartmouth, Dighton, Easton, Fairhaven, Fall River, Freetown, Mansfield, New Bedford, North Attleborough, Norton, Raynham, Rehoboth, Seekonk, Somerset, Swansea, Taunton, and Westport.

DUKES -- Chilmark, Edgartown, Gayhead, Gosnold, Oak Bluffs, Tisbury, and West Tisbury.

ESSEX -- Amesbury, Andover, Beverly, Boxford, Danvers, Essex, Georgetown, Gloucester, Groveland, Hamilton, Haverhill, Ipswich, Lawrence, Lynn, Lynnfield, Manchester, Marblehead, Merrimac, Methuen, Middleton, Nahant, Newburyport, North Andover, Peabody, Rockport, Rowley, Salem, Salisbury, Saugus, Swampscott, Topsfield, Wenham, and West Newbury.

FRANKLIN -- Ashfield, Bernardston, Buckland, Charlemont, Colrain, Conway, Deerfield, Erving, Gill, Greenfield, Hawley, Heath, Leverett, Leyden, Monroe, Montague, New Salem, Northfield, Orange, Rowe, Shelburne, Shutesbury, Sunderland, Warwick, Wendell, and Whately.

HAMPDEN -- Agawam, Blandford, Brimfield, Chester, Chicopee, East Longmeadow, Granville, Hampden, Holland, Holyoke, Longmeadow, Ludlow, Monson, Montgomery, Palmer, Russell, Southwick, Springfield, Tolland, Wales, Westfield, West Springfield, and Wilbraham.

HAMPSHIRE -- Amherst, Belchertown, Chesterfield, Cummington, Easthampton, Goshen, Granby, Hadley, Hatfield, Huntington, Middlefield, Northampton, Pelham, Plainfield, South Hadley, Southampton, Ware, Westhampton, Williamsburg, and Worthington.

MIDDLESEX -- Acton, Arlington, Ashby, Ashland, Ayer, Bedford, Belmont, Billerica, Boxborough, Burlington, Cambridge, Carlisle, Chelmsford, Concord, Dracut, Dunstable, Everett, Framingham, Groton, Holliston, Hopkinton, Hudson, Lexington, Lincoln, Littleton, Lowell, Malden, Marlborough, Medford, Melrose, Natick, Newton, North Reading, Pepperell, Reading, Sherborn, Shirley, Somrville, Stoneham, Stow, Sudbury, Tewksbury, Townsend, Tyngsborough, Wakefield, Waltham, Watertown, Wayland, Westford, Weston, Wilmington, Winchester, and Woburn.

NANTUCKET -- Nantucket.

NORFOLK -- Avon, Bellingham, Braintree, Brookline, Canton, Cohasset, Dedham, Dover, Foxborough, Franklin, Holbrook, Medfield, Medway, Millis, Milton, Needham, Norfolk, Norwood, Plainville, Quincy, Randolph, Sharon, Stoughton, Walpole, Wellesley, Westwood, Weymouth, and Wrentham.

PLYMOUTH -- Abington, Bridgewater, Brockton, Carver, Duxbury, East Bridgewater, Halifax, Hanover, Hanson, Hingham, Hull, Kingston, Lakeville, Marion, Marshfield, Mattapoisett, Middleborough, Norwell, Pembroke, Plymouth, Plympton, Rochester, Rockland, Scituate, West Bridgewater, Wareham, and Whitman.

SUFFOLK -- Boston, Chelsea, Revere, and Winthrop.

WORCESTER -- Ashburnham, Athol, Auburn, Barre, Berlin, Blackstone, Bolton, Boylston, Brookfield, Charlton, Clinton, Douglas, Dudley, East Brookfield, Fitchburg, Gardner, Grafton, Hardwick, Harvard, Holden, Hopedale, Hubbardston, Lancaster, Leicester, Leominster, Lunenburg, Mendon, Milford, Millbury, Millville, New Braintree, North Borough, Northbridge, North Brookfield, Oakham, Oxford, Paxton, Petersham, Phillipston, Princeton, Royalston, Rutland, Shrewsbury, Southborough, South Bridge, Spencer, Sterling, Sturbridge, Sutton, Templeton, Upton, Uxbridge, Warren, Webster, Westborough, West Brookfield, West Boylston, Westminster, Winchendon, and Worcester.

MASSACHUSETTS TOWNS ORGANIZED
Before 1800

BARNSTABLE COUNTY -- Barnstable, 1638, Chatham, 1712, Dennis, 1798; Eastham, 1651; Falmouth, 1694; Harwich, 1694; Nauset, 1643; Orleans, 1747; Provincetown from Eastham, Sandwich, 1630; Suckanasset, 1670; Truro, 1709; Wellfleet, 1763; Yarmouth, 1639.

BERKSHIRE COUNTY -- Adams, 1778; Alford, 1773; Becket, 1765; Chesshire, 1793; Clarksburg, 1798; Dalton, 1784; Egremont, 1760; Gagesborough, 1771; Great Barrington, 1761; Hancock, 1776; Lanesborough, 1765; Lee, 1777; Lenox, 1767; Loudon, 1773; Mount Washington, 1779; New Ashford, 1781; New Marlborough, 1759; Partridgefield, 1771; Pittsfield, 1771; Richmont, 1766; Richmond, 1785; Sandisfield, 1762; Savoy, 1797; Sheffield, 1733; Stockbridge, 1739; Tyringham, 1762; Washington, 1777; W. Stockbridge, 1774; Williamtown, 1765; Windsor, 1778.

BRISTOL COUNTY -- Attleboro, 1694; Berkley, 1735; Dartmouth, 1652; Dighton, 1712; Easton, 1725; Freetown, 1683; Mansfield, 1770; New Bedford, 1787; Norton, 1710; Raynham, 1731; Rehoboth, 1645; Somerset, 1790; Swansea, 1668; Taunton, 1639; Westport, 1787.

DUKES COUNTY -- Chilmark, 1695; Edgartown, 1671; Tisbury, 1671; Orig. Middletowne.

ESSEX COUNTY -- Amesbury, 1668, name changed from Salisbury-new-town; Andover, 1646; Beverly, 1668; Boxford, 1694; Bradford, 1675; Danvers, 1752; Gloucester, 1642; Hamilton, 1793; Haverhill, 1641; Ipswick, 1634; Lynn, 1637; Lynnfield, 1782; Manchester, 1645; Marblehead, 1633; Methuen, 1725; Middletown, 1728; Newbury, 1635; Newburyport, 1764; Rowley, 1639; Salem, 1630; Salisbury, 1640; Saugus, 1631, name changed to Lynn; 1782; Topsfield, 1648; Wenham, 1643.

FRANKLIN COUNTY -- Ashfield, 1765; Bernardstown, 1765; Buckland, 1779; Charlemont, 1765; Colrain, 1761; Conway, 1767; Deerfield, 1677; Gill, 1793; Greenfield, 1753; Hawley, 1792; Heath, 1785; Huntstown, 1736; Leverett, 1774; Leyden, 1784; Montague, 1754; New Salem, 1753; Northfield, 1714; Orange, 1783; Rowe, 1785; Sherburne, 1786; Shutesbury, 1761; Sunderland, 1718; Warwick, 1763; Wendall, 1781; Whateley, 1771.

HAMPDEN COUNTY -- Blandford, 1741, Orig. Glasgow; Brimfield, 1714; Chester, 1783; Orig. Murrayfield; Granville, 1754; Longmeadow, 1783; Ludlow, 1774; Monson, 1760; Montgomery, 1780; Murrayfield, 1765; Palmer, 1752; Russell, 1792; South Brimfield, 1762; Southwick, 1770; Springfield, 1641; Westfield, 1669; West Springfield, 1774; Wilbraham, 1763.

HAMPSHIRE COUNTY -- Amherst, 1759; Belchertown, 1761; Chesterfield, 1762; Cummington, 1779; Easthampton, 1785; Goshen, 1781; Granby, 1768; Greenwich, 1754; Hadley, 1661; Hatfield, 1670; Middlefield, 1783; Northampton, 1656; Norwich, 1773; Pelham, 1743; Plainfield, 1785; Southampton, 1753; South Hadley, 1783; Ware, 1761; Westhampton, 1775; Williamsburg, 1771; Worthington, 1768.

MIDDLESEX COUNTY -- Acton, 1755; Ashby, 1767; Bedford, 1729; Billerica, 1655; Boxborough, 1783; Burlington, 1799; Cambridge, 1630; Carlisle, 1780; Charlestown, 1630; Chelmsford, 1655; Concord, 1635; Dracut, 1702; Dunstable, 1680; E. Sudbury, 1780; Framingham, 1675; Groton, 1655; Holliston, 1724; Hopkinston, 1715; Lexington, 1713; Littleton, 1715; Malden, 1649; Marlborough, 1660; Medford, 1630; Natick, 1661; Newton, 1691; Pepperell, 1733; Reading, 1644; Sherburn, 1674; Shirley, 1753; Stoneham, 1725; Stow, 1683; Sudbury, 1639; Tewksbury, 1734; Townsend, 1732; Tynesborough, 1732; Waltham, 1738; Watertown, 1630; Westford, 1729; Weston, 1713; Wilmington, 1730; Woburn, 1642.

NANTUCKET COUNTY Orig. 1695 (Island) -- Nantucket, 1795; Sherburn, 1687.

NORFOLK COUNTY -- Bellingham, 1719; Braintree, 1640; Brookline, 1705; Canton, 1797; Cohasset, 1700; Dedham, 1636; Dorchester, 1630; Dover, 1784; Foxsborough, 1778; Franklin, 1778; Medfield, 1650; Medway, 1713; Milton, 1652; Needham, 1711; Quincy, 1792; Randolph, 1793; Roxbury, 1630; Sharon, 1783; Stoughton, 1726; Stoughtonham, 1765; Walpole, 1724; W. Roxbury, 1772; Weymouth, 1635; Wrentham, 1673.

PLYMOUTH COUNTY -- Abington, 1712; Bridgewater, 1656; Carver, 1790; Duxbury, 1637; Halifax, 1734; Hanover, 1727; Hingham, 1635; Hull, 1644; Kingston, 1726; Marshfield, 1642; Middleborough, 1669; Pembroke, 1712; Plymouth, 1620; Plympton, 1707; Rexhame, 1642, name changed to Marshfield. Rochester, 1686; Scituate, 1633; Wareham, 1739.

SUFFOLK COUNTY -- Boston, 1630; Chelsea, S. 1739.

WORCESTER COUNTY -- Ashburnham, 1765; Athol, 1762; Barre, 1776, Berlin, 1784; Bolton, 1738; Boyleston, 1786; Brookfield, 1673; Charlton, 1755; Douglas, 1746; Dudley, 1732; Fitchburg, 1764; Gardner, 1785; Gerry, 1786; Grafton, 1735; Hardwick, 1739; Harvard, 1732; Holden, 1741; Hubbardtown, 1767; Hutchinson, 1774; Lancaster, 1653; Leicester, 1713; Leominster, 1740; Luenberg, 1728; Mendon, 1667; Milford, 1780; New Braintree, 1751; New Sherburn, 1745; Northborough, 1766; Northbridge, 1772; Oakham, 1693; Oxford, 1693; Paxton, 1765; Petersham, 1754; Princeton, 1759; Royalston, 1765; Rutland, 1714; Shrewsbury, 1720; Southborough, 1727; Spencer, 1753; Sterling, 1781; Sturbridge, 1738; Sutton, 1714; Templeton, 1762; Upton, 1735; Uxbridge, 1727, Westborough, 1717; Western, 1742; Westminister, 1759; Winchenden, 1754; Worcester, 1684.

Genealogical Archives, Libraries, Societies, and Publications

Attleboro Public Library, 74 N. Main St., Attleboro, MA 02703.

Berkshire Athenaeum, The, 1 Wendell Ave., Pittsfield, MA 01201.

Berkshire Chapter, Massachusetts Society of Genealogists, Inc., Box 1437, Pittsfield, MA 01201.

Bristol Chapter, Massachusetts Society of Genealogists, Inc., 16 R. Trim, Rehoboth, MA 02769.

Boston Public Library, P.O. Box 286, Boston, MA 02117.

Brockton Public Library, 304 Main St., Brockton, MA 02401.

Danvers Historical Society, Danvers, MA 01923.

Dedham Historical Society, 612 High St., Dedham, MA 02026.

Eastham Public Library, Box 338, Samoset Rd., Eastham, MA 02642.

Essex Society of Genealogists, c/o Public Library, Lynnfield, MA 01940.

Essex Institute, 132 Essex St., Salem, MA 01970.

Forbes Library, 20 West St., Northampton, MA 01060.

Greenfield Public Library, 402 Main St., Greenfield, MA 01301.

Hampden Chapter, Massachusetts Society of Genealogists, G.P.O. Box 294, Chicopee, MA 01021.

Haverhill Public Library, 99 Main St., Haverhill, MA 01830.

Jones Library, 43 Amity St., Amherst, MA 01002.

Lynn Public Library, 5 N. Common St., Lynn, MA 01902.

Lynnfield Public Library, 18 Summer St., Lynnfield, MA 01940.

Massachusetts Historical Society, 1154 Boylston St., Boston, MA 02215.

Massachusetts Society of Genealogists, Inc., Box 215, Ashland, MA 01721.

Massachusetts State Library, Beacon Hill, Boston, MA 02155.

Medford Historical Society, 10 Governors Ave., Medford, MA 02155.

Middleborough Historical Association, Inc., Jackson St., Middleboro, MA 02346.

Middlesex (Southern), Chapter, Massachusetts Society of Genealogists, 33 Bigelow Road, Waltham, MA 02154.

New Bedford Massachusetts City Library, Pleasant St., New Bedford, MA 02740.

New England Historic Genealogical Society, 101 Newbury St., Boston, MA 02116.

Norfolk Chapter Massachusetts Society of Genealogists, Inc., Box 55, Walpole, MA 02081.

Old Colony Historical Society, 66 Church Green, Taunton, MA 02780.

Peabody Historical Society, 35 Washington Street, Peabody, MA 01960.

Springfield City Library, 220 State Street, Springfield, MA 01103.

Sturgis Library, Main St., Barnstable, MA 02630.

Swansea Free Public Library, 69 Main St., Swansea, MA 02777.

Western Massachusetts Genealogical Society, P.O. Box 206, Forest Park Station, Springfield, MA 01108.

Winchester Historical Society, c/o Mrs. Robert Bairnsfather, 1 Copley Street, Winchester, MA 01890.

Yarmouth Library, 297 Main St., Yarmouth Port, MA 02675.

Essex Genealogist, The, M. W. Wiswall, Editor, c/o Lynnfield Public Library, 18 Summer St., Lynnfield, MA 01940.

Massog, publication of the Massachusetts Society of Genealogists, Inc., Box 215 Ashland, MA 01721.

New England Historical and Genealogical Register, The, New England Historic Genealogical Society, 101 Newbury St., Boston, MA 02116.

Printed Census Records and Mortality Schedules

State Indexes-1790, 1800, 1810, 1820, 1830, 1840, 1850

Printed Census Records

Hampden County-1790, 1800
1620-1720-Pioneers
1623-1627-Plymouth Colony
1779-Short Census of Massachusetts

Valuable Printed Sources

Atlases and Gazetteers

Gannett, Henry. *A Geographic Dictionary of Massachusetts.* Originally published in 1894. Reprint. Baltimore: Genealogical Publishing Company (1978).

Nason, Rev. Elias. *A Gazetteer of the State of Massachusetts.* Boston: B. B. Russell (1874).

Place Names

Guzzi, Paul. *Historical Data Relating to Counties, Cities and Towns in Massachusetts.* The Commonwealth of Massachusetts (1975).

Guides To Genealogical Research

Barlow, Claude W. *New England Genealogy: A Research Guide with Special Emphasis on Massachusetts and Connecticut,* 1976.

New England Library Association. *Genealogist's Handbook for New England Research.* Lynnfield, Massachusetts: Bibliography Committee, 1980.

Wright, Norman E. *Genealogy in America: Massachusetts, Connecticut, and Maine.* Salt Lake City: Deseret Book, (1968).

Histories

Barber, John Warner. *Historical Collections, Relating to the History and Antiquities of Every Town in Massachusetts with Geographical Descriptions.* Worcester, Massachusetts: Dorr, Howland and Company, 1840.

Encyclopedia of Massachusetts. Chicago: The American Historical Society, 13 Vols.

Hutchinson, Thomas. *The History of the Colony and Province of Massachusetts Bay.* Cambridge, Massachusetts: Harvard University Press, 1936. 3 Vols.

Genealogical Sources

Bailey, Frederic W. *Early Massachusetts Marriages.* Baltimore: Genealogical Publishing Company, reprinted 1968.

Boston Public Library Collection includes Colonial and Massachusetts newspapers; an index to the Boston Evening Transcript Genealogical Column with micro-cards of the columns; the Hartford Times genealogical columns; passenger lists; microfiche collection of city directories for Boston and other cities; indexes and probate court records for Suffolk and Middlesex Counties.

Copies of early Massachusetts newspapers - American Antiquarian Society, Massachusetts Historical society and other libraries.

D.A.R.; S.A.R.; and other lineage societies have compiled records for the colonial period in printed books and on microfilm.

Jones, E. Alfred. *The Loyalists of Massachusetts Their Memorials, Petitions and Claims.* Baltimore: Genealogical Publishing Company, reprinted 1969.

Lists of Persons Whose Names Have Been Changed in Massachusetts 1780-1892. Boston: Wright and Potter Printing Company State Printers, 1893.

Massachusetts Soldiers and Sailors of the Revolutionary War, 17 Vols. A Compilation from the Archives prepared and published by the Secretary of the Commonwealth 1896-1908. Boston: Wright and Potter Printing Co. State Printers.

New England Historic Genealogical Society Collection includes family genealogies, local histories, manuscript collection, indexes, and periodicals.

Bibliographies

Haskell, John D. Jr. ed. *Massachusetts: A Bibliography of Its History.* Boston: G. K. Hall and Company, 1976.

New England Library Association Bibliography Committee. *A Genealogist's Handbook For New England Research,* 1980. Lynnfield, Massachusetts.

COUNTY MAP FOR THE STATE OF MASSACHUSETTS

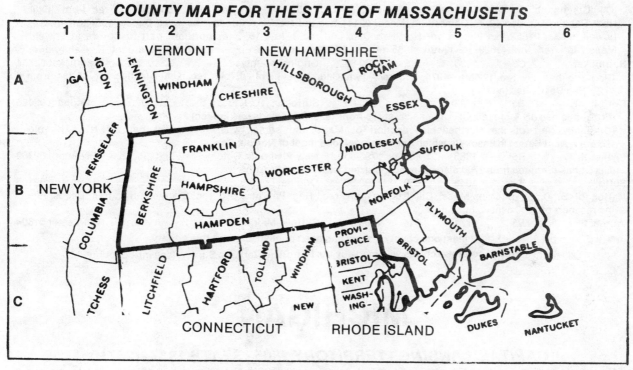

MASSACHUSETTS COUNTY HISTORIES
(Population figures to nearest thousand - 1980 U. S. Census)

Name	Map Index	Date Created	Pop. By M 1980	U.S. Cen Reports Available	Parent County or Territory From Which Organized	County Seat
* Barnstable	B6	1685	148	1790-80	New Plymouth Colony	Barnstable 02630
(Clk Cir Ct has div & civ ct rec from 1828)						
* Berkshire	B2	1760	145	1790-80	Hampshire	Pittsfield 01201
(Clk Cts has div rec from 1761 to 1922, civ ct rec from 1761; Pro Judge has div rec from 1922 & pro rec from 1761)						
* Bristol	C5	1685	474	1790-80	New Plymouth Colony	Taunton 02780
						New Bedford 02740 & Fall River 02720
(Clk Cts has civ ct rec from 1796, also naturalization rec; bur rec are at cem; b, m, d rec are at city offices; Pro Ct has div rec from 1921 also pro rec)						
* Dukes	C5	1695	9	1790-80	(Martha's Vineyard)	Edgartown 02539
(Clk Cts has div rec & sup ct rec from 1859; Pro Ct has pro rec; Twn Clks have b, m, d & bur rec)						

Name	Map Index	Date Created	Pop. By M 1980	U.S. Cen Reports Available	Parent County or Territory From Which Organized	County Seat
*§ Essex	A4	1643	632	1790-80	Original county . . . . Lawrence 01842 Newburyport 01950 & Salem 01970	
* Franklin	B2	1811	64	1820-80	Hampshire . . . . Greenfield 01301	

(Clk Cts has div rec from 1811 in concurrent jurisdiction with pro ct; Clk Cts has civ ct rec from 1811 in concurrent jurisdiction with Dis Ct & Sup Judicial Ct; Reg Pro has pro rec; Reg Deeds has lnd rec)

* Hampden	B2	1812	443	1820-80	Hampshire . . . . Springfield 01103	

(Clk Cts has most div rec from 1812 to 1932 & civ ct rec)

* Hampshire	B2	1662	139	1790-80	Middlesex . . . . Northampton 01061	

(City Clks have b, m & d rec; Hampshire Sup Ct or Pro Ct has div rec; Pro Ct has pro rec; Sup Ct has civ ct rec)

* Middlesex	B4	1643	1,367	1790-80	Original county . . . . Cambridge 02141 & Lowell 01850	

(Clk Cts has b rec 1632-1745, m rec 1651-1793, d rec 1651-1689, div rec from 1888, civ ct rec from 1648; Rcdr Deeds, P.O. Box 68, E. Cambridge, Mass. 02141 has lnd rec for Southern Dis.; Reg Deeds, 360 Gorham St., Lowell, Mass. 01852 has lnd rec for Northern Dis.; Lnd rec 1 July 1855 for northern part of Co are at Lowell, Mass., lnd rec from 1639 to 1 July 1855 for all of Co and then up to the present are at E. Cambridge)

* Nantucket	C6	1695	5	1790-80	Original county . . . . Nantucket 02554	

(Reg Pro has div rec 1922 to 1979, pro rec; Twn Clks have b, m, d, bur rec; Clk Cts has civ ct rec from 1721; Reg Deeds has lnd rec)

* Norfolk	B5	1793	604	1800-80	Suffolk . . . . Dedham 02026	

(Pro Judge has div & pro rec; Clk Cts has civ ct rec from 1928; Reg Deeds has lnd rec)
(Originally part of the Northeastern section of Mass and some twns at present part of NH, The old rec are now at Salem in Essex Co which originally included most of Norfolk Co)

* Plymouth	B5	1685	405	1790-80	New Plymouth Colony . . . . Plymouth 02362	

(Clk Ct has civ ct rec from 1700 also div rec concurrent with Reg of Pro)

* Suffolk	B4	1643	650	1790-80	Original county . . . . Boston 02108	

(Reg of B, D, M, Boston, Mass; Clk Cts has div rec; Reg Pro has pro rec & civ ct rec; Reg Deeds has lnd rec; part of 1800 census missing)

* Worcester	B3	1731	644	1790-80	Suffolk, Middlesex . . . . Worcester 01604	

* - At least one county history has been published about this county.

§ - Inventory of county archives was made by the Historical Records Survey. (see introduction)

MICHIGAN

CAPITAL, LANSING - TERRITORY 1805 - STATE 1837 - (26TH)

For some time after France obtained possession of American territory, a considerable outpost had been maintained at Detroit. This regime came to an end in 1763. Michigan then became part of Quebec Territory, under which jurisdiction it remained for twenty years.

It was in 1783 that it was again under the claim of America. For a short time, the Indians, urged on by the British, inflicted considerable damage to the Americans in that section. This ended about 1795 when American troops under the command of General Anthony Wayne cleared up the situation by herding the Indians farther west.

From 1787 until 1800 the Michigan section was part of the Northwest Territory, and from 1800 to 1805 it was connected with the Ohio and the Indian Territories.

Although the first American settlers began coming to Michigan from New England about 1796, it was not until about twenty-two years later that any appreciable influx of settlers was noted. Many came in 1818 to participate in the first public land sales. The commencing of work on the Erie Canal in that year drew many New Englanders to the Michigan sections. The completion of that important canal in 1825 added new stimula to the migrations. That same year many came to work on the road construction headed toward Chicago.

With the construction of the territorial road through the Kalamazoo Valley in 1829, many

New Englanders established themselves in the Jackson, Calhoun, Kalamazoo, and Allegan Counties. The following year saw the Saginaw Valley, including the counties of Shiawassee, Saginaw and Bay, beginning to fill up with permanent residents. The growth was so constant and rapid during the first years of the new century that by 1836 fourteen counties were established in the territory.

By 1840 the immigration increased to such an extent that about half of the southern peninsula was cultivated by eager land seekers who came from New York, the New England section, and from Germany.

A fifty-year boom, from 1840 to 1890, attracted tens of thousands of workers into the lumber camps and the mining camps of Michigan, where they extracted the valuable and plentiful copper and iron ores from the rich mineral deposits of the state.

To secure the needed manpower to work these rich deposits men were induced to come there from Canada, Ireland, Finland, Norway, Sweden, Wales, Poland, Italy and England. The tin mines of Cornwall, England, transplanted hundreds of expert miners into the Michigan mining camps.

Also during that time large groups of religious refugees from Holland settled around Grand Rapids and the western coast of the state.

Birth, marriage, and death records before 1867 are handled by the Clerk of the Circuit Court where incident occurred, since then at the State Department of Public Health, P.O. Box 30035, Lansing, Michigan 48909, and at the Office of the County Clerk. The Clerk of the Probate Court supervises all court records, such as wills, and probate matters. The Register of Deeds of each county handles all matters pertaining to land titles. County Clerks have many vital records, see county histories.

Genealogical Archives, Libraries, Societies, and Publications

Archives & Regional History Collections, Western Michigan University, Kalamazoo, MI 49001.

Bentley Historical Library, Michigan Historical Collections, University of Michigan, Ann Arbor 48104.

Bay County Genealogical Society, P.O. Box 27, Essexville, MI 48732.

Burton Historical Collection of the Detroit Public Library, 5201 Woodward Avenue, Detroit, MI 48202.

Central Michigan University Library, Mt. Pleasant, MI 48858.

Clarke Historical Library, Central Michigan University, Mt. Pleasant, MI 48858.

Clinton County Genealogical Society, 110 Lewis Street, St. Johns, MI 48879.

Dearborn Genealogical Society, P.O. Box 1112, Dearborn, MI 48121.

Detroit Society for Genealogical Research, Detroit Public Library, 5201 Woodward Ave., Detroit, MI 48202.

Flat River Historical Society, 302 S. Lafayette St., Greenville, MI 48838.

Flint Genealogical Society, P.O. Box 1217, Flint, MI 48501.

Flint Public Library, 1026 E. Kearsley, Flint, MI 48502.

Genealogical Association of Southwestern Michigan, Box 573, St. Joseph, MI 49085.

Genealogical Society of Monroe County, Michigan, 126 S. Monroe Street, Monroe, MI 48161.

Genealogical Society of Washtenaw County, Michigan, Inc., P.O. Box 7155, Ann Arbor, MI 48107.

Grand Rapids Public Library, 60 Library Plaza, N.E., Grand Rapids, MI 49502.

Herrick Public Library, 300 River Ave., Holland, MI 49423.

Jackson Public Library, 244 W. Michigan Ave., Jackson, MI 49201.

Kalamazoo Valley Genealogical Society, 315 So. Rose St., Kalamazoo, MI 49006.

Macomb County Genealogy Group, Mount Clemens Public Library, 150 Cass Ave., Mount Clemens, MI 48043.

Mason County Historical Society, 1687 S. Lake Shore Drive, Ludington, MI 49431.

Michigan Army National Guard, Retirement Section, 2500 S. Washington Ave., Lansing, MI 48909 W.W.I + records.

Michigan Historical Comm., 505 State Office Bldg., Lansing, MI 48913.

Michigan State Library, 735 East Michigan Ave., Lansing, MI 48933.

Midland County Historical Society, 1710 W. St. Andrews Dr., Midland, MI 48640.

Midland Genealogical Society, 1201 Glendale, Midland, MI 48640.

Mid-Michigan Genealogical Society, c/o 3800 Glasgow Drive, Lansing, MI 48910.

Monroe County, Michigan Genealogical Society, 126 S. Monroe Street, Monroe, MI 48161.

Mt. Clemens Public Library, 150 Cass Ave., Mt. Clemens, MI 48403.

Northeast Michigan Genealogical Society, c/o Jesse Besser Museum, 491 Johnson Street, Alpena, MI 49707.

North Oakland Genealogical Society, 845 S. Lapeer Road, Lake Orion Library, Lake Orion, MI 48035.

Northwest Oakland County Historical Society, 423 N. Saginaw St., Holly, MI 48442.

Oakland County Genealogical Society, c/o Royal Oak Public Library, 211 East 11 Mile Road, Royal Oak, MI 48068.

Ogemaw Genealogical and Historical Society, c/o West Branch Public Library, West Branch, MI 48661.

Peter White Public Library, 217 N. Front, Marquette, MI 49855.

Pontiac Area Historical and Genealogical Society, 35 Huron Street, Furlong Building, Pontiac, MI 48056.

Saginaw Genealogical Society, c/o Saginaw Public Library. 505 Janes Ave., Saginaw, MI 48507.

Shiawassee County Genealogical Society, P.O. Box 145, Owosso, MI 48867.

Shiawassee County Historical Society, Room 302, Mathews Building, Owosso, MI 48867.

Sturgis Public Library, N. Nottawa at West St., Sturgis, MI 49091.

Webster Memorial Library, 200 Phelps St., Decatur, MI 49045.

Western Michigan Genealogical Society, Ryerson Library Bldg., Grand Rapids, MI 49502.

Western Wayne County Genealogical Society, P.O. Box 63, Livonia, MI 48152.

Westland Michigan Genealogical Library, P.O. Box 70, Westland, MI 48185.

Detroit Society For Genealogical Research Magazine, The, c/o Burton Historical Collection, Detroit Public Library, 5201 Woodward Ave., Kirby, Detroit, MI 48202.

The Flint Genealogical Quarterly, P.O. Box 1217, Flint, MI 48501.

Heir-Lines, North Oakland Genealogical Society, Lake Orion Library, Lake Orion, MI 48035.

Michigan Newsletter, publication of the Kalamazoo Valley Genealogical Society, 315 South Rose Street, Kalamazoo, MI 49006.

Pioneer Record, Midland Genealogical Society, 1201 Glendale, Midland, MI 48640.

Timbertown Log, Saginaw Genealogical Society, Saginaw Public Library, 505 Janes Ave., Saginaw, MI 48607.

Printed Census Records and Mortality Schedules

Territory and State Indexes-1820, 1830, 1840, 1850

Printed Census Records (Counties):

Allegan-1840	Livingston-1850	Ontonagon-1850
Berrien-1830	Mackinac-1850	Saginaw-1850
Detroit-1860	Macomb-1880	Saint Clair-1850
Eaton-1850	Manistee-1850	Saint Joseph-1850;1845
Emmet-1884	Marquette-1850	Sanilac-1850
Gladwin-1850	Mason-1850, 1860, 1870	Schoolcraft-1850
Hillsdale-1850	Mecosta-1880	Shiawassee-1850,1860
Huron-1850	Michilimackinac-1850	Tuscola-1850
Ingham-1840, 1850	Midland-1850	Van Buren-1840, 1850, 1860
Kalamazoo-1850;1837	Neewago-1850	Washtenaw-1827-1834, 1845
Lenawee-1830, 1850	Oceana-1850	Wayne-1850, 1860; 1799, 1806, 1827

Family Trails, Winter Issue 1968/69 featured an article "Census Record Transcriptions Available at the Michigan State Library".

Mortality Schedules (Printed): 1850

Valuable Printed Sources

Atlases and Gazetteers

Blois, John T. *Gazetteer of the State of Michigan.* Detroit: S. L. Rood and Company (1839).

Miles, William. *Michigan Atlases and Plat Books: A Check List 1872-1973.* Lansing: Michigan Department of Education State Library Services (1975), (Out of print)

Books On Early Place Names

Romig, Walter. *Michigan Place Names.* Grosse Pointe, Michigan: W. Romig 1972

Welch, Richard. *County Evolution in Michigan 1790-1897.* Lansing, Michigan: State Library, 1972.

William, Ethel W. *The Counties and Townships of Michigan Past and Present.* Kalamazoo: Published privately (1973) (Out of print but available in genealogical libraries).

Guides to Genealogical Research In Michigan

Anderson, Alloa and Polly Bender. *Genealogy in Michigan What, When, Where.* Ann Arbor: Published privately (1977).

Kellog, Lucy Mary. *Guide to Ancestral Trails in Michigan.* Detroit: Detroit Society for Genealogical Research. (1961) Revised 1970, 1981 in progress.

Michigan Cemetery Compendium. Spring Arbor, Michigan: HAR-AL, Inc. 1979.

Histories and Biographies

Michigan Pioneer and Historical Collections. Lansing: 1874-1929. 42 Volumes.

Michigan Biography Index, 10 Volumes. Detroit: Detroit Public Library, 1946. (Typescript. Located in a few large Michigan libraries.)

Moore, Charles. *History of Michigan.* Chicago: Lewis Publishing Company, 1915.

Genealogical Sources

Genealogy of the French Families of the Detroit River Region. Detroit: Detroit Society for Genealogical Research, 1976. Two Volumes.

Michigan Newspapers on Microfilm. Lansing: Michigan State Library, 1975.

Record of Service of Michigan Volunteers in the Civil War. Lansing: State of Michigan, ca 1915. 48 Volumes.

Stevens, Wystan, ed. *Directory of Historical Collections and Society in Michigan.* Ann Arbor: Historical Society of Michigan (1973).

Warner, Robert M. and Ida C. Brown. *Guide to Manuscripts in the Michigan Historical Collections of the University of Michigan.* Ann Arbor (1963).

Bibliographies

Michigan County Histories A Bibliography. Lansing: Michigan State Library, 1978.

The Michigan Unit, Department of Education, State Library Services, offers the following:

The Michigan Unit:

Maintains a research and circulating collection of historical and current books, pamphlets, maps, ephemera and newspapers which provide information on all aspects of Michigan and the Great Lakes.

Provides access to State of Michigan publications by acquiring and distributing state documents to selected Michigan libraries and by issuing a quarterly index on microfiche titled *Michigan Documents.*

Assists in using magazines published in Michigan by subscribing to over 300 titles and by issuing a quarterly index on microfiche titled *Michigan Magazine Index.*

Supplies, through the State Library's Audio-Visual Unit, films, filmstrips, cassettes and slides about Michigan and the Great Lakes.

Compiles, publishes and distributes publications such as *Michigan in Books* (semi-annual), *Family Trails* (semi-annual), *Michigan in Brief,* and bibliographies like *Michigan County Histories, Native Americans of Michigan* and *Selected List of Recommended Michigan Books and Pamphlets.*

Advises consultants, teachers, librarians and media specialists in developing collections of Michigan materials and courses relating to Michigan.

The Michigan Unit Genealogy Sources:

Contains an extensive collection of local histories, census schedules, copies of records, family histories and other genealogical material to assist students discover their family background.

Does not circulate out of the building (except for several handbooks, manuals and filmstrips), but staff members will assist students and adults who come to the library to use the material.

Staff will work with teachers and students in developing a family heritage program for their school.

Compiled, published and distributes free of charge a "Selected Bibliography, Genealogical Research For Young People."

The *Michigan Genealogical Council* is the coordinating body for organized genealogical socieites in the state. It publishes only an internal newsletter but does publish other publications from time to time. Its mailing address is the Michigan State Library, P.O. Box 30007, 735 E. Michigan Ave., Lansing, MI 48909.

MICHIGAN COUNTY HISTORIES
(Population figures to nearest thousand - 1980 U. S. Census)

Name	Map Index	Date Created	Pop. By M 1980	U.S. Cen Reports Available	Parent County or Territory From Which Organized	County Seat
Aishcum (changed to Lake, 1843)						
* Alcona	C4	1840	10	1860-80	Alpena, Cheboygan	Harrisville 48740
(Co Clk has b, m, d, div, pro, civ ct rec from 1870, also bur rec from 1940)						
*§ Alger	B2	1885	9		Schoolcraft	Munising 49862
(Co Clk has b, d & Ind rec from 1884, m rec from 1887, div & civ ct rec from 1885)						
* Allegan	E3	1831	81	1840-80	Kalamazoo	Allegan 49010
(Co Clk has b & d rec from 1867, m rec from 1836, civ ct rec from 1837 & div rec from 1850)						
*§ Alpena	C4	1840	32	1860-80	Cheboygan	Alpena 49707
(Co Clk has b, m, d, div rec from 1870; Pro Judge has pro rec; Reg Deeds has Ind rec)						
Anamickee (changed to Alpena, 1843)						
Antrim	C4	1840	16	1860-80	Grand Traverse	Bellaire 49615
(Co Clk has b, m, d, div & civ ct rec from 1867; Pro Judge has pro rec from 1863; Reg Deeds has Ind rec)						
Arenac	D4	1883	15		Bay, Saginaw	Standish 48658
(Co Clk has b, m, d, div, civ ct rec from 1883, bur rec from 1952)						
§ Baraga	B2	1875	8	1880	Houghton	L'Anse 49946
(Co Clk has b, m, d, div & civ ct rec from 1875 & bur rec from 1950)						
* Barry	E4	1829	45	1840-80	St. Joseph, Kalamazoo	Hastings 49058
(Co Clk has b, d rec from 1867, m rec from 1839, div rec from 1869, civ ct rec from 1845; Pro Ct has pro rec; Reg Deeds has Ind rec)						
*§ Bay	D4	1857	120	1860-80	Saginaw, Midland	Bay City 48706
(Co Clk has b rec from 1868, m rec from 1857, d rec from 1867, div rec from 1883; civ ct rec from 1965; Pro Ct has pro rec; Reg Deeds has Ind rec)						
Benzie	C3	1863	11	1870-80	Grand Traverse, Leelanau	Beulah 49617
(Co Clk has b & d rec from 1868, m & civ ct rec from 1869, div & pro rec from 1870, naturalization rec from 1871, bur rec from 1934)						
* Berrien	E3	1829	171	1830-80	Cass	St. Joseph 49085
(Co Clk has b & d rec from 1867, m rec from 1831, div & civ ct rec)						
Bleeker (changed to Menominee, 1863)						
* Branch	E4	1829	40	1840-80	St. Joseph, Lenawee	Coldwater 49036
(Co Clk has b, d rec from 1867, m rec from 1833, div, civ ct rec from 1848; City and Township clks have bur rec; Pro Ct has pro rec; Reg Deeds has Ind rec)						
*§ Calhoun	E4	1829	141	1840-80	St. Joseph, Kalamazoo	Marshall 49068
(Co Clk has b, d, m rec from 1867, bur rec 1952-1978, div, civ ct rec from 1867, naturalization rec from 1918, military discharge rec from 1919, election rec from 1972; Pro Ct has pro rec)						
* Cass	E3	1829	50	1830-80	Lenawee	Cassopolis 49031
(Co Clk has b & d rec from 1867, m rec from 1831, div & civ ct rec from 1830)						
Charlevoix	C4	1869		1870-80	Emmet	Charlevoix 49720
(Co Clk has b rec from 1867, m & d rec from 1868, div & civ ct rec from 1869; Pro Judge has pro rec from 1881; Reg Deeds has Ind rec from 1869)						
*§ Cheboygan	C4	1840	21	1860-80	Mackinac	Cheboygan 49721
(Co Clk has b, m, d rec from 1867, div, civ ct rec from 1884; Reg of Pro has pro rec from 1854; Reg of Deeds has Ind rec from 1854)						

COUNTY MAP FOR THE STATE OF MICHIGAN

Name	Map Index	Date Created	Pop. By M 1980	U.S. Cen Reports Available	Parent County or Territory From Which Organized	County Seat
Cheonoquet (changed to Montmorency, 1843)						
Chippewa	B4	1826	29	1830-80	Mackinac	Sault Ste. Marie 49783

(Co Clk has b rec from 1869, m rec from 1868, d rec from 1870, div rec from 1891, bur rec; Pro Judge has pro rec; Dis Judge has civ ct rec; Reg Deeds has Ind rec)

Clare	D4	1840	24	1870-80	Isabella, Midland, Mecosta	Harrison 48625

(Co Clk has b, m, d, bur, div, civ ct & Ind rec)

* Clinton	D4	1818	56	1850-80	Shiawssee, Kent	St. Johns 48879

(Co Clk has b, d rec from 1867, m rec from 1840, div rec from 1839, civ ct rec)

Crawford	C4	1818	9	1820-80	Cheboygan, Antrim, Kalkaska	Grayling 49738

(Co Clk has b rec from 1879, m rec from 1887, d rec from 1878, div, civ ct rec from 1881; City Office has bur rec; Pro Judge has pro rec)

Delta	B2	1843	39	1860-80	Mackinac	Escanaba 49829

(Co Clk has b, m, d, bur, div & civ ct rec from 1862; Pro Judge has pro rec)

Des Moines		1834			Disorganized	
* Dickinson	B2	1891	26		Marquette, Menominee	Iron Mountain 49801

(Co Clk has b, m, d, div, civ ct, Ind rec, naturalization, articles of corporation and crim rec from 1891; Pro Ct has pro rec)

* Eaton	E4	1837	88	1840-80	St. Joseph, Kalamazoo, Calhoun	Charlotte 48813

(Co Clk has b & d rec from 1867, m rec from 1838, div & civ ct rec 1847; Pro Judge has pro rec)

* Emmet	C4	1853	23	1860-80	Mackinac	Petoskey 49770

(Co Clk has b, m, d rec from 1867, div rec from 1875, pro, civ ct rec from 1867, Ind rec from 1843, naturalization 1875-1975)

*§ Genesee	D4	1835	450	1840-80	Lapeer	Flint 48502

(Co Clk has b, d rec from 1867, m rec from 1835, div rec from 1890 civ ct, crim rec from 1835; Pro Judge has pro rec; Cem custodians have bur rec)

Gladwin	D4	1855	20	1860-80	Saginaw, Midland	Gladwin 48624

(Co Clk has b, m, d, bur, div & civ ct rec from 1880)

Gogebic	B1	1881	20		Ontonagon	Bessemer 49911

(Co Clk has b, m, d, div, civ ct & naturalization rec from 1887)

* Grand Traverse	C3	1851	55	1860-80	Mackinac	Traverse City 49684

(Co Clk has b, d rec from 1867, m rec from 1853, div, civ ct rec from 1882; Townships have bur rec; Title Companies have Ind rec)

* Gratiot	D4	1855	40	1860-80	Saginaw, Clinton	Ithaca 48847

(Co Clk has b, m, d, div & civ ct rec from 1867)

* Hillsdale	E4	1835	42	1840-80	Lenawee	Hillsdale 49242
Houghton	B1	1845	38	1850-80	Marquette, Schoolcraft, Ontonagon	Houghton 49931

(Co Clk has b, d rec from 1867, m rec from 1848, div, civ ct rec from 1853, Ind rec from 1850; citizenship rec from 1848, inquests from 1890, military rec - few CW, 1 bk WWI, many bks WWII)

* Huron	D5	1840	36	1850-80	Saginaw, St. Clair, Sanilac	Bad Axe 48413

(rec prior 1867 destroyed by fire) (Co Clk has b, m, d, div & civ ct rec from 1867, bur rec; Pro Judge has pro rec; Reg Deeds has Ind rec)

* Ingham	E4	1838	272	1840-80	Washtenaw, Jackson, Eaton	Mason 48854

(Co Clk has b & d rec from 1867, m rec from 1838, div & civ ct rec from 1839; bur rec are with Twnship & City Clks; Pro Ct has pro rec)

* Ionia	D4	1831	52	1840-80	Kent	Ionia 48846

(Co Clk has b & d rec from 1867, m rec from 1837, div rec from 1897 & civ ct rec)

*§ Iosco	C4	1857	28	1860-80	Saginaw, Cheboygan	Tawas City 48763

(Co clk has b rec from 1867, m rec from 1862, d rec from 1868, bur rec 1961-1978, div, civ ct rec from 1859, naturalization rec from 1894 to 1903, declaration of intention 1859-1906)

§ Iron	B2	1885	14		Marquette, Menominee	Crystal Falls 49920

(Co Clk has b, m, d, div, civ ct rec from 1895; Pro Ct has pro rec; Reg Deeds has Ind rec; Townships and cities have bur rec)

* Isabella	D4	1831	54	1860-80	Saginaw, Midland	Mt. Pleasant 48858

(Co Clk has b, m, d, div, civ ct rec from 1880, bur rec from 1950)

Isle Royal		1875		1880	Disorganized 1897	

(attached 1885 to Houghton, 1897 to Keweenaw where rec now are held)

Name	Map Index	Date Created	Pop. By M 1980	U.S. Cen Reports Available	Parent County or Territory From Which Organized	County Seat
*§ Jackson	E4	1832	151	1840-80	Washtenaw	Jackson 49201

(Co Clk has b & d rec from 1867, m rec from 1867, also m rec from 1833 to 1850 not available to public only by request, bur rec from 1957, div & civ ct rec)

| * Kalamazoo | E3 | 1829 | 212 | 1840-80 | St. Joseph | Kalamazoo 49006 |

(Co Clk has b & d rec from 1867, m rec from 1831, div & civ ct rec from 1800's; Pro Judge has pro rec; Reg Deeds has Ind rec)

| * Kalkaska | C3 | 1870 | 11 | 1870-80 | Grand Traverse, Antrim | Kalkaska 49646 |

(Co Clk has b, m, d, div & civ ct rec from 1871 & bur rec; Pro Judge has pro rec; Reg Deeds has Ind rec)

Kanotin (changed to Iosco, 1843)

Kautawaubet (changed to Wexford, 1843)

Kaykakee (changed to Clare, 1843)

| * Kent | D3 | 1836 | 444 | 1840-80 | Kalamazoo | Grand Rapids 49502 |

(Co Clk has b, d, div & civ ct rec from 1867, m rec from 1845, bur rec from 1959)

| Keweenaw | A2 | 1861 | 2 | 1870-80 | Houghton | Eagle River 49924 |

(Co Clk has b, m, d, rec from 1867, div, civ ct rec, Ind rec from 1861; Pro Judge has pro rec)

| Lake | D3 | 1870 | 8 | 1870-80 | Oceana, Mason, Newaygo | Baldwin 49304 |

(Co Clk has b, d rec from 1870, m, Ind rec from 1872, civ ct rec from 1871; Pro Ct has pro rec; Township clks have bur rec)

| * Lapeer | D5 | 1835 | 70 | 1840-80 | Oakland | Lapeer 48446 |

(Co Clk has b & d rec from 1868, m, div & civ ct rec from 1835)

| Leelanau | C3 | 1840 | 14 | 1860-80 | Grand Traverse | Leland 49654 |

(Co Clk has b, m & d rec from 1867, div rec from 1870 & civ ct rec; Pro Judge has pro rec)

| * Lenawee | E4 | 1822 | 90 | 1830-80 | Wayne | Adrian 49221 |

(Co Clk has b, m & d rec from 1867, div & civ ct rec from 1870; Courthouse burned 1852)

| * Livingston | D4 | 1836 | 100 | 1840-80 | Shiawassee, Washtenaw | Howell 48843 |

(Co clk has b, d, div, civ ct rec from 1867, m rec from 1836; Pro Judge has pro rec; Reg Deeds has Ind rec)

| * Luce | B3 | 1887 | 7 | | Chippewa, Mackinac | Newberry 49868 |

(Co Clk has b, m, d, div, civ ct, Ind rec from 1887; Pro Judge has pro rec)

| * Mackinac | B3 | 1818 | 10 | 1820-80 | Wayne and the French | St. Ignace 49781 |

(This county first called Michilimackinac, changed in 1849 to Mackinac. Co Clk has b, d rec from 1873, m rec from 1863, civ ct rec from 1808, div rec)

| * Macomb | D5 | 1818 | 694 | 1820-80 | Wayne | Mt. Clemens 48043 |

(Co Clk has b, d, bur rec from 1867, m rec from 1848, div rec from 1847, Ind rec; Pro Ct has pro rec)

| * Manistee | C3 | 1855 | 23 | 1860-80 | Mackinac, Ottawa, Oceana, Grand Traverse | Manistee 49660 |

(Co Clk has b & d rec from 1867, m rec from 1855, div rec from 1856, civ ct rec from 1855)

| Manitou | | 1855 | | 1860-80 | Disbanded 1895 | |

| § Marquette | B2 | 1851 | 73 | 1860-80 | Chippewa, Houghton | Marquette 49855 |

(Co Clk has b, d rec from 1867, m rec from 1851, div, civ ct rec from 1852, naturalization rec from 1855)

| Mason | D3 | 1840 | 26 | 1850-80 | Ottawa, Oceana | Ludington 49431 |

(Co Clk has b, m, d, div, civ ct rec from 1867; City Clks have bur rec; Pro Ct has pro rec; Reg Deeds has Ind rec)

| * Mecosta | D4 | 1840 | 37 | 1860-80 | Newaygo | Big Rapids 49307 |

(Co clk has b, m, d, div rec; Pro Ct has pro rec; Reg Deeds has Ind rec; Clk Cir Ct has civ ct rec)

Meegisee (changed to Antrim, 1843)

| * Menominee | C2 | 1863 | 26 | 1870-80 | Marquette | Menominee 49858 |

(Co Clk has b, m, d, div, civ ct rec from 1861; Pro Judge has pro rec; Reg Deeds has Ind rec)

Michilimackinac (changed to Mackinac, 1849)

| * Midland | D4 | 1850 | 74 | 1850-80 | Saginaw | Midland 48640 |

(Co Clk has b rec from 1869, m rec from 1868, d rec from 1867, div, civ ct rec from 1916; Township Clks have bur rec)

Mikenauk (changed to Roscommon, 1843)

| * Missaukee | C4 | 1840 | 10 | 1870-80 | Antrim, Grand Traverse | Lake City 49651 |

(Co Clk has b, m, d, bur, div, civ ct & Ind rec from 1871; Pro Judge has pro rec) (some rec destroyed by fire 1944)

| * Monroe | E5 | 1817 | 134 | 1820-80 | Wayne | Monroe 48161 |

(Co Clk has b rec from 1874, m rec from 1818, d rec from 1867, bur rec 1923-1979, div rec from 1917, civ ct rec from 1950; Pro Ct has pro rec; Reg Deeds has Ind rec)

Name	Map Index	Date Created	Pop. By M 1980	U.S. Cen Reports Available	Parent County or Territory From Which Organized	County Seat
* Montcalm	D4	1831	48	1850-80	Ionia	Stanton 48888

(Co Clk has b, m, d, div & civ ct rec; Pro Judge has pro rec; Reg Deeds has Ind rec)

| Montmorency | C4 | 1881 | 7 | | Cheboygan, Alpena | Atlanta 49709 |

(most rec lost in fire 1942, still has vital rec others start 1943)

| *§ Muskegon | D3 | 1859 | 157 | 1860-80 | Ottawa | Muskegon 49440 |

(Co Clk has b, m, d, div & pro rec from 1867, civ ct rec from 1859 & Ind rec)

Neewago (changed to Alcoma, 1843)

| * Newaygo | D3 | 1840 | 33 | 1850-80 | Kent, Muskegon, Oceana | White Cloud 49349 |

(Co Clk has b, d, civ ct rec from 1867, m rec from 1851, div rec from 1854)

Notipekago (changed to Mason, 1843)

| * Oakland | D5 | 1819 | 1,007 | 1820-80 | Wayne | Pontiac 48053 |

(Co Clk has b & d rec from 1867, m rec from 1827, naturalization rec from 1827)

| * Oceana | D3 | 1831 | 22 | 1840-80 | Ottawa | Hart 49420 |

(Co Clk has b, m, d rec from 1867 & div rec from 1897)

| Ogemaw | C4 | 1875 | 16 | 1880 | Saginaw, Bay | West Branch 48661 |

(Co Clk has b rec from 1879, m, d, civ ct rec from 1876, div rec from 1877; Pro ct has pro rec; Reg Deeds has Ind rec)

Okkuddo (changed to Otsego, 1843)

| Ontonagon | B1 | 1848 | 10 | 1850-80 | Chippewa, Houghton | Ontonagon 49953 |

(Co Clk has b, d rec from 1868, m rec from 1861, div, civ ct rec from 1854, Ind rec from 1850; Pro Ct has pro rec; Cem associations have bur rec)

| * Osceola | D3 | 1840 | 19 | 1860-80 | Mason, Newaygo, Mecosta | Reed City 49677 |

(Co Clk has b & m rec from 1869, d & div rec from 1870, civ ct rec from 1963 & bur rec; Pro Judge has pro rec; Treas. has Ind rec)

| Oscoda | C4 | 1840 | 7 | 1870-80 | Cheboygan, Alpena, Alcona | Mio 48647 |

(Co Clk has b, m, d, bur, div & civ ct rec from 1881, Ind rec from 1850; Pro Judge has pro rec)

| Otsego | C4 | 1875 | 15 | 1880 | Mackinac, Alpena, Cheboygan, Antrim | Gaylord 49735 |

(Co Clk has b, m, d, div, civ ct, Ind rec from 1875)

| * Ottawa | D3 | 1837 | 157 | 1840-80 | Kent | Grand Haven 49417 |

(Co Clk has b & d rec from 1867, m & civ ct rec from 1847 & div rec from 1863)

| Presque Isle | C4 | 1840 | 14 | 1860-80 | Mackinac | Rogers City 49779 |

(Co Clk has b & d rec from 1871, m rec from 1872 & div rec from 1900)

Reshkauko (changed to Charlevoix, 1843)

| Roscommon | C4 | 1875 | 16 | 1880 | Cheboygan, Midland | Roscommon 48653 |

(Co Clk has b & d rec from 1874, m, div, pro, civ ct & Ind rec from 1875)

| * Saginaw | D4 | 1835 | 227 | 1840-80 | Oakland | Saginaw 48602 |

(Co Clk has b, m rec from 1867, d rec from 1868, div rec from 1886, civ ct rec from 1843)

| * St. Clair | D5 | 1822 | 137 | 1830-80 | Wayne | Port Huron 48060 |

(Co Clk has b rec from 1867, m rec from 1834, d rec from 1868, div, civ ct rec from 1849)

| * St. Joseph | E4 | 1829 | 56 | 1830-80 | Wayne | Centreville 49032 |

(Co Clk has d rec from 1867, b rec from 1867, m rec from 1844, div rec from 1850, pro rec from 1832 & civ ct rec from 1842)

| Sanilac | D5 | 1848 | 41 | 1850-80 | Oakland, St. Clair, Lapeer | Sandusky 48471 |

(Co Clk has b, d rec from 1860, m rec from 1870, div rec from 1900, civ ct rec; Pro Ct has pro rec)

| Schoolcraft | B3 | 1848 | 9 | 1850-80 | Chippewa, Houghton, Marquette | Manistique 49854 |

(Co Clk has b, m, d, div, civ ct, Ind rec from 1870; Pro Ct has pro rec from 1870)

Shawano (changed to Crawford, 1843)

| * Shiawassee | D4 | 1822 | 71 | 1840-80 | Oakland, Genesee | Corunna 48817 |

(Co Clk has b, m & d rec from 1867, div & civ ct rec from 1848; Pro Judge has pro rec; Reg Deeds has Ind rec; fire destroyed many rec 1867)

Tonedagana (changed to Emmet, 1843)

| * Tuscola | D5 | 1840 | 57 | 1850-80 | Saginaw | Caro 48723 |

(Co Clk has b & d rec from 1866, div rec from 1884, civ ct rec from 1887 & m rec from 1851)

Unwattin (changed to Osceola, 1843)

| * Van Buren | E3 | 1829 | 67 | 1830-80 | Cass | Paw Paw 49079 |

(Co Clk has b & d rec from 1867, m rec from 1837, bur rec from 1949, div rec from 1837, civ ct rec from 1844; Village & Cities are also holders of b & d rec)

Name	Map Index	Date Created	Pop. By M 1980	U.S. Cen Reports Available	Parent County or Territory From Which Organized	County Seat
Wabassee (changed to Kalkaska, 1843)						
* Washtenaw	E4	1826	258	1830-80	Wayne	Ann Arbor 48108
(Co Clk has b, m & d rec from 1867, div, civ ct & Ind rec, naturalization & supervisors rec from 1835)						
* Wayne	E5	1815	2,331	1820-80	Original county	Detroit 48226
* Wexford	C3	1840	25	1870-80	Manistee	Cadillac 49601
(Co Clk has b rec from 1868, m, d, div, civ ct rec from 1869)						

* - At least one county history has been published about this county.

§ - Inventory of county archives was made by the Historical Records Survey. (see introduction)

MINNESOTA

CAPITAL, ST. PAUL - TERRITORY 1849 - STATE 1858 - (32ND)

Minnesota, with its more than ten thousand lakes, began to attract sturdy Scandinavian settlers to its borders shortly after 1851 when the land west of the Mississippi was procured from the Indians. Several years prior to that, Yankees from the east and northeast, largely from Maine, were pulled there by its infant lumber industry, which in succeeding decades drew thousands to its borders. When the Scandinavian influx began, it is estimated that less than 5,000 persons lived in the territory.

The earliest white people to visit the section were the Catholic missionaries and fur traders. Chief among the missionaries was Father Hennepin, who has been honored by having a county and one of the main streets in Minneapolis named after him. He came there about 1680 and floated down the Mississippi in a canoe.

The Minnesota region passed to Britain after the French and Indian War of 1763. Its eastern part was included by the U.S. in the Northwest Territory (1787), and the rest was acquired in the Louisiana Purchase (1803). Real effort in settlement started in 1805.

When the northern iron mines began to be developed in the 1880's, Finns and Slavs came there by the tens of thousands. Poland, Lithuania and the Balkans furnished much of the labor for the rapidly growing packing plants around the Twin Cities at the beginning of the present century.

The progenitors of the present Minnesota generation came mainly from Sweden, Norway, Denmark, Germany, Canada. Finland, Poland and Russia.

Birth and death records before 1908 and all marriage records are in the offices of the clerks of the District Court in the respective counties. The birth and death records after 1908 are in the office of Minnesota Department of Health, Birth and Death Records, 717 Delaware Street, SE, Minneapolis, MN 55440.

Records of wills, and all probate of estates are in the office of the clerk of the Probate Court in the county courthouse, while the records of deeds and mortgages are handled by the register of deeds in the county seat.

Birth and death records for events occurring within the city limits of St. Paul or Minneapolis are on file with the respective city health department.

Genealogical Archives, Libraries, Societies, and Publications

Anoka County Genealogical Society, 1900 Third Ave., Anoka, MN 55303.

Blue Earth County Historical Society, 606 South Broad Street, Mankato, MN 56001.

Brown County Historical Society, New Ulm, MN 56073.

Fillmore County Historical Society, County Courthouse, Preston, MN 55965.

Folke Bernadette Memorial Library, Gustavus Adolphus College, St. Peter, MN 56082.

Freeborn County Genealogical Society, P.O. Box 403, Albert Lea, MN 56007.

Heart O'Lakes Genealogical Society, 419 W. Holmes St., Detroit Lakes, MN 56501.

Minneapolis Public Library, 300 Nicolet Ave., Minneapolis, MN 55401.

Minnesota Genealogical Society, P.O. Box 16069, St. Paul, MN 55116.

Minnesota Historical Society, 690 Cedar St., St. Paul, MN 55101.

Mower County Genealogical Society, The, P.O. Box 145, Austin, MN 55912.

Nobles County Historical Society, P.O. Box 213, Worthington, MN 56187.

Northwest Territory French and Canadian Heritage Institute, P.O. Box 26372, St. Louis Park, MN 55426.

Olmsted County Genealogical Society, P.O. Box 6411, Rochester, MN 55901.

Olmsted County Historical Society, 3103 S.W. Salem Rd., Rochester, MN 55901.

The Prairieland Genealogical Society, 703 North Sixth St., Marshall, MN 56258.

Public Library, 90 West 4th, St. Paul, MN 55102.

Range Genealogical Society, Box 278, Buhl, MN 55713.

Rochester Public Library, Broadway at First Street, S.E., Rochester, MN 55901.

Rolvaag Memorial Library, St. Olaf College, Northfield, MN 55057.

Stearns County Historical Society, Box 702, St. Cloud, MN 56301.

Swift County Historical Society, Box 39, Benson, MN 56215.

University of Minnesota Library, Minneapolis, MN 55455.

Cousins et Cousines, P.O. Box 26372, St. Louis Park, MN 55426.

Crow Wing County Genealogy Newsletter, the Crow Wing County, Minnesota Genealogical Society, 402 4th Ave., N.E., Brainerd, MN 56401.

Minnesota Genealogist, P.O. Box 16069, St. Paul, MN 55116.

Prairieland Register, 703 North Sixth St., Marshall, MN 56258.

Printed Census Records and Mortality Schedules

State Indexes-1850, 1860, 1870, 1849

Printed Mortality Schedules - 1850, 1860, 1870, 1880

The Minnesota State Census Records 1865 to 1895 are available on microfilm at the Genealogical Society Library of the Church of Jesus Christ of Latter-day Saints. The original records are located at the Minnesota State Archives, St. Paul, Minnesota.

Mortality Records of Minnesota by Counties from the Territorial Period 1850 through 1870, and St. Louis County, Minnesota years ending 31 Dec. 1872, 1873, 1874, 1878 1881, 1882, 1883 transcribed by Edith H. Jannssen, St. Paul Chapter of D.A.R. are available on microfilm at Genealogical Society of the Church of Jesus Christ of Latter-day Saints.

Minnesota Historical Society, St. Paul has indexes for the 1850 and 1860 census records

The 1836 Iowa Territory census includes present Minnesota.

Valuable Printed Sources

Atlas

Illustrated Historical Atlas of the State of Minnesota. Chicago: A. T. Andreas 1874.

Place Names

Upham, Warren. *Minnesota Geographic Names: Their Origin and Historic Significance* St. Paul: Minnesota Historical Society (Reprinted 1969)

Guides To Genealogical Research

Hage, George S. *Newspapers on the Minnesota Frontier 1849-1860.* St. Paul: Minnesota Historical Society (1967)

Pope, Wiley R. and Alissa L. Wiener. *Tracing Your Ancestors in Minnesota - A Guide to the Sources.* St. Paul: Minnesota Family Trees, 2nd edition, 1980.

Histories

Brook, Michael. *Reference Guide to Minnesota History.* St. Paul: Minnesota Historical Society (1974)

Burnquist, Joseph A. *Minnesota and Its People.* Chicago: S. J. Clark, (1924)

Follwell, William Watts. *A History of Minnesota.* St. Paul: Minnesota Historical Society (1921)

Genealogical Sources: Indexes and Guides

Kane, Lucille M. and Kathryn A. Johnson. *Manuscripts Collections of the Minnesota Historical Society* Guide #2. St. Paul: Minnesota Historical Society 1955.

Lareau, Paul J. and Elmer Courteau, *French-Canadian Families of the North Central States - A Genealogical Dictionary.* 8 Volumes. St. Paul: Northwest Territory French and Canadian Heritage Institute, 1980-1981.

Nute, Grace Lee and Gertrude W. Ackermann. *Guide to the Personal Papers in the Manuscript Collections of the Minnesota Historical Society.* St. Paul: Minnesota Historical Society (1935)

MINNESOTA COUNTY HISTORIES
(Population figures to nearest thousand - 1980 U. S. Census)

Name	Map Index	Date Created	Pop. By M 1980	U.S. Cen Reports Available	Parent County or Territory From Which Organized	County Seat
§ Aitkin	C3	1857	13	1860-80	Cass, Itasca	Aitkin 56431

(Clk Dis Ct has b rec from 1883, m rec from 1885, d rec from 1887, div rec from 1886, pro, civ ct rec, naturalization rec from 1885; Co Rcdr has Ind rec)
Andy Johnson (changed from Toombs 1858 & to Wilkin, 1868)

Name	Map Index	Date Created	Pop. By M 1980	U.S. Cen Reports Available	Parent County or Territory From Which Organized	County Seat
*§ Anoka	D3	1857	195	1857-80	Ramsey	Anoka 55303

(Clk Dis Ct has b & d rec from 1870, m rec from 1865, div, civ ct & Ind rec from 1866; Pro Judge has pro rec)

Name	Map Index	Date Created	Pop. By M 1980	U.S. Cen Reports Available	Parent County or Territory From Which Organized	County Seat
* Becker	C2	1858	29	1860-80	Indian Lands	Detroit Lakes 56501
*§ Beltrami	B2	1866	29	1870-80	Unorg. Terr.	Bemidji 56601

(Beltrami was attached to Becker County for many years for record purposes.) (Clk Dis Ct has b, m, d, bur, div, pro, civ ct recom from 1894)

Name	Map Index	Date Created	Pop. By M 1980	U.S. Cen Reports Available	Parent County or Territory From Which Organized	County Seat
§ Benton	D2	1849	25	1850-80	Original county	Foley 56329

(Clk Dis Ct has b rec from 1871, m rec from 1850, d rec from 1865, div, civ ct rec from 1852, pro rec)

Name	Map Index	Date Created	Pop. By M 1980	U.S. Cen Reports Available	Parent County or Territory From Which Organized	County Seat
*§ Big Stone	D1	1862	8	1870-80	Pierce	Ortonville 56278

(Clk Dis Ct has b, m, d rec from 1881, div, civ ct rec from 1885; Ct Judge has pro rec; Co Rcdr has Ind rec)

Name	Map Index	Date Created	Pop. By M 1980	U.S. Cen Reports Available	Parent County or Territory From Which Organized	County Seat
*§ Blue Earth	F2	1853	52	1857-80	Unorg. Terr.	Mankato 56001

(Clk Dist Ct has b, d rec from 1870, m rec from 1865, div, civ ct rec from 1854, pro rec from 1858; Reg Deeds has Ind rec)

Name	Map Index	Date Created	Pop. By M 1980	U.S. Cen Reports Available	Parent County or Territory From Which Organized	County Seat
Breckenridge				1860	See Clay, Toombs & Wilkin	
* Brown	E2	1855	29	1857-80	Nicollett, Blue Earth	New Ulm 56073

(Clk Dis Ct has b & d rec from 1870, m rec from 1857, div rec from 1856, civ ct rec from 1885 & naturalization rec from 1870)

Name	Map Index	Date Created	Pop. By M 1980	U.S. Cen Reports Available	Parent County or Territory From Which Organized	County Seat
Buchanan				1857-60	Discontinued	
* Carlton	C3	1857	30	1857-80	Pine, St. Louis	Carlton 55718

(Clk Dis Ct has b, m, d, bur, div, pro, civ ct rec from 1872, immigration rec from 1872; Co Rcdr has Ind rec)

Name	Map Index	Date Created	Pop. By M 1980	U.S. Cen Reports Available	Parent County or Territory From Which Organized	County Seat
* Carver	E3	1855	37	1857-80	Hennepin	Chaska 55318

(Clk Dis Ct has b, m, d rec from 1870, div, pro, civ ct rec from 1856; Reg Deeds has Ind rec)

Name	Map Index	Date Created	Pop. By M 1980	U.S. Cen Reports Available	Parent County or Territory From Which Organized	County Seat
*§ Cass	C2	1851	21	1857-80	Original county	Walker 56484

(Clk Dis Ct has b, d rec from 1896, m rec from 1897, div rec from 1899, civ ct rec from 1898, pro rec; Co Rcdr has Ind rec; City or township clks have bur rec)

Name	Map Index	Date Created	Pop. By M 1980	U.S. Cen Reports Available	Parent County or Territory From Which Organized	County Seat
*§ Chippewa	E2	1862	15	1870-80	Pierce	Montevideo 56265

(Clk Dis Ct has b, m, d, div, pro, civ ct rec from 1870; Co Rcdr has Ind rec from 1870; City Clks have bur rec)

Name	Map Index	Date Created	Pop. By M 1980	U.S. Cen Reports Available	Parent County or Territory From Which Organized	County Seat
Chisago	D3	1851	26	1857-80	Washington	Center City 55012

(Clk Dis Ct has b & d rec from 1870, m rec from 1852, civ ct rec from 1880 & div rec; Pro Judge has pro rec; Reg Deeds has Ind rec)

Name	Map Index	Date Created	Pop. By M 1980	U.S. Cen Reports Available	Parent County or Territory From Which Organized	County Seat
* Clay	C1	1858	49	1870-80	Formerly Breckenridge (changed 1862)	Moorhead 56560

(Clk Dis Ct has b, m, d, div & civ ct rec from 1872)

Name	Map Index	Date Created	Pop. By M 1980	U.S. Cen Reports Available	Parent County or Territory From Which Organized	County Seat
* Clearwater	B2	1902	9		Beltrami	Bagley 56621

(Clk Dis Ct has b, m, d, div, pro, civ ct rec from 1903; Town Clks have bur rec; Co Rcdr has Ind rec)

Cook	B4	1874	4	1880	Lake	Grand Marais 55604

(Clk Dis Ct has b rec from 1879, m, d, div, civ ct rec from 1901; Co Rcdr has Ind rec)

* Cottonwood	F2	1857	15	1857-80	Brown	Windom 56101

(Clk Dis Ct has b, m, d, div & civ ct rec from 1871)

* Crow Wing	C2	1857	42	1857-80	Cass, Aitkin	Brainerd 56401
*§ Dakota	E3	1849	194	1850-80	Original county	Hastings 55033

(Clk Dis Ct has b & d rec from 1870, m rec from 1857, div & civ ct rec from 1853)

*§ Dodge	F3	1855	15	1857-80	Olmstead	Mantorville 55955

(Clk Dis Ct has b, d, div, civ ct rec from 1870, m rec from 1865, pro rec from 1858, school rec from 1917)

Doty (see St. Louis & Lake)

*§ Douglas	D2	1858	28	1860-80	Todd	Alexandria 56308

(Clk Dis Ct has b rec from 1869, m rec from 1866, d, div & civ ct rec from 1870) (attached to Stearns until 1866)

*§ Faribault	F2	1855	20	1857-80	Blue Earth	Blue Earth 56013

(Clk Dis Ct has b & d rec from 1870, m, div & civ ct rec from 1856; Pro Judge has pro rec; Reg Deeds has Ind rec)

*§ Fillmore	F4	1853	22	1857-80	Wabasha	Preston 55965

(Clk Dis Ct has b, d, div, civ ct rec from 1870, m rec from 1838, pro rec from 1860; Co Rcdr has Ind rec)

*§ Freeborn	F3	1857	36	1857-80		Albert Lea 56007

(Clk Dis Ct has b & d rec from 1870, m & civ ct, crim rec from 1857; Co Rcdr has Ind rec from 1854; Pro office has pro rec from 1866)

*§ Goodhue	E3	1853	39	1857-80	Wabasha	Red Wing 55066

(Clk Dis Ct has b & d rec from 1870, m, div, civ ct rec from 1854)

*§ Grant	D1	1868	7	1870-80	Stearns	Elbow Lake 56531

(Clk Dis Ct has b & d rec from 1877, m rec from 1869, div & civ ct rec from 1883; Pro Judge has pro rec; Reg Deeds has Ind rec)

* Hennepin	E3	1852	940	1857-80	Dakota	Minneapolis 55415

(Clk Dis Ct has b & d rec from 1870, m, div & civ ct rec from 1853)

*§ Houston	F4	1854	19	1857-80	Fillmore	Caledonia 55921

(Clk Dis Ct has b & d rec from 1870, m rec from 1854, civ ct rec from 1856 & div rec; Pro Judge has pro rec; Reg Deeds has Ind rec)

§ Hubbard	C2	1883	14		Cass	Park Rapids 56470

(Clk of Ct has b, m rec from 1890, d rec from 1888, pro rec from 1894, div, civ ct rec; Co Rcdr has Ind rec)

* Isanti	D3	1857	23	1857-80	Anoka	Cambridge 55008

(Clk Dis Ct has b rec from 1869, m rec from 1871, d rec from 1873, bur rec 1900-1908, 1941-1979, div, civ ct rec from 1872, pro rec from 1892; Co Rcdr has Ind rec)

* Itasca	B3	1849	43	1850-80	Original county	Grand Rapids 55744

(Clk Dis Ct has b, m, d, div & civ ct rec from 1880)

*§ Jackson	F2	1857	14	1857-80	Unorg. Terr.	Jackson 56143

(Clk Dis Ct has b, m, d, div, civ ct, naturalization rec from 1870, pro rec from 1867; Co Rcdr has Ind rec; local funeral directors have bur rec)

Johnson (see Wilkin)

*§ Kanabec	D3	1858	12	1860-80	Pine	Mora 55051

(Clk Dis Ct has b, d rec from 1883, m, div, civ ct rec from 1882, pro rec from 1891; Co Rcdr has Ind rec; Mora City Hall has bur rec)

* Kandiyohi	E2	1858	37	1860-80	Meeker	Willmar 56201

(Clk Dis Ct has b, m, d, div, civ ct rec from 1870)

* Kittson	A1	1862	7	1880	Unorg. Terr., formerly Pembina	Hallock 56728

(Clk Dis Ct has b, m, d, div, civ ct rec from 1880)

Koochiching	B3	1906	18		Itasca	International Falls 56649

(Clk Dis Ct has b, m, d, div, civ ct, pro rec from 1907)

* Lac qui Parle	E1	1871	11	1870-80	Brown, Redwood	Madison 56256
* Lake	B4	1856	13	1857-80	Formerly Doty	Two Harbors 55616

(Clk Dis Ct has b rec from 1898, m & d rec from 1891, div & civ ct rec from 1892; City Clk has bur rec; Pro Judge has pro rec)

COUNTY MAP FOR THE STATE OF MINNESOTA

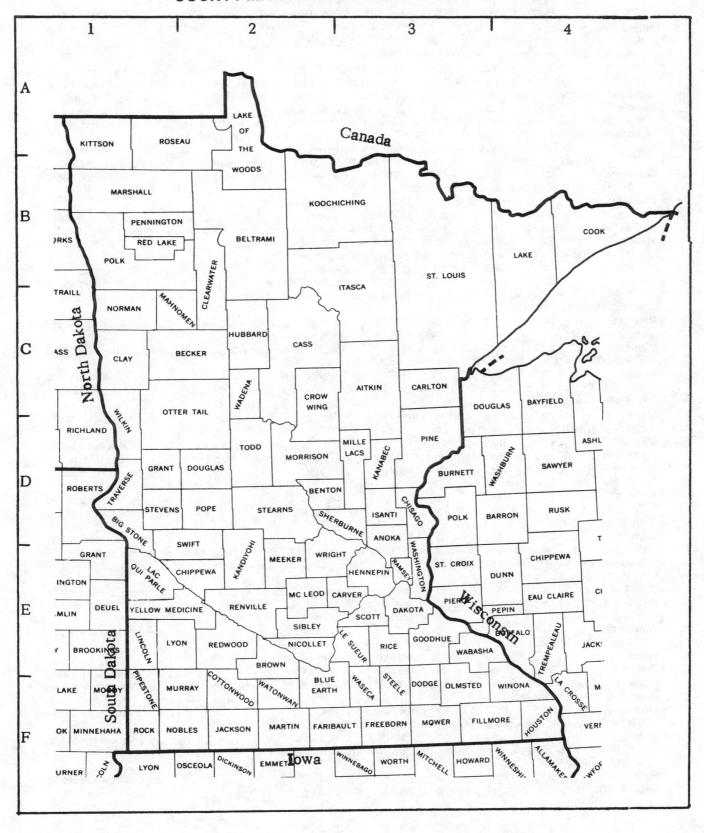

Name	Map Index	Date Created	Pop. By M 1980	U.S. Cen Reports Available	Parent County or Territory From Which Organized	County Seat
Lake of the Woods	A2	1922	4		Beltrami	Baudette 56623

(Clk Dis Ct has b, m, d, div, pro civ ct rec from 1923)

* Le Sueur	E3	1853	23	1857-80	Unorg. Terr.	Le Center 56057

(Clk Dis Ct has b & d rec from 1870, m rec from 1854, div & civ ct rec from 1880; Pro Judge has pro rec from 1855; Reg Deeds has Ind rec from 1850)

*§ Lincoln	E1	1866	8	1880	Lyon	Ivanhoe 56142

(Clk Dis Ct has b & m rec from 1879, d & civ ct rec from 1880, div rec from 1891; Pro Judge has pro rec from 1877; Reg Deeds has Ind rec from 1873)

* Lyon	E1	1868	25	1880	Redwood	Marshall 56258

(Clk Dis Ct has b, d rec from 1874, m rec from 1872, div, pro, civ ct rec from 1880; Co Rcdr has Ind rec)

Mahnomen	C1	1906	6	1857-80	Becker, Norman	Mahnomen 56557

(Clk dis Ct has b, m, d, div & civ ct rec from 1908)

Mankahta				1850	Discontinued	
§ Marshall	B1	1879	13	1880	Kittson	Warren 56762

(Clk Dis Ct has b & d rec from 1884, m rec from 1880, div rec from 1900 & civ ct rec from 1898)

*§ Martin	F2	1857	25	1857-80	Faribault, Brown	Fairmont 56031

(Clk Dis Ct has b, m, d, div, civ ct rec from 1884; pro, naturalization rec)

* McLeod	E2	1856	30	1857-80	Carver	Glencoe 55336
*§ Meeker	E2	1856	21	1857-80	Wright, Stearns	Litchfield 55355

(Clk Dis Ct has b, m, d, div, civ ct rec from 1870, pro rec from 1858, school rec, naturalization rec from 1884; Co Rcdr has Ind rec)

§ Mille Lacs	D3	1857	18	1860-80	Kanabec	Milaca 56353
Monongalia				1860-70	Discontinued	
*§ Morrison	D2	1856	29	1857-80	Benton, Stearns	Little Falls 56345

(Clk Dis Ct has b & d rec from 1870, m, div, civ ct rec from 1860)

* Mower	F3	1855	40	1857-80	Fillmore, Freeborn	Austin 55912

(Clk Dis Ct has b, d rec from 1870, m rec from 1865, div, civ ct rec from 1900, pro rec from 1856; Co Rcdr has Ind rec)

§ Murray	F2	1857	11	1857-80	Lyon	Slayton 56172

(Clk Dis Ct has b, m, d, div & civ ct rec)

*§ Nicollet	E2	1853	27	1857-80	Unorg. Terr.	Saint Peter 56082

(Clk Dis Ct has b, d rec from 1870, m rec from 1856, div, pro, civ ct rec from 1853; Co Rcdr has Ind rec)

*§ Nobles	F2	1857	22	1857-80	Jackson	Worthington 56187

(Clk Dis Ct has b, m & d rec from 1872, div rec from 1882 & civ ct rec from 1874; Pro Judge has pro rec)

* Norman	C1	1881	9		Polk	Ada 56510

(Clk Dis Ct has b & d rec from 1881, m rec from 1882, some div rec & civ ct rec; Pro Judge has pro rec)

*§ Olmsted	F3	1855	92	1857-80	Unorg. Terr.	Rochester 55901

(Clk Dis Ct has incomplete b, d rec from 1871, m rec from 1855, div rec from 1860, civ ct rec from 1858; Coroner and Dept of Health have bur rec; Co Ct has pro rec; Dept of Health, Div of Vit Statistics, St. Paul, also has b, m, d rec)

*§ Otter Tail	C2	1858	52	1860-80	Pembina, Cass	Fergus Falls 56537

(Clk Dis Ct has b, d rec from 1870, m rec from 1869, div rec from 1897, pro, civ ct rec from 1872)

Pembina				1850-70	(changed to Kittson, 1878)	
Pennington	B1	1910	15		Red Lake	Thief River Falls 56701

(Clk Dis Ct has b, m, d, div, pro, civ ct rec from 1910; Co Rcdr has Ind rec)

Pierce				1857-60	Disorganized	
* Pine	D3	1856	20	1857-80	Unorg. Lands	Pine City 55063

(Clk Dis Ct has b rec from 1874, d rec from 1879, m, div & civ ct rec from 1871; Pro Judge has pro rec; Reg Deeds has Ind rec)

*§ Pipestone	F1	1857	12	1857-80	Murray	Pipestone 56164

(Clk Dis Ct has b, m, d, div, pro, civ ct rec from 1877; Co Rcdr has Ind rec)

* Polk	B1	1858	33	1860-80	Indian Lands	Crookston 56716

(Clk Dis Ct has b, m & d rec from 1875, div rec from 1890, civ ct rec from 1875 & naturalization rec from 1879 to 1955)

* Pope	D2	1862	12	1870-80	Pierce	Glenwood 56334

(Clk Dis Ct has b, m, d rec from 1870, div, civ ct rec from 1880, pro rec from 1867)

Name	Map Index	Date Created	Pop. By M 1980	U.S. Cen Reports Available	Parent County or Territory From Which Organized	County Seat
* Ramsey	E3	1849	458	1850-80	Original county	Saint Paul 55102

(Clk dis Ct has b & d rec from 1870, m, div & civ ct rec from 1849; Pro Judge has pro rec)

Red Lake	B1	1896	5		Polk	Red Lake Falls 56750

(Clk Dis Ct has b, m, d, div, pro, civ ct rec from 1897; Co Rcdr has Ind rec)

*§ Redwood	E2	1862	19	1870-80	Brown	Redwood Falls 56283

(Clk Dis Ct has b, d rec from 1870, m rec from 1865, div rec from 1871, civ ct rec from 1867, pro rec from 1877; Co Rcdr has Ind rec from 1865)

*§ Renville	E2	1855	20	1857-80	Unorg. Terr.	Olivia 56277

(Clk Dis Ct has b, m, d rec from 1870, div, pro, civ ct rec; Co Rcdr has Ind rec)

*§ Rice	E3	1853	46	1857-80	Original county	Faribault 55021

(Clk Dis Ct has b, d, div, pro, civ ct rec from 1870; m rec from 1856, bur rec; Co Rcdr has Ind rec)

*§ Rock	F1	1857	11	1857-80	Nobles as Unorg. Co. Brown	Luverne 56156

(Clk Dis Ct has b, m, d, div & civ ct rec from 1872)

* Roseau	A1	1894	13		Kittson	Roseau 56751

(Clk Dis Ct has b, m, d, div & civ ct rec from 1895; Pro Judge has pro rec from 1895; Reg Deeds has Ind rec)

* Saint Louis	B3	1856	217	1857-80	Doty (now Lake)	Duluth 55802

(Clk Dis Ct has b, d, m rec from 1870, bur permits from 1938, div, civ ct rec from 1859, Ind rec from 1859; Co Ct has pro rec) (Branch courthouses also at Virginia and Hibbing, Minn.)

§ Scott	E3	1853	44	1857-80	Dakota	Shakopee 55379
§ Sherburne	D3	1856	30	1857-80	Benton	Elk River 55330

(Clk Dis Ct has b, d, civ, civ ct rec from 1870, m rec from 1858, pro rec; Co Rcdr has Ind rec)

* Sibley	E2	1853	15	1857-80	Unorg. Terr.	Gaylord 55334

(Clk Dis Ct has b, d, div, civ ct rec from 1870, m rec from 1856, pro rec; Co Rcdr has Ind rec)

*§ Stearns	D2	1855	108	1857-80	Indian Lands	Saint Cloud 56301

(Clk Dis Ct has b, d rec from 1870, m rec from 1868, div, civ ct rec from 1865, pro rec; Co Rcdr has Ind rec)

* Steele	F3	1855	30	1857-80	Unorg. Terr., Dodge	Owatonna 55060

(Clk Dis Ct has b & d rec from 1870, m rec from 1855, div & civ ct rec from 1858)

* Stevens	D1	1862	11	1870-80	Pierce, Big Stone	Morris 56267

(Clk Dis Ct has b, d rec from 1872, m rec from 1869, div, civ ct rec from 1873, pro rec from 1901; Co Rcdr has Ind rec from 1871; cem sexton has bur rec)

Superior (changed to Saint Louis, 1855)

* Swift	E1	1870	13	1880	Chippewa, Unorg. Lands	Benson 56215

(Clk Dis Ct has b rec from 1870, m, div, civ ct rec from 1871, d rec from 1872, pro rec; Co Rcdr has Ind rec)

* Todd	D2	1855	25	1857-80	Stearns	Long Prairie 56347

(Clk Dis Ct has b, d rec from 1870, m rec from 1867, div rec from 1880, civ ct rec from 1874, pro rec, school cen from 1914, naturalization rec from 1870; cem associations have bur rec; Co Rcdr has Ind rec)

Toombs (changed to Andy Johnson Co, 1858; changed to Wilkin Co, 1868)

*§ Traverse	D1	1862	6	1870-80	Toombs	Wheaton 56296

(Clk Dis Ct has b, m, d, bur, div, pro, civ ct rec from 1881)

*§ Wabasha	E3	1849	19	1850-80	Original county	Wabasha 55981

(Clk Dis Ct has b & d rec from 1870, m rec from 1868, div & civ ct rec)

Wadena	C2	1858	14	1870-80	Cass, Todd	Wadena 56482

(Clk Dis Ct has b, m & d rec from 1873, div & civ ct rec from 1881)

Wahnata				1850	Disorganized	
* Waseca	F3	1857	18	1857-80	Steele	Waseca 56093

(Clk Dis Ct has b & d rec from 1870, m, div, civ ct rec from 1857 & bur rec from 1880)

*§ Washington	E3	1849	114	1850-80	Original county	Stillwater 55082

(Clk Dis Ct has b, d rec from 1870, m rec from 1845, div, civ ct rec from 1847, pro rec from 1850)

* Watonwan	F2	1860	12	1870-80	Brown	Saint James 56081

(Clk Dis Ct has b, m & d rec from 1863, div & civ ct rec from 1865; Pro Judge has pro rec; Reg Deeds has Ind rec)

Wilkin	D1	1858	8	1870-80	Cass, Toombs, Johnson	Breckenridge 56520

(Clk Dis Ct has b rec from 1874, m & div rec from 1890, d rec from 1875, civ ct rec from 1858; Pro Judge has pro rec)

* Winona	F4	1854	46	1857-80	Unorg. Terr.	Winona 55987

(Clk Dis Ct has b & d rec from 1870, m, div & civ ct rec from 1856)

Name	Map Index	Date Created	Pop. By M 1980	U.S. Cen Reports Available	Parent County or Territory From Which Organized	County Seat
*§ Wright	E3	1855	59	1857-80	Hennepin	Buffalo 55313

(Clk Dis Ct has b & d rec from 1871, m rec from 1866, div & civ ct rec from 1870; Pro Judge has pro rec; Reg Deeds has Ind rec)

*§ Yellow Medicine	E1	1871	14	1880	Redwood	Granite Falls 56241

(Clk Dis Ct has b, m rec from 1872, d, div, pro, civ ct rec, naturalization rec from 1872; Co Rcdr has Ind rec)

* - At least one county history has been published about this county.

§ - Inventory of county archives was made by the Historical Records Survey. (see introduction)

MISSISSIPPI

CAPITAL, JACKSON - TERRITORY 1798 - STATE 1817 - (20TH)

French and Spanish adventurers, less interested in establishing homes in the New World than in finding easy wealth to take home to their native lands, came to the Mississippi regions in the sixteenth century. Few evidences of their sojourn remain.

The French established colonies on the Gulf Coast at Old Biloxi in 1699 and on the Mississippi River at Natchez in 1716. The province was ceded to Great Britain in 1763 and the British settlers who followed established permanent homes. Land grants in the vicinity of Natchez to retired English army and navy officers spurred a migration of Protestants, land-loving settlers who contrasted greatly with the remaining Roman Catholic settlers of the French period. When the Thirteen Colonies revolted in 1776, the Natchez District remained loyal to the Crown, and a number of Tories of the seaboard colonies, unwilling to participate in the forced resistance, moved their families to the district. Between 1779 and 1781 Spain asserted her authority and took over the government of the Natchez District.

By 1798 pro-American sentiment had overthrown the rule of Spain and on April 7 of that year the Mississippi Territory was created by act of Congress. Natchez was the first territorial capital, having served also as a seat of government for the district during the British and Spanish regimes.

The opening of the Mississippi River following the completion of the Louisiana Purchase in 1803 and the relinquishment of her claims to the western lands by the State of Georgia, brought about a land boom in the Mississippi Territory. Thousands of settlers came from the eastern and the northern states to claim the new lands. Petitions for statehood soon began and on 10 December 1817 the State of Mississippi was created, the eastern half of the territory having been sheared off to create the Alabama Territory.

Another tremendous migration came in 1837, after the last of the Indian lands in Mississippi had been opened for settlement.

By 1850 Mississippi's population was more or less stabilized and is little changed basically today. The white people of the state are mostly Anglo-Saxon who trace their ancestry to the British Isles. Exceptions to this rule may be found in the families of southern European extraction who were brought to Biloxi as laborers in the fishing industry, and small colonies of thrifty Germans and Italians in various localities. In addition, the Greek restaurateur is a fixture in almost every town of any size throughout the state and in the northwest section the Chinese grocer is an institution.

Genealogical information about Mississippi may be gained from records in the Mississippi Department of Archives and History at Dept. of Archives and History, War Memorial Bldg., 120 No. State St., Jackson, MS 39201, which has early censuses and tax rolls, newspaper files, microfilm copies of the Federal Censuses of Mississippi, records of Mississippi's

Confederate soldiers and an excellent pamphlet "Research in the Mississippi Department of Archives and History". Many helpful suggestions are given in foreign, territorial, state and federal archives. Wills, deeds and probate files are held by the Chancery Clerks of the various counties. Marriage records are kept by the Circuit Clerks. Records of births and deaths since 1912 are at Vital Records, Mississippi State Board of Health, P.O. Box 1700, Jackson, MS 39205.

The limited staff of the Department of Archives and History, Jackson, is happy to supply any information that is indexed or readily accessible but cannot undertake detailed research or microfilm census checking due to the time involved. They are glad to recommend persons outside of the Department who do this sort of work for a reasonable fee.

Genealogical Archives, Libraries, Societies, and Publications

Attala County Library, 328 Goodman St., Kosciusko, MS 39090.

Biloxi Public Library, P.O. Box 467, Biloxi, MS 39533.

Columbus Public Library, 314 N. 7th St., Columbus, MS 39701.

Dept. of Archives and History, Archives History Bldg., Capitol Green, Jackson, MS 39205.

Evans Memorial Library, Aberdeen, MS 39730.

Greenwood-Leflore Public Library, 408 W. Washington, Greenwood, MS 38930.

Gulfport-Harrison County Public Library, Box 4018, 14th St., & 21st Ave., Gulfport, MS 39501.

Jackson-George Regional Library System, headquarters in Pascagoula City Library, 3214 Pascagoula Street, P.O. Box 937, Pascagoula, MS 39567.

Jennie Stephens Smith Library, Box 846, Court Ave. & Main St., New Albany, MS 38652.

Lauren Rogers Memorial Library and Museum, P.O. Box 1108, 5th at 7th St., Laurel, MS 39440.

Marks-Quitman County Library, 315 E. Main, Marks, MS 38646.

Meridian Public Library, 2517 7th St., Meridian, MS 39301.

Mississippi Coast Genealogical and Historical Society, P.O. Box 513, Biloxi, MS 39530.

Mississippi Dept. of Archives and History, P.O. Box 571, Jackson, MS 39205.

Mississippi Genealogical Society, P.O. Box 5301, Jackson, MS 39216.

Northeast Mississippi Historical and Genealogical Society, P.O. Box 434, Tupelo, MS 38801.

Northeast Regional Library, 1023 Fillmore, Corinth, MS 38834.

Ocean Springs Genealogy Society, P.O. Box 300, Ocean Springs, MS 39564.

Public Library, 341 Main St., Greenville, MS 38701.

Public Library, Vicksburg, MS 39180.

Union county, Library, P.O. Box 22, New Albany, MS 38652.

University of Mississippi Library, The, University, MS 38652.

Mississippi Genealogical Exchange, P.O. Box 16609, Jackson, MS 39206.

Mississippi Genealogy and Local History, P.O. Box 9114, Shreveport, LA 71109.

Northeast Mississippi Historical and Genealogical Society Newsletter, P.O. Box 434, Tupelo, MS 38801.

Printed Census Records and Mortality Schedules

State Indexes-1810, 1820, 1830, 1840, 1850, 1860, 1880

Printed Census Records (Counties):

Adams-1816, 1840	Greene-1840	Leake-1840
Amite-1820, 1840, 1860	Hancock-1820, 1840	Lowndes-1830, 1840, 1850
Attala-1840	Harrison-1850	Madison-1830, 1840
Bolivar-1840	Holmes-1840	Marion-1830, 1840, 1850, 1860; 1816
Carroll-1840	Issaquena-1860	Marshall-1840
Chickasaw-1840, 1860	Itawamba-1840, 1850	Monroe-1840, 1850, 1860, 1870
Choctaw-1840	Jackson-1840	Neshoba-1840, 1860
Claiborne-1840, 1860	Jasper-1840	Newton-1840, 1860
Clarke-1840	Jefferson Davis-1840	Noxubee-1840, 1860
Coahoma-1840	Jones-1840; 1837	Oktibbeha-1840
Copiah-1830, 1840, 1860	Kemper-1840	Panola-1840
Covington-1840	Lafayette-1840	Perry-1840; 1821
DeSoto-1840	Lauderdale-1840, 1850	Pike-1830, 1840
Franklin-1820, 1840	Lawrence-1820, 1840	Pontotoc-1840

Printed Census Records (Counties) continued

Rankin-1840
Scott-1840, 1860
Simpson-1830, 1840, 1860
Smith-1860
Tallahatchie-1840
Tippah-1840, 1900

Tishomingo-1840
Tunica-1840, 1860; 1841
Warren-1840
Washington-1830, 1840
Wayne-1810, 1840

Webster-1880
Wilkinson-1840
Winston-1840
Yalobusha-1840
Yazoo-1840

Natchez District-1792, 1805, 1810, 1816

Mortality Schedules
State indexes-1850, 1860

Counties:
Harrison-1850
Marion-1850, 1860

Valuable Printed Sources

Atlas

Ladd, Edward Johnson. *Atlas and Outline History of Southeastern United States Fort Worth, Texas:* Miran Publishers (Reprint from *Gone to Alabama Vol. II* 1973)

Maps

Mississippi Maps 1816-1873. Jackson, Mississippi: Mississippi Historical Society (1974)

Place Names

Brieger, James F., Jackson, Mississippi. *Hometown, Mississippi* #20.

Oakley, Bruce C. *A Postal History of Mississippi Stampless Period 1799-1860.* Baldwyn, Mississippi: Magnolia Publishers (1969)

Guides To Genealogical Research in Mississippi

Lackey, Richard S. *Cite Your Sources.* A Manual for Documenting Family Histories & Genealogical Records. Published 1980, Polyanthos, Inc., New Orleans, Louisiana.

Stryker-Rodda, Kenn ed. *Genealogical Research - Methods and Sources Vol. 2* (Chapter XII Mississippi by Richard Stephen Lackey page 201). Washington D.C.: The American Society of Genealogists (1960)

Wright, Norman Edgar, comp. *North American Genealogical Sources - Southern States.* Provo, Utah: B.Y.U. Press (1968) (Information on Mississippi pages 145-157)

Histories

Biographical and Historical Memoirs of Mississippi. Chicago: Goodspeed Publishing Company (1891). Index published 1961 by Norman E. Gillis.

Lowry, Robert and William H. McCardle. *A History of Mississippi.* Jackson, Mississippi: R. H. Henry and Company (1891)

McLemore, Richard Avery. *A History of Mississippi* (2 Vols). University and College Press of Mississippi 1973.

Genealogical Sources

King, J. Estelle Stewart. *Mississippi Court Records 1799-1835.* Baltimore: Genealogical Publishing Company (1969)

Mississippi Cemetery and bible Records, publications of the Mississippi Genealogical (1954-1979) 18 Vols.

Rowland, Mrs. Dunbar. *Mississippi Territory in the War of 1812.* Baltimore: Genealogical Publishing Company, 1968.

Welch, Alice Tracy. *Family Records Mississippi Revolutionary Soldiers.* Mississippi Society of D.A.R.

Bibliographies

Survey of Records in Mississippi Court Houses. Jackson, Mississippi. Mississippi Genealogical Society (1967)

MISSISSIPPI COUNTY HISTORIES
(Population figures to nearest thousand - 1980 U. S. Census)

Name	Map Index	Date Created	Pop. By M 1980	U.S. Cen Reports Available	Parent County or Territory From Which Organized	County Seat
* Adams	E1	1799	38	1820-80	Natchez District	Natchez 39120
Alcorn	A4	1870	33	1870-80	Tippah, Tishomingo	Corinth 38834

(Clk Chan Ct has div rec from 1913 & chan ct rec; Clk Cir Ct has civ ct rec from 1860)

Name	Map Index	Date Created	Pop. By M 1980	U.S. Cen Reports Available	Parent County or Territory From Which Organized	County Seat
*§ Amite	E1	1809	13	1820-80	Wilkinson	Liberty 39645
* Attala	C3	1833	20	1840-80	Choctaw Cession	Kosciusko 39090

(Clk Cir Ct has m rec; Clk Chan Ct has div, pro, Ind & old newspapers)

Name	Map Index	Date Created	Pop. By M 1980	U.S. Cen Reports Available	Parent County or Territory From Which Organized	County Seat
Benton	A3	1870	8	1880	Marshall, Tippah	Ashland 38603

(Chan Clk has div, pro, deeds & wills from 1871)

Name	Map Index	Date Created	Pop. By M 1980	U.S. Cen Reports Available	Parent County or Territory From Which Organized	County Seat
* Bolivar	B1	1836	46	1840-80	Choctaw Cession	Rosedale 38769 & Cleveland 38732

(Clk Cir Ct, Cleveland Miss has m & civ ct rec; Clk Chan Ct has div, pro & Ind rec) (Clk Cir Ct, Rosedale Miss has m rec from 1866, civ ct rec from 1870; Clk Chan Ct has div, pro & Ind rec) (Chan & Cir Clks office in both Courthouses. Rosedale rec go back about 20 years further than Cleveland, it being the older of the two towns)

Name	Map Index	Date Created	Pop. By M 1980	U.S. Cen Reports Available	Parent County or Territory From Which Organized	County Seat
* Calhoun	B3	1852	16	1860-80	Lafayette, Valobusha	Pittsboro 38951

(Clk Chan Ct has div, pro & Ind rec from 1923)

Name	Map Index	Date Created	Pop. By M 1980	U.S. Cen Reports Available	Parent County or Territory From Which Organized	County Seat
Carroll	B2	1833	10	1840-80	Choctaw Cession	Carrollton 38917 & Vaiden 39176

(Co Clk has m, div, pro, civ ct & Ind rec from 1870)

Name	Map Index	Date Created	Pop. By M 1980	U.S. Cen Reports Available	Parent County or Territory From Which Organized	County Seat
Chickasaw	B3	1836	18	1840-80	Chickasaw Cession of 1832	Houston 38851 & Okolona 38860

(Clk Cir Ct, Houston has m, div, pro, civ ct rec & all Ind rec for Co) (Clk Cir Ct, Okolona has m rec from 1877 & civ ct rec; Clk Chan Ct has div & pro rec from 1886)

Name	Map Index	Date Created	Pop. By M 1980	U.S. Cen Reports Available	Parent County or Territory From Which Organized	County Seat
Choctaw	C3	1833	9	1840-80	Chickasaw Cession of 1832	Ackerman 39735

(Clk Cir Ct has m, div, pro, civ ct, Ind rec from 1881)

Name	Map Index	Date Created	Pop. By M 1980	U.S. Cen Reports Available	Parent County or Territory From Which Organized	County Seat
Claiborne	D1	1802	12	1820-80	Jefferson	Port Gibson 39150

(Chan Clk has m rec from 1816, div rec from 1856, pro & civ ct rec 1802)

Name	Map Index	Date Created	Pop. By M 1980	U.S. Cen Reports Available	Parent County or Territory From Which Organized	County Seat
Clarke	D4	1812	17	1840-80	Washington	Quitman 39355

(Chan Clk has div & pro rec from 1875)

Name	Map Index	Date Created	Pop. By M 1980	U.S. Cen Reports Available	Parent County or Territory From Which Organized	County Seat
* Clay	B4	1871	21	1880	Chickasaw, Lowndes, Monroe, Oktibbeha (formerly Colfax)	West Point 39773

(Clk Cir Ct has m, civ ct rec; Clk Chan Ct has div, pro, Ind rec from 1872; Bur Vit Statistics, Jackson, has b, d rec)

Name	Map Index	Date Created	Pop. By M 1980	U.S. Cen Reports Available	Parent County or Territory From Which Organized	County Seat
Coahoma	A2	1836	37	1840-80	Chickasaw Cession 1836	Clarksdale 38614

(Clk Cir Ct has m, civ ct rec from 1848; crim ct rec, voter rec from 1949; Clk Chan Ct has div, pro, Ind rec; Bur Vit Statistics, Jackson has b, d rec)

Name	Map Index	Date Created	Pop. By M 1980	U.S. Cen Reports Available	Parent County or Territory From Which Organized	County Seat
Colfax		1871			Name changed to Clay, 1876	
* Copiah	D2	1823	26	1830-80	Hinds	Hazlehurst 39083

(Clk Chan Ct has div, pro, civ ct & mtg rec from 1823)

Name	Map Index	Date Created	Pop. By M 1980	U.S. Cen Reports Available	Parent County or Territory From Which Organized	County Seat
Covington	E3	1819	16	1820-80	Lawrence, Wayne	Collins 39428

(Clk Chan Ct has m, div & pro rec from 1900, civ ct rec & Ind rec from 1860)

Name	Map Index	Date Created	Pop. By M 1980	U.S. Cen Reports Available	Parent County or Territory From Which Organized	County Seat
DeSoto	A2	1836	54	1840-80	Indian Lands	Hernando 38632

(Clk Chan Ct has div, pro & Ind rec)

Name	Map Index	Date Created	Pop. By M 1980	U.S. Cen Reports Available	Parent County or Territory From Which Organized	County Seat
§ Forrest	E3	1906	66		Perry	Hattiesburg 39401
Franklin	E1	1809	8	1820-80	Adams	Meadville 39653
George	F4	1910	15		Greene, Jackson	Lucedale 39452

(Clk Cir Ct has m rec & civ ct rec from 1911; Clk Chan Ct has div, pro & Ind rec from 1911)

Name	Map Index	Date Created	Pop. By M 1980	U.S. Cen Reports Available	Parent County or Territory From Which Organized	County Seat
Greene	E4	1811	10	1820-80	Amita, Franklin, Wayne	Leakesville 39451
§ Grenada	B2	1870	21	1870-80	Carroll, Yalobusha, Choctaw, Talahatchie, Webster, Montgomery	Grenada 38901

(Clk Cir Ct has m rec, div, pro rec from 1870, Ind rec from 1835; State Board of Health, Jackson, has b, d rec)

Name	Map Index	Date Created	Pop. By M 1980	U.S. Cen Reports Available	Parent County or Territory From Which Organized	County Seat
* Hancock	F3	1812	25	1820-80	Mobile District	Bay St. Louis 39520

(Clk Cir Ct has m & civ ct rec; Clk Chan Ct has div, pro & Ind rec)

Name	Map Index	Date Created	Pop. By M 1980	U.S. Cen Reports Available	Parent County or Territory From Which Organized	County Seat
Harrison	F3	1841	15	1850-80	Hancock, Jackson	Gulfport 39501

(Clk Cir Ct has m rec from 1841 & civ ct rec; Clk Chan Ct has div, pro & Ind rec)

Name	Map Index	Date Created	Pop. By M 1980	U.S. Cen Reports Available	Parent County or Territory From Which Organized	County Seat
* Hinds	D2	1821	248	1830-80	Choctaw Cession 1820	Jackson 39201

(Clk Cir Ct has m rec from 1823, civ ct rec from 1930; Clk Chan Ct has div, pro, Ind rec)

| Holmes | C2 | 1833 | 23 | 1840-80 | Yazoo | Lexington 39095 |

(Chan Clk has div & pro rec from 1894, also deeds, wills from 1833 & bur rec; Clk Cir Ct has m, civ ct rec)

| § Humphreys | C2 | 1918 | 14 | | Holmes, Washington, Yazoo, Sunflower | Belzoni 39038 |

(Clk Cir Ct has b & m rec; Clk Chan Ct has div, pro & Ind rec from 1918)

| Issaquena | C1 | 1844 | 3 | 1850-80 | Washington | Mayersville 39113 |

(Clk Chan Ct has m rec from 1866, div, pro, civ ct & Ind rec from 1850)

| Itawamba | A4 | 1836 | 20 | 1840-80 | Chickasaw Cession 1832 | Fulton 38843 |

(Clk Chan Ct has m, div, pro, civ ct & Ind rec)

| * Jackson | F4 | 1812 | 118 | 1820-80 | Mobile District | Pascagoula 39567 |

(Clk Chan Ct has div & pro rec from 1875, also justice of the peace dockets & license of physicians & dentists from 1875; Clk Cir Ct has m rec from 1875)

| Jasper | D3 | 1833 | 17 | 1840-80 | Indian Lands | Bay Springs 39422 & Paulding 39348 |

(Co Clk has div, pro & civ ct rec from 1906; Cir Clk has m rec)

| Jefferson | E1 | 1799 | 9 | 1820-80 | Natchez, originally Pickering | Fayette 39069 |

(Clk Chan Ct has m rec from 1798, div rec from 1860, pro & Ind rec from 1798)

| Jefferson Davis | E2 | 1906 | 14 | | Covington, Lawrence | Prentiss 39474 |
| Jones | E3 | 1826 | 62 | 1830-80 | Covington, Wayne | Ellisville 39437 & Laurel 39440 |

(Clk Cir Ct has m rec from 1882 & civ ct rec from 1907; Clk Chan Ct at Laurel & Ellisville, Miss has div & Ind rec)

| Kemper | C4 | 1833 | 10 | 1840-80 | Choctaw Cession, 1832 | DeKalb 39328 |

(Clk Cir Ct has m rec from 1912; Clk Chan Ct has div, pro, civ ct & Ind rec from 1912)

| Lafayette | A3 | 1836 | 31 | 1840-80 | Chickasaw Cession | Oxford 38655 |

(Chan Clk has m, div, pro & civ ct rec)

| § Lamar | E3 | 1904 | 24 | | Marion, Pearl River | Purvis 39475 |

(Clk Cir Ct has m rec; Clk Chan Ct has div, pro & Ind rec from 1900's; J P has civ ct rec)

| * Lauderdale | D4 | 1833 | 76 | 1840-80 | Choctaw Cession | Meridian 39301 |

(Clk Chan Ct has div, pro & Ind rec; Co Health has b & d rec; Clk Cir Ct has m & civ ct rec)

| Lawrence | E2 | 1814 | 13 | 1820-80 | Marion | Monticello 39654 |

(Clk Cir Ct has m & civ ct rec; Clk Chan Ct has div, pro & Ind rec from 1815)

| Leake | C3 | 1833 | 19 | 1840-80 | Choctaw Cession | Carthage 39051 |

(Clk Chan Ct has m rec, div, pro rec from 1871, civ ct rec, Ind rec from 1833, wills from 1840, mil discharge rec from 1918)

| Lee | A4 | 1866 | 57 | 1870-80 | Itawamba, Pontotoc | Tupelo 38801 |

(Clk Chan Ct has div & pro rec from 1866)

| Leflore | B2 | 1871 | 42 | 1880 | Carroll, Sunflower, Tallahatchie | Greenwood 38930 |

(Clk Cir Ct has m & civ ct rec; Clk Chan Ct has div & pro rec from 1871 & Ind rec from 1834)

| Lincoln | E2 | 1870 | 30 | 1870-80 | Franklin, Lawrence, Copiah, Pike, Amite | Brookhaven 39601 |

(Clk Chan Ct has div, pro & civ ct rec from 1893; Clk Dis Ct has m rec from 1893)

| * Lowndes | C4 | 1830 | 57 | 1830-80 | Monroe | Columbus 39701 |

(m, div, pro, civ ct, Ind rec from 1830 to 1900 are at the Lowndes Co Dept of Archives and History, also Bible rec, manuscripts, cen rec. All recs for this county are complete from 1830 to date)

| * Madison | C2 | 1828 | 41 | 1830-80 | Yazoo | Canton 39046 |

(Clk Chan Ct has m, div, pro, civ ct & Ind rec from 1828)

| Marion | E2 | 1811 | 26 | 1820-80 | Amite, Wayne, Franklin | Columbia 39429 |

(Clk Chan Ct has m, div, pro, civ ct & Ind rec)

| Marshall | A3 | 1836 | 29 | 1840-80 | Chickasaw Cession, 1832 | Holly Springs 38635 |

(Clk Chan Ct has div, pro & deeds from 1836)

| * Monroe | B4 | 1821 | 36 | 1820-80 | Chickasaw Cession, 1821 | Aberdeen 39730 |

(Clk Cir Ct has m & civ ct rec; Clk Chan Ct has div rec, pro & Ind rec from 1821)

COUNTY MAP FOR THE STATE OF MISSISSIPPI

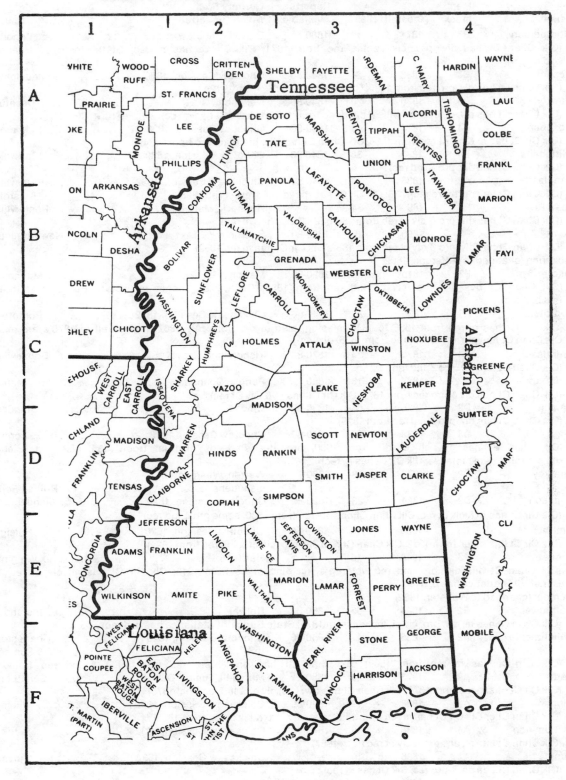

Name	Map Index	Date Created	Pop. By M 1980	U.S. Cen Reports Available	Parent County or Territory From Which Organized	County Seat
Montgomery	B3	1871	13	1880	Carroll, Choctaw	Winona 38967

(Clk Chan Ct has div, pro, civ ct, Ind rec from 1871; Clk Cir Ct has m rec; State Board of Health has b, d rec)

| Neshoba | C3 | 1833 | 24 | 1840-80 | Choctaw Cession, 1830 | Philadelphia 39350 |

(Clk Chan Ct has div, pro rec from 1890; Clk Cir Ct has m rec from 1912)

| * Newton | D3 | 1836 | 20 | 1840-80 | Neshoba | Decatur 39327 |

(Clk Chan Ct has div, pro, civ ct, wills & deed rec from 1876; Clk Cir Ct has m rec)

| Noxubee | C4 | 1833 | 13 | 1840-80 | Choctaw Cession, 1830 | Macon 39341 |

(Clk Cir Ct has m & civ ct rec from 1834; Clk Chan Ct has div, pro & Ind rec from 1834)

| * Oktibbeha | B4 | 1833 | 36 | 1840-80 | Choctaw Cession, 1830 | Starkville 39759 |

(Clk Chan Ct has div, pro & Ind rec)

| Panola | A2 | 1836 | 28 | 1840-80 | Chickasaw Cession, 1832 | Batesville 38606 & Sardis 38666 |

(Clk Chan Ct has div & pro rec 1836; Clk Cir Ct has m rec 1885, civ ct rec 1836)

| § Pearl River | F3 | 1890 | 34 | | Hancock, Marion | Poplarville 39470 |

(Clk Chan Ct has div, pro & civ ct rec from 1890; Clk Cir Ct has m rec)

| Perry | E3 | 1820 | 10 | 1820-80 | Greene | New Augusta 39462 |

(Clk Chan Ct has div, pro & civ ct rec from 1882; Clk Cir Ct has m rec 1882)

Pickering (changed to Jefferson, 1802)

| * Pike | E2 | 1815 | 36 | 1820-80 | Marion | Magnolia 39652 |

(Clk Chan Ct has div, pro, civ ct, Ind rec from 1882; Clk Cir Ct has m rec, State Bur of Vit Statistics has b, d rec)

| Pontotoc | A3 | 1836 | 21 | 1840-80 | Chickasaw Cession, 1832 | Pontotoc 38863 |

(Clk Cir Ct has m rec from 1836 to 1840 missing, also m rec from July 1867 through all of 1870's are missing; Clk Chan Ct has pro, civ ct, Ind rec from 1836, div rec)

| * Prentiss | A4 | 1870 | 24 | 1870-80 | Tishomingo | Booneville 38829 |

(Clk Chan Ct has div, pro & Ind rec)

| Quitman | A2 | 1877 | 13 | 1880 | Panola, Coahoma | Marks 38646 |

(Clk Chan Ct has div & pro rec from 1877; Clk Cir Ct has m & Civ Ct rec)

| Rankin | D2 | 1828 | 68 | 1830-80 | Hinds | Brandon 39042 |

(Clk Chan Ct has div, pro & Ind rec from 1829)

| Scott | D3 | 1833 | 24 | 1840-80 | Choctaw Cession 1832 | Forest 39074 |

(Clk Chan Ct has div, civ ct rec from 1900, pro, deeds, deeds of trust from 1835, also Ind & chattel, old church & cem plots rec; Clk Cir Ct has m rec)

| Sharkey | C2 | 1876 | 8 | 1880 | Warren, Washington, Issaquena | Rolling Fork 39159 |

| Simpson | D2 | 1824 | 23 | 1830-80 | Choctaw Cession, 1820 | Mendenhall 39114 |

(Clk Cir Ct has m & civ ct rec; Clk Chan Ct has div rec from 1880, some pro & Ind rec)

| * Smith | D3 | 1833 | 15 | 1840-80 | Choctaw Cession, 1820 | Raleigh 39153 |

(Clk Cir Ct has m rec from 1912; Clk Chan Ct has div, pro, civ ct & Ind rec from 1892)

| Stone | F3 | 1916 | 10 | | Harrison | Wiggins 39577 |

(Clk Chan Ct has div, pro, Ind rec, veteran's mil discharges from 1916; Clk Cir Ct has m, civ ct rec; State Bur of Vit Statistics has b, d rec)

Sumner (changed to Webster, 1882)

| Sunflower | B2 | 1844 | 35 | 1850-80 | Bolivar | Indianola 38751 |

(Clk Chan Ct has m, div, pro, civ ct, Ind rec from 1871; State Bur of Vit Statistics has b, d rec)

| Tallahatchie | B2 | 1833 | 17 | 1840-80 | Choctaw Cession, 1820 | Charleston 38921 & Sumner 38957 |

(Clk Cir Ct has m rec from 1909; Clk Chan Ct has div & pro rec from 1909 & Ind rec from 1858)

| Tate | A2 | 1873 | 20 | 1880 | Marshall, Tunica, DeSoto | Senatobia 38668 |

(Clk Cir Ct has m rec from 1873; Clk Chan Ct has div, pro, civ ct & Ind rec from 1873)

| § Tippah | A3 | 1836 | 19 | 1840-80 | Chickasaw Cession, 1832 | Ripley 38663 |

(Clk Chan Ct or Clk Cir Ct has m rec from 1856, also div, pro & civ ct rec from 1856)

| * Tishomingo | A4 | 1836 | 18 | 1840-80 | Chickasaw Cession, 1832 | Iuka 38852 |

(Clk Chan Ct has m, div, pro & civ ct rec from 1887)

| § Tunica | A2 | 1836 | 10 | | Chickasaw Cession, 1832 | Tunica 38676 |

(Clk Chan Ct has div & pro rec; Clk Ct has m rec)

| * Union | A3 | 1870 | 22 | 1880 | Pontotoc, Tippah | New Albany 38652 |

(Clk Chan Ct has div, pro & civ ct rec; Clk Cir Ct has m rec)

Name	Map Index	Date Created	Pop. By M 1980	U.S. Cen Reports Available	Parent County or Territory From Which Organized	County Seat
§ Walthall	E2	1910	14		Marion, Pike	Tylertown 39667

(Clk Cir Ct has m rec from 1914; Clk Chan Ct has div, pro, civ ct, Ind rec from 1914)

* Warren	D2	1809	52	1820-80	Natchez District	Vicksburg 39180
* Washington	C1	1827	72	1820-80	Warren, Yazoo	Greenville 38701

(Clk Cir Ct has m rec from 1858, civ ct rec from 1890; Clk Chan Ct has div rec from 1856, pro, Ind rec from 1831)

Wayne	E4	1809	19	1820-80	Washington	Waynesboro 39367
Webster	B3	1874	10		Montgomery, Chickasaw, Choctaw, Oktibbeha	Walthall 39771

(Originally Summer, named changed 1882) (Clk Cir Ct has m, civ ct rec; Clk Chan Ct has div, pro, Ind rec from 1880)

Wilkinson	E1	1802	10	1820-80	Adams	Woodville 39669

(Clk Chan Ct has m, div, pro, ct & Ind rec)

Winston	C3	1833	20	1840-80	Choctaw Cession, 1830	Louisville 39339
Yalobusha	B3	1833	13	1840-80	Choctaw Cession, 1830	Coffeyville 38922 & Water Valley 38965

(Clk Cir Ct, Coffeyville has m rec; Clk Chan Ct has div, pro, civ ct & Ind rec) (Clk Chan Ct, Water Valley has div, pro, civ ct & Ind rec)

* Yazoo	C2	1823	27	1830-80	Hinds	Yazoo City 39194

(m rec date from 1820)

* - At least one county history has been published about this county.

§ - Inventory of county archives was made by the Historical Records Survey. (see introduction)

MISSOURI

CAPITAL, JEFFERSON CITY - TERRITORY 1812 - STATE 1821 - (24TH)

The Mississippi River, five hundred miles of which is the eastern border of Missouri, was first seen by a white man in 1541 when the Spanish explorer, Hernando or Fernando De Soto, saw that mighty river. It was 132 years later that two French explorers, Marquette and Joilet, were the first to see the Missouri River. Only nine years later, in 1682, another French explorer, Robert Cavelier de La Salle, took possession of the section as part of Louisiana and claimed it for France. A Catholic mission has established on the present site of St. Louis about 1700. The first permanent Missouri settlement was established about 1750 by the French. It was located along the Mississippi River about 50 miles south of St. Louis and was called Sainte Genevieve.

The first actual American settlement in Missouri was in 1787 when one John Dodge established himself in Ste. Genevieve County. He was followed there by Israel Dodge in 1790, and three years later by Dr. Jesse Bryan. A John Moore is said to have made his home in 1790 in what since then has become Perry County which borders Ste. Genevieve County on the southeast. In 1795 American settlements were established on Femme Osage creek in what is now St. Charles County, north of St. Louis. It was then called Upper Louisiana or New Spain. Authority for these statements comes from *Pioneer Families of Missouri,* published in 1876 by Wm. S. Bryan and Robert Rose, and reprinted in 1935 with an introduction by W. W. Elwang.

From 1682 until 1803 control over the Missouri section was passed back and forth between France and Spain. In the Louisiana Purchase, consummated in 1803, ownership passed into the hands of the United States.

In 1805 Missouri became part of the Territory of Louisiana and remained so until 1812 when it became a territory in its own name. At that time it claimed a population of 20,000. Most of its early settlers came from Kentucky and Virginia, and some from North and South Carolina, Maryland, Pennsylvania, and Tennessee. In those early days, Indian tribes, enticed by the British, constantly scourged the Missouri settlers in severe plundering raids. It was not until about 1815 that these raids were halted through peace treaties with the various Indian tribes within the territory.

Missouri became a state in 1821. Then it had about 56,000 white settlers. She became the twenty-fourth state in the Union. At present she has 114 counties and one independent city, St. Louis.

For many decades after 1830 a steady stream of European immigrants came into the state, as a result of which St. Louis has a distinct German flavor. Many Irish, English, Polish, Swiss, Bohemian and Italian natives settled in various parts of the state. In his *Creoles of St. Louis*, (1893), Paul Beckwith does full justice to the early French immigration, the so-called Creoles, the Chouteaus, Gratiots, Cabannes, Papins, Pauls, etc.

Throughout the Civil War, numerous skirmishes and bloody battles were fought in Missouri which was one of the important battle grounds of the conflict, keeping the population in constant excitement and fear.

Missouri Department of Social Services, Division of Health, Broadway State Office Building, P.O. Box 570, Jefferson City, Missouri 65102 reports that births and deaths were not recorded in this office prior to 1910, although for a brief period (1883-1893) county clerks were required to register births and deaths and some counties and cities kept these records for other years. Any of the vital statistic records which are still available must be obtained from the county clerk of the county where the birth or death occurred or from Records Management and Archives Service, 1001 Industrial Drive, Post Office Box 778, Jefferson City, Missouri 65101. Records Management and Archives Service is currently receiving microfilm copies of county records. The Vital Records office has no provisions for checking of genealogical sources elsewhere.

The Missouri State Historical Society, Corner of Hitt and Lowry Streets, Columbia, Missouri 65201 does not have birth and death certificates as such; however, it is possible that they may be able to furnish researchers with other evidence from their resources which will serve as a record.

Information on some marriages from 1825 to date may be had at the office of the Recorder of Deeds in each county. In those offices are also the records of deeds. Wills are in the Probate Courts. Taxpayer lists are in the offices of the county assessors. War service records are under the care of the Adjutant General at Jefferson City, MO 65101. A law originating in 1863 makes it permissible for the Recorder of Deeds in each county to file birth information on request. The first death recording began in St. Louis in 1841.

Many of the county courthouses in Missouri have been lost through fire. With them were lost at the same time many old records.

Among organizations and institutions able to give much genealogical information are the Nancy Hunter Chapter, Daughters of the American Revolution, Cape Giardeau, MO 63701, Ann Haynes chapter, DAR, Kirksville, MO 63501.

Genealogical Archives, Libraries, Societies, and Publications

Andrew County Historical Society, Box 12, Savannah, MO 64485.

Boonslick Regional Library, Sedalia, MO 63501.

Camden County, Missouri Historical Society, Linn Creek, MO 65052.

Cape Girardeau County Missouri Genealogical Society, 204 S. Union Ave., Jackson, MO 63755.

Cass County Historical Society, 400 E. Mechanic, Harrisonville, MO 64701.

Clay County Museum Assn. Library, 14 North Main Street, Liberty, MO 64086.

Cole County Museum, 109 Madison, Jefferson City, MO 65101.

Concordia Historical Institute, 301 DeMun Ave., St. Louis, MO 63105.

Dallas County Historical Society, R. 2, Box 126, Buffalo, MO 65622.

Eastern Jackson County, Missouri Genealogical Society, P.O. Box 7791, Independence, MO 64084.

Genealogical Society of Central Missouri, P.O. Box 26, Columbia, MO 65205.

Graham Historical Society, P.O. Box 72, Graham, MO 64455.

Heart of American Genealogical Society, c/o Public Library, 311 East 12th St., Kansas City, MO 64101.

Heritage Library, Johnson County Historical Society, 135 E. Pine St., Warrensburg, MO 64093.

Kansas City Public Library, 311 East 12th St., Kansas City, MO 64106.

Kent Library, Southeast Missouri State College, Cape Girardeau, MO 63701.

Keytesville Library, 110 Bridge Street, Keytesville, MO 65261.

Lawrence County Historical Society, P.O. Box 406, Mt. Vernon, MO 65712.

Mid-Missouri Genealogical Society, Inc., P.O. Box 715, Jefferson City, MO 65102.

Missouri Baptist Historical Society, William Jewell College Library, Liberty, MO 64068.

Missouri Historical Society, Jefferson Memorial Bldg., Forest Park, St. Louis, MO 63112.

Missouri State Genealogical Association, 4302 Barth Drive, St. Louis, MO 63125.

Missouri State Library, 308 East High St., Jefferson City, MO 65101.

Missouri Territorial Pioneers, 3920 Milton Drive, Independence, MO 64055.

Moniteau County Missouri Historical Society, California, MO 65018.

Morgan County Missouri Historical Society, P.O. Box 177, Versailles, MO 65084.

Newton County Historical Society, 504 Joy, Neosho, MO 64850.

Nodaway County Genealogical Society, Maryville, MO 64468.

Northwest Missouri Genealogy Society, P. O. Box 68, Station E. St. Joseph, MO 64505.

Old Mines Area Historical Society, Route 1, Box 300Z, Cadet, Old Mines, MO 63630.

Oregon County Genealogical Society, Courthouse, Alton, MO 65606.

Ozarks Genealogical Society, Box 3494 G.S., Springfield, MO 65804.

Platte County Missouri Genealogical Society, P.O. Box 103, Platte City, MO 64079.

Records and Archives, Office of Sec. of State Capitol Bldg., Jefferson, MO 65101.

Riverside Regional Library, The, P.O. Box 389, Jackson, MO 63755.

St. Charles County Genealogical Society, P.O. Box 715, St. Charles, MO 63301.

St. Louis Genealogical Society, 1695 Brentwood Blvd., Suite 203, St. Louis, MO 63144.

St. Louis Public Library, 1301 Olive St., St. Louis, MO 63103.

Shelbina Carnegie Public Library, Box 247, 102 N. Center St., Shelbina, MO 63468.

Springfield Public Library, Reference Department and Shepard Room, 397 E. Central St., Springfield, MO 65801.

State Historical Society of Missouri, Hitt and Lowry Sts., Columbia, MO 65201.

Vernon County Historical Society, c/o W. R. Hamblin, 127 E. Cherry, Nevada, MO 64772.

White River Valley Historical Society, Box 565, Point Lookout, MO 65726.

Genealogia, newsletter of the Mid-Missouri Genealogical Society, P.O. Box 715, Jefferson City, MO 65101.

Kansas City Genealogist, The, The Heart of America Genealogical Society, c/o Missouri Valley Room, Kansas City Public Library, 311 East 12th St., Kansas City, MO 64106.

Northwest Missouri Genealogical Society Journal, P.O. Box 68, Station E, St. Joseph, MO 64505.

Ozar'kin, quarterly publication of the Ozarks Genealogical Society, Box 3494, Springfield, MO 65804.

Pioneer Times, Journal Mid-Missouri Genealogical Society, P.O. Box 715, Jefferson City, MO 65101.

Pioneer Trails, Genealogy Society of Eastern Jackson County, Missouri, P.O. Box 7791, Independence, MO 64084.

Platte County Historical Society Bulletin, Platte County, Missouri Genealogical Society, P.O. Box 103, Platte City, MO 64079.

Printed Census Records and Mortality Schedules

State Indexes! 1830, 1840, 1850

Printed Census Records (Counties):

Adair-1850
Allen-1850
Andrew-1850, 1860, 1870, 1880, 1890
Atchison-1850, 1890
Audrain-1840, 1850
Barry-1840, 1850
Bates-1850
Benton-1840, 1850; 1876
Boone-1830, 1840, 1850, 1860, 1870, 1880
Buchanan-1840, 1850, 1860, 1880
Butler-1850, 1860

Caldwell-1840, 1850
Callaway-1840, 1850
Camden-1850
Cape Girardeau-1840, 1850; 1876
Carroll-1840, 1850
Cass-1850
Cedar-1850, 1860
Chariton-1840, 1850
Christian-1876
Clark-1840, 1850, 1880
Clay-1840

Clinton-1840, 1850
Cole-1840, 1850
Cooper-1840, 1850
Crawford-1830, 1840, 1850
Dade-1850, 1860, 1870, 1880
Dallas-1850
Daviess-1840, 1850
DeKalb-1850
Dunklin-1850, 1860, 1870, 1880
Franklin-1840, 1850
Gasconade-1840, 1850, 1860; 1864

Printed Census Records (Counties) continued:

Gentry-1850
Greene-1840, 1850
Grundy-1850, 1860, 1890
Harrison-1850
Henry-1840, 1850
Hickory-1850
Holt-1850
Howard-1840, 1850
Jackson-1830, 1840, 1850, 1860
Jasper-1850, 1860, 1880
Jefferson-1840, 1850
Johnson-1840, 1850
Knox-1850
Laclede-1850, 1860
Lafayette-1840, 1850
Lawrence-1850
Lewis-1840, 1850
Lincoln-1840, 1850
Linn-1840, 1850
Livingston-1840, 1850
Macon-1840, 1850
Madison-1850, 1880
Marion-1850
McDonald-1850
Mercer-1850
Miller-1840, 1850

Mississippi-1850
Moniteau-1850, 1860
Monroe-1840, 1850
Montgomery- 1840, 1850
Morgan-1840, 1850
New Madrid- 1840, 1850, 1860; 1796, 1797, 1803
Newton-1840, 1850, 1860
Nodaway-1850
Oregon-1850
Osage-1850
Ozark-1850
Perry-1850; 1821
Pettis-1850
Pike-1850
Platte-1840, 1850
Polk-1830, 1840, 1850
Pulaski-1830, 1840, 1850
Putnam-1850
Ralls-1840, 1850
Randolph-1830, 1840, 1850, 1860, 1870, 1880
Ray-1810, 1830, 1840, 1850, 1860
Reynolds-1850, 1860
Ripley-1840, 1850, 1860, 1870

Rives-1840, 1860
St. Charles-1840
St. Clair-1850
St. Francois-1840, 1850
St. Louis-1840, 1850
St. Joseph-1880
St. Geneviere-1840, 1850
Saline-1850
Schuyler-1850, 1880
Scotland-1850, 1860
Scott-1840, 1850
Shannon-1850
Shelby-1840, 1850
Stoddard-1840, 1850
Stone-1850, 1860
Sullivan-1850, 1860
Taney-1840, 1850, 1860
Texas-1850, 1860
Warren-1820, 1850
Washington-1820, 1850, 1860
Wayne-1840, 1850, 1860
Webster-1860, 1880
Wright-1850, 1860, 1870, 1880

Mortality Schedules- (Printed) 1850, 1860
Counties:

Andrew-1850, 1860, 1870, 1880
New Madrid-1850, 1860, 1870, 1880

Ripley-1850, 1860, 1870, 1880
Dunklin-1850, 1860, 1870, 1880

Valuable Printed Sources

Gazetteers

Beck, Lewis Caleb. *A Gazetteer of the States of Illinois and Missouri.* New York: Arno Press (1975) reprint of 1823 edition.

Campbell, Robert Allen ed. *Campbell's Gazetteer of Missouri.* St. Louis: R.A. Campbell (1875).

Place Names

Ramsay, Robert Lee. *Our Storehouse of Missouri Place Names.* Columbia: University of Missouri (1952)

Guides To Genealogical Research

Parkin, Robert E. *Guide to Tracing your Family Tree in Missouri.* St. Louis: Genealogical R. and P. (1979)

Williams, Betty H. *A Genealogical Tour Through the Courthouses and Libraries of Missouri.* Warrensburg, Mo. Privately published (1972)

Williams, Jacqueline Hogan and Betty Harvey Williams compilers. *Resources for Genealogical Research in Missouri.* Warrensburg, Missouri Privately published (1969).

Histories

Conard, Howard L. *Encyclopedia of the History of Missouri.* St. Louis: Southern History Company (1901).

Williams, Walter. *A History of Northwest Missouri.* 3 Vols. Chicago and New York: Lewis Publishing Company, 1915.

History of Southeast Missouri. Chicago: Goodspeed Publishing Company, 1888.

Genealogical Sources

Carter, Mrs. J. R. *Early Missouri Marriages to 1840.* Sedalia, Missouri: Privately published.

Ellsberry, Elizabeth Prather. *Bible Records of Missouri.* Chillicothe, Missouri: Privately published (1963)

Revolutionary Soldiers and Their Descendants - Genealogical Records, Missouri Edition. New York: American Historical Publishing Company.

Taft, William Howard, comp. *Missouri Newspapers: When and Where 1808.* Columbia: University of Missouri (1964).

MISSOURI COUNTY HISTORIES
(Population figures to nearest thousand - 1980 U. S. Census)

Name	Map Index	Date Created	Pop. By M 1980	U.S. Cen Reports Available	Parent County or Territory From Which Organized	County Seat
* Adair	C1	1841	25	1850-80	Macon	Kirksville 63501

(Co Rcdr has m & Ind rec; Clk Cir Ct has div rec; Pro Judge has pro rec; Co Clk has school enum rec)

Allen (changed to Atchison, 1845)

| * Andrew | E1 | 1841 | 14 | 1850-80 | Platte Purchase | Savannah 64485 |

(Co Clk has b & d rec from 1883 to 1900; Clk Cir Ct has m, div & civ ct rec from 1841, Ind & mil ser rec; Pro Judge has pro rec from 1841)

| Arkansas | | 1813 | | | New Madrid | |

(abolished 1819 when terr of Arkansas was formed)

Ashley (changed to Texas, 1845)

| Atchison | E1 | 1843 | 9 | 1850-80 | Holt | Rockport 64482 |

(part of Platte Purchase; attached to Holt Co until 1854; lost 10-mile strip to Iowa, 1848) (Clk Cir Ct has m, div & Ind rec; Pro Judge has pro & civ ct rec)

| * Audrain | C2 | 1831 | 26 | 1840-80 | Monroe | Mexico 65265 |

(created in 1831, but remained attached to Callaway, Monroe & Ralls Cos until 1836. In 1842 gained an additional 31 sq miles from Monroe Co) (Co Clk has b rec from 1883 to 1886; Rcdr Deeds has m & Ind rec; Clk Cir Ct has div & civ ct rec; Pro Judge has pro rec)

| * Barry | D5 | 1835 | 24 | 1840-80 | Greene | Cassville 65625 |

(error in survey, rectified in 1876, established the western line 2½ miles east of previous boundary; in 1872 many rec in Cir Clks office were destroyed by fire) (Rcdr Deeds has m & Ind rec; Clk Cir Ct has div & civ ct rec; Pro Judge has pro rec)

| Barton | D4 | 1855 | 11 | 1860-80 | Jasper | Lamar 64759 |

(Courthouse burned in 1860. Co Clk has b, d rec 1883 to 1897; Rcdr Deeds has div, Ind rec; Pro Ct has pro rec; Magistrate Ct, division 2 has civ ct rec)

| * Bates | D3 | 1841 | 16 | 1850-80 | Cass, Van Buren, Jackson | Butler 64730 |

(Feb 22, 1855, the three southern tiers of twnships in Cass Co were added to Bates; Courthouse burned in 1861; some rec prior to 1861) (Co Clk has b & d rec from 1883 to 1887; Co Rcdr has m rec from 1860 & Ind rec from 1840; Clk Cir Ct has div rec from 1860; Pro Judge has pro rec)

| * Benton | D3 | 1835 | 12 | 1840-80 | Pettis, St. Clair | Warsaw 65355 |

(Benton remained unorganized until Jan. 1837, in 1845, 24 sq miles of northwest part of Benton became parts of Pettis, and Hickory Co was created, reducing Benton to its present size. Co Clk has b, d rec from 1883, m rec from 1839; Clk Cir Ct has div, civ ct rec; Pro Ct has pro rec; Rcdr of Deeds has Ind rec)

| Bollinger | A4 | 1851 | 10 | 1860-80 | Cape Girardeau, Stoddard, Wayne | Marble Hill 63764 |

(In 1866 courthouse destroyed by fire, in 1884 courthouse burned while occupied only by the Co Clk's office) (Co Clk has b, d rec from 1882 to 1892; Clk Cir Ct and Rcdr has m, div, Ind rec; Cir Judge has pro rec)

| * Boone | C2 | 1820 | 100 | 1830-80 | Howard | Columbia 65201 |

(Co Clk has m, div, pro, civ ct & Ind rec from 1821)

| * Buchanan | E2 | 1838 | 88 | 1840-80 | Platte Purchase | Saint Joseph 64501 |

(Rcdr Deeds has m rec; Clk Cir Ct has div rec; Pro Judge has pro rec; Mag Ct has civ ct rec; Co Asr has Ind rec)

| * Butler | B5 | 1849 | 38 | 1850-80 | Wayne | Poplar Bluff 63901 |

Name	Map Index	Date Created	Pop. By M 1980	U.S. Cen Reports Available	Parent County or Territory From Which Organized	County Seat
* Caldwell	D2	1836	9	1840-80	Ray	Kingston 64650

(April 19, 1860 courthouse destroyed by fire, all recs destroyed except those of the pro ct; Nov. 28, 1896 courthouse destroyed by fire) (Rcdr Office has m, Ind rec; Clk Cir Ct has div rec; Division two Cir Ct has pro rec; Division one Cir Ct has civ ct rec)

* Callaway	C3	1820	32	1830-80	Montgomery	Fulton 65251

(Co Clk has b & d rec from 1883 to 1888; Co Rcdr has m & Ind rec; Clk Cir Ct has div rec; Pro Judge has pro rec)

* Camden	C3	1841	18	1850-80	Benton, Pulaski	Camdenton 65020

(organized as Kinderhook, renamed Feb 23, 1843; line between Camden & Miller changed in 1845) (Co Rcdr has m & div rec from 1902; Pro Judge has pro rec from 1902; Clk Cir Ct has civ ct rec from 1902; Tompkins Abstract Office has Ind rec; Courthouse burned 1902)

Cape Girardeau	A4	1812	59	1830-80	Original District	Jackson 63755

(present size of county since Mar. 5, 1849, courthouse burned in 1870) (Co Clk has b, d rec 1883 to 1893, Ind rec 1821 to 1859; Co Rcdr has m rec; Clk Cir Ct has div, civ ct rec; Pro Judge has pro rec)

* Carroll	D2	1833	12	1840-80	Ray	Carrollton 64633

(Co Clk has b rec 1883 to 1895, d rec 1883 to 1890; Clk Cir Ct has div, civ ct rec from 1833, naturalization rec 1843 to 1919; Rcdr Deeds has m rec, Ind rec from 1833; Pro Office has pro rec)

Carter	B4	1859	5	1860-80	Ripley, Shannon	Van Buren 63965
*§ Cass	D3	1835	51	1850-80	Jackson	Harrisonville 64701

(Organized as Van Buren, renamed Feb. 19, 1849; three southern tiers of townships relinquished to Bates Co Feb. 22, 1855; Co Clk has partial b rec 1883 to 1896, m rec from 1835, div rec from 1830's, pro, civ ct rec from 1837; Ind rec from 1837)

* Cedar	D4	1845	12	1850-80	Dade, St. Clair	Stockton 65785

(Co Clk has m, div & Ind rec from 1845, pro & civ ct rec)

* Chariton	C2	1820	10	1830-80	Howard	Keytesville 65261

(Courthouse burned Sept 20, 1864, only a few rec lost) (Co Clk has b rec from 1883 to 1887, m & div rec from 1821, pro rec from 1876, Ind rec from 1827 & wills from 1865)

Christian	D4	1859	22	1860-80	Greene, Taney, Webster	Ozark 65721

(Sources differ on date organized, some say Mar. 8, 1859, others say Mar. 8, 1860; Co seat, Ozark, selected May 1859; Courthouse burned 1865. Cir Clk and Rcdr has m, div, civ ct, Ind rec; Pro Office has pro rec; Bur Vit Statistics, Jefferson City has b, d rec)

Clark (old)		1818			Arkansas	

(never organized; abolished in 1819 when terr of Arkansas was created)

Clark	C1	1836	8	1840-80	Lewis	Kahoka 63445

(Co Clk has m, div, pro, civ ct & Ind rec from 1836)

* Clay	D2	1822	136	1830-80	Ray	Liberty 64068

(Rcdr Deeds has m rec; Clk Cir Ct has div & civ ct rec; Pro Judge has pro rec; Co Asr has Ind rec)

* Clinton	D2	1833	16	1840-80	Clay	Plattsburg 64477

(Co Clk has m, div, civ ct, Ind rec from 1833, service rec from WWI; Pro Judge has pro rec)

*§ Cole	C3	1820	57	1830-80	Cooper	Jefferson City 65101

(Clk Cir Ct has div & civ ct rec from 1821; Pro Judge has pro rec from 1821; Rcdr Deeds has m rec from 1821)

* Cooper	C3	1818	15	1830-80	Howard	Boonville 65233
Crawford	B3	1829	18	1830-80	Gasconade	Steelville 65565

(1829-1835 Co Ct rec lost; Courthouse burned Feb 15, 1873; Courthouse burned Jan 5, 1884) (Co Clk has m, div, civ ct & Ind rec from 1832; Pro Judge has pro rec from 1889)

* Dade	D4	1841	7	1850-80	Greene	Greenfield 65661

(lost 10-mile strip on northern boundary to Cedar Co & 9-mile strip on southern boundary to Lawrence Co, reducing it to its present limits, Mar 28, 1845; Courthouse burned in 1863, but rec had been removed to safety) (Co Rcdr has m rec from 1867 & Ind rec; Clk Cir Ct has div rec from 1867; Pro Judge has pro & civ ct rec)

§ Dallas	D4	1841	12	1850-80	Polk	Buffalo 65622

(organized 1842 as Niangua Co; in 1844 boundaries slightly changed & name changed to Dallas; Courthouse burned Oct 18, 1863; second courthouse burned Jul 30, 1864 & rec destroyed; the replaced rec were burned Sept 3, 1867) (Co Rcdr has b, m, d, bur, div, pro, civ ct & Ind rec)

* Daviess	D1	1836	9	1840-80	Ray	Gallatin 64640
DeKalb	D2	1845	8	1850-80	Clinton	Maysville 64469

(In 1878 courthouse burned, many rec being destroyed, but rec of cir clks office were preserved along with a few papers of other offices; Co Rcdr has m & div rec; Co Clk has b rec from 1880 to 1902; Pro Judge has pro rec)

COUNTY MAP FOR THE STATE OF MISSOURI

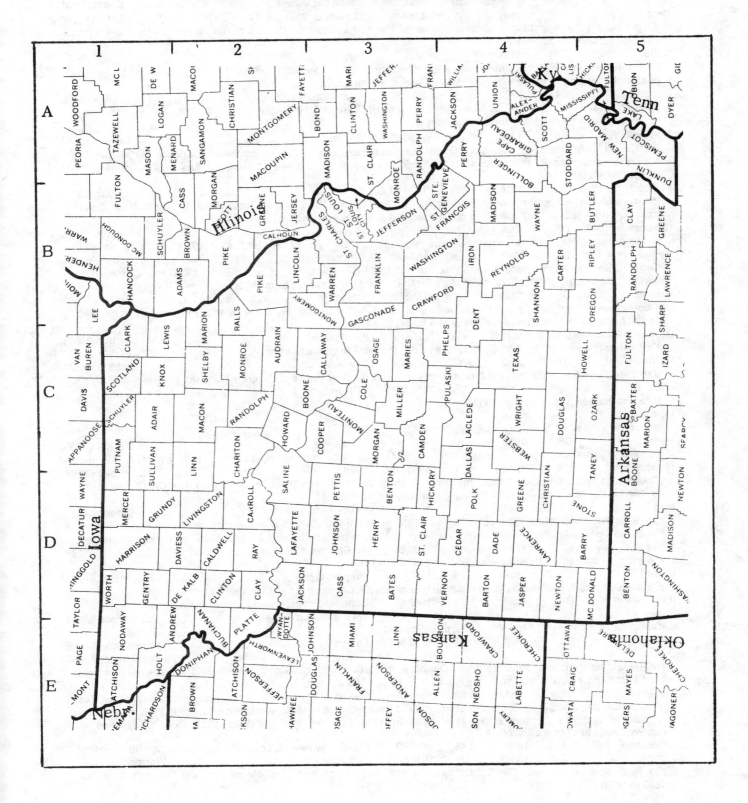

Name	Map Index	Date Created	Pop. By M 1980	U.S. Cen Reports Available	Parent County or Territory From Which Organized	County Seat
Dent	B4	1851	15	1860-80	Crawford, Shannon .... Salem 65560	

(Courthouse burned in 1864, destroying some of the ct rec) (Clk Cir Ct has m, div & civ ct rec; Clk Mag Ct has pro rec; Co Rcdr has Ind rec)

| Dodge | | 1851 | | 1850 | Putnam | |

(discontinued in 1853; had lost terr when Iowa boundary was established, bringing its area below the constitutional limit of 400 sq miles; its terr was added to Putnam Co)

| * Douglas | C4 | 1857 | 12 | 1860-80 | Ozark, Taney .... Ava 65608 | |

(terr increased in 1864 by addition of portions of Taney & Webster Cos) (Clk Cir Ct & Rcdr have m, div & civ ct rec; Pro & Mag Judge have pro rec)

| * Dunklin | A5 | 1845 | 36 | 1850-80 | Stoddard .... Kennett 63857 | |

(In 1853 a strip one mile wide was taken from Stoddard and added to northern boundary of Dunklin Co) (Courthouse burned in 1872, all rec lost) (Rcdr Deeds has m, Ind rec; Clk Cir Ct has div, civ ct rec; Pro Judge has pro rec)

| * Franklin | B3 | 1818 | 71 | 1830-80 | St. Louis .... Union 63084 | |

(boundaries not accurately defined until 1845; Co Clk has b & d rec from 1883 to 1887; Rcdr Deeds has m rec from 1883 to 1887; Clk Cir Ct has div rec; Pro Judge has pro rec)

| Gasconade | B3 | 1820 | 13 | 1830-80 | Franklin .... Hermann 65041 | |

(In 1869 relinquished 36 sq miles to Crawford Co); Co Clk has b rec 1867 to 1897, d rec 1883 to 1901

| * Gentry | D1 | 1841 | 8 | 1850-80 | Clinton .... Albany 64402 | |

(Organization completed 1843; courthouse burned 1885) (Co Clk has b, d rec 1883 to 1893, m rec from 1885; Clk Cir Ct has m, div, civ ct, Ind rec from 1885; Cir Ct Division II has pro rec from 1885)

| * Greene | D4 | 1833 | 184 | 1840-80 | Crawford .... Springfield 65802 | |

(Courthouse burned 1861; no mention of fate of rec; Clk Cir Ct has div & civ ct rec; Pro Judge has pro rec; Co Clk has a few old b & d rec; Rcdr Deeds has m rec)

| * Grundy | D1 | 1841 | 12 | 1850-80 | Livingston .... Trenton 64683 | |

(Co Clk has b, d rec 1881 to 1890, Co Rcdr has m, div, Ind rec; Pro Office has pro rec)

| * Harrison | D1 | 1845 | 10 | 1850-80 | Daviess .... Bethany 64424 | |

(Jan 1874 Courthouse burned; Ind bks, ct rec, pro rec & most of the co rec were saved; tax bks were destroyed; Co Clk has some b rec from 1883 to 1893; Clk Cir Ct has m & div rec from 1858 & civ ct rec from 1845; Pro Judge has pro rec from 1853)

| Hempstead | | 1818 | | | Arkansas | |

(abolished 1819 when terr of Arkansas was created)

| *§ Henry | D3 | 1834 | 20 | 1850-80 | Lafayette .... Clinton 64735 | |

(originally Rives Co; name changed Oct 15, 1841; Co Rcdr has b, m, bur, div, pro, civ ct & Ind rec)

| * Hickory | D3 | 1845 | 6 | 1850-80 | Benton, Polk .... Hermitage 65668 | |

(Courthouse burned 1852 and 1881; many rec destroyed; Co Clk has b rec 1883 to 1898; Clk Cir Ct has m rec 1872, div rec 1858 & civ ct rec 1858; Pro Judge has pro rec from 1845)

| * Holt | E1 | 1841 | 7 | 1850-80 | Platte Purchase .... Oregon 64473 | |

(Co Rcdr has incomplete b, d rec 1883 to 1893, m rec from 1841, div, Ind rec from 1841; Clk Cir Ct has civ ct rec from 1841; Pro Judge has pro rec from 1849) (Courthouse burned 20 Jan. 1965, most rec undamaged)

| * Howard | C2 | 1816 | 10 | 1830-80 | St. Charles, St. Louis .... Fayette 65248 | |

(Courthouse burned 1887; rec were saved & some date to 1816)

| Howell | C5 | 1857 | 29 | 1860-80 | Oregon, Ozark .... West Plains 65775 | |

(Courthouse destroyed during CW no mention fate of rec) (Co Clk has b rec 1883 to 1895)

| Iron | B4 | 1857 | 11 | 1860-80 | Dent, Madison, Reynolds, St. Francis, Washington, Wayne .... Ironton 63650 | |

(Co Clk has b rec from 1883 to 1885, m, div, pro & Ind rec)

| * Jackson | D2 | 1826 | 628 | 1830-80 | Lafayette .... Kansas City 64106 Independence 64050 | |

(nearly all its terr was acquired from Osage & Kansas Indians, June 2, 1825) (Rcdr Deeds has m rec; Clk Cir Ct has div & civ ct rec; Pro Judge has pro rec; Co Asr has Ind rec)

| *§ Jasper | D4 | 1841 | 87 | 1850-80 | Newton .... Carthage 64836 | |

(Courthouse destroyed in 1863; rec had been removed were returned in 1865; Courthouse burned in 1883; no mention of fate of rec) (Co Clk has b rec from 1883 to 1900 & d rec from 1883 to 1891: Rcdr Deeds has m rec; Pro Judge has pro rec & civ ct rec)

| * Jefferson | B3 | 1818 | 146 | 1830-80 | Ste. Genevieve, St. Louis .... Hillsboro 63050 | |
| *§ Johnson | D3 | 1834 | 39 | 1840-80 | Lafayette .... Warrensburg 64093 | |

(Co Rcdr has m, Ind rec; Clk Cir Ct has div rec; Pro Judge has pro, civ ct rec; Co Clk has b, d rec 1883 to 1893)

Name	Map Index	Date Created	Pop. By M 1980	U.S. Cen Reports Available	Parent County or Territory From Which Organized	County Seat
Kinderhook		1841			Benton, Pulaski	

(renamed Camden Feb 23, 1843)

* Knox	C1	1845	6	1850-80	Scotland	Edina 63537
* Laclede	C4	1849	24	1850-80	Camden, Pulaski, Wright	Lebanon 65536

(Co Rcdr has m rec; Clk Cir Ct has div & civ ct rec; Pro Judge has pro rec; Co Asr has Ind rec)

* Lafayette	D2	1820	30	1830-80	Cooper	Lexington 64067

(Originally called Lillard, changed Feb. 16, 1825. Co Rcdr has m, div, pro, civ ct, Ind rec from 1821)

Lawrence old)		1815			New Madrid	

(abolished 1818)

* Lawrence	D4	1845	29	1850-80	Barry, Dade	Mount Vernon 65712

(Rcdr Deeds has m & Ind rec from 1846; Clk Cir Ct has div & civ ct rec from 1846; Pro Judge has pro rec from 1846; Rcdr Deeds has Ind rec from 1846)

* Lewis	C1	1833	11	1840-80	Marion	Monticello 63457

(Clk Cir Ct has m, div & Ind rec; Pro Judge has pro & civ ct rec)

Lillard		1820			Cooper	

(Changed to Lafayette Feb 16, 1825)

* Lincoln	B2	1818	22	1830-80	St. Charles	Troy 63379

(Co Rcdr has m rec from 1825; Pro Judge pro rec from 1823; Co Rcdr has d & bur rec; Clk Cir Ct has div rec)

*§ Linn	C2	1837	16	1840-80	Chariton	Linneus 64653

(Co Clk has incomplete b, d rec 1883 to 1888; Co Rcdr has m, Ind rec from 1842; local funeral homes have bur rec; Clk Cir Ct has div rec from 1837; Pro Office has pro rec from 1840)

* Livingston	D2	1837	16	1840-80	Carroll	Chillicothe 64601
§ Macon	C2	1837	16	1840-80	Randolph	Macon 63552

(Co Clk has b, d rec 1883 to 1893; Co Rcdr has m, Ind rec; Clk Cir Ct has div rec; Cir Ct Division II has pro rec)

Madison	B4	1818	11	1830-80	Cape Girardeau, Ste. Genevieve	Fredericktown 63645

(Co Clk has b rec from 1883 to 1900, d rec from 1883 to 1892; Clk Cir Ct has m, div & civ ct rec; Clk Mag Ct has pro rec; Co Asr has Ind rec)

Maries	C3	1855	8	1860-80	Osage, Pulaski	Vienna 65582

(In 1859 and 1868 small tracts of land were exchanged with Phelps Co, Courthouse burned Nov. 6, 1868 nearly all rec destroyed) (Clk Cir Ct has m rec from 1873, div, civ ct rec from 1866, Ind rec from 1855, school rec from 1911; Pro Division has pro rec from 1880)

*§ Marion	C2	1822	29	1830-80	Ralls	Palmyra 63461

(Clk Cir Ct has m & div rec from 1827; City Clk Hannibal, Mo has b, d rec; Pro Judge has pro rec; Mag Ct has civ ct rec)

*§ McDonald	D5	1849	15	1850-80	Newton	Pineville 64856

(In 1876 an error in survey was corrected, establishing a new eastern line which annexed a 2½ mile strip previously included in Barry Co; in 1863 Courthouse & rec were burned) (Rcdr Deeds has m rec; Clk Cir Ct has div, civ ct & Ind rec; Pro Judge has pro rec)

* Mercer	D1	1845	5	1850-80	Grundy	Princeton 64673

(Courthouse burned 24 Mar. 1898, nearly all rec of the Cir Clk & Rcdr, Treas and Sheriff were destroyed or badly damaged, rec in office of Pro Judge and Co Clk were saved, but many were badly damaged; Co Clk has b rec 1883 to 1894, d rec 1883 to 1891; Clk Cir Ct has m, div, pro, civ ct, Ind rec; Cir Ct Division 2 has pro rec; local register has bur rec)

* Miller	C3	1837	19	1840-80	Cole	Tuscumbia 65082

(line between Camden or Miller changed 1845; terr from Morgan annexed 1860; minor changes in 1868; (Co Clk has b rec from 1883 to 1891; Co Rcdr has m & div rec; Pro Judge has pro rec; Clk Cir Ct has civ ct rec)

Mississippi	A4	1845	16	1850-80	Scott	Charleston 63834

(Clk Cir Ct has m, div & civ ct rec; Pro Judge has pro rec; Co Rcdr has Ind rec)

* Moniteau	C3	1845	12	1850-80	Cole, Morgan	California 65018
* Monroe	C2	1831	10	1840-80	Ralls	Paris 65275

(Clk Cir Ct has m, div & civ ct rec; Pro Judge has pro rec; Co Asr has Ind rec)

* Montgomery	B3	1818	12	1830-80	St. Charles	Montgomery City 63361

(Co rec burned 1864; Clk Cir Ct has m rec from 1864; div & civ ct rec from 1886; Pro Judge has pro rec from 1890; Mag Ct has rec from 1947)

* Morgan	C3	1833	14	1840-80	Cooper	Versailles 65084

(Courthouse burned 1887; rec were saved)

New Madrid	A5	1812	23	1830-80	Original district	New Madrid 63869

(Rcdr Deeds has m rec; Clk Cir Ct has div & civ ct rec; Pro Clk has pro rec)

Name	Map Index	Date Created	Pop. By M 1980	U.S. Cen Reports Available	Parent County or Territory From Which Organized	County Seat
* Newton	D4	1838	40	1840-80	Barry	Neosho 64850

(In 1846 a strip two miles wide was detached from Newton & attached to Jasper; Courthouse burned 1862; no mention of fate of rec) (Co Clk has m, div, pro, civ ct & Ind rec)

| Niangua | | 1842 | | | Polk | |

(boundaries slightly changed & name changed to Dallas Dec 10, 1844)

| * Nodaway | D1 | 1841 | 22 | 1850-80 | Andrew | Maryville 64468 |

(Clk Cir Ct has div rec; Pro Ct Clk has pro rec)

| Oregon | B5 | 1845 | 10 | 1850-80 | Ripley | Alton 65606 |

(Courthouse burned during CW; rec were removed and most of them saved) (Clk Cir Ct has m, div & civ ct rec; Pro Judge has pro rec; Rcdr Deeds has Ind rec)

| Osage | C3 | 1841 | 12 | 1850-80 | Gasconade | Linn 65051 |

(Mar 1, 1855 boundaries between Osage & Pulaski defined. Nov 15, 1880, Courthouse burned; fireproof vaults saved rec)

| Ozark | C5 | 1841 | 8 | 1850-80 | Taney (changed to Decatur 1843, back to Ozark, 1845) | Gainesville 65655 |
| Pemiscot | A5 | 1851 | 25 | 1860-80 | New Madrid | Caruthersville 63830 |

(Courthouse & contents burned 1883) (Rcdr Deeds has m & Ind rec from 1883; Clk Cir Ct has div & civ ct rec from 1890; Pro Judge has pro rec; Rcdr Deeds has Ind rec from 1883)

Perry	A4	1820	17	1830-80	Ste. Genevieve	Perryville 63775
*§ Pettis	D3	1833	36	1840-80	Cooper, Saline	Sedalia 65301
Phelps	C4	1857	34	1860-80	Crawford, Pulaski, Maries	Rolla 65401

(Co Clk has m, div, civ ct, Ind rec from 1857, pro rec)

| *§ Pike | B2 | 1818 | 17 | 1830-80 | St. Charles | Bowling Green 63334 |

(Courthouse burned 1864; no mention of fate of rec)

| * Platte | E2 | 1838 | 46 | 1840-80 | Platte Purchase | Platte City 64079 |

(attached to Clay for civil & mil purpose from Dec 1836 to Dec 31, 1838) (Co Clk has b rec from 1883 to 1887, d rec from 1883 to 1888; Rcdr Deeds has m & Ind rec; Clk Cir Ct has div rec; Pro Judge has pro & civ ct rec)

| Polk | D4 | 1835 | 19 | 1840-80 | Greene | Bolivar 65613 |

(Co Rcdr has m rec from 1835 & Ind rec from 1836; Clk Cir Ct has div & civ ct rec 1857; Pro Judge has pro rec from 1947)

| Pulaski (old) | | 1818 | | | Franklin | |

(organization not perfected & much of its terr became Gasconade in 1820; abolished 1819 when terr of Arkansas was created)

| Pulaski | C4 | 1833 | 42 | 1840-80 | Crawford | Waynesville 65583 |

(Co Clk has m, div, pro & civ ct rec from 1903)

| Putnam | C1 | 1843 | 6 | 1850-80 | Linn | Unionville 63565 |

(when Iowa boundary was established, the areas of both Putnam & Dodge were below the constitutional limit; Dodge disorganized in 1853 & its terr was regained by Putnam) (Clk Cir Ct has b rec from 1878 to 1903, m rec from 1854, div rec from 1855, civ ct rec from 1855 & Ind rec from 1848; Pro Judge has pro rec from 1848)

| * Ralls | B2 | 1820 | 9 | 1830-80 | Pike | New London 63459 |

(Co Clk has b & d rec from 1883 to 1886; Clk Cir Ct has m, div rec; Pro Judge has pro & civ ct rec; Co Asr has Ind rec)

| * Randolph | C2 | 1829 | 25 | 1830-80 | Chariton | Huntsville 65259 |

(a few rec lost when Courthouse burned 1880) (Co Rcdr has m rec; Clk Cir Ct has div rec)

| * Ray | D2 | 1820 | 21 | 1830-80 | Howard | Richmond 64085 |

(Rec of interest to genealogists obtainable from Ray Co Historical Society, Richmond, Mo. 64085, write for rates) (Co Clk has b, d rec 1883 to 1884; Rcdr of Deeds has m, Ind rec; Clk Cir Ct has div, civ ct rec; Pro Judge has pro rec)

| § Reynolds | B4 | 1845 | 7 | 1850-80 | Shannon | Centerville 63633 |

(Courthouse burned 1872, all rec lost; Co Clk has b rec from 1883, m, div, pro & civ ct rec from 1872)

| § Ripley | B5 | 1833 | 12 | 1840-80 | Wayne | Doniphan 63935 |
| Rives | | 1834 | | 1840 | Lafayette | |

(name changed to Henry Oct 15, 1841)

| * St. Charles | B3 | 1812 | 144 | 1830-80 | Original district | St. Charles 63301 |
| St. Clair | D3 | 1841 | 9 | 1850-80 | Rives (later Henry) | Osceola 64776 |

(Co Clk has b rec from 1885 to 1887, d rec from 1855 to 1892; Clk Cir Ct has div, civ ct & Ind rec from 1841; Pro Judge has pro rec from 1865)

| St. Francois | B4 | 1821 | 43 | 1830-80 | Jefferson, Ste. Genevieve, Washington | Farmington 63640 |
| * St. Louis | B3 | 1812 | 967 | 1830-80 | Original district | Clayton 63105 |

(Co Clk has b rec from 1877 to 1910) (Rcdr Deeds has m & Ind rec; Clk Cir Ct has div & civ ct rec; Co Clk has inc of cities, twns etc, proceedings of Co Ct since 1887, old & new road files)

| St. Louis City | B3 | 1764 | 450 | 1830-80 | | St. Louis 63105 |

Name	Map Index	Date Created	Pop. By M 1980	U.S. Cen Reports Available	Parent County or Territory From Which Organized	County Seat
* Ste. Genevieve	B4	1812	15	1830-80	Original district	Ste. Genevieve 63670

(Co Clk has b, d rec 1883 to 1892; Cir Clk-Rcdr has m, div, civ ct, Ind rec; Cir Ct Judge has pro rec; various churches in Co have bur rec)

Name	Map Index	Date Created	Pop. By M 1980	U.S. Cen Reports Available	Parent County	County Seat
* Saline	D2	1820	25	1830-80	Cooper, Howard	Marshall 65340

(Courthouse burned 186? but rec were saved)

| Schuyler | C1 | 1845 | 5 | 1850-80 | Adair | Lancaster 63548 |

(Co Clk has b & d rec from 1883 to 1893; Clk Cir Ct has m & div rec; Pro Judge & Mag Cts have pro & civ ct rec)

| * Scotland | C1 | 1841 | 5 | 1850-80 | Lewis | Memphis 63555 |

(Co Clk has b & d rec from 1883 to 1889; Clk Cir Ct has m, div, civ ct & Ind rec from 1841; Pro Judge has pro rec from 1841)

| * Scott | A4 | 1821 | 40 | 1830-80 | New Madrid | Benton 63736 |

(Rcdr Deeds has m & Ind rec; Clk Cir Ct has div & civ ct rec; Pro Judge has pro rec)

| Shannon | B4 | 1841 | 8 | 1850-80 | Ripley, Washington | Eminence 65466 |

(Courthouse destroyed during CW; Co Clk has m rec from 1881, div, pro, civ ct & Ind rec from 1872; Courthouse burned 1863, 1871, 1938, Rcdr Office burned 1893; some Ind rec in Ironton, Mo prior to 1872)

| § Shelby | C2 | 1835 | 8 | 1840-80 | Marion | Shelbyville 63469 |

(Rcdr Deeds has m & Ind rec; Clk Cir Ct has div rec; Pro Ct has pro rec; Clk Mag Ct has civ ct rec)

| * Stoddard | A4 | 1835 | 29 | 1840-80 | Cape Girardeau | Bloomfield 63825 |

(Courthouse burned 1864 but rec had been removed to safety; Co Clk has b rec from 1883 to 1886; Rcdr Deeds has m rec; Clk Cir Ct has div rec; Pro Judge has pro rec; Clk Mag Ct has civ ct rec; Co Clk has mil service rec)

| Stone | D5 | 1851 | 16 | 1860-80 | Taney | Galena 65656 |

(Co Clk has m, Ind rec from 1851, pro, civ ct rec from 1800, discharge rec from 1918)

| * Sullivan | C1 | 1843 | 7 | 1850-80 | Linn | Milan 63556 |

(Rcdr Deeds has b rec from 1867 to 1895 inc, m rec from 1845 & d rec from 1883 to 1896, Ind rec from 1845; Clk Cir Ct has div & civ ct rec from 1845; Pro Judge has pro rec from 1845)

| * Taney | D5 | 1837 | 20 | 1840-80 | Greene | Forsyth 65653 |

(Clk Cir Ct has m, div, civ ct & Ind rec; Pro Judge has pro rec; Co Clk has voter registration rec from 1961; Courthouse burned 1885)

| Texas | C4 | 1845 | 21 | 1850-80 | Shannon, Wright (formerly Ashley, changed to Texas 1845) | Houston 65483 |

(Co Clk has b & d rec from 1881 to 1889)

| Van Buren | | 1835 | | 1840 | Jackson | |

(name changed to Cass Feb 19, 1849)

| Vernon | D4 | 1851 | 20 | 1860-80 | Bates | Nevada 64772 |

(Vernon created Feb. 15, 1851, but act was declared unconstitutional since its territory was exactly that of Bates; legally created Feb. 27, 1855; reorganized Oct. 17, 1865 after total suspension of civil order during CW; Courthouse destroyed during that period, but clk had taken the rec with him when he joined the army and all rec were later recovered except one deed book. Co Clk has b, d rec 1883 to 1904; Rcdr of Deeds has m, Ind rec; Clk Cir Ct has div, civ ct rec; Pro Ct has pro rec; Co Hist Soc has bur rec)

| Warren | B3 | 1833 | 15 | 1840-80 | Montgomery | Warrenton 63383 |
| Washington | B3 | 1813 | 18 | 1830-80 | Ste. Genevieve | Potosi 63664 |

(Co Clk has b rec 1883 to 1891, d rec 1883 to 1886, 1875 to present; Clk Cir Ct has m, div, civ ct, Ind rec from 1825; Pro Office has pro rec from 1814; Funeral homes have bur rec)

| Wayne | B4 | 1818 | 11 | 1830-80 | Cape Girardeau | Greenville 63944 |

(Courthouse burned with all the rec 1854) (Co Clk has b & d rec from various dates to 1940; Rcdr Office has m rec; Cir Clk has div rec; Pro Judge has pro rec)

| * Webster | C4 | 1855 | 20 | 1860-80 | Greene, Wright | Marshfield 65706 |

(Courthouse burned 1863 but rec were saved with the exception of tax rolls & election returns) (Co Rcdr has m rec & Ind rec; Clk Cir Ct has div & civ ct rec; Pro Judge has pro rec)

| Worth | D1 | 1861 | 3 | 1870-80 | Gentry | Grant City 64456 |

(Co Clk has b rec from 1883 to 1893, m, div & civ ct rec from 1861)

| Wright | C4 | 1841 | 16 | 1850-80 | Pulaski | Hartville 65667 |

(1864 Courthouse burned, destroying many rec; 1897 Courthouse destroyed with all its rec) (Clk Cir Ct has m, div & civ ct rec; Pro Judge has pro rec; Co Rcdr has Ind rec)

* - At least one county history has been published about this county.

§ - Inventory of county archives was made by the Historical Records Survey. (see introduction)

MONTANA

CAPITAL, HELENA - TERRITORY 1864 - STATE 1889 - (41ST)

At least sixteen tribes of Indians roamed over Montana when white explorers first came into the section. Traders from France, Scotland and England were the first whites to visit Montana.

The eastern part of Montana was part of the Louisiana Purchase in 1803. Members of the Lewis and Clark Expedition crossed the state in 1805 enroute west and on the return trip in 1806.

The western part of Montana was included in the section that came to the United States in 1846 through the Oregon Treaty.

The first influx of people really attracted to Montana was in 1862 when gold was discovered in what is now Madison County, southeast of Butte. About twenty years later, copper and silver were found in the Butte region. To work the resulting mines, many workers were shipped in from Ireland, Germany, Austria, Poland, and Czechoslovakia.

In 1864 Montana became an organized territory. Prior to this, various parts of the section had belonged at sundry times to surrounding territories, including those of Missouri, Nebraska, Oregon, Washington, and Idaho.

Birth and death records from June 1907 to the present are at the Bureau of Records and Statistics, Montana Department of Health and Environmental Sciences, Capitol Station, Helena, Montana 59620.

The Gallatin County Clerk and Recorder does have information on births and deaths dating back to the 1890's; however, these are in the form of a quarterly report and are not complete.

The Cascade County Clerk and Recorder has birth and death reports back to 1887.

The Lewis and Clark County Clerk and Recorder has birth reports only back to 1895. The file is limited to approximately 45 certificates.

The records in Silver Bow County have now been incorporated with those of Butte and the new governmental unit is known as Butte-Silver Bow. The records of the former Silver Bow County have now been placed in the archives.

Genealogical Archives, Libraries, Societies, and Publications

Carbon County Historical Society, Box 476, Red Lodge, MT 59068.

Central Montana Genealogy Society, 701 W. Main Street, Lewistown, MT 59457.

Gallatin Genealogy Society, P.O. Box 2020, Bozeman, MT 59715.

Great Falls Genealogy Society, Paris Gibson Square, 1400 First Avenue North, Great Falls, MT 59401.

Mineral County Historical Society, SR1, Box 38, Superior, MT 59872.

Montana Historical Society, 225 N. Roberts St., Helena, MT 59601.

Parmly Billings Library, 501 N. Broadway, Billings, MT 59101.

Public Library, 106 W. Broadway St., Butte, MT 59701.

Public Library, Great Falls, MT 59401.

Public Library, Pine and Pattee Sts., Missoula, MT 59801.

University of Montana Mansfield Library, Missoula, MT 59812.

Western Montana Genealogical Society, P.O. Box 8946, Missoula, MT 59807.

Yellowstone Genealogy Forum, c/o Parmly Billings Library, 501 N. Broadway, Billings, MT 59101.

Treasure State Lines, Great Falls Genealogical Society, Paris Gibson Square, 1400 First Avenue North, Great Falls, MT 59401.

Western Montana Genealogical Society Bulletin, Western Montana Genealogical Society, P.O. Box 8946, Missoula, MT 59807.

Printed Census Records and Mortality Schedules

Indexes (Territory)-1870, 1871

Printed Census Indexes (Counties):

Big Horn-1870
Dawson-1880

1860 Census-Bitter Root Valley and Ponderay Mountain Area of Washington Territory now Montana. The Bitter Root Valley in 1860 was in Spokane County, Washington Territory and enumerated on NARS microfilm (M653 Roll No. 1398). (Reference: Montana's Genealogical and Local History Records)

1862-1863 Census List of Early Settlers: A List of All Persons (except Indians) who were in what is now Montana during the winter of 1862-1863. List is not complete "We ask for information enabling us to make it perfect". Contributions to the Historical Society of Montana, 2nd Edition. Helena, Montana: Rocky Mountain Publishing Company.

Mortality Schedules (Printed): 1870, 1880

Valuable Printed Sources

Place Names

Cheney, Roberta Carkeek. *Names on the Face of Montana.* Missoula, Montana: University of Montana Publications in History, 1971.

Guides To Genealogical Research

Richards, Dennis, comp. *Montana's Genealogical and Local History Records.* Detroit: Gale Research Company, 1981.

Histories

Burlingame, Merrill C. and K. Ross Toole, *A History of Montana.* New York: Lewis Historical Publishing Company, 1957.

Miller, Joaquin. *An illustrated History of The State of Montana.* Chicago: Lewis Publishing Company, 1894.

Sanders, James U. *Society of Montana Pioneers.* Akron, Ohio: Wermer Company, 1899.

Sanders, Helen Fitzgerald, *A History of Montana.* Chicago and New York: The Lewis Publishing Company, 1913.

Progressive Men of the State of Montana. Chicago: A. W. Bowen and Co.

Bibliographies

John, Henry. *Bibliography of Montana Local Histories.* Montana Library Association, 1977.

Walter, David A. "Montana Mosaic: A Teacher's Guide to Montana Local History Materials," *Montana Historican.* Vol. 8, number 2, May 1978, pages 20-70.

MONTANA COUNTY HISTORIES
(Population figures to nearest thousand - 1980 U. S. Census)

Name	Map Index	Date Created	Pop. By M 1980	U.S. Cen Reports Available	Parent County or Territory From Which Organized	County Seat
§ Beaverhead	E4	1865	8	1860-80	Original county	Dillon 59725
					(Co Clk has b rec from 1902, d rec from 1901, Ind, mining, lease, mtg rec from 1864 & voting rec; Clk Dis Ct has div, pro & civ ct rec)	
Big Horn	B4	1913	11	1860-80	Rosebud, Yellowstone	Hardin 59034
					(Co Clk has b, d rec from 1913, Ind rec; Clk Dis Ct has m, div, pro, civ ct rec)	

Name	Map Index	Date Created	Pop. By M 1980	U.S. Cen Reports Available	Parent County or Territory From Which Organized	County Seat
* Blaine	C2	1912	7		Chouteau, Hill	Chinook 59523
(Co Clk has b, d & Ind rec from 1912; Clk Dis Ct has m, div, pro & civ ct rec)						
Broadwater	D3	1897	3		Jefferson, Meagher	Townsend 59644
(Co Clk has b & d rec from 1907; Clk Ct has m, div, pro & civ ct rec)						
*§ Carbon	C4	1895	8		Park, Yellowstone	Red Lodge 59068
(Co Clk has b, m, d, bur, div, pro, civ ct & Ind rec from 1895)						
Carter	A4	1917	2		Custer	Ekalaka 59324
(Co Clk has b, d & Ind rec from 1917; Clk Cts has m, div, pro & civ ct rec)						
Cascade	D2	1887	81		Chouteau, Meagher	Great Falls 59401
(Co Clk has b, d, Ind rec from 1887, mil service rec from 1918; Clk Cts has m, div, pro rec; J P has civ ct rec)						
Chouteau	D2	1865	6	1860-80	Original county	Fort Benton 59442
(Co Clk has b & d rec from 1895, m rec from 1887, div, pro & civ ct rec 1879)						
Custer	A3	1865	13	1880	Original county	Miles City 59301
(Co Clk has b, d rec from 1907, Ind rec from 1909; Clk Dis Ct has m, div, pro rec; J P has civ ct rec; cem associations have bur rec; Bur Vit Statistics, Helena, has b, d rec)						
* Daniels	A1	1920	3		Valley, Sheridan	Scobey 59263
(Co Clk has b, d, Ind rec from 1820; Clk of Ct has m, div, pro, civ ct rec from 1920; funeral home has bur rec)						
Dawson	A2	1869	12	1860-80	Original county	Glendive 59330
(Co Clk has b, d rec from 1895, Ind rec from 1888; Clk of Ct has m, div, civ ct rec from 1880)						
Deer Lodge	E3	1865	13	1860-80	Original county	Anaconda 59711
Fallon	A3	1913	4		Custer	Baker 59313
(Co Clk has b rec from 1887, d rec from 1919, Ind rec; Clk of Ct has m, div, pro, civ ct rec)						
§ Fergus	C2	1885	13		Meagher	Lewistown 59457
(Co Clk has b & d rec; Clk Cts has m, div, pro & civ ct rec; Co Asr has Ind rec)						
§ Flathead	E1	1893	51		Missoula	Kalispell 59901
(Co Clk has b rec from 1885, m rec from 1893 & d rec from 1897)						
* Gallatin	D3	1865	43	1860-80	Original county	Bozeman 59715
(Co Clk has b, d & Ind rec; Clk Dis Ct has m, div & pro rec)						
Garfield	B2	1919	2		Valley, McCone	Jordan 59337
(Co Clk has b rec from 1919)						
Glacier	E1	1919	10		Teton	Cut Bank 59427
(Co Clk has b, d & Ind rec from 1919; Clk Cts has m, div, pro & civ ct rec)						
Golden Valley	C3	1920	1		Musselshell	Ryegate 59074
(Co Clk & Rcdr has b, d & Ind rec; Clk Cts has m, div, pro & civ ct rec)						
Granite	E3	1893	3		Deer Lodge	Philipsburg 59858
(Co Clk & Rcdr has b & Ind rec; Clk Cts has m, div, pro & civ ct rec)						
Hill	D1	1912	18		Chouteau	Havre 59501
(Co Clk & Rcdr has b, d & Ind rec; Clk Cts has m, div, pro & civ ct rec)						
Jefferson	E3	1866	7	1860-80	Original county	Boulder 59632
(Co Clk has b & d rec from 1907 & Ind rec from 1865; Clk Dis Ct has m, div, pro & civ ct rec)						
Judith Basin	D2	1920	3		Fergus, Cascade	Stanford 59479
(Co Clk and Rcdr has b, d rec from 1920; Clk Dis Ct has m, div, pro, civ ct rec from 1920; Co Asr has Ind rec from 1920)						
§ Lake	E2	1923	19		Flathead, Missoula	Polson 59860
(Co Clk has b, d, bur, Ind rec from 1923; Clk Cts has m, div, pro, civ ct rec from 1923)						
Lewis & Clark	E2	1865	43	1860-80	Original county	Helena 59601
(Co Clk has b rec from 1907, d rec from 1895 & Ind rec from 1865; Clk Dis Ct has m, div, pro & civ ct rec)						
Liberty	D2	1920	2		Chouteau, Hill	Chester 59522
(Co Clk has b, d, Ind rec from 1920; Clk Dis Ct has m rec from 1920, div, pro, civ ct rec)						
§ Lincoln	F1	1909	18		Flathead	Libby 59923
(Co Clk has b, d & Ind rec from 1909; Clk Dis Ct has m, div, pro & civ ct rec; Co Clk also has some transcribed b & d rec prior to 1909)						
§ Madison	E4	1865	5	1860-80	Original county	Virginia City 59755
(Co Clk has b & d rec from 1900 & Ind rec from 1864; Clk Cts has m, div, pro & civ ct rec)						
McCone	A2	1919	3		Dawson, Richland	Circle 59215
(Co Clk & Rcdr has b, d, bur & Ind rec from 1919; Clk Cts has m, div, pro & civ ct rec)						
* Meagher	D3	1867	2	1860-80	Original county	White Sulpher Springs 59645
(Co Clk & Rcdr has b & d rec from 1896, bur rec from 1884 & Ind rec from 1866; Clk Cts has m & pro rec from 1866, div & civ ct rec from 1867 & naturalization rec from 1867)						
§ Mineral	F2	1914	4		Missoula	Superior 59872
(Co Clk & Rcdr has b, d, bur & Ind rec from 1914; Clk Dis Ct has m, div, pro & civ ct rec from 1914)						
§ Missoula	E2	1865	73	1860-80	Original county	Missoula 59801
(Co Clk has b & d rec from 1895 & Ind rec; Clk Cts has m, div, pro & civ ct rec)						
Musselshell	C3	1911	4		Fergus, Yellowstone	Roundup 59072
(Co Clk has b, d & Ind rec from 1911; Clk Cts has m, div, pro & civ ct rec)						

COUNTY MAP FOR THE STATE OF MONTANA

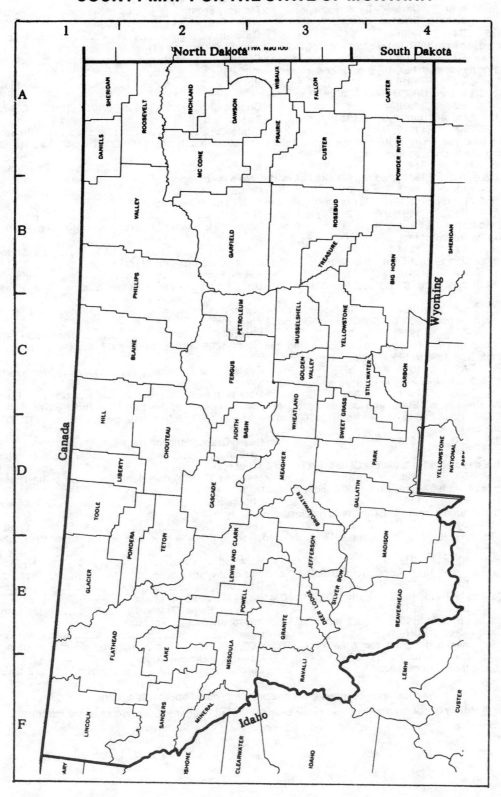

Name	Map Index	Date Created	Pop. By M 1980	U.S. Cen Reports Available	Parent County or Territory From Which Organized	County Seat
§ Park	D4	1887	13		Gallatin	Livingston 59047
(Co Clk has b, d rec from 1907, Ind rec from 1887; Clk Dis Ct has m, div, pro, civ ct rec)						
* Petroleum	C2	1924	1		Fergus, Garfield	Winnett 59087
(Director of Rec has b, m, d, bur, div, pro, civ ct & Ind rec from 1925)						
Phillips	B2	1915	5		Valley	Malta 59538
(Co Clk has b, d & Ind rec; Clk Cts has m, div, pro & civ ct rec)						
Pondera	E2	1919	7		Chouteau	Conrad 59425
(Co Clk has b, d & Ind rec from 1919; Clk Cts has m, div, pro & civ ct rec)						
* Powder River	A4	1919	3		Custer	Broadus 59317
(Co Clk has b, d rec from 1919, Ind rec from 1890's, election rec from 1919; Clk Dist Ct has m, div rec from 1919, pro, civ ct, crim rec from 1882)						
Powell	E2	1901	7		Missoula	Deer Lodge 59722
(Co Clk has b & d rec from 1907 & Ind rec; Clk Cts has m, div, pro & civ ct rec)						
Prairie	A3	1915	2		Custer	Terry 59349
(Co Clk has b, d & Ind rec from 1915; Clk Cts has m, div, pro & civ ct rec from 1915)						
§ Ravalli	F3	1893	22		Missoula	Hamilton 59840
(Co Clk & Rcdr has b, d rec from 1911, Ind rec from 1894, deeds, mortgages, voter reg from 1937; Clk Ct has m, div, pro, civ ct rec)						
Richland	A2	1914	12		Dawson	Sidney 59270
(Co Clk has b rec from 1910, d & Ind rec from 1914; Clk Dis Ct has m, div, pro & civ ct rec)						
Roosevelt	A2	1919	10		Valley, Richland	Wolf Point 59201
(Co Clk & Rcdr has b, d & Ind rec from 1919; Clk Dis Ct has m, div, pro rec from 1919; J P has civ ct rec)						
* Rosebud	B3	1901	10		Custer	Forsyth 59327
(Co Clk has b & d rec from 1900; Clk Dis Ct has m, div, pro & civ ct rec)						
§ Sanders	F2	1905	9		Missoula	Thompson Falls 59873
(Co Clk & Rcdr has b, m, div, pro, civ ct & Ind rec from 1906, d rec from 1907 & sale of twn lots of Thompson Falls from 1895 to 1955)						
* Sheridan	A1	1913	5		Custer	Plentywood 59254
(Co Clk has b, d, bur, Ind rec from 1913)						
§ Silver Bow	E3	1881	38		Deer Lodge	Butte 59701
(May 2, 1977 the city of Butte and county of Silver Bow were unified to form the Butte-Silver Bow government. Co Clk & Rcdr has b, d rec from 1890, Ind rec from 1881, mil discharge rec from 1932; Clk Cts has m, div, pro, civ ct rec)						
§ Stillwater	C4	1913	6		Sweet Grass, Yellowstone, Carbon	Columbus 59019
(Co Clk has b & d rec from 1913; Clk Dis Ct has m, div, pro & civ ct rec)						
§ Sweet Grass	D3	1895	3		Meagher, Park, Yellowstone	Big Timber 59011
(Co Clk has b rec from 1907, d rec from 1900 & Ind rec from 1895)						
Teton	E2	1893	6		Chouteau	Choteau 59422
(Co Clk has b, d & bur rec from 1899; Clk Dis Ct has m, div, pro & civ ct rec)						
*§ Toole	D1	1914	6		Teton	Shelby 59474
(Co Clk & Rcdr has b, d & bur from 1914 & Ind rec from 1890; Clk Cts has m rec from 1914, div, pro & civ ct rec)						
* Treasure	B3	1918	1		Rosebud	Hysham 59038
(Co Clk has b, d rec from 1917, Ind rec from 1879; Clk Dis Ct has m, div, pro rec)						
* Valley	B2	1893	10		Dawson	Glasgow 59230
(Co Clk & Rcdr has b, d & Ind rec from early 1900's; Clk Cts has m, div, pro & civ ct rec)						
Wheatland	D3	1917	2		Meagher, Sweet Grass	Harlowton 59036
(Co Clk & Rcdr has b rec from 1917, d, bur & Ind rec; Clk Cts has m, div, pro & civ ct rec)						
Wibaux	A3	1914	1		Dawson	Wibaux 59353
(Co Clk & Rcdr has b, bur, Ind rec from 1914, d rec; Clk Dist Ct has m, div, pro, civ ct rec from 1914)						
* Yellowstone	C3	1883	108		Gallatin, Meagher, Custer, Carbon	Billings 59101
(Co Clk has b, d & Ind rec from 1883)						

* - At least one county history has been published about this county.

§ - Inventory of county archives was made by the Historical Records Survey. (see introduction)

NEBRASKA

CAPITAL, LINCOLN - TERRITORY 1854 - STATE 1867 - (37TH)

Nebraska was, for a long time, a choice spot for several rather belligerent Indian tribes. The first settlers were stragglers of the California Gold Rush days and the Oregon migration. Others unused to the mountain terrain returned to the level lands of Nebraska which had formed a delightful picture in their memory as they were westward bound. Nebraska was passed to the possession of the United States by the Louisiana Purchase of 1803.

The first settlement was established in 1823. It was called Bellevue, and is situated less than ten miles below Omaha on the Missouri River.

Nebraska was part of the Missouri Territory before 1820. In 1834 it was carved into three sections and placed under the supervision of Arkansas, Michigan and the state of Missouri. Twenty years later it became a territory in its own name, including sections of Colorado, Montana, North and South Dakota, and Wyoming.

All during the 1850's many Germans settled in Nebraska. Twenty years later a large contingent of Germans came out of Russia and settled Lancaster and nearby counties. Many Scandinavians established homes there after the adoption of the Homestead Act of 1862.

In 1867 Nebraska was admitted to the Union— the thirty-seventh state. Many Civil War veterans secured cheap land after the close of that struggle.

Most Nebraskans of today are of German, Czech, Swedish or Russian descent.

Birth and death records since 1904 and marriage records since 1909 are at the Bureau of Vital Statistics, State Department of Health, Lincoln, Nebraska 68509. Prior to those dates, the birth, death and marriage records are available at the offices of the county clerks, where wills and probate matters are recorded.

Land records, such as deeds, mortgages and all land titles are recorded in the office of the Register of Deeds in the various county seats.

Genealogical Archives, Libraries, Societies, and Publications

Adams County Genealogical Society, P.O. Box 424, Hastings, NE 68901.

Alliance Public Library, 202 West 4th St., Alliance, NE 69301.

Bayard Public Library, Bayard, NE 69334.

Big Springs Public Library, Big Springs, NE 69122.

Bridgeport Public Library, Bridgeport, NE 69336.

Broadwater Public Library, Broadwater, NE 69125.

Chadron Public Library, Chadron, NE 69337.

Chappell Public Library, Chappell, NE 69129.

Cherry County Genealogical Society, Box 380, Valentine, NE 69201.

Cheyenne County Genealogical Society, Box 802, Sidney, NE 69162.

Columbus Public Library, Columbus, NE 68601.

Cozad Genealogy Club (Dawson County), Cozad Library, Drawer C, Cozad, NE 69130.

Cravath Memorial Library, Hay Spring, NE 69347.

Crawford Public Library, Crawford, NE 69339.

Dalton Public Library, Dalton, NE 69131.

Eastern Nebraska Genealogical Society, P.O. Box 541, Fremont, NE 68025.

Fort Kearny Genealogical Society, Box 22, Kearney, NE 68847.

Gage County Historical Society, Box 793, Beatrice, NE 68310.

Gering Public Library, Gering, NE 69341.

Gordon Public Library, Gordon, NE 69343.

Grand Island Public Library, 211 S. Washington, Grand Island, NE 68801.

Greater Omaha Genealogical Society, P.O. Box 4011, Omaha, NE 68104.

Greater York Area Genealogical Society, c/o Levitt Library, York College, York, NE 68467.

Hemingford Public Library, Hemingford, NE 69348.

Holt County Historical Society, Box 231, O'Neill, NE 68763.

Kearney Public Library, Kearney, NE 68847.

Kimball Public Library, Kimball, NE 69145.

Lewellen Public Library, Lewellen, NE 69147.

Lincoln-Lancaster County Genealogy Society, P.O. Box 30055, Lincoln, NE 68503.

Lisco Library, Lisco, NE 69148.

Lyman Public Library, Lyman, NE 69352.

Minatare Public Library, Minatare, NE 69356.

Morrill Public Library, Morrill, NE 69358.

Nancy Fawcett Memorial Library, Lodgepole, NE 69149.

Nebraska D.A.R. Library, 202 West 4th St., Alliance, NE 69301.

Nebraska State Genealogical Society, Box 62, Fremont, NE 68025.

Nebraska State Historical Society Library, 1500 R. St., Lincoln, NE 68508.

Nebraska State Law Library, Third Floor, Nebraska State Capitol Bldg., 1445 K, Lincoln, NE 68508.

Norfolk, Nebraska Public Library, North 4th Street, Norfolk, NE 68701.

North Platte Genealogical Society, c/o North Platte Public Library, 4th and Vine, North Platte, NE 69101.

Northeastern Nebraska Genealogical Society (NENGS), P.O. Box 249, Lyons, NE 68038.

Northern Antelope County Genealogical Society, Box 267, Orchard, NE 68764.

Northern Nebraska Genealogical Society, Box 362, O'Neill, NE 68763.

Northwest Genealogical Society, P.O. Box 6, Alliance, NE 69301.

Omaha Public Library, 215 South 15th St., Omaha, NE 68102.

Oshkosh Public Library, Oshkosh, NE 69154.

Pawnee Genealogy Scouters (Boone County), Box 112, Albion, NE 68620.

Plains Genealogical Society, c/o Kimball Public Library, 208 South Walnut Street, Kimball, NE 69145.

Potter Public Library, Box 317, Potter, NE 69156.

Prairie Pioneer Genealogical Society (Hall County), Box 1122, Grand Island, NE 68801.

Public Library, 136 South 14th St., Lincoln, NE 68508.

Quivey Memorial Library, Mitchell, NE 69357.

Rebecca Winters Genealogical Society, c/o Mrs. Earl Smith, Rt. 1, Box 251, Scottsbluff, NE 69361.

Rushville Public Library, Rushville, NE 69360.

Scottsbluff Public Library, Scottsbluff, NE 69361.

Southeast Nebraska Genealogical Society, P.O. Box 562, Beatrice, NE 68301.

Southwest Nebraska Genealogical Society, Box 6, McCook, NE 69001.

University of Nebraska Library, Lincoln, NE 68503.

Valley County Genealogical Society, 619 S. 10th, Ord, NE 68862.

Washington County Genealogical Society, c/o Blair Public Library, Blair, NE 68008.

Wayne Public Library, 410 Main St., Wayne, NE 68787.

Ancestors Unlimited, Southwest Nebraska Genealogical Society, P.O. Box 6, McCook, NE 69001.

Nebraska Ancestree, quarterly publication of Nebraska State Genealogical Society, Box 62, Fremont, NE 68025.

Northwest Genealogical Society Quarterly, Northwest Genealogical Society, P.O. Box 6, Alliance, NE 69301.

Westward Into Nebraska, publication of the Greater Omaha Genealogical Society, P.O. Box 4011, Omaha, NE 68104.

The Wagoner, publication of the Northwest Genealogical Society, P.O. Box 6, Alliance, NE 69301.

Printed Census Records and Mortality Schedules

Indexes (Territory): 1854, 1855, 1856, 1860

State Indexes: 1870

Printed Census Records(Counties):

Adams-1870	Dawson-1870	Lincoln-1870
Blackbird-1870	Dixon-1870	Madison-1870
Buffalo-1870	Dodge-1870; 1855, 1856	Merrick-1870
Burt - 1856	Douglas-1870; 1855, 1856	Nemaha - 1855, 1856
Butler-1870; 1869	Fillmore-1870	Otoe - 1855, 1856, 1865
Cass-1870; 1855, 1856	Gage- 1870	Pawnee-1870; 1854, 1855, 1856
Cedar-1870	Hall-1870	Platte-1856
Cheyenne-1870	Hamilton-1870	Polk-1860
Clay - 1870; 1856, 1865	Jefferson-1870	Richardson-1890; 1854, 1855, 1856
Colfax-1870	Johnson-1870; 1885	Stanton-1869
Cuming - 1870; 1856, 1865	Kearney-1870; 1885	Washington-1855, 1856
Custer-1880	Lancaster-1870; 1856	Winnebago Indian Reservation-1870
Dakota-1870; 1856	L'Eau Qui Court-1870	

Nebraska Territory Mortality Schedule - 1860, 1870, 1880

Valuable Printed Sources

Maps

Nimmo, Sylvia. *Maps Showing the County Boundaries of Nebraska 1854-1925.* Papillion, Nebraska: Privately published. (n.d.)

Place Names

Fitzpatrick, Lilian L. *Nebraska Place Names.* Lincoln: University of Nebraska Press (1967)

Guides To Genealogical Research

Cox, E. Evelyn. *Ancestree Climbing in the Midwest.* Ellensburg, Washington: Privately Published (1977)

McCallson, Ilene. *Research in Nebraska.* Article published in *The Genealogical Helper,* July-August 1977, pages 378-380.

Histories

Andreas, A.T. *History of the State of Nebraska.* The Western Historical Company (1882). Evansville: Unigraphic Reprint 1975.

Morton, J. Sterling. *Illustrated History of Nebraska.* Lincoln: Jacob North and Company (1907)

Rosicky, Rose. *A History of Czechs (Bohemians) in Nebraska.* Reprint from 1926 edition, plus index. Fremont, NE.

Genealogical Sources

Diffendal, Anne P. *A Guide to the Newspaper Collection of the State Archives.* Lincoln: State Historical Society (1977).

Luebke, Frederick C. *Immigrants and Politics, The Germans of Nebraska 1880-1900.* Lincoln: University of Nebraska Press.

See pages VIII and X of the introduction for more information on the state of Nebraska.

NEBRASKA COUNTY HISTORIES
(Population figures to nearest thousand - 1980 U. S. Census)

Name	Map Index	Date Created	Pop. By M 1980	U.S. Cen Reports Available	Parent County or Territory From Which Organized	County Seat
* Adams	C3	1867	31	1870-80	Clay	Hastings 68901
(Co Judge has m & pro rec; Clk Dis Ct has div & Ind rec)						
* Antelope	B2	1871	9	1880	Pierce	Neligh 68756
* Arthur	E2	1887	1	1880	Unorg. Terr.	Arthur 69121
(Arthur County was formed in 1887, but it did not become a county until 1913, before 1913, records were kept at McPherson County) (Co Clk has Ind rec from 1913, Co Ct has m, pro, civ ct rec from 1913; Clk Dis Ct has div rec from 1913; Dept Vit Statistics has b, d rec; Co Cem Sexton has bur rec; Co Supt of Schools has school cen from 1913)						
Banner	F2	1888	1		Cheyenne	Harrisburg 69345
(b and d rec must be certified from Nebr. Dept of Health, 301 Centennial Mall South, Lincoln, Nebr) Co Clk has b rec from 1920, Ind rec from 1890; Co Ct has m, pro, civ ct rec from 1890; Dept of Health has bur, div rec)						
* Blaine	D2	1885	1		Custer	Brewster 68821
(Co Judge has b, m, pro & civ ct rec; Co Clk has div & Ind rec from 1885)						
Blackbird				1870	See Thurston	
Boone	B2	1871	7	1880	Platte	Albion 68620
* Box Butte	F2	1887	14		Unorg. Terr.	Alliance 69301
(Co Judge has m, div, pro & civ ct rec; Co Clk has Ind rec)						
* Boyd	C1	1891	3		Holt	Butte 68722
(Co Clk has b, d rec from 1917, div, civ ct, Ind rec from 1897; Co Judge has m rec, civ ct rec from 1894) (Certified b, d rec from Nebr. Dept of Health, Lincoln)						
* Brown	D2	1883	4		Unorg. Terr.	Ainsworth 69210
(attached to Holt Co Nebr prior 1883) (Co Judge has m, pro & civ ct rec from 1883; Clk Dis Ct has div rec from 1883; Co Clk has Ind rec; Co Supt of schools has school census rec from 1883)						

Name	Map Index	Date Created	Pop. By M 1980	U.S. Cen Reports Available	Parent County or Territory From Which Organized	County Seat
* Buffalo	C3	1855	35	1860-80	Original county	Kearney 68847

(Co Judge has m & pro rec from 1872; Clk Dis Ct has div, civ ct & Ind rec)

| * Burt | A2 | 1854 | 9 | 1860-80 | Original county | Tekamah 68061 |

(Co Clk has bur rec; Co Judge has m, pro & civ ct rec; Clk Dis Ct has div & civ ct rec)

| * Butler | B3 | 1856 | 9 | 1860-80 | Unorg. Terr. | David City 68632 |

(Co Clk has Ind rec from 1869; Co Ct has m, pro rec; Dis Ct has div, civ ct rec; Nebr. Dept of Health has b, d, bur rec)

| Calhoun | | | | 1860 | Changed to Saunders 8 Jan, 1862 | |
| * Cass | A3 | 1854 | 20 | 1860-80 | Original county | Plattsmouth 68048 |

(Nebr. Dept of Health, Lincoln, has b, d rec from 1904; Co Ct has m rec from 1855, pro, civ ct rec from 1854; cem board has bur rec; Clk Dis Ct has div rec from 1855; Co Surveyor has Ind rec from 1857)

| * Cedar | B1 | 1857 | 11 | 1860-80 | Original county | Hartington 68739 |

(Co Judge has m, pro & civ ct rec; Co Clk has d, bur & Ind rec; Clk Dis Ct has div rec)

| * Chase | E3 | 1873 | 5 | 1880 | Unorg. Terr. | Imperial 69033 |

(Co Judge has m, pro & civ ct rec from 1886; Clk Dis Ct has div rec from 1886; Co Clk has Ind rec from 1886)

| Cherry | E2 | 1883 | 7 | | Unorg. Terr. | Valentine 69201 |

(Co Clk has m, div, civ ct rec, some bur rec, Ind rec from 1884; Nebr. Dept of Health, Lincoln, has b, d rec)

| * Cheyenne | F3 | 1867 | 10 | 1870-80 | Unorg. Terr. | Sidney 69162 |
| * Clay | B3 | 1855 | 8 | 1860-80 | Original county | Clay Center 68933 |

(Co Clk has b, d rec 1917-1918, Ind rec from 1871; Co Judge has m, pro, civ ct rec; Clk Dis Ct has div rec)

| * Colfax | B2 | 1869 | 10 | 1870-80 | Dodge | Schuyler 68661 |

(Co Judge has m rec from 1869, pro rec from 1886 & civ ct rec from 1885; Clk Dis Ct has div rec from 1881; Co Clk has Ind rec from 1860)

| * Cuming | B2 | 1855 | 12 | 1860-80 | Burt | West Point 68788 |

(Co Judge has m, pro rec from 1866, civ ct rec from 1960, school cen; Clk Dis Ct has div rec from 1869)

| * Custer | D3 | 1877 | 14 | 1880 | Unorg. Terr. | Broken Bow 68822 |

(Co Clk has b rec from 1910, d rec from 1915 inc, obituaries from 1877, pioneer biographical data; Custer Co Hist soc has many other rec; Co Judge has m rec from 1878, pro & civ ct rec from 1887; Clk Dis Ct has div rec from 1881; Reg Deeds has Ind rec from 1880)

| * Dakota | A2 | 1855 | 17 | 1860-80 | Original county | Dakota City 68731 |

(Co Judge has m rec from 1859, pro rec from 1864, civ ct rec from 1872 & guardianship rec; Clk Dis Ct has div rec from 1866; Co Clk has Ind rec)

| Dawes | F1 | 1885 | 10 | | Sioux | Chadron 69337 |

(Co Clk has Ind rec from 1880; Co Judge has m, pro rec; Clk Dis Ct has div rec)

| * Dawson | D3 | 1860 | 22 | 1860-80 | Buffalo | Lexington 68850 |

(Co Judge has m, div & pro rec; Reg Deeds has Ind rec)

| * Deuel | E3 | 1888 | 2 | | Cheyenne | Chappell 69129 |

(Co Judge has m & pro rec; Co Clk has bur, div & Ind rec, dis ct rec from 1890)

| * Dixon | B2 | 1856 | 7 | 1860-80 | Original county | Ponca 68770 |

(Co Clk has b, d & bur rec from 1919 but they are not public & Ind rec from 1871)

| * Dodge | B2 | 1854 | 36 | 1860-80 | Original county | Fremont 68025 |

(Co Clk has b & d rec from 1919; Co Judge has m, div & pro rec; Reg Deeds has Ind rec)

| * Douglas | A3 | 1854 | 395 | 1860-80 | Original county | Omaha 68102 |

(Co Judge has m & pro rec; Clk Dis Ct has div rec; Co Clk has service discharges)

| Dundy | E4 | 1873 | 3 | 1880 | Unorg. Terr. | Benkelman 69021 |

(Co Clk has b rec from 1907, d rec from 1904, also bur, div & civ ct rec; Co Judge has pro rec)

| Emmet (changed from L'eau qui court 18 Feb 1867. Changed to Knox 21 Feb 1873) | | | | | | |
| * Fillmore | B3 | 1856 | 8 | 1860-80 | Unorg. Terr. | Geneva 68361 |

(Co Clk has m, bur, div, pro, civ ct & Ind rec)

Forney (changed to Nemaha)						
Franklin	C4	1867	4	1870-80	Kearney Org. 1871	Franklin 68939
* Frontier	D3	1872	4	1880	Unorg. Terr.	Stockville 69042

(Co Judge has m & pro rec; Co Clk has div & Ind rec; Supt Schools has school census)

| * Furnas | D4 | 1873 | 6 | 1880 | Unorg. Terr. | Beaver City 68926 |

(Co Judge has m, pro & civ ct rec; Clk Dis Ct has div rec; Co Clk has Ind rec from 1873)

| * Gage | A4 | 1855 | 24 | 1860-80 | Original county | Beatrice 68310 |

(Co Judge has m, pro rec from 1860; Clk Dis Ct has div rec)

| Garden | D2 | 1887 | 3 | | Cheyenne, Deuel | Oshkosh 69154 |

(Co Judge has m, pro & civ ct rec; Clk Dis Ct has div rec; Co Clk has Ind rec)

| * Garfield | C2 | 1884 | 2 | | Wheeler | Burwell 68823 |

(Co Judge has m, div & pro rec)

| *§ Gosper | D4 | 1873 | 2 | | Unorg. Terr. | Elwood 68937 |

(Co Judge has m & pro rec from 1891, civ ct rec from 1920; Co Clk has div rec from 1880 & Ind rec)

COUNTY MAP FOR THE STATE OF NEBRASKA

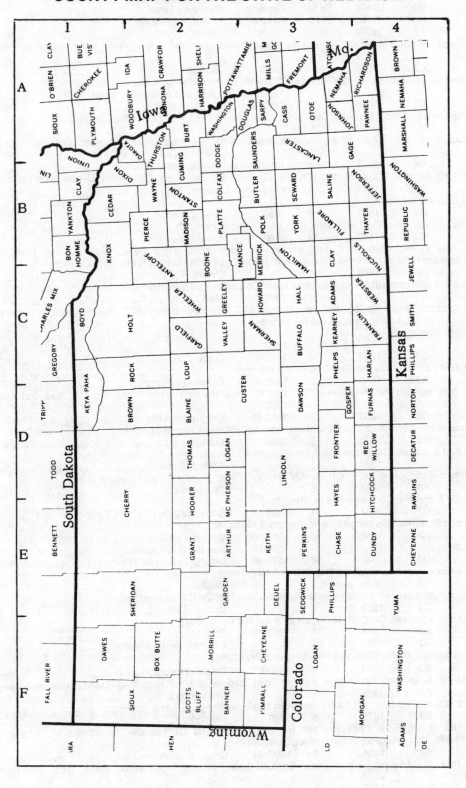

Name	Map Index	Date Created	Pop. By M 1980	U.S. Cen Reports Available	Parent County or Territory From Which Organized	County Seat
Grant	E2	1887	1		Unorg. Terr.	Hyannis 69350

(Co Judge has m, div, pro, civ ct, Ind rec from 1888, bur rec from 1941; Nebr. Dept of Health, Lincoln, has b, d rec)

| *§ Greeley | C2 | 1871 | 3 | 1880 | Boone | Greeley 68842 |

(Co Judge has m, pro, Ind rec, div rec from 1880's; Nebr. Dept of Health, Lincoln, has b, d rec)

| Greene | | | | 1860 | Changed to Seward 3 Jan, 1862 | |
| * Hall | C3 | 1858 | 48 | 1860-80 | Original county | Grand Island 68801 |

(Co Judge has m & pro rec from 1860; Clk Dis Ct has div, civ ct rec; Reg Deeds has Ind rec)

| * Hamilton | B3 | 10 | | 1870-80 | York | Aurora 68818 |

(Co Clk has b, d rec from 1906, Ind rec from 1870; Co Judge has m rec; Clk Dis Ct has div, pro, civ ct rec)

| Harlan | C4 | 1871 | 4 | 1880 | Unorg. Terr. | Alma 68920 |

(Co Judge has m, pro & civ ct rec; Clk Dis Ct has div rec from 1870; Reg Deeds has Ind rec from 1870)

| * Hayes | D3 | 1877 | 1 | 1880 | Unorg. Terr. | Hayes Center 69032 |

(Co Clk has d, bur & Ind rec)

| Hitchcock | D4 | 1873 | 4 | 1880 | Unorg. Terr. | Trenton 69044 |

(Co Judge has m & pro rec; Co Clk has div, dis ct & Ind rec from 1873)

| Holt | C2 | 1860 | 14 | 1880 | Knox (see West) | O'Neill 68763 |

(Co Judge has m rec from 1878, pro, civ ct rec from 1882; Regr Deeds has Ind rec from 1879; Clk Dis Ct has div rec from 1879; mortuaries have bur rec; Nebr. Dept of Health, Lincoln, has b, d rec)

| * Hooker | E2 | 1889 | 1 | | Unorg. Terr. | Mullen 69152 |

(Co Clk has b & d rec from 1919 & Ind rec from 1889; Co Judge has m & pro rec)

| *§ Howard | C3 | 1871 | 7 | 1880 | Hall | Saint Paul 68873 |

(Co Judge has m, pro, civ ct, Ind rec from 1872, div rec from 1873, naturalization papers from 1872; Nebr. Dept of Health, Lincoln, has b, d rec from 1915)

Izard (changed to Stanton)						
Jackson				1870		
* Jefferson	B4	1856	10	1870-80	Gage	Fairbury 68352

(Co Judge has m, pro & civ ct rec; Reg Deeds has Ind rec)

| * Johnson | A3 | 1855 | 5 | 1860-80 | Original county | Tecumseh 68450 |

(Co Judge has m, pro & civ ct rec; Clk Dis Ct has div rec from 1850; Co Clk has Ind rec from 1857)

| Jones | | | | 1860 | | |
| * Kearney | C3 | 1860 | 7 | 1860-80 | Original county | Minden 68959 |

(Co Judge has m rec from 1872, pro & civ ct rec from 1876; Co Clk has Ind rec)

| Keith | E3 | 1873 | 9 | 1880 | Lincoln | Ogallala 69153 |

(Co Clk has b, d & Ind rec; Co Judge has m rec; Clk Dis Ct has div, pro & civ ct rec)

| * Keya Paha | D1 | 1884 | 1 | | Brown, Rock | Springview 68778 |

(Co Clk has m, div, pro, civ ct, Ind rec from 1885; Nebr. Dept of Health, Lincoln, has b, d rec)

| Kimball | F3 | 1888 | 5 | | Cheyenne | Kimball 69145 |

(Co Clk has div & pro rec; Co Judge has m, civ ct rec)

| * Knox | B1 | 1857 | 11 | 1880 | See L'Eau Qui Court & Emmet | Center 68724 |

(Co Clk has b, d & bur rec; Co Judge has m, div, pro & civ ct rec)

* Lancaster	A3	1856	193	1860-80	Original county	Lincoln 68508
L'Eau Qui Court				1860-70	See Knox & Emmet	
* Lincoln	D3	1860	36	1870-80	Unorg. Terr. (see Shorter)	North Platte 69101

(Co Judge has m, div, pro & civ ct rec; Reg Deeds has Ind rec)

| Logan | D2 | 1885 | 1 | | Custer | Stapleton 69163 |

(Co Judge has m, div, pro, civ ct rec from 1885, partial bur rec; Co Clk has Ind rec)

| § Loup | C2 | 1855 | 1 | | Unorg. Terr. | Taylor 68879 |

(Co Judge has m & pro rec; Co Clk has div, civ ct & Ind rec from 1887)

| Madison | B2 | 1856 | 31 | 1860-80 | Platte | Madison 68748 |
| McPherson | D2 | 1887 | 1 | | Lincoln, Keith, Logan | Tryon 69167 |

(Co Clk has m, bur & Ind rec; Co Judge has div, pro & civ ct rec)

| *§ Merrick | B3 | 1858 | 9 | 1860-80 | Original county | Central City 68826 |

(Co Clk has b & d rec; Co Judge has m, div, pro & civ ct rec; Reg Deeds has Ind rec from 1873)

| Morrill | F2 | 1908 | 6 | | Cheyenne | Bridgeport 69336 |

(Co Clk has b, d & bur rec from 1917 & Ind rec from 1909; Co Judge has m & pro rec)

| Nance | B3 | 1879 | 5 | 1880 | Merrick | Fullerton 68638 |

(Co Judge has m rec from 1880, pro rec from 1887; Clk Dis Ct has div, civ ct rec from 1880; Co Clk has Ind rec from 1880, chronological list of b, d rec from 1919)

| * Nemaha | A3 | 1854 | 8 | 1860-80 | Original county | Auburn 68305 |

(Co Judge has m, div, pro, civ ct rec; Co Clk has Ind rec from 1853; Nebr. Dept of Health, Lincoln, has b, d rec)

| * Nuckolls | B4 | 1860 | 7 | 1860-80 | Clay | Nelson 68961 |

(Co Judge has m & pro rec; Clk Dis Ct has div & civ ct rec; Co Clk has Ind rec from 1900 obtained only with description of Ind in question)

Name	Map Index	Date Created	Pop. By M 1980	U.S. Cen Reports Available	Parent County or Territory From Which Organized	County Seat
* Otoe	A3	1854	15	1860-80	Original county	Nebraska City 68410

(Co Judge has m & pro rec; Co Clk has Ind rec)

| * Pawnee | A4 | 1855 | 4 | 1860-80 | Original county | Pawnee City 68420 |

(Co Judge has m rec from 1870 & pro rec; Co Clk has Ind rec)

| Perkins | E3 | 1887 | 4 | | Keith | Grant 69140 |

(Co Clk has b & d rec from 1919 & dis ct rec from 1888; Co Judge has div, pro & civ ct rec)

| * Phelps | C3 | 1873 | 10 | 1880 | Unorg. Terr. | Holdrege 68949 |

(Co Judge has m rec from 1877, pro rec from 1895; Clk Dis Ct has div rec from 1880)

| * Pierce | B2 | 1856 | 8 | 1870-80 | Madison | Pierce 68767 |

(Co Judge has m, pro & civ ct rec; Clk Dis Ct has div rec; Co Clk has Ind rec)

| * Platte | B2 | 1856 | 29 | 1860-80 | Original county | Columbus 68601 |

(Co Judge has m & pro rec; Clk Dis Ct has div & civ ct rec; Co Asr has Ind rec)

| * Polk | B3 | 1856 | 6 | 1860-80 | Original county | Osceola 68651 |

(Co Judge has m & pro rec; Co clk has Ind rec)

| Red Willow | D4 | 1873 | 13 | 1880 | Frontier | McCook 69001 |

(Co Judge has m, pro & civ ct rec; Clk Dis Ct has div rec; Co Clk has Ind rec ca 1870)

| * Richardson | A4 | 1854 | 11 | 1860-80 | Original county | Falls City 68355 |

(Co Clk has b, d rec from 1918; Co Judge has m rec from 1800's, pro, civ ct rec; Reg Deeds has Ind rec; local cemeteries have bur rec; Clk Dis Ct has div rec)

| Rock | C2 | 1857 | 2 | | Brown | Bassett 68714 |

(Co Judge has m rec; Co Clk has div rec from 1889, pro, civ ct, Ind rec from 1889)

| * Saline | B3 | 1855 | 13 | 1860-80 | Gage, Lancaster | Wilber 68465 |

(Co Clk has b, d from 1976, Ind rec from 1886; Co Ct has m rec from 1886, pro rec from 1870; Clk Dist Ct has div, civ ct rec from 1886)

| * Sarpy | A3 | 1857 | 85 | 1860-80 | Original county | Papillion 68046 |

(Co Judge has m & pro rec; Co Clk has Ind rec)

| * Saunders | A3 | 1856 | 19 | | Sarpy, Douglas | Wahoo 68066 |

(Co Clk has m, bur, div, pro, civ ct & Ind rec)

| * Scotts Bluff | F2 | 1881 | 38 | | Cheyenne | Gering 69341 |

(Co Clk has m, div, pro & civ ct rec from 1889)

| *§ Seward | B3 | 1855 | 16 | 1870-80 | Greene | Seward 68434 |

(Co Ct has m, pro rec from 1869; Co Clk has Ind rec from 1866; Clk Dis Ct has div rec from 1868, civ ct rec from 1869; cem associations have bur rec; Nebr. Dept of Health, Lincoln, has b, d rec from 1904)

| Sheridan | E2 | 1885 | 8 | | Sioux | Rushville 69360 |

(Bureau of Vit Stat, Lincoln, Nebr has b, d & bur rec; Co Judge has m, pro & civ ct rec; Clk Dis Ct has div rec)

| * Sherman | C3 | 1871 | 4 | 1880 | Buffalo | Loup City 68853 |

(Co Clk has b, d & div rec, m rec from 1873, pro rec from 1877, civ ct rec from 1889; Co Rgstr has b, d & bur rec)

| Shorter | | | | 1860 | Changed to Lincoln 11 Dec, 1861 | |
| Sioux | F2 | 1877 | 2 | 1880 | Unorg. Terr. | Harrison 69346 |

(Co Judge has m rec, pro & civ ct rec from 1887; City Clk has bur rec; Clk Dis Ct has div rec)

| * Stanton | B2 | 1855 | 7 | 1870-80 | Dodge (formerly Izard) | Stanton 68779 |

(Co Judge has m, pro & civ ct rec; Co Clk has Ind rec from 1878)

| Taylor | | | | 1870 | | |
| * Thayer | B4 | 1871 | 8 | 1880 | Jefferson | Hebron 68370 |

(Co Judge has m, pro & civ ct rec; Clk Dis Ct has div rec; Co Clk has Ind rec)

| * Thomas | D2 | 1887 | 1 | | Blaine | Thedford 69166 |

(Co Judge has m & pro rec; Clk Dis Ct has div & civ ct rec; Co Clk has Ind rec)

| Thurston | A2 | 1865 | 7 | 1870-80 | Burt (see Blackbird Co) | Pender 68047 |

(Co Judge has m & pro rec from 1889; Clk Dis Ct has div & civ ct rec from 1889; Co Clk has Ind rec from 1885) (Thurston Co was originally an Indian res & prior to organization was called Blackbird. From 1884 to 1889 it was administered by Dakota Co according to Co Clk)

| * Valley | C2 | 1871 | 6 | 1880 | Unorg. Terr. | Ord 68862 |

(Co Judge has m & pro rec; Clk Dis Ct has div & civ ct rec; Co Clk has Ind rec from 1883)

| * Washington | A2 | 1854 | 16 | 1860-80 | Original county | Blair 68008 |

(Co Clk has b, d, bur & Ind rec; Judge's Office has m, pro & civ ct rec; Clk Dis Ct has div rec)

| * Wayne | B2 | 1871 | 10 | 1870-80 | Thurston | Wayne 68787 |

(Co Judge has m, pro & civ ct rec from 1871; Clk Dis Ct has div rec; Co Clk has Ind rec from 1870)

| *§ Webster | C4 | 1867 | 5 | 1880 | Unorg. Terr. | Red Cloud 68970 |

(Co clk has b rec from 1919, partial d rec, div & Ind rec from 1871; Co Judge has m & pro rec)

| West (changed to Holt 9 Jan, 1862) | | | | | | |
| Wheeler | C2 | 1877 | 1 | 1880 | Boone | Bartlett 68622 |

(Co Clk has civ ct, Ind rec)

| Winnebago Indian Reservation | | | | 1870 | | |

Name	Map Index	Date Created	Pop. By M 1980	U.S. Cen Reports Available	Parent County or Territory From Which Organized	County Seat
* York	B3	1855	15	1860-80	Original county	York 68467

(Co Judge has m & pro rec; Clk Dis Ct has div & civ ct rec; Co Clk has Ind rec from 1870)

* - At least one county history has been published about this county.

§ - Inventory of county archives was made by the Historical Records Survey. (see introduction)

NEVADA

CAPITAL, CARSON CITY - TERRITORY 1861 - STATE 1864 - (36TH)

Apparently the first whites to enter Nevada arrived in the mid-1820's. Jedediah S. Smith, Peter S. Ogden, Kit Carson and John C. Fremont explored much of Nevada. During the 1849 gold rush, numerous wagon trains rumbled through on their way to California.

After the Mexican War, the region was ceded to the U.S. (1848), and in 1850 most of the present-day Nevada was included in the new Utah Territory. Genoa (formerly Mormon Station) was the first permanent settlement in 1851.

Twelve years after the Mormon pioneers reached the Great Salt Lake, gold and silver were found in the Comstock Mine in Virginia City, Nevada, midway - twenty or twenty-five miles - between Reno and Carson City. The strike was rich enough to turn California gold seekers eastward. Almost overnight, the Nevada population, which up to that time had stood around a thousand, doubled over and over again. Among Europeans attracted by the rich mineral discovery were people from all sections of Britain, Italy, Scandinavia, Germany and France. Many Mexicans came also.

Nevada became a territory in 1861 and three years later was admitted into the Union as the thirty-sixth state.

Birth and death records from 1887 to 30 June 1911, marriage records from 1864 to date, deeds and land records from 1864 to date are all in the office of the Recorder of each county.

Birth and death files from 1 July 1911 to date are at the Nevada State Department of Health, Division of Vital Statistics, Carson City, Nevada 89710.

Marriage banns are not filed.

Wills from 1864 to date are in the office of the clerk of each county.

Tax payers lists from 1864 are at the office of the Assessor of each county.

Genealogical Archives, Libraries, Societies, and Publications

Las Vegas Public Library, 400 E. Mesquite Ave., Las Vegas, NV 89101.

Nevada State Historical Society Library, P.O. Box 1192, Reno, NV 89501.

Northeastern Nevada Genealogical Society, P.O. Box 1903, Elko, NV 89801.

University of Nevada Library, Reno, NV 89507.

Washoe County Library, Reno, NV 89507.

Chart and Quill, Northeastern Nevada Genealogical Society, P.O. Box 1903, Elko, NV 89801.

Prospector, The, publication of the Clark County Nevada Genealogical Society, 4333 El Cid Circle, Las Vegas, NV 89121.

Printed Census Records and Mortality Schedules

State Indexes: 1870, 1880

Mortality Schedule (Printed): 1870

Valuable Printed Sources

Place Names

Averett, Walter R. *Directory of Southern Nevada Place Names.* Privately published (1963)

Carlson, Helen S. *Nevada Place Names, A Geographical Dictionary.* Reno: University of Nevada Press (1974).

History

Nevada, The Silver State. Carson City: Western States Historical Publishers (1970).

Genealogical Sources

Paterson, Mrs. Chester A. *Genealogical Records.* Compiled by various chapters, Nevada Daughters of the American Revolution. Salt Lake City: Genealogical Society (1954).

Bibliography

Lingenfelter, Richard E. *The Newspapers of Nevada 1858-1958; A History and Bibliography.* San Francisco: John Howell - Books (1964).

NEVADA COUNTY HISTORIES
(Population figures to nearest thousand - 1980 U. S. Census)

Name	Map Index	Date Created	Pop. By M 1980	U.S. Census Reports Available	Parent County or Territory From Which Organized	County Seat
Carson				1860	(see Utah) discontinued	
Churchill	C2	1861	14	1870-80	Original county	Fallon 89406
(Co Clk has m, div, pro & civ ct rec from 1905)						
Clark	F4	1909	462		Lincoln	Las Vegas 89101
(Co Clk has m, div, pro & civ ct rec from 1909; Co Rcdr has Ind rec)						
§ Douglas	C1	1861	20	1870-80	Original county	Minden 89423
(Co Clk has m, div, pro & civ ct rec)						
§ Elko	A4	1869	17	1870-80	Lander	Elko 89801
(Co Clk has m applications, div, pro, civ ct rec from 1876; Co Rcdr has b, d, bur, Ind rec.)						
Esmeralda	D2	1861	1	1870-80	Original county	Goldfield 89013
(Co Clk has b rec from 1900, m, d, bur rec from 1898, div rec from 1908, civ ct rec from 1907)						
§ Eureka	B3	1873	1		Lander	Eureka 89316
(Co Rcdr has b, m, d, bur rec; Co Clk has div, pro, civ ct rec from 1874.)						
Humboldt	A2	1861	9	1860-80	Original county	Winnemucca 89445
(Co Clk has m rec from 1881, div & civ ct rec from 1863, pro rec from 1900, naturalization rec from 1864, inquests 1862; see Utah 1860 cen; Rcdr & State Dept of Health have b & d rec)						
Lander	B3	1862	4	1870-80	Original county	Austin 89310
(Co Clk has m rec from 1867, div rec, pro & civ ct rec from 1865; Aud has some b rec)						
Lincoln	D4	1866	4	1870-80	Nye	Pioche 89043
(Co Clk has m, div, pro & civ ct rec from 1873)						
Lyon	C1	1861	14	1870-80	Original county	Yerington 89447
(Co Rcdr has m & Ind rec from 1862; Co Clk has div, pro & civ ct rec from 1890)						
§ Mineral	D2	1911	6		Esmeralda	Hawthorne 89415
(Co Clk has m applications, div, pro & civ ct rec from 1911; Co Rcdr has Ind rec)						
*§ Nye	D3	1864	9	1870-80	Esmeralda	Tonopah 89049
(Co Clk has m, div, pro & civ ct rec from 1860; Co Rcdr has Ind rec)						
Ormsby	C1	1861	8	1870-80	Original county	Carson City 89701
(Co Clk has m, div, pro & civ ct rec)						
Pahute				1870	Discontinued	
Pershing	B2	1919	3		Humboldt	Lovelock 89419
(Co Clk has m, div, pro & civ ct rec from 1919)						
Roop				1870	Discontinued	
St. Mary's				1860	(see Utah) discontinued	
Storey	C1	1861	1	1870-80	Original county	Virginia City 89440
(Co Rcdr has b, m & d rec from 1875; Co Clk has div & civ ct rec from 1861 & pro rec from 1875)						
§ Washoe	B1	1861	194	1870-80	Original county	Reno 89505
(Dis Health Dept has b, d, bur rec from 1900; Co Clk-Rcdr has m rec from 1871; Co Clk has div, pro, civ ct rec from 1862; Co Rcdr has Ind rec from 1862.						
White Pine	C4	1869	8	1870-80	Lincoln	Ely 89301
(Co Clk has m rec from 1885, div, pro & civ ct rec from 1907; Co Rcdr has Ind rec from 1885)						

* - At least one county history has been published about this county.

§ - Inventory of county archives was made by the Historical Records Survey. (see introduction)

COUNTY MAP FOR THE STATE OF NEVADA

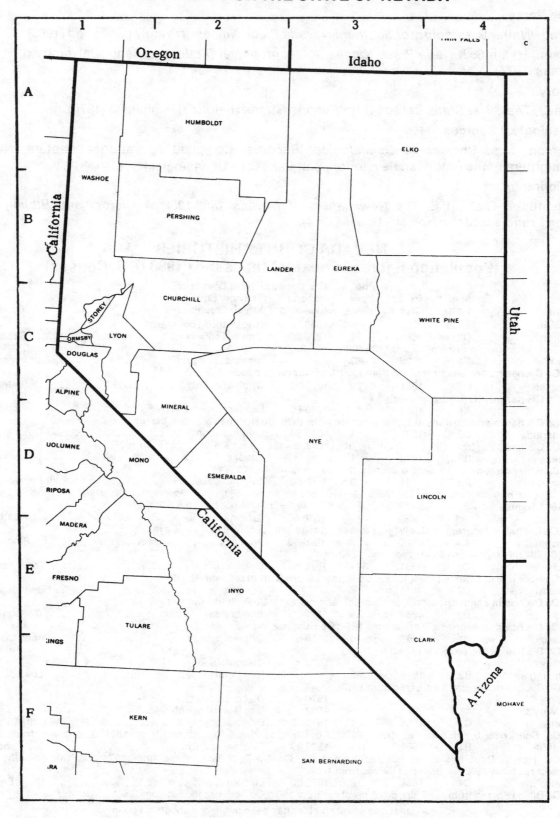

NEW HAMPSHIRE

CAPITAL, CONCORD - STATE 1788 - (9TH)

New Hampshire, in the northeastern corner of the United States, is one of the thirteen original colonies. Its history dates back to 1603 when an Englishman, Martin Pring, anchored in Piscataqua harbor. The French explorer, Samuel de Champlain, discovered the Isles of Shoals in 1605 while sailing along the coast of New Hampshire. In 1614 Captain John Smith landed on its shores. It was settled about 1623 at Rye (Little Harbor) and shortly afterwards at Dover and Portsmouth. This was only three years after the landing of the Pilgrim fathers in Massachusetts. A little later settlements were made at Exeter and Hampton. These places were on or near the coast, or on a river bank near its mouth. After these first settlements, little effort was put forth to establish new settlements for almost a hundred years. The fear of Indians kept the settlers from moving inland.

New Hampshire became part of the Massachusetts colony in 1641, and continued so, with brief interruptions, for about thirty-eight years. In 1679 it became a Royal British Province and remained so until the Revolutionary War.

The boundaries of New Hampshire were not definite until 1764. Prior to that date there were many bitter disputes, especially with Massachusetts and New York, as to where the lines should be.

A large part of the early settlers came from Massachusetts and Connecticut. The Connecticut River is the western boundary of the state. Apparently it was much easier to go up the river than to cut long roads through the forests from the eastern shore. Many of the river towns, as a result, are much older than those in the interior. If the ancestry of the early settlers of one of those towns is sought, it will more than likely be found in Connecticut or western Massachusetts.

Of New Hampshire, Archibald F. Bennett, former secretary of the Genealogical Society of Utah, has said: "In the great migration to the west, New Hampshire and Vermont were stopping places for a few years for one or more generations of families now established far from there. Many families from their homelands in Massachusetts and Connecticut seemed to pause here briefly, and then resume their westward trek. Their residence in New Hampshire was often during the pioneer period when records were not kept too regularly. Then they removed so early that almost all trace of their presence in those localities is obliterated. Consequently, many ancestral lines of western families are followed back to New Hampshire or Vermont, and then are hopelessly lost. Yet, there are actually many sources which can assist in the solution of such problems."

During the first two hundred years or more of its history, it was mainly people from England who came to New Hampshire. During the next seventy-five years, tens of thousands came into the state from the Scandinavian countries and from Greece, Italy and France.

New Hampshire entered the Union in 1788, the ninth state to ratify the constitution.

Vital statistics have been kept in the towns since 1640, though they are not complete. Copies of all statistics records since that date have been made. They include town records, church records, cemetery records, and all other available old records. These have all been indexed, and may be searched for a small fee. These records are available at the office of the Registrar of Vital Statistics, State House, Concord, NH 03303, and at some of the offices of the town clerks. Wills are in the charge of the clerks of the probate courts of the ten counties. The Registrars of deeds are in charge of deeds and land titles. The State Library at Concord has charge of the Census Records. Cemetery records are handled by the cemetery superintendents or selectmen of the towns. Tax papers are handled by the town and city clerks throughout the state.

Almost all towns have town histories. Many of these contain much genealogical information about the early settlers. In the genealogical departments of the public libraries will be found many books with valuable information about the town families.

NEW HAMPSHIRE TOWNS
Organized Before 1800

BELKNAP COUNTY -- Alton,- 1770; Barnstead, 1727; Belmont; Center Harbor, 1797; Gilmanton, 1761; Meredith, 1748; New Hampton, 1765; Sanbornton, 1764.

CARROLL COUNTY -- Albany, 1766; Bartlett, 1790; Brookfield, 1794; Conway, 1765, Chatham, 1767; Eaton, 1766; Effingham, 1749; Hart's Location, 1772; Jackson, 1778; Madison 1785; Moultonborough, 1763; Ossipee, 1765; Sandwich, 1763; Tamworth, 1766; Tuftonboro, 1750; Wakefield, 1774; Wolfeboro 1759.

CHESHIRE COUNTY -- Alstead, 1763; Chesterfield, 1761; Dublin, 1752; Fitzwilliam, 1752; Gilsum, 1764; Jaffrey, 1752; Keene, 1754; Marlborough, 1752; Marlow, 1753; Nelson, 1767; Rindge, 1754; Richmond, 1758; Stoddard, 1769; Sullivan, 1760; Swanzey, 1753; Surry, 1769; Walpole, 1749; Westmoreland, 1741; Winchester, 1732.

COOS COUNTY -- Berlin, 1771; Colebrook, 1762; Columbia, 1762; Cambridge, 1793; Drummer, 1773; Dalton, 1764; Jefferson, 1765; Lancaster, 1763; Milan, 1771; Northumberland 1767; Randolph, 1772; Stark, 1788; Shelburne, 1770; Stratford, 1775.

GRAFTON COUNTY -- Alexandria, 1782; Benton, 1764; Bath, 1765; Bethlehem, 1799; Bridgewater, 1788; Canaan, 1761; Compton, 1765; Danbury, 1795; Dorchester, 1761; Enfield, 1761; Ellsworth, 1769; Franconia, 1754; Grafton, 1772; Groton, 1761; Hanover, 1765; Haverhill, 1763; Holderness, 1751; Hebron, 1792; Landaff, 1764; Lebanon, 1761; Lisbon, 1763; Littleton, 1764; Lyme, 1764; Lyman, 1761; Lincoln, 1764; Orange, 1790; Oxford, 1765; Pierpont, 1768; Plymouth, 1764; Rumney, 1705; Thornton, 1770; Warren, 1767; Wentworth, 1766; Woodstock, 1763.

HILLSBORO COUNTY -- Amherst, 1760; Antrim, 1744; Bedford, 1736; Brookline, 1769; Deering, 1765; Francestown, 1720; Lyndeborough, 1759, Manchester, 1751; Mason, 1768; Merrimack, 1722; Milford, 1740; Nashua, 1673; New Boston, 1720; Lyndeborough, 1759; Manchester, 1751; Mason, 1768; Merrimack 1722; Milford, 1740; Nashua, 1673; New Boston, 1735; New Ipswich, 1735; Petersboro, 1749; Pellham, 1745; Sharon, 1791; Temple, 1750; Weare, 1735; Wilton, 1749; Windsor, 1798.

MERRIMACK COUNTY -- Allenstown, 1747; Andover, 1761; Boscowan, 1760; Bow, 1727; Bradford, 1771; Canterbury, 1723-50; Chichester, 1727; Concord, 1727; Danbury, 1795; Dunbarton, 1746; Epsom, 1727; Henniker, 1760; Hill, 1768; Hopkinton, 1740; Loudon, 1765; Newbury, 1762; New London, 1758; Northfield, 1760; Pembroke, 1728; Pittsfield, 1782; Salisbury, 1750; Sutton, 1767; Warner, 1773.

ROCKINGHAM COUNTY -- Arkinson, 1728; Auburn, 1734; Brentwood, 1742; Candia, 1748; Chester, 1720; Danville, 1738; Deerfield, 1750; E. Kingston, 1738; Epping, 1741; Exeter, 1638; Fremont, 1764; Greenland, 1704; Hempstead, 1728; Hampton, 1635; Hampton Falls, 1726; Kensington, 1737; Kingston, 1694; Londonderry, 1719; Newcastle, 1693; Newington, 1670; Newfields, 1681; Newmarket, 1727; Newton, 1749; North Hampton, 1690; Northwood, 1763; Nottingham, 1722; Plaistow, 1642; Portsmouth, 1623; Raymond, 1764; Rye, 1635; Sandown, 1756; Seabrook, 1758; South Hampton, 1742; Stratham, 1629; Windham, 1741.

STRAFFORD COUNTY -- Barrington, 1762; Dover, 1623; Durham, 1623; Farmington, 1798; Lee, 1766; Madbury, 1755; Middleton, 1778; Milton, 1760; New Durham, 1749; Rochester, 1722; Somersworth, 1754.

SULLIVAN COUNTY -- Acworth, 1767; Charlestown, 1735; Claremont, 1764; Cornish, 1765; Croydon, 1766; Goshen, 1761; Grantham, 1761; Langdon, 1773; Lempster, 1785; Newport, 1765-6; Plainfield, 1765; Springfield, 1772; Unity, 1754; Washington, 1768.

Genealogical Archives, Libraries, Societies, and Publications

Baker Memorial Library, Dartmouth College, Hanover, NH 03755.

City Library, Carpenter Memorial Bldg., 405 Pine St., Manchester, NH 03104.

Dartmouth College Archives, Baker Library, Hanover, NH 03755.

Dover Public Library, 73 Locust St., Dover, NH 03820.

New Hampshire Historical Society, Library, 30 Park St., Concord, NH 03301.

New Hampshire Society of Genealogists (NHSOG), P.O. Box 633, Exeter, NH 03833.

New Hampshire State Library, 20 Park St., Concord, NH 03303.

Portsmouth Athenaeum, 9 Market Street, Portsmouth, NH 03801.

Rockingham County chapter, NHSOG, P.O. Box 81, Exeter, NH 03833.

Strafford County Chapter, NHSOG, P.O. Box 322, Dover, NH 03820.

Genealogical Record, The, publication of the Strafford County Chapter of the New Hampshire Society of Genealogists, P.O. Box 322, Dover, New Hampshire.

Printed Census Records and Mortality Schedules

State Indexes: 1790, 1800, 1810, 1820, 1830, 1840, 1850, 1880

Printed Census Records (Counties):

Cheshire-1800, 1810	Rockingham-1800
Grafton-1800, 1840	Strafford-1800
Hillsboro-1800	

Mortality Schedules

State-1850

Other Printed Census Records:

1633-1699 Residents	1776-Colony
1732-Colony	

Valuable Printed Sources

Gazetteers

Farmer, John and Jacob B. Moore. *A Gazetteer of the State of New Hampshire.* Concord: J. B. Moore (1823).

Hayward, John. *A Gazetteer of New Hampshire.* Boston: J. P. Jewett (1849).

Maps

Hurd, D. H. and Company. *Town and City Atlas of the State of New Hampshire.* Boston: 1892.

Place Names

New Hampshire State Planning and Development Commission. *Communities, Settlements and Neighborhood Centers in the State of New Hampshire.* Concord: (1937) reprinted 1954.

Guides To Genealogical Research

Genealogists Handbook for New England Research. New England Library Association, 1980.

New England Historical and Genealogical Register, Oct. 1976, Vol. 130 page 244. New Hampshire Genealogy: A Perspective - David C. Dearborn.

Histories

Squires, James Duane. *The Granite State of the United States: A History of New Hampshire from 1623 to the present.* New York: The American Historical Company (1956)

Genealogical Sources

Hammond, Isaac W. *Rolls of the Soldiers in the Revolutionary War,* 4 Vols. Concord: State Printer, 1885-1889)

Noyes, Sybil. *Genealogical Dictionary of Maine and New Hampshire.* Originally published in Portland, Maine 1928-1939, reprinted Baltimore: Genealogical Publishing Company (1976).

Probate Records of the Province of New Hampshire (State Papers Series Volumes 31 to 39) State of New Hampshire, 9 Vols., 1907-1941.

Provincial and State Papers. *Documents and Records Relating to the Province of New Hampshire* Vols. 1 to 40. Concord: George E. Jenks State Printer.

Stearns, Ezra S. *Genealogical and Family History of the State of New Hampshire.* 4 Volumes. New York: Lewis Publishing Company, 1908.

Bibliographies

Haskell, John D. Jr. ed. *New Hampshire: A Bibliography of Its History.* Boston: G.K. Hall and Company (1979).

COUNTY MAP FOR THE STATE OF NEW HAMPSHIRE

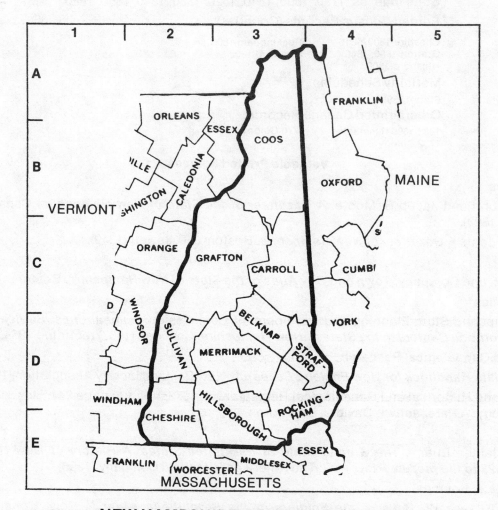

NEW HAMPSHIRE COUNTY HISTORIES
(Population figures to nearest thousand - 1980 U. S. Census)

Name	Map Index	Date Created	Pop. By M 1980	U.S. Cen Reports Available	Parent County or Territory From Which Organized	County Seat
*§ Belknap	D3	1840	43	1850-80	Strafford, Merrimac	Laconia 03246

(Twn or City Clks have b, m & d rec; Clk Sup Ct has div & civ ct rec; Pro Judge has pro rec from 1841; Reg Deeds has Ind rec from 1841)

| *§ Carroll | C3 | 1840 | 28 | 1850-80 | Strafford | Ossipee 03864 |

(Clk Ct has div & civ ct rec from 1859; Twn Clk of each twn has b, m, d & bur rec; Pro Judge has pro rec)

| *§ Cheshire | E2 | 1769 | 62 | 1790-80 | Original county | Keene 03431 |

(Twn or City Clks have b, m, d & bur rec; Co Clk has div & civ ct rec; Reg Pro has pro rec; Reg Deeds has Ind rec)

| *§ Coos | A3 | 1803 | 35 | 1810-80 | Grafton | Lancaster 03584 |

(Twn or City Clks have b, m, d & bur rec; Clk Sup Ct has div & civ ct rec from 1887; Reg Pro has pro rec; Reg Deeds has Ind rec)

| *§ Grafton | C2 | 1769 | 66 | 1790-80 | Original county | Woodsville 03785 |

(1820 census missing? Clk Ct has div & civ ct rec; Pro Judge has pro rec; Vit Stat, Concord, NH has b, m, d & bur rec)

| * Hillsboro | D3 | 1769 | 276 | 1790-80 | Original county | Nashua 03060 and Manchester 03101 |

(Co Clk has div & pro rec from 1771)

| *§ Merrimack | D3 | 1823 | 98 | 1830-80 | Rockingham, Hillsboro | Concord 03302 |

(Co Clk has div rec from 1840, civ ct rec from 1823; Twn or City Clk or Bureau of Vit Stat, Concord, NH has b, m, d & bur rec; Pro Judge has pro rec from 1823)

Name	Map Index	Date Created	Pop. By M 1980	U.S. Cen Reports Available	Parent County or Territory From Which Organized	County Seat
* Rockingham	D4	1769	190	1790-80	Original county	Exeter 03833
(Clk Ct has div & civ ct rec from 1769)						
* Strafford	D4	1769	85	1790-80	Original county	Dover 03820
(Twn or City Clks have b, m, d & bur rec; Clk Sup Ct has div rec; Reg Pro has pro rec; Reg Deeds has Ind rec from 1773)						
* Sullivan	D2	1827	36	1830-80	Cheshire	Newport 03773
(Twn or City Clks have b, m, d & bur rec; Clk Sup Ct has div & civ ct rec from 1827; Reg Pro has pro rec; Reg Deeds has Ind rec; other rec of interest to genealogists at Richards Library, Newport, NH)						

* - At least one county history has been published about this county.

§ - Inventory of county archives was made by the Historical Records Survey. (see introduction)

NEW JERSEY

CAPITAL, TRENTON - STATE 1787 - (3RD)

French explorers sailed along the New Jersey coast as early as 1524. In the service of Holland, Henry Hudson sailed up the Hudson River in 1609. Nine years later the Dutch had settlers opposite the present upper New York City. Commissioned by their King, Swedish adventurers established a colony in the Delaware Valley, shortly after the Dutch came to the area. This New Sweden colony was annexed by the Dutch in 1655 and in 1664 the entire area was captured by the British.

With the experience gained in colonizing southern sections of America, two English court favorites, Lord Berkeley and Sir George Carteret, induced the Duke of York to grant them the area between the Hudson and the Delaware Rivers. They named the colony New Jersey after the English Channel home of Carteret. Throwing the territory open to land seekers in 1664, the promoters made tempting offers to those willing to come. To the small Dutch communities along the Hudson came folks from every section of Britain. Puritans came down from Connecticut and established Newark. Scotch-Irish Presbyterians poured into the eastern counties, and English Quakers came into the fertile regions of the Delaware.

While differing strongly in their religious convictions, the settlers were solidly united against the tax and monetary ideas of the Crown and the proprietors. Disgusted with the lack of financial returns in the venture, the proprietors sold out to William Penn and his Quaker Friends.

In the intervening years difficulties were erased and more unity ensued. In the early part of the eighteenth century, New Jersey and New York had the same royal governor, but this ended in 1738. During the next 49 years New Jersey had a governor and a legislature of its own.

New Jersey became the third state to ratify the constitution of the United States in 1778. Three years later, the first U.S. Census gave New Jersey a population of 184,139. The majority of these were English from the Old World as well as from New England. The Dutch and the Swedes were also represented by large numbers. In the western part of the state there were many French and Scottish.

Before William Penn acquired Pennsylvania, he and a company of Quakers settled West Jersey. The early Swedish and Dutch settlers continued to live there. Hence, a New Jersey pedigree may trace back to the English Quakers, the Puritans from New England, the Swedes who waged war on the early English settlers, the Dutch settlers who came from New Amsterdam (New York) and the Huguenots who fled from France in search of religious liberty and peace.

Research conditions are not so favorable in New Jersey as in some other states. Since they were not required by law to keep a record of births and deaths, the family Bible was about the only place where these things were recorded. And yet, researchers willing to search into available records can find a wealth of information.

The State Registrar's office, State of New Jersey, Department of Health, John Fitch Plaza, P.O. Box 1540, Trenton, NJ 08625 maintains birth, death, and marriage records from 1878 to the present date. Marriage licenses are issued by Registrars of Vital Statistics in each of every incorporated municipality having a Registrar of Vital Statistics, who serves as the licensing official. In those municipalities having a population of 5,000 or less, the City Clerk automatically serves as the Registrar of Vital Statistics. Records preceding 1878 to 1848 are stored in the Bureau of Archives and History, Department of Education, State Street, Trenton, New Jersey.

Divorce records are kept in the Superior Court, Chancery Division, at the State House in Trenton.

The federal circuit and district courts and the State Supreme court, all in Trenton and the county circuit courts have records of naturalization proceedings. Records of Deeds in New Jersey may be found as follows: From 1664 to 1703 in New Jersey Archives, Vol. XXI; From 1664 to 1790 in Secretary of State's Office; From 1790 to the present in the County Clerk's Offices (A few of earlier dates are included); In Gloucester County deeds recorded before 1786 were destroyed by fire, deeds recorded after that date (even though dated earlier) are extant.

Most of the churches in the state have records of their respective memberships for many years back.

The originals of wills and probate matters, together with early guardianship and orphans' court proceedings are in the custody of the Secretary of State in Trenton. Copies of wills and administrations of estates beginning in 1804 are at the county courthouses. Wills and administrations of estates from 1682 to 1805 have been digested and published in the State Archives. There are ten volumes, each completely indexed. The state also published an index of New Jersey Wills, three volumes. These wills extend to a much later date than those given in the Archives. Many libraries have a complete set of the Archives of New Jersey.

Genealogical Archives, Libraries, Societies, and Publications

Atlantic City Free Public Library, Illinois and Pacific Aves., Atlantic City, NJ 08401.

Burlington County Library, Woodlane Rd., Mt. Holly, NJ 08060.

Camden County Historical Society, Euclid Ave. and Park Blvd., Camden, NJ 08103.

Cape May Historical Society, Courthouse, Cape May, NJ 08204.

Genealogical Society of New Jersey, P.O. Box 1291, New Brunswick, NJ 08903.

Genealogical Society of The West Field, c/o Westfield Memorial Library, 425 East Broad St., Westfield, NJ 07090.

Glassboro State College, Glassboro, NJ 08028.

Gloucester County Historical Society Library, 17 Hunter St., Woodbury, NJ 08096.

Hunterdon County Historical Society, Hiram E. Deats Memorial Library, 114 Main Street, Flemington, NJ 08822.

Joint Free Public Library of Morristown and Morris Township, Box 267M, 1 Miller Rd., Morristown, NJ 07960.

Monmouth County Historical Association, 70 Court St., Freehold, NJ 07728.

Neptune Township Historical Society, 25 Neptune Blvd., Neptune, NJ 07753.

New Jersey Historical Society, 230 Broadway, Newark, NJ 07104.

New Jersey State Library, Archives and History Bureau, 185 West State St., Trenton, NJ 06618.

North Jersey Highlands Historical Society, MS Vi Hill, 177 Valley Road, Wayne, NJ 07470.

Passaic County Historical Society, The, Lambert Castle Garret Mt. Reservation, Paterson, NJ 07509.

Princeton University Library, The Princeton, NJ 08540.

Rutgers University Library, New Brunswick, NJ 08903.

Salem County New Jersey Historical Society, 81-83 Market St., Salem, NJ 08079.

Vineland Historical and Antiquarian Society, 108 So. Seventh St., Vineland, NJ 10028.

Westfield Memorial Library, 425 East Broad St., Westfield, NJ 07090.

Bergen County Genealogy Society Quarterly, 16 Beech Street, Westwood, NJ 07675.

Printed Census Records and Mortality Schedules

State Indexes: 1830, 1840, 1850

Printed Census Records (Counties):

Atlantic-1850, 1860
Bergen-1850
Burlington-1830, 1850
Cape May-1830

Cumberland-1800, 1850
Gloucester-1850; 1782 (twp. Gallaway)
Hudson-1850
Hunterdon-1830, 1850

Ocean-1850
Somerset-1830
Sussex-1850

Other printed census records:

1693-Census of New Sweden
1773-1784 Revolutionary War Census
1793-State census of males between ages 18 and 45.

Valuable Printed Sources

Gazetteer

Gordon, Thomas F. *A Gazetteer of the State of New Jersey.* Trenton: Daniel Fenton (1834).

Place Names

Gannett, Henry. *A Geographic Dictionary of New Jersey.* Originally published 1894, reprinted Baltimore: Genealogical Publishing Company (1978).

Guides To Genealogical Research

National Genealogical Society Quarterly Vol. 48 #2 June 1960. *That Genealogical Quagmire: New Jersey.*

Stryker-Rodda, Kenn. *New Jersey: Digging for Ancestors in the Garden State.* Detroit: The Detroit Society for Genealogical Research (1970), 1978.

Stryker-Rodde, Kenn. *Genealogical Spadework in the Garden State.* Proceedings of the New Jersey Historical Society: A Magazine of New Jersey History Vol. 79 Oct. 1961 pages 264-281.

Histories

Chambers, Theodore F. *The Early Germans of New Jersey, Their History, Churches and Genealogies.* Baltimore: Genealogical Publishing Company, reprinted 1969.

Kull, Irving S. *New Jersey, A History.* New York: The American Historical Society (1930).

Genealogical Sources

New Jersey Index of Wills, 3 Vols. (Originally published, 1912, by State of New Jersey, 1912.) Reprinted Baltimore: Genealogical Publishing Company, 1969.

New Jersey Historical Society in Newark, New Jersey *Charles R. Hutchinson Collection.*

Office of the Adjutant General, comp. *Records of Officers and Men of New Jersey in Wars 1791-1815.* Trenton: State Gazette Publishing Company, 1909.

Rutgers University: *John P. Dornan Collection. Charles C. Gardiner Collection.* New Brunswick, New Jersey.

Schlam, Rebecca and Kenneth W. Richards. *Genealogical Research, A Guide to Source Materials in the New Jersey State Library and other State Agencies.* Trenton: State of New Jersey Division of the State Library (1961).

State of New Jersey. *New Jersey Archives.* Trenton, New Jersey. First Series 42 Vols., Second Series 5 Vols. (1880-1949).

Bibliographies

Stryker-Rodda, Kenn. *Bibliographies and Genealogical Research in New York and New Jersey.* Presented at the annual meeting of the Iowa Genealogical Society in Nov. 1975.

COUNTY MAP FOR THE STATE OF NEW JERSEY

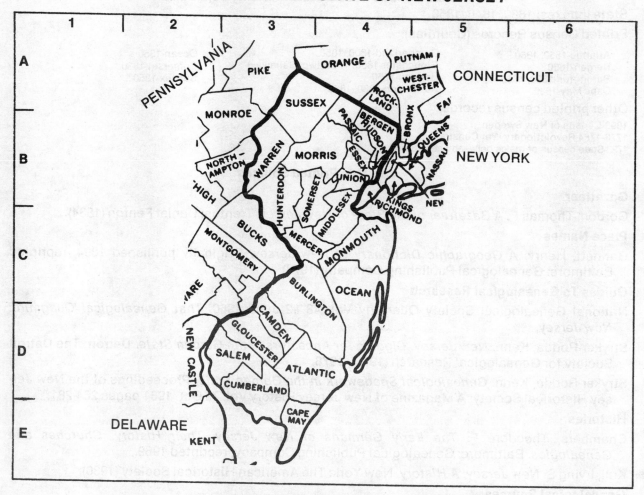

NEW JERSEY COUNTY HISTORIES
(Population figures to nearest thousand - 1980 U. S. Census)

Name	Map Index	Date Created	Pop. By M 1980	U.S. Cen Reports Available	Parent County or Territory From Which Organized	County Seat
* Atlantic	D4	1837	189	1840-80	Gloucester	Mays Landing 08330
(Co Clk has div rec from 1949, civ ct, Ind & cem rec from 1837; Co Surr has pro rec)						
*§ Bergen	B4	1683	845	1830-80	Prov East Jersey	Hackensack 07602
(Co Clk has div rec from 1955, civ ct & Ind rec)						
* Burlington	C3	1694	361	1830-80	Original county	Mt. Holly 08060
(Co Clk has div rec from 1966, pro & Ind rec from 1785 & civ ct rec from 1880)						
* Camden	D3	1844	471	1850-80	Glouc	Camden 08101
* Cape May	E3	1692	82	1830-80	Cumberland	Cape May Courthouse 08210
(Settled 1682; Co Clk has m rec from 1795 to 1826, pro & civ ct rec; also deeds & wills from 1692; Surr has pro rec)						
* Cumberland	D3	1748	132	1830-80	Salem	Bridgeton 08302
(Co Clk has div rec also civ ct rec from 1903 & Ind rec from 1787; Co Surr has pro rec)						
Essex	B4	1683	851	1830-80	Prov East Jersey	Newark 07102
(Co Clk has m rec from 1795 to 1879, div, civ ct rec from 1948, naturalizations from 1779-1929; City Clks have b, d rec Co Surr has pro rec; Reg Deeds has Ind rec)						
* Gloucester	D3	1686	199	1830-80	Original county	Woodbury 08096
(Co Clk has civ ct & Ind rec from about 1787; Surr Ct has pro rec; Clk Sup Ct has div rec; Courthouse burned 1786; early rec preserved at Surveyor General's office, Burlington & Sec of State Office, Trenton)						
* Hudson	B4	1840	555	1840-80	Bergen	Jersey City 07306

Name	Map Index	Date Created	Pop. By M 1980	U.S. Cen Reports Available	Parent County or Territory From Which Organized	County Seat
* Hunterdon	B3	1714	87	1830-80	Burlington	Flemington 08822

(Co Clk has m rec from 1795 to 1875, civ ct rec from 1714, deeds & mtg from 1716; Surr Ct has pro rec; Sup Ct has div rec)

| * Mercer | C3 | 1838 | 306 | 1840-80 | Somerset, Middlesex, Hunterdon, Burlington | Trenton 08607 |

(Co Surr has pro rec; Co Clk has civ ct & Ind rec from 1838 also judgements, tax maps, business name rec & corporation rec)

| * Middlesex | B4 | 1683 | 595 | 1830-80 | Prov. East Jersey | New Brunswick 08903 |

(Co Clk has m, div, civ ct & Ind rec)

| * Monmouth | C4 | 1683 | 496 | 1830-80 | Prov. East Jersey | Freehold 07728 |

(Co Clk has m rec from 1795 to 1892 & Ind rec from 1667)

| *§ Morris | B3 | 1739 | 407 | 1830-80 | Hunterdon | Morristown 07960 |

(Co Clk has m rec 1796-1969, civ ct rec 1739-1978, Ind rec from 1787; Bur Vit Statistics, Trenton, has b, d rec; Municipal Clks have bur rec; Clk Sup Ct has div rec; Surrogate has pro rec.)

| *§ Ocean | C4 | 1850 | 344 | 1850-80 | Monmouth | Toms River 08753 |

(Co Clk has pro & civ ct rec from 1850)

| *§ Passaic | A4 | 1837 | 448 | 1840-80 | Bergen, Essex | Paterson 07505 |

(Co Clk has div rec from 1947, civ ct rec from 1900, also Ind rec)

| * Salem | D3 | 1694 | 65 | 1830-80 | Original county | Salem 08079 |

(Co Clk has m rec 1795-1956, civ ct rec from 1875, Ind rec from 1786; Co Surr has pro rec; City Clks have b, d, bur rec.)

| * Somerset | B4 | 1688 | 202 | 1830-80 | Middlesex | Somerville 08876 |

(Co Clk has civ ct rec from 1777 & Ind rec from 1785)

| *§ Sussex | A3 | 1753 | 116 | 1830-80 | Morris | Newton 07860 |

(Co Clk has slave b rec, m rec 1795-1878, civ ct rec from 1753, Ind rec from 1800, crim rec from 1753, naturalizations, road returns from 1780, jury lists from 1805)

| * Union | B4 | 1857 | 503 | 1860-80 | Essex | Elizabeth 07207 |

(Clk Sup Ct has div rec from 1848, civ ct rec; Surrogate has pro rec from 1857; State Board of Health has b, m, d rec; Reg Deeds has Ind rec.)

| * Warren | B3 | 1824 | 86 | 1830-80 | Sussex | Belvidere 07823 |

(Municipal Clks have b, d rec; Co Clk has m, Ind rec from 1825, div, civ ct rec; Surr office has pro rec.)

* - At least one county history has been published about this county.

§ - Inventory of county archives was made by the Historical Records Survey. (see introduction)

NEW MEXICO

CAPITAL, SANTA FE - TERRITORY 1850 - STATE 1912 - (47TH)

Until 1821 when the 780-mile Santa Fe Trail was opened from Independence, Missouri to Santa Fe, New Mexico, few Americans or Europeans had made their homes in New Mexico. For years, the region belonged to Mexico and was inhabited mainly by Indians and Spanish-Americans. Its main city, Santa Fe, had been the capital of the Mexican Territory since 1609. At that early date and for the next 150 years or more, its connections were more with Mexico than the United States. Indians and Spanish-Americans were its only inhabitants until the first part of 1800.

New Mexico became part of the United States in 1848. In 1850 when it was created a territory, it included most of its present domain, plus Arizona and Colorado. The Gadsden Purchase in 1854 included within its boundaries the Gila Valley in Catron and Grant Counties.

The Colorado section was taken from New Mexico in 1861 and made into a separate territory. Two years later, Arizona was also withdrawn and created into a separate territory.

After operating for 62 years under territorial laws, New Mexico became a state in 1912, when it was made the forty-seventh in the Union.

Birth, death, and fetal death records from 1919 are at the Vital Statistics Bureau, P.O. Box 968, Santa Fe, NM 87501. Delayed birth certificates are available from 1867 and are not complete.

Copies available (for a fee) only to registrant, family member, or by court order. County Clerks in each of 32 county seats have records of marriage, wills, property deeds, and administration of records.

Land grants are in the State Land Office, Santa Fe, New Mexico. Historical land grant records are in the State Records Center and Archives and are not complete.

Tax payers lists are at the office of the County Assessor. War service records are at the New Mexico Veterans Service Commission in Santa Fe (and field offices in larger cities statewide).

Perpetual care cemetery records of incorporation are at the State Corporation Commission with individual records at cemetery offices.

Proceedings of divorce, guardianship, and adoption are at the office of the district court clerk in each of the 32 counties. Confidentiality provisions apply to adoptions.

Genealogical Archives, Libraries, Societies, and Publications

Deming Public Library, Deming, NM 88030.

Eddy County Genealogical Society, P.O. Box 461, Carlsbad, NM 88220.

Genealogy Club, The, Albuquerque Public Library, 423 Central N.E., Albuquerque, NM 87102.

History Library Museum of New Mexico Palace of the Governors, Santa Fe, NM 87501.

Lea County Genealogical Society, P.O. Box 1044, Lovington, NM 88260.

Lovington Public Library, 103 North First Street, Lovington, NM 88260.

New Mexico Genealogical Society, P.O. Box 8734, Albuquerque, NM 87103.

New Mexico State Library Commission, 301 Don Gasper, Santa Fe, NM 87501.

Portales Public Library, 218 S. Ave. B, Portales, NM 88130.

Public Library, 423 East Central Ave., Albuquerque, NM 87101.

Southern New Mexico Genealogical Society, 2501 Chaparral Street, Las Cruces, NM 88001.

University of New Mexico Library, Albuquerque, NM 87106.

New Mexico Genealogist, The, Box 8330, Albuquerque, NM 87198-8330.

Pecos Trails, the Eddy County Genealogical Society, P.O. Box 461, Carlsbad, NM 88220.

Printed Census Records and Mortality Schedules

Indexes (Territory): 1850, 1860

Printed Census Records (Counties)
Bernalillo-1850
Colfax-1870, 1880
Rio Arriba-1850

New Mexico Spanish and Mexican Colonial Census Records, 1790-1823-1845

Valuable Printed Sources

Atlas

Beck, Warren A. and Ynez D. Haase. *Historical Atlas of New Mexico.* Norman: University of Oklahoma Press (1969).

Place Names

Pearce, T. M. *New Mexico Place Names, A Geographical Dictionary.* Albuquerque: University of New Mexico Press (1965).

Guides To Genealogical Research

Jenkins, Myra Ellen. *Tracing Spanish-American Pedigrees in the Southwestern United States: New Mexico, Texas and Colorado.* Salt Lake City: Genealogical Society of Utah (1969).

Historical Services Division, NM State Records Center and Archives, 404 Montezuma, Santa Fe, NM 87503. *Guides to the Spanish, Mexican, and Territorial Archives of New Mexico.* On microfilm.

Histories

Beck, Warren A. *New Mexico; A History of Four Centuries.* Norman: University of Oklahoma Press (1962).

Chavez, Fray Angelico. *Origins of New Mexico Families in the Spanish Colonial Period.* Santa Fe: The Historical Society of New Mexico, 1954.

Read, Benjamin M. *Illustrated History of New Mexico,* Sante Fe: New Mexico Printing, ca 1912.

Twitchell, Ralph Emerson. *The Leading Facts of New Mexican History.* Cedar Rapids, Iowa: The Torch Press, 1911.

Bibliographies

Grove, Pearce S., Becky L. Barnett and Sandra J. Hansen. *New Mexico Newspapers: A Comprehensive Guide to Bibliographical Entries and Locations.* Albuquerque: University of New Mexico Press (1975).

NEW MEXICO COUNTY HISTORIES
(Population figures to nearest thousand - 1980 U.S. Census)

Name	Map Index	Date Created	Pop. By M 1980	U.S. Cen Reports Available	Parent County or Territory From Which Organized	County Seat
§ Bernalillo	B2	1852	415	1850-80	Original county	Albuquerque 87101

(Co Clk has m rec from 1885 & pro rec from 1895; Clk Dis Ct has div & civ ct rec)

Catron	C1	1921	3		Socorro	Reserve 87830

(Co Clk has m, pro & Ind rec from 1921)

Chaves	C3	1887	51		Lincoln	Roswell 88201

(Co Clk has m & pro rec from 1887; Clk Dis Ct has div & civ ct rec)

§ Colfax	A3	1869	13	1870-80	Taos	Raton 87740

(Co Clk has m rec from 1890, pro rec from 1903 & Ind rec from 1864; Clk Dis Ct has div & civ ct rec)

* Curry	B4	1909	42		Quay, Roosevelt	Clovis 88101

(Co Clk has m rec from 1905 informal pro rec from 1909, Ind rec from 1903; Dis Ct has div rec and formal pro rec; Vital Statistics Bureau, Santa Fe has b, d rec)

De Baca	C3	1917	2		Chaves, Guadalupe, Roosevelt	Fort Sumner 88119

(Co Clk has m, div, pro, civ ct, real estate, deeds & mtgs from 1917)

§ Dona Ana	D2	1852	96	1860-80	Original county	Las Cruces 88001

(Co Clk has b & m rec from 1816, pro rec from 1901, deeds from 1886, liens from 1850 & mtgs from 1860)

*§ Eddy	D4	1889	48		Lincoln	Carlsbad 88220

(Co Clk has m, pro, Ind rec & newspapers from 1891; Clk Dis Ct has div & civ ct rec)

§ Grant	D1	1868	26	1870-80	Dona Ana	Silver City 88061

(Co Clk has m rec from 1872, pro rec from 1884, Ind rec from 1871, newspaper rec from 1900; Dis Ct Clk has div rec; Municipal Ct has civ ct rec; Vital Ststistics Bureau, Santa Fe has b, d rec)

Guadalupe	B3	1891	5		Lincoln, San Miguel	Santa Rosa 88435

(Co Clk has m, div & pro rec from 1900)

Harding	A4	1921	1		Mora, Union	Mosquero 87733

(Co Clk has m, div, pro, civ ct & Ind rec from 1921)

*§ Hidalgo	D1	1919	6		Grant	Lordsburg 88045

(Co Clk has m, pro & Ind rec from 1920; Clk Dis Ct has div & civ ct rec)

Lea	D4	1917	56		Chaves, Eddy	Lovington 88260

(Co Clk has m & pro rec from 1917, also Ind rec)

Lincoln	C3	1869	11	1870	Socorro, Dona Ana	Carrizozo 88301

(Co Clk has m rec from 1882, pro rec from 1880, newspapers from 1890)

Los Alamos	B2	1949	18		Sandoval, Santa Fe	Los Alamos 87544

(Co Clk has m, pro & Ind rec from 1949 & bur rec from 1961; Clk Dis Ct has div & civ ct rec)

*§ Luna	D2	1901	16		Dona Ana, Grant	Deming 88030

(Co Clk has m, pro & Ind rec from 1901, Deming newspapers from 1901)

* McKinley	B1	1899	56		Bernalillo, Valencia, San Juan, Rio Arriba	Gallup 87301

(Co Clk has b rec from 1907 to 1958, m, pro & Ind rec from 1901, also voters reg; Clk Dis Ct has div rec)

§ Mora	A3	1860	4	1860-80	Taos	Mora 87732

(Co Clk has m & pro rec from 1891, d rec from 1957; Clk Dis Ct has div rec)

§ Otero	D3	1899	45		Dona Ana, Lincoln, Socorro	Alamogordo 88310

(Co Clk has m, pro & Ind rec from 1899, voters reg certif from 1939; Clk Dis Ct has div & civ ct rec from 1899)

Quay	B4	1903	11		Guadalupe	Tucumcari 88401

(Co Clk has m, pro, Ind rec from 1893)

Rio Arriba	A2	1852	29	1850-80	Original county	Tierra Amarilla 87575

(Co Clk has m & pro rec from 1852)

Roosevelt	C4	1903	16		Chaves, Guadalupe	Portales 88130

(Co Clk has m, pro, Ind rec from 1903, discharges from 1919, newspapers published in county; Dis Ct Clk has div, civ ct rec; Vital Statistics Bureau, Santa Fe has b, d rec.)

COUNTY MAP FOR THE STATE OF NEW MEXICO

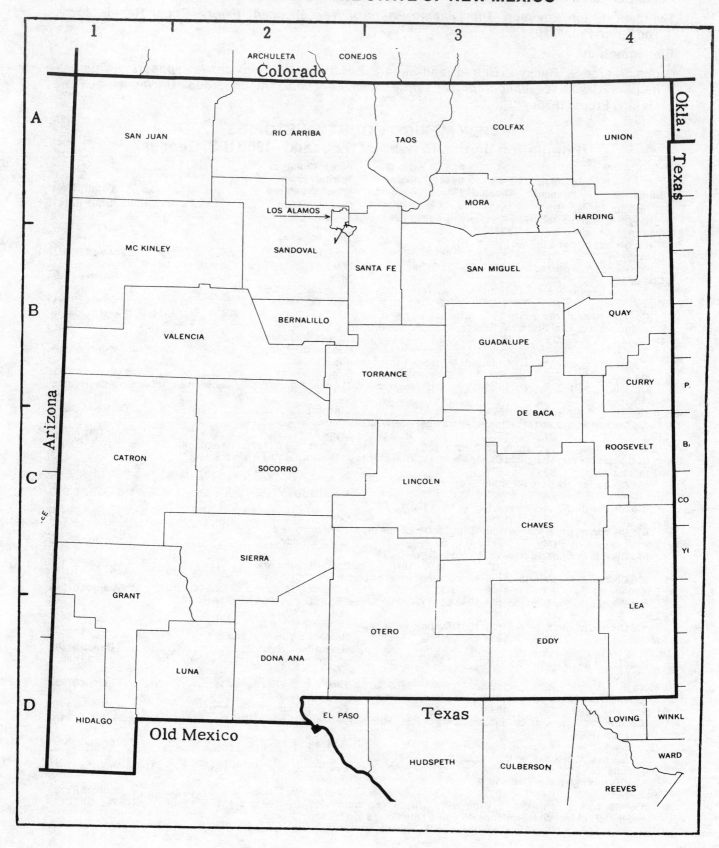

Name	Map Index	Date Created	Pop. By M 1980	U.S. Cen Reports Available	Parent County or Territory From Which Organized	County Seat
Sandoval	B2	1903	34		Bernalillo	Bernalillo 87004
* San Juan	A1	1887	81		Rio Arriba	Aztec 87410

(Co Clk has m, Ind rec from 1887, pro rec from 1899; Dis Ct Clk has div, civ ct rec; city cem associations have bur rec; Vital Statistics Bureau, Santa Fe has b, d rec)

§ San Miguel	B3	1852	23	1850-80	Original county	Las Vegas 87701

(Co Clk has m rec from 1880, pro rec from 1939, Ind rec from 1800; Clk Dis Ct has div, civ ct rec from 1882)

Santa Ana		1844			Original County	(abolished by 1880)
*§ Santa Fe	B3	1852	75	1860-80	Original county	Santa Fe 87501

(Co Clk has m rec from 1900, pro rec from 1894 & Ind rec from 1848)

Sierra	C2	1884	8		Socorro	Truth or Consequences 87901

(Co Clk has m, Ind rec from 1884; pro rec from 1919; Clk Dis Ct has div rec; Magistrate Ct has civ ct rec; Vital Statistics Bureau, Santa Fe has b, d rec)

* Socorro	C2	1852	12	1860-80	Original county	Socorro 87801

(Co Clk has m rec from 1887, pro rec from 1920, Ind rec from 1882, army discharge rec)

§ Taos	A3	1852	19	1850-80	Original county	Taos 87571

(Co Clk has b, m, d, bur & pro rec from 1846)

* Torrance	B3	1903	8		Lincoln, San Miguel, Socorro, Santa Fe, Valencia	Estancia 87016

(Courthouse burned in 1910) (Co Clk has m, informal pro, Ind rec from 1911; Clk Dis Ct has div, civ ct rec; Vital Statistics Bureau, Santa Fe has b, d rec)

§ Union	A4	1893	5		Colfax, Mora, San Miguel	Clayton 88415

(Co Clk has m rec from 1894 & Ind rec from 1884, also div, pro & civ ct rec)

§ Valencia	B1	1852	61	1850-80	Original county	Los Lunas 87031

(Co Clk has m rec from 1865, pro rec from 1900; Clk Dis Ct has div & civ ct rec)

* - At least one county history has been published about this county.

§ - Inventory of county archives was made by the Historical Records Survey. (see introduction)

NEW YORK

CAPITAL, ALBANY - STATE 1788 - (11TH)

The Dutch settled New York in 1624 when they established a colony at Albany, then called Fort Orange. In 1626 other settlers from Holland came to New York City, then New Amsterdam. Previously, at least two explorers, Hudson and Champlain, had looked over the territory.

In the next few years the Dutch induced individuals from Scandinavia, Great Britain, and Germany to come with them to the New World.

Many Puritan families in Massachusetts and Connecticut drifted south into New York around 1640. Some sixty years later German families came into the Mohawk Valley looking for places in which to build their homes. About the same time French settlers were straggling into the new section from Canada. Other French families, together with some Spaniards and Portuguese, disturbed by the uprisings in the West Indies, where they had been for some time, sought refuge in New York.

The total population of the colony in 1740 was established at only 50,000. About that time many former Connecticut dwellers went across the sound and settled in Long Island. Others came into Dutchess, Westchester and Orange counties. A population check previous to the outbreak of the Revolutionary War found settlers on Long Island, on the banks of the Hudson River, a few Palatine Germans along the Mohawk River and some New Englanders in the extreme southeastern part of the state.

In 1776 New York broke with the Mother Country, and joined the other colonies in their fight for freedom. This struggle continued until 1781. Seven years later New York became the eleventh state in the Union by ratifying the constitution.

New York is described as a land of many tongues, not less than sixty languages being heard. The predominating nationalities are Italian, Russian, German, Polish, Irish, Austrian, English, Hungarian, Swedish, Norwegian, Czech, Greek, French, Finish, and Danish.

The Bureau of Vital Records, State Department of Health, ESP Tower Building, Albany, New York 12237 has birth and death records since 1880, except the five boroughs of New York City. These records do not include births and deaths which occurred in the cities of Albany, Buffalo, or Yonkers. These records are filed with the Registrar of Vital Statistics in the appropriate city from 1914.

Birth and deaths records for New York City are available from 1898 and can be obtained by writing the New York City Department of Health, 125 Worth Street, New York City, New York 10013.

The local Registrar of vital statistics for the city, town or village in which birth or death occurred has office copies of these records generally beginning in 1880, except Albany, Buffalo, or Yonkers who have original records beginning in 1914.

The Bureau of Vital Records also has marriage records from 1880 except for New York City and records prior to 1908 for Albany, Buffalo and Yonkers. For these records write to the City Clerk in Albany or Buffalo and the Registrar of Vital Statistics in Yonkers.

City and town clerks where marriage license was issued have office copies of marriage records generally beginning about 1880.

New York City Clerk, Chambers and Centre Street, New York, New York 10007 has marriage records from 1866.

The Municipal Archives and Records Retention Center, 31 Chambers Street, New York, New York 10007 has birth and death records from 1866 to 1897 and marriage records from 1847 to 1865.

A number of old church, cemetery, and marriage records are on file with the New York State Library, Department of Education, Manuscripts and History Section, Albany, New York. They also have some published genealogies, local histories, and the decennial federal censuses of New York State, 1800-1870.

The New York State Archives, Cultural Education Center, Empire State Plaza, Albany, New York 12230 has vital records - birth, death, marriage - scattered among the holdings of local government records. Most of these vital records date from before 1880. The archives has early vital records for the following localities: Albany County: Towns of Coeymans, Guilderland and Westerlo. Delaware County: Town of Stamford. Dutchess County: Town of Amenia. Herkimer County: Towns of Fairfield and Wilmut. Montgomery County: Town of Root. Onondaga County: Towns of Pompey and Tully. Orange County: Town of Deerpart. Saratoga County: Town of Greenfield. Sullivan County: Town of Liberty. Ulster County: Town of Olive.

Additional vital records may be found in the microfilm copies of local records in the Archives. An inventory of these records is available upon request from the Archives. "Marriage Bonds 1753-1783" recorded with the Department of State, although extensively damaged in the 1911 fire, have been largely restored.

The Archives holds census returns from the 1915 and 1925 statewide censuses and also original returns for Albany County for 1855, 1860, 1865, 1870, 1875, 1880 and 1892.

Military service, pension, and landgrant records for soldiers who served in the Revolution and the War of 1812, though incomplete, are available at the Archives. Record series which are particularly helpful include: Comptroller's Office, Revolutionary Manuscripts, 1775-1880; Audited Accounts of the State Auditor, 1782-1794; NYS Dept. Audit and Control Accounts, 1783-1858; Claims of Soldiers of the War of 1812.

Deeds, assessment and tax rolls, and maps dating from 1643 may be searched at the archives for information on purchasers or other recipients of land under Colonial and State Governments. Specific record groups are: N.Y. Colonial Manuscripts, Land Papers, 1643-1802; Surveyor General Maps, ca 1775-1900; Albany City records, deeds, leases and maps, 1731-1810.

Wills, Surrogate Court Records, and related probate records are found in: Albany County Surrogates Court Papers, 1800-1840; Assembly Papers, Volumes 39-31 "Estates of Deceased Persons, 1779-1831"; and Forfeited Estates, Volumes 25-28; Albany County Court Records, "Wills and Actions of Surrogates Court, 1935."

New York State's Public Health Law, SS 4173, 4174 states the following: "Information from records of birth and death on file in the State Department of Health or on file with a local registrar of vital statistics may be provided for genealogical research in the form of an uncertified copy or abstract upon written application and payment of the fees specified in subdivision three of section 4174 of the Public Health Law. The search of the files may be conducted only by authorized employees of the State Department of Health and locally by registrar, deputy registrar, or an authorized employee of the registrar, subject to the following limitations: No information shall be issued from a record of birth unless a record has been on file for at least 75 years or more (1881 to 1906); No information may be issued from a record of death unless the record has been on file for at least 50 years or more (1880 to 1931); No information shall be issued from a record of marriage unless the record has been on file for at least 50 years (1880 to 1931)."

Genealogical Archives, Libraries, Societies, and Publications

Adirondack Genealogical-Historical Society, 100 Main Street, Saranac Lake, NY 12983.

Adriance Memorial Library, 93 Market St., Poughkeepsie, NY 12601.

Blauvelt Free Library, 86 S. Western Hwy., Blauvelt, NY 10913.

Buffalo and Erie County Public Library, Lafayette Square, Buffalo, NY 14203.

Cayuga-Owasco Lakes Historical Society, Box 241, Moravia, NY 13118.

Central New York Genealogical Society, Box 104, Colvin Station, Syracuse, NY 13205.

Columbia University, Journalism Library, New York, NY 10027.

DeWitt Historical Society, 121 East Court St., Ithaca, NY 14850.

Dutchess County Genealogical Society, P.O. Box 88, Poughkeepsie, NY 12602.

Dutchess County Historical Society, c/o Adriance Memorial Library, 93 Market Street, Poughkeepsie, NY 12601.

East Hampton Free Library, 159 Main St., East Hampton, NY 11937.

Flower Memorial Library, Genealogical Committee, Watertown, NY 13601.

Franklin County Historical and Museum Society, 51 Milwaukee Street, Malone, NY 12953.

General Society of Colonial Wards, 122 East 58th St., New York, NY 10022.

Genesee County Library, Department of History, 131 West Main Street, Batavia, NY 14020.

Geneva Free Library, 244 Main St., Geneva, NY 14456.

Guernsey Memorial Library, 3 Court St., Norwich, NY 13815.

Hamilton Public Library, 13 Broad St., Hamilton, NY 13346.

Holland Society, 122 E. 58th St., New York, NY 14304.

Historical Society of Middletown and Walkill Precinct, Inc., 25 East Ave., Middletown, NY 10940.

Huguenot Historical Society, 14 Forest Glen Rd., New Paltz, NY 12561.

Huntington Historical Society, Conklin House Library and Educational Service, 2 High St., Huntington, Long Island, NY 11743.

Institute for Jewish Research, 1048 Fifth Ave., New York, NY 10028.

Jefferson County Historical Society, 228 Washington St., Watertown, NY 13601.

John Lont Research Center, P.O. Box 732, Adams Basin, NY 14410.

John M. Olin Library, Cornell University, Ithica, NY 14853.

Johnstown Public Library, 38 S. Market St., Johnstown, NY 12095.

Kodak Genealogical Society, Dr. Stanley R. Ames, P.O. Box 1911, Rochester, NY 14603.

Leo Baeck Institute, German-Jewish families, 129 East 73 St., New York, NY 10021.

Little Nine Partners, The Historical Society, Box 243, Pine Plains, NY 12567.

Long Island Historical Society, Pierpont St., Corner Clinton St., Brooklyn, NY 11201.

Minisink Valley Historical Society, Port Jervis, NY 12771.

Moore Memorial Library, 59 Genesee St., Greene, NY 13778.

Newburgh Free Library, 124 Grand Street, Newburgh, NY 12550.

New City Free Library, 125 South Main Street, New City, NY 10956.

New York Genealogical and Biographical Society, 122-126 East 58th St., New York, NY 10022.

New York Historical Association, 170 Central Park, West, New York, NY 10024.

New York Public Library, 5th Ave. and 42nd Sts., New York, NY 10016.

New York State Historical Association, Fenimore House, Lake Rd., Cooperstown, NY 13326.

New York State Library, Albany, NY 12224.

Oneida Library, 220 Broad St., Oneida, NY 13421.

Onondaga County Public Library, Local History and Genealogy Department, 335 Montgomery Street, Syracuse, NY 13202.

Onondaga Historical Association, 311 Montgomery St., Syracuse, NY 13202.

Ontario County Historical Society, Canadaigua, NY 14424.

Patterson Library, 40 S. Portage St., Westfield, NY 14757.

Port Chester Public Library, 1 Haseco Ave., Port Chester, NY 10573.

Queens Borough Public Library, 89-11 Merrick Blvd., Jamaica, NY 11432.

Rochester Genealogical Society, c/o Mrs. Doris Andrus, 156 Nob Hill, Rochester, NY 14617.

Rochester Public Library, Local History Division, 115 South Avenue, Rochester, NY 14607.

Roswell P. Flower Genealogy Library, 229 Washington St., Watertown, NY 13601.

Schenectady County Historical Society, 32 Washington Avenue, Schenectady, NY 12305.

Schuyler County Historical Society and Library, 108 North Catherine St., Rte. 14, Montour Falls, NY 14865.

Southhold Historical Society, Southhold, Long Island, NY 11971.

Staten Island Historical Society, Richmondtown, Staten Island, NY 10301.

Steuben County Historical Society, P.O. Box 349, Bath, NY 14810.

Suffolk County Historical Society, Riverhead, Long Island, NY 11901.

Tioga County Historical Society, Museum, 110-112 Front St., Owego, NY 13827.

Twin Tiers Genealogical Society, 230 Devonshire Dr., Elmira, NY 14903.

Ulster County Genealogical Society, RD 1, Box 84, Stone Ridge, NY 12484.

Utica Public Library, 303 Genesee St., Utica, NY 13501.

Wayne County Historical Society, 21 Butternut St., Lyons, NY 14489.

Westchester County Historical Society, 43 Read Ave., Tuckahoe, NY 10707.

Western New York Genealogical Society, P.O. Box 338, Hamburg, NY 14075.

New York Genealogical and Biographical Record, The, The New York Genealogical Biographical Society, 122 East 58th St., New York, NY 10022.

Western New York Genealogical Society Journal, P.O. Box 338, Hamburg, NY 14075.

Yesteryears Magazine, 3 Seymour St., Auburn, NY 13021.

Printed Census Records and Mortality Schedules

State Indexes: 1790, 1800, 1810, 1820, 1830, 1840, 1850

Printed Census Records (Counties):

Albany-1790, 1800	Herkimer-1800, 1810, 1820	Otsego-1800
Broome-1850	Jefferson-1810, 1820	Oswego-1800
Cattaraugus-1840	Oneida-1800, 1810	St. Lawrence-1790, 1800, 1810, 1820
Cayuga-1800, 1810	Ontario-1800, 1810	Tioga-1820; 1855
Delaware-1800	Orange-1850 (Warwick);	Warren-1850
Dutchess-1810	1702 (list of inhabitants)	Yates- 1855

Valuable Printed Sources

Gazetteer

French, John Homer. *Gazetteer of the State of New York.* Syracuse: R. P. Smith (1860).

Place, Frank II, comp. Index of Personal Names in J. H. French's Gazetteer of the State of New York (1860). Cortland, New York: Cortland County Historical Society (1962).

Maps

Catalogue of Maps and Surveys in the Offices of the Secretary of State, State Engineer and Surveyor and Comptroller and the New York State Library. Albany: Charles Van Benthuysen (1859).

Place Names

Spafford, Horatio Gates. *A Gazetteer of the State of New York: Embracing an Ample Survey and Description of Its Counties, Towns, Cities.* Albany: B. D. Packard (1824).

Guides To Genealogical Research

Bailey, Rosalie Fellows. *Guide to Genealogical and Biographical Sources for New York City (Manhattan) 1783-1898.* New York: Privately published (1954).

Clint, Florence. *New York Area Key.* Elizabeth, Colorado: Keyline Publishers (1979).

Wright, Norman Edgar comp. *North American Genealogical Sources: Mid Atlantic States and Canada.* Provo, Utah: B.Y.U. Press (1968).

Histories

Flick, A. C. *The History of the State of New York.* Port Washington: Ira J. Friedman Inc., (1962).

Genealogical Sources

D.A.R. Collection*

Haigh, Roger M. ed. *Finding Aids to the Microfilmed Manuscript Collection of the Genealogical Society of Utah: Descriptive Inventory of the New York Collection* by Arlene H. Eakle and L. Ray Gunn, Salt Lake City: University of Utah Press (1980).

New York Public Library, *The Research Libraries Dictionary Card Catalog of the Local History and Genealogy Division.* Boston: G. K. Hall and Company.

Vosburgh, Royden, W. *Vosburgh Collection: Church Records of New York State.* Hartford, Connecticut: Connecticut State Library.*

Bibliographies

Fairbisoff, Sylvia and Lois Bryson O'Connor. *A Bibliography of Newspapers in Fourteen New York State Counties.*

Klein, Milton M. comp. *New York in the American Revolution, A Bibliography.* Albany, New York State American Revolution Bicentennial Commission.

---

*Microfilm - Genealogical Society of The Church of Jesus Christ of Latter-day Saints, Salt Lake City, Utah.

NEW YORK COUNTY HISTORIES
(Population figures to nearest thousand - 1980 U. S. Census)

Name	Map Index	Date Created	Pop. By M 1980	U.S. Cen Reports Available	Parent County or Territory From Which Organized	County Seat
*§ Albany	B3	1683	286	1790-80	Original county	Albany 12207
* Allegany	D2	1806	52	1810-80	Genesee	Belmont 14813
(Co Clk has m rec from 1908 to 1935, div & civ ct rec, also Ind rec from 1807)						
Bronx	B4	1912	1,163		New York	Bronx 10451
(Co Clk has m, div, sup civ ct rec from 1914)						
*§ Broome	C3	1806	213	1810-80	Tioga	Binghamton 13901
(Co Clk has m rec from 1908, civ ct, Ind rec from 1806, mil rolls from 1808, naturalization rec from 1860, div rec; Surrogate Ct has pro rec from 1806, guardianship rec from 1860; town and city clks have b, m, d, bur rec from 1880)						
*§ Cattaraugus	E2	1808	85	1810-80	Genesee	Little Valley 14755
(Co Clk has div rec, Ind rec from 1817; Town and city clks have b, m, d, bur rec; Surr Ct has pro rec)						
* Cayuga	C2	1799	79	1800-80	Onondaga	Auburn 13022
(Co Clk has pro, civ ct rec from 1799, Ind rec from 1794, DAR county cem rec 1790-1960; Town or city clks have b, m, rec)						
Charlotte		1772			Albany (renamed Washington, 1784)	
*§ Chautauqua	E2	1808	147	1810-80	Genesee	Mayville 14757
(Co Clk has m rec from 1908, div, civ ct, Ind rec from 1811; Surr Ct has pro rec; Town or city clks have b, m, d, bur rec)						
*§ Chemung	D2	1836	98	1850-80	Tioga	Elmira 14901
(Co Clk has m rec from 1908 to 1936, div, civ ct & Ind rec; Surr Ct has pro rec; Twn Clks have m rec)						
* Chenango	C2	1798	49	1800-80	Herkimer, Tioga	Norwich 13815
(Co Clk has m, div, civ ct & Ind rec; Surr Ct has pro rec; Twn Clks have b, m & d rec)						
* Clinton	A1	1788	81	1790-80	Washington	Plattsburg 12901
(Co Clk has m rec from 1908 to 1935, div rec from 1869 & Ind rec from 1778; Surr Ct has pro rec; Co Ct has civ ct rec; Twn Clks have b, m & d rec)						
* Columbia	B3	1786	59	1790-80	Albany	Hudson 12534
(Co Clk has m rec from 1908, div rec from 1882, pro rec from 1787, Ind rec from 1786, naturalization rec from 1853, lists of gravestone inscriptions)						
* Cortland	C2	1808	49	1820-80	Onondaga	Cortland 13045
(Co Clk has m rec from 1910 to 1935, div rec, civ ct rec from 1808, Ind rec from 1808, Surr Ct has pro rec Town and city clks have b, m, d rec)						
* Delaware	B3	1797	47	1800-80	Ulster, Otsego	Delhi 13753
(Co Clk has m rec from 1908 to 1931, div, civ ct, Ind rec from 1797; Town clks have b, m, d, bur rec)						
* Dutchess	B3	1683	244	1790-80	Original county	Poughkeepsie 12601
(Co Clk has m rec 1908 to 1935, div, civ ct rec from 1847, Ind rec from 1718; Surr Ct has pro rec) (Town or city clks have b, m, d rec. Co Clk has state and federal cen rec for 1865, 1870, 1875, 1880, 1892, 1915, 1925)						

Name	Map Index	Date Created	Pop. By M 1980	U.S.Cen Reports Available	Parent County or Territory From Which Organized	County Seat
* Erie	D2	1821	1,015	1830-80	Niagara	Buffalo 14202

(Co Clk has m rec from 1820 to 1935, div & civ ct rec from 1809 & Ind rec from 1810)

| * Essex | A2 | 1799 | 36 | 1800-80 | Clinton | Elizabethtown 12932 |

(Co Clk has m rec from 1908 to 1936, div, pro, civ ct & Ind rec from 1799)

| * Franklin | A1 | 1808 | 45 | 1810-80 | Clinton | Malone 12953 |

(Co Clk has m rec from 1908 to 1935, some div rec from 1808 & civ ct rec from 1808; Surr Ct has pro rec; various twns hold b, m & d rec)

| * Fulton | B2 | 1838 | 55 | 1840-80 | Montgomery | Johnstown 12095 |

(Co Clk has m rec from 1900 to 1926)

| * Genesee | D1 | 1802 | 59 | 1810-80 | Ontario | Batavia 14020 |

(Co Clk has m rec 1908 to 1934, div, civ ct rec, Ind rec from 1802; Surr Ct has pro rec; Town and city clks have b, d rec; Co Clk has NY state cen rec for 1860, 1870, 1880, 1875, 1892, 1905, 1915, 1925)

| * Greene | B3 | 1800 | 40 | 1800-80 | Ulster, Albany | Catskill 12414 |

(Co Clk has m rec from 1900 to 1935, div, civ ct & Ind rec from 1800; Surr Ct has pro rec; Twn Clks have b, m & d rec)

| Hamilton | B2 | 1816 | 5 | 1820-80 | Montgomery | Lake Pleasant 12108 |

(Co Clk has m rec 1908 to 1936, div, civ ct, Ind rec; Surr Ct has pro rec; Town and city clks have b, m, d, bur rec)

| * Herkimer | B2 | 1791 | 1800-80 | 1800-80 | Montgomery | Herkimer 13350 |

(Co Clk has m rec from 1908 to 1934, div & civ ct rec)

| * Jefferson | B1 | 1805 | 88 | 1810-80 | Oneida | Watertown 13601 |

(Co Clk has m rec from 1908 to 1933, civ ct rec from 1847, deeds Oneida 1795, Jefferson 1805, many other rec & censuses)

| * Kings | B4 | 1683 | 2,218 | 1790-80 | Original county | Brooklyn 11201 |

(Dept of Health, Brooklyn Borough Office, 295 Flatbush Ave Extension, Brooklyn, N.Y. 11201 has b, d & bur rec; City Clk, Mun. Bldg. Brooklyn, N.Y. 11201 has m rec; Co Clk, Sup Ct Bldg. 360 Adams St, Brooklyn, N.Y. 11201 has div rec; Surr Ct, Sup Ct Bldg., 360 Adams St, Brooklyn, N.Y. 11201 has pro rec; Clk Civ Ct, 120 Schermerhorn St, Brooklyn, N.Y. has civ ct rec; Co Reg, Municipal Bldg, Joralemon & Court Streets, Brooklyn, N.Y. 11201 has Ind rec)

| * Lewis | B1 | 1805 | 25 | 1810-80 | Oneida | Lowville 13367 |

(Co Clk has m rec from 1908 to 1935, div rec from 1847, civ ct rec from 1907, Ind rec from 1805, naturalization rec from 1808 to 1906, military rolls from 1862 to 1866; Surr Ct has pro rec)

| * Livingston | D2 | 1821 | 57 | 1830-80 | Genesee, Ontario | Geneseo 14454 |

(Co Clk has div, civ ct, Ind rec from 1821)

| * Madison | C2 | 1806 | 65 | 1810-80 | Chenango | Wampsville 13163 |

(Co Clk has m rec from 1905 to 1934, div rec from 1900, civ ct rec from 1889 & Ind rec from 1806; Surr Ct has pro rec; Twn Clks have b, m, d & bur rec)

| * Monroe | D1 | 1821 | 702 | 1830-80 | Genesee, Ontario | Rochester 14614 |

(Co Clk has m rec from 1908 to 1935, div & civ ct rec from 1860, pro & Ind rec from 1821; Twn Clks have m & bur rec; Health Dept, 111 Westfall Rd, Rochester, N.Y. 14620 has b & d rec; Historians Office, 39 Main St, W., Rochester, N.Y. has some cem inscriptions, indexes to old co histories & biography files)

| * Montgomery | B2 | 1772 | 53 | 1790-80 | Albany (as Tryon to 1784) | Fonda 12068 |

(Co Clk has m rec from 1908 to 1926, div rec from 1880)

| * Nassau | B4 | 1898 | 1,320 | | Queens | Mineola 11501 |

(Co Clk has m rec from 1907 to 1935, div, civ ct, Ind, business names from 1899; Surr Ct has pro rec; Town clks have b, m, d rec)

| * New York | B4 | 1683 | 1,418 | 1790-80 | Original county | New York 10007 |

(Co Clk has div rec from 1800, naturalization rec from late 1900's to 1925, state cen rec 1870, 1885, 1905, 1915, 1925)

| * Niagara | D1 | 1808 | 227 | 1810-80 | Genesee | Lockport 14094 |

(Co Clk has m rec 1908 to 1935; div rec from 1850, civ ct, Ind rec; Surr Ct has pro rec; Town and city clks have b, m, d, bur rec)

| * Oneida | B2 | 1798 | 253 | 1800-80 | Herkimer (see Jefferson) | Rome 13440 & Utica 13501 |

(Co Clk has div rec, also Ind rec from 1791; Surr Ct has pro rec; Twn Clks have b, m, d & bur rec)

| * Onondaga | C2 | 1794 | 464 | 1800-80 | Herkimer | Syracuse 13202 |

(Co Clk & Twn Clks have m rec from 1908 to 1935; Co Clk has div rec from 1849, civ ct rec from 1799 & Ind rec from 1794; Surr Ct has pro rec; Co Clk has census rec from 1850 to 1925)

| * Ontario | D2 | 1789 | 89 | 1790-80 | Montgomery | Canadaigua 14424 |

(Co Clk has civ ct, Ind rec from 1789, immigration and citizenship rec; Surr Ct has pro rec; Town and city clks have b, m, d, bur rec) (Co Clk has state cen rec for 1850, 1855, 1860, 1865, 1870, 1875, 1880, 1892, 1915, 1925)

| * Orange | B4 | 1683 | 259 | 1790-80 | Original county | Goshen 10924 |

(Co Clk has m rec from 1908 to 1933, div & civ ct rec from 1852, Ind rec from 1703 & census rec for 1820, 1825, 1835, 1845, 1850, 1855, 1860, 1865, 1870, 1875, 1880 & other old rec)

COUNTY MAP FOR THE STATE OF NEW YORK

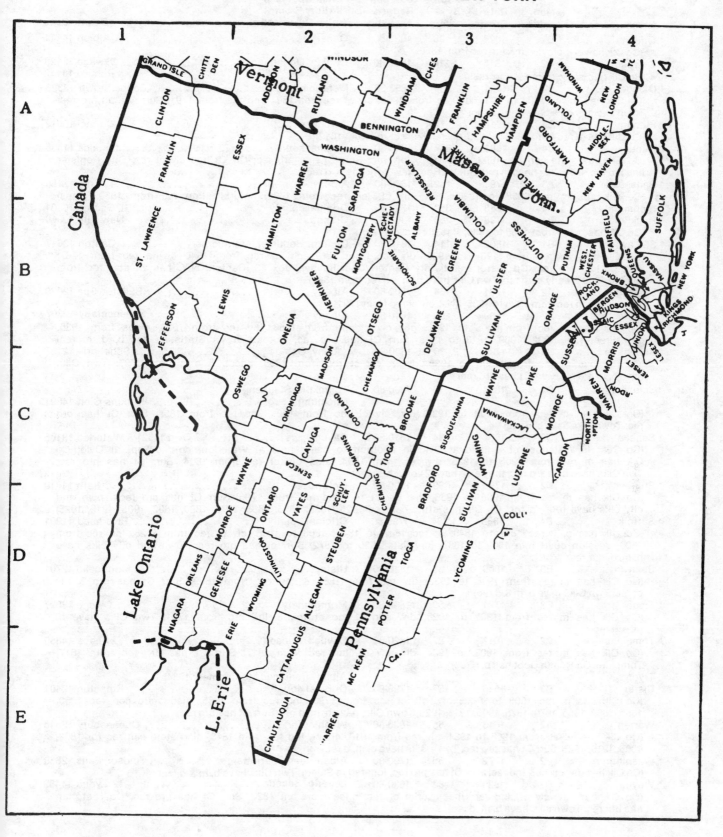

Name	Map Index	Date Created	Pop. By M 1980	U.S. Cen Reports Available	Parent County or Territory From Which Organized	County Seat
* Orleans	D1	1824	38	1830-80	Genesee	Albion 14411

(Co Clk has div, pro civ ct & Ind rec from 1850)

| * Oswego | C2 | 1816 | 114 | 1820-80 | Oneida, Onondaga | Oswego 13126 & Pulaski 13142 |

(Co Clk has m rec from 1907 to 1935)

| * Otsego | B2 | 1791 | 59 | 1850-80 | Montgomery | Cooperstown 13326 |

(Co Clk has m rec 1908 to 1936, div rec from 1900, civ ct rec from1891, Ind rec from 1791; Surr Ct has pro rec; Town and city clks have b, m, d rec)

| * Putnam | B4 | 1812 | 77 | 1820-80 | Dutchess | Carmel 10512 |

(Co Clk has m rec from 1908 to 1935, div rec & civ ct rec from 1812)

| * Queens | B4 | 1683 | 1,887 | 1790-80 | Original county | Jamaica 11435 |

(Co Clk has state cen rec 1892, 1905, 1915, div rec; Surr Ct has pro rec; Civ Ct has civ ct rec; City Register has Ind rec; City Clks have m rec; Bur Vit Rec, New York has b, d rec)

| * Rensselaer | A3 | 1791 | 152 | 1800-80 | Albany | Troy 12180 |

(Co Clk has m rec 1908 to 1930's, div, civ ct, Ind rec from 1791, naturalization rec from 1830; maps)

| * Richmond | B4 | 1683 | 350 | 1790-80 | Original county | St. George 10301 |
| * Rockland | B4 | 1798 | 260 | 1800-80 | Orange | New City 10956 |

(Co Clk has m rec from 1908 to 1935, also div & civ ct rec)

| * St. Lawrence | B1 | 1802 | 114 | 1810-80 | Clinton, Herkimer, Montgomery | Canton 13617 |

(Co Clk has m rec from 1908 to 1935, div rec from 1867, civ ct rec from 1840 & Ind rec from 1787; Surr Ct has pro rec; Co Historian, History Center (Courthouse), Box 43, Canton, N.Y. has vit stat rec from 1847 to 1850 & early cem rec; Twn Clks have b, m & d rec from 1881)

| * Saratoga | A2 | 1791 | 154 | 1800-80 | Albany | Ballston Spa 12020 |

(Co Clk has m rec from 1908 to 1935, div & civ ct rec from 1791)

| Schenectady | B2 | 1809 | 150 | 1810-80 | Albany | Schenectady 12307 |

(Co Clk has m rec from 1908 to 1930, div, civ ct rec from 1858, Ind rec from 1630, maps from 1630, city directories, 1892, 1909, 1913 to 1968; Surr Ct has pro rec; Bureau of Vit Statistics has b, d, m rec)

| * Schoharie | B3 | 1795 | 30 | 1800-80 | Albany, Ostego | Schoharie 12157 |

(Co Clk has m rec from 1908 to 1935, div & civ ct rec from 1898, deeds & mtg from 1797; Twn Clks have b, m & d rec; Surr Ct has pro rec)

| Schuyler | D2 | 1854 | 18 | 1860-80 | Tompkins, Steuben, Chemung | Watkins Glen 14891 |

(Co Clk has m rec from 1908 to 1935, div, civ ct rec from 1921, Ind rec from 1855; Surr Ct has pro rec; Town clks have b, d rec)

| * Seneca | C2 | 1804 | 34 | 1810-80 | Cayuga | Ovid 14521 & Waterloo 13165 |

(Co Seat is Waterloo, ct is held at Ovid in addition to being held at Waterloo, no rec kept at Ovid; Co Clk has m rec from 1908 to 1925, div rec from 1804, also civ ct rec from 1804; Surr Ct has pro rec; Twn Clks have b, m & d rec, they also have 2 vol of hist rec)

| * Steuben | D2 | 1796 | 99 | 1800-80 | Ontario | Bath 14810 |

(Co Clk has m rec from 1908 to 1936, div, civ ct rec, Ind rec from 1796; Surr Ct has pro rec; Town and city clks have b, m, d rec; Co Clk has state cen rec 1825, 1835, 1855, 1865, 1875, 1880, 1892, 1905, 1915, 1925)

| * Suffolk | B4 | 1683 | 1,284 | 1790-80 | Original county | Riverhead 11901 |

(Co Clk has b, d rec 1847 to 1849; m rec 1847 to 1849, 1908 to 1935, civ ct rec from 1725, Ind rec from 1666, session court min 1669 to 1687, jury lists 1820 to 1872; Surr ct has pro rec; Town and city clks have b, m, d, bur rec)

| * Sullivan | B3 | 1809 | 65 | 1810-80 | Ulster | Monticello 12701 |

(Co Clk has m rec from 1908 to 1933, div rec from 1885 & Ind rec from 1809; Surr Ct has pro & civ ct rec; Twn Clks have b, m & d rec)

| * Tioga | C3 | 1791 | 50 | 1800-80 | Montgomery | Owego 13827 |

(Co Clk has m rec from 1902 to 1926, div, sup ct, co ct rec & Ind rec from 1791; Twn Clks have b, m, & d rec)

| * Tompkins | C2 | 1817 | 87 | 1820-80 | Cayuga, Seneca | Ithaca 14850 |

(Co Clk has m rec from 1908 to 1934; div, civ ct, Ind rec from 1817; Surr Ct has pro rec from 1817; Tompkins Co Health Dept has b, d rec)

| * Tryon | | 1772 | | | Albany (renamed Montgomery 1784) | |
| * Ulster | B3 | 1683 | 157 | 1790-80 | Original county | Kingston 12401 |

(Co Clk has m rec 1908 to 1925, div, civ ct rec from 1793, Ind rec from 1685, also state cen rec 1850, 1855, 1860, 1865, 1870, 1875, 1905, 1915, 1925; Town Clks have b, m, d rec; Surr Ct has pro rec)

| * Warren | A2 | 1813 | 55 | 1820-80 | Washington | Queensbury 12845 |

(Co Clk has m rec from 1908 to 1934, div rec from 1918, civ ct, Ind rec from 1813, also state cen rec for 1892, 1905, 1915, 1925; Surr Ct has pro rec; Town Clks have b, m, d rec)

| * Washington | A2 | 1772 | 55 | 1790-80 | Albany (see Charlotte) | Hudson Falls 12839 |

(Co Clk has div, civ ct & Ind rec; Surr Ct has pro rec, located in Salem; Twn Clks have b, m & d rec)

| * Wayne | C2 | 1823 | 84 | 1830-80 | Ontario, Seneca | Lyons 14489 |

(Co Clk has div, civ ct, Ind rec, maps, crim ct rec, misc rec from 1823; Surr Ct has pro rec; Co Historian has bur rec; Town clks have b, m, d rec)

Name	Map Index	Date Created	Pop. By M 1980	U.S. Cen Reports Available	Parent County or Territory From Which Organized	County Seat
* Westchester	B4	1683	864	1790-80	Original county	White Plains 10601
(Co Clk has m rec from 1908 to 1935, div & Ind rec from 1847; Twn Clks have b, m & d rec)						
* Wyoming	D2	1841	40		Genesee	Warsaw 14569
(Co Clk has m rec from 1908 to 1933, div, civ ct & Ind rec from 1841, also state census reports for 1915 & 1925; Surr Ct has pro rec)						
* Yates	D2	1823	21	1830-80	Ontario, Steuben	Penn Yan 14527
(Co Clk has m rec from 1908 to 1933, div, civ ct rec, state cen rec for 1835, 1925; Surr Ct has pro rec)						

* - At least one county history has been published about this county.

§ - Inventory of county archives was made by the Historical Records Survey. (see introduction)

NORTH CAROLINA

CAPITAL, RALEIGH - STATE 1789 - (12TH)

The first permanent settlement in North Carolina territory was established in 1653 when groups of settlers came south from Virginia to occupy the section north of the Albemarle Sound. The influx of new settlers was so limited that in an eighty-year period the population had increased only to about 14,000. After 1691 the province was called North Carolina and from then until 1711 it was administered by deputy governors from South Carolina.

For several years after 1746, Highland Scot immigrants were arriving frequently in North Carolina . Most of them established themselves in the southeast section. So rapidly did they arrive that in a few years there were more than 20,000 of them in that territory.

When large groups of Scotch-Irish departed from Pennsylvania down the Shenandoah Valley to settle in Virginia, many continued on into North Carolina. For religious reasons they had been banished from Scotland, where their strong Protestant views irked the religious leaders. Thousands of them were transplanted into Ireland, where they remained long enough to get an opportunity to come to the new world. Many of them established homes in the western section of the state, around the present region of Iredell County.

Many Germans came into North Carolina in the early days. In 1760 there were about 15,000 in Forsyth and Guilford Counties. A colony of English speaking Quakers from Virginia, Pennsylvania, and Nantucket, Massachusetts, settled in Rockingham, Guilford, and Chatham Counties. Disliking slavery, they later moved to Ohio and Indiana. However, some of them remained and their descendants are still in North Carolina.

Before the Revolution, the Church of England was the established church in North Carolina as in Virginia. Until 1767, only the ordained ministers of that church and civil officials were permitted by law to perform marriage ceremonies, although ministers of other denominations married couples. After 1741, those who wished to marry could have "banns" published or announced from the pulpit or they could buy a license. Those married by license had to furnish a bond. Surviving marriage bonds except for Granville and Davie Counties are now in the North Carolina State Archives. They contain the name of the groom, the name of the bride, the name of the other bondsman, and the name of the witness; only rarely do they contain other genealogical information.

None of the parish registers containing records of births, deaths, and marriages for the colonial period have survived and none are known to exist prior to about 1820 when the Episcopal Church re-entered North Carolina as an organized denomination.

Virtually all county records useful for genealogical research to about 1910 are now in the North Carolina State Archives, 109 East Jones Street, Raleigh, NC 27611. For a detailed description see *Guide to Research Materials in the North Carolina State Archives; Section B: County Records,* 7th edition (1979).

Genealogical Archives, Libraries, Societies, and Publications

Genealogical Society of Davidson County, P.O. Box 1665, Lexington, NC 27292.

Genealogical Society of Iredell County, P.O. Box 946, Statesville, NC 28677.

Guilford County Genealogical Society, P.O. Box 9575, Greensboro, NC 27408.

Johnston County Genealogical Society, c/o Public Library of Johnston County and Smithfield, Smithfield, NC 27577.

Lincoln County Historical Association, Inc., Rt. 1, Box 315, Denver, NC 28037.

North Carolina Department of Cultural Resources, Raleigh, NC 27611.

North Carolina Division of Archives and History, 109 East Jones Street, Raleigh, NC 27611.

North Carolina Genealogical Society, The. P.O. Box 1492, Raleigh, NC 27602.

North Carolina State Library, 109 E. Jones St., Raleigh, NC 27611.

Old Buncombe County Genealogical Society, P.O. Box 2122, Asheville, NC 28802.

Pack Memorial Public Library, 8 S. Pack St., Asheville, NC 28801.

Public Library of Charlotte and Mecklenburg Counties, 310 No. Tyron St., Charlotte, NC 28202.

Richard H. Thornton, Memorial Library, Box 339, Main & Spring Sts., Oxford, NC 27565.

Robeson County Public Library, Box 1346, 101 N. Chestnut St., Lumberton, NC 28358.

Rowan Public Library, 201 W. Fisher St., Box 1009, Salisbury, NC 28144.

Sandhill Regional Library, Box 548, 1104 E. Broad Ave., Rockingham, NC 28379.

Southern Historical Collection, University of North Carolina Library, Chapel Hill, NC 27514.

Thomas Hackney Braswell Memorial Library, 334 Falls Rd., Rocky Mount, NC 27801.

Union County Public Library, 316 E. Windsor, Monroe, NC 28110.

University of North Carolina, Drawer 870, Chapel Hill, NC 27514.

Wilkes Genealogical Society, Inc., P.O. Box 1629, North Wilkesboro, NC 28659.

Journal, The, North Carolina Genealogical Society, P.O. Box 1492, Raleigh, NC 27602.

North Carolina Historical Review. 109 East Jones Street, Raleigh, NC 27611.

North Carolina Genealogy (J), formerly called *North Carolinian,* published 1955-1975 by the late W. P. Johnson, Raleigh, NC.

North Carolina Genealogical Society Journal, 1975--, published by the North Carolina Genealogical Society, P.O. Box 1492, Raleigh NC 27602.

Printed Census Records and Mortality Schedules

State Indexes-1790, 1800, 1810, 1820, 1830, 1840, 1850

Printed Census Records (Counties)

Anson-1800, 1820, 1850
Ashe-1800, 1820
Beaufort-1800, 1820
Bertie-1800, 1820
Bladen-1790, 1800, 1810, 1820, 1850
Brunswick-1800, 1820
Buncombe-1800, 1820
Burke-1800, 1820
Cabarrus-1800, 1820
Camden-1820, 1850
Carteret-1800, 1820, 1850
Caswell-1800, 1820, 1786
Chatham-1820
Chowan-1820
Cleveland-1870
Columbus-1810, 1820
Craven-1820, 1850
Cumberland-1800, 1820
Duplin-1820
Edgecombe-1820
Franklin-1810

Gates-1820
Granville-1820, 1850
Greene-1820, 1850
Guilford-1820
Halifax-1820
Haywood-1820
Hertford-1810, 1820
Hyde-1800, 1820
Iredell-1820
Jackson-1860
Johnston-1820
Jones-1820; 1786
Lenoir-1820
Lincoln-1820
Martin-1800
Mecklenburg-1820
Moore-1820
Nash-1820, 1860
New Hanover-1820
Northampton-1790, 1810, 1820
Onslow-1820

Orange-1820
Pasquotank-1820
Perquimans-1820
Person-1820
Pitt-1820
Randolph-1850, 1860
Richmond-1820
Robeson-1820
Rockingham-1820
Rowan-1800, 1820, 1830
Rutherford-1800, 1810, 1820, 1850
Sampson-1800, 1820
Stokes-1820
Surry-1820; 1771 (tax list)
Tyrrell-1820, 1850
Warren-1790, 1810, 1800, 1830
Washington-1820
Wayne-1820
Wilkes-1800, 1810, 1820, 1850, 1860; 1782, 1787

Mortality Schedule

Rowan County-1850

State Census: 1784-1787

Valuable Printed Sources

Atlases and Gazetteers

Clay, James W., Douglas M. Orr, Jr., Alfred W. Stuart, eds. *North Carolina Atlas.* Chapel Hill: University of North Carolina Press, 1975.

Corbitt, David LeRoy. *The Formation of the North Carolina Counties, 1663-1943.* Raleigh: State Department of Archives and History, 1975.

Powell, William S. *The North Carolina Gazetteer.* Chapel Hill: University of North Carolina Press.

Guides To Genealogical Research

Leary, Helen F. M. and Maurice R. Stirewalt eds. *North Carolina Research: Genealogy and Local History.* Raleigh: The North Carolina Genealogical Society, 1980.

Histories

Lefler, Hugh Talmage, and Alfred Ray Newsome. *The History of a Southern State: North Carolina,* 3rd edition. Chapel Hill: University of North Carolina Press, 1973.

Genealogical Sources - Microfilm

Cemetery Inscription Card Index (Surname indexes for persons who died prior to 1914; arranged by name of deceased. Also card index arranged by county, town and cemetery name). Raleigh: North Carolina State Archives*

D.A.R. Collection. Washington D.C.: D.A.R. Library*

Eller Collection. Jefferson: Ashe County Public Library.

McCubbins Collection. Salisbury: Rowan County Library.*

Outlaw Collection. Kenansville: Liberty Hall.

Printed Sources - Abstracts of Records

Grimes, J. Bryan. *Abstracts of North Carolina Wills, 1690-1760.* Baltimore: Genealogical Publishing Company, 1975.

Hofmann, Margaret M. *Province of North Carolina, 1663-1729, Abstracts of Land Patents.* Weldon, North Carolina: Noanoke News Company, 1979.

Manarin, Louis H., and W. T. Jordan, Jr. *North Carolina Troops, 1861-1865: A Roster.* Raleigh: Division of Archives and History, 1966--).

Neal, Lois S. *Abstracts of Vital Records from Raleigh, North Carolina,* Newspapers, 1799-. Spartanburg, South Carolina: Reprint Company, 1979-.

Olds, Fred A. *An Abstract of North Carolina Wills, 1760-1800.* Baltimore: Genealogical Publishing Company, 1968.

Powell, William S., ed. *Dictionary of North Carolina Biography.* Chapel Hill: Southern Historical Collection, 1979--).

Bibliographies - Guides and Check Lists

Davis, Richard C. and Linda Angle Miller, eds., *Guide to the Cataloged Collections in the Manuscript Department of the William R. Perkins Library, Duke University.* Santa Barbara: Clio Books, 1980.

Jones, Roger C. ed. *North Carolina Newspapers on Microfilm: A Checklist of North Carolina Newspapers Available on Microfilm from the Division of Archives and History,* 5th edition. Raleigh: Division of Archives and History, 1981.

---

*Microfilm - Genealogical Society of The Church of Jesus Christ of Latter-day Saints, Salt Lake City, Utah.

NORTH CAROLINA COUNTY HISTORIES
(Population figures to nearest thousand - 1980 U.S. Census)

Name	Map Index	Date Created	Pop. By M 1980	U.S. Cen Reports Available	Parent County or Territory From Which Organized	County Seat
*§ Alamance	D1	1849	99	1850-80	Orange	Graham 27253

(Clk Sup Ct has div, pro & civ ct rec from 1849; Reg of Deeds has b, m & d rec)

Name	Map Index	Date Created	Pop. By M 1980	U.S. Cen Reports Available	Parent County or Territory From Which Organized	County Seat
Albemarle		1663			1 of 3 original cos. discontinued in 1739	
* Alexander	E1	1847	25	1850-80	Iredell, Caldwell & Wilkes	Taylorsville 28681

(Reg Deeds has b, m, d & bur rec; Clk Sup Ct has div, pro & civ ct rec)

| Alleghany | E1 | 1859 | 10 | 1860-80 | Ashe .... | Sparta 28675 |

(Clk Sup Ct has b & d rec from 1914, m rec from 1868, also div rec, pro rec from 1883, civ ct rec from 1860)

| * Anson | D2 | 1750 | 25 | 1790-80 | Bladen............................. | Wadesboro 28170 |

(Reg Deeds has b rec from 1913, m rec from 1869, d rec & Ind rec; Clk Sup Ct has div rec from 1868, pro rec from 1750 & civ ct rec from 1770; Courthouse burned 1868)

| Ashe | E1 | 1799 | 22 | 1800-80 | Wilkes .... | Jefferson 28640 |

(Clk has b & d rec from 1913, m rec from 1853, div, pro & civ ct rec from 1800)

| Archdale | | 1705 | | | Changed to Beaufort 1712 .... | |
| Avery | E1 | 1911 | 14 | | Caldwell, Mitchell, Watauga .... | Newland 28657 |

(Clk Sup Ct has div, pro civ ct & Ind rec from 1911)

Bath		1696			Discontinued in 1739	
* Beaufort	B2	1712	40	1790-80	Bath (formerly Archdale)...............	Washington 27889
Bertie	B1	1722	21	1790-80	Chowan	Windsor 27983

(Reg Deeds has b, m & d rec; Clk Sup Ct has div & civ ct rec from 1869 & pro rec from 1763)

| * Bladen | C3 | 1734 | 30 | 1790-80 | New Hanover, Bath .... | Elizabethtown 28337 |

(Reg Deeds has b & d rec from 1914, m rec from 1893 & Ind rec from 1734; Clk Sup Ct has div & civ ct rec from 1893 & pro rec from 1734; Courthouse burned 1800-1893)

| Brunswick | C3 | 1764 | 35 | 1790-80 | New Hanover, Bladen .... | Bolivia 28422 |

(Reg of Deeds has b, m, d & bur rec; Clk Sup Ct has div rec from 1900, pro rec & wills from 1858, civ ct rec from 1882)

| * Buncombe | F2 | 1791 | 160 | 1800-80 | Burke, Rutherford .... | Asheville 28807 |

(Courthouse burned 1830-35; Reg Deeds has b, m, d, bur & Ind rec; Clk Sup Ct has div & pro rec from 1832 & civ ct rec)

| Burke | E2 | 1777 | 72 | 1790-80 | Rowan .... | Morganton 28655 |

(Reg Deeds has b, d & bur rec from 1913, m & Ind rec from 1865; Clk Sup Ct has div, pro & civ ct rec from 1865)

| Bute | | 1764 | | | Discontinued in 1779 | |
| Cabarrus | D2 | 1792 | 86 | 1800-80 | Mecklenburg............................. | Concord 28025 |

(Courthouse burned 1874; Clk Sup Ct has div, pro & civ ct rec)

| * Caldwell | E1 | 1841 | 67 | 1850-80 | Burke, Wilkes .... | Lenoir 28645 |

(Reg Deeds has b, m, d & Ind rec; Clk Sup Ct has div, civ ct & pro rec from 1841)

| * Camden | A1 | 1777 | 6 | 1790-80 | Pasquotank............................. | Camden 27921 |

(Clk Sup Ct has div & civ ct rec from 1896, pro rec from 1912)

| * Carteret | B2 | 1722 | 41 | 1790-80 | Craven .... | Beaufort 28516 |

(Reg Deeds has b, m, d & Ind rec; Clk Sup Ct has div, pro & civ ct rec)

| Caswell | D1 | 1777 | 21 | 1800-80 | Orange................................. | Yanceyville 27379 |

(Clk Sup Ct has div, pro & civ ct rec)

| * Catawba | E2 | 1842 | 105 | 1850-80 | Lincoln .... | Newton 28658 |

(Clk Sup Ct has div, pro & civ ct rec from 1843)

| * Chatham | D2 | 1770 | 33 | 1790-80 | Orange .... | Pittsboro 27312 |

(Reg Deeds has b & d rec from 1913, m & Ind rec from 1771; Clk Sup Ct has div rec from 1913, pro rec from 1771 & civ ct rec from 1869)

| * Cherokee | G2 | 1839 | 19 | 1840-80 | Macon .... | Murphy 28906 |

(Clk Sup Ct has div, pro & civ ct rec)

| * Chowan | B1 | 1670 | 12 | 1790-80 | Albermarle .... | Edenton 27932 |
| * Clay | G2 | 1861 | 7 | 1870-80 | Cherokee .... | Hayesville 28904 |

(Reg Deeds has b, m, d, pro & Ind rec)

| * Cleveland | E2 | 1841 | 83 | 1850-80 | Rutherford, Lincoln .... | Shelby 28150 |

(Reg Deeds has b & d rec from 1913, m rec from 1851, also Ind rec; Clk Sup Ct has div, pro & civ ct rec from 1841)

| § Columbus | C3 | 1808 | 51 | 1810-80 | Bladen, Brunswick .... | Whiteville 28472 |

(Reg Deeds has b & d rec from 1913, m rec from 1867; Clk Sup Ct has div & civ rec from 1868, pro rec from 1817)

| *§ Craven | B2 | 1712 | 71 | 1790-80 | Prec. Bath Co .... | New Bern 28560 |

(1810 census missing) (Reg Deeds has b & d rec from 1914, m & pro rec from 1780, civ ct rec from 1915 & Ind rec from 1710; City Clk has bur rec from 1800; Clk Sup Ct has div rec from 1915)

| * Cumberland | C2 | 1754 | 246 | 1790-80 | Bladen............................. | Fayetteville 28301 |

(Reg Deeds has b, m, d & bur rec; Clk Sup Ct has div rec from 1930, pro rec from 1850 & civ ct rec from 1900)

| Currituck | A1 | 1670 | 11 | 1790-80 | Albemarle............................. | Currituck 27929 |

(1820 census missing; Courthouse burned 1842) (Reg Deeds has b, m, d & Ind rec; Clk Sup Ct has div, pro & civ ct rec)

| Dare | A2 | 1870 | 12 | 1870-80 | Currituck, Tyrell, Hyde .... | Manteo 27954 |

(Reg Deeds has b & d rec from 1913, m rec from 1870; Clk Sup Ct has div, pro & civ ct rec from 1870)

| * Davidson | D2 | 1822 | 113 | 1830-80 | Rowan .... | Lexington 27292 |

(Reg Deeds has b, m, d, bur & Ind rec from 1823; Clk Sup Ct has div, pro & civ ct rec from 1823)

COUNTY MAP FOR THE STATE OF NORTH CAROLINA

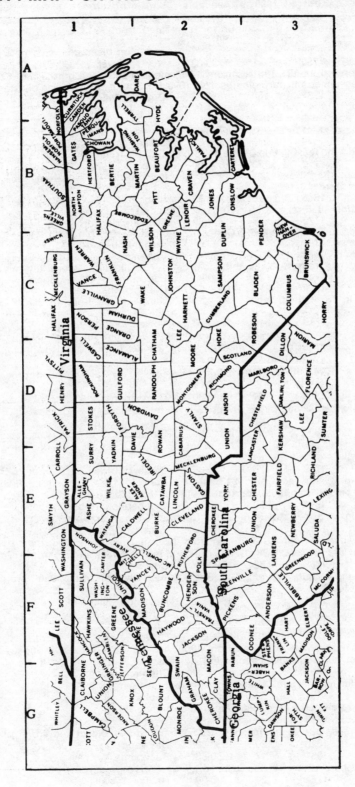

Name	Map Index	Date Created	Pop. By M 1980	U.S. Cen Reports Available	Parent County or Territory From Which Organized	County Seat
* Davie	D1	1836	24	1840-80	Rowan	Mocksville 27028

(Reg Deeds has b rec from 1913, d & bur rec combined from 1913 & m & Ind rec from 1836; Clk Sup Ct has div rec from 1831, civ ct & pro rec from 1837)

Dobbs		1758			Johnston, discontinued 1791	
* Duplin	C2	1750	41	1790-80	New Hanover	Kenansville 28349

(Reg Deeds has b, d rec from 1913, m rec from 1749, maps, deeds, Ind grants and deeds of trust from 1749, corporations, assumed names and partnerships from 1899; Clk Sup Ct has wills, Ind division rec)

* Durham	C1	1881	150		Orange, Wake	Durham 27701

(Co Health Dept has b, d & bur rec; Reg Deeds has m & Ind rec; Clk Sup Ct has div, pro & civ ct rec from 1881)

* Edgecombe	B1	1741	56	1790-80	Bertie	Tarboro 27886
* Forsyth	D1	1849	243	1850-80	Stokes	Winston-Salem 27102

(Reg Deeds has b, m, d & Ind rec; Clk Sup Ct has div, pro & civ ct rec from 1849)

Franklin	C1	1779	30	1800-80	Bute	Louisburg 27549

(1820 census missing) (Reg Deeds has b & d rec from 1913, m rec from 1869, Ind rec from 1779 & pro rec; Clk Sup Ct has div rec)

* Gaston	E2	1846	161	1850-80	Lincoln	Gastonia 28052

(Reg Deeds has b rec from 1846, m, d, notary & Ind rec; Clk Sup Ct has div rec)

Gates	B1	1779	9	1790-80	Chowan, Hertford, Perquimans	Gatesville 27938

(Reg Deeds has b, m, d, bur & Ind rec; Clk Sup Ct has div, pro & civ ct rec from 1780)

Glasgow		1791			Discontinued 1799	
Graham	G2	1872	7	1880	Cherokee	Robbinsville 28771

(Reg Deeds has b, d rec from 1913, m, Ind rec from 1873; Clk Sup Ct has div, civ ct, pro rec from 1872)

Granville	C1	1746	34	1800-80	Edgecombe, Orig. Glasgow	Oxford 27565
Greene	B2	1799	16	1800-80	Dobbs or Glasgow	Snow Hill 28580

(Courthouse burned in 1876) (Reg deeds has b, m, d, bur, Ind rec from 1876; Clk Sup Ct has div, civ ct, pro rec from 1876)

* Guilford	D1	1770	315	1790-80	Rowan, Orange	Greensboro 27402

(Reg Deeds has b, d, bur rec from 1913, m rec from 1872, Ind rec from 1771, pro rec from 1771; Clk Sup Ct has div, civ ct rec from 1840) (Courthouse burned 1872, many older rec still available)

* Halifax	B1	1758	54	1790-80	Edgecombe	Halifax 27839

(Reg Deeds has b & d rec from 1913, m rec from 1867, div, pro & spec proceedings from 1868, civ ct rec from 1893, Ind rec from 1729 & mil dis from 1918)

* Harnett	C2	1855	59	1860-80	Cumberland	Lillington 27546

(Reg Deeds has b, m & d rec; Clk Sup Ct has div, pro & civ ct rec from 1894)

* Haywood	F2	1808	46	1810-80	Buncombe	Waynesville 28786
* Henderson	F2	1838	58	1840-80	Buncombe	Hendersonville 28739

(Reg Deeds has b, d rec from 1914, m rec from 1800; Clk Sup Ct has div, pro, civ ct rec from 1841, Ind rec from 1835, special proceedings rec)

* Hertford	B1	1759	23	1790-80	Bertie, Chowan, Northampton, Gates	Winton 27986

(Reg Deeds has b, d & bur rec from 1913, m rec from 1884, Ind rec from 1866; Clk Sup Ct has div & civ ct rec from 1883, pro rec from 1869; Courthouse burned 1832-1862)

* Hoke	C2	1911	20		Cumberland, Robeson	Raeford 28376

(Reg Deeds has b, m, d & bur rec from 1911; Clk Sup Ct has div, pro, civ ct & crim ct rec from 1911)

* Hyde	A2	1712	6	1790-80	Wickham, Pres. Bath Co	Swanquarter 27885

(Reg Deeds has b, d, bur rec from 1913, m rec from 1850, Ind rec from 1736, marr bonds from 1735 to 1867, delayed birth cert from late 1800's; Clk Sup Ct has div, civ ct rec from 1868, pro rec from 1774)

Iredell	E2	1788	82	1790-80	Rowan	Statesville 28677

(Reg Deeds has b, m, d, bur, Ind rec; Clk Sup Ct has Div rec from 1820, pro, civ ct rec from 1788) (Courthouse burned in 1854)

* Jackson	F2	1851	26	1860-80	Haywood, Macon	Sylva 28779

(Reg Deeds has b, m, d, bur, & Ind rec; Clk Sup Ct has div, pro, civ ct & rec of estates from 1851)

* Johnston	C2	1746	70	1790-80	Craven	Smithfield 27577
* Jones	B2	1778	10	1790-80	Craven	Trenton 28585

(Reg Deeds has b, d rec from 1913, m rec from 1850, Ind rec from 1779; Clk Sup Ct has div rec from 1869, pro rec from 1779, civ ct rec) (Courthouse burned in 1862)

Lee	C2	1907	37		Chatham, Moore	Sanford 27330

(Reg Deeds has b, d & Ind rec; Clk Sup Ct has m, div, pro & civ ct rec from 1907)

Lenoir	B2	1791	59	1800-80	Dobbs	Kinston 28501

(Clk Sup Ct has div, pro & civ ct rec from 1880; Courthouse burned 1878)

* Lincoln	E2	1778	42	1790-80	Tryon	Lincolnton 28092

(Reg Deeds has b, m, d, bur & Ind rec; Clk Sup Ct has div & civ ct rec from 1920, pro rec from 1869)

* Macon	F2	1828	20	1830-80	Haywood	Franklin 28734
Madison	F2	1851	17	1860-80	Buncombe, Yancey	Marshall 28753

(Reg Deeds has b, m, d, bur, Ind rec; Clk Sup Ct has div, pro, civ ct rec from 1851)

Martin	B2	1774	26	1790-80	Halifax, Tyrrell	Williamston 27892

(Courthouse burned in 1884; 1820 cen missing; Clk Sup Ct has div, pro, civ ct, Ind rec from 1885, wills from 1774)

Name	Map Index	Date Created	Pop. By M 1980	U.S. Cen Reports Available	Parent County or Territory From Which Organized	County Seat
McDowell	F2	1842	35	1850-80	Burke, Rutherford	Marion 28752

(Reg Deeds has b, m, d & Ind rec; Clk Sup Ct has div, pro & civ ct rec from 1842)

* Mecklenburg	E2	1762	401	1790-80	Anson	Charlotte 28202

(Reg Deeds has b & d rec from 1913, m rec from 1850 & Ind rec from 1763; Clk Sup Ct has div, pro & civ ct rec from 1930)

Mitchell	F1	1861	14	1870-80	Burke, Caldwell, McDowell, Watauga, Yancey	Bakersville 28705

(Clk Sup Ct has div & pro rec from 1861, civ ct rec from 1912)

Montgomery	D2	1779	22	1790-80	Anson	Troy 27371

(Courthouse burned 1835; 1820 census missing) (Reg Deeds has b, m, d, bur, pro & Ind rec; Clk Sup Ct has div & civ ct rec from 1842)

*§ Moore	D2	1784	50	1790-80	Cumberland	Carthage 28327

(Courthouse burned in 1889) (Reg Deeds has b, m, d, bur, Ind rec; Clk Sup Ct has div, pro, civ ct rec)

*§ Nash	C1	1777	67	1790-80	Edgecombe	Nashville 27856

(Reg Deeds has b & d rec from 1913, m rec from 1872; Clk Sup Ct has div & civ ct rec from 1876, pro & Ind rec from 1869; oldest wills in Dept of Archives, Raleigh, N.C.)

* New Hanover	C3	1729	103	1790-80	Craven	Wilmington 28401

(Courthouse burned 1798, 1819 & 1840; 1810 cen missing; Reg of Deeds has b, m & d rec; Clk Sup Ct has div, pro & civ ct rec)

Northampton	B1	1741	22	1790-80	Bertie	Jackson 27845

(Reg Deeds has b, m, d & Ind rec; Clk Sup Ct has div rec from 1800, pro & civ ct rec from 1761)

* Onslow	B2	1734	112	1790-80	Preceding Bath	Jacksonville 28540

(Reg Deeds has b, d rec from 1914, m rec from 1893, Ind rec from 1734; Clk Sup Ct has div, pro, civ ct rec from 1915, prior rec in Archives and History, Raleigh, NC 27602)

* Orange	C1	1752	77	1800-80	Bladen, Granville, Johnston	Hillsboro 27278

(Courthouse burned 1789; Reg Deeds has b & d rec from 1913, m & Ind rec from 1754, div rec from 1869, pro rec from 1756 & civ ct rec from 1865)

Pamlico	B2	1872	10	1880	Beaufort, Craven	Bayboro 28515

(Reg Deeds has b rec from 1913, m, d & Ind rec from 1872; Clk Sup Ct has div, pro & civ ct rec from 1872)

* Pasquotank	B1	1670	26	1790-80	Prec. Albemarle	Elizabeth City 27909

(Courthouse burned 1862; Clk Sup Ct has div rec from 1900, pro rec & wills recorded from 1765, civ ct rec from 1765)

Pender	B3	1875	22	1880	New Hanover	Burgaw 28425

(Reg Deeds has b, m, d & Ind rec; Clk Sup Ct has div, pro & civ ct rec)

* Perquimans	B1	1670	9	1790-80	Prec. Albermarle	Hertford 27944

(Perquimans Co was known as Berkeley Precinct from 1671 to 1681)

* Person	C1	1791	29	1800-80	Caswell	Roxboro 27573

(Reg Deeds has b, m, d & Ind rec; Clk Sup Ct has div, pro & civ ct rec from 1791)

* Pitt	B2	1760	88	1790-80	Beaufort	Greenville 27834

(Courthouse burned 1857; Reg Deeds has b & d rec from 1913, m rec from 1866, real estate rec from 1762; Clk Sup Ct has div, pro, civ ct & Ind rec from 1885)

* Polk	F2	1855	13	1860-80	Henderson, Rutherford	Columbus 28722

(Clk Sup Ct has div rec from 1932, pro, civ ct rec from 1872)

* Randolph	D2	1779	92	1790-80	Guilford	Asheboro 27203

(1820 cen missing; Reg Deeds has b, d rec from 1913, m rec from 1800; Clk Sup Ct has div rec from 1869, pro, civ ct rec from 1913, Ind rec from 1779)

Richmond	D2	1779	45	1790-80	Anson	Rockingham 28379

(Reg Deeds has b & d rec from 1913, m rec from 1870, Ind rec from 1784; Clk Sup Ct has div rec from 1913, pro rec from 1782)

* Robeson	C3	1787	101	1790-80	Bladen	Lumberton 28358

(Reg Deeds has b rec from 1913, m rec from 1787, d rec from 1915; Ind rec from 1799; Clk Sup Ct has div, civ ct rec from 1920; pro rec from 1868)

* Rockingham	D1	1785	83	1790-80	Guilford	Wentworth 27375

(Courthouse burned 1906; Reg of Deeds has m rec from 1868, deeds from 1787, b & d rec from 1913; Clk Sup Ct has wills from 1804; N.C. Hist Com has m rec from 1741 to 1868)

* Rowan	D2	1753	99	1790-80	Anson	Salisbury 28144

(Reg Deeds has b, m, d & Ind rec; Clk Sup Ct has div rec from 1881, pro & civ ct rec)

* Rutherford	E2	1779	53	1790-80	Burke, Tyron	Rutherfordton 28139

(Clk Sup Ct has wills from 1790; Courthouse burned 1857)

* Sampson	C2	1784	49	1790-80	Duplin, New Hanover	Clinton 28328

(Courthouse burned 1921)

Scotland	D2	1899	32		Richmond	Laurinburg 28352

(Reg Deeds has b rec from 1913, m, d, bur rec from 1899; Clk Sup Ct has div, pro & civ ct rec from 1899)

Name	Map Index	Date Created	Pop. By M 1980	U.S. Cen Reports Available	Parent County or Territory From Which Organized	County Seat
Stanly	D2	1841	48	1850-80	Montgomery	Albemarle 28001
Stokes	D1	1789	33	1800-80	Surry	Danbury 27016
* Surry	E1	1770	59	1790-80	Rowan	Dobson 27017

(Reg Deeds has b, m, d, bur, Ind rec; Clk Sup Ct has div, civ ct rec, pro rec from 1771)

| Swain | G2 | 1871 | 10 | 1880 | Jackson, Macon | Bryson City 28713 |

(Reg Deeds has b & d rec 1913, m rec 1907; Clk Sup Ct has div & civ ct rec from 1900)

| Transylvania | F2 | 1861 | 23 | 1870-80 | Henderson, Jackson | Brevard 28712 |

(Clk Sup Ct has div, pro & civ ct rec)

| Tryon | | 1768 | | | Discontinued 1779 (see Lincoln) | |
| Tyrrell | A1 | 1729 | 4 | 1790-80 | Bertie, Chowan, Currituck, Pasquotank | Columbia 27925 |

(Reg Deeds has b & d rec from 1913, m rec from 1862; Clk Sup Ct has div rec, pro, wills from 1730 & civ ct rec from 1900)

| * Union | D2 | 1842 | 70 | 1850-80 | Anson, Mecklenburg | Monroe 28110 |

(Reg Deeds has b, m, d & bur rec; Clk Sup Ct has div rec, pro & civ ct rec from 1843)

| * Vance | C1 | 1881 | 36 | | Franklin, Granville, Warren | Henderson 27536 |

(Clk Sup Ct has div, pro, civ ct rec)

| * Wake | C2 | 1770 | 298 | 1790-80 | Cumberland, Johnston, Orange | Raleigh 27611 |

(1810 & 1820 cen missing)

| * Warren | C1 | 1779 | 16 | 1790-80 | Bute, Discontinued 1779 | Warrenton 27589 |

(Reg Deeds has b & d rec from 1913, m rec from 1867, Ind rec from 1764; Clk Sup Ct has div rec, pro rec from 1776 & civ ct rec from 1864)

| Washington | B2 | 1799 | 15 | 1790-80 | Tyrrell | Plymouth 27962 |

(Reg Deeds has b & d rec from 1913, m rec from 1800, Ind rec from 1799; Clk Sup Ct has div rec, also pro, civ ct rec & wills from 1871) (Courthouse burned 1862-1869-1873)

| * Watauga | E1 | 1849 | 32 | 1850-80 | Ashe, Caldwell, Wilkes, Yancey | Boone 28607 |

(Reg Deeds has b & d rec from 1914, m rec from 1872; Clk Sup Ct has div, pro & civ ct rec from 1872)

| * Wayne | C2 | 1779 | 97 | 1790-80 | Craven, Dobbs | Goldsboro 27530 |

(Reg Deeds has b, m, d, bur & Ind rec; Clk Sup Ct has div, pro & civ ct rec)

| * Wilkes | E1 | 1777 | 58 | 1790-80 | Surry | Wilkesboro 28697 |

(Reg Deeds has b, d rec from 1913, m rec from 1750, Ind rec, wills from 1778; Clk Sup Ct has div, pro, civ ct rec)

| Wilson | C2 | 1855 | 63 | 1860-80 | Edgecombe, Johnston, Nash, Wayne | Wilson 27893 |

(Reg Deeds has b, m, d & Ind rec; Clk Sup Ct has div & civ ct rec from 1868, pro rec from 1855)

| * Yadkin | E1 | 1850 | 28 | 1860-80 | Surry | Yadkinville 27055 |

(Reg Deeds has b, d rec from 1913, m, Ind rec from 1850; Clk Sup Ct has div, civ ct rec; pro rec from 1850)

| § Yancey | F2 | 1833 | 15 | 1840-80 | Buncombe, Burke | Burnsville 28714 |

(Reg Deeds has b, m, d, bur rec; Clk Sup Ct has div rec from 1875, pro, Ind rec from 1870, civ ct rec from 1870. Archives and History in Raleigh, NC has older rec)

* - At least one county history has been published about this county.

§ - Inventory of county archives was made by the Historical Records Survey. (see introduction)

NORTH DAKOTA

CAPITAL, BISMARCK - TERRITORY 1861 - STATE 1889 - (39TH)

Many Indian tribes roamed the Dakota plains when the white man began to build the mid-section of the American continent. Although explorers had visited the section off and on since the early 1700's it was not until 1851 that the region was thrown open for settlement.

The first settlers were attracted there by the highly productive Red River district soil. That river is the boundary line between North Dakota and Minnesota. Some hearty Scottish pioneers arrived as early as 1812 in Pembina. Farm folk from the northern European countries, especially from Norway, came there in large numbers in the mid 1800's. In the early days of the section, bloody skirmishes between the Indians and the settlers were common place occurences.

The Dakota Territory was organized in 1861. It embraced the two Dakotas and Montana and Wyoming. In 1864 the Wyoming and Montana parts of the territory were formed into a separate section as the Montana Territory. The remaining Dakota Territory was divided about equally, north and south, into North Dakota and South Dakota about 1873. In 1889 North Dakota became the thirty-ninth state in the Union.

It was the vision of homes and fertile acres, big barns and cattle, that drew the poor peasants of northern and middle Europe to North Dakota. From Norway they came in the largest numbers, scattering over the state. They were accompanied by large groups of Swedes, Danes, and Icelanders, while numbers of Czechs, Poles and Dutch also came at that time. Previously French-Canadians came down from the north following the Red River. Many Germans and other Europeans settled around Bismarck and the south central counties indicated by the many German place names in that area, like Leipzig, Strassburg, and Danzig.

Local registrars (Clerks of District Court of the various counties of North Dakota) are authorized to issue certified copies of death and fetal death certificates; however, they are not authorized to issue certified copies or furnish information from birth certificates. Only the state registrar is authorized to issue certified copies of birth certificates. The North Dakota State Department of Health, State Capitol, Bismarck, North Dakota 58505 has authorized those local registrars who have requested same to issue certified copies of death and fetal death certificates. At present (February, 1981) only 22 of the 53 local registrars have requested such authorization.

The first law requiring registration of births and deaths in North Dakota was enacted effective July 1, 1893, but was repealed in 1895 and not re-enacted until 1899. Even though the law required registration of all births and deaths, registration was poorly done in the early years and it was not until about 1923 that registration became quite complete.

Original licenses and certificates of marriage are filed in the office of the county judge of the county where the license was issued. Since July 1, 1925 copies of licenses and certificates of marriage have been forwarded to the State Registrar for statistical purposes and for maintaining a state-wide index. The state office is also authorized to issue certified copies.

Clerks of the District Courts have charge of Civil Court, divorce and probate matters. The Register of deeds has charge of deeds and land titles.

Genealogical Archives, Libraries, Societies, and Publications

Bismarck - Mandan Historical and Genealogical Society, Box 485, Bismarck, ND 58501.

Minot Public Library, 516 Second Avenue, S.W., Minot, ND 58701.

Mouse River Loop Genealogy Society, Box 1391, Minot, ND 58701.

Public Library, Fargo, ND 58102.

Public Library, Grand Forks, ND 58201.

Public Library, Minot, ND 58701.

State Historical Society of North Dakota, Liberty Memorial Bldg., Bismarck, ND 58501.

State Library, Bismarck, ND 58501.

University of North Dakota Library, Grand Forks, ND 58201.

North Central North Dakota Genealogical Record, publication of the Mouse River Loop Genealogy Society, Box 1391, Minot, ND 58701.

Printed Census Records and Mortality Schedules

Indexes (Territory): 1870, 1880, 1885

1836 Iowa Territorial Census includes North Dakota

Mortality Schedule (Printed) Dakota Territory: 1880

Valuable Printed Sources

Atlases - County Plat Books

The State Historical Society of North Dakota collection of county plat books date from 1884 to the present and includes at least one volume for most counties. These books show land ownership within each township in the county and, occasionally a directory of county residents is included. A list, with publication dates for each volume, is available on request from the State Historical Society.

Place Names

Williams, Mary Ann Barnes. *Origins of North Dakota Place Names.* Washburn: North Dakota (1966).

Histories

Lounsberry, Clement A. *North Dakota History and People.* Washington D.C.: Liberty Press (1919).

Rath, George. *The Black Sea Germans in the Dakotas.* Peru, Nebraska: Privately published (1977).

Genealogical Sources

State Historical Society of North Dakota Collections. Bismarck: State Historical Society.

The Division's library contains many resources to assist persons conducting genealogical research. These materials are non-circulating and must be used in the Divisional Reading Room. Some of the sources include:

Anniversary and jubilee editions of newspapers.

Cemetery lists compiled by the Red River Valley Genealogy Society.

City Directories - dating from 1884.

County and local history book collection. (Most contain biographical sections).

Newspaper abstract file. (Includes citations for many obituaries and surnames from 1905 to present).

The State Historical Society of North Dakota provided the following information: Standard histories of North Dakota with biographical sections:

Andreas. *Historical Atlas of Dakota* (1884) Short biographical section, arranged by county of residence. (No index).

Compendium of History and Biography of North Dakota. 1900. indexed.

Crawford, Lewis F. *History of North Dakota*, 1931. Volumes 2 and 3. Biographical sketches, indexed.

Hennessey, W.B. *History of North Dakota.* 1910, indexed.

History of the Red River Valley, Past and Present. 1909. Short biographical section in Volume 2, indexed.

Lounsberry, Clement A. *North Dakota: History and People.* 1917. Volumes 2 and 3 consist entirely of biographica sketches - index at end of each volume.

(Most of these books can be commonly found in North Dakota libraries)

1. Census schedules for the following:
   Minnesota 1850 (includes Pembina County, North Dakota).
   Pembina County - 1850, 1857.
   1860, 1870, 1880 Dakota Territory
   1885 Dakota Territory (Northern half of Territory only - not indexed - no South Dakota counties)
   1900 North Dakota - soundex index and population schedules.
   1915 State census records (not indexed).
2. Historical Data Project biography files. Indexed by surname and county of residence.
3. *Lineage Books* published by the National Society of the Daughters of the American Revolution. The Division has volumes 1 through 166; and published indexes for volumes 1 through 160.
4. North Dakota newspapers - "The Division has files of most newspapers published in the state since 1905 and many for earlier years back to the 1870's." Some of these newspapers (Microfilm copies) are available for use through interlibrary loan.

NORTH DAKOTA COUNTY HISTORIES
(Population figures to nearest thousand - 1980 U. S. Census)

Name	Map Index	Date Created	Pop. By M 1980	U.S. Cen Reports Available	Parent County or Territory From Which Organized	County Seat
Adams	C2	1907	4		Stark, comprising part of old Hettinger	Hettinger 58639

(Clk Dis Ct has m, div, pro & civ ct rec from 1907 & Ind rec from 1904)

Allred (see McKenzie)

| Barnes | B4 | 1875 | 14 | 1880 | Cass (Burbank, disorganized) | Valley City 58072 |

(Clk Dis Ct has b, d, bur & civ ct rec; Co Judge has m & pro rec)

| Benson | B4 | 1883 | 8 | | Ramsey | Minnewaukan 58351 |

(Clk Dis Ct has b, d rec from late 1800's, m rec from 1889, bur rec from early 1900's, div, pro, civ ct rec from early 1900's; Reg Deeds has Ind rec)

| Billings | B1 | 1879 | 1 | 1880 | Unorg. Terr. | Medora 58645 |

(Clk Dis Ct has m rec from 1893, bur rec from 1922, div rec, pro rec from 1895, civ ct rec from 1890 & Ind rec from 1886)

| Bottineau | A3 | 1873 | 9 | 1884 | Unorg. Terr. | Bottineau 58318 |

(Clk Dis Ct has b, d, bur rec from 1943, m rec from 1887, div, pro, civ ct rec from 1889, naturalization rec from 1884; Reg deeds has Ind rec)

| Bowman | C1 | 1883 | 4 | | Billings | Bowman 58623 |

(Clk Dis Ct has m rec from 1907, div rec, pro & civ ct rec from 1908, Ind rec from 1896 & bur rec)

| Buffalo | | | | 1880 | Disorganized 1873 | |

(see Burleigh, Kidder, Logan, McHenry, Rolette & Sheridan)

Burbank (disorganized & transfered to Traill & Griggs)

| * Burke | A2 | 1910 | 4 | | Ward | Bowbells 58721 |

(Clk Dis Ct has b, d, bur rec from 1900, m, div, pro, civ ct, Ind rec from 1910, homestead patents from 1903)

| Burleigh | B3 | 1873 | 55 | 1880 | Buffalo - discontinued | Bismarck 58501 |
| Cass | B5 | 1873 | 88 | 1880 | Original county | Fargo 58102 |

(Clk Dis Ct has div & civ ct rec from 1885)

| Cavalier | A4 | 1873 | 8 | | Pembina | Langdon 58249 |

(Clk Dis Ct has m, pro & civ ct rec from 1881, div rec from 1888)

| * Dickey | C4 | 1881 | 7 | | La Moure | Ellendale 58436 |

(Clk Dis Ct has b & d rec from 1943, m & pro rec from 1883, bur rec from 1932, div rec from 1885, pro rec from 1883 & civ ct rec from 1884)

| * Divide | A1 | 1910 | 3 | | Williams | Crosby 58730 |

(Clk Dis Ct has b, d & bur rec also civ ct rec from 1910; Co Judge has m rec from 1910 & pro rec; Reg Deeds has Ind rec)

| * Dunn | B2 | 1908 | 5 | | Stark, Mercer | Manning 58642 |

(Clk Dis Ct has m rec from 1908, bur rec from 1943, div, pro & civ ct rec)

Dunn, old (formed from part of Howard (discontinued) in 1883 & annexed to Stark in 1897)

| Eddy | B4 | 1885 | 4 | | Foster | New Rockford 58356 |
| Emmons | C3 | 1879 | 6 | 1880 | Unorg. Terr. | Linton 58552 |

(Clk Dis Ct has b rec from 1889, m rec from 1888, d, bur, div & civ ct rec from 1890, pro rec from 1884 & naturalization rec from 1886; Reg Deeds has Ind rec)

| Foster | B4 | 1873 | 5 | 1880 | Pembina | Carrington 58421 |

(Clk Dis Ct has b & d rec from 1900, m, div, pro & civ ct rec 1884; Reg Deeds has Ind rec)

| § Golden Valley | B1 | 1912 | 2 | | Billings | Beach 58621 |

(Clk Dis Ct has b, m, d, bur, div, pro, civ ct, Ind rec from 1912)

| * Grand Forks | B5 | 1873 | 66 | 1880 | Pembina | Grand Forks 58201 |

(Clk Dis Ct has b rec from 1903, d rec from 1908, div rec from 1878, bur & civ ct rec, adoption rec & change of name; Co Judge has m rec from 1887, pro rec from 1880)

| Grant | C2 | 1916 | 4 | | Morton | Carson 58529 |

(Clk Dis Ct has b rec from 1945, m, d, bur, div, pro & civ ct rec from 1916; Reg of Deeds has Ind rec)

| Griggs | B4 | 1881 | 4 | | Foster, Burbank, Traill | Cooperstown 58425 |

(Clk Dis Ct has b rec from 1901, m, pro rec from 1883, d rec from 1901, div, civ ct rec from 1887; Reg Deeds has Ind rec from 1880)

| Gringras | | 1872 | | | Buffalo & Dakota Terr. | |

(name changed to Wells, 1881)

| Hettinger | C2 | 1883 | 4 | | Stark | Mott 58646 |

(Clk Dis Ct has b, d, bur rec from 1943, m, div, pro, civ ct rec from 1907; Reg deeds has Ind rec)

| * Kidder | B3 | 1873 | 4 | 1880 | Buffalo | Steele 58482 |

(Clk Dis Ct has b, d & bur rec from 1943, div, civ ct rec from 1885; Co Judge has m rec from 1887, pro rec from 1883; Reg Deeds has Ind rec from 1881)

| La Moure | C4 | 1873 | 6 | 1880 | Pembina | La Moure 58458 |

(Clk Dis Ct has b, m, d, bur, div, pro & civ ct rec from 1881)

| Logan | C4 | 1873 | 3 | | Buffalo | Napoleon 58561 |

(Clk Dis Ct has b, d, pro rec from 1893, m, div, civ ct rec from 1890, bur rec from 1927, naturalization, citizenship rec from 1909; Reg Deeds has Ind rec; Catholic Church, St. Philip Neri, Napoleon, ND has many bur rec)

Name	Map Index	Date Created	Pop. By M 1980	U.S. Cen Reports Available	Parent County or Territory From Which Organized	County Seat
McHenry	A3	1873	8		Buffalo	Towner 58788

(Clk Dis Ct has m rec from 1903, div, pro & civ ct rec from 1900; Reg Deeds has Ind rec)

Name	Map Index	Date Created	Pop. By M 1980	U.S. Cen Reports Available	Parent County or Territory From Which Organized	County Seat
* McIntosh	C4	1883	5		Logan	Ashley 58413
* McKenzie	B1	1905	7		Billings, Stark (comprising the unorganized cos of Allred, Old McKenzie & Wallace	Watford City 58854

(Clk Dis Ct has b, d rec from 1943, m, div, pro, civ ct rec from 1905, bur rec; Reg Deeds has Ind rec)

Name	Map Index	Date Created	Pop. By M 1980	U.S. Cen Reports Available	Parent County or Territory From Which Organized	County Seat
McKenzie (old		1883	6		Howard (annexed to Billings, 1897)	
* McLean	B2	1883	12		Stevens	Washburn 58577

(Clk Dis Ct has m rec from 1887, bur rec from 1920, div, civ ct rec from 1891, pro rec from 1900; Reg Deeds has Ind rec; Division Vital Statistics, Bismarck, has b, d rec)

Name	Map Index	Date Created	Pop. By M 1980	U.S. Cen Reports Available	Parent County or Territory From Which Organized	County Seat
*§ Mercer	B2	1875	9		Original county	Stanton 58571

(Clk Dis Ct has b, d, bur rec from 1942, m rec from 1894, div, civ ct rec from 1906, pro rec from 1898; Reg Deeds has Ind rec)

Name	Map Index	Date Created	Pop. By M 1980	U.S. Cen Reports Available	Parent County or Territory From Which Organized	County Seat
Morton	C2	1873	25	1880	Original county	Mandan 58554

(Clk Dis Ct has b rec from 1883, m rec from 1888, d rec from 1873, bur rec from 1943, div, pro rec from 1900's, civ ct rec from late 1800's; Reg Deeds has Ind rec from late 1800's)

Name	Map Index	Date Created	Pop. By M 1980	U.S. Cen Reports Available	Parent County or Territory From Which Organized	County Seat
Mountrail	A2	1909	8	1880	Ward	Stanley 58784

(Old Mountrail formed 1873, annexed to Ward in 1891. Clk Dis Ct has b rec, m, d, div, pro, civ ct, citizenship rec from 1909, incomplete bur rec)

Name	Map Index	Date Created	Pop. By M 1980	U.S. Cen Reports Available	Parent County or Territory From Which Organized	County Seat
Nelson	B4	1883	5		Foster, Grand Forks	Lakota 58344

(Clk Dis Ct has b, d, bur rec from 1940, m, pro, Ind rec from 1880, div, civ ct rec)

Name	Map Index	Date Created	Pop. By M 1980	U.S. Cen Reports Available	Parent County or Territory From Which Organized	County Seat
Oliver	B2	1885	3		Mercer	Center 58530

(Clk Dis Ct has m rec from 1915, also d rec; Co Judge has pro & civ ct rec; Reg Deeds has Ind rec)

Name	Map Index	Date Created	Pop. By M 1980	U.S. Cen Reports Available	Parent County or Territory From Which Organized	County Seat
* Pembina	A5	1867	10	1880	Indian Lands	Cavalier 58220

(Clk Dis Ct has b & d rec from 1893, a few m rec from 1872, bur rec from 1943, div rec from 1883, pro rec from 1875 & civ ct rec from 1883)

Name	Map Index	Date Created	Pop. By M 1980	U.S. Cen Reports Available	Parent County or Territory From Which Organized	County Seat
* Pierce	A3	1887	6		De Smet	Rugby 58368

(Clk Dis Ct has b, d, bur rec from 1943, m rec from 1888, div, civ ct rec from 1900, pro rec from 1898; Reg Deeds has Ind rec)

Name	Map Index	Date Created	Pop. By M 1980	U.S. Cen Reports Available	Parent County or Territory From Which Organized	County Seat
Ramsey	A4	1873	13	1880	Pembina	Devils Lake 58301

(Clk Dis Ct has b, d & bur rec from 1890, div & civ ct rec; Co Judge has m & pro rec; Reg Deeds has Ind rec)

Name	Map Index	Date Created	Pop. By M 1980	U.S. Cen Reports Available	Parent County or Territory From Which Organized	County Seat
* Ransom	C5	1873	7	1880	Pembina	Lisbon 58054

(Clk Dis Ct has b & d rec from 1943, m from 1882, div, pro & civ ct rec)

Name	Map Index	Date Created	Pop. By M 1980	U.S. Cen Reports Available	Parent County or Territory From Which Organized	County Seat
Renville	A2	1910	4		Ward (see Renville, old)	Mohall 58761

(Clk Dis Ct has m, bur, div, pro, civ ct & Ind rec from 1910)

Renville, old (formed 1873 from part of Buffalo Co, Dakota Terr; part taken to form Ward in 1885 & parts annexed to Bottineau & Ward in 1894)

Name	Map Index	Date Created	Pop. By M 1980	U.S. Cen Reports Available	Parent County or Territory From Which Organized	County Seat
Richland	C5	1873	19	1880	Original county	Wahpeton 58075

(Clk Dis Ct has b, d, bur rec from 1943, div, civ ct rec from 1883; Co Judge has m rec from 1890, pro rec from 1876; Reg Deeds has Ind rec)

Name	Map Index	Date Created	Pop. By M 1980	U.S. Cen Reports Available	Parent County or Territory From Which Organized	County Seat
* Rolette	A3	1873	12		Buffalo	Rolla 58367

(Clk Dis Ct has b, d & bur rec from 1943, m, div, civ ct rec from 1887, pro rec from 1896)

Name	Map Index	Date Created	Pop. By M 1980	U.S. Cen Reports Available	Parent County or Territory From Which Organized	County Seat
Sargent	C5	1883	6		Ransom	Forman 58032

(Clk Dis Ct has b, d rec from 1943, m rec from 1886, bur rec from 1948, pro rec from 1883, div, civ ct rec)

Name	Map Index	Date Created	Pop. By M 1980	U.S. Cen Reports Available	Parent County or Territory From Which Organized	County Seat
Sheridan	B3	1909	3		McLean (see Sheridan, old)	McClusky 58463

(Co Clk has b, d rec from 1943, m, div, pro, civ ct, Ind rec from 1909, bur rec)

Sheridan, old (formed 1873 from part of Buffalo Co, Dakota Terr; part taken to form part of church in 1887; annexed to McLean in 1891)

Name	Map Index	Date Created	Pop. By M 1980	U.S. Cen Reports Available	Parent County or Territory From Which Organized	County Seat
Sioux	C3	1915	4		Standing Rock Reservation	Fort Yates 58538

(Clk Dis Ct has m rec from 1916, bur, div, pro, civ ct & Ind rec)

Name	Map Index	Date Created	Pop. By M 1980	U.S. Cen Reports Available	Parent County or Territory From Which Organized	County Seat
Slope	C1	1915	1		Billings	Amidon 58620

(Clk Dis Ct has m, d, bur, div, pro, civ ct rec from 1915, Ind rec; Division Vital Statistics, Bismarck has b rec)

Name	Map Index	Date Created	Pop. By M 1980	U.S. Cen Reports Available	Parent County or Territory From Which Organized	County Seat
Stark	B2	1879	24		Unorg. Terr.	Dickinson 58601

(Clk Dis Ct has b & d rec from 1898, bur rec, div & civ ct rec from 1887 & naturalization rec from 1887 to 1963)

Name	Map Index	Date Created	Pop. By M 1980	U.S. Cen Reports Available	Parent County or Territory From Which Organized	County Seat
Steele	B5	1883	3		Grand Forks, Griggs	Finley 58230

(Clk Dis Ct has b & d rec from 1894 to 1896, 1900 to 1901, div & civ ct rec from 1886; Co Judge has m rec from 1883, pro rec from 1886)

Name	Map Index	Date Created	Pop. By M 1980	U.S. Cen Reports Available	Parent County or Territory From Which Organized	County Seat
Stutsman	B4	1873	24	1880	Pembina	Jamestown 58401

(Clk Dis Ct has b, pro & civ ct rec; Reg Deeds has Ind rec; Co Judge has m rec)

Name	Map Index	Date Created	Pop. By M 1980	U.S. Cen Reports Available	Parent County or Territory From Which Organized	County Seat
* Towner	A4	1883	4		Rolette, Cavalier	Cando 58324

(Clk Dis Ct has m rec from 1888, div rec from 1890, pro rec from 1886, civ ct rec from 1889, Ind rec from 1884 & bur rec)

COUNTY MAP FOR THE STATE OF NORTH DAKOTA

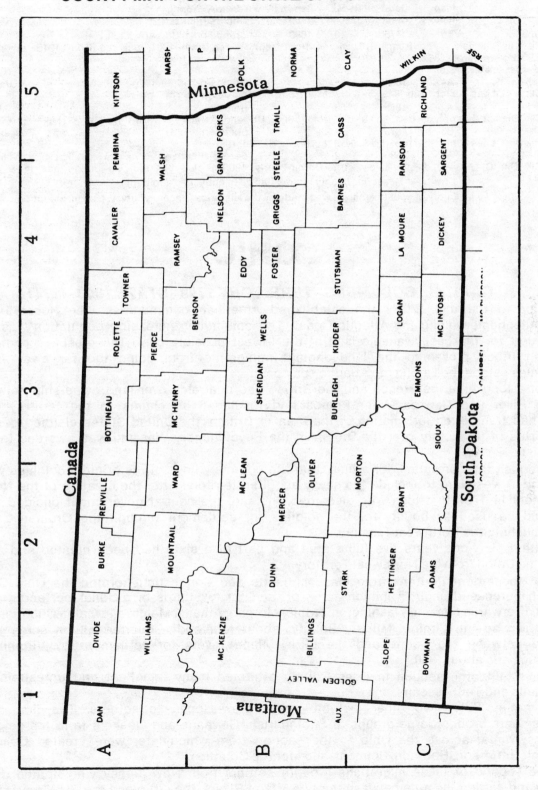

Name	Map Index	Date Created	Pop. By M 1980	U.S. Cen Reports Available	Parent County or Territory From Which Organized	County Seat
Traill	B5	1875	10	1880	Grand Forks, Burbank, Cass	Hillsboro 58045

(Clk Dis Ct has b rec from 1910, m rec from 1887, d rec from 1907, bur rec from 1915, div rec from 1890 & pro rec from 1882)

| Wallace (see McKenzie) | | | | | | |
| * Walsh | A4 | 1881 | 15 | | Grand Forks .... | Grafton 58237 |

(Clk Dis Ct has bur rec from 1943, div & civ ct rec from 1884; Co Judge has m & pro rec)

| Ward | A2 | 1885 | 58 | | Renville .... | Minot 58701 |

(Clk Dis Ct has b, d, bur rec & div from 1900; Co Judge has m & pro rec; Reg Deeds has Ind rec)

| * Wells | B3 | 1873 | 7 | | Sheridan .... | Fessenden 58438 |

(Clk Dis Ct has b, m, d, bur, div, pro & civ ct rec) (formerly Gingras)

| § Williams | A1 | 1890 | 22 | | Buford, Flannery .... | Williston 58801 |

(Clk Dis Ct has b, d, div & civ ct rec from early 1900's, also bur rec; Co Judge has m & pro rec)

* - At least one county history has been published about this county.

§ - Inventory of county archives was made by the Historical Records Survey. (see introduction)

OHIO

CAPITAL, COLUMBUS - TERRITORY 1799 - STATE 1803 - (17TH)

Prior to the mid 1700's the established American communities were located east of the Alleghenies along the Atlantic Coast. The constantly increasing population was ever on the alert for the best available land at the lowest possible cost. The presence of numerous Indian tribes prevented the land-longing immigrants from going too far away from the colonies established along the Atlantic sea coast.

For a long time the French and the British had quarreled over land ownership between the Ohio River and Canada. After France had rescinded all claims to the territory in 1763, and had transferred jurisdiction of the area to Britain, the United States claimed possession by virtue of its victory over the British in the Revolutionary War and was awarded the region in 1783.

The idea then prevailed, for a time, that the boundary lines of the original colonies would be extended westward to include the newly acquired territory. After the creation of the Northwest Territory in 1787 that idea was discarded. Instead, the central government decided the land should be used as bounty for the soldiers for settlement through the Ordinance of 1787 establishing the Northwest Territory.

Within sixty-one years five full states and part of a sixth had been created and admitted into the Union from the Northwest Territory.

Not too ardent Puritans from Massachusetts and Connecticut formed the Ohio Company which purchased about a million acres of land for two-thirds of a dollar per acre, including what afterwards became Washington, Noble, Morgan, Athens, Meigs, and Gallia Counties.

Known as the Virginia Military Bounty, about four and a quarter million acres were set aside between the Scioto and the Little Miami Rivers for settlement by Virginians and Kentuckians about 1800.

The Chillicothe section in Ross County attracted many impatient and unrestrained Kentuckians and Tennesseans.

Sometime later two other districts were thrown open to settlers. The first of these movements brought large groups of Scotch-Irish, Germans and Quakers from the neighboring Pennsylvania, across the Ohio to the section from which later were created Columbiana, Carroll, Jefferson, Harrison, Belmont, and Monroe Counties.

The second of these migrations brought settlers from New Jersey who floated down the Ohio and settled the area between the two Miami Rivers, the Little and the Big. They, and some Scotch-Irish and Dutch, began the cultivation of some 300,000 acres in that southwestern corner of Ohio. Cincinnati became an important part of that colonization.

After General Anthony Wayne and his United States forces had driven the hostile Indian tribes westward from the Lake Erie section in 1794, another four-million-acre tract, known as the Western Reserve, was opened for settlement in the northeast corner of Ohio, along Lake Erie. It was settled mainly by former Connecticut residents. Closely allied with that project was the settlement of the half a million acres in what became Erie and Huron Counties just south of Lake Erie. The settlers of that tract were also former Connecticut residents whose holdings had been burned out by the British during the Revolutionary War. For that reason that section was often referred to as the "Fire Lands."

The "Refugee Tract" was set aside by Congress for Canadians who had aided the American cause in the Revolution and who lost their lands in Canada. It was a tract 4½ miles wide (north and south) and extended eastward from the Scioto River to near the Muskingum River. It was the proximity of Franklin, Licking and Perry Counties. It was created 1801, effective 1802.

After 1815 the large northwestern section of the state was thrown open to settlers who flocked there from east and south. The opening of the Erie Canal in 1825 brought more settlers along the route from the northeastern states.

In 1799 Ohio was organized as a territory included in what was the Indiana section. The very next year Indiana was organized as a territory, and in 1803 Ohio became a state, the seventeenth in the Union.

State of Ohio Department of Health, Division of Vital Statistics, Ohio Departments Building, Room G-20, 65 South Front Street, Columbus, Ohio 43215 started to file births and deaths beginning December 20, 1908. Any records registered before that time were filed in the probate court of the county where the event occurred.

The certified copy of a marriage record may be obtained from the probate court of the county that issued the marriage license. The certified copy of a divorce record may be obtained from the Clerk of Courts of the county in which the divorce decree was granted.

Certified abstracts of marriages and divorces are on file at this office beginning September 1949.

Each County Recorder has charge of land records within the county.

Genealogical Archives, Libraries, Societies, and Publications

Adams County Genealogical Society, P.O. Box 231, West Union, OH 45693.

Allen County Historical Society, Elizabeth M. MacDonall Memorial Library, 620 West Market Street, Lima, OH 45801.

Akron Public Library, 55 South Main St., Akron, OH 44309.

American Jewish Archives, Clifton Ave., Cincinnati, OH 45220.

Ashland Chapter, Ohio Genealogical Society, 625 Center Street, Apt. 302, Ashland, OH 44805.

Ashtabula County Genealogical Society, c/o Henderson Library, 54 E. Jefferson Street, Jefferson, OH 44047.

Auglaize County Chapter, OGS, P.O. Box 2021, Wapakoneta, OH 45895.

Belmont County Chapter, OGS, c/o Betsy Hartley, R. #2, Barnesville, OH 43713.

Brown County Genealogical Society, Box 83, Georgetown, OH 45121.

Cadiz Public Library, Court House, Cadiz, OH 43907.

Carnegie Library, 520 Sycamore St., Greenville, OH 45331.

Carnegie Public Library, 127 S. North St., Washington Court House, OH 43160.

Chillicothe and Ross County Public Library, 140 S. Paint St., Chillicothe, OH 45601.

Cincinnati Historical Society, Eden Park, Cincinnati, OH 45202.

Cincinnati Public Library, 800 Vine St., Cincinnati, OH 45202.

Clermont County Genealogical Society, c/o Clermont County Public Library, 3rd and Broadway, Batavia, OH 45103.

Cleveland Public Library, 325 Superior Ave., Cleveland, OH 44114.

Crawford County Genealogical Society, P.O. Box 523, Galion, OH 44833.

Cuyahoga-East County, Ohio, Chapter of The Ohio Genealogical Society, P.O. Box 24182, Lyndhurst, OH 44124.

Dayton and Montgomery Counties Public Library, 215 East third St., Dayton, OH 45406.

Fairfield County Chapter, OGS, P.O. Box 203, Lancaster, OH 43130.

Firelands Historical Society, Norwalk, OH 44587.

Franklin County Chapter, OGS, P.O. Box 09324, Columbus, OH 43209.

Fulton County Genealogical Society, 305 Chestnut St., Swanton, OH 43558.

Gallia County Historical Society, 16 State Street, Gallipolis, OH 45631.

Glendover Warren County Museum, Lebanon, OH 45036.

Granville Public Library, 217 E. Broadway, Granville, OH 43023.

Greater Cleveland Genealogical Society, P.O. Box 9639, Cleveland, OH 44140.

Greene County District Library, 194 E. Church Street, Xenia, OH 45385.

Guernsey County District Public Library, 800 Steubenville Ave., Cambridge, OH 43725.

Hamilton County Chapter, Ohio Genealogical Society, P.O. Box 15185, Cincinnati, OH 45215.

Hardin County Genealogy and Historical Society, P.O. Box 503, Kenton, OH 43326.

Highland County Historical Society, 151 E. Main St., Hillsboro, OH 45133.

Jefferson County Historical Association, RD 6, Box 625, Steubenville, OH 43952.

Johnstown Genealogy Society, P.O. Box 345, Johnstown, OH 43031.

KYOWVA Genealogical Society, P.O. Box 1254, Huntington, WV 25715.

Lake County Chapter Ohio Genealogical Society, Morley Public Library, 184 Phelps St., Painesville, OH 44077.

Lakewood Public Library, 15425 Detroit Avenue, Lakewood, OH 44107.

Licking County Genealogical Society, P.O. Box 215, Newark, OH 43055.

Logan County Genealogical Society, Box 296, Bellefontaine, OH 43311.

Lorain Public Library, 351 6th St., Lorain, OH 44052.

Marion County Chapter, OGS, P.O. Box 844, Marion, OH 43302.

Mennonite Historical Library, Bluffton College, Bluffton, OH 45817.

Miami Valley Genealogical Society, P.O. Box 1365, Dayton, OH 45401.

Middletown Public Library, 1320 1st Ave., Middletown, OH 45042.

Monroe County Historical Society, P.O. Box 538, Woodsfield, OH 43793.

Montgomery County Chapter of the Ohio Genealogical Society, P.O. Box 1584, Dayton, OH 45401.

Morley Library, 184 Phelps St., Painesville, OH 44077.

Norwalk Public Library, 46 W. Main St., Norwalk, OH 44857.

Ohio Genealogical Society, 419 West Third St., P.O. Box 2625, Mansfield, OH 44906.

Ohio Historical Society Library, 1-17 and 17th Avenue, Columbus, OH 43211.

Ohio Records and Pioneer Families, 36 N. Highland Ave., Akron, OH 44303.

Ohio State Library, 65 South Front St., Columbus, OH 43215.

Portsmouth Public Library, 1220 Gallia St., Portsmouth, OH 45662.

Public Library of Cincinnati and Hamilton County, The, Eighth and Vine Sts., Cincinnati, OH 45202.

Public Library of Youngstown and Mahoning County, The, 305 Wick Ave., Youngstown, OH 44503.

Ross County Genealogical Society, P.O. Box 395, Chillicothe, OH 45601.

Sandusky County Historical Society, Genealogy Division, 1337 Hayes Ave., Fremont, OH 43520.

Sidney Public Library, 230 E. North St., Sidney, OH 45365.

South Central Ohio Genealogical Society, Box 33, Chillicothe, OH 45601.

Stark County Chapter, Ohio Genealogical Society, 7300 Woodcrest NE, North Canton, OH 44721.

Stark County District Library, 236 3rd St., SW, Canton, OH 44702.

Toledo Public Library, Local Historical and Genealogical Department, 325 Michigan St., Toledo, OH 43624.

Twinsburg Historical Society, Twinsburg, OH 44087.

Tuscarawas County Genealogical Society, P.O. Box 141, New Philadelphia, OH 44663.

University of Cincinnati Library, Cincinnati, OH 45221.

Warder Public Library, 137 E. High St., Springfield, OH 45502.

Warren County Genealogical Society, 12 W. South Street, Lebanon, OH 45036.

Wayne County Historical Society, 722 Quimby Ave., Wooster, OH 44691.

Wayne County Public Library, 304 N. Market St., Wooster, OH 44691.

West Augusta Historical and Genealogical Society, 1510 Prairie Dr., Belpre, OH 45714.

Western Reserve Historical Society, 10825 East Blvd., Cleveland, OH 44106.

Ancestor Hunt, publication of the Ashtabula County Genealogical Society, Jefferson, OH 44047.

Clermont County Genealogical Society Newsletter, c/o Clermont County Public Library, Third and Broadway, Batavia, OH 45103.

Ohio Records and Pioneer Families, The Ohio Genealogical Society, P.O. Box 2625, Mansfield, OH 44906.

Printed Census Records and Mortality Schedules

State Indexes: 1800, 1810, 1820, 1830, 1840, 1850, 1860

Printed Census Records (Counties):

Athens-1850	Hamilton-1817	Monroe-1850, 1860
Butler-1807	Hancock-1850, 1860, 1870	Montgomery-1850
Clermont-1820, 1830	Huron-1820	Pike-1870
Columbiana-1850, 1860	Jackson-1820	Preble-1900
Cuyahoga-1850	Knox-1860	Trumball-1820
Fayette-1850	Lorain-1850	Washington-1800, 1820
Gallia-1820, 1830, 1840	Meigs-1820, 1830, 1840	Wayne-1850, 1880; 1795-1820

Mortality Schedule (Printed): 1850

Valuable Printed Sources

Gazetteer

Kilbourn, John. *The Ohio Gazetteer.* Columbus: J. Kilbourn (1826).

Maps

Brown, Lloyd Arnold. *Early Maps of the Ohio Valley: A Selection of Maps, Plans and Views Made by Indians and Colonials from 1673 to 1783.* University of Pittsburg Press (1959).

Guides To Genealogical Research

Douthit, Ruth Long. *Ohio Resources for Genealogists with some References for Genealogical Searching in Ohio.* Detroit: Detroit Society for Genealogical Research (1971).

Flavell, Carol Willsey and Florence Clint. *Ohio Area Key.* Denver: Area Keys (1977).

McCay, Betty L. *Sources for Genealogical Searching in Ohio.* Indianapolis: Privately published (1973).

Histories

Biographical Encyclopedia of Ohio. Cincinnati: Galaxy Publishing, 1875.

Howe, Henry. *Historical Collections of Ohio, An Encyclopedia of the State.* Columbus: Henry Howe and Sons.

Randall, Emilius O. *History of Ohio.* New York: The Century History Company (1912).

Genealogical Sources

Adams, Marilyn. *Southeastern Ohio Local and Family History Sources in Print.* Atlanta: Heritage Research (1979).

Daughters of the American Revolution Collection.*

Flavell, Carol Willsey, *Ohio Genealogical Periodical Index: A County Guide.* Youngstown, Ohio: Privately published (1979).

Gutgesell, Stephen. *Guide to Ohio Newspapers 1793-1973, Union Bibliography of Ohio Newspapers Available in Ohio Libraries.* Columbus: Ohio Historical Society (1974).

Khouw, Petta and State Library of Ohio. *County by County in Ohio Genealogy.* Columbus: The State Library of Ohio (1978).

Pike, Kermit J. *A Guide to the Manuscripts and Archives of the Western Reserve Historical Society.* Cleveland: Western Reserve Historical Society (1972).

Smith, Clifford N. *The Federal Land Series.* Chicago: American Library Association, 1972-1978. (Index to sale of Federal Lands in Ohio).

The Ohio Network of American History Research Centers was established in 1970. The regional centers collect manuscripts, newspapers, printed materials and local government records of Ohio. The Network consists of the following institutions:

Bowling Green State University Library Archival Collections, Bowling Green, Ohio.

Kent State University Library, Kent, Ohio.

Ohio Historical Society, Archives- Manuscript Division, Columbus, Ohio.

Ohio University Library, Special Collections, Athens, Ohio.

University of Akron, Bierce Library Archives, Akron, Ohio.

University of Cincinnati Main Library, Special Collections, Cincinnati, Ohio.

Western Reserve Historical Society, Cleveland, Ohio.

Wright State University Library, Department of Archives, Dayton, Ohio.

---

*Microfilm - Genealogical Society of The Church of Jesus Christ of Latter-day Saints, Salt Lake City, Utah.

OHIO COUNTY HISTORIES
(Population figures to nearest thousand - 1980 U. S. Census)

Name	Map Index	Date Created	Pop. By M 1980	U.S. Cen Reports Available	Parent County or Territory From Which Organized	County Seat
§ Adams	D2	1797	24	1820-80	Hamilton	West Union 45693

(Courthouse burned in 1910, some rec saved, some as early as 1796, others to 1799; rec of several adjacent cos prior to their formation included; Clk Cts has b, d rec 1888 to 1893, m, div, pro, civ ct rec from 1910, Ind rec from 1797; County Health Department has b rec after 1910)

| *§ Allen | B1 | 1820 | 112 | 1830-80 | Shelby | Lima 45801 |

(Pro Ct has b & d rec 1867, m rec 1831; Clk Cts has div & civ ct rec 1831)

| *§ Ashland | B3 | 1846 | 46 | 1850-80 | Wayne, Richland, Huron, Lorain | Ashland 44805 |

(Clk Cts has div & civ ct rec from 1846)

| * Ashtabula | A4 | 1808 | 104 | 1820-80 | Trumbull, Geauga | Jefferson 44047 |
| *§ Athens | C3 | 1805 | 56 | 1820-80 | Washington | Athens 45701 |

(Pro Judge has b, m & pro rec; Clk Cts has div & civ rec from 1800; Rcdr has Ind rec)

| * Auglaize | B1 | 1848 | 42 | 1850-80 | Allen, Mercer, Darke, Hardin, Logan, Shelby, Van Wert | Wapakoneta 45895 |

(Pro Judge has b, m, d & pro rec; Clk Cts has div & civ ct rec from 1848; Co Rcdr has Ind rec)

| *§ Belmont | C4 | 1801 | 82 | 1820-80 | Jefferson, Washington | St. Clairsville 43950 |

(Clk Cts has div & civ ct rec from 1820; Pro Ct has b, m, d & pro rec; Co Health Dept has bur rec)

| *§ Brown | D2 | 1818 | 32 | 1820-80 | Adams, Clermont | Georgetown 45121 |

(Pro Judge has b, m & pro rec from 1800's; Co Health has d rec from 1800's; Clk Cts has div & civ ct rec from 1800's; Co Rcdr has Ind rec)

| * Butler | C1 | 1803 | 258 | 1820-80 | Hamilton | Hamilton 45011 |

(Co Health has b & d rec; Pro Judge has m & pro rec; Clk Cts has div & civ ct rec; Co Aud Ind rec)

| * Carroll | B4 | 1833 | 25 | 1840-80 | Columbiana, Stark,Harrison, Jefferson, Tuscarawas | Carrollton 44615 |

(Clk Cts has div & civ ct rec from 1833; Pro Judge has pro rec; Co Rcdr has Ind rec)

| * Champaign | C2 | 1805 | 34 | 1820-80 | Greene, Franklin | Urbana 43078 |

(Pro Judge has b, m & pro rec; Co Health has d rec; Co Aud has bur rec; Clk Cts has d & civ ct rec; Co Rcdr has Ind rec)

| * Clark | C2 | 1818 | 150 | 1820-80 | Champaign, Madison, Greene | Springfield 45502 |

(Clark Co Hist Soc., Memorial Hall, Springfield, Ohio 45502 may assist you in your work, also Warder Public Lib., Springfield)

| * Clermont | D2 | 1800 | 128 | 1820-80 | Hamilton | Batavia 45103 |

(Clk Cts has div rec from 1861 & civ ct rec from 1803)

| * Clinton | C2 | 1810 | 35 | 1820-80 | Highland, Warren | Wilmington 45177 |

(Pro Ct has b, d rec bef 1908, Co Health Office has b, d rec aft 1908, Pro Ct has b, d rec from 1867 to 1908; Pro Judge has m, pro rec from 1810; Clk Cts has div, civ ct rec from 1810; Co Rcdr has Ind rec from 1810)

| *§ Columbiana | B4 | 1803 | 113 | 1820-80 | Jefferson, Washington | Lisbon 44432 |

(Clk Cts has div & civ ct rec)

| * Coshocton | B3 | 1810 | 36 | 1820-80 | Muskingum, Tuscarawas | Coshocton 43812 |

(Pro Ct has b, m, pro rec; City Health Board has d rec; County Trustees have bur rec; Clk Cts has div, civ ct rec; Co Rcdr has Ind rec)

| * Crawford | B2 | 1820 | 50 | 1830-80 | Delaware | Bucyrus 44820 |

(Co Health Dept has b, d rec for Crestline, Ohio and the Rural Routes of Crawford Co 1908 to present, Bucyrus City Health Dept has same rec for City of Bucyrus, Galion City Health Dept has same rec for City of Galion; Pro Judge has b, d rec 1867 to 1908, m, pro rec from 1831; Co Rcdr has Ind rec; Clk Cts has div, civ ct rec from 1834)

| *§ Cuyahoga | A3 | 1808 | 1,496 | 1820-80 | Geauga | Cleveland 44113 |

(Pro Judge has b, m, d & pro rec; Clk Cts has div & civ ct rec from 1810; Co Aud has Ind rec)

| * Darke | C1 | 1809 | 55 | 1820-80 | Miami | Greenville 45331 |

(Pro Judge has b, d rec from 1867 to 1908, m rec from 1817; Clk Cts has div, civ ct rec from 1820; Co Rcdr has Ind rec from 1816, bur rec (veterans graves) from 1832)

COUNTY MAP FOR THE STATE OF OHIO

Name	Map Index	Date Created	Pop. By M 1980	U.S. Cen Reports Available	Parent County or Territory From Which Organized	County Seat
* Defiance	A1	1845	40	1850-80	Williams, Henry, Paulding	Defiance 43512

(Clk Cts has div & civ ct rec from 1845; General Health Dis has d & bur rec; Pro Judge has b & m rec from 1845)

* Delaware	B2	1808	53	1820-80	Franklin	Delaware 43015

(Chan Ct has div & civ ct rec from 1825)

* Erie	A3	1838	79	1840-80	Huron, Sandusky	Sandusky 44870

(Co Health has b rec from 1908, d & bur rec; Pro Judge has m & pro rec; Clk Cts has div & civ ct rec from 1870; Co Rcdr has Ind rec)

* Fairfield	C3	1800	94	1820-80	Ross, Washington	Lancaster 43130

(Pro Judge has b rec from 1803 to 1907, m, d, pro rec; Clk Cts has div rec from 1860, civ ct rec from 1800; Co Rcdr has Ind rec from 1803)

*§ Fayette	C2	1810	27	1820-80	Ross, Highland	Washington C.H. 43160

(Clk Cts has div rec from 1853 & civ ct rec from 1828)

*§ Franklin	C2	1803	865	1830-80	Ross	Columbus 43215

(Pro Ct has b, d rec prior to 1908, m, pro rec; Bureau vital Statistics has b, d rec after 1908; Clk Cts has div, civ ct rec from 1803; Co Auditor has Ind rec)

* Fulton	A2	1850	38	1850-80	Lucas, Henry, Williams	Wauseon 43567

(Clk Cts has div, civ ct, b, m, d, bur & pro rec)

* Gallia	D3	1803	30	1820-80	Washington, Adams	Gallipolis 45631

(Pro Judge has b, m, d & pro rec; Co Health has bur rec; Clk Cts has div & civ ct rec from 1850; Co Rcdr has Ind rec)

*§ Geauga	A3	1806	74	1820-80	Trumbull	Chardon 44024

(Pro Judge has b, m, d & pro rec; Co Health has bur rec; Clk Cts has div & civ ct rec from 1806; Co Rcdr has Ind rec)

* Greene	C2	1803	130	1820-80	Hamilton, Ross	Xenia 45385

(Pro Judge has b rec from 1869 to 1908, pro & m rec 1803; Clk Cts has div, civ ct & crim rec 1802; Co Rcdr has deeds & plat maps 1803; Aud has tax rec 1803)

* Guernsey	C3	1810	42	1820-80	Belmont, Muskingum	Cambridge 43725

(Clk Cts has div rec from 1850, civ ct rec from 1810; Pro Judge has b, m & pro rec; City-Co Health Dept has d rec)

*§ Hamilton	D1	1790	867	1820-80	Original county	Cincinnati 45202

(Pro Judge has m, bur & pro rec; Co Health has d rec; Clk Cts has div & civ ct rec from 1900; Co Rcdr has Ind rec)

*§ Hancock	B2	1820	64	1830-80	Logan	Findlay 45840
* Hardin	B2	1820	33	1820-80	Logan	Kenton 43326
* Harrison	B4	1813	18	1820-80	Jefferson, Tuscarawas	Cadiz 43907

(Clk Cts has div, civ ct rec from 1813; Pro Judge has b rec to 1917, m, pro rec; Health Office has b rec from 1917, d, bur rec)

* Henry	A2	1820	28	1830-80	Shelby	Napoleon 43545

(Pro Judge has b, d rec from 1867 to 1908, m, pro rec from 1847; Clk Cts has div, civ ct rec from 1864; Co Rcdr has Ind rec from 1847)

* Highland	D2	1805	33	1820-80	Ross, Adams, Clermont	Hillsboro 45133

(Pro Judge has b, m & pro rec; Co Health has d rec; Clk Cts has div rec from 1807 & civ ct rec from 1805; Co Rcdr has Ind rec)

Hocking	C3	1818	24	1820-80	Athens, Ross, Fairfield	Logan 43138

(Pro Judge has b, m & pro rec; Co Health has d rec; Clk Cts has div & civ ct rec from 1873; Co Rcdr has Ind rec)

* Holmes	B3	1824	29	1830-80	Coshocton, Wayne, Tuscarawas	Millersburg 44654

(Pro Judge has b, d & pro rec; Clk Cts has div & civ ct rec from 1825; Co Rcdr has Ind rec)

* Huron	B3	1815	54	1820-80	Portage, Cuyahoga	Norwalk 44857

(Pro Judge has b, d rec from 1867 to 1908, m rec from 1815, estate and guardianship rec from 1815, naturalizations from 1859 to 1900; Health Dept has b, d rec from 1908 to present except for city of Bellevue, Ohio, those rec are in its Health Dept; Co Clk has common pleas ct rec from 1815, div and naturalizations to 1859; Co Rcdr has Ind and mortgage rec from 1808, Connecticut Fire Sufferers rec 1792 to 1808, mil discharge rec from 1865; Co Auditor has tax rec from 1820; Co Hist Lib has Infirmary rec from 1848 to 1900, tax rec from 1815 to 1825, Co Commissioners Journals from 1815, Ind partition rec from 1815 to 1920, co militia lists 1864, 1865, indigent soldier bur rec 1880 to 1920)

*§ Jackson	D3	1816	31	1820-80	Scioto, Gallia, Athens, Ross	Jackson 45640

(Pro Judge has b, m & pro rec; Co Health has d & bur rec; Clk Cts has div & civ ct rec; Co Rcdr has Ind rec)

* Jefferson	B4	1797	91	1820-80	Washington	Steubenville 43952

(Pro Judge has m, pro, naturalization rec; Clk Cts has div, civ ct rec from 1797, Co Rcdr has Ind rec from 1797; Board of Health, Steubenville, has b, d rec)

*§ Knox	B3	1808	46	1820-80	Fairfield	Mt. Vernon 43050

(Co Health has b rec from 1908, d & bur rec; Pro Judge has m rec from 1803 & pro rec; Clk Cts has div & civ ct rec from 1810; Co Rcdr has Ind rec)

Name	Map Index	Date Created	Pop. By M 1980	U.S. Cen Reports Available	Parent County or Territory From Which Organized	County Seat
*§ Lake	A3	1840	212	1840-80	Geauga, Cuyahoga	Painesville 44077

(Clk Cts has civ ct rec from 1840)

| * Lawrence | D3 | 1815 | 64 | 1820-80 | Gallia, Scioto | Ironton 45638 |
| * Licking | C3 | 1808 | 121 | 1820-80 | Fairfield | Newark 43055 |

(Pro Judge has b, m & pro rec; Co Health has d rec; Clk Cts has div rec from 1876 & civ ct rec from 1872; Co Rcdr has Ind rec)

| * Logan | B2 | 1818 | 39 | 1820-80 | Champaign | Bellefontaine 43311 |

(Pro Judge has b, m & pro rec; Clk Cts has div & civ ct rec from 1818; Co Rcdr has Ind rec)

| *§ Lorain | A3 | 1822 | 273 | 1830-80 | Huron, Cuyahoga, Medina | Elyria 44035 |

(Pro Judge has b, m & pro rec; Clk Cts has div rec from 1850 & civ ct rec from 1824; Co Rcdr has Ind rec; the Elyria Public Lib & Lorain Co Hist Soc both have some bks of this locality of genealogical interest)

| *§ Lucas | A2 | 1835 | 472 | 1840-80 | Wood, Sandusky, Henry | Toledo 43624 |

(Clk Cts has div, civ ct rec from 1850; Pro Judge has b rec from 1865 to 1908, pro rec; Pro Judge has d rec aft 1935)

| *§ Madison | C2 | 1810 | 33 | 1820-80 | Franklin | London 43140 |

(Co Health has b & d rec; Pro Judge has m & pro rec; Clk Cts has div rec from 1800's & civ ct rec; Co Rcdr has Ind rec)

| * Mahoning | B4 | 1846 | 289 | 1850-80 | Columbiana, Trumbull | Youngstown 44503 |

(Co Health has b & d rec; Pro Judge has m & pro rec; Clk Cts has div & civ ct rec; Co Aud has Ind rec)

| * Marion | B2 | 1820 | 68 | 1830-80 | Delaware | Marion 43302 |

(Pro Judge has b, m & pro rec; Co Health has d rec; Clk Cts has div & civ ct rec; Co Rcdr has Ind rec)

| * Medina | B3 | 1812 | 113 | 1820-80 | Portage | Medina 44256 |

Pro Judge has m, pro rec; Co Health Dept has b, d rec; Clk Cts has div, civ ct rec; Co Rcdr has Ind rec)

| * Meigs | D3 | 1819 | 24 | 1820-80 | Gallia, Athens | Pomeroy 45769 |

Pro Judge has b, m, d rec; Clk Cts has div, civ ct rec from 1819; Co Rcdr has Ind rec)

| Mercer | B1 | 1820 | 38 | 1820-80 | Darke | Celina 45822 |

(Pro Judge has b & d rec from 1867 to 1908, m rec from 1830, pro rec from 1829; Clk Cts has div & civ ct rec from 1824)

| * Miami | C1 | 1807 | 90 | 1820-80 | Montgomery | Troy 45373 |

(Clk Cts has div & civ ct rec from 1807; Pro Judge has m, d & pro rec; Co Health has b rec)

| Monroe | B4 | 1813 | 17 | 1820-80 | Belmont, Wash., Guernsey | Woodsfield 43793 |

(Clk Cts has div, civ ct rec from early 1800's)

| *§ Montgomery | C1 | 1803 | 568 | 1820-80 | Hamilton, Wayne Co., Mich | Dayton 45402 |

(Clk Cts has div & civ ct rec)

| * Morgan | C3 | 1817 | 14 | 1820-80 | Washington, Guernsey, Muskingum | McConnelsville 43756 |
| * Morrow | B2 | 1848 | 26 | 1850-80 | Knox, Marion, Delaware, Richland | Mt. Gilead 43338 |

(Co Health has b rec; Pro Judge has m, d & pro rec; Clk Cts has div & civ ct rec from 1800; Co Rcdr has Ind rec)

| * Muskingum | C3 | 1804 | 83 | 1820-80 | Washington, Fairfield | Zanesville 43701 |

(Pro Judge has b, d rec from 1867, m, pro rec from 1804; Co Rcdr has Ind rec from 1803; Clk of Com Pleas Ct has div, civ ct rec from 1804)

| * Noble | C3 | 1851 | 11 | 1860-80 | Monroe, Washington, Morgan, Guernsey | Caldwell 43724 |

(Clk Cts has div, civ ct rec from 1851)

| Ottawa | A2 | 1840 | 40 | 1840-80 | Erie, Sandusky, Lucas | Port Clinton 43452 |

(Co Health Dept has b, d, bur rec; Pro Judge has m, pro rec; Clk Cts has div, civ ct rec, crim rec, from 1840; naturalizations from 1905 to 1929; Co Rcdr has Ind rec)

| * Paulding | B1 | 1820 | 21 | 1830-80 | Darke | Paulding 45879 |

(Co Health has b & d rec; Pro Judge has m & pro rec; Clk Cts has div rec; Co Judge has civ ct rec; Co Aud has Ind rec)

| * Perry | C3 | 1818 | 31 | 1820-80 | Washington, Fairfield, Muskingum | New Lexington 43764 |

(Pro Ct has b, d rec from 1867, m rec from 1818)

| Pickaway | C2 | 1810 | 44 | 1820-80 | Ross, Fairfield, Franklin | Circleville 43113 |
| § Pike | D2 | 1815 | 23 | 1820-80 | Ross, Scioto, Adams | Waverly 45690 |

(Pro Judge has b, m & pro rec; Clk Cts has div & civ ct rec from 1815; Co Rcdr has Ind rec)

| * Portage | B3 | 1808 | 136 | 1820-80 | Trumbull | Ravenna 44266 |

(Mayor's Office has b, d & bur rec; Pro Judge has m & pro rec; Clk Cts has div & civ ct rec from 1820; Co Treas Ind rec)

| * Preble | C1 | 1808 | 38 | 1820-80 | Montgomery, Butler | Eaton 45320 |

(Pro Judge has b & d rec from 1867, pro rec from 1800 & m rec from 1808; Clk Cts has div & civ ct rec from 1850; Co Rcdr has Ind rec from 1804)

| Putnam | B1 | 1820 | 33 | 1830-80 | Shelby | Ottawa 45875 |

(Clk Cts has div & civ ct rec from 1834)

Name	Map Index	Date Created	Pop. By M 1980	U.S. Cen Reports Available	Parent County or Territory From Which Organized	County Seat
* Richland	B3	1808	131	1820-80	Fairfield	Mansfield 44902

(Clk Cts has div & civ ct rec from 1815)

| *§ Ross | C2 | 1798 | 65 | 1820-80 | Adams, Washington | Chillicothe 45601 |

(Pro Judge has b, m, d & pro rec; Clk Cts has div from late 1800's & civ ct rec; Co Rcdr has Ind rec)

| * Sandusky | A2 | 1820 | 62 | 1820-80 | Huron | Fremont 43420 |

(Co Health has b, d & bur rec; Pro Judge has m & pro rec; Clk Cts has div rec from 1820 & civ ct rec; Co Rcdr has Ind rec)

| *§ Scioto | D2 | 1803 | 85 | 1820-80 | Adams | Portsmouth 45662 |

(Clk Cts has div & civ ct rec from 1817)

| *§ Seneca | B2 | 1820 | 62 | 1830-80 | Huron | Tiffin 44883 |

(Pro Judge has b, m & pro rec; Co Health has d rec; Clk Cts has div & civ ct rec from 1826; Co Rcdr has Ind rec)

| * Shelby | B1 | 1819 | 43 | 1820-80 | Miami | Sidney 45365 |

(Clk Cts has civ ct rec from 1819; Pro Judge has b, m, d, estates, guardianships, trusteeships from 1825; Co Rcdr has Ind rec from 1819)

*§ Stark	B3	1808	378	1820-80	Columbiana	Canton 44702
*§ Summit	B3	1840	524	1840-80	Portage, Medina, Stark	Akron 44308
*§ Trumbull	A4	1800	240	1820-80	Jefferson, Wayne Co. Mich	Warren 44481

(Clk Cts has div, civ ct & citizenship rec from 1800)

| * Tuscarawas | B3 | 1808 | 84 | 1820-80 | Muskingum | New Philadelphia 44663 |

(Pro Judge has b, m, d, pro rec; Clk Cts has div, civ ct rec from 1808, immigration naturalization rec from 1907; Co Rcdr has Ind rec)

| * Union | B2 | 1820 | 30 | 1820-80 | Franklin, Madison, Logan, Delaware | Marysville 43040 |
| * Van Wert | B1 | 1820 | 30 | 1830-80 | Darke | Van Wert 45891 |

(Clk Cts has div & civ ct rec; Pro Judge has m & pro rec; Dis Board of Health has b, d & bur rec)

| * Vinton | C3 | 1850 | 12 | 1850-80 | Gallia, Athens, Ross, Jackson, Hocking | McArthur 45651 |

(Pro Judge has b, d rec from 1867 to 1950, m rec from 1850, pro rec from 1867; Co Health Dept has b rec aft 1950; Clk Cts has div, civ ct, Ind rec from 1850)

| * Warren | C1 | 1803 | 96 | 1820-80 | Hamilton | Lebanon 45036 |

(Pro Judge has b & d rec from 1867, m & pro rec from 1803; Clk Cts has div & civ ct rec; Co Rcdr has Ind rec)

| *§ Washington | C3 | 1788 | 64 | 1820-80 | Original county | Marietta 45750 |

(Pro Judge has b, d rec from 1867, m, pro rec from 1789; Clk Cts has div, civ ct rec from 1795; Co Rcdr has Ind rec)

| * Wayne | B3 | 1808 | 97 | 1820-80 | Columbiana | Wooster 44691 |

(the original Wayne Co was established 15 Aug 1796, this co disappears from Ohio in 1803 when Ohio became a state; it ultimately became Wayne Co Michigan; the present Wayne Co Ohio was erected 13 Feb 1808)

| * Williams | A1 | 1820 | 36 | 1830-80 | Darke | Bryan 43506 |

(Clk Cts has div & civ ct rec)

| * Wood | A2 | 1820 | 107 | 1830-80 | Logan | Bowling Green 43402 |

(Clk Cts has div rec from 1851, also civ ct rec; Pro Judge has b, m & pro rec; Health Dept has d & bur rec)

| * Wyandot | B2 | 1845 | 23 | 1850-80 | Marion, Crawford, Hardin, Hancock | Upper Sandusky 43351 |

(Co Health has b rec from 1845 to 1908; Pro Judge has m rec from 1845, d rec from 1845 to 1908, bur rec from 1845 to 1908 & pro rec from 1845; Clk Cts has div & civ ct rec from 1845; Co Rcdr has Ind rec from 1845)

* - At least one county history has been published about this county.

§ - Inventory of county archives was made by the Historical Records Survey. (see introduction)

OKLAHOMA

CAPITAL, OKLAHOMA CITY - TERRITORY 1890 - STATE 1907 - (46TH)

"Westward" for the red man ended with Oklahoma when it became the last gathering place of the displaced Indian. Here the Indian gave up the nomadic existance of his forefathers and accepted the white man's mode of living.

Little significance attaches to the fact that Spanish and French explorers, in search of the proverbial pot of gold at the end of the rainbow, traversed the Oklahoma section time and again from 1590.

While the territory was still dedicated for the use of the Indians, white settlers came there in such hordes to secure land that eventually they had to be driven away by United States soldiers. The clamor for more land became so vociferous that the government purchased from the Indians about two million acres in the section adjacent to Logan and Oklahoma Counties.

During the influx of new settlers, Illinois, Iowa and Kansas farmers seemed to favor the western and the northwestern sections of the state, while those from Arkansas, Missouri and Texas preferred the southern and the eastern parts of the state.

After Oklahoma became part of the United States with the Louisiana Purchase in 1803, it was included in the Indiana Territory. In 1812 it was combined with the Missouri Territory, and in 1819 with the Arkansas Territory. For several years, most of Oklahoma was included in what was called the Indian Territory, which continued until about 1893 when the section was divided into the Indian Territory and the Oklahoma Territory, the latter being thrown open to white settlements.

In 1890 the territorial government was established with Guthrie as its first capital. Two new counties were formed in 1891, and in 1892 six more were formed. The Cherokee Outlet in the northwest section of the state, next to the panhandle, was opened for white settlers in 1893. A court decision and an act of Congress awarded Greer County to Oklahoma in 1896. Prior to that time it had been claimed by both Oklahoma and Texas. In 1906 Congress passed the enabling act. Oklahoma became the forty-sixth state to enter the Union when it was admitted 16 November 1907. The capital was moved from Guthrie to Oklahoma City in 1910.

The first seven counties of the Oklahoma Territory were designated First, Second, Third, Fourth, Fifth, Sixth and Seventh, thereafter as other counties were added they were named after the letters of the alphabet. Later on by vote of the people they were given their present names. The original seven counties took the following names when this change was accomplished: Logan, Cleveland, Oklahoma, Canadian, Kingfisher, Payne and Beaver.

Birth and death records since 1908 are obtainable at the Department of Health, Division of Vital Statistics, N.E. 10th and Stonewall, Oklahoma City, Oklahoma 73105.

Marriage records may be obtained from the respective County Court Clerks, who also have supervision of all court and land records.

All of Oklahoma except the extreme southwestern tip (Greer County) and No Man's Land and possibly the Unassigned Lands were Indian Territory until 22 April 1889. On this date the Unassigned Lands were thrown open for settlement in 'Run of 89'. Out of this 2,000,000 acres were formed Logan, Oklahoma, Cleveland, Canadian, Kingfisher and Payne Counties by Act of 2 May 1890 when Oklahoma Territory was authorized and at the same time Beaver County (No Man's Land) was made a part of it.

The Iowa, Sac, Fox, and Pottawatomie, Shawnee Reservations were opened to form Lincoln and Pottawatomie Counties in the 'Run of 1891'.

In 1892 the Cheyenne and Arapho Lands were opened and Day, Roger Mills, Beckham, Dewey, Custer, Washita and Blain Counties were organized out of it.

The "Strip" (Cherokee Outlet) opened in the "Run of 1893", to form Woodward, Woods, Grant, Garfield, Kay, Noble and Pawnee Counties. In 1901 the Wichita-Caddo and Comanche, Kiowa and Apache lands were opened and formed the counties of Caddo, Kiowa and Comanche.

Generally this is the way things remained until 1907 when Oklahoma was admitted as the 46th state. When this happened there were some readjustments of county boundaries or new counties were added by carving them out of existing counties. In the case of Day County, it no longer existed after statehood. A part of it and a part of Woodward County formed the new Ellis County. Roger Mills was formed out of a part of Beckham (and perhaps a part of Day). Woodward and Woods were reduced in area to form Harper, Alfalfa and Major. Out of a part of Comanche, Cotton County was formed, also the Jackson County was formed out of Greer. (In 1908 or 1909 Harmon County was also formed out of Greer).

In that part of Oklahoma which has been an Indian Territory, before statehood called the "Indian Nations", only the Osage and Seminole Nations were designated single counties of the same name. The other four Indian Nations were carved into the following counties:

CHEROKEE NATION: Washington, Rogers, Nowata, Craig, Mayes, Cherokee, Sequoyah, Adair, Delaware and part of Ottawa.

CREEK NATION: Creek, Okfuskee, Hughes, McIntosh, Okmulgee, Muskogie, Wagoner and Tulsa.

CHOCTAW NATION: Bryan, Atoka, Coal, Pittsburg, Haskell, Leflore, Latimer, Pushmataha, Choctaw and McCurtain.

CHICKASAW NATION: Grady, McClain, Pontotoc, Stephens, Murray, Johnston, Marshall, Love, Jefferson, and Carter.

In 1908, as previously stated, Harmon County was created out of Greer and Jackson and thus were formed the 77 counties of Oklahoma as they exist today.

Genealogical Archives, Libraries, Societies, and Publications

Arbuckle Historical Society, 201 S. 4th, Davis, OK 73030.

Broken Arrow Oklahoma Genealogical Society, P.O. Box 1244, Broken Arrow, OK 74012.

Canadian County Genealogical Society, P.O. Box 866, El Reno, OK 73036.

Carnegie Public Library, Fifth and B St., Lawton, OK 73501.

Cherokee City-County Public Library, 602 S. Grand Ave., Cherokee OK 73728.

Coal County Historical and Genealogical Society, Box 322 Coalgate, OK 74538.

Cushing Public Library, Box 551, 215 N. Steele, Cushing, OK 74203.

Garfield County Genealogists, Inc., P.O. Box 427, Enid, OK 73701.

Grant County Historical Society, Box 127, Medford, OK 73759.

Kiamichi Genealogical Society, Route 3, Box 53, Wilburton, OK 74578.

Love County Historical Society, P.O. Box 134, Marietta, OK 73448.

Northeast Oklahoma Genealogical Society, P.O. Box 484, Vinita, OK 74301.

Northwest Oklahoma Genealogical Society, 708 Main, Woodward, OK 73801.

Oklahoma City Library, 131 N.W. Third St., Oklahoma City, OK 73102.

Oklahoma Genealogical Society, P.O. Box 314, Oklahoma City, OK 73101.

Oklahoma Historical Society, Historical Bldg., Lincoln Blvd. at N.E. 19 St., Oklahoma City, OK 73105.

Oklahoma State Historical Society, 2100 N. Lincoln, Oklahoma City, OK 73105.

Oklahoma State Library, 109 Capitol, Oklahoma City, OK 73105.

Ottawa County Genealogical Society, Box 1383, Miami, OK 74354.

Pawhuska Oklahoma Genealogical Society, P.O. Box 807, Pawhuska, OK 74056.

Pioneer Genealogical Society, P.O. Box 1839, Ponca City, OK 74601.

Poteau Valley Genealogical Society, Inc., P.O. Box 1031, Poteau, OK 74953.

Public Library, Muskogee, OK 74401.

Public Library, 220 So. Cheyenne, Tulsa, Ok 74103.

Sapulpa Public Library, 27 W. Dewey, Sapulpa, OK 74066.

State D.A.R. Library, Historical Bldg., Oklahoma City, OK 73102.

Tulsa Central Library, 400 Civic Center, Tulsa, OK 74103.

Tulsa Genealogical Society, P.O. Box 585, Tulsa, OK 74101.

University of Oklahoma Library, Norman, OK 73069.

Vinita Public Library, Maurice Haynes Memorial Building, 211 W. Illinois, Vinita, OK 74301.

Chronicles of Oklahoma Historical Society, The, Historical Bldg., Lincoln Blvd. at N.E. 19 St., Oklahoma City, OK 73105.

Green Country Quarterly, published by the Broken Arrow Genealogical Society, P.O. Box 1244, Broken Arrow, OK 74012.

Oklahoma Genealogical Society Quarterly, P.O. Box 314, Oklahoma City, OK 73101.

Tree Tracers, The, Southwest Oklahoma Genealogical Society, Inc., P.O. Box 5044, Lawton, OK 73501.

Printed Census Records and Mortality Schedules

Indexes (Territory): 1860, 1890

Printed Census Records:

1851 Census Drennen Roll of Cherokee and Court Claims Records. Tulsa, Oklahoma: Indian Nations Press.

1860 Census of Indian Lands West of Arkansas. Huntsville, Arkansas: Century Enterprises, 1964

1880 and 1890 Census Canadian District, Cherokee Nation, Indian Territory Oklahoma City: Oklahoma Genealogical Society, 1978.

1885 Anoka County, Choctaw Nation Indian Territory,

Valuable Printed Sources

Atlas

Morris, John W. and Edwin C. McReynolds. *Historical Atlas of Oklahoma.* Norman: University of Oklahoma Press (1976).

Place Names

Morris, John W. *Ghost Towns of Oklahoma.* Norman: University of Oklahoma Press (1978).

Shirk, George H. *Oklahoma Place Names.* Norman: University of Oklahoma Press (1974).

Guide To Genealogical Research

Brown, Jean c. Oklahoma. *Research The Twin Territories.* Sapulpa, Oklahoma: Privately Published (1975).

Histories

Hill, Luther B. *A History of the State of Oklahoma,* 2 Volumes. New York: Lewis Publishing Company, 1909.

Litton, Gaston. *History of Oklahoma at the Golden Anniversary of Statehood.* New York: Lewis Historical Publishing Company (1957).

McReynolds, Edwin C. *Oklahoma: A History of the Sooner State.* Norman: University of Oklahoma Press (1964).

Genealogical Sources (Guides)

Blessing, Patrick Joseph. *Oklahoma: Records and Archives.* University of Tulsa Publications in American Social History (1978).

Gibson, A.M. *A Guide to Regional Manuscript Collections in University of Oklahoma Library.* Norman, Oklahoma: University of Oklahoma Press, 1960.

Oklahoma State Historical Society, Oklahoma City
Stallings, H.C. *Index of Surname and Miscellaneous Files of the Laura Pierce Kendall Manuscript Collection of Genealogical Notes and References.*

Portrait and Biographical Record of Oklahoma. Chicago: Chapman Publishing Company, 1901.

OKLAHOMA COUNTY HISTORIES
(Population figures to nearest thousand - 1980 U. S. Census)

Name	Map Index	Date Created	Pop. By M 1980	U.S. Cen Reports Available	Parent County or Territory From Which Organized	County Seat
* Adair	A2	1907	19		Cherokee Lands	Stilwell 74960
(Clk Cts has m, div, pro & civ ct rec from 1907; Co Asr has Ind rec)						
Alfalfa	D1	1907	7		Woods	Cherokee 73728

Name	Map Index	Date Created	Pop. By M 1980	U.S. Cen Reports Available	Parent County or Territory From Which Organized	County Seat
*§ Atoka	B3	1907	13		Choctaw Lands	Atoka 74525

(Clk Cts has m rec from1897, div, pro & civ ct rec from 1913; Co Clk has Ind rec)

| Beaver | E1 | 1890 | 7 | | Original county (Public Lands) | Beaver 73932 |

(Clk Cts has m, div & civ ct rec from 1890, pro rec from 1891)

| § Beckham | E3 | 1907 | 19 | | Roger Mills | Sayre 73662 |
| Blaine | D2 | 1892 | 13 | | Original county | Watonga 73772 |

(Clk Ct has m, div, pro, civ ct rec from 1892; Co Clk has Ind rec; Dept Vital Statistics, Oklahoma City, has b, d rec)

| Bryan | B4 | 1907 | 30 | | Choctaw Lands | Durant 74701 |

(Clk Ct has m, div, pro & civ ct rec from 1902)

| * Caddo | D3 | 1901 | 31 | | Original Lands | Anadarko 73005 |

(Clk Ct has m, div, pro & civ ct rec from 1902)

(Wichita-Caddo Lands)

| Canadian | C2 | 1889 | 56 | | Original county | El Reno 73036 |

(Clk Ct has m rec from 1890, div, pro & civ ct rec from 1900, voting rec 1909)

| Carter | C4 | 1907 | 44 | | Chickasaw Lands | Ardmore 73401 |
| *§ Cherokee | A2 | 1907 | 30 | | Cherokee Lands | Tahlequah 74464 |

(Clk Ct has m, div & civ ct rec from 1907; Co Clk has Ind rec)

| Choctaw | B4 | 1907 | 17 | | Choctaw Lands | Hugo 74743 |

(Clk Ct has m, div, pro & civ ct rec from 1907; Co Clk has Ind rec)

| *§ Cimarron | G1 | 1907 | 4 | | Beaver | Boise City 73933 |

(Clk Ct has m, div, pro, civ ct rec from 1908; Co Clk has Ind rec from1908; Dept Vital Statistics, Oklahoma City, has b, d rec)

| Cleveland | C3 | 1889 | 133 | | Unassigned Lands | Norman 73069 |

(Co Clk has Ind rec)

| Coal | B3 | 1907 | 6 | | Choctaw Lands | Coalgate 74538 |

(Clk Ct has m, div, pro & civ ct rec from 1907; Co Clk has Ind rec)

| Comanche | D3 | 1901 | 112 | | Kiowa, Comanche, Apache Lands | Lawton 73501 |

(Clk Ct has m, div, pro & civ ct rec from 1901)

| Cotton | D4 | 1912 | 7 | | Comanche | Walters 73572 |

(Clk Cts has m, div, pro & civ ct rec from 1912; Co Clk has Ind rec)

| * Craig | B1 | 1907 | 15 | | Cherokee Lands | Vinita 74301 |

(Clk Ct has m rec from 1902, div, pro & civ ct rec from 1907; Co Clk has Ind rec)

| Creek | B2 | 1907 | 58 | | Creek Lands | Sapulpa 74066 |

(Clk Ct has m rec from 1907, div, pro & civ ct rec)

| * Custer | D2 | 1890-08 | 26 | | Cheyenne, Arapaho Lands | Arapaho 73620 |

(Co Clk has m, div, pro rec from 1899, civ ct rec from 1894, real-estate, deeds, mtgs & releases, army & U.S. service rec from 1892, school cen from 1913 & co reg of electors from 1916; Cem Assn has bur rec for each city)

Day		1892			Cheyenne-Arapaho lands discontinued 1906	
* Delaware	A1	1907	24		Cherokee	Jay 74346
Dewey	D2	1892	6		Original county	Taloga 73667
					(Cheyenne-Arapaho Lands)	

(Clk ct has m rec from 1893, div, civ ct rec from 1894; Co Clk has Ind rec; Dept Vital Statistics, Oklahoma City has b, d rec)

| Ellis | E2 | 1907 | 6 | | Day, Woodward | Arnett 73832 |

(Clk Ct has m rec from 1892, div rec from 1893, pro rec from 1908 & civ ct rec from 1896; Co Clk has Ind rec from 1898)

| * Garfield | C2 | 1893 | 63 | | Originally "O" changed to Garfield 1901 (Cherokee Outlet) | Enid 73701 |

(Clk Dis Ct has m, div, pro & civ ct rec from 1893; Reg Deeds has Ind rec from 1893)

| Garvin | C3 | 1907 | 28 | | Chickasaw Lands | Pauls Valley 73075 |

(Clk Ct has m, div, pro & civ ct rec from 1908)

| Grady | C3 | 1907 | 39 | | Caddo, Comanche | Chickasha 73018 |

(Clk Ct has m, div, civ ct, pro rec from 1907)

| Grant | C1 | 1893 | 7 | | Original county | Medford 73759 |
| | | | | | (Cherokee Outlet) | |

(Clk Ct has m, div, pro & civ ct rec from 1893)

| Greer | E3 | 1890 | 7 | | Org. by Texas, to Okla. by court decision | Mangum 73554 |

(organized as Greer Co, Texas in 1886; an act of Congress on May 4, 1896 declared it Greer Co, Okla; a fire in 1901 destroyed the co rec; Clk Ct has m, div, pro & civ ct rec from 1901; Co Clk has Ind rec)

| Harmon | E3 | 1909 | 5 | | Greer, Jackson | Hollis 73550 |

(Clk Ct has m, div, pro & civ ct rec from1909)

| Harper | E1 | 1907 | 5 | | Indian Lands, Woods, Woodward | Buffalo 73834 |

(Clk Ct has div, pro & civ ct rec)

COUNTY MAP FOR THE STATE OF OKLAHOMA

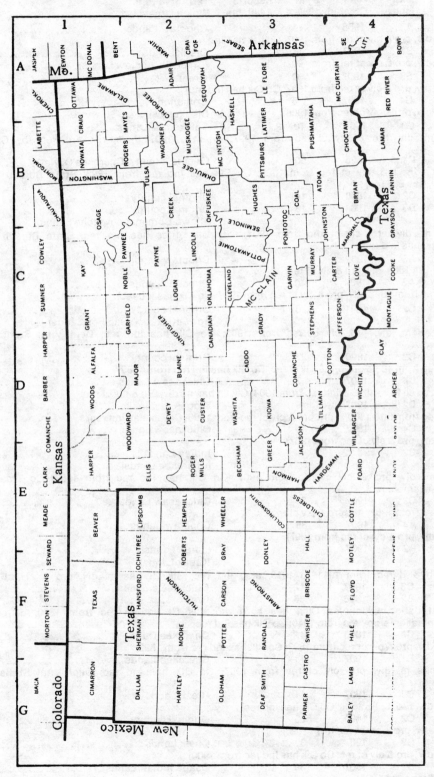

Name	Map Index	Date Created	Pop. By M 1980	U.S. Cen Reports Available	Parent County or Territory From Which Organized	County Seat
§ Haskell	A3	1908	11		Choctaw Lands	Stigler 74462

(Clk Ct has m, div, pro & civ ct rec from 1907; Co Clk has Ind rec)

Hughes	B3	1907	14		Creek Lands	Holdenville 74848

(Clk Ct has m, div, pro & civ ct rec from 1907)   (Creek & Choctaw Lands)

Jackson	E3	1907	30		Greer	Altus 73521

(Clk Ct has m, div, pro & civ ct rec from 1907; Co Clk has Ind rec)

* Jefferson	C4	1907	8		Comanche	Waurika 73573

(Clk Ct has m, div, pro & civ ct rec from 1908)   Chickasaw)

Johnston	C3	1907	10		Chickasaw Lands	Tishomingo 73460

(Clk Ct has m, div, pro & civ ct rec from 1907; prior to 1907 these rec are kept by Clk Dis Ct, Ardmore, Okla)

* Kay	C1	1895	50		Original county (Cherokee Outlet)	Newkirk 74647

(Clk Ct has m, div, pro, civ ct rec from 1893; Co Clk has Ind rec from 1893; State Bureau Vital Statistics, Oklahoma City, has b, d rec)

Kingfisher	C2	1890	14		Original county	Kingfisher 73750
Kiowa	D3	1901	13		Original county	Hobart 73651

(Kiowa-Comanche-Apache Lands)

(Clk Ct has m, div, pro, civ ct rec from 1901; City Clk office has bur rec; State Bureau Vital Statistics, Oklahoma City, has b, d rec)

Latimer	A3	1902	10		Choctaw Lands	Wilburton 74578

(Clk Ct has m from 1906, div, pro & civ ct rec)

Le Flore	A3	1907	40		Choctaw Lands	Poteau 74953

(Clk Ct has m rec from 1898, div, pro & civ ct rec from 1907; Co Clk has Ind rec)

§ Lincoln	C2	1891	26		Original county	Chandler 74834

(Iowa-Kickapoo-Sac-Fox Lands)

(Clk Dis Ct has m, div, pro, civ ct rec from 1900; Co Clk has Ind rec; Dept Vital Statistics, Oklahoma City, has b, d rec)

Logan	C2	1890	27		Original county	Guthrie 73044

(Clk Ct has m rec from 1889, div, pro & civ ct rec; Co Clk has Ind rec from 1889)

Love	C4	1907	7		Chickasaw Lands	Marietta 73448

(Co Clk has b & d rec from 1958 & Ind rec from 1904; Clk Ct has m, div, pro & civ ct rec)

Major	D2	1907	9		Woods	Fairview 73737

(Clk Ct has m rec from late 1800's, div, pro & civ ct rec from 1908; Co Clk has Ind rec)

Marshall	C4	1907	10		Chickasaw Lands	Madill 73446

(Clk Ct has m, div, pro & civ ct rec from 1907)

§ Mayes	B2		32		Indian Lands	Pryor 74361

(Cherokee Lands)

(Clk Ct has m, div, pro & civ ct rec from 1907; Co Clk has Ind rec from 1907; Co Treas has tax rec; Co Asr has assessment rec)

McClain	C3	1907	20		Chickasaw Lands	Purcell 73080

(Clk Ct has m rec from 1907, div, pro & civ ct rec)

* McCurtain	A4	1907	36		Choctaw Lands	Idabel 74745

(Clk Ct has m, div, pro & civ ct rec from 1907)

*§McIntosh	B2	1907	15		Indian Lands	Eufaula 74432

(Creek Lands)

(Co Clk has b & d rec from 1911 to 1918, also Ind rec; Clk Ct has m, div, pro & civ ct rec from 1907)

Murray	C3	1907	12		Chickasaw Lands	Sulphur 73086
*§ Muskogee	B2	1898	66		Creek	Muskogee 74401

(Dept Vital Statistics, Oklahoma City, has b, d rec; Clk Ct has m rec from 1890, div, pro, civ ct rec from 1907, criminal or felony rec from 1940; Co Clk has Ind rec)

* Noble	C2	1893	12		Cherokee Outlet	Perry 73077

(Clk Ct has m, div, pro & civ ct rec from 1893; Co Clk has Ind rec from 1893)

* Nowata	B1	1907	11		Cherokee Lands	Nowata 74048

(Clk Dis Ct has m, div, pro, civ ct rec from 1907; Co Clk has Ind rec; Dept Vital Statistics, Oklahoma City, has b, d rec)

Okfuskee	B2	1907	11		Creek Lands	Okemah 74859

(Clk Ct has m, div, pro & civ ct rec; Co Clk has Ind rec)

Oklahoma	C2	1890	566		Original county	Oklahoma City 73102

(Co Clk has m, div, pro & civ ct rec from 1890)

Okmulgee	B2	1907	39		Creek Lands	Okmulgee 74447

(Clk Ct has m, div, pro & civ ct rec from 1907; Co Clk has Ind rec from 1900)

Osage	B1	1907	39		Osage Indian Lands	Pawhuska 74056

(Co Clk has Ind rec from 1907)

* Ottawa	A1	1907	33		Cherokee Nation	Miami 74354

(Clk Ct has m, div, pro & civ ct rec; Co Clk has Ind rec)

Name	Map Index	Date Created	Pop. By M 1980	U.S. Cen Reports Available	Parent County or Territory From Which Organized	County Seat
Pawnee	C2	1893	14		Cherokee Outlet	Pawnee 74058

(Clk Ct has m rec from 1893, div & civ ct rec from 1894, pro rec from 1911)

* Payne	C2	1890	62		Original county	Stillwater 74074

(Clk Ct has m, div, pro, civ ct rec from 1894; Co Clk has Ind rec; Dept Vital Statistics, Oklahoma City, has b, d rec)

* Payne	C2	1890	62		Original county	Stillwater 74074

(Clk Ct has m, div, pro, civ ct rec from 1894; Co Clk has Ind rec; Dept Vital Statistics, Oklahoma City, has b, d rec)

§ Pittsburg	B3	1907	40		Choctaw Lands	McAlester 74501

(Co Health has b, d & bur rec; Clk Ct has m, div, pro & civ ct rec from 1890; Co Clk has Ind rec)

Pontotoc	C3	1907	33		Chickasaw Lands	Ada 74820

(Clk Ct has m, div, pro & civ ct rec from 1907)

* Pottawatomie	C3	1891	54		Original county Pottawatomie-Shawnee Lands)	Shawnee 74801

(Clk Ct has m, div, pro & civ ct rec; Co Clk has Ind rec from 1892)

§ Pushmataha	B3	1907	12		Choctaw Lands	Antlers 74523
* Rogers Mills	E2	1892	5		Cheyenne-Arapaho Lands	Cheyenne 73628
* Rogers	B2	1907	46		Cherokee Nation (Coo-wee-Scoowee Dist)	Claremore 74017

(Clk Ct has m, div, pro & civ ct rec from 1907)

Seminole	B3	1907	28		Seminole Indian Lands	Wewoka 74884

(Clk Ct has m, div, pro & civ ct rec from 1907)

* Sequoyah	A2	1907	30		Cherokee Indian Lands	Sallisaw 74955

(Clk Ct has m, div, pro & civ ct rec from 1907)

Stephens	C3	1907	43		Comanche County	Duncan 73533
Texas	F1	1907	18		Beaver	Guymon 73942

(Clk Ct has m, div, pro, civ ct rec from 1907; Co Clk has Ind rec; Dept Vital Statistics, Oklahoma City, has b, d rec)

Tillman	D3	1907	12		Comanche Indian Lands	Frederick 73542

(Clk Ct has m, div, pro & civ ct rec from 1907; Co Clk has Ind rec from 1907)

Tulsa	B2	1905	462		Creek Lands	Tulsa 74103

(Clk Ct has m, div, pro & civ ct rec from 1907)

* Wagoner	B2	1908	42		Creek Lands	Wagoner 74467

(Clk Ct has m, div, pro & civ ct rec from 1908)

* Washington	B1	1897	48		Cherokee Lands	Bartlesville 74003

(Clk Ct has m, div, pro & civ ct rec from 1907)

Washita	D3	1900	14		Cheyenne-Arapaho Lands	Cordell 73632

(Clk Ct has m, div, pro, civ ct rec from 1900; Dept Vital Statistics, Oklahoma City, has b, d rec)

* Woods	D1	1893	11		Cherokee Outlet	Alva 73717

(Clk Ct has m, div, pro & civ ct rec)

Woodward	D2	1893	21		Cherokee Outlet	Woodward 73801

* - At least one county history has been published about this county.

§ - Inventory of county archives was made by the Historical Records Survey. (see introduction)

OREGON

CAPITAL, SALEM - TERRITORY 1848 - STATE 1859 - (33RD)

John Astor's Pacific Fur Company originally settled the Oregon country in 1811. They were bought out by the Northwest Company of Montreal in 1813. This company was absorbed in the Hudson Bay Company in 1821. The earliest settlers were Canadian British and American who intermarried with the Indian population.

Simultaneously as the Mormon pioneers were headed for the then uninviting Utah valleys as a refuge from religious persecutions, and the gold seekers were rushing toward California, thousands of sturdy tillers of the soil who already had broken virgin soil in three or four different states were trekking toward the northwest with the same enthusiasm as those participating in the other movements. A steady stream of these prairie schooners headed toward the Oregon country for several years, attracted there by a generous offer. In 1850 the Territorial Legislature of Oregon guaranteed settlers ownership of considerable tracts of land if for four years they would live on and cultivate those farm lands. At the time there were in Oregon slightly more than 13,000 people. The attractiveness of the free land offer is evident in the four-fold increase in population during the following ten-year period. Not only did people from many sections of the United States change their residences to Oregon, but people came there from all parts of the world. Among European countries whose people came there in large numbers are, in order of their numerical contributions to its citizenry, Germany, Sweden, England, Norway, Russia, Finland, Italy, Denmark, Ireland, Austria, Greece, and Czechoslovakia.

Oregon became a territory in 1848 when it also embraced all of the present Washington, Idaho and parts of Montana and Wyoming. It remained so for eleven years and in 1859 became the 33rd state in the Union. At that time it had been shrunk to its present size.

The State Registrar, State Board of Health, 1400 SW 5th Ave., Portland, Oregon 97204, has birth and death records since 1903 and marriage records since 1907. The County Clerks in the respective counties have marriage records since creation of county in some instances. The County Clerk also has custody of the records of wills and the administration of estates, deeds, and matters pertaining to real estate ownership.

Genealogical Archives, Libraries, Societies, and Publications

Albany Public Library, Albany, OR 97321.

Coos Bay Genealogical Forum, P.O. Box 1067, North Bend, OR 97459.

Cottage Grove Genealogical Society, c/o W.A. Woodard Memorial Library, 40 South 16th Street, Cottage Grove, OR 97424.

Curry Genealogical Society, P.O. Box 1336, Gold Beach, OR 97444.

Genealogical Forum of Portland, 1410 S.W. Morrison, Room 812, Portland, OR 97205.

Genealogical Society of Douglas County, Oregon, P.O. Box 579, Roseburg, OR 97470.

Grants Pass Genealogical Society, P.O. Box 1834, Grants Pass, OR 97526.

Klamath County Library, 126 South Third Street, Klamath Falls, OR 97601.

Lebanon City Library, 626 2nd St., Lebanon, OR 97355.

Mid-Columbia Genealogical Society, c/o The Dalles Public Library, 722 Court Street, The Dalles, OR 97058.

Mid-Valley Genealogical Society, 3960 N.W. Elizabeth Pl., Corvallis, OR 97330.

Mt. Hood Genealogical Forum, P.O. Box 208, Oregon City, OR 97045.

Oregon Genealogical Society, P.O. Box 1214, Eugene, OR 97440.

Oregon Historical Society Library, 1230 S.W. Park Ave., Portland, OR 97201.

Oregon State Archives, 1005 Broadway N.E., Salem, OR 97301.

Oregon State Library, State Library Building, Summer and Court Sts., Salem, OR 97310.

Portland Library Association, 801 S.W. Tenth Ave., Portland, OR 97205.

Public Library, 100 West 13th Ave., Eugene, OR 97401.

Public Library, LaGrande, OR 97850.

Rogue Valley Genealogical Society, Inc., 643 Ipson Drive, Medford, OR 97501.

Umatilla County Historical Society, Box 253, Pendleton, OR 97801.

University of Oregon Library, Eugene, OR 97403.

Willamette Valley Genealogical Society, P.O. Box 2083, Salem, OR 97308.

Beaver Briefs, Willamette Valley Genealogical Society, P.O. Box 2083, Salem, OR 97308.

Bulletin of The Genealogical Forum of Portland, Oregon, Inc., Headquarters and Library, Room 812, 1410 S.W. Morrison, Portland, OR 97205.

Curry Roots, Curry Genealogical Society, P.O. Box 1336, Gold Beach, OR 97444.

Oregon Genealogical Society Bulletin, P.O. Box 1214 Eugene, OR 97440.

Printed Census Records and Mortality Schedules

Index (Territory) 1850, 1845, 1854

State Indexes: 1860

Printed Census Records (Counties):

Baker- 1870
Benton- 1850, 1860, 1870; 1854
Champoeg- 1860
Clackamas- 1850, 1860, 1870; 1845, 1856, 1857
Clark- 1850
Clatsop- 1850, 1860, 1870
Columbia- 1860, 1870

Coos- 1860, 1870
Curry- 1860, 1870
Douglas- 1860, 1870, 1880
Grant- 1870, 1880
Jackson- 1860, 1870, 1880
Josephine- 1870, 1880, 1900
Lake- 1880

Lane- 1860, 1870
Lewis- 1850
Linn- 1850, 1860, 1870; 1905
Marion- 1850, 1860, 1870
Multnomah- 1860, 1870
Polk- 1850, 1870; 1856
Tillamook- 1860, 1870

Printed Census Records (Counties) cont.

Umatilla- 1870
Umpqua- 1860, 1870
Union- 1870

Wasco- 1870, 1880
Washington- 1850, 1860, 1870, 1880

Yamhill- 1850, 1860, 1870, 1880
1870 - City of Portland

Mortality Schedules (Printed): 1850, 1860, 1870

Valuable Printed Sources

Atlases, Gazetteers, Maps

Brown, Erma Skyles. *Oregon County Boundary Change Maps 1843-1916.* Lebanon, Oregon: End of Trail Researchers, 1970.

Historical Oregon, Overland Stage Routes, Old Military Roads, Indian Battle Grounds, Old Forts, Old Gold Mines. Corvallis, Oregon: Western Guide Publishers, 1972.

Oregon Genealogical Society, comp. *Oregon, Oregon Country 1819-1890.* n.d.

Place Names

McArthur, Lewis A. *Oregon Geographic Names.* Portland: Binfords and Mort for the Oregon Historical Society, 1965.

Guides To Genealogical Research

Members of the Genealogical Forum of Portland, Oregon. *Genealogical Research in Oregon. National Genealogical Society Quarterly,* Vol. 47, page 115 ff.

Histories

Carey, Charles Henry. *History of Oregon.* Chicago: The Pioneer Historical Publishing Company, 1922. 3 Vols.

Hines, Rev. H. K. *An Illustrated History of the State of Oregon.* Chicago: Lewis Publishing Company, 1893.

Wojcik, Donna M. *The Brazen Overlanders of 1845.* Portland: Privately published, 1976.

Genealogical Sources

Brandt, Patricia and Nancy Gilford. *Oregon Biography Index.* Corvallis: Oregon State University Press, 1976.

D.A.R. Collection*

Genealogical Material in Oregon Donation Land Claims - Abstracted from Applications. Portland: Genealogical Forum of Portland, Oregon, 1957-1975.

Munnick, Harriet D. and Mikell D. Warner. *Catholic Church Records of The Pacific Northwest.* 1839-1898, 2 Vols.

Oregon Historical Society - Index file of Oregon Pioneers to 1859.

Biographies

Bibliography of Pacific Northwest. Portland: Oregon Historical Society.

---

*Microfilm - Genealogical Society of The Church of Jesus Christ of Latter-day Saints, Salt Lake City, Utah.

OREGON COUNTY HISTORIES
(Population figures to nearest thousand - 1980 U. S. Census)

Name	Map Index	Date Created	Pop. By M 1980	U.S. Cen Reports Available	Parent County or Territory From Which Organized	County Seat
* Baker	A2	1862	16	1905	Wasco	Baker 97814
(Co Clk has m, div, pro & civ ct rec from1862)						
*§ Benton	E2	1847	68	1850-80	Polk	Corvallis 97330
(Co Clk has b & d rec from 1907, m, div, pro, civ ct & Ind rec from 1850 & mil dis from 1919)						
Champoeg		1843	237		Orig. Co (name changed to Marion)	
* Clackamas	D1	1843	237	1850-80	Original county	Oregon City 97045
(Co Clk has m, div, pro, civ ct, Ind rec from 1859; State Board of Health has b, d, bur rec; State Archivist has custody of some old county rec)						

Name	Map Index	Date Created	Pop. By M 1980	U.S. Cen Reports Available	Parent County or Territory From Which Organized	County Seat
Clark				1850	Now part of state of Washington	
§ Clatsop	E1	1844	32	1850-80	Twality	Astoria 97103

(Co Clk has m, Ind rec from ca 1860, div, civ ct rec from ca 1875, pro rec from ca 1880; Dept of Vital Statistics has b, d rec; City of Astoria has bur rec)

Columbia	E1	1854	36	1860-80	Washington	St. Helens 97051

(Co Clk has m, div, pro & civ ct rec from 1854)

*§ Coos	F3	1853	64	1860-80	Umpqua, Jackson	Coquille 97423

(Co Clk has m rec from 1864, div, pro, civ ct, Ind rec from 1854; County Health Dept, Portland, has b, d rec)

Crook	C2	1882	13		Wasco	Prineville 97754

(Co Clk has b rec from 1907 to 1941, d rec from 1907 to 1939, m rec from 1883, div, pro rec from 1883, civ ct, Ind rec from 1882)

* Curry	F4	1855	17	1860-80	Coos	Gold Beach 97444

(Co Clk has m, div, pro, civ ct rec; Vital Statistics, Portland, has b, d rec)

Deschutes	D3	1916	62		Crook	Bend 97701

(Co Clk has m, div, pro & civ ct rec from 1916)

Douglas	E3	1852	93	1860-80	Umpqua 1852 & 1862	Roseburg 97470

(Co Clk has m, Ind rec from 1852, div, pro, civ ct rec from 1862; State Dept of Health, Portland, has b, d rec)

Gilliam	C1	1885	2		Wasco	Condon 97823

(Co Clk has m, div, pro, civ ct, Ind rec from 1885; State Vital Statistics, Portland, has b, d rec; local cem districts has bur rec)

Grant	B2	1864	8	1870	Wasco, Umatilla	Canyon City 97820

(Co Clk has b, d rec from 1916 to 1944, m, div, pro, civ ct, Ind rec from 1864)

* Harney	B3	1889	8		Grant	Burns 97720

(Co Clk has m, div, pro & civ ct rec from 1889 & Ind rec from 1870)

§ Hood River	D1	1908	16		Wasco	Hood River 97031

(Co Clk has m, div, pro, civ ct rec from 1908, Ind rec from 1895; Oregon Board of Health, Portland, has b, d rec; cem associations have bur rec)

* Jackson	E4	1852	131	1860-80	Umpqua	Medford 97501

(Co Clk has m rec from 1863, pro rec from 1833, Ind rec from 1853, voter registration from 1952)

* Jefferson	D2	1914	12		Crook	Madras 97741

(Co Clk has m, div, pro, civ ct, Ind rec from 1914; Vital Statistics, Portland, has b, d rec)

§ Josephine	E4	1856	53	1860-80	Jackson	Grants Pass 97526

(Co Clk has m, div, pro, ct & Ind rec from 1857)

*§ Klamath	D4	1882	59		West part of Lake Co.	Klamath Falls 97601
Lake	C4	1874	8	1880	Jackson, Wasco	Lakeview 97630

(Co Clk has m, div, pro, civ ct & Ind rec from 1875)

* Lane	E3	1845	271	1860-80	Linn, Douglas, Benton, Klamath, Deschutes, Lincoln	Eugene 97401

(Co Clk has m rec from 1852, Ind rec from 1855, div, pro, civ ct rec from 1853; State Board of Health, Portland, has b, d rec)

Lewis				1850	Now part of state of Washington	
* Lincoln	E2	1893	35		Benton, Polk	Newport 97365

(Co Clk has m, div, pro, civ ct, Ind rec from 1893; Bureau Vital Statistics, Portland, has b, d rec)

*§ Linn	E2	1847	88	1850-80	Champoeg	Albany 97321

(Co Clk has m rec from 1850, div, pro & civ ct rec from 1854, mil enum of 1905)

* Malheur	A3	1887	27		Baker	Vale 97918

(Co Clk has m, div & civ ct rec from 1887, also pro & Ind rec)

* Marion	E2	1843	204	1850-80	Orig. Co. name changed from Champoeg	Salem 97301

(Co Clk has m rec from 1870, div, pro & civ ct rec from 1851; Co Rcdr has Ind rec)

§ Morrow	C1	1885	8	1870-80	Umatilla	Heppner 97836

(Co Clk has m, pro, div & civ ct rec from 1885)

§ Multnomah	E1	1854	559	1860-80	Washington, Clackamas	Portland 97204

(Co Clk has div, civ ct & Ind rec from 1854)

* Polk	E2	1845	45	1850-80	Yamhill	Dallas 97338

(Co Clk has m, pro & Ind rec; Clks office cannot make researches, will assist otherwise)

* Sherman	C1	1889	2		Wasco	Moro 97039

(Co Clk has m & pro rec from 1889, b rec from 1904 to 1939, d rec from 1905 to 1952 & civ ct rec from 1894)

*§ Tillamook	E1	1853	21	1860-80	Clatsop, Polk, Yamhill	Tillamook 97141

(Co Clk has m rec from 1862, div, pro & civ ct rec from 1860)

Twality		Changed to Washington 1849				
*§ Umatilla	B1	1862	59	1870-80	Wasco	Pendleton 97801

(Co Clk has m, div, pro, civ ct & Ind rec from 1862)

Umpqua		1851		1860	Benton & Linn (absorbed by Douglas 1863)	

COUNTY MAP FOR THE STATE OF OREGON

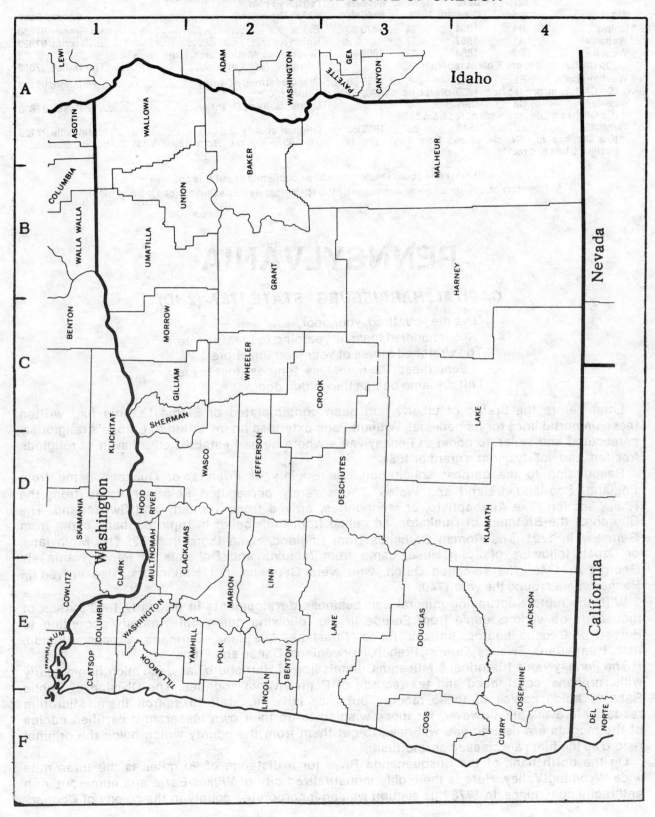

Name	Map Index	Date Created	Pop. By M 1980	U.S. Cen Reports Available	Parent County or Territory From Which Organized	County Seat
* Union	B1	1864	24	1870-80	Baker	La Grande 97850
Wallowa	A1	1887	7		Union	Enterprise 97828
§ Wasco	D2	1854	22	1860-80	Clackamas, Marion, Linn, Lane, Douglas, Jackson	The Dalles 97058
(Co Clk has m, div, pro & civ ct rec from 1854)						
§ Washington	E1	1843	246	1850-80	Orig Co formerly Twality	Hillsboro 97123
(Co Clk has m, pro rec from 1850, div rec from 1890, civ ct rec from 1862)						
Wheeler	C2	1899	2		Crook, Gilliam, Grant	Fossil 97830
(Co Clk has m, div, pro & civ ct rec from 1899)						
* Yamhill	E2	1843	55	1850-80	Original county	McMinnville 97128
(Co Clk has m, div, civ ct rec from 1857, pro rec from 1852, Ind rec from 1854; Vital Statistics Bureau, Portland, has b, d rec)						

* - At least one county history has been published about this county.

§ - Inventory of county archives was made by the Historical Records Survey. (see introduction)

PENNSYLVANIA

CAPITAL, HARRISBURG - STATE 1787 - (2ND)

Give me your tired, your poor,
Your huddled masses yearning to breathe free,
The wretched refuse of your teeming shore.
Send these, the homeless, tempest-tost to me.
I lift my lamp beside the golden door.

Long before the Statue of Liberty had been contemplated or Emma Lazarus had written these immortal lines for its pedestal, William Penn extended an invitation to Europe's religiously persecuted and exiled to come to Pennsylvania where he had established a haven of religious freedom and liberty under a grant of 1681.

Responding to the earnest solicitation, the Society of Friends, or Quakers, came from England, Scotland, Ireland and Wales. The severely persecuted Palatines came from the Rhine section. The Anabaptists, or Mennonites, arrived from Germany and Switzerland. The Church of the Brethren, or Dunkards, so called from their belief in triple baptism, came from Germany in 1721. The Roman Catholics from England came there in 1732. The Moravians, or Czech followers of John Huss, came from Moravia and Bohemia to Pennsylvania via Georgia in 1740. The so-called Dutch, who were Germans, not Hollanders, also arrived in Pennsylvania around the year 1740.

With the rapidly advancing mineral and business developments in the early 1800's, tens of thousands of workers came from Europe in the following numerical strength, according to Bureau of Census figures: Italians, Poles, Russians, Austrians, Germans, Czechs, English, Irish, Hungarians, Swedes, Greeks, French, Norwegians, Danes and Finns.

The Pennsylvania Historical & Museum Commission of Harrisburg has been microfilming early wills, orphans' court, deed and tax records of Pennsylvania counties. The Division of Public Records holds copies of these records but they have no staff to search them. Microfilm readers are available, however, for those wishing to do their own research. If certified copies of the records are desired you will have to get them from the county which holds the original record as the films are classed as unofficial.

On the north bank of the Susquehanna River for a distance of 20 miles is the three mile wide Wyoming Valley. Here is the highly industrialized city of Wilkes-Barre and numerous rich anthracite coal mines. In 1778 this section was an incorporated county in the colony of Connecticut. More than 200 settlers were killed that year in the Pennamite-Yankee War fought between the colonists of Connecticut and Pennsylvania. The dispute was finally settled by Congress in 1782 in what is known as the Decree of Trenton. Researchers looking for material from the Wyoming Valley prior to 1782 must search for it in Hartford, Connecticut.

Marriage licenses were first issued in Pennsylvania about 1883. Birth and death records have been kept since 1892. Until 1906 these records were kept in their respective counties, since then they have been under the direction of the Division of Vital Statistics, P.O. Box 1528, New Castle, PA 16103. The marriage licenses are kept at the offices of the clerks of the respective counties. From 1852 to 1856 birth and death records were also recorded in the counties. The birth records give the names of other children in the family.

Genealogical Archives, Libraries, Societies, and Publications

Adams County Pennsylvania Historical Society, Drawer A, Gettysburg, PA 17325.

Altoona Public Library, "The Pennsylvania Room," 1600 Fifth Ave., Altoona, PA 16602.

American Swedish Historical Foundation, 1900 Pattiso Ave., Philadelphia, PA 19145.

Beaver County Genealogical Society, c/o Historical Research Office, 699 5th St., Beaver, PA 15009.

Berks County Genealogical Society, P.O. Box 777, Reading, PA 19603.

Blair County Genealogical Society, P.O. Box 855, Altoona, PA 16603.

Bloomsburg Public Library, 225 Market St., Bloomsburg, PA 17815.

Bucks County Historical Society, Pine and Ashland St., Doylestown, PA 18901.

Cambria County Historical Society, West High St., Ebensburg, PA 15931.

Carnegie Library, 4400 Forbes Ave., Pittsburgh, PA 15213.

Central Pennsylvania Genealogical Society, P.O. Box 1135, State College, PA 16801.

Centre County Library and Historical Museum, 203 N. Allegheny St., Bellefonte, PA 16823.

Chester County Historical Society, 225 N. High St., West Chester, PA 19015.

Clarion County Historical Society, Courthouse, Clarion, PA 16214.

Clearfield County Historical Society, 104 East Pine St., Clearfield, PA 16830.

Connellsville Area Historical Society, 410 East Cedar Avenue, Connellsville, PA 15425.

Clinton County Historical Society, East Water St., Lock Haven, PA 15370.

Cornerstone, Genealogical Society, P.O. Box 547, Waynesburg, PA 15370.

Coyle Free Library, 102 N. Main St., Chambersburg, PA 17201.

Crawford County Genealogical Society, 848 North Main Street, Meadville, PA 16335.

Cumberland County Historical Society, 21 No. Pitt St., Carlisle, PA 17013.

Delaware County Historical Society, Box 1036 Widener College, Chester, PA 19013.

Easton Area Public Library, 6th & Church Sts., Easton, PA 18042.

Elk County Historical Society, The County Courthouse, Ridgway, PA 15853.

Erie City and County Library, 3 S. Perry Square, Erie PA 10511.

Erie Society for Genealogical Research, The, P.O. Box 1403, Erie, PA 16512.

Fackenthal Library, Franklin and Marshall College, Lancaster, PA 17602.

Ford City Public Library, 1136 4th Ave., Ford City, PA 16226.

Franklin Institute Library, Benjamin Franklin Parkway and 20th Street, Philadelphia, PA 19103.

Free Library of Philadelphia, The, Logan Square, Philadelphia, PA 19141.

Friends Historical Association, Haverford College, Haverford, PA 19041.

Genealogical Society of Pennsylvania, 1300 Locust St., Philadelphia, PA 19107.

Genealogical Society of Southwestern Pennsylvania, P.O. Box 894, Washington, PA 15301.

Green Free Library, 134 Main St., Wellsboro, PA 16901.

Historical and Genealogical Society of Indiana County Pennsylvania, 6th and Wayne, Ave., Indiana, PA 15701.

Historical and Genealogical Society of Somerset County, Inc., Box 533, Somerset, PA 15501.

Historical Society of Berks County, 940 Centre Ave., Reading, PA 19605.

Historical Society of Cocalico Valley, 249 West Main St., Ephrata, PA 17522.

Historical Society of Pennsylvania, 1300 Locust St., Philadelphia, PA 19107.

Historical Society of Perry County Headquarters and Museum, 129 North Second St., Newport, PA 17074.

Historical Society of Schuylkill County, 14 N. Third St., Pottsville, PA 17901.

Historical Society of Western Pennsylvania, 4338 Bieglow Blvd., Pittsburgh, PA 15213.

Historical Society of York County, The, 250 East Market St., York, PA 17403.

Huntingdon County Historical Society, P.O. Box 305, Huntingdon, PA 16652.

James V. Brown Library, The, 19 East 4th St., Williamsport, PA 17701.

Juniata County Historical Society, c/o Mr. David Shellenberger, Star Route, Mifflintown, PA 17059.

Lackawanna County Historical Society, 232 Monroe Ave., Scranton, PA 18510.

Lancaster Mennonite Conference Historical Society, 2215 Millstream Road, Lancaster, PA 17602.

Lebanon County Historical Society, 924 Cumberland St., Lebanon, PA 17042.

Lehigh County Historical Society, The, 414 Walnut St., Allentown, PA 18102.

Ligonier Valley Historical Society, Star Route East, Ligonier, PA 15658.

Lutheran Historical Society Library, The, Gettysburg, PA 17325.

Methodist Historical Center, 326 New St., Philadelphia, PA 19106.

Mifflin County Historical Society, 17 North Main St., Lewistown, PA 17044.

Monroe County Historical Society, 9th and Main St., Stroudsburg, PA 18360.

Mt. Lebanon Public Library, 16 Castle Shannon Blvd., Pittsburgh, PA 15228.

Muncy Historical Society and Museum of History, 131 So. Main St., Muncy, PA 17756.

Myerstown Community Library, Box 242, 199 N. College St., Myerstown, PA 17067.

Northampton County Historical and Genealogical Society, 101 So. 4th St., Easton, PA 18042.

Northumberland County Historical Society, 1150 N. Front St., Sunbury, PA 17801.

Oil City Library, 2 Central Ave., Oil City, PA 16301.

Osterhout Free Public Library, 71 So. Franklin St., Wilkes-Barre, PA 18701.

Pennsylvania Genealogical Society, 1300 Locust St., Philadelphia, PA 19107.

Pennsylvania German Society, The, Box 97, Breinigsville, PA 18031.

Pennsylvania Historical and Museum Commission Division of Archives and Manuscripts, Box 1026, Harrisburg, PA 17108.

Pennsylvania State Library, Walnut and Commonwealth Ave., Education Bldg., Harrisburg, PA 17126.

Pittsburgh History and Landmarks Foundation, The Old Post Office, One Landmarks Square, Pittsburgh, PA 15212.

Presbyterian Historical Society, 425 Lombard St., Philadelphia, PA 19147.

Reading Public Library, Fifth and Franklin Sts., Reading, PA 19607.

Schlow-Memorial Library, The, 100 E. Beaver Ave., State College, PA 16801.

Snyder County Historical Society, 30 East Market St., P.O. Box 276, Middleburg, PA 17842.

South Central Pennsylvania Genealogical Society, P.O. Box 1824, York, PA 17405.

Susquehanna County Historical Society, Montrose, PA 18801.

Tulpehocken Settlement Historical Society, Box 53, Womelsdorf, PA 19567.

University Library, The Pennsylvania State University, University Park, PA 16802.

University of Pennsylvania Library, Central Bldg. 34th St. below Woodland, Philadelphia, PA 19104.

Warren County Historical Society, 210 Fourth Ave., Box 427, Warren, PA 16365.

Washington County Historical Society and Library, LeMoyne House, 49 East Maiden St., Washington, PA 15301.

Western Pennsylvania Genealogical Society, 4338 Bigelow Boulevard, Pittsburgh, PA 15213.

Westmoreland County Historical Society, 221 North Main St., Greensburg, PA 15601.

Whitehall Township Public Library, 3700 Mechanicsville Rd., Whitehall, PA 18052.

Wyoming Historical and Genealogical Society, 69 So. Franklin St., Wilkes-Barre, PA 18701.

York County Historical Society Library, 250 East Market St., York, PA 17403.

Der Reggeboge (The Rainbow), quarterly publication of the Pennsylvania German Society, Box 97, Breinigsville, PA 18031.

Keyhole to the West, The Genealogical Society of Southwestern Pennsylvania, P.O. Box 894, Washington, PA 15301.

Old Westmoreland, published quarterly by the Southwest Pennsylvania Genealogical Services, P.O. Box 253, Laughlintown, PA 15655.

Pennsylvania Genealogical Magazine, The, The Genealogical Society of Pennsylvania, 1300 Locust St., Philadelphia, PA 19107.

Pennsylvania Mennonite Heritage, quarterly publication of the Lancaster Mennonite Conference Historical Society, 2215 Millstream Road, Lancaster, PA 17602.

Pennsylvania Traveler - Post, The, P.O. Box 307, Danboro, PA 18916.

Printed Census Records and Mortality Schedules

State Indexes: 1790, 1800, 1810, 1820, 1830, 1840, 1850, 1880

Printed Census Records (Counties):

Allegheny-1850, 1860, 1870
Berks-1850
Bucks-1850
Centre-1790, 1800
Crawford-1790, 1800, 1810, 1820
Fayette-1810
Greene-1810

Juniata-1790
Lancaster-1850
Luzerne-1850
Mifflin-1790, 1800
Northampton-1840, 1850
Susquehanna-1830
Tioga-1820, 1830, 1840, 1850, 1860, 1870, 1880

Union-1850
Venango-1790, 1800, 1810, 1820
Westmoreland-1810, 1850
Wyoming-1850
York- 1790

1761-Pittsburg, Allegheny County
1850-City of Philadelphia

Mortality Schedule (Printed): 1870

Valuable Printed Sources

Gazetteer

Gordon, Thomas F. *A Gazetteer of the State of Pennsylvania* 1832. New Orleans: Polyanthos (reprinted 1975).

Maps

Morris, Jean S. *Maps Showing the Development of Pennsylvania.* Pittsburgh: (reprinted by permission of the Land Office Bureau, Department of Internal Affairs 1979).

Place Names

Espenshade, A. Howry. *Pennsylvania Place Names.* Baltimore, Maryland: Genealogical Publishing Company (reprinted 1970).

Guides To Genealogical Sources

Bell, Raymond Martin Bell. *Searching in Western Pennsylvania.* Detroit: Detroit Society for Genealogical Research, 1968, reprinted 1977.

Clint, Florence. *Pennsylvania Area Key.* Denver: Area Keys (1970).

Hoenstine, Floyd G. *Guide to Genealogical and Historical Research in Pennsylvania.* Hollidaysburg: Published Privately (1978).

McCay, Betty L. *Sources for Genealogical Searching in Pennsylvania.* Indianapolis: Privately published (1970).

Weikel, Sally A. comp. *Genealogical Research in the Published Pennsylvania Archives.* Harrisburg: State Library of Pennsylvania, 1974.

Histories

Donehoo, George P. *Pennsylvania A History.* Chicago and New York: Lewis Historical Publishing Company (1926).

Shenk, Hiram H. *Encyclopedia of Pennsylvania.* Harrisburg: National Historical Association, 1932.

Genealogical Sources

Descriptive List of the Map Collection in the Pennsylvania State Archives: Catalogue of Maps in the Principal Map Collection.

Historical and Museum Commission - Harriburg
Guide to Published Archives of Pennsylvania: Covering 138 Vols. of Colonial Records and Pennsylvania Archives.

Jordan, Wilfred. *Colonial and Revolutionary Families of Pennsylvania.* Vols. 1-3. New York: Lewis Historical Publishing Company, 1911-1934.

Molitor, Albert J. *Genealogical Sources, Southeastern Pennsylvania.* Abington, Pennsylvania: Old York Road Genealogical Society (1980).

Myers, Albert Cook. *Immigration of the Irish Quakers into Pennsylvania.* Baltimore: Genealogical Publishing Company, 1969.

Pennsylvania Archives and Colonial Records are valuable for early Pennsylvania Research. The Genealogical Publishing Company has reprinted some of the important records. Some of these records include the following:

Muster Rolls of the Pennsylvania Volunteers in the War of 1812-1814.

Names of Foreigners Who Took the Oath of Allegiance to the Province and State of Pennsylvania 1727-1775 with the Foreign Arrivals 1786-1808.

Pennsylvania Marriages Prior to 1790.

Pennsylvania Marriages prior to 1810.

Rupp, I. Daniel. *Thirty Thousand Names of Immigrants.* Reprinted. Baltimore: Genealogical Publishing Company, 1965.

Strassburger, Ralph Beaver. *Pennsylvania German Pioneers.* Reprinted, Baltimore: Genealogical Publishing Company, 1966. 2 Vols.

Bibliographies

Dructor, Robert M. *A Guide to Genealogical Sources at the Pennsylvania State Archives.* Harrisburg: Pennsylvania Historical and Museum Commission (1980).

Salisbury, Ruth ed. *Pennsylvania Newspapers, A Bibliography and Union List.* Pennsylvania Library Association (1969).

Wall, Carol. *Bibliography of Pennsylvania History: A supplement.* Harrisburg: Historical and Museum Commission (1976)

Wilkinson, Norman B. *Bibliography of Pennsylvania History.* Harrisburg: Historical and Museum Commission (1957).

PENNSYLVANIA COUNTY HISTORIES
(Population figures to nearest thousand - 1980 U. S. Census)

Name	Map Index	Date Created	Pop. By M 1980	U.S. Cen Reports Available	Parent County or Territory From Which Organized	County Seat
*§ Adams	C3	1800	68	1800-80	York	Gettysburg 17325

(Clk of Ct has b, d rec from 1852 to 1855, 1893 to 1905, m rec 1852 to 1855, 1856 to present; Prothonotary Office has div, civ ct rec from 1800; Co Rcdr has pro, Ind rec from 1800)

Name	Map Index	Date Created	Pop. By M 1980	U.S. Cen Reports Available	Parent County or Territory From Which Organized	County Seat
* Allegheny	C1	1788	1,448	1790-80	Westmoreland, Washington	Pittsburgh 15219

(Reg Wills has m rec; Prothonotary's Office, 1st floor, City Co Bldg has div rec; Clk Ct has pro & civ ct rec; Rcdr Deeds has Ind rec)

Name	Map Index	Date Created	Pop. By M 1980	U.S. Cen Reports Available	Parent County or Territory From Which Organized	County Seat
* Armstrong	B1	1800	77	1800-80	Allegheny, Lycoming, Westmoreland	Kittanning 16201

(Co Reg & Rcdr has b, d & bur rec from 1893 to 1905, m rec from 1895, pro, deeds, petitions & plan of lots from 1805)

Name	Map Index	Date Created	Pop. By M 1980	U.S. Cen Reports Available	Parent County or Territory From Which Organized	County Seat
*§ Beaver	B1	1800	204	1800-80	Allegheny, Washington	Beaver 15009

(Co Clk has b rec from 1893 to 1907, m rec 1885, d rec 1834, bur rec from 1852 to 1855 & 1893 to 1907, div rec 1805, pro rec 1800 & civ ct rec 1797)

Name	Map Index	Date Created	Pop. By M 1980	U.S. Cen Reports Available	Parent County or Territory From Which Organized	County Seat
* Bedford	C2	1771	47	1790-80	Cumberland	Bedford 15522

(Prothonotary has b rec from 1852 to 1854, from 1893 to 1906, m rec from 1852 to 1854 and from 1885, d rec from 1852 to 1854, from 1893 to 1906, div rec from 1804, pro rec from 1771, civ ct rec from 1771 & warrants from 1771)

Name	Map Index	Date Created	Pop. By M 1980	U.S. Cen Reports Available	Parent County or Territory From Which Organized	County Seat
*§ Berks	B4	1752	313	1790-80	Bucks, Lancaster, Philadelphia	Reading 19601

(Co Clk has b, d rec from 1894 to 1905, m rec from 1885, pro rec from 1752; Prothonotary Office has div, civ ct rec; Rcdr of Deeds has Ind rec)

Name	Map Index	Date Created	Pop. By M 1980	U.S. Cen Reports Available	Parent County or Territory From Which Organized	County Seat
*§ Blair	C2	1846	136	1850-80	Huntingdon, Bedford	Hollidaysburg 16648

(Prothontary has b & d rec from 1893 to 1905, m rec from 1885, div, pro & civ ct rec from 1846)

Name	Map Index	Date Created	Pop. By M 1980	U.S. Cen Reports Available	Parent County or Territory From Which Organized	County Seat
*§ Bradford	A3	1812	63	1820-80	Luzerne, Lycoming	Towanda 18848

(Clk Orph Ct has b & d rec from 1892 to 1906 & m rec; Co Clk has div rec from 1878 & civ ct rec from 1850; Reg Wills has pro rec; Rcdr Deeds has Ind rec; name changed from Ontario 1812)

Name	Map Index	Date Created	Pop. By M 1980	U.S. Cen Reports Available	Parent County or Territory From Which Organized	County Seat
* Bucks	B4	1682	478	1790-80	Original county	Doylestown 18901

(Orph Ct has b & d rec from 1893 to 1906, m rec from 1885; Prothonotary has div rec from 1878, civ ct rec from 1682; Reg Wills has pro rec from 1684)

Name	Map Index	Date Created	Pop. By M 1980	U.S. Cen Reports Available	Parent County or Territory From Which Organized	County Seat
* Butler	B1	1800	148	1800-80	Allegheny	Butler 16001

(Co Clk has b, d rec from 1893 to 1906, m rec from 1885, div rec from 1805, Orphan's Ct has pro rec from 1804; Prothonotary Office has civ ct, Ind rec from 1804; Co Clk has naturalization rec from 1804)

Name	Map Index	Date Created	Pop. By M 1980	U.S. Cen Reports Available	Parent County or Territory From Which Organized	County Seat
*§ Cambria	B2	1804	183	1810-80	Somerset, Bedford, Huntingdon	Ebensburg 15931

(Co Clk has b & d rec from 1893 to 1906, m rec from 1885, div rec from 1866, pro rec from 1819, civ ct rec from 1849 & Ind rec from 1846)

Name	Map Index	Date Created	Pop. By M 1980	U.S. Cen Reports Available	Parent County or Territory From Which Organized	County Seat
* Cameron	A2	1860	7	1870-80	Clinton, Elk, McKean, Potter	Emporium 15834

(Co Clk has b & d rec from 1860 to 1905, m div, pro, civ ct & Ind rec from 1860)

Name	Map Index	Date Created	Pop. By M 1980	U.S. Cen Reports Available	Parent County or Territory From Which Organized	County Seat
* Carbon	B4	1842	53	1850-80	Northampton, Monroe	Jim Thorpe 18229

(Co Clk has b rec from 1894 to 1905, d rec from 1890 to 1904, m rec from 1885, pro rec from 1843; Prothonotary has div rec; Clk Cts has civ ct rec; Rcdr Deeds has Ind rec)

COUNTY MAP FOR THE STATE OF PENNSYLVANIA

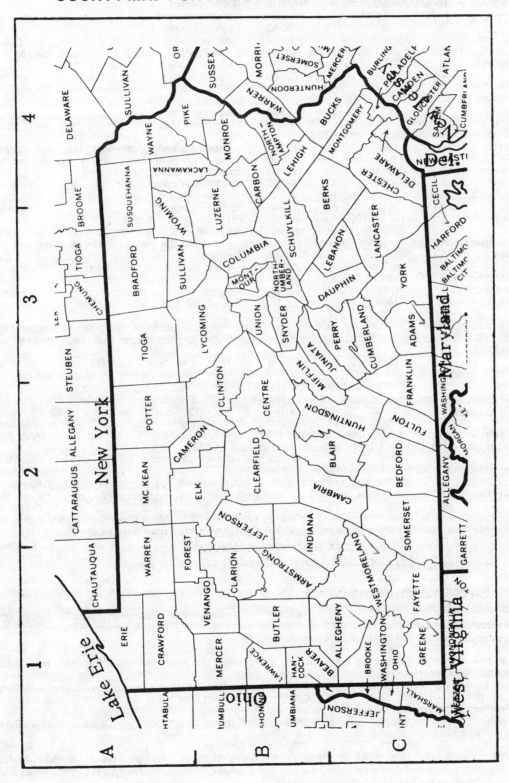

Name	Map Index	Date Created	Pop. By M 1980	U.S. Cen Reports Available	Parent County or Territory From Which Organized	County Seat
* Centre	B2	1800	113	1800-80	Lycoming, Mifflin, Northumberland	Bellefonte 16823

(Co Clk has b, d rec from 1893 to 1905, m rec from 1885; Prothonotary Office has div rec from 1890, civ ct rec from 1800; Reg of Wills has pro rec from 1800; Rcdr of Deeds has Ind rec from 1801)

| * Chester | C4 | 1682 | 316 | 1790-80 | Original county | W. Chester 19380 |

(Co Clk has b rec from 1893 to 1906, d rec from 1893 to 1905, m rec from 1885, div rec from 1893, pro rec from 1714)

| * Clarion | B1 | 1839 | 44 | 1850-80 | Venango, Armstrong | Clarion 16214 |

(Register and Rcdr has b, d rec from 1893 to 1906, m rec from 1885, pro, Ind rec from 1840; Prothonotary Clk has div rec from 1880, civ ct rec from 1874)

| * Clearfield | B2 | 1804 | 83 | 1810-80 | Northumberland, Lycoming | Clearfield 16830 |

(Co Reg & Rcdr has b & d rec from 1893 to 1905 & m rec from 1885; Prothonotary has div rec from 1867, civ ct & naturalization rec from 1863; Co Rcdr has pro rec from 1875; Co Comm has Ind rec)

| * Clinton | B2 | 1839 | 39 | 1840-80 | Lycoming, Centre | Lock Haven 17745 |

(Co Clk has b, m, d, div, pro, civ ct & Ind rec)

| * Columbia | B3 | 1813 | 62 | 1820-80 | Northumberland | Bloomsburg 17815 |

(Co Clk has b & d rec from 1893 to 1905, m rec from 1888, civ ct rec from 1814 & div rec)

| * Crawford | A1 | 1800 | 88 | 1800-80 | Allegheny | Meadville 16335 |

(Co Clk has b, d & bur rec from 1893 to 1905, m rec from 1885, div rec, pro, civ ct & Ind rec from 1800)

| * Cumberland | C3 | 1750 | 179 | 1790-80 | Lancaster | Carlisle 17013 |

(Reg Wills has b & d rec from 1894 to 1905, m rec from 1885 & pro rec from 1750; Prothonotary has div & civ ct rec from 1751; Rcdr Deeds has Ind rec from 1751)

| * Dauphin | C3 | 1785 | 232 | 1790-80 | Lancaster | Harrisburg 17101 |

(Co Clk has b rec from 1893 to 1906, m rec from 1885, d rec from 1852 to 1906 & pro rec from 1785)

| *§ Delaware | C4 | 1789 | 554 | 1790-80 | Chester | Media 19063 |

(Co Clk has b, d rec from 1893 to 1906, m rec from 1885, div rec from 1927, pro rec from 1790, civ ct rec from 1897, Ind rec from 1789, administration rec from 1790, Orphan Ct rec from 1865, delayed b rec from 1875 to 1900)

| * Elk | A2 | 1843 | 38 | 1850-80 | Jefferson, McKean, Clearfield | Ridgway 15853 |

(Clk Orph Ct has b & d rec from 1893 to 1906, m rec from 1895, pro rec from 1847 & Ind rec from 1861)

| *§ Erie | A1 | 1800 | 279 | 1800-80 | Allegheny | Erie 16501 |

(Co Clk has b, d rec from 1893 to 1906, m rec from 1885; Prothonotary has div, civ ct rec from 1823; Reg Wills has pro rec from 1823; Co Rcdr has Ind rec from 1823; Courthouse burned 1823 all rec destroyed)

| *§ Fayette | C1 | 1783 | 159 | 1790-80 | Westmoreland | Uniontown 15401 |

(Clk Orph Ct has b & d rec from 1893 to 1905, m rec from 1885 & pro rec from 1784; Prothontary has div rec also civ ct rec from 1784; Rcdr Deeds has Ind rec from 1784)

| § Forest | A1 | 1848 | 5 | 1860-80 | Jefferson, Venango | Tionesta 16353 |

(Co Reg & Rcdr has b rec from 1893 to 1906, m, div & Ind rec)

| * Franklin | C2 | 1784 | 114 | 1790-80 | Cumberland | Chambersburg 17201 |

(Co Clk has b, d rec from 1894 to 1906, m rec from 1885, div rec from 1884, pro, Ind rec from 1785)

| * Fulton | C2 | 1850 | 13 | 1850-80 | Bedford | McConnellsburg 17233 |

(Clk Orphan Ct has b, d rec from 1895 to 1905, m rec from 1885, Orphan rec from 1850; Prothonotary has div, civ ct rec from 1850; Reg Will has pro rec from 1850; Rcdr Deeds has Ind rec from 1850)

| *§ Greene | C1 | 1796 | 40 | 1800-80 | Washington | Waynesburg 15370 |

(Co Clk has b & d rec from 1893 to 1915, m rec from 1885; Prothonotary has div rec from 1816 & civ ct rec from 1797; Co Reg has pro rec from 1796; Rcdr Deeds has Ind rec from 1796)

| * Huntingdon | C2 | 1787 | 42 | 1790-80 | Bedford | Huntingdon 16652 |

(Co Clk has b rec from 1894 to 1906, m rec from 1885, d rec from 1894 to 1905, div pro & civ ct rec from 1787)

| * Indiana | B2 | 1803 | 92 | 1810-80 | Westmoreland, Lycoming | Indiana 15701 |

(Co Orphan Ct has b, d rec from 1893 to 1906, m rec from 1884, pro rec from 1894, Ind rec from 1803; Prothonotary Ct has div rec from 1879, civ ct rec from 1894)

| * Jefferson | B2 | 1804 | 48 | 1810-80 | Lycoming | Brookville 15825 |

(Co Clk has b rec from 1893 to 1906, m rec from 1885, div rec from 1880, pro rec from 1828, civ ct rec from 1831 & Ind rec from 1828)

| * Juniata | B3 | 1831 | 19 | 1840-80 | Mifflin | Mifflintown 17059 |

(Co Rcdr has b rec from 1893 to 1907; Co Clk has d rec from 1893 to 1907, bur rec & Ind rec from 1831; Prothontary has div & pro rec)

| * Lackawanna | A4 | 1878 | 225 | 1880 | Luzerne | Scranton 18503 |

(Co Comm Office has m, div, pro & civ ct rec from 1878)

| *§ Lancaster | C3 | 1729 | 362 | 1790-80 | Chester | Lancaster 17602 |

(Reg Wills has b rec from 1893 to 1905, m rec from 1885, d, div, pro, civ ct & Ind rec from 1729. Prothontary Ct has rec of Common Pleas, div rec; Clk Orphans Ct has orphan rec; Rcdr Deeds has Ind rec from 1729; Ct Common Pleas has d rec from 1894 to 1927)

Name	Map Index	Date Created	Pop. By M 1980	U.S. Cen Reports Available	Parent County or Territory From Which Organized	County Seat
*§ Lawrence	B1	1850	105	1850-80	Beaver, Mercer	New Castle 16101

(Co Clk has b, d rec from 1893 to 1905, m rec from 1885, civ ct rec from 1849, div rec; Reg of Wills & Rcdr has pro, Ind rec)

| * Lebanon | C3 | 1813 | 109 | 1820-80 | Dauphin, Lancaster | Lebanon 17042 |

(Clk Orph Ct has b rec from 1893 to 1906, m rec from 1885; Prothonotary has div rec from 1888; Reg Wills has pro rec from 1813)

| *§ Lehigh | B4 | 1812 | 272 | 1820-80 | Northampton | Allentown 18105 |

(Clk Orphan Ct has b rec from 1895 to 1905, d rec from 1893 to 1904, m rec from 1885; Prothonotary Ct has div, civ ct rec from 1812; Reg of Wills has pro rec from 1812; Rcdr of Deeds has deed rec from 1812)

| *§ Luzerne | B3 | 1786 | 336 | 1790-80 | Northumberland | Wilkes-Barre 18702 |

(Reg Wills has b, d & bur rec from 1893 to 1906, m rec from 1885, pro rec from 1786; Prothonotary has div & civ ct rec; Rcdr Deeds has Ind rec)

| * Lycoming | B3 | 1795 | 119 | 1800-80 | Northumberland | Williamsport 17701 |

(Co Clk has b rec from 1893 to 1905, d rec from 1893 to 1898, m rec from 1885; pro rec from 1850, Ind rec from 1795; Prothonotary Ct has div, civ ct rec from 1795; The James V. Brown Library, 19 E. Fourth St., Williamsport, PA is the major source for Lycoming Co genealogical information)

| * McKean | A2 | 1804 | 51 | 1810-80 | Lycoming | Smethport 16749 |
| * Mercer | B1 | 1800 | 128 | 1800-80 | Allegheny | Mercer 16137 |

(Co Clk has b & d rec from 1893 to 1905, m rec from 1885, pro rec from 1800; Prothonotary Officer has div & civ ct rec)

| * Mifflin | B2 | 1789 | 47 | 1790-80 | Cumberland, Northumberland | Lewistown 17044 |

(Co Clk has b rec from 1893 to 1905, m rec from 1885, pro & Ind rec from 1789; Prothonotary has pro & civ ct rec)

| * Monroe | B4 | 1836 | 67 | 1840-80 | Pike, Northampton | Stroudsburg 18360 |

(Co Clk has m rec from 1885, div rec from 1844, pro & civ ct rec from 1836)

| * Montgomery | C4 | 1784 | 640 | 1790-80 | Philadelphia | Norristown 19404 |

(Clk Orph Ct has b & d rec from 1893 to 1915, m rec from 1885; Rcdr Deeds has bur & Ind rec from 1784; Prothonotary has div & civ ct rec from 1784; Reg Wills has pro rec from 1784; Rcdr Deeds has Ind rec from 1784)

| * Montour | B3 | 1850 | 17 | 1850-80 | Columbia | Danville 17821 |

(Prothonotary & Clk Cts has b & d rec from 1893 to 1905, m rec from 1885, div, civ ct rec from 1850)

| * Northampton | B4 | 1752 | 225 | 1790-80 | Bucks | Easton 18042 |

(Clk Orphan Ct has b rec from 1893 to 1936, m rec from 1885; Prothonotary Office has div, civ ct rec; Reg Wills has pro rec; Rcdr Deeds has Ind rec)

| * Northumber-
land | B3 | 1772 | 100 | 1790-80 | Lancaster, Berks, Cumberland | Sunbury 17801 |

(Reg and Rcdr has b, d rec from 1893 to 1905, m rec from 1885, pro, Ind rec from 1772; Prothonotary Office has div, civ ct rec)

Ontario (see Bradford)

| * Perry | C3 | 1820 | 36 | 1820-80 | Cumberland | New Bloomfield 17068 |

(Co Clk has b rec from 1893 to 1918, m rec from 1870 & Ind rec from 1820)

| Philadelphia | C4 | 1682 | 1,681 | 1790-80 | Original county | Philadelphia 19107 |

(Clk Orph Ct has m rec; Prothonotary has div & civ ct rec from 1874; Reg Wills has pro rec; Dept Rec has Ind rec)

| Pike | A4 | 1814 | 13 | 1820-80 | Wayne | Milford 18337 |

(Clk Comm has b & d rec from 1885 to 1905, m rec from 1885, div, pro, civ ct & Ind rec from 1814)

| * Potter | A2 | 1804 | 18 | 1810-80 | Lycoming | Coudersport 16915 |

(Prothonotary has b, d & bur rec from 1893 to 1905, m rec from 1885, div rec from 1885)

| * Schuylkill | B3 | 1811 | 159 | 1820-80 | Berks, Northampton | Pottsville 17901 |

(Clk Comm has b & d rec from 1893 to 1905, m rec from 1885, div rec from 1878, pro, civ ct & Ind rec from 1811)

| * Snyder | B3 | 1855 | 34 | 1860-80 | Union | Middleburg 17842 |

(Clk Cts has b, d & bur rec from 1893 to 1905, m from 1885, div, civ ct rec from 1855; Co Reg & Rcdr has pro & Ind rec)

| * Somerset | C2 | 1795 | 81 | 1800-80 | Bedford | Somerset 15501 |

(Reg Wills has b, d rec from 1893 to 1906, m rec from 1885, pro rec from 1795; Prothonotary Office has div, immigration rec; Clk of Cts has civ ct rec; Rcdr of Deeds has Ind, army discharge rec)

| * Sullivan | A3 | 1847 | 6 | 1850-80 | Lycoming | Laporte 18626 |

(Clk Orph Ct has b & d rec from 1893 to 1905, m rec from 1885; Prothonotary has div rec from 1847, civ ct rec from 1847; Reg Wills has pro rec 1847)

| * Susquehanna | A4 | 1810 | 38 | 1820-80 | Luzerne | Montrose 18801 |

(Co Clk has div & civ ct rec from 1812)

| * Tioga | A3 | 1804 | 41 | 1810-80 | Lycoming | Wellsboro 16901 |

(Co Clk has b & d rec from 1893 to 1906, m rec from 1885, pro & Ind rec from 1806; Prothonotary has div & civ ct rec)

| * Union | B3 | 1813 | 33 | 1820-80 | Northumberland | Lewisburg 17837 |

(Co Clk has b & d rec from 1893 to 1905, m rec from 1885, div & civ ct rec from 1813)

Name	Map Index	Date Created	Pop. By M 1980	U.S. Cen. Reports Available	Parent County or Territory From Which Organized	County Seat
* Venango	B1	1800	64	1800-80	Allegheny, Lycoming	Franklin 16323

(Clk Cts & Rcdr Deeds has b & d rec from 1893 to 1905, m rec from 1885, pro rec from 1806 & Ind rec from 1800)

*§ Warren	A1	1800	48	1800-80	Allegheny, Lycoming	Warren 16365

(Reg and Rcdr has b, d rec from 1893 to 1906, m rec from 1885, pro, Ind rec from 1819; Prothonotary Office has div, civ ct rec)

*§ Washington	C1	1781	217	1790-80	Westmoreland	Washington 15301

(Chief Clk has b & d rec from 1893 to 1906, m rec from 1885, bur, civ ct & Ind rec from 1850, div & pro rec from 1843)

§ Wayne	A4	1796	34	1800-80	Northampton	Honesdale 18431

(Prothonotary has b & d rec from 1893 to 1906, m rec from 1885, div rec from 1900 & civ ct rec from 1798; Co Reg & Rcdr has pro & Ind rec from 1798)

*§ Westmoreland	C1	1773	392	1790-80	Bedford	Greensburg 15601

(Co Clk has b rec from 1893 to 1905, m rec from 1893 & pro rec from 1800; Prothonotary has div rec; Clk Cts has civ ct rec; Reg Deeds has Ind rec)

* Wyoming	A3	1842	25	1850-80	Luzerne	Tunkhannock 18657

(Clk Cts has b, d rec from 1893 to 1905, m rec from 1885, div, pro, civ ct, Ind rec from 1842.)

* York	C3	1749	312	1790-80	Lancaster	York 17401

(Co Clk has b, d rec from 1893 to 1907, m rec from 1885, div, civ ct, Ind rec from 1749)

* - At least one county history has been published about this county.

§ - Inventory of county archives was made by the Historical Records Survey. (see introduction)

RHODE ISLAND

CAPITAL, PROVIDENCE - STATE 1790 - (13TH)

Giovanni de Verrazano, a 44-year-old Florentine navigator, in 1524 visited Block Island and the site of the present Newport on Aquidneck Island, both part of today's Rhode Island. He was then a privateer in the French service.

In 1636 Roger Williams, a 30-year-old Englishman, and some of his followers established the first Rhode Island settlement at Providence. His religious pronouncements, too advanced for the clergy to accept, led to his banishment from Massachusetts. An uncompromising advocate of freedom, he held that difference of opinion is not a bar to friendship. All land he settled or tilled was purchased from the Indians.

The banishment of Williams from Massachusetts was soon followed by others including Anne Marbury Hutchinson, John Clarke, and William Coddington. They established a colony at Portsmouth in 1638. Later Clarke and Coddington settled Newport, after their attempt to establish a government based on the Jewish nation had failed. A fourth colony was established at Warwick in 1642. In 1663 by Royal charter of Charles II, the unified Colony of Rhode Island and Providence Plantations was created.

Many Quakers found a haven in Rhode Island in the early days. The large majority of the people who came into Rhode Island were former residents of Massachusetts.

New England researchers have an abundance of material at their command. The state and the cities have large genealogical libraries or genealogical sections in their public libraries. The Rhode Island Historical Society has a wonderful assortment of books at 52 Power St., Providence, Rhode Island 02906. The Society has one of the largest genealogical collections in New England, probably the third largest. Many people from various sections, searching for the progenitors among Rhode Island families, have attained splendid results in the library of the Rhode Island Historical Society.

Among Rhode Island's large numbers of industrial workers are members of almost every nationality. Those with the largest numbers are the Italians, English, Irish, Polish, Russians, Swedes, Germans, and Austrians.

All vital statistics are in the custody of the town or city clerks. Birth and death records since 1853 are in the office of the Registrar of Vital Statistics, Providence, RI 02903.

Rhode Island Towns
Organized Before 1800

BRISTOL COUNTY -- Barrington, 1717; Bristol, 1681; Warren, 1746-7.

KENT COUNTY -- Coventry, 1741; East Greenwich, 1677; Warwick, 1642-3; West Greenwich, 1741.

NEWPORT COUNTY -- Jamestown, 1678; Little Compton, 1746-7; Middletown, 1743; Newport, 1639; New Shoreham, 1672; Portsmouth, 1638; Tiverton, 1746-7.

PROVIDENCE COUNTY -- Cranston, 1754; Cumberland, 1746-7; Foster, 1781; Glocester, 1730-1; Johnston, 1759; North Providence, Providence, 1636; Scituate, 1730-1; Smithfield, 1730-1.

WASHINGTON COUNTY -- Charlestown, 1738; Exeter, 1742-3; Hopkinton, 1757; North Kingston, 1641; Richmond, 1747; South Kingston, 1657-8; Westerly, 1669.

Note: The State of Rhode Island does not have the county system of keeping records. For information write to the individual cities.

Genealogical Archives, Libraries, Societies, and Publications

East Greenwich Free Library, 82 Pierce St., East Greenwich, RI 02818.

John Hay Library, Brown University, Providence, RI 02912.

Newport Historical Society, 82 Touro St., Newport, RI 02840.

Providence Public Library, 229 Washington St., Providence, RI 02903.

Rhode Island Genealogical Society, Box 207, Mapleville, RI 02839.

Rhode Island State Archives, 314 State House, Providence, RI 02900.

Rhode Island State Historical Society, 52 Power St., Providence, RI 02906.

Rhode Island State Library, 82 Smith, State House, Providence, RI 02903.

Westerley Public Library, Box 356, Broad St., Westerly, RI 02891.

Rhode Island Genealogical Register, Beaman Road, Princeton, MA 01517.

R.I. Roots, publication of the Rhode Island Genealogical Society, Box 207, Mapleville, RI 02839.

Printed Census Records and Mortality Schedules

State Indexes: 1790, 1800, 1810, 1820, 1830, 1840, 1850; 1885

Other Printed Census Records:

Macgunnigle, Bruce C., comp. *Rhode Island Freemen 1747-1755, A Census of Registered voters.* Baltimore, Maryland: Genealogical Publishing Company, 1977.

Bartlett, John R. comp. indexed by E. E. Brownell. *1774 Census of the Inhabitants of the Colony of Rhode Island and Providence Plantations* Baltimore, Maryland: Genealogical Publishing Company, 1969 (reprinted)

Valuable Printed Sources

Atlases

Beers, Daniel G. *Atlas of the State of Rhode Island and Providence Plantations.* Philadelphia, 1870.

Rhode Island. *Rhode Island Boundaries, 1636-1936.* By John Hutchins Cady. Providence, 1936.

Wright, Marion I. *Rhode Island Atlas.* Providence: Rhode Island Publications Society, 1980.

Place Names

Gannett, Henry. *A Geographic Dictionary of Connecticut and Rhode Island.* 2 Vols. in 1. 1894. Reprint. Baltimore: Genealogical Publishing Co., 1978.

Pease, John C. and John M. Niles. *A Gazetteer of the States of Connecticut and Rhode Island.* Hartford: William S. Marsh, 1819.

Guides To Genealogical Research

Farnham, Charles W. *Rhode Island Colonial Records.* Salt Lake City: Genealogical Society, 1969.

Rubincam, Milton, ed. *Genealogical Research: Methods and Sources.* Washington, D.C.: American Society of Genealogists, 1980.

Histories

Arnold, Samuel G. *History of the State of Rhode Island and Providence Plantations.* 2 Vols. 1859-60. Reprint, 1970.

McLoughlin, William G. *Rhode Island: A Bicentennial History.* New York: W. W. Norton and Co., 1978.

Monahan, Clifford P. *Rhode Island, A Students' Guide to Localized History.* New York: Teachers College Press, Columbia University, 1974.

Genealogical Sources

Arnold, James N. *Vital Record of Rhode Island, 1636-1850.* 21 Vols. Providence: Narragansett Historical Publishing co., 1891-1911.

Austin, John Osborne. *The Genealogical Dictionary of Rhode Island.* 1887. Reprint. Baltimore: Genealogical Publishing Co., 1978.

Bates Collection consists of abstracts of deeds, wills, probates, and town and other records. It is available at the Rhode Island Historical Society.*

Beaman, Alder G. *Rhode Island Vital Records, New Series.* Princeton, Mass.: The compiler, 1976-.

Daughters of the American Revolution genealogical collections for Rhode Island.*

MacGunnigle, Bruce C. *Rhode Island Freemen, 1747-1755, A Census of Registered Voters.* Baltimore: Genealogical Publishing Co., 1977.

Providence, R.I. *The Early Records of the Town of Providence.* 21 Vols. Providence, 1892-1915.

Rhode Island. *Records of the Colony of Rhode Island and Providence Plantations in New England.* Edited by John R. Bartlett. 10 Vols. Providence, 1856-65.

Smith, Joseph J. *Civil and Military List of Rhode Island, 1647-1850.* 2 Vols. Providence, 1900-1901.
_____.

*On microfilm at the Genealogical Society Library of The Church of Jesus Christ of Latter-day Saints, Salt Lake City, Utah.

RHODE ISLAND COUNTY HISTORIES
(Population figures to nearest thousand - 1980 U.S. Census)

Name	Map Index	Date Created	Pop. By M 1980	U.S. Cen Reports Available	Parent County or Territory From Which Organized	County Seat
* Bristol	B3	1747	47	1790-80	..........Bristol 02809, Warren 02885 & Barrington 02806	

(There is no Co Clk in Bristol Co, the twns of Bristol, Warren & Barrington have b, m, d, bur & pro rec; Providence, R.I. has div rec; 5th Dis Ct Warren has civ ct rec) (four twns in Bristol Co)

Name	Map Index	Date Created	Pop. By M 1980	U.S. Cen Reports Available	Parent County or Territory From Which Organized	County Seat
* Kent	B2	1750	154	1790-80	Providence ....E. Greenwich 02818	

(Twn Clk, E. Greenwich has b, m, d & Ind rec from 1677, bur & pro rec; contact City or Twn Clk in each of 5 twns in Kent Co to get rec)

Name	Map Index	Date Created	Pop. By M 1980	U.S. Cen Reports Available	Parent County or Territory From Which Organized	County Seat
* Newport	C3	1703	81	1790-80	Original county ....Newport 02840	

(Newport County was incorporated June 22, 1703 as Rhode Island County; June 16, 1729, incorporated as Newport County and included then Newport, Portsmouth, Jamestown and New Shoreham. 1746-47 Eastern boundary adjusted under decree of the King of England incorporating Tiverton and Little Compton into County. June 16, 1743, Town of Middletown was taken from the Town of Newport and became part of County. On September 17, 1963, New Shoreham joined Washington County. Land area is 104.9 sq. mil. 5 Towns and 1 city in Newport County. City of Newport settled in 1639. Line between Newport and Portsmouth established September 14, 1640. Incorporated as a city June 1, 1784. City Charter repealed March 27, 1787. City incorporated the second time May 6, 1853 and the Charter accepted May 20, 1853. A new City Charter was drawn up under the provisions of the Home Rule Amendment to the State Constitution providing for Council-Manager form of government approved by the voters November 4, 1952 and enacted November 1, 1953. City Clk Office, Newport has b rec from 1670, m rec from 1693, d rec from 1697; local cem offices have bur rec; Fam & Sup Cts have div rec; pro ct has pro rec from 1784; Dist Ct has civ ct rec; Rcdr Deeds has Ind rec from 1780; Newport Hist Soc, 82 Touro St., Newport, RI has early ch rec, Ind rec, pro rec, and cen reports of City of Newport 1820, 1840, 1880)

Name	Map Index	Date Created	Pop. By M 1980	U.S. Cen Reports Available	Parent County or Territory From Which Organized	County Seat
* Providence	A2	1703	57	1790-80	Original county	Providence 02903

(City Clk of Providence reports as follows: Family Ct has div rec; Pro Judge has pro rec; Municipal Ct has civ ct rec; Rcdr Deeds has Ind rec) (22 twns in Providence Co)

| * Washington | C2 | 1729 | 93 | 1790-80 | Newport (For. Naragannset) .... | So. Kingston 02879 |

(Town Clk, South Kingston, Town Hall, Wakefield, RI 02879 has b, m, d, pro, Ind rec from 1723, bur rec from 1926; Family Ct has div rec; Clk Sup Ct has civ ct rec. South Kingstown, County of Washington, State of Rhode Island incorporated 1723. Twenty towns in Washington Co)

* - At least one county history has been published about this county.

COUNTY MAP FOR THE STATE OF RHODE ISLAND

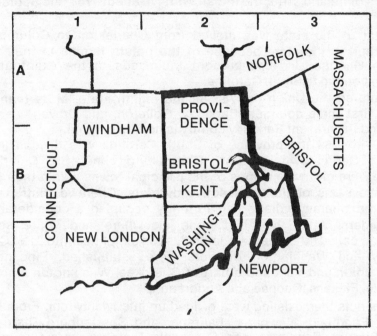

SOUTH CAROLINA

CAPITAL, COLUMBIA - STATE 1788 - (8TH)

Several attempts by the Spaniards and the French to establish settlements in what is now South Carolina between 1526 and 1664 failed.

The first colony was established on the Ashley River in the southeastern part of the state in 1671. The settlers were a group of English people direct from the Old World, and another group, the members of which had been living on the Barbados Island, the south-easternmost island in the West Indies group. They called their settlement Charles Town. A few months later some Dutch families, who had left New York after the English had taken over there established themselves along the Ashley River. They were later joined by many families direct from Holland.

In 1675 a group of Quakers came into the territory. In 1680 about 45 families of Huguenots also established homes there. Quite a colony of dissenters from the Episcopal Church came in 1683 from Somersetshire to the present site of Charleston. In that year came also an Irish colony that settled along the Ashley River. In 1684 ten families of Scotch Presbyterians established themselves at Port Royal. In 1713 the southern Carolina region was separated from North Carolina and was recognized as a royal colony in 1723.

Immigrants continued to come in large streams until by 1730 there were gathered "on the banks of the Santee, the Edisto, and the Combahee Rivers some of the best elements of the European nations. The Huguenot, the Scottish Presbyterian, the English dissenter, the loyalist and High Churchmand, the Irish adventurer, and the Dutch mechanic composed the powerful material out of which soon grew the beauty and renown of the Palmetto State." (Ridpath's History of the United States.)

From 1732 until 1736 a number of families from England, Scotland, Ireland, Wales, Switzerland, and Germany came into the central section of South Carolina. Some of the first settlements in the so-called "Up Country," the western half of the state, were created from 1745 to 1760 by immigrants from the Rhine section of Germany, the northern American colonies, and the Ulster section of Ireland. After the Indian Wars, in about 1761, the Scotch Irish immigrants came.

In 1790 the capital of the state was moved from Charleston to Columbia. From 1845 to 1850 many Irish settled in the state because of the potato famine in their own country. The political struggle in Germany in 1848 brought thousands of the expatriates to the United States, many of them coming to South Carolina.

South Carolina entered the Union in 1788 as the eighth state. More than a hundred years before, in 1683, the first three counties, Berkeley, Colleton, and Craven, were established. All were discontinued and the present Berkeley county is not the original.

By an act ratified in 1769 the province of South Carolina was divided into seven judicial districts: Charleston, Georgetown, Beaufort, Orangeburg, Ninety-Six, Camden and Cheraws. The first six of these were given the names of the principal towns within their borders and those towns were made the seats of their respective districts. Cheraws District derived its name from the fact that the Cheraw Indians had formerly occupied a considerable portion of the land within its borders. After they had gone elsewhere and white settlers moved in, the section was at first called "the Cheraws' lands", soon simplified into "The Cheraws".

In 1795 Pinckney and Washington Districts were established. Pinckney embraced the present counties of Union and York and a part of Cherokee. Washington embraced the present counties of Greenville, Pickens, Oconee and Anderson.

In 1798 the nine districts then existing were divided up into twenty-four. From Ninety-Six District, (in 1795) Abbeville, Edgefield, Newberry, Laurens, and Spartanburg Districts were formed. From Washington District, Pendleton and Greenville Districts were formed. From Pinckney District, Union and York Districts were formed. From Camden District, Chester, Lancaster, Fairfield, Kershaw and Sumter Districts were formed. From Cheraws District, Chesterfield, Darlington and Marlborough Districts were formed. Ninety-Six, Washington, Pinckney, Camden and Cheraw were discarded as district names. Georgetown District was divided into Georgetown and Marion Districts; Charleston into Charleston and Colleton; and Orangeburg into Orangeburg and Barnwell.

In 1799 Richland District was formed from Kershaw. In 1802 Horry and Willamsburg Districts were formed from parts of Georgetown. In 1804 Lexington was formed from Orangeburg. In 1826 Pendleton District was formed into Pickens and Anderson Districts and the name Pendleton was discarded as a district name. In 1855 Clarendon District was formed from a part of Sumter.

South Carolina Districts were formed as follows: Abbeville, 1795; Anderson, 1826; Barnwell, 1798; Beaufort, 1769; Berkeley, 1683; Camden, 1769; Cartaret, 1683; Charleston, 1769; Cheraws, 1769; Chester, 1798; Chesterfield, 1798; Clarendon, 1785; Colleton, 1798; Darlington, 1798; Dorchester, 1785; Edgefield, 1795; Fairfield, 1798; Georgetown, 1769; Granville, 1700; Greenville, 1798; Horry, 1802; Kershaw, 1798; Lancaster, 1798; Laurens, 1798; Lexington, 1804; Marion, 1798; Marlboro, 1798; Newberry, 1795; Ninety-Six, 1795; Orangeburg, 1769; Pendleton, 1798; Pickens, 1826; Pinckney, 1795; Richland, 1799; Spartanburg, 1798; Sumter, 1798; Union, 1798; Washington, 1795; Williamsburg, 1802; and York, 1798.

Birth and death records from 1915 to the present are in the office of the South Carolina Department of Health and Environmental Control, Columbia, South Carolina 29201. Marriage records from 1 July 1950 to the present are also at that office. Marriages from 1 July 1911 to the present are at the office of the Probate Judge, County Court House in the respective county seats.

Birth records kept at the city of Charleston are available since 1877 at the City Health Department. They also have available death records from 1821 to the present.

South Carolina's Department of Health also houses divorce records for the state since July, 1962. Records of divorce occurring from April, 1949 to the present may be obtained from the Clerk of Court's office in the county where the petition was filed.

Disclosure of information from South Carolina's Department of Health is restricted to authorized parties only. In the case of birth records, issuance is restricted to the registrant, parent or guardian, or their respective legal representatives. Death records are issued only to surviving relatives of the deceased or their respective legal representatives. Copies of marriage and divorce records are issued to the parties married or divorced, their adult children, or their legal representatives.

The Judge of Probates office in Charleston has records of wills and estates back to 1692. They are recorded in chronological volumes, with indexes.

Records of deeds and other estate matters are available from 1719 in Charleston. Those prior to 1719 are in the office of the Historical Commission of South Carolina in Columbia.

What few marriage bonds are available from those early days have been printed in the *South Carolina Historical and Genealogical Magazine.* Between 1778 and 1911 no marriage bonds or licenses were required in South Carolina, and only for brief intervals were such records kept.

Records of land grants earlier than 1695 are in the office of the Historical Commission of South Carolina in Columbia. The Secretary of State in Columbia has records of land grants from 1695 to the present time, and a plat to land grants from 1688, warrants for entry and surveys made and certified before the corresponding final grants or patents were issued. The plat records and grant records in the Secretary of State's office are in separate books. There are sets of index books for plats and index books for grants.

The Clerk of the Court in the various counties has charge of wills, deeds, and land grants. Dates will vary with the different counties.

War service records are in the custody of Adjutant General in Columbia, South Carolina.

Genealogical Archives, Libraries, Societies, and Publications

Abbeville-Greenwood Regional Library, N. Main St., Greenwood, SC 29646.

Calhoun County Museum, Archives Library, 303 Butler Street, St. Matthews, SC 29135.

Columbia Chapter, South Carolina Genealogical Society, P.O. Box 11353, Columbia, SC 29211.

Free Library, 404 King St., Charleston, SC 29407.

Greenville County Library, 300 College St., Greenville, SC 29601.

Huguenot Society of South Carolina, 94 Church St., Charleston, SC 29401.

Pee Dee Chapter, South Carolina Genealogical Society, P.O. Box 236, Latta, SC 29565.

Public Library, Rock Hill, SC 29730.

Public Library, So. Pine St., Spartanburg, SC 29302.

Richland County Public Library, 1400 Sumter St., Columbia, SC 29201.

Rock Hill Public Library, Box 32, 325 S. Oakland Ave., Rock Hill, SC 29730.

South Carolina Archives Dept., 1430 Senate St., Columbia, SC 29201.

South Carolina Historical Society, 100 Meeting St., Charleston, SC 29401.

South Carolina State Library, 1500 Senate St., Columbia, SC 29201.

University South Carolina Society, The, Columbia, SC 29208.

South Carolina Historical Magazine, The, South Carolina Historical Society, 1500 Old Town Road, Charleston, SC 29407.

South Carolina Magazine of Ancestral Research, Box 21766, Columbia, SC 29221.

Printed Census Records and Mortality Schedules

State Indexes: 1790, 1800, 1810, 1820, 1830, 1840, 1850

Printed Census Records (Counties):

Abbeville-1800, 1810, 1830, 1850
Anderson-1800, 1830
Barnwell-1830
Beaufort-1830
Berkeley-1830
Chester-1820
Chesterfield-1800, 1820, 1830
Colleton-1820, 1830
Darlington-1800, 1830
Edgefield-1790, 1800, 1830
Fairfield.1810, 1820, 1830

Georgetown-1810, 1830
Greenville-1800, 1820, 1830
Horry-1810, 1830, 1850
Kershaw-1800, 1810, 1820, 1830
Lancaster-1810, 1820, 1830
Laurens-1810, 1830; 1829
Lexington-1800, 1830
Marion-1830
Marlboro-1830
Newberry-1800, 1830, 1860

Oconee-1800
Orangeburg-1830, 1850
Pendleton-1800, 1810, 1820
Pickens-1800, 1830, 1850
Richland-1830
Spartanburg-1830, 1860
Sumter-1830, 1850
Union-1800, 1830, 1850
Williamsburg-1830, 1850
York-1830

Valuable Printed Sources

Place Names

Neuffer, Claude Henry, ed. *Names in South Carllina* 27 Vols. Columbia: University of South Carolina, Department of English (1954 - published in November)

Guides To Genealogical Research

Black, James M. "The Counties and Districts of South Carolina". *Genealogical Journal,* Vol. 5, No. 3, pages 100-113. Salt Lake City: Utah Genealogical Association, 1976.

Frazier, Evelyn McDaniel. *Hunting Your Ancestors in South Carolina.* Jacksonville: Florentine Press, 1977.

Holcomb, Brent H. *A Brief Guide to South Carolina Genealogical Research and Records.* Columbia: Author, 1979.

Lee, Charles E. *South Carolina Archives of the South Carolina Public Records: Comstock Lode for Genealogists and Historians.* Salt Lake City: World Conference on Records. Genealogical Seminar Paper I-33, 1969.

McCay, Bettly L. comp. *State Outline for South Carolina Sources.* Indianapolis: Privately published (1970).

Wakefield, Roberta P. *Genealogical Source Material in South Carolina.* Washington D.C.: Special Publication of the National Genealogical Society (1962). Published in National Genealogical Society Quarterly Vol. XL No. 3 pages 81-89.

Histories

McCrady, Edward. *The History of South Carolina.* New York: Paladin Press (1969)

Ramsey, David. *History of South Carolina.* Newberry, South Carolina: W. J. Duffie (1858)

Genealogical Sources

Andrea, Leonardo, comp. *Index to Genealogical Folders in the Leonardo Andrea Collection.* Columbia, South Carolina.*

Burns, Annie Walker. *South Carolina Pension Abstracts of the Revolutionary War; War of 1812 and Indian Wars.* Washington D.C.: privately published.

Chandler, Marion C. and Earl W. Wade. *The South Carolina Archives: A Temporary Summary Guide.* Columbia: South Carolina Department of Archives and History, 1976.

Holcomb, Brent H. *South Carolina Marriages 1688-1799.* Baltimore: Genealogical Publishing Company, 1980.

Houston, Martha Lou. *Indexes to the County Wills of South Carolina.* Baltimore: Genealogical Publishing Company, 1964.

McCall, James. *Revolutionary Claims Files in South Carolina* between August 20, 1783 and August 31, 1786.

Moore, Carolina T. and Agatha Aimar. *Abstracts of the Wills of the State of South Carolina 1670-1740.* Columbia: R.L. Bryan Company, 1960.

Revill, Janie. *A Compilation of the Original Lists of Protestant Immigrants to South Carolina 1763-1773.* Baltimore: Genealogical Publishing Company, 1974 (reprint of 1939 edition).

Salley, A. S. Jr. *Marriage Notices in the South Carolina Gazette and its Successors 1732-1801.* Baltimore: Genealogical Publishing Company, 1965.

Salley, A. S. Jr. *Stub Entries to Indents Issued in Payment of Claims Against South Carolina Growing Out of the Revolutions.* Columbia: State Company. 12 Vols.

Stephenson, Jean. *Scotch-Irish Migration to South Carolina, 1772.* Strasburg, Virginia: Shenandoah Publishing House, 1971.

South Carolina Department of Archives and History, Columbia, South Carolina.

South Caroliniana Library - University of South Carolina, Columbia, South Carolina.

The South Carolina Historical Society: County Wills and tombstone inscriptions.
"Each (tombstone) entry is on an alphabetized card that was transcribed by local chapter members of the South Carolina Genealogical Society from the volumes compiled by the W.P.A. in the late 1930's . . . There are over 30 counties and several hundred graveyards represented.

Bibliographies and Guides To Resources

Cote, Richard. *South Carolina Family and Local History: A Bibliography.* Easley, South Carolina: Southern Historical Press, 1981.

Moore, John Hammond. *Research Material in South Carolina, A Guide.* Columbia: University of South Carolina Press (1967).

SOUTH CAROLINA COUNTY HISTORIES
(Population figures to nearest thousand - 1980 U.S. Census)

Name	Map Index	Date Created	Pop. By M 1980	U.S. Cen Reports Available	Parent County or Territory From Which Organized	County Seat
§ Abbeville	B1	1785	23	1800-80	District 96	Abbeville 29620
(Clk Ct has Ind rec from 1873, div & civ ct rec)						
§ Aiken	B2	1871	105	1880	Edgefield, Orangeburg, Barnwell, Lexington	Aiken 29801
(Co Health has b & d rec; Pro Judge has m rec from 1911 & pro rec from 1875; Clk Ct has div, civ ct & Ind rec)						
§ Allendale	C2	1919	11		Barnwell, Hampton	Allendale 29810
*§ Anderson	A1	1826	131	1830-80	Pendleton District	Anderson 29621
(Co Health Dept has b, d, bur rec; Pro Judge has m, pro rec; Clk Ct has div rec from 1949, Ind rec from 1788, civ ct rec)						
Bamberg	B3	1897	18		Barnwell	Bamberg 29003
(Clk Ct has div & civ ct rec; Pro Judge has pro & m rec; Co Health has b & d rec)						
Barnwell	B2	1798	20	1800-80	Orangeburg Dist	Barnwell 29812
(Co Clk has b & d rec from 1915, div rec from 1950, also civ ct rec; Pro Judge has m & pro rec)						
* Beaufort	C3	1769	64	1790-80	Original Dist	Beaufort 29902
(Co Clk has b & d rec from 1915)						
Berkeley	B3	1882	86		Charleston	Moncks Corner 29461
(Clk Ct has div & civ ct rec; Pro Judge has m & pro rec; Co Health Dept has b, d & bur rec)						
Berkeley		1683		(Discontinued)	Original Co not present Berkeley Co	
* Calhoun	B3	1908	12		Lexington, Orangeburg	St. Matthews 29135
(Co Health has b & d rec from 1915; Pro Judge has m rec from 1911, pro rec from 1908; Clk Ct has civ ct rec from 1908, div rec from 1949; Hist Commission has Ind, Bible, cem & gen col from 1735)						
Camden Dist.		1769			1 Original Dist (discontinued)	
Carteret Dist		1683			Name changed to Granville 1700	
* Charleston	C3	1769	269	1800-80	Original District	Charleston 29401
(Co Health has b & d rec; Pro Judge has m, pro & civ ct rec; Clk Ct has div rec; Co Reg has Ind rec)						
Cheraws Dist.		1769			Original Dist (discontinued)	
§ Cherokee	A2	1897	41		Union, York, Spartanburg	Gaffney 29340
(Co Health has b & d rec; Pro Judge has m & pro rec; Clk Ct has div, civ ct & Ind rec)						

Name	Map Index	Date Created	Pop. By M 1980	U.S. Cen Reports Available	Parent County or Territory From Which Organized	County Seat
Chester	A2	1785	30	1800-80	Craven, Camden Dist	Chester 29706

(Pro Judge has pro rec from 1789, m rec from 1911; Clk Ct has deeds from 1785, div & civ ct rec)

| * Chesterfield | A3 | 1798 | 38 | 1800-80 | Cheraws District | Chesterfield 29709 |

(Clk Ct has b, d, bur, div, pro & civ ct rec; Pro Judge has m rec)

| Claremont | | | | 1800-10 | | |
| Clarendon | B3 | 1855 | 27 | 1800-80 | Sumter District | Manning 29102 |

(Cen schedules missing for 1820, 1830, 1840 & 1850) (Co Health has b, d & bur rec from 1915; Pro Judge has m rec from 1911 & pro rec from 1856; Clk Ct has div rec from 1947, civ ct & Ind rec from 1856)

| Colleton | C3 | 1798 | 31 | 1800-80 | Charleston District | Walterboro 29488 |

(Pro Judge has m & pro rec; Clk Ct has div rec, also civ ct & Ind rec from 1864)

Colleton, Old		1683			Discontinued	
Craven, Old		1683			Discontinued	
Darlington	A3	1798	63	1800-80	Cheraws District	Darlington 29532

(Co Clk has m rec from 1912, div rec from 1950, civ ct rec, Ind rec from 1806)

| § Dillon | A4 | 1910 | 31 | | Marion | Dillon 29536 |

(Clk Cts has civ ct rec, deeds, real estate & mtgs from 1910)

| Dorchester | B3 | 1897 | 57 | | Berkeley, Colleton | St. George 29477 |

(Co Clk has b rec from 1915)

| * Edgefield | B2 | 1785 | 18 | 1800-80 | District 96 | Edgefield 29824 |

(Co Health has b, d & bur rec; Pro Judge has m & pro rec; Clk Ct has div, civ ct & Ind rec from 1839, judgements & crim rec from 1839 & plats rec from 1907; small portion of Aiken Co added to Edgefield 1966)

| * Fairfield | A2 | 1798 | 21 | 1800-80 | Camden District | Winnsboro 29180 |

(Co Health has b & d rec; Pro Judge has m & pro rec; Clk Ct has div rec from 1947, civ ct & Ind rec from 1795)

| *§ Florence | B3 | 1888 | 110 | | Marion, Darlington, Clarendon, Williamsburg | Florence 29501 |

(Co Health has b & d rec; Pro Judge has m & pro rec; Clk Ct has div, civ ct & Ind rec)

| Georgetown | B4 | 1769 | 42 | 1790-80 | Original District | Georgetown 29440 |

(Co Health Dept has b, d rec; Pro Judge has m rec from 1911, pro rec; Clk Ct has div rec from 1949, civ ct rec, Ind rec from 1866)

| Granvill Dist. (see Carteret) | | | | | | |
| * Greenville | A1 | 1798 | 286 | 1800-80 | Washington Dist. | Greenville 29601 |

(Clk Ct has b & d rec from 1915, m rec from 1911, div & pro rec)

| Greenwood | B2 | 1897 | 57 | | Abbeville, Edgefield | Greenwood 29646 |

(Co Health has b & d rec; Pro Judge has m & pro rec; Clk Ct has div rec from 1949, civ ct & Ind rec from 1897)

| Hampton | C2 | 1878 | 17 | 1880 | Beaufort | Hampton 29924 |

(Co Health Dept has b, d rec; Clk Ct has civ ct rec from 1878; Pro Judge has m rec from 1911)

| Horry | B4 | 1802 | 101 | 1810-80 | Georgetown Dist. | Conway 29526 |

(Co Health has b & d rec; Pro Judge has m & pro rec; Clk Ct has div, civ ct & Ind rec)

| *§ Jasper | C2 | 1912 | 14 | | Beaufort, Hampton | Ridgeland 29936 |

(Co Health has b & d rec; Pro Judge has m & pro rec; Clk Ct has div, civ ct & Ind rec)

| * Kershaw | A3 | 1798 | 39 | 1800-80 | Camden District | Camden 29020 |

(Clk Ct has div rec from 1949, civ ct & Ind rec from 1791)

| * Lancaster | A3 | 1798 | 53 | 1800-80 | Camden District | Lancaster 29720 |

(Co Health has b & d rec; Pro Judge has m & pro rec; Clk Ct has div rec from 1958, civ ct rec from 1800 & Ind rec from 1762)

| Laurens | A2 | 1785 | 51 | 1800-80 | District 96 | Laurens 29360 |

(Co Health has b & d rec; Pro Judge has m & pro rec; Clk Ct has div rec also civ ct rec from 1900 & Ind rec from 1790)

| *§ Lee | B3 | 1902 | 19 | | Darlington, Sumter, Kershaw | Bishopville 29010 |

(Co Health has b rec from 1915, d rec from 1902; Pro Judge has m & pro rec from 1902; Clk Ct has div rec from 1949, civ ct & Ind rec from 1902)

| Lexington | B2 | 1804 | 136 | 1800-80 | Orangeburg Dist. | Lexington 29072 |

(Co Health has b & d rec; Pro Judge has m & pro rec; Clk Ct has div rec from 1949, Ind rec from 1839 & civ ct rec)

| Liberty | | | | 1800 | | |
| * Marion | A4 | 1798 | 34 | 1800-80 | Georgetown Dist. | Marion 29571 |

(Co Health has b, d & bur rec; Pro Judge has m & pro rec; Clk Ct has div rec from 1948, civ ct & Ind rec from 1800)

| * Marlboro | A3 | 1798 | 32 | 1800-80 | Cheraws District | Bennettsville 29512 |

(Co Clk has b, d, bur, div & civ ct rec; Pro Judge has m & pro rec)

COUNTY MAP FOR THE STATE OF SOUTH CAROLINA

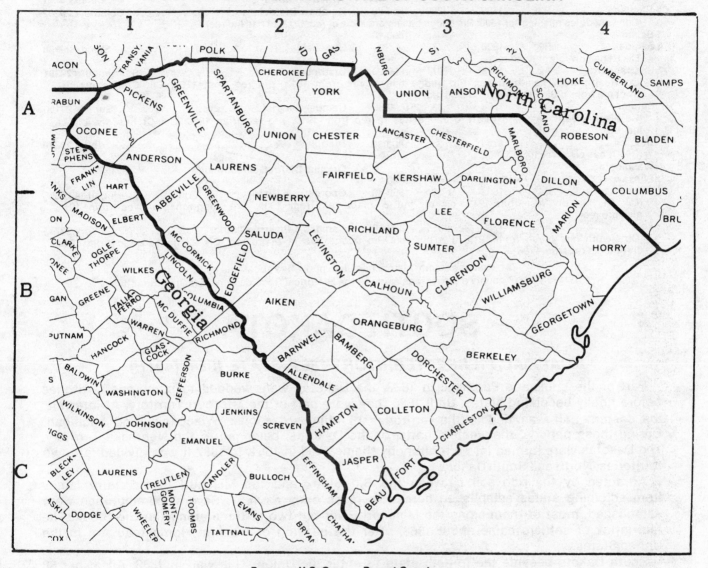

Name	Map Index	Date Created	Pop. By M 1980	U.S. Cen Reports Available	Parent County or Territory From Which Organized	County Seat
§ McCormick	B1	1916	8		Greenwood, Abbeville	McCormick 29835
				(Co Health Dept has b rec from 1912, d rec from 1916; Pro Judge has m, pro rec from 1916; Clk Ct has div rec from 1948, civ, Ind rec from 1916; Co Treas has tax rec from 1916)		
* Newberry	B2	1785	31	1800-80	District 96	Newberry 29108
				(Clk Ct has b & d rec from 1915, m rec from 1911, div rec from 1949, pro, civ ct & Ind rec from 1776)		
Ninety-Six Dist.		1769			Original Dist (discontinued)	
§ Oconee	A1	1868	49	1870-80	Pickens	Wahalla 29691
				(Co Health Dept has b, d rec from 1915; Pro Judge has m rec from 1911, pro rec from 1868; Clk Ct has div rec from 1949, civ ct, Ind rec from 1868)		
Orange				1800		
* Orangeburg	B3	1769	77	1800-80	Original District	Orangeburg 29115
				(Clk Ct has div rec from 1949, civ ct & Ind rec from 1865)		
Pendleton		1798		1800-20	Washington Dist (discontinued 1826) See Pickens & Anderson	
*§ Pickens	A1	1825	79	1830-80	Pendleton District	Pickens 29671
				(Clk Ct has b & d rec from 1915, div rec from 1949, civ ct rec from 1868; Pro Judge has m & pro rec)		
Pickney District		1793			Original District (discontinued)	

Name	Map Index	Date Created	Pop. By M 1980	U.S. Cen Reports Available	Parent County or Territory From Which Oranized	County Seat
*§ Richland	B3	1799	260	1810-80	Kershaw District	Columbia 29202
(Cen schedules missing for 1800; Pro Judge has m, pro & civ ct rec; Co Aud has Ind rec)						
Salem				1800-10		
§ Saluda	B2	1896	16		Edgefield	Saluda 29138
(Clk Ct has div, civ ct & Ind rec)						
* Spartanburg	A2	1785	197	1800-80	District 96	Spartanburg 29301
(Co Health Dept has b, d rec; Pro Judge has m rec from 1911, pro rec from 1700; Clk Ct has div rec, civ ct rec from 1785; RMC office has Ind rec)						
* Sumter	B3	1798	88	1800-80	Camden District	Sumter 29150
(Co Health Dept has b, d rec; Pro Judge has m rec from 1910, pro rec from 1900; Clk Ct has div, civ ct, Ind rec)						
* Union	A2	1798	31	1800-80	District 96	Union 29379
(Clk Ct has civ ct rec from 1785)						
Washington		1793			Original District (discontinued)	
Winyaw				1800		
* Williamsburg	B4	1802	38	1800-80	Georgetown District	Kingstree 29556
(Clk Ct has div rec from 1948, civ ct, Ind & plats rec from 1806; Pro Judge has m rec from 1911, also pro rec)						
York	A2	1785	105	1800-80	Camden & Pickney District	York 29745
(Co Health has b rec from 1915, d & bur rec; Pro Judge has m & pro rec; Clk Ct has div rec from 1942, civ ct & Ind rec from 1786)						

* - At least one county history has been published about this county.
§ - Inventory of county archives was made by the Historical Records Survey. (see introduction)

SOUTH DAKOTA

CAPITAL, PIERRE - TERRITORY 1861 - STATE 1889 - (40TH)

Part of the Louisiana Purchase in 1803, the Dakotas were wedded to numerous territories before finally becoming states. Until 1820 they were part of the Missouri Territory. At intervals, the eastern half was tied to the territories of Minnesota, Iowa, Wisconsin, and Michigan. During those periods, the western parts, or the Dakotas, belonged to the Nebraska Territory. The Dakotas were formed into a territory by themselves in 1861. In 1887 it was divided into two territories, North and South Dakota.

Attracted by the rich soil between the Big Sioux and the Missouri Rivers, farm family from adjoining states established homes there as early as 1857. Several communities were established, most of them along the Missouri River but two or three along the Big Sioux. The real influx of settlers came about 1863, after the passing of the first Homestead Act in the United States.

South Dakota became the fortieth state to enter the Union. This was in 1889. All of her 68 counties, with the exception of three were already organized at that time.

The predominating nationality in South Dakota is Norwegian. Other nationalities represented among its citizenry, in the order of their predominance, are the German, Russian, Swedish, Danish, Czechoslovakian, English, Austrian, Irish, Finnish, Polish, Greek and Italian.

Records of births, marriages, divorces and deaths from 1905 to the present are on file at the Department of Health, Vital Records Program, Joe Foss Office Building, Pierre, South Dakota 57501.

Wills and probate matters are in the offices of the Clerk of the Court in each county. County Treasurers have marriage records since 1905.

All land records are at the office of the Register of Deeds in the county of filing. Land grants are at the office of the Commissioner of School and Public Lands, Pierre, South Dakota 57501.

Taxpayers lists are at the offices of the County Treasurer of each county.

The war service records are under the direction of the Register of Deeds of each county. The Sexton of each cemetery is supervisor of the records of the respective cemeteries.

Genealogical Archives, Libraries, Societies, and Publications

Aberdeen Area Genealogical Society, c/o Alexander Mitchell Library, 519 S. Kline Street, Aberdeen, SD 57401.

Alexander Mitchell Public Library, 21 Sixth Ave., S.E., Aberdeen, SD 57401.

Brookings Area Genealogical Society, 524 Fourth Street, Brookings, SD 57006.

Pierre-Ft. Pierre Genealogical Society, 301 E. Missouri, Pierre, SD 57501.

Rapid City Society For Genealogical Research, P.O. Box 1495, Rapid City, SD 57701.

Sioux Valley Genealogical Society, P.O. Box 655, Sioux Falls, SD 57101.

State Historical Society Library, Memorial Bldg., Pierre, SD 57501.

Tri-State Genealogical Society, 719 11th Avenue, Belle Fourche, SD 57717.

University of South Dakota Library, Vermillion, SD 57069.

Black Hills Nuggets, Rapid City Society for Genealogical Research, P.O. Box 1495, Rapid City, SD 57701.

Printed Census Records and Mortality Schedules

Indexes (Territory): 1860, 1870, 1880, 1885

1836 Iowa Territorial Census includes South Dakota

Hudson, Alice M. compiler and publisher. *An 1893 Census of Landowners Minnehaha County, South Dakota.* Edgemont, South Dakota, 1978.

Valuable Printed Sources

Guides To Genealogical Research

Historic Sites Committee. *Clay County Place Names.* Vermillion, South Dakota: Clay County Historical Society (1976)

Histories

Kingsbury, George W. *History of Dakota Territory.* Chicago: S. J. Clarke (1915).

Robinson, Doane. *History of South Dakota.* B. F. Bowen and Company, (1904)

Schell, Herbert S. *History of South Dakota.* Lincoln, Nebraska: University of Nebraska Press (1968)

SOUTH DAKOTA COUNTY HISTORIES
(Population figures to nearest thousand - 1980 U. S. Census)

Name	Map Index	Date Created	Pop. By M 1980	U.S. Cen Reports Available	Parent County or Territory From Which Organized	County Seat
Aurora	B4	1879	4	1880	Brule	Plankinton 57368
(Clk Cts has b & d rec from 1905, m rec from 1883, bur, div, pro & civ ct rec from 1879)						
* Beadle	B4	1879	19	1880	Spink, Clark	Huron 57350
(Clk Cts has b & d rec from 1905, m rec from 1880, bur rec from 1941, div rec from 1884, pro & civ ct rec from 1893 & Ind rec)						
§ Bennett	C2	1909	3		Indian Lands	Martin 57551
(attached to Fall River Co until 1911) (Clk Cts has b, d & bur rec from 1923, m rec from 1912, div, pro & civ ct rec from 1914)						
Bon Homme	C4	1862	8	1860-80	Charles Mix	Tyndall 57066
(Clk Cts has b rec from 1905, m rec from 1887, d rec from 1909, bur rec from 1935, pro rec from 1900, civ ct rec from 1878 & div rec)						
* Brookings	B5	1862	24	1860-80	Unorg. Terr.	Brookings 57006
(Clk Cts has b, m, d, bur, div, pro & civ ct rec; Reg Deeds has Ind rec)						
* Brown	A4	1879	37	1880	Beadle	Aberdeen 57401
(Clk Cts has b, m, d, bur, div, pro & civ ct rec; Reg Deeds has Ind rec)						
* Brule	B4	1875	5	1880	Old Buffalo (disc.)	Chamberlain 57325
(Reg of Deeds has b, d rec from 1905, bur rec from 1941, Ind rec from 1880; Treasurer has m rec from 1882; Co Clk has div rec from 1885, pro rec from 1880, civ ct rec from 1882, naturalization, citizenship rec from 1880)						
*§ Buffalo	B3	1873	2	1880	Territorial County	Gannvalley 57341
(Reg Deeds has b, d rec from 1905, bur rec from 1941, Ind rec; Treasurer has m rec from 1887; Co Clk has div rec from 1915, pro, civ ct rec from 1885)						
Butte	B1	1883	8		Harding	Belle Fourche 57717
(Reg Deeds has b, d rec from 1905, bur rec from 1930, Ind rec; Treasurer has m rec from 1890; Clk of Ct has div rec from 1890, pro rec from 1884, civ ct rec from 1892)						

Name	Map Index	Date Created	Pop. By M 1980	U.S. Cen Reports Available	Parent County or Territory From Which Organized	County Seat
Campbell	A3	1873	2	1880	Buffalo	Mound City 57646

(Reg of Deeds has b, d rec from 1905, Ind rec; Treasurer has m rec from 1888; Clk of Ct has div, civ ct rec from 1885, pro rec from 1890; Co Auditor has school rec)

| Charles Mix | C4 | 1862 | 10 | 1860-80 | Original District | Lake Andes 57356 |

(Clk Cts has b, m & d rec from 1905, bur rec, div, pro & civ ct rec from 1890)

| § Clark | B4 | 1873 | 5 | 1880 | Hanson | Clark 57225 |

(Clk Cts has b & d rec from 1905, m rec from 1886, div rec from 1900, pro rec from 1885 & civ ct rec)

| * Clay | C5 | 1862 | 14 | 1860-80 | | Vermillion 57069 |

(Reg Deeds has b, d rec from 1905; Treasurer has m rec from 1880; Clk Ct has pro rec from 1875, civ ct rec from 1866, div rec from 1889)

| * Codington | B5 | 1877 | 21 | 1880 | Indian Lands | Watertown 57201 |

(Clk Cts has b, d, bur & div rec from 1905, m rec from 1900, pro rec from 1893 & civ ct rec from 1883)

| Corson | A2 | 1909 | 5 | | Boreman, Dewey | McIntosh 57641 |

(Reg Deeds has b, d, Ind rec from 1909; Treasurer has m rec; Clk Ct has div, pro, civ ct rec)

| * Custer | C1 | 1875 | 6 | 1880 | Indian Lands | Custer 57730 |

(Clk Cts has b & d rec from 1905, m rec from 1887, div, pro & civ ct rec from 1890)

| Davison | B4 | 1873 | 18 | 1880 | Hanson | Mitchell 57301 |

(Reg Deeds has b, d, bur rec; Treasurer has m rec; Clk Ct has div, pro, civ ct rec from 1880)

| * Day | A4 | 1879 | 8 | 1880 | Clark | Webster 57274 |

(Reg Deeds has b, d rec from 1905, Ind rec from 1879 bur rec from 1930; Treasurer has m rec from 1880; Clk Ct has div, civ ct rec from 1885, pro rec from 1898)

| Deuel | B5 | 1862 | 5 | 1880 | Brookings | Clear Lake 57226 |

(Reg Deeds has b rec from 1876, d rec from 1905, bur rec from 1941; Treasurer has m rec from 1887; Clk Ct has div, pro rec from 1889, civ ct rec from 1880. Deuel County has 1860-70 federal cen)

| Dewey | A3 | 1910 | 5 | | Indian Res., Armstrong (see Rusk) | Timber Lake 57656 |

(Reg Deeds has b, d, Ind rec from 1910, bur rec from 1941; Treasurer has m rec from 1910; Clk Ct has pro, civ ct, div rec from 1910)

| * Douglas | C4 | 1873 | 4 | 1880 | Charles Mix | Armour 57313 |

(Clk Cts has b & d rec from 1905, m rec from 1884, bur rec from 1941, div & pro rec from 1887, civ ct rec from 1884)

| Edmunds | A3 | 1873 | 5 | | Buffalo | Ipswich 57451 |

(Reg Deeds has b rec from 1905, d rec from 1887, Ind rec from 1883, bur rec from 1941; Treasurer has m rec from 1887; Clk Ct has div rec from 1887, civ ct, pro rec from 1884)

| Fall River | C1 | 1883 | 8 | | Custer | Hot Springs 57747 |

(Clk Cts has b & d rec from 1905, m, div, pro & civ ct rec from 1890)

| *§ Faulk | A4 | 1873 | 3 | 1880 | | Faulkton 57438 |

(Reg Deeds has b rec from 1888, d rec from 1900, Ind rec from 1888, bur rec from 1900; Treasurer has m rec from 1888; Clk Ct has div, civ ct rec from 1900, pro rec from 1888)

| * Grant | A5 | 1873 | 9 | 1880 | Codington, Deuel | Milbank 57252 |

(Clk Cts has b & d rec from 1905, m rec from 1890, div, pro, civ ct rec from 1897, newspapers from 1880; Reg Deeds has Ind rec)

| Gregory | C3 | 1862 | 6 | | Yankton | Burke 57523 |

(Reg Deeds has b, d, Ind rec from 1905, bur rec; Treasurer has m rec; Clk Ct has div, pro, civ ct rec from 1899)

| § Haakon | B2 | 1914 | 3 | | Stanley | Philip 57567 |

(Clk Cts has b, m, d, bur, div, pro, civ ct, mental ill, guardian & adoption rec from 1915)

| * Hamlin | B5 | 1873 | 5 | 1880 | Deuel | Hayti 57241 |

(Reg Deeds has b, d, bur rec from 1905, Ind rec; Treasurer has m rec from 1879; Clk Ct has div, civ ct rec from 1885, pro rec from 1890, naturalization rec from 1880; Co Auditor has school cen from 1903, school rec from 1890)

| Hand | B4 | 1873 | 5 | 1880 | Buffalo | Miller 57362 |

(Reg Deeds has b, d rec from 1905, bur, Ind rec; Treasurer has m rec from 1883; Clk Ct has div rec from late 1800's, pro rec from 1880's, civ ct rec from 1889)

| Hanson | B4 | 1871 | 3 | 1880 | Buffalo, Deuel | Alexandria 57311 |

(Clk Cts has b, m, d, bur, div, pro & civ ct rec from 1905)

| * Harding | A1 | 1909 | 2 | | Unorg. Terr. | Buffalo 57720 |

(Reg Deeds has b, d, bur, Ind rec from 1909; Treasurer has m rec from 1909; Clk Ct has div, pro, civ ct, school cen rec from 1909)

| * Hughes | B3 | 1874 | 14 | 1880 | Buffalo | Pierre 57501 |

(Clk Cts has b & d rec from 1905, m, pro rec from 1890, div, civ ct rec from 1880)

| * Hutchinson | C4 | 1862 | 9 | 1860-80 | Unorg. Terr. | Olivet 57052 |

(Reg Deeds has b, d rec from 1905, bur rec from 1941, Ind rec from 1876; Treasurer has m rec from 1887; Clk Ct has div, civ ct rec from 1883, pro rec from 1899, naturalization rec from 1876; Co Auditor has school rec from 1924)

COUNTY MAP FOR THE STATE OF SOUTH DAKOTA

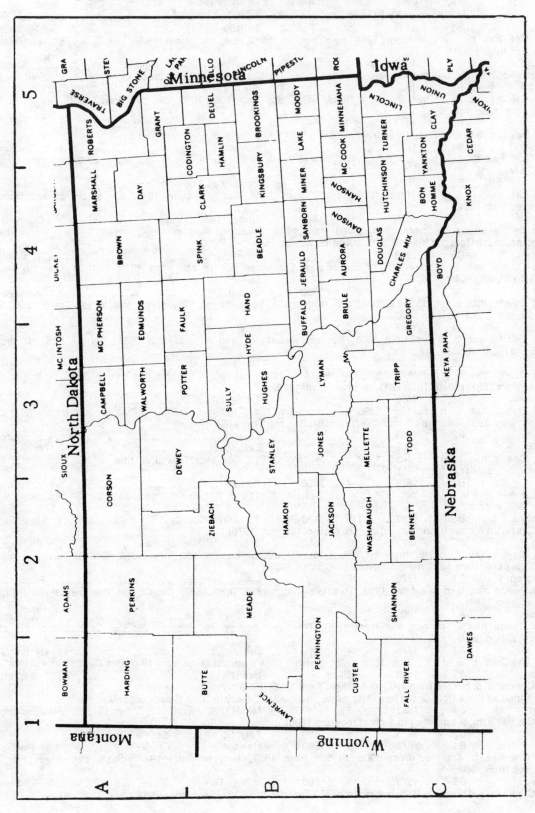

Name	Map Index	Date Created	Pop. By M 1980	U.S. Cen Reports Available	Parent County or Territory From Which Organized	County Seat
* Hyde	B3	1873	2		Buffalo	Highmore 57345

(Clk Cts has b & d rec from 1905, m rec from 1887, bur rec from 1936, div & civ ct rec from 1884 & pro rec from 1892)

| § Jackson | B2 | 1915 | 3 | | Stanley | Kadoka 57543 |

(Reg Deeds has b, d, bur, Ind rec; Treasurer has m rec; Clk Ct has div, pro, civ ct rec)

| * Jerauld | B4 | 1883 | 3 | | Aurora | Wessington Springs 57382 |

(Clk Cts has b, d & bur rec from 1905, m & pro rec from 1890, div rec from 1900, civ ct rec from 1895 & cir ct rec from 1889)

| Jones | B3 | 1917 | 1 | | Lyman | Murdo 57559 |

(Reg Deeds has b, d, Ind rec; Treasurer has m rec; Clk Ct has div, pro, civ ct rec from 1917)

| Kingsbury | B4 | 1873 | 7 | | Hanson | De Smet 57231 |

(Clk Cts has b, d & bur rec from 1905, m rec from 1890, div & civ ct rec from 1920, pro rec & naturalization rec)

| Lake | B5 | 1873 | 11 | 1880 | Brookings, Hanson | Madison 57042 |

(Clk Cts has b & d rec from 1905, m rec from 1874, bur rec from 1941, div & civ ct rec from 1881 & pro rec from 1884)

| * Lawrence | B1 | 1875 | 18 | 1880 | Unorg. Terr. | Deadwood 57732 |

(Reg Deeds has b rec from 1905, d rec from 1906; Treasurer has m rec from 1887; Clk Ct has div, pro, civ ct rec, real estate rec from 1895; City Auditor has bur rec)

| Lincoln | C5 | 1862 | 14 | | Minnehaha | Canton 57013 |

(Reg Deeds has b, d rec from 1905, bur rec; Treasurer has m rec from 1890; Clk Ct has pro rec from 1890, civ ct, div rec from 1872)

| Lyman | B3 | 1873 | 4 | 1880 | Unorg. Terr. | Kennebec 57544 |

(Reg Deeds has b rec from 1905, d rec from 1920, bur, Ind rec; Treasurer has m rec from 1905; Clk Ct has div, pro, civ ct rec from 1880)

| * Marshall | A4 | 1885 | 7 | | Day | Britton 57430 |

(Reg Deeds has b, d rec from 1905, bur rec; Treasurer has m rec from 1887; Clk Ct has div rec from 1888, pro rec from 1889, civ ct rec)

| * McCook | B5 | 1873 | 6 | 1880 | Hanson | Salem 57058 |

(Reg Deeds has b, d rec from 1905, bur rec from 1895, Ind rec; Treasurer has m rec from 1882; Clk Ct has div rec from 1887, pro rec from 1881, civ ct rec from 1880)

| * McPherson | A3 | 1873 | 4 | | Buffalo | Leola 57456 |

(Reg Deeds has b, d rec from 1905, bur rec from 1941, Ind rec; Treasurer has m rec from 1887; Clk Ct has pro from 1893, civ ct rec from 1889, Naturalization rec from 1884, div rec)

| Meade | B2 | 1889 | 21 | | Lawrence | Sturgis 57785 |
| *§ Mellette | C3 | 1909 | 2 | | Lyman | White River 57579 |

(Reg Deeds has b, d rec from 1912, bur rec from 1913, Ind rec; Treasurer has m rec from 1912; Clk Ct has div, pro, civ ct rec from 1911)

| *§ Miner | B4 | 1873 | 4 | 1880 | Hanson | Howard 57349 |

(Reg Deeds has b, d rec from 1905, bur rec; Ind rec; Treasurer has m rec from 1886; Clk Ct has pro, civ ct rec from 1886, div rec)

| * Minnehaha | B5 | 1862 | 110 | 1860-80 | Territorial County | Sioux Falls 57102 |

(Clk Cts has b & d rec from 1905, m, div, pro & civ ct rec from 1876)

| Moody | B5 | 1873 | 7 | 1880 | Brookings, Minnehaha | Flandreau 57028 |

(Reg Deeds has b, d rec from 1905, bur rec; Treasurer has m rec from 1873; Clk Ct has pro rec from 1890, civ ct rec from 1905, div rec, newspapers since 1880's)

| Pennington | B1 | 1875 | 70 | 1880 | Unorg. Terr. | Rapid City 57701 |

(Reg Deeds has b, d rec from 1905; Treasurer has m rec from 1887; Clk Ct has div, civ ct rec from 1877, pro rec from 1884)

| * Perkins | A2 | 1909 | 5 | | Harding, Butte | Bison 57620 |

(Reg Deeds has b, d, bur, rec from 1909; Treasurer has m rec from 1909; Clk Ct has pro, civ ct, div, naturalization rec from 1909)

| * Potter | A3 | 1875 | 4 | | Buffalo | Gettysburg 57442 |

(Clk Cts has b & d   from 1885, civ ct rec from 1884 & adoption rec from 1941; Reg Deeds has Ind rec)

| Roberts | A5 | 1883 | 11 | | Grant | Sisseton 57262 |

(Clk Cts has b, d, bur rec from 1905, m & div rec from 1890, pro & civ ct rec from 1889)

Rusk (formed as Rusk from unorg terr 1873; name changed to Dewey in 1883, Dewey organized 1910)

| Sanborn | B4 | 1883 | 3 | | Miner | Woonsocket 57385 |

(Clk Cts has b, m, d, bur, div, pro & civ ct rec from 1905)

| Shannon | C2 | 1875 | 9 | 1880 | Terr. Co. - Attached to Fall River County | |
| * Spink | B4 | 1873 | 9 | 1880 | Hanson | Redfield 57469 |

(Clk Cts has b & d rec from 1905, m rec from 1887, bur rec from 1941, div & civ ct rec from 1882 & pro rec from 1880)

| Stanley | B3 | 1873 | 3 | 1880 | Unorg. Terr. | Ft. Pierre 57532 |

(Clk Cts has b & d rec from 1905, bur rec from 1892, m, div, pro & civ ct rec from 1890)

Name	Map Index	Date Created	Pop. By M 1980	U.S. Census Reports Available	Parent County or Territory From Which Organized	County Seat
* Sully	B3	1873	2	1880	Potter	Onida 57564

(Clk Ct has b, m, d, bur, div, pro, civ ct, old rec from Ft. Sully & old newspapers; Reg Deeds has Ind rec)

Todd	C3	1909	7	1860-80	Attached to Tripp County	

(Though created by legislative act 9 March 1909, Todd has never been organized. It was formed from parts of Lugenbeel, Meyer, Tripp & Washabaugh; part of the unorg co of Bennett, comprising part of Rosebud Indian Reservation, annexed in 1911; within the limits of Rosebud Indian Reservation)

Tripp	C3	1873	7		Unorg. Terr.	Winner 57580

(Reg Deeds has b, rec from 1909, bur rec from 1941; Treasurer has m rec from 1909; Clk Ct has civ, pro, civ ct rec from 1912)

* Turner	C5	1871	9	1880	Lincoln	Parker 57053

(Clk Cts has b & d rec from 1905, m rec from 1872, div rec from 1907, pro rec from 1886, civ ct rec from 1900)

* Union	C5	1862	11	1880	Unorg. Terr.	Elk Point 57025

(formerly Cole, named changed 7 Jan 1864)

* Walworth	A3	1873	7	1880	Buffalo	Selby 57472

(Reg Deeds has b, d, bur rec from 1905, Ind rec; Treasurer has m rec from 1889; Clk Ct has div rec from 1889, pro, civ ct rec from 1892, criminal rec)

§ Washabaugh	C2	1883	2		Attached to Jackson County	

(unorg: formed from part of Lugenbeel; within limits of Pine Ridge Indian Reservation; part taken to form parts of Bennett, Mellette & Todd in 1909 & part comprising part of Rosebud Indian Reservation, annexed to Mellette in 1911)

Washington (unorg; formed from part of Sahnnon in 1883; within limits of Pine Ridge Indian Reservation; part taken to form part of Bennett in 1909)

* Yankton	C5	1862	19	1860-80	Unorg. Terr.	Yankton 57078

(Reg Deeds has b, d rec from 1905, bur rec; Treasurer has m rec from 1900; Clk Ct has div, pro, civ ct rec from 1900; Director Assessments has Ind rec)

Ziebach	B2	1911	2		Schnasse, Sterling, Armstrong (within limits of Cheyenne River Indian Res)	Dupree 57623

(Clk Cts has b, m, d, bur, div, pro & civ ct rec from 1911; Reg Deeds has Ind rec from 1911)

* - At least one county history has been published about this county.

§ - Inventory of county archives was made by the Historical Records Survey. (see introduction)

TENNESSEE

CAPITAL, NASHVILLE - STATE 1796 - (16TH)

Four or five hostile Indian tribes inhabited Tennessee up to as late as 1800. Explorers, representing Spain, France, and England, visited the territory intermittently from about 1540 until the early part of the 1700's.

The Blue Ridge Mountains, which form the boundary between North Carolina and Tennessee, are barriers to travel. They were more so in the early days than now. For that reason it was easier to come into Tennessee from the north than from the east. Many of the settlers, therefore, came into Tennessee from Virginia. It was in fact thought by some that it was part of that state.

Also, starting as early as 1768, several families came into the northeast corner of Tennessee from the Uplands of North Carolina. They banded together as the Watauga Association in 1771 and spread over the eastern part of the section. In 1776 North Carolina accepted the district as Washington County which eventually embraced all of the present Tennessee. To secure federal protection for that territory, North Carolina handed it to the national government as a present. Apparently no one in Washington became enthusiastic about the gift, refusing even to acknowledge it. After it had been ignored for four or five years some of the settlers retaliated by organizing the territory into a new state, Franklin. But even that action received cold treatment from Washington, and eventually vanished into the air.

Almost as many early settlers in Tennessee came from North Carolina as came from South Carolina and Virginia. Many of the Tennessee counties were settled by Scotch-Irish immigrants coming into the state via the Shenandoah Valley. Many German families settled in several of the counties west of Chattanooga where many of their descendants still live.

Many present Tennessee counties were settled years before they were formed into counties. Some of those sections and the dates of their earliest settlement are as follows: Johnson, 1770; Washington, 1772; Robertson, 1776; Greene, 1778; Sumner, 1779; Hawkins, Hamilton, Davidson, Montgomery, 1780; Hamblen, Jefferson, Cooke, Jackson, 1783; Grainger, Williamson, 1784; Blount, 1786; Smith, 1787; Cheatham, 1790; Dickson, Stewart, 1793; Claiborne, 1794; Hancock, 1795; Campbell, 1796; De Kalb, Wilson, 1797; Houston, Trousdale, 1798; Anderson, Franklin, Humphreys, Moore, Van Buren, 1800; Lincoln, 1806; Morgan, Lewis, Marshall, Maury, 1807; Lawrence, Henderson, 1815; Marion, Meiga, Benton, 1817; McMinn, Gibson, Hardeman, Hardin, Henry, Madison, McNairy, Obion, Shelby, Weakley, 1819; Carroll, Decatur, Lauderdale, 1820; Haywood, 1821; Fayette, 1822; Crockett, 1823; Lake, 1825; Polk, 1836.

In 1790, perhaps earlier, Tennessee had seven counties, each one embracing the following present counties: SULLIVAN - Johnson and Sullivan; WASHINGTON - Washington, Carter and Unicoi; HAWKINS - Hawkins, Hamblen, Grainger, Hancock, Claiborne, Campbell, Union, Anderson, Jefferson, Knox, Roane, Rhea, and Hamilton; GREENE - Greene, Cocke, corner of Jefferson, Blount, Loudon, southwest corner of Roane, Monroe, M'Minn, Polk, Meigs, Bradley, James, southeast corner of Hamilton; SUMNER - eastern third of Robertson, Sumner, Macon, Clay, Pickett, western half of Fentress, Overton, Jackson, Smith, Trousdale, Wilson, DeKalb, western two-thirds of White, Warren, northwest half of Coffee, and Cannon; DAVIDSON - Bedford, Marshall, Maury, Williamson, Rutherford, Davidson, Cheatham, and about middle third of Robertson; TENNESSEE - Stewart, Houston, Humphreys, Hickman, Dickson, Montgomery, and western third of Robertson. The rest of the territory was included in the Indian Country.

It should be noted that the counties to be settled first were in the East and the Middle Tennessee districts, the East district rather leading the Middle. The West Tennessee district was the last to be settled.

Official registration of births and deaths began in Tennessee in 1914. Central registration of marriages and divorces began July 1, 1945. Certified copies of these records may be secured from the Division of Vital Records, Department of Public Health, Nashville, Tennessee 37219.

Certified copies of records of births and deaths that occurred in Nashville, Knoxville, and Chattanooga, Tennessee between the years 1881-1914 may be secured from the address given above. Certified copies of records of births and deaths that occurred in Memphis, Tennessee may be secured from the Memphis / Shelby County Health Department, 814 Jefferson Avenue, Memphis, Tennessee 37202. Other delayed certificates of birth have been filed by the individuals for births that occurred prior to 1914 or for whom no certificate was filed at the time of birth. Certified copies of records of the District School Enumeration Census for the years 1908-1912 are available from the Division of Vital Records, Tennessee Department of Public Health, Nashville, Tennessee 37219.

Certificates of marriage prior to July 1, 1945 may be secured from the Clerk of the County Court in the county in which the license was secured. Copies of divorces granted prior to July 1, 1945 may be secured from the Clerk of the Court in the county in which the divorce was granted.

The counties maintain records of wills, deeds, taxpayers lists, guardianship and other court proceedings in the respective county courthouses. Some of these records have been transcribed and are in the State Library.

Genealogical Archives, Libraries, Societies, and Publications

Blount County Library, 300 E. Church St., Maryville, TN 37801.

Chattanooga Public Library, 601 McCallie Ave., Chattanooga, TN 37403.

Coffee County Historical Society, P.O. Box 524, Manchester, TN 37355.

Cossitt-Goodwyn Library, 33 So. Front St., Memphis, TN 38103.

East Tennessee Historical Society, Lawson McGhee Library, 217 Market St., Knoxville, TN 37902.

H. B. Stamps Memorial Library, 415 W. Main St., Rogersville, TN 37857.

Highland Rim Regional Library Center, 2102 Mercury Blvd., Murfreesboro, TN 37130.

Jackson-Madison County Library, 433 E. Lafayette, Jackson, TN 38301.

Lawson McGhee Library, 500 W. Church Ave., Knoxville, TN 37902.

Maury County Tennessee Historical Society, P.O. Box 147, Columbia, TN 38401.

McClung Historical Collection, Lawson McGhee Library, Knoxville Public Library System, 217 Market St., Knoxville, TN 37902.

Memphis Public Library and Information Center, 1850 Peabody, Memphis, TN 38104.

Memphis State University Library, Mississippi Valley Collection, Memphis, TN 38104.

Mid-West Tennessee Genealogical Society, P.O. Box 3343, Jackson, TN 38301.

Morristown-Hamblen Library, 417 W. Main St., Morristown, TN 37814.

Public Library of Knoxville and Knox County, McClung Historical Collection, 217 Market St., Knoxville, TN 37902.

Public Library of Nashville and Davidson County, 222 8th Ave. No., Nashville, TN 37203.

Tennessee Genealogical Society, P.O. Box 12124, Memphis, TN 38112.

Tennessee State Library and Archives, 403 7th Ave. N., Nashville, TN 37219.

Upper Cumberland Genealogical Association, Putnam Library, 48 East Broad St., Cookeville, TN 38501.

Watauga Association of Genealogists, P.O. Box 117, Johnson City, TN 37601.

Ansearchin News, P.O. Box 12124, Memphis, TN 38112. Published by The Tennessee Genealogical Society.

Family Findings, Mid-West Tennessee Genealogical Society, P.O. Box 3343, Jackson, TN 38301.

Historic Maury, annual publication of the Maury County Tennessee Historical Society, P.O. Box 147, Columbia, TN 38401.

River Counties, The, 610 Terrace Dr., Columbia, TN 38401.

Printed Census Records and Mortality Schedules

State Indexes: 1810, 1820, 1830, 1840, 1850, 1860, 1880

Printed Census Records (Counties):

Anderson-1830, 1880
Bedford-1820, 1830, 1850, 1880
Benton-1840, 1850, 1860, 1870, 1880
Bledsoe-1830, 1850, 1870, 1880
Blount-1830, 1880
Bradley-1840, 1880
Campbell-1830, 1880
Cannon-1850
Carroll-1830, 1850, 1860, 1870
Carter-1830, 1880
Cheatham-1880
Claiborne-1830
Clay-1880
Cocke-1830, 1840
Coffee-1840, 1850, 1860
Davidson-1830, 1850
Decatur-1850
DeKalb-1850
Dickson-1820, 1830, 1850
Dyer-1830, 1850, 1860
Fayette-1830, 1850, 1860, 1870
Fentress-1830, 1840, 1850, 1870, 1880
Franklin-1820, 1830, 1850, 1860
Gibson-1830, 1850, 1860, 1880
Giles-1820, 1830, 1840, 1850
Grainger-1810, 1830, 1860
Greene-1830

Hamilton-1830
Hardeman-1830
Hardin-1820, 1830, 1840, 1850
Hawkins-1830
Haywood-1830, 1850
Henderson-1830, 1850
Henry-1830
Hickman-1830
Humphreys-1820, 1830, 1850, 1860, 1870
Jackson-1830, 1850
Jefferson-1830, 1850
Johnson-1840, 1850, 1860
Knox-1830, 1850
Lauderdale-1840
Lawrence-1810, 1820, 1830, 1840, 1850, 1860, 1870
Lewis-1850
Lincoln-1820, 1830, 1840, 1850
Madison-1830, 1840, 1850
Marion-1830, 1850
Marshall-1850
Maury-1820, 1830, 1850, 1860, 1880
McMinn-1830, 1850
McNairy-1830, 1850, 1860
Meigs-1840, 1850
Monroe-1830
Montgomery-1820, 1830, 1850

Morgan-1830, 1850
Obion-1830, 1850
Overton-1830
Perry-1820, 1830, 1850
Polk-1840
Rhea-1830, 1840
Roane-1830, 1850
Robertson-1820, 1830, 1850
Rutherford-1800, 1810, 1820, 1830, 1840, 1850, 1860
Scott-1850
Sevier-1830, 1850
Shelby-1820, 1830, 1840
Smith-1830, 1850
Stewart-1830
Sullivan-1830, 1850
Sumner-1820, 1830, 1850
Tipton-1830, 1850, 1860
Van Buren-1850
Warren-1830, 1850
Washington-1830
Wayne-1820, 1830, 1850, 1860
Weakley-1830, 1850
White-1830
Williamson-1820, 1830, 1850
Wilson-1830, 1840, 1850, 1860, 1870

Mortality Schedules (Printed)
State-1850
Counties:
Benton-1840
Cocke-1850, 1860, 1870
Fayette-1850

Other printed Census records:
East Tennessee-1830
Middle Tennessee-1830
West Tennessee-1830

1850 Census Records (Surnames)
Aaron-Childress
Childs-Gary
Gaskell-Jones
Jones-Murley
Murpha-Rudd
Ruddell-Wallace
Walland-Zumbro

1850 Census-City of Norfolk
1850 Census-City of Nashville

Valuable Printed Sources

Gazetteers and Maps

McBride, Robert M. *Eastin Morris Tennessee Gazetteer, 1834 and Matthew Rhea's Map of the State of Tennessee, 1832.* Nashville: Gazetteer Press (1971).

Memphis Public Library has early Tennessee Gazetteers - 1834, 1860, 1870, 1880, 1890 and old maps of Shelby County and parts of West Tennessee.

Place Names

Fullerton, Ralph O. *Place Names of Tennessee.* Nashville: Department of Conversation Division of Geology (1974).

Guides To Genealogical Research

Hailey, Naomi M. *A Guide to Genealogical Research in Tennessee.* Evansville, Indiana: Cook and McDowell Publication (1979)

Hathaway, Beverly West. *Genealogical Research Sources in Tennessee.* West Jordan: All States Research Company (1972).

McCay, Betty L. comp. *Sources for Searching in Tennessee.* Indianapolis: Privately published (1970).

Schweitzer, George K. *Tennessee Genealogical Research.* Knoxville: United Printers, 1981.

Histories

Folmsbee, Stanley J. *History of Tennessee.* New York: Lewis Historical Publishing Company (1960) 4 Vols.

Ray, Worth S. *Tennessee Cousins, A History of Tennessee People.* (1950). Baltimore, Maryland: Genealogical Publishing Company (reprinted 1971) 1977.

Genealogical Sources

D.A.R. collection*

Mississippi Valley Collection. Memphis State University, Memphis, Tennessee.

Bibliographies

Smith, Sam B. ed. and comp. *Tennessee History, A Bibliography.* Knoxville, Tennessee: The University of Tennessee Press (1974).

Tennessee Newspapers, A Cumulative List of Microfilmed Tennessee Newspapers in the Tennessee State Library and Archives. Nashville: Tennessee State Library and Archives (1978).

TENNESSEE COUNTY HISTORIES
(Population figures to nearest thousand - 1980 U. S. Census)

Name	Map Index	Date Created	Pop. By M 1980	U.S. Census Reports Available	Parent County or Territory From Which Organized	County Seat
*§ Anderson	C2	1801	67	1830-80	Knox	Clinton 37716
(Co Clk has m & pro rec)						
*§ Bedford	D2	1807-8	28	1820-80	Rutherford	Shelbyville 37160
(Courthouse destroyed by fire and by a tornado in the past. Co Clk has m rec from 1863, pro rec; Clk Cir Ct has div rec)						
Benton	E2	1835	15	1840-80	Henry, Humphreys	Camden 38320
(Co Clk has m rec from 1836, pro rec from 1840; Clk Cir Ct has div & civ ct rec; Reg Deeds has Ind rec)						
* Bledsoe	C2	1807	9	1830-80	Roane	Pikeville 37367
(Courthouse burned in 1908. Co Clk has m, pro rec from 1908)						
*§ Blount	B2	1795	78	1830-80	Knox	Maryville 37801
(Co Clk has m & pro rec from 1795; Clk Cir Ct has div rec; Reg Deeds has Ind rec)						
*§ Bradley	C3	1836	67	1840-80	Indian Lands	Cleveland 37311
(Courthouse destroyed by fire in Nov. 1864. Co Clk has m, pro rec from 1864; Cir and Sessions Ct has div, civ ct rec; Reg Deeds has Ind rec; Vital Records, Nashville, has b, d rec)						

COUNTY MAP FOR THE STATE OF TENNESSEE

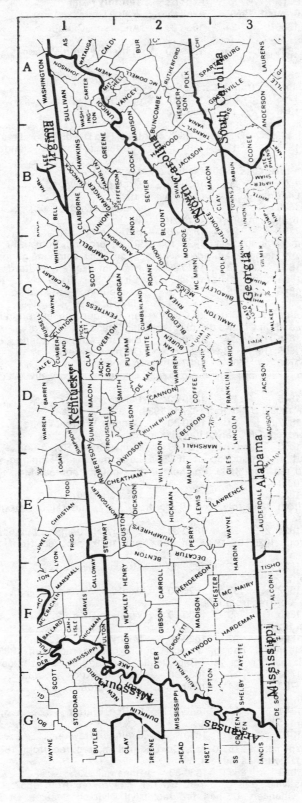

Name	Map Index	Date Created	Pop. By M 1980	U.S. Cen Reports Available	Parent County or Territory From Which Organized	County Seat
* Campbell	C1	1806	34	1830-80	Anderson, Claiborne	Jacksboro 37757
(Co Clk has m rec from 1838)						
* Cannon	D2	1836	10	1840-80	Coffee, Warren, Wilson	Woodbury 37190
(Co Clk has m rec from 1838)						
Carroll	F2	1821	28	1830-80	Western District	Huntingdon 38344
(Co Clk has m rec from 1838, pro rec from 1826; Co Reg has Ind rec)						
* Carter	A1	1796	50	1830-80	Washington	Elizabethton 37643
*§ Cheatham	E2	1856	22	1860-80	Davidson, Dickson, Montgomery	Ashland City 37015
(Co Clk has m & pro rec from 1865; Clk Cir Ct has div & civ ct rec; Reg Deeds has Ind rec)						
* Chester	F3	1875	13	1881	Hardeman, Madison, Henderson, McNairy	Henderson 38340
(Co Clk has m & pro rec from 1890; Clk Cir Ct has div & civ ct rec)						
Claiborne	B1	1801	25	1830-80	Grainger, Hawkins	Tazewell 37879
(Co Clk has m rec; Clk Cir Ct has div rec; Reg Deeds has Ind rec)						
Clay	D1	1870	7	1880	Jackson, Overton	Celina 38551
(Co Clk has b rec from 1909 to 1929, m, pro, civ ct rec from 1871)						
* Cocke	B2	1797	29	1830-80	Jefferson	Newport 37821
(Co Clk has b, d rec from 1909 to 1911, 1928 to 1930, m, pro rec from 1877; Cir Ct has civ, civ ct rec; Reg Deeds has Ind rec; Stokely Memorial Library, Newport, Tenn. has a complete genealogical section)						
* Coffee	D2	1836	38	1840-80	Franklin, Warren, Bedford	Manchester 37355
(Co Clk has m rec from 1854, pro rec from 1836; Clk Cir Ct has div & civ ct rec; Reg Deeds has Ind rec)						
§ Crockett	F2	1845	15	1880	Lauderdale, Dyer, Madison, Gibson, Haywood	Alamo 38001
(Many early cen rec of residents of Crockett County can be found in surrounding counties. Co Clk has m, pro rec from 1872; Chancery and Cir Ct have div, civ ct rec; Reg Deeds has Ind rec)						
* Cumberland	C2	1856	28	1860-80	Bledsoe, Morgan, Roane	Crossville 38555
(Co Clk has m, pro rec from 1905; Clerk & Master and Cir Ct Clk have div rec)						
* Davidson	E2	1783	460	1820-80	Washington	Nashville 37201
(Co Clk has m rec from 1789, pro rec from 1783; Clk Cir Ct has div & civ ct rec; Reg Deeds has Ind rec)						
* Decatur	E2	1845	11	1850-80	Perry	Decaturville 38329
(Co Clk has m & pro rec from 1869 & b rec from 1927 to 1939)						
* DeKalb	D2	1837-8	14	1840-80	Cannon, Warren, White	Smithville 37166
(Co Clk has m from 1848 & pro rec; Clk Chan Ct has div rec)						
* Dickson	D2	1803	30	1820-80	Montgomery, Robertson	Charlotte 37036
(Courthouse was destroyed by tornado about 1835, a large number of the rec were destroyed. Co Clk has m rec from 1839, wills, Ind rec from 1803. For help in this county contact Mrs. Ron Kilgore at the Historical Society, Charlotte, Tenn. 37036)						
Dyer	F2	1823	34	1830-80	Western District	Dyersburg 38024
(Co Clk has m, pro rec from 1850, div, civ ct rec from 1927, funeral rec from 1914 to 1956; Reg Deeds has Ind rec)						
* Fayette	F3	1824	25	1830-80	Shelby, Hardeman	Somerville 38068
(Co Clk has b, d rec from 1925 to 1939, m rec from 1838, pro rec from 1824, m rec 1918 to 1925 lost in fire)						
* Fentress	C1	1823	15	1830-80	Morgan, Overton	Jamestown 38556
(Co Clk has m rec from 1905)						
* Franklin	D3	1807	32	1820-80	Bedford, Warren	Winchester 37398
(Co Clk has m rec from 1838 & pro rec from 1808)						
Gibson	F2	1823	49	1830-80	Western District	Trenton 38382
(Co Clk has m & pro rec from 1824)						
* Giles	E3	1809	25	1820-80	Maury	Pulaski 38478
(Bureau Vital Statistics, Nashville, has b, d rec; Co Clk has m rec from 1865, pro rec; Clk and Master Office has div rec; Cir Ct has civ ct rec; Reg Deeds has Ind rec. Courthouse burned during Civil War)						
Grainger	B1	1796	17	1830-80	Hawkins, Knox	Rutledge 37861
* Greene	B1	1783	54	1830-80	Washington	Greenville 37743
(Co Clk has m rec from 1789)						
Grundy	D2	1844	14	1850-80	Coffee, Warren	Altamont 37301
(Co Clk has m & pro rec from 1850)						
Hamblen	B1	1870	49	1880	Grainger, Hawkins	Morristown 37814
(Bureau Vit Statistics, Nashville, has b, d rec; Co Clk has m, pro rec from 1870; Clk and Master has div rec; Cir Ct has civ ct rec; Reg Deeds has Ind rec)						
*§ Hamilton	C3	1819	283	1830-80	Rhea	Chattanooga 37402
(Bureau Vit Statistics, Nashville, has b, d rec; Co Clk has m rec from 1857; Cir Ct and Clk and Master has div rec; Pro Division Chancery Ct has pro rec; Civil Division Session Ct and Cir Ct has civ ct rec; Reg Deeds has Ind rec)						

Name	Map Index	Date Created	Pop. By M 1980	U.S. Census Reports Available	Parent County or Territory From Which Organized	County Seat
Hancock	B1	1844	7	1850-80	Claiborne, Hawkins	Sneedville 37869

(Co Clk has m, pro rec from 1930)

* Hardeman	F3	1823	24	1830-80	Western District	Bolivar 38008

(Bureau Vit Statistics, Nashville, has b, d rec; Co Clk has m, pro rec from 1823, tax lists from 1824; Reg Deeds has Ind rec. Bur rec are published in book, *Cem Records of Hardeman County, Tenn.,* by Davidson, Owens, Boyd, in six vols from cem listings)

* Hardin	E3	1819	22	1820-80	Western District	Savannah 38372

(Co Clk Ct has m rec from 1860, div, pro & civ ct rec, settlements, wills & Ind grants from 1865)

Hawkins	B1	1786	44	1830-80	Sullivan	Rogersville 37857

(Co Clk has m rec from 1789 & pro rec; Clk Cir Ct has div & civ ct rec; Reg Deeds has Ind rec)

§ Haywood	F2	1823	20	1830-80	Western District	Brownsville 38012

(Co Clk has m rec from 1859, div rec from 1941 to 1965 & pro rec from 1826)

* Henderson	F2	1821	21	1830-80	Western District	Lexington 38351

(Clk Chan Ct has b rec; Co Ct has m & pro rec; Clk Cir Ct has div & civ ct rec; Reg Deeds has Ind rec; Courthouse burned 1863 & 1895, some rec saved)

* Henry	F2	1821	29	1830-80	Western District	Parish 38242
* Hickman	E2	1807	15	1820-80	Dickson	Centerville 37033

(Courthouse burned 1865, all rec lost. Bureau Vit Statistics, Nashville, has b, d rec; Co Clk has m, pro rec from 1867; Cir Ct Clk has div rec, civ ct rec; Reg Deeds has Ind rec from 1807)

* Houston	E2	1871	6	1880	Dickson, Stewart	Erin 37061

(Co Clk has m rec; Clk Cir Ct has div & civ ct rec; Co Ct has pro rec; Reg Deeds has Ind rec)

Humphreys	E2	1809	16	1820-80	Stewart, Smith	Waverly 37185

(Courthouse burned in 1876 & in 1898, great lack of rec, Ind rec are only thing that is com; Co Clk has deed rec from 1809, m from 1861, wills & inventories from 1838)

* Jackson	D1	1801	9	1820-80	Smith	Gainesboro 38562

(Co Clk has m & pro rec from 1870)

* Jefferson	B2	1792	31	1830-80	Green, Hawkins	Dandridge 37725

(Bureau Vit Statistics, Nashville, has b, d rec; Co Clk has m, pro, wills from 1792; Clk and Master has div rec; Cir Ct Clk has civ ct rec; Reg Deeds has Ind rec)

Johnson	A1	1836	14	1840-80	Carter	Mountain City 37683

(Co Clk has m & pro rec from 1836; Chan Ct has div & civ ct rec)

* Knox	B2	1792	319	1830-80	Greene, Hawkins	Knoxville 37902

(Bureau Vit Statistics, Nashville, has b, d rec; Co Clk has m rec, pro, wills from 1700; Cir and Chancery Cts have div rec; Reg Deeds has Ind rec)

Lake	F2	1870	7	1870-80	Obion	Tiptonville 38079

(Co Clk has m rec from 1870 & pro rec)

* Lauderdale	G2	1835	24	1840-80	Dyer, Tipton	Ripley 38063

(Bureau Vit Statistics, Nashville, has b, d rec; Co Clk has m rec from 1838, pro rec; Chancery Ct has div rec; General Sessions Ct has civ ct rec; Reg Deeds has Ind rec)

Lawrence	E3	1817	33	1820-80	Hickman, Maury	Lawrenceburg 38464

(Co Health has b rec; Co Clk has m rec from 1818 & pro rec from 1829; Clk Cir Ct has div rec; Reg Deeds has Ind rec)

Lewis	E2	1843	9	1850-80	Hickman, Maury, Wayne, Lawrence	Hohenwald 38462

(Co Clk has m rec from 1881, pro rec from 1940 & general sessions ct rec; Clk Cir Ct has div rec; Reg Deeds has Ind rec) (this co completely abolished for one year following the CW, for that year rec will be found in Maury, Lawrence, Hickman & Wayne Cos; Guardian bonds & court minutes begin 1846)

* Lincoln	D3	1809	26	1820-80	Bedford	Fayetteville 37334

(Co Clk has m & pro rec; Clk Cir Ct has div rec; Clk & Master has civ ct rec; Reg Deeds has Ind rec)

§ Loudon	C2	1870	28	1880	Blount, Monroe, Roane, McMinn	Loudon 37774

(Co Clk has m rec from 1870; Clk Cir Ct has div & civ ct rec from 1870; Reg Deeds has Ind rec from 1870)

* Macon	D1	1842	16	1850-80	Smith, Sumner	Lafayette 37083

(Co Clk has b rec from 1908 to 1912, m rec from 1901, pro rec from 1900; Clk Cir Ct has div, civ ct rec; Reg Deeds has Ind rec)

* Madison	F2	1821	75	1830-80	Western District	Jackson 38301

(Co Clk has m rec from 1838 & pro rec from 1825)

* Marion	D3	1817	24	1830-80	Indian Lands	Jasper 37347

(Co Clk has m rec from 1919, pro rec from 1874; Courthouse burned 1822, m rec destroyed)

Marshall	D2	1836	20	1840-80	Bedford, Lincoln, Giles, Maury	Lewisburg 37091

(Co Clk Ct has m rec & pro rec from 1836)

Maury	D2	1807	51	1820-80	Williamson	Columbia 38401

(Co Clk has b & d rec from 1908 to 1910 - 1914 to 1940, m rec from 1807; Clk Cir Ct has div, pro & civ ct rec; Reg Deeds has Ind rec)

* McMinn	C2	1819	42	1830-80	Indian Lands	Athens 37303

(Co Clk has m rec from 1879; Clk Cir Ct has div rec)

Name	Map Index	Date Created	Pop. By M 1980	U.S. Cen Reports Available	Parent County or Territory From Which Organized	County Seat
* McNairy	F3	1823	22	1830-80	Hardin	Selmer 38375

(Co Clk has b rec from 1882 to 1937, m rec from 1862, pro rec from 1873; Clk Cir Ct has div rec; Reg Deeds has Ind rec)

Meigs	C2	1836	7	1840-80	Hamilton, McMinn, Rhea	Decatur 37322

(Co Clk has m & pro rec from 1836; Clk Cir Ct has div & civ ct rec; Reg Deeds has Ind rec)

Monroe	C2	1819	29	1830-80	Roane	Madisonville 37354

(Co Clk has m rec from 1838, pro rec 1853, wills 1833 & co ct rec 1868)

* Montgomery	E1	1796	83	1820-80	Tennessee	Clarksville 37040

(Bureau Vit Statistics, Nashville, has b, d rec; Co Clk has m rec from 1838, pro rec from 1797; Clk Cir Ct has div rec; Criminal Ct Clk has civ ct rec; Reg Deeds has Ind rec)

Moore	D3	1871	5	1880	Bedford, Franklin	Lynchburg 37352
Morgan	C2	1817	17	1830-80	Roane	Wartburg 37887

(Co Clk has b rec from 1908 to 1912, m rec from 1862, div, pro rec also Ind rec from 1818)

* Obion	F2	1823	33	1830-80	Western District	Union City 38261

(Bureau Vit Statistics, Nashville, has b, d rec; Co Clk has m rec from 1824, pro rec from 1833; Cir and Chancery Ct has div rec; Cir and General Sessions Ct has civ ct rec; Reg Deeds has Ind rec)

* Overton	C1	1806	18	1820-80	Jackson	Livingston 38570

(Bureau Vit Statistics, Nashville, has b, d rec; Co Clk has m, pro rec from 1867; Cir Ct has div, civ ct rec; Reg Deeds has Ind rec)

Perry	E2	1818	6	1820-80	Hickman	Linden 37096

(Co Clk has b rec from 1908 to 1912 - 1925 to 1939 & m rec from 1899)

* Pickett	C1	1879	4		Fentress, Overton	Byrdstown 38549

(Co Health has b rec; Co Clk has m & pro rec from 1935; Clk & Master & Clk Cir Ct has div rec; Clk Cir Ct has civ ct rec; Reg Deeds has Ind rec)

* Polk	C3	1839	14	1840-80	Bradley, McMinn	Benton 37307
* Putnam	D2	1854	47	1860-80	White, Jackson, Overton, Dekalb	Cookeville 38501

(Courthouse burned in 1899. Co Clk has b, d rec from 1925 to 1940, partial b, d rec from 1908 to 1912; m rec from 1879, pro rec from 1900, wills from 1876; Chancery Ct as div, civ ct rec from 1900; Reg Deeds has Ind rec from 1854; Cir Ct Clk has Cir Ct Rec from 1900; Pat Franklin, County Historian, Rte. 2, Box 408, Cookeville, Tenn. 38501 has misc co rec)

* Rhea	C2	1807	24	1830-80	Roane	Dayton 37321

(Co Clk has m rec from 1808)

* Roane	C2	1801	48	1830-80	Knox, Blount	Kingston 37763

(Co Clk has m & pro rec from 1801)

Robertson	E1	1796	36	1820-80	Tennessee	Springfield 37172

(Co Clk has m rec from 1839, pro rec from 1796; Clk Cir Ct has div & civ ct rec)

*§ Rutherford	D2	1803	84	1810-80	Davidson	Murfreesboro 37130

(Co Clk has m & pro rec from 1804)

* Scott	C1	1849	19	1850-80	Fentress, Morgan, Anderson	Huntsville 37756
* Sequatchie	C2	1858	8	1860-80	Hamilton, Bledsoe, Marion	Dunlap 37327

(Co Clk has b, m, d, pro rec from 1858; Cir Ct Clk has div, civ ct rec; Reg Deeds has Ind rec)

* Sevier	B2	1794	41	1830-80	Jefferson	Sevierville 37862

(Co Clk has m rec from 1856 & pro rec from 1900, wills from 1850)

* Shelby	G3	1819	774	1820-80	Hardin	Memphis 38103

(Co Health has b, d & bur rec; Co Clk has m rec from 1820; Clk Cir Ct has div rec; Pro Judge has pro rec; Gen Sessions Ct has civ ct rec; Reg Deeds has Ind rec)

* Smith	D2	1799	15	1820-80	Sumner	Carthage 37030
* Stewart	E1	1803	9	1820-80	Montgomery	Dover 37058

(Co Clk has m & pro rec from 1898; Reg Deeds has Ind rec & deeds from 1803; Courthouse burned during CW)

*§ Sullivan	A1	1779	144	1830-80	Washington	Blountville 37617

(Co Clk has m & pro rec from 1863)

* Sumner	D1	1786	85	1820-80	Davidson	Gallatin 37066

(Co Clk has m & pro rec)

Tennessee		1788			Co. surrendered name when state became Tennessee 1796	
*§ Tipton	G3	1823	32	1830-80	Western District	Covington 38019

(Co Clk has m, div & pro rec; Clk Cir Ct has civ ct rec)

* Trousdale	D1	1870	6	1880	Macon, Smith, Wilson	Hartsville 37074

(Co Clk has m, pro rec from 1906; Clk Cir Ct has div, civ ct rec; Reg Deeds has Ind rec)

Unicoi	A1	1875	16	1880	Carter, Washington	Erwin 37650

(Co Clk has m, pro rec from 1875; Clk Cir Ct and Chan Ct has div, civ ct rec; Reg Deeds has Ind rec from 1875)

Union	B1	1850	12	1860-80	Anderson, Campbell, Claiborne, Grainger, Knox	Maynardville 37807

(Co Clk has m & pro rec; Co Asr has Ind rec)

Name	Map Index	Date Created	Pop. By M 1980	U.S. Cen Reports Available	Parent County or Territory From Which Organized	County Seat
Van Buren	D2	1840	5	1850-80	Bledsoe, Warren, White	Spencer 38585

(Co Clk has b rec from 1925 to 1938, d rec from 1926 to 1938, m & pro rec from 1840; Clk & Master has div rec from 1840; Gen Sessions Ct has civ ct rec from 1840; Reg Deeds has Ind rec from 1840)

* Warren	D2	1807	32	1820-80	White	McMinnville 37110

(Co Clk has m rec from 1852, pro rec from 1827; Cir Ct Clk has div, civ ct rec; Reg Deeds has Ind rec)

Washington	A1	1777	89	1830-80	Covered present state. Many counties from section	Jonesboro 37659

(This co also embraced parts of present N.C. Cos) (Co Clk has b rec from 1908 to 1912 & from 1925 to 1938, m rec from 1787, pro rec from 1780 & wills from 1779)

Wayne		1785			Abolished 1788	

(This Wayne Co created under the state of Franklin. Included present Carter Co & part of Johnson Co)

Wayne	E3	1817	14	1820-80	Hickman	Waynesboro 38485

(Co Clk has m rec from 1857 & pro rec from 1848)

Weakley	F2	1823	33	1830-80	Western District	Dresden 38225

(Co Clk has m rec from 1840, pro rec & wills from 1828; Clk Cir Ct has div rec)

* White	C2	1806	19	1820-80	Overton, Jackson, Smith	Sparta 38583

(Co Clk has m rec from 1838, about two dozen before that from 1809, wills, settlements, deeds & inventories from 1806)

Williamson	E2	1799	58	1820-80	Davidson	Franklin 37064

(Co Clk has m rec from 1800, tax, wills, minutes, deeds from 1799)

§ Wilson	D2	1799	54	1820-80	Sumner	Lebanon 37087

(Co Clk has m rec from 1802, pro rec from 1800; Clk and Master and Cir Ct Clk has div rec; Reg Deeds has Ind rec)

* - At least one county history has been published about this county.

§ - Inventory of county archives was made by the Historical Records Survey. (see introduction)

TEXAS

CAPITAL, AUSTIN - STATE 1845 - (28TH)

Texas has been under the jurisdiction of six separate governments since 1685, those of France, Spain, Mexico, the Republic of Texas, the Confederacy, and the United States.

In 1820 the white settlers of Texas could be counted in four digits. Shortly afterwards former residents of Alabama, Louisiana, Mississippi, and Tennessee were brought into the section under the leadership of Moses Austin and his son, Stephen. By 1830 more than 20,000 Americans had become tillers of Texas soil.

Austin has been the capital of Texas since statehood. Other cities which have been the capitals of Texas are Sen Felip de Austin, Washington-on-the-Brazos, Harrisburg, Galveston, Velasco and Columbia during the Revolution, 1835, 1836; Houston, 1837-1839; Austin, 1839; Houston, Washington-on-the-Brazos, 1842-1845; Austin since 1845.

From 1903 to 1909 attendants filed reports of birth and death with the county clerk. About 1916 some of the county clerks, but not all, transmitted to the Texas Department of Health, Bureau of Vital Statistics, 1100 West 49th Street, Austin, Texas 78756 their records of 1903-1909 births and deaths.

In 1910 the Bureau of Vital Statistics commenced receiving records on timely filed reports of birth and death.

From 1911 to 1929 the law did not require a local registrar of an incorporated city or town to file a copy of a certificate with the county clerk, but did require that the original records be forwarded to the Bureau of Vital Statistics.

From 1911 to 1927 the county clerk continued to record and transmit to the Bureau certificates of births and deaths occurring outside the limits in an incorporated city or town.

Since 1927 justice precincts have become registration districts. The precinct registrars receive and transmit to the Bureau of Vital Statistics certificates of birth and death and they are required to file a copy with the county clerk.

From 1929 to 1951 the city registrars, serving incorporated cities or towns having a population of 2,500 or more, received and transmitted to the Bureau of Vital Statistics, certificates relating to births and deaths occurring inside the city limits and were also required to file a copy of the certificate with the county clerk.

Since 1951, the city registrars, in cities having an ordinance requiring that a copy of the certificate be filed in the office of the city registrar, do not file a copy with the county clerk. The original certificate is transmitted to the Bureau of Vital Statistics by the city registrars and justices of the peace.

Copies of marriage applications were not filed with the Bureau of Vital Statistics until January 1, 1966. For a marriage record filed prior to that time, contact the County Clerk of the county in which the license was obtained.

Reports of divorce or annulment of marriage were not filed with the Bureau of Vital Statistics until January 1, 1968. For events occurring prior to that time, application should be made to the District Clerk of the county in which the decree was issued.

Genealogical Archives, Libraries, Societies, and Publications

Amarillo Genealogical Society, c/o Amarillo Public Library, 300 East 4th, P.O. Box 2171, Amarillo, TX 79101.

Amarillo Public Library, Box 2171, 10th and Polk Sts., Amarillo, TX 79105.

Anderson County Genealogical Society, 502 N. Queen St., Palestine, TX 75801.

Arlington Public Library, 101 E. Abram, Arlington, TX 76010.

Austin Genealogical Society, P.O. Box 774, Austin, TX 78767.

Beaumont Public Library, Box 3827, 800 Pearl St., Beaumont, TX 77704.

Belton Carnegie Library, Box 89, 301 E. 1st St., Belton, TX 76513.

Bryan Public Library, 201 E. 26th St., Bryan, TX 77801.

Calhoun County Genealogical Society, P.O. Box 1150, Port Lavaca, TX 77979.

Carnegie Public Library, Local History / Genealogy Department, 125 South College Avenue, Tyler, TX 75702.

Castro County Genealogical Society, P.O. Box 911, Dimmitt, TX 79027.

Central Texas Genealogical Society, Waco McLennan County Library, 1717 Austin Ave., Waco, TX 76701.

Chaparral Genealogical Library, Tomball Municipal Building, Tomball, TX 77375.

Chaparral Genealogical Society, P.O. Box 606, Tomball, TX 77375.

City-College Library, 1825 May St., Brownsville, TX 78520.

Clayton Library for Genealogical Research, 5300 Caroline, Houston, TX 77004.

Coastal Bend Genealogical Society, La Retama Library, 505 Mesquite Street, Corpus Christi, TX 78401.

Corsicana Public Library, 100 N. 12th St., Corsicana, TX 75110.

Cross Timbers Genealogical Society, Inc., P.O. Box 197, Gainesville, TX 76240.

Dallas Genealogical Society, P.O. Box 12648, Dallas, TX 75225.

Dallas Public Library, Texas History and Genealogy Dept., 1954 Commerce St., Dallas, TX 75201.

Deaf Smith County Genealogical Society, 211 E. 4th St., Hereford, TX 79045.

Denton County Genealogical Society, P.O. Box 23322, TWU Station, Denton, TX 76204.

East Texas Genealogical Society, P.O. Box 6967, Tyler, TX 75711.

Ector County Library, 622 N. Lee, Odessa, TX 79760.

Ellis County Genealogical Society, Box 385, Waxahachie, TX 75165.

El Paso Genealogical Library, 3651 Douglas, El Paso, TX 79903.

El Paso Public Library, Document Genealogy Dept., 501 N. Oregon St., El Paso, TX 79901.

El Progreso Memorial Library, 129 W. Nopal, Uvalde, TX 78801.

Fort Worth Genealogical Society, Box 9767, Fort Worth, TX 76107.

Fort Worth Public Library, 300 Taylor Street, Fort Worth, TX 76102.

Genealogical Society of Van Zandt County, P.O. Box 434, Willis Point, TX 75169.

Grand Prairie Memorial Library, 326 W. Main, Grand Prairie, TX 75050.

Harlingen Public Library, 504 E. Tyler Ave., Harlingen, TX 78550.

Harris County Genealogical Society, P.O. Box 3329, Pasadena, TX 77501.

Henderson County Historical Society, P.O. Box 943, Athens, TX 75751.

High Plains Genealogical Society, Cornette Library, Lecture Room, West Texas State University, Canyon, TX 79015.

Houston Area Genealogical Association, 2507 Tannehill, Houston, TX 77008.

Houston Public Library, 500 McKinney Ave., Houston, TX 77004.

Hutchinson County Genealogical Society, Hutchinson County Library, 625 Weatherly St., Borger, TX 79007.

Kent County Genealogical and Historical Society, Box 414, Jayton, TX 79528.

Kurth Memorial Library, 101 Calder Square, Lufkin, TX 75901.

Lamesa Area Genealogical Society, Box 1090, Lamesa, TX 79331.

Lancaster Genealogical Society, P.O. Box 185, Lancaster, TX 75146.

La Retama Public Library, 505 N. Mesquite Street, Corpus Christi, TX 78401.

Leon County Genealogical Society, Centerville, TX 75833.

Lubbock City-County Library, 1306 9th St., Lubbock, TX 79401.

McLennan County Library, 1717 Austin Ave., Waco, TX 76701.

Mesquite Historical and Genealogical Society, P.O. Box 165, Mesquite, TX 75149.

Mesquite Public Library, 300 Grubb Dr., Mesquite, TX 75149.

Mid-Cities Genealogical Society, P.O. Box 171, Bedford, TX 76021.

Midland Genealogical Society, Box 1191, Midland, TX 79702.

Mirabeau B. Lamar Library, University of Texas, Austin, TX 78712.

Montgomery County Genealogical Society, Inc., P.O. Box 751, Conroe, TX 77301.

Montgomery County Library, Box 579, San Jacinto and Phillips, Conroe, TX 77301.

Mt. Pleasant Municipal Library, Box 1285, 213 N. Madison, Mt. Pleasant, TX 75455.

Nacogdoches Genealogical Society, P.O. Box 4634, Nacogdoches, TX 75962.

Navarro County Genealogical Society, P.O. Box 821, Corsicana, TX 75110.

Northeast Texas Genealogical Society, P.O. Box 240, Mineola, TX 75773.

Pampa Genealogical and Historical Society, 430 N. Summer St., Pampa, TX 79065.

Parker County Genealogical Society, 1214 Charles St., Weatherford, TX 76086.

Permian Basin Genealogical Society, c/o Ector County Library, 622 N. Lee, Odessa, TX 79761.

Pilot Point Community Library, 105 South Jefferson St., Pilot Point, TX 76258.

Public Library, The, Longview, TX 75601.

San Angelo Genealogical and Historical Society, Inc., P.O. Box 3453, San Angelo, TX 76901.

San Antonio Genealogical and Historical Society, P.O. Box 5907, San Antonio, TX 78201.

San Antonio Public Library, 203 S. St., Mary's St., San Antonio, TX 78205.

San Augustine Public Library, 413 E. Columbia, San Augustine, TX 75972.

Scarborough Library of Genealogy, History and Biography of South and Southwest, c/o McMurry College Library, McMurry Station, Abilene, TX 79605.

South Plains Genealogical Society, 4215 University Ave., Lubbock, TX 79408.

Southeast Texas Genealogical and Historical Society, c/o Tyrrell Historical Library, P.O. Box 3827, Beaumont, TX 77704.

Southwest Genealogical Society, c/o San Antonio College Library, 1300 San Pedro Ave., San Antonio, TX 78212.

Southwest Texas Genealogical Association, 308 Ave. K, Del Rio, TX 78840.

Temple Public Library, 101 North Main Street, Temple, TX 76501.

Texarkana Public Library, 901 State Line Ave., Texarkana, TX-AR 75501.

Texarkana USA Genealogy Society, (Bowie County), P.O. Box 2323, Texarkana, TX 75501.

Texas State Genealogical Society, 220 West 32nd Street, Houston, TX 77018.

Texas State Historical Association, Box 8011, University Station, Austin, TX 78712.

Texas State Library, 1201 Brazos St., Box 12927 Capitol St., Austin, TX 78711.

Tip O'Texas Genealogical Society, Harlingen Public Library, Harlingen, TX 78550.

Tyrell Public Library, 695 Pearl St., Beaumont, TX 77701.

Victoria County Genealogical Society, 302 N. Main St., Victoria, TX 77901.

Van Zandt County Genealogical Society, Box 434, Wills Point, TX 75169.

Waco Public Library, 1717 Austin Ave., Waco, TX 76701.

Weatherford Public Library, 1214 Charles St., Weatherford, TX 76086.

West Texas Historical and Scientific Society, Inc., Alpine, TX 79830.

Footprints, Fort Worth Genealogical Society, Box 864, Ft. Worth, TX 76101.

Our Heritage, published quarterly by the Genealogical Society of Van Zandt County, P.O. Box 434, Wills Point, TX 75169.

Reflections, quarterly publication of the Coastal Bend Genealogical Society, 505 Mesquite Street, Corpus Christi, TX 78401.

Searchers and Researchers, publication of the Ellis County Genealogical Society, P.O. Box 385, Waxahachie, TX 75165.

Stalkin' Kin, San Angelo Genealogical and Historical Society, Inc., P.O. Box 3453, San Angelo, TX 76901.

Stirpes, publication of the Texas State Genealogical Society, 2410 47th Street, Lubbock, TX 79412.

Yellowed Pages, Southeast Texas Genealogical and Historical Society, 2870 Driftwood Lane, Beaumont, TX 77703.

Printed Census Records and Mortality Schedules

Indexes before and after statehood: 1830, 1840, 1850, 1860, 1870, 1880

Printed Census Records (Counties):

Anderson-1850
Angelina-1850
Atascosa-1826
Austin-1850, 1870
Bastrop-1850
Bexar-1850
Bosque-1860
Bowie-1850, 1860
Brazoria-1850, 1860
Brazos-1850, 1860; 1841
Brown-1860
Burleson-1850
Burnet-1860
Caldwell-1850
Calhoun-1850, 1860, 1870, 1880
Cameron-1850, 1860, 1870
Cass-1850
Cherokee-1850, 1880
Collin-1850, 1860
Colorado-1850
Comal-1850
Comanche-1860
Cooke-1850
Dallas-1850
Denton-1850
DeWitt-1850
Eastland-1880
Ellis-1850
Falls-1850
Fannin-1850, 1870
Fayette-1850
Fort Bend-1850
Franklin-1880

Galveston-1850
Gillespie-1850
Goliad-1850
Gonzales-1850
Grayson-1850
Grimes-1850
Guadalupe-1850
Harris-1850
Harrison-1850
Hays - 1850, 1860
Henderson-1850
Hood-1880
Hopkins-1850
Houston-1850
Hunt-1850, 1860, 1870
Jack-1870
Jackson-1850, 1860, 1870
Jasper-1850
Jefferson-1850, 1870
Kaufman-1850
Lamar-1850
Lavaca-1850
Leon-1850
Liberty-1850, 1860, 1870, 1880; 1826
Limestone-1850
Mason-1860, 1870, 1880
Matagorda-1850, 1860, 1880
Medina-1850
Menard-1860, 1880
Milam-1850, 1880
Mitchell-1880
Montgomery-1850

Nacogdoches-1850, 1860, 1870
Navarro-1850
Newton-1850
Nueces-1850
Panola-1850, 1860
Polk-1850
Presidio-1870
Red River-1850
Refugio-1850
Robertson-1850
Rockwall-1880
Runnels-1860
Rusk-1850
Sabine-1850, 1880
San Augustine-1850
San Patricio-1850
Shelby-1850
Smith-1850, 1870
Starr-1850
Tarrant-1850
Titus-1850
Travis-1850, 1860
Tyler-1850
Upshur-1850
Van Zandt-1850
Victoria-1850
Walker-1850
Washington-1850, 1860
Webb-1850
Wharton-1850
Williamson-1850
Young-1860, 1870, 1880

Mortality Schedules (Printed)

State-1850, 1860

Counties: 1860

Anderson
Angelina
Atascosa
Austin
Bandera
Bee
Bell
Baxar
Blanco
Bowie
Brazoria
Burleson
Burnet
Caldwell
Calhoun
Cass
Chambers
Cherokee
Collin
Colorado
Comal
Comanche
Cooke

Coryell
Dallas
Denton
DeWitt
Ellis
El Paso
Erath
Falls
Fannin
Fayette
Fort Bend
Freestone
Galveston
Gillespie
Goliad
Gonzales
Grayson
Grimes
Guadalup
Hardin
Harris
Harrison
Hays

Henderson
Hopkins
Houston
Hunt
Jack
Jackson
Jasper
Jeffersons
Johnson
Karnes
Kaufman
Kerr
Lamar
Lampasas
Lavaca
Leon
Liberty
Limestone
Live Oak
Llano
Madison
Marion
Mason

Matagorda
Maverick
McLennan
Medina
Milam
Montague
Montgomery
Nacogdoches
Navarro
Newton
Nueces
Orange
Palo Pinto
Panola
Parker
Polk
Presidio
Red River
Refugio
Robertson
Rusk
Sabine
St. Augustine

San Patricio
San Saba
Shackeford
Shelby
Smith
Starr
Titus
Travis
Trinity
Tyler
Upshur
Uvalde
Van Zandt
Victoria
Walker
Washington
Webb
Wharton
Williamson
Wise
Wood
Young
Zapata

Other printed census records

1829-1836

1821-1845 Texas Citizens Lists and other early records of the Republic of Texas (National Genealogical Society Special Publication No.22)

Valuable Printed Sources

Atlas and Gazetteer

Gannett, Henry. *A Gazetteer of Texas.* Washington D.C.: Government Printing Office (1904 United States Geological Survey Bulletin Number 224)

Pool, William C. *A Historical Atlas of Texas.* Austin: Encino Press (1975).

Maps

Day, James M. comp. *Maps of Texas 1527-1900; the Map Collection of the Texas State Archives.* Austin Pemberton Press (1974).

Wheat, Jim. *More Ghost Towns of Texas.* Garland, Texas: The Lost and Found (1980)

Place Names

Bartholomew, Ed. *800 Texas Ghost Towns.* Fort Davis, Texas: Frontier Book Publishers (1971).

Wheat, Jim. *Postmasters and Post Offices of Texas, 1846-1930.* Garland, Texas: The Lost and Found (1974)

Guides To Genealogical Research

Winfrey, Dorman H. *"Gone to Texas" - Sources for Genealogical Research in the Lone Star State.* Salt Lake City: Genealogical Society of Utah (1969 World Conference on Records I31)

Histories

Brown, John Henry. *History of Texas from 1685-1892.* St. Louis: L. E. Daniell (1893).

Wharton, Clarence R. *Texas Under Many Flags.* Chicago and New York; American Historical Society, Inc. (1930).

Genealogical Sources

D.A.R. Collection*

Gracy, Alice Duggan. *Early Texas Birth Records, 1838-1878.* Austin, Texas: Privately published, 1969.

Miller, Thomas Lloyd. *Bounty and Donation Land Grants of Texas, 1835-1888.* Austin: University of Texas Press, 1967.

Source Index

Crofford-Gould, Sharry. *Texas Cemetery Inscriptions: A Source Index.* San Antonio, Texas: Limited Editions (1977).

TEXAS COUNTY HISTORIES
(Population figures to nearest thousand - 1980 U. S. Census)

Name	Map Index	Date Created	Pop. By M 1980	U.S. Cen Reports Available	Parent County or Territory From Which Organized	County Seat
* Anderson	E9	1846	38	1850-80	Houston	Palestine 78801
(Dis Clk has div rec; Co Clk has b & d rec from 1903, m, pro & Ind rec from 1846, also civ ct rec)						
Andrews	D4	1875	13		Bexar	Andrews 79714
(Co Clk has b, m & civ ct rec from 1910, pro rec from 1911 & Ind rec from 1884; Dis Clk has div rec)						
* Angelina	E10	1846	64	1850-80	Nacogdoches	Lufkin 75901
(Co Clk has some b rec from 1875 to 1979, d rec from 1903, m, pro, Ind rec from 1846; Dis Clk has div rec; Co Clk and Dis Clk have civ ct rec from 1920)						
* Aransas	H8	1871	14	1880	Refugio	Rockport 78382
(Co Clk has b & d rec from 1901, m, pro, civ ct rec & deeds from 1871)						
* Archer	C7	1858	7	1880	Fannin	Archer City 76351
(Co Clk has b rec from 1880, m, d, bur, div, pro, civ ct, Ind rec)						
* Armstrong	B5	1876	2	1880	Bexar	Claude 79019
(Co Clk has b & d rec from 1903, m & pro rec from 1890, civ ct rec from 1898 & deeds from 1883; Clk Cir Ct has div rec)						
Atascosa	G7	1856	25	1860-80	Bexar	Jourdanton 78026
(Co Clk has b rec from 1890, d rec from 1903, m, pro & Ind rec from 1856, civ ct rec from 1860; Dis Clk has div rec)						

Name	Map Index	Date Created	Pop. By M 1980	U.S. Cen Reports Available	Parent County or Territory From Which Organized	County Seat
* Austin	F9	1837	18	1850-80	Old Mexican Municipality	Bellville 77418

(Co Clk has b, d rec from 1903, m rec from 1824, pro rec from 1835, civ ct rec from 1877 and Ind rec from 1828, naturalization rec from 1896, declaration rec from 1876)

| * Bailey | C4 | 1876 | 8 | | Bexar | Muleshoe 79347 |

(Co Clk has b, m, pro & civ ct rec from 1918, Ind rec from 1882; Dis Clk has div rec)

| *§ Bandera | G7 | 1856 | 7 | | Uvalde, Bexar | Bandera 78003 |

(Co Clk has b & d rec from 1904, m, div, pro, civ ct & Ind rec from 1856, also cattle brands from 1856)

| *§ Bastrop | F8 | 1836 | 24 | 1850-80 | Old Mexican Municipality | Bastrop 78602 |

(Co Clk has b & d rec from 1903, m rec from 1860, pro rec from 1850, civ ct rec from 1890, Ind rec from 1837; Dis Clk has div rec)

| Baylor | C7 | 1858 | 5 | 1880 | Fannin | Seymour 76380 |

(Co Clk has b & d rec from 1903, m rec from 1879, div rec from 1881, pro & civ ct rec from 1880)

| * Bee | H8 | 1857 | 26 | 1860-80 | Goliad, Refugio, Live Oak, San Patricio | Beeville 78102 |

(Co Clk has b & d rec from 1903, m, pro & Ind rec from 1858, civ ct rec from 1876; Dis Clk has div rec)

| * Bell | F8 | 1850 | 158 | 1860-80 | Milam | Belton 76513 |

(Co Clk has b & d rec from 1903, m, pro, civ ct & Ind rec from 1850)

| Bexar | G7 | 1836 | 987 | 1850-80 | Old Mexican Municipality established 1718 | San Antonio 78204 |

(Co Clk has b rec from 1838, m rec from 1837, d rec from 1903, pro rec from 1843, Ind rec from 1700's, Spanish church rec from 1737 to 1859, minutes of Spanish City Council from 1815 to 1820)

| * Blanco | F7 | 1858 | 5 | 1870-80 | Gillespie, Comal, Burnet, Hays | Johnson City 78636 |

(Co Clk has b, d rec from 1903, m, div, pro, civ ct, Ind rec from 1876)

| Borden | D5 | 1876 | 1 | 1880 | Bexar | Gail 79738 |

(Co Clk has b & d rec from 1903, m, div & civ ct rec from 1891, pro rec from 1894)

| Bosque | E8 | 1854 | 13 | 1860-80 | McLennan, Milam District | Meridian 76665 |

(Co Clk has b, d rec from 1902, m, pro, Ind rec from 1854, civ ct rec; Dis Clk has div rec)

| Bowie | C10 | 1840 | 75 | 1850-80 | Red River | Boston 75557 |

(Co Clk has b, m, d, pro, civ ct rec & deeds from 1889)

| Brazoria | G9 | 1836 | 167 | 1850-80 | Old Mexican Municipality | Angelton 77515 |

(Co Clk has b rec from 1901, d rec from 1903, m rec from 1829, pro, civ ct, Ind rec from 1800's, mil rec from 1900, crim, delayed b certificates, election rec from 1800's)

| * Brazos | F9 | 1841 | 93 | 1850-80 | Washington, Robertson | Bryan 77801 |

(originally Navasota Co - changed to Brazos 1842; Co Clk has m rec from 1841, b & d rec from 1900, pro rec from 1844, civ ct rec from 1959, some civ ct rec earlier)

| Brewster | F4 | 1887 | 8 | | Presidio | Alpine 79830 |

(Co Clk has b & d rec from 1903, m, div, pro & civ ct rec from 1887)

| Briscoe | C5 | 1876 | 3 | 1880 | Bexar | Silverton 79257 |

(Co Clk has b rec from 1906, m, div, pro & civ ct rec from 1892, d rec from 1902)

| Brooks | I7 | 1911 | 9 | | Starr, Zapata, Hidalgo | Falfurrias 78355 |

(Co Clk has b, m, d, pro & civ ct rec from 1911)

| *§ Brown | E7 | 1856 | 33 | 1860-80 | Travis, Comanche | Brownwood 76801 |

(Co Clk has b, m, d, pro, civ ct, Ind, cattle brands from 1880; Dis Clk has div rec)

| Buchanan | | | | 1860 | Changed to Stephens 1861 | |

| * Burleson | F9 | 1846 | 12 | 1850-80 | Milam, Washington | Caldwell 77836 |

(Co Clk has b, d rec from 1903, m, pro, civ ct, Ind rec from 1845; Dis Clk has div rec from 1845)

| Burnet | F7 | 1852 | 18 | 1860-80 | Travis, Bell, Williamson | Burnet 78611 |

(Co Clk has b, d rec from 1903, m, bur, pro, Ind rec from 1852, civ ct rec from 1876; Dis Clk has div rec)

| *§ Caldwell | F8 | 1848 | 23 | 1850-80 | Gonzales | Lockhart 78644 |

(Co Clk has b & d rec from 1903, m & Ind rec from 1848 & civ ct rec; Dis Clk has div rec)

| § Calhoun | H9 | 1846 | 20 | 1850-80 | Victoria, Matagorda, Jackson | Port Lavaca 77979 |

(Co Clk has b & d rec from 1903, m & deeds from 1846, pro rec from 1849, civ ct rec from 1850, crim rec from 1909 & discharge rec from 1919)

| Callahan | D6 | 1858 | 11 | 1880 | Bexar, Travis, Bosque | Baird 79504 |

(Co Clk has b, d rec from 1903, m, pro, Ind rec from 1877; Dis Clk has div, civ ct rec)

| * Cameron | J8 | 1848 | 208 | 1850-80 | Nueces | Brownsville 78520 |

(Co Clk has b & d rec from 1929, m, pro, civ ct & Ind rec from 1848, marks & brands, mil dis & comm ct rec from 1848, also assumed names)

| Camp | D10 | 1874 | 9 | 1880 | Upshur | Pittsburg 75686 |

(Co Clk has b, d rec from 1903, m, pro, civ ct rec from 1874, Ind rec from 1854, marks and brands from 1874)

| Carson | B5 | 1876 | 7 | | Bexar | Panhandle 79068 |

(Co Clk has b, d rec from 1903, m rec from 1888, div rec from 1902, pro rec from 1907, Ind rec from 1883)

| Cass | D10 | 1846 | 29 | 1850-80 | Bowie | Linden 75563 |

(Name changed to Davis 1861, renamed Cass 1871) (Co Clk has b, d rec from 1903, m rec from 1847, pro rec from 1846, Ind rec from 1846; Dis Clk has div, civ ct rec)

Name	Map Index	Date Created	Pop. By M 1980	U.S. Cen Reports Available	Parent County or Territory From Which Organized	County Seat
Castro	C4	1876	11		Bexar	Dimmitt 79027

(Co Clk has b, m, d, div, pro, civ ct & Ind rec)

* Chambers	G10	1858	18	1860-80	Jefferson, Liberty	Anahuac 77514

(Co Clk has b rec from 1903, d rec from 1908, m, pro, civ ct, Ind rec from 1875, div rec from 1910)

* Cherokee	E10	1846	38	1850-80	Nacogdoches	Rusk 75785

(Co Clk has b & d rec from 1903, m, pro & civ ct rec from 1846)

Childress	C6	1876	7	1880	Bexar, Youngland District	Childress 79201

(Co Clk has b, m, d, bur, pro, Ind rec from 1886, div, civ ct rec from 1900)

Clay	C7	1857	10	1860-80	Cooke	Henrietta 76365

(Co Clk has b, d rec from 1903, m rec from 1874, pro, Ind rec from 1873, civ ct rec from 1876)

* Cochran	C4	1876	5		Bexar	Morton 79346

(Co Clk has b, d, div, pro & civ ct rec from 1926, m rec from 1924, Ind rec from 1884, cattle brands from 1921)

Coke	E6	1889	3		Tom Green	Robert Lee 76945

(Co Clk has b, d rec from 1903, m, div, pro, civ ct, Ind rec from 1890)

* Coleman	E6	1858	10	1870-80	Travis, Brown	Coleman 76834
* Collin	D8	1846	144	1850-80	Fannin	McKinney 75069

(Co Clk has b & d rec from 1903, m, pro & civ ct rec; Dis Clk has div & Ind rec)

* Collingsworth	B6	1876	5	1880	Bexar, Youngland District	Wellington 79095

(Co Clk has b rec from 1891, m rec from 1890, d rec from 1892, div & civ ct rec from 1903)

Colorado	G9	1837	19	1850-80	Old Mexican Municipality	Columbus 78934

(Co Clk has b & d rec from 1903, m & pro rec from 1837; Dis Clk has div & civ ct rec)

Comal	F7	1846	36	1850-80	Bexar, Gonzales, Travis	New Braunfels 78130
* Comanche	E7	1856	13	1860-80	Bosque, Coryell	Comanche 76442

(Co Clk has b, d & bur rec from 1903, m rec from 1882, pro rec from 1897, civ ct rec from 1934 & Ind rec from 1859)

* Concho	E6	1858	3	1880	Bexar	Paint Rock 76866

(Co Clk has b, m, d, div, pro, civ ct & Ind rec from 1888)

* Cooke	C8	1848	28	1850-80	Fannin	Gainesville 76240

(Co Clk has b, d rec from 1903, m, pro, civ ct, Ind rec from 1850; Dis Clk has div rec)

* Coryell	E7	1854	56	1860-80	Bell	Gatesville 76528

(Co Clk has b & d rec from 1903, m, pro, civ ct & Ind rec from 1854)

* Cottle	C6	1876	3	1880	Fannin	Paducah 79248

(Co Clk has b, m, d, bur, div, pro, civ ct & Ind rec from 1892)

Crane	E4	1887	5		Tom Green	Crane 79731

(Co Clk has b rec from 1928, m, d, div, pro, civ ct & Ind rec from 1927 & bur rec from 1953)

Crockett	F5	1875	5	1880	Bexar	Ozona 76943

(Co Clk has b, d rec from 1903, div, pro, civ ct rec from 1892, bur rec after Jan. 1, 1980)

* Crosby	C5	1876	9	1880	Bexar District (org 1886)	Crosbyton 79322

(Co Clk has b, d rec from 1903, m, pro, civ ct, Ind rec from 1886; Dis Clk has div rec)

Culberson	E3	1911	3		El Paso	Van Horn 79855

(Co Clk has b, m, d, div, pro, civ ct, Ind rec from 1911, bur rec from 1972)

* Dallam	A4	1876	7		Bexar	Dalhart 79022

(Co Clk has b, d rec from 1903, m, civ ct rec from 1891, div rec from 1892, pro rec from 1900, Ind rec from 1876)

* Dallas	D8	1846	1,551	1850-80	Nacogdoches, Robertson	Dallas 75202

(Co Clk has b & d rec from 1903, m rec from 1846, pro & civ ct rec; Dis Ct has div rec)

Davis				1870	Changed to Cass 1871	
* Dawson	D5	1876-58	16	1860-80	Bexar (org. 1905)	Lamesa 79331

(Co Clk has b, m, d, bur, pro, civ ct & Ind rec; Dis Clk has div rec)

Deaf Smith	B4	1876	21	1880	Bexar	Hereford 79045

(Co Clk has b, d rec from 1903, m, pro, civ ct rec from 1891, Ind rec from 1882, brand rec, discharge rec from 1919; funeral homes have bur rec; Dis Clk has div rec, doctor recs from 1903)

* Delta	D9	1870	5		Hopkins, Lamar	Cooper 75432

(Co Clk has b, pro & civ ct rec from 1903, m rec from 1870, d rec from 1916 & Ind rec)

*§ Denton	D8	1846	142	1850-80	Fannin	Denton 76201

(Co Clk has b, d & bur rec from 1903, m, pro, civ ct & Ind rec from 1876; Dis Clk has div rec from 1876; Courthouse burned 1875, a few prior rec saved)

§ DeWitt	G8	1846	19	1850-80	Goliad, Gonzales, Victoria	Cuero 77954

(Co Clk has b & d rec from 1903, m, pro, civ ct, Ind rec & cattle brands from 1846, CW muster roll for home guard groups from 1861)

Dickens	C6	1876	4	1880	Bexar	Dickens 79229

(Co Clk has b, m, d, bur, div, pro, civ ct & Ind rec from 1891)

* Dimmit	H6	1858	11	1880	Uvalde, Bexar, Maverick, Webb	Carrizo Springs 78834

(Co Clk has b & d rec from 1903, m & civ ct rec from 1881, pro rec from 1882 & Ind rec; Dis Clk has div rec)

Name	Map Index	Date Created	Pop. By M 1980	U.S. Cen Reports Available	Parent County or Territory From Which Organized	County Seat
* Donley	B5	1881	4	1881	Jack	Clarendon 79226

(Co Clk has b, d & bur rec from 1903, m, div, pro & civ ct rec from 1881)

| Duval | H7 | 1858 | 13 | 1870-80 | Live Oak, Starr, Neuces | San Diego 78384 |

(Co Clk has b & d rec from 1903, m, pro & Ind rec from 1877 also civ ct rec)

| * Eastland | D7 | 1858 | 19 | 1860-80 | Bosque, Coryell, Travis | Eastland 76448 |

(Co Clk has b, d rec from 1903 to 1930, 1940 to 1950, m, pro, Ind rec from 1873; Dis Ct has div rec from 1903)

| Ector | E4 | 1887 | ·115 | | Tom Green | Odessa 79760 |

(Co Clk has b, m, d, bur, pro, civ ct, Ind rec from 1896; Dist Clk has div rec)

| Edwards | F6 | 1858 | 2 | 1880 | Bexar | Rocksprings 78880 |

(Co Clk has b & d rec from 1903, m, div, pro, civ ct rec & deeds from 1884)

| * Ellis | D8 | 1849 | 60 | 1850-80 | Navarro | Waxahachie 75165 |
| * El Paso | E1 | 1850 | 479 | 1860-80 | Bexar | El Paso 79901 |

(Co Clk has b, d & bur rec from 1903, m rec from 1880, pro, civ ct & Ind rec, also mil dis rec from 1919)

| Encinal | | | | 1860-70 | Discontinued | |
| * Erath | D7 | 1856 | 22 | 1860-80 | Bosque, Coryell | Stephenville 76401 |

(Co Clk has b, d rec from 1903, m rec from 1869, pro rec from 1876, Ind rec from 1867)

| * Falls | E8 | 1850 | 18 | 1860-80 | Limestone, Milam | Marlin 76661 |

(Co Clk has b, d rec from 1903, m rec from 1854, pro, Ind rec)

| * Fannin | C9 | 1837 | 24 | 1850-80 | Red River | Bonham 75418 |

(Co Clk has b rec from 1903, a few from 1874 to 1876, d rec from 1903, m rec from 1850, pro & Ind rec from 1838, civ ct rec from 1914)

| *§ Fayette | F8 | 1837 | 19 | 1850-80 | Bastrop, Colorado | La Grange 78945 |

(Co Clk has b, d rec from 1903, m, pro, Ind rec from 1838; Dis Clk has div rec from 1838)

| Fisher | D6 | 1876 | 6 | 1880 | Bexar | Roby 79543 |

(Co Clk has b, d & m rec from 1903, pro, civ ct & Ind rec from 1886)

| * Floyd | C5 | 1876 | 10 | 1880 | Bexar (org. 1890) | Floydada 79235 |

(Co Clk has b, d rec from 1903, m, pro, civ ct, Ind rec from 1891; Dis Clk has div rec)

| * Foard | C6 | 1891 | 2 | | Hardman, Knox, King, Cottle | Crowell 79227 |

(Co Clk has b & d rec from 1903, m, div, pro, civ ct & Ind rec from 1891)

| * Fort Bend | G9 | 1837 | 131 | 1850-80 | Austin | Richmond 77469 |

(Co Clk has b, d rec from 1903, m, Ind rec from 1838, pro rec from 1836 civ ct rec from 1876)

| Franklin | D9 | 1875 | 7 | 1880 | Titus | Mt. Vernon 75457 |

(Co Clk has b, d rec from 1903, m, pro rec from 1875, Ind rec from 1846)

| * Freestone | E9 | 1850 | 15 | 1860-80 | Limestone | Fairfield 75840 |

(Co Clk has b, d rec from 1903, m, pro, Ind rec from 1851)

| Frio | G7 | 1858 | 14 | 1860-80 | Atascosa, Bexar, Uvalde | Pearsall 78061 |

(Co Clk has b, d rec from 1903, m rec from 1876, pro rec from 1874, civ ct rec from 1907, Ind rec from 1871)

| Gaines | D4 | 1876 | 13 | 1880 | Bexar | Seminole 79360 |

(Co Clk has b, m, d, bur, pro & civ ct rec from 1905)

| Galveston | G10 | 1838 | 195 | 1850-80 | Brazoria | Galveston 77550 |

(Co Clk has b & d rec from 1903 to 1910 - 1941 to 1951, m, pro & Ind rec from 1838, civ ct rec from 1875)

| Garza | D5 | 1876 | 5 | 1880 | Bexar (org. 1907) | Post 79356 |

(Co Clk has b, m, d, div, pro & civ ct rec from 1907)

| *§ Gillespie | F7 | 1848 | 13 | 1850-80 | Bexar, Travis | Fredericksburg 78624 |

(Co Clk has incomplete b, m, d, pro, civ ct, Ind rec from 1848; Dis Clk has div rec)

| * Glasscock | E5 | 1887 | 1 | | Tom Green | Garden City 79739 |

(Co Clk has b, d rec from 1903, m, civ ct rec from 1893, pro rec from 1895, Ind rec from 1883; Dis Clk has div rec; Co Judge has recent bur rec)

| Goliad | H8 | 1836 | 5 | 1850-80 | Old Mexican Municipality | Goliad 77963 |

(Co Clk has b & d rec from 1903, m, pro, civ ct & Ind rec from 1870 & div rec)

| Gonzales | G8 | 1836 | 17 | 1850-80 | Old Mexican Municipality | Gonzales 78629 |

(Co Clk has b, d rec from 1903, m, pro, Ind rec, brands from 1829; Dis Clk has div rec)

| * Gray | B5 | 1876 | 26 | 1880 | Bexar | Pampa 79065 |

(Co Clk has b rec from 1903, m, d, pro, civ ct rec from 1902, bur rec from 1930, Ind rec from 1887, discharge rec from 1919, marks and brands from 1902; Dis Clk has div rec)

| * Grayson | C8 | 1846 | 89 | 1850-80 | Fannin | Sherman 75090 |

(Co Clk has b & d rec from 1900, m, pro, civ ct & Ind rec from 1846; Dis Clk has div rec)

| *§ Gregg | D10 | 1873 | 98 | 1880 | Rusk, Upshur | Longview 75601 |

(Co Clk has b, m, civ ct, Ind rec from 1873, d rec from 1900, pro rec)

| * Grimes | F9 | 1846 | 14 | 1850-80 | Montgomery | Anderson 77830 |

(Co Clk has b, d & civ ct rec from 1903, m & pro rec from 1848 & Ind rec from 1843)

| *§ Guadalupe | G8 | 1846 | 47 | 1850-80 | Bexar, Gonzales | Seguin 78155 |

(Co Clk has b, d & bur rec from 1935, m & pro rec from 1838, also civ ct & Ind rec; Dis Clk has div rec)

COUNTY MAP FOR THE STATE OF TEXAS

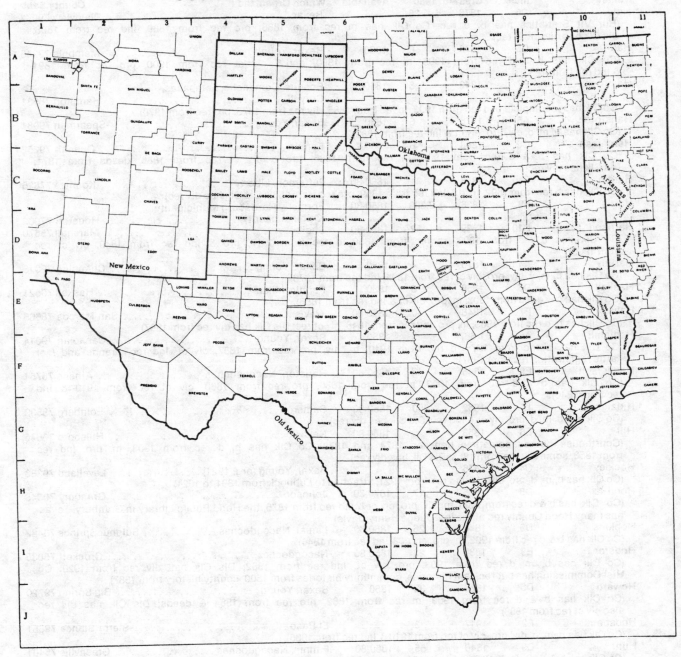

Name	Map Index	Date Created.	Pop. By M 1980	U.S. Cen Reports Available	Parent County or Territory From Which Organized	County Seat
* Hale	C5	1876	38		Bexar	Plainview 79072

(Bur Vit Statistics has b, d rec; Co Clk has m rec from 1888, pro rec from 1889, Ind rec from 1888; Dis Clk has div, civ ct rec)

| * Hall | C6 | 1876 | 6 | 1880 | Bexar, Young | Memphis 79245 |

(Co Clk has b & d rec from 1903, m rec from 1890, div & civ ct rec from 1900, pro rec from 1891 & Ind rec from 1833)

| Hamilton | E7 | 1842 | 8 | 1860-80 | Bosque, Comanche, Lampasas, Coryell | Hamilton 76531 |

(Co Clk has incomplete b, d rec from 1903, m rec from 1885, div rec from 1875, pro rec from 1870)

| * Hansford | A5 | 1876 | 6 | 1880 | Bexar, Young | Spearman 79081 |

(Co Clk has b, m, d, div, pro, civ ct & Ind rec from 1889)

| * Hardeman | C6 | 1858 | 6 | 1880 | Fannin | Quanah 79252 |

(Co Clk has b & d rec from 1903, m rec from 1885, pro & civ ct rec from 1886, deeds from 1871; Dis Clk has div rec)

| Hardin | F10 | 1858 | 41 | 1860-80 | Jefferson, Liberty | Kountze 77625 |

(Co Clk has b rec from 1892, m, d & Ind rec from 1859, pro rec from 1888; Dis Clk has div rec)

| * Harris | F9 | 1836 | 2,399 | 1850-80 | Formerly Harrisburg Municipality (Original county) | Houston 77002 |

| * Harrison | D10 | 1839 | 52 | 1850-80 | Shelby | Marshall 75670 |

(Co Clk has b rec from 1903, m rec from 1850, d rec from 1917, pro & Ind rec from 1840, civ ct rec from 1900)

| * Hartley | A4 | 1876 | 4 | 1880 | Bexar, Young | Channing 79018 |

(Co Clk has b, m, d, div, pro, civ ct rec from 1891, Ind rec from 1876)

| * Haskell | D6 | 1858 | 8 | 1880 | Fannin, Milam | Haskell 79521 |

(Co Clk has b & d rec from 1903, m, pro, civ ct & Ind rec from 1885)

| *§ Hays | F7 | 1848 | 40 | 1850-80 | Travis | San Marcos 78666 |

(Co Clk has b, d rec from 1903, m, pro, Ind rec from 1848, civ ct rec; Dis Clk has div rec from 1897)

| Hemphill | A6 | 1,887 | 5 | 1880 | Bexar, Young | Canadian 79014 |

(Co Clk has b rec from 1876, d rec from 1910, m, div, pro rec from 1887, civ ct, Ind rec, brands and / or cattle registration rec from 1887)

| * Henderson | E9 | 1846 | 42 | 1850-80 | Houston, Nacogdoches | Athens 75751 |

(Co Clk has b & d rec from 1903, m rec from 1880, pro rec from 1860, civ ct rec from 1910 & Ind rec from 1846)

| * Hidalgo | I7 | 1852 | 280 | 1860-80 | Cameron | Edinburg 78539 |

(Co Clk has b, m, d, pro, civ ct & Ind rec; Dis Clk has div rec)

| * Hill | E8 | 1853 | 25 | 1860-80 | Navarro | Hillsboro 76645 |

(Courthouse burned sometime between 1874 and 1878. Co Clk has b, d rec from 1903, m, pro, Ind rec from 1853, some bur rec from 1853; Dis Clk has div rec)

| * Hockley | C4 | 1876 | 23 | | Bexar, Young (org. 1921) | Levelland 79336 |

(Co Clk has b, m, d, pro, civ ct & Ind rec from 1921; attached to Lubbock from 1891 to 1921)

| *§ Hood | D8 | 1865 | 17 | 1870-80 | Johnson | Granbury 76048 |

(Co Clk has b & d rec from 1903, m, div, pro, civ ct & Ind rec from 1875; the Hood Public Library in Granbury, Texas has many Hood County rec of the late Judge Henry Davis)

| * Hopkins | D9 | 1846 | 25 | 1850-80 | Lamar, Nacogdoches | Sulphur Springs 75482 |

(Co Clk has b & d rec from 1903, m, pro, civ ct & Ind rec from 1846)

| * Houston | E9 | 1837 | 22 | 1850-80 | Nacogdoches | Crockett 75835 |

(Co Clk has b, m, d rec from 1903, pro, civ ct, Ind rec from 1882; Dis Clk has div rec from 1920; Co Hist Commission has bur rec, fam histories, community histories from 1800, county history from 1687)

| Howard | D5 | 1876 | 33 | 1880 | Bexar, Young | Big Spring 79720 |

(Co Clk has b & d rec from 1903, m rec from 1882, pro rec from 1884 & deeds; Dis Clk has div rec also civ ct rec from 1883)

| Hudspeth | E2 | 1917 | 3 | | El Paso | Sierra Blanca 79851 |

(Co Clk has b, m, d, div, pro, civ ct rec from 1918 & Ind rec from 1836)

| * Hunt | D9 | 1846 | 55 | 1850-80 | Fannin, Nacogdoches | Greenville 75401 |

(Co Clk has b & d rec from 1903, m rec 1858, pro rec 1896 & deeds 1846)

| * Hutchinson | A5 | 1876 | 26 | | Bexar District | Stinnett 79083 |

(Co Clk has m, pro, civ ct, Ind rec from 1901; b, d rec complete to 1952; Dis Clk has div rec)

| Irion | E5 | 1 | | | Tom Green | Mertzon 76941 |

(Co Clk has b, d, bur, div, pro & civ ct rec from 1903, m rec from 1889)

| * Jack | D7 | 1856 | 7 | 1860-80 | Cooke | Jacksboro 76056 |

(Co Clk has b & d rec from 1903, pro rec from 1857 & Ind rec from 1860, also m & civ ct rec; Dis Clk has div rec)

| *§ Jackson | G9 | 1836 | 13 | 1850-80 | Old Mexican Municipality | Edna 77957 |

(Co Clk has b & d rec from 1903, m, pro, Ind rec from 1836, civ ct rec from 1910; Dis Clk has div rec)

| Jasper | F10 | 1836 | 31 | 1850-80 | Old Mexican Municipality | Jasper 75951 |

Name	Map Index	Date Created	Pop. By M 1980	U.S. Cen Reports Available	Parent County or Territory From Which Organized	County Seat
Jeff Davis	F3	1887	2		Presidio	Fort Davis 79734

(Co Clk has b & d rec from 1903, m, div, pro, civ ct & Ind rec from 1887)

| Jefferson | F10 | 1836 | 251 | 1850-80 | Old Mexican Municipality | Beaumont 77704 |

(Co Clk has b, d rec from 1903, m, pro, civ ct, Ind rec from 1836; Dis Clk has div rec)

| Jim Hogg | I7 | 1913 | 5 | | Brooks, Duval | Hebbronville 78361 |
| * Jim Wells | H7 | 1911 | 36 | | Nueces | Alice 78332 |

(Co Clk has b, d, m, pro, civ ct rec from 1911, Ind rec from 1848; Dis Clk has div rec)

| * Johnson | D8 | 1854 | 67 | 1860-80 | Ellis, Hill, Navarro | Cleburne 76031 |

(Co Clk has m, Ind, pro rec from 1854, b, d rec from 1903, wills from 1897; Dist Ct has div rec)

| Jones | D6 | 1858-61 | 17 | 1880 | Bexar, Bosque (org. 1881) | Anson 79501 |

(Co Clk has b & d rec from 1903, m rec & deeds from 1881, pro rec from 1882; Dis Clk has div rec)

| Karnes | G8 | 1854 | 14 | 1860-80 | Bexar | Karnes City 78118 |

(Co Clk has b, d, pro rec from 1900, m, Ind rec from 1875; Dis Clk has div rec from 1858)

| * Kaufman | D9 | 1848 | 39 | 1850-80 | Henderson | Kaufman 75142 |

(Co Clk has b & d rec from 1903, m & pro rec from 1850)

| Kendall | F7 | 1862 | 11 | 1870-80 | Kerr, Blanco | Boerne 78006 |
| Kenedy | I8 | 1921 | 1 | | Willacy, Hidalgo, Cameron | Sarita 78385 |

(Co Clk has b rec from 1926, m rec from 1923, d rec from 1929, div, civ ct rec from 1914, pro, Ind rec)

| Kent | D6 | 1876 | 1 | | Bexar, Young | Jayton 79528 |

(Co Clk has b rec from 1903, also m, d, bur, div, pro & civ ct rec from 1893)

| * Kerr | F6 | 1856 | 29 | 1860-80 | Bexar | Kerrville 78028 |

(Co Clk has b, d & bur rec from 1903, m, pro & Ind rec from 1856, co ct rec from 1900; Dis Clk has div rec)

| * Kimble | F6 | 1858 | 4 | 1870-80 | Bexar | Junction 76849 |

(Co Clk has b, d & bur rec from 1903, m, div, pro, civ ct & Ind rec from 1884)

| King | C6 | 1876 | .5 | 1880 | Bexar | Guthrie 79236 |

(Co Clk has b, div, civ ct rec from 1914, m rec from 1891, d rec from 1925, pro rec from 1915 & Ind rec from 1878)

| * Kinney | G6 | 1850 | 2 | 1860-80 | Bexar | Brackettville 78832 |

(Co Clk has b, d rec from 1903, m rec from 1872, div, pro, civ ct, Ind rec from 1873; St. Mary's Catholic Church, Brackettville, Tex. has bur rec)

| * Kleberg | I8 | 1913 | 33 | | Nueces | Kingsville 78363 |

(Co Clk has b, m, d, pro, civ ct & Ind rec from 1913; Dis Clk has div rec)

| Knox | C6 | 1858 | 5 | 1880 | Young, Bexar | Benjamin 79505 |

(Co Clk has b rec from 1905, m rec from 1886, d rec from 1917, div rec from 1900's, pro, civ ct, Ind rec from 1887)

| * Lamar | C9 | 1840 | 42 | 1850-80 | Red River | Paris 75460 |

(Co Clk has b & d rec from 1903, m, pro, civ ct & Ind rec from 1843; Dis Clk has div rec)

| * Lamb | C4 | 1876 | 19 | | Bexar | Littlefield 79339 |

(Co Clk has b, m, d, pro rec from 1920, Ind rec from 1915, also civ ct rec)

| * Lampasas | E7 | 1856 | 12 | 1860-80 | Bell, Travis | Lampasas 76550 |

(Co Clk has b rec from 1895, d rec from 1910, m rec from 1879, pro rec from 1876, civ ct rec from 1899 & Ind rec from 1872)

| La Salle | H7 | 1858-80 | 6 | 1870-80 | Bexar, Webb | Cotulla 78014 |

(Co Clk has b, d rec from 1900, m, div, pro, civ ct, Ind rec from 1880, marks and brand rec from 1881)

| * Lavaca | G8 | 1846 | 19 | 1850-80 | Colorado, Victoria, Jackson, Gonzales | Hallettsville 77964 |

(Co Clk has b, d rec from 1903, m, pro, civ ct rec from 1860, Ind rec from 1846)

| Lee | F8 | 1874 | 11 | 1880 | Bastrop, Burleston, Washington, Fayette | Giddings 78942 |

(Co Clk has b & d rec from 1903, m, pro, civ ct & Ind rec from 1874; Dis Clk has div rec)

| * Leon | E9 | 1846 | 10 | 1850-80 | Robertson | Centerville 75833 |

(Co Clk has b & d rec from 1903, m rec from 1885, pro rec from 1846, also civ ct & Ind rec)

| * Liberty | F10 | 1836 | 47 | 1850-80 | Old Spanish Municipality | Liberty 77575 |

(Courthouse burned 11 Dec. 1874, rec destroyed. Co Clk has b, d rec from 1903, m, pro, civ ct, Ind rec from 1875; Dis Clk has div rec)

| * Limestone | E9 | 1846 | 20 | 1850-80 | Robertson | Groesbeck 76642 |

(Co Clk has b & d rec from 1903, bur rec from 1914, m & Ind rec from 1873, pro rec from 1890 & civ ct rec; Dis Clk has div rec)

| Lipscomb | A6 | 1876 | 4 | 1880 | Bexar | Lipscomb 79056 |

(Co Clk has b, m, d, div, pro, civ ct, Ind rec from 1887)

| * Live Oak | H7 | 1856 | 10 | 1860-80 | Nueces, San Patricio | George West 78022 |

(Co Clk has b & d rec from 1903, m & Ind rec from 1856, pro rec from 1857 & civ ct rec; Dis Clk has div rec)

| Llano | F7 | 1856 | 10 | 1860-80 | Bexar | Llano 78643 |

(Co Clk has b & d rec from 1903 to 1924, m rec from 1880, div, pro, civ ct & Ind rec)

Name	Map Index	Date Created	Pop. By M 1980	U.S. Cen Reports Available	Parent County or Territory From Which Organized	County Seat
* Loving	E3	1887	.1		Tom Green	Mentone 79754

(Co Clk has b, m, d, div, pro, civ ct rec from 1931, Ind rec from 1920; Reorg 1931 having been attached to Reeves Co for judicial purposes)

Lubbock	C5	1876	212	1880	Bexar, Crosby	Lubbock 79408

(Co Clk has b & d rec from 1903, m rec from 1891, pro & civ ct rec from 1904; at one time attached to Crosby)

Lynn	D5	1876	9	1880	Bexar	Tahoka 79373

(Co Clk has b, m, d, bur & civ ct rec from 1903, pro rec from 1905 & Ind rec from 1879)

Madison	F9	1854	11	1860-80	Leon, Grimes, Walker	Madisonville 77864
*§ Marion	D10	1860	10	1860-80	Cass	Jefferson 75657

(Co Clk has b, d rec from 1903, m, pro, Ind rec from 1860)

Martin	D5	1876	5	1880	Bexar	Stanton 79782

(Co Clk has b & d rec from 1910, m, civ ct, div & pro rec from 1885)

* Mason	F7	1858	4	1860-80	Gillespie	Mason 76856

(Co Clk has b, d & bur rec from 1903, m, div, pro, civ ct rec from 1877 & Ind rec from 1850)

Matagorda	G9	1836	38	1850-80	Old Mexican Municipality	Bay City 77414
Maverick	G6	1856	31	1860-80	Kenedy	Eagle Pass 78852

(Co Clk has b & d rec from 1903, m rec from 1871, pro & civ ct rec)

* McCulloch	E6	1856	9	1870-80	Bexar	Brady 76825

(Co Clk has b, d, pro & co ct rec from 1903, m & Ind rec from 1879; Dis Clk has div rec)

* McLennan	E8	1850	171	1860-80	Milam	Waco 76703

(Co Clk has b & d rec from 1929, m, pro, civ ct & Ind rec from 1850; Dis Clk has div rec)

McMullen	H7	1858	1	1870-80	Bexar, Live Oak, Atascosa	Tilden 78072
Medina	G7	1848	23	1850-80	Bexar	Hondo 78861

(Co Clk has b, d rec from 1903, m, pro, Ind rec from 1848, civ ct rec from 1876)

* Menard	F6	1858	2	1870-80	Bexar	Menard 76859

(Co Clk has b & civ ct rec from 1900, m rec from 1878, d rec from 1917, div rec from 1889, pro & Ind rec from 1880)

Midland	E5	1885	82		Tom Green	Midland 79701

(Co Clk has b rec from 1917 also d rec, m & Ind rec from 1885, pro rec from 1886, civ ct rec from 1929 & mil dis from 1919; Dis Clk has div rec)

*§ Milam	F8	1836	23	1850-80	Old Mexican Municipality	Cameron 76520

(Co Clk has b, m, d, pro, civ ct & Ind rec)

*§ Mills	E7	1887	5		Comanche, Brown, Hamilton, Lampasas	Goldthwaite 76844

(Co Clk has b & d rec from 1903, m, div, pro, civ ct & Ind rec from 1887)

* Mitchell	D5	1876	9	1880	Bexar	Colorado City 79512

(Co Clk has b, m, d, pro & civ ct rec)

* Montague	C8	1857	17	1860-80	Cooke	Montague 76251

(Co Clk has b & d rec from 1903, m, pro & civ ct rec from 1873)

Montgomery	F9	1837	128	1850-80	Washington	Conroe 77301

(Co Clk has b, m, d, pro & Ind rec from 1838 & civ ct rec; Dis Clk has div rec from 1914)

Moore	A5	1876	17		Bexar	Dumas 79029

(Co Clk has b, d, bur, pro, civ ct rec from 1901, Ind rec from 1877, m rec from 1894; Dis Clk has div rec)

Morris	D10	1875	14	1880	Titus	Daingerfield 75638

(Co Clk has b & d rec from 1903, m, pro & Ind rec from 1875)

Motley	C6	1876	2	1880	Bexar (org. 1891)	Matador 79244

(Co Clk has b & d rec from 1903, m, div, pro, civ ct rec from 1891, also Ind rec from 1891 & a few prior)

* Nacogdoches	E10	1836-7	47	1880	Old Mexican Municipality	Nacogdoches 75961

(Co Clk has b, d rec from 1903, m rec from 1824, pro rec from 1845, Ind rec from 1833, civ ct rec; Dis Clk has div rec)

* Navarro	E8	1846	35	1850-80	Robertson	Corsicana 75110

(Co Clk has b & d rec from 1903, m rec from 1846, pro & Ind rec from 1850 & civ ct rec; Dis Clk has div rec)

Navasota (name changed to Brazos in 1842)

Newton	F10	1846	13	1850-80	Jasper	Newton 75966

(Co Clk has b & d rec from 1903, m rec from 1846, pro rec from 1870, also civ ct rec)

* Nolan	D6	1876	17	1880	Young, Bexar	Sweetwater 79556

(Co Clk has b rec from 1903, m, d, pro, civ ct rec from 1900, Ind rec from 1881; Dis Clk has div rec; Co Justice of Peace has bur rec)

* Nueces	H8	1846	267	1850-80	San Patricio	Corpus Christi 78401
* Ochiltree	A5	1876	10		Bexar	Perryton 79070

(Co Clk has b rec from 1903, d rec from 1904, m & civ ct rec from 1889, pro rec from 1884; Dis Clk has div rec)

Name	Map Index	Date Created	Pop. By M 1980	U.S. Cen Reports Available	Parent County or Territory From Which Organized	County Seat
* Oldham	B4	1876	2	1880	Bexar (org. 1880)	Vega 79092

(Co Clk has b rec from 1917, d rec from 1918, m & div rec from 1881, bur & pro rec from 1887, civ ct rec from 1911, Ind rec from 1878)

| § Orange | F11 | 1852 | 84 | 1860-80 | Jefferson | Orange 77630 |

(Co Clk has b rec from 1903, m, d, pro, civ ct, Ind rec from 1852; Dis Clk has div rec)

| * Palo Pinto | D7 | 1856 | 24 | 1860-80 | Navarro, Bosque | Palo Pinto 76072 |

(Co Clk has b & d rec from 1903, m & Ind rec from 1857, pro & civ ct rec from 1860; Dis Clk has div rec from 1900)

| * Panola | E10 | 1846 | 20 | 1850-80 | Harrison, Shelby | Carthage 75633 |

(Co Clk has b & d rec from 1903, m rec from 1846, pro, civ ct & Ind rec)

| * Parker | D8 | 1855 | 44 | 1860-80 | Bosque, Navarro | Weatherford 76086 |

(Co Clk has b, d rec from 1903, m, pro, Ind rec from 1874, civ ct rec; Dis Clk has div rec; Library, Weatherford, has bur rec)

| Parmer | C4 | 1876 | 11 | | Bexar | Farwell 79325 |

(Co Clk has b, m & d rec from 1906 also pro, civ ct & Ind rec; Dis Clk has div rec)

| Pecos | F4 | 1871 | 15 | 1880 | Presidio | Fort Stockton 79735 |

| * Polk | F10 | 1846-50 | 24 | 1850-80 | Liberty | Livingston 77351 |

(Co Clk has b, d rec from 1903, m, pro Ind rec from 1846, civ ct rec, Conf. State Army and Navy Roster 1861-1865, comm ct and tax assessments; Dis Clk has div rec)

| * Potter | B5 | 1876 | 99 | 1880 | Bexar | Amarillo 79101 |

(Co Clk has b, d rec from 1903 to 1910, from 1941 to 1951, m rec from 1888, pro rec from 1896, civ ct rec from 1889, Ind rec from 1878; Dis Clk has div rec)

| * Presidio | F3 | 1850 | 5 | 1860-80 | Bexar | Marfa 79843 |

(Co Clk has b rec from 1900, m, d, bur, div, pro, civ ct & Ind rec from 1886)

| * Rains | D9 | 1870 | 5 | 1880 | Hopkins, Hunt, Wood | Emory 75440 |

(Co Clk has b rec from 1902, d rec from 1903, m, div, Ind rec from 1880 & pro rec from 1894)

| * Randall | B5 | 1876 | 75 | | Bexar | Canyon 79015 |

(Co Clk has m, pro, civ ct & Ind rec; Dis Clk has div rec)

| * Reagan | E5 | 1903 | 4 | | Tom Green | Big Lake 76932 |

(Co Clk has b, m, d, div, pro, civ ct & Ind rec from 1903, some rec from 1883 transferred from Tom Green Co)

| Real | G6 | 1913 | 2 | | Bandera, Kerr, Edwards | Leakey 78873 |

(Co Clk has b, m, d, div, pro & civ ct rec from 1913)

| * Red River | C10 | 1836 | 16 | 1850-80 | Old Mexican Municipality | Clarksville 75426 |

(Co Clk has b, d rec from 1903, m rec from 1845, pro, Ind rec from 1835, brand rec from 1843; Dis Clk has div, civ ct rec)

| Reeves | E3 | 1883 | 16 | | Pecos | Pecos 79772 |

(Co Clk has b rec from 1903, m, d, pro, co ct & Ind rec from 1885, also deferred b rec some to the 1800's)

| * Refugio | H8 | 1836 | 9 | 1850-80 | Old Mexican Municipality | Refugio 78377 |

(Co Clk has b & d rec from 1903, m rec from 1851, pro rec from 1840, co ct & Ind rec from 1881)

| Roberts | A5 | 1876 | 1 | | Bexar | Miami 79059 |

(Co Clk has b & d rec from 1903, m, div, pro & civ ct rec from 1889)

| *§ Robertson | F9 | 1837 | 15 | 1850-80 | Milam | Franklin 77856 |

(Co Clk has b & d rec from 1903, m & pro rec from 1837 & Ind rec; Dis Clk has div & civ ct rec)

| *§ Rockwall | D8 | 1873 | 14 | 1880 | Kaufman | Rockwall 75087 |

(Co Clk has b rec from 1885, d rec from 1900, m rec from 1875, pro rec from 1877, Ind rec & deeds from 1873)

| * Runnels | E6 | 1858 | 12 | 1880 | Bexar, Travis (org. 1880) | Ballinger 76821 |

(Co Clk has b, d, civ ct rec from 1903, m, pro, Ind rec from 1880, cattle brands 1971 to date, soldiers discharge rec from 1918, school cen 1925 to 1970; Dis Clk has div rec)

| * Rusk | E10 | 1843 | 41 | 1850-80 | Nacogdoches | Henderson 75652 |

(Co Clk has b & d rec from 1903, m, pro, civ ct & Ind rec from 1844)

| § Sabine | E11 | 1836 | 9 | 1850-80 | Old Mexican Municipality | Hemphill 75948 |

(Co Clk has b & d rec from 1903, m rec from 1880, div, pro, civ ct & Ind rec)

| * San Augustine | E10 | 1836 | 6 | 1850-80 | Old Mexican Municipality | San Augustine 75972 |

(Co Clk has b, d rec from 1903, m, pro, Ind rec from 1837; Dis Clk has div, civ ct rec from 1837)

| San Jacinto | F10 | 1870 | 11 | 1880 | Liberty, Polk, Montgomery, Walker | Coldspring 77331 |

(Co Clk has b rec from 1903, d rec from 1905, m, div, pro, civ ct, Ind rec from 1870)

| * San Patricio | H8 | 1836 | 58 | 1850-80 | Old Mexican Municipality | Sinton 78387 |

(Co Clk has b rec from 1893, d rec from 1903, m rec from 1858, pro rec from 1847, civ ct rec from 1876 & Ind rec from 1848)

| * San Saba | E7 | 1856 | 6 | 1860-80 | Bexar | San Saba 76877 |

(Co Clk has b, d rec from 1903, m, div, civ ct, Ind rec from 1856, pro rec from 1890)

| * Schleicher | F6 | 1887 | 3 | | Crockett | Eldorado 76936 |

(Co Clk has b, d rec from 1903, m, div, pro, civ ct rec from 1901, Ind rec from 1889)

Name	Map Index	Date Created	Pop. By M 1980	U.S. Cen Reports Available	Parent County or Territory From Which Organized	County Seat
* Scurry	D5	1876	18	1880	Bexar	Snyder 79549

(Co Clk has b, d rec from 1903, m, pro rec from 1884, civ ct, Ind rec; Dis Clk has div rec)

Shackelford	D6	1858	4	1860-80	Bosque	Albany 76430

(Co Clk has b rec from 1903, m, Ind rec from 1874, d, pro rec from 1875, civ ct rec from 1899, div rec)

Shelby	E10	1836	23	1850-80	Old Mexican Municipality	Center 75935

(Co Clk has b, m, pro, civ ct & Ind rec from 1882, d & bur rec from 1903; Dis Clk has div rec)

Sherman	A5	1876	3		Bexar	Stratford 79084

(Co Clk has b, d, pro, civ ct rec from 1903, m, Ind rec from 1901, bur rec from 1895, div rec from 1914, Commission's Court Minutes from 1889, Crim rec from 1891, Cattle and Ranch Brands Register 1892)

* Smith	D9	1846	127	1850-80	Nacogdoches	Tyler 75701

(Co Clk has b & d rec from 1903, m rec from 1848, pro rec from 1847, civ ct rec & deeds rec from 1846)

*§ Somervell	E8	1875	4	1880	Hood, Johnson	Glen Rose 76043

(Co Clk has b & d rec from 1903, m rec from 1885, div, civ ct rec from 1898, pro & Ind rec from 1875)

Starr	I7	1848	27	1850-80	Nueces	Rio Grande City 78582

(Co Clk has b, d rec from 1903, m rec from 1847, pro, Ind rec from 1848, civ ct rec from 1885, marks and brands from 1874, Intentions to become citizens 1883 to 1898, soldier's discharge rec from 1919)

* Stephens	D7	1858	10	1870-80	Bosque	Breckenridge 76024

(Co Clk has b, d rec from 1903, m rec from 1876, pro rec from 1886, Ind rec from 1858; Dis Clk has div, civ ct rec. Originally Buchanan, changed to Stephens County 1861)

* Sterling	E5	1891	1		Tom Green	Sterling City 76951

(Co Clk has b & d rec from 1909, m, div, pro, civ ct rec from 1892 & Ind rec from 1891)

* Stonewall	D6	1876	2		Bexar	Aspermont 79502

(Co Clk has b, m, d, div, pro, civ ct & Ind rec from ca 1900)

Sutton	F6	1890	5		Crockett	Sonora 76950

(Co Clk has b, d rec from 1903, m, div, pro, civ ct, Ind rec from Dec. 1890)

Swisher	C5	1876	10		Bexar, Young	Tulia 79088

(Co Clk has b rec from 1904, m, d, bur rec from 1900, div rec from 1905, pro & civ ct rec from 1890, Ind rec from 1888)

* Tarrant	D8	1849	859	1850-80	Navarro (1860 cen missing)	Fort Worth 76102

(Co Clk has b, m, pro rec from 1876, d rec from 1900; Dis Clk has div & civ ct rec)

Taylor	D6	1858	111	1880	Bexar, Travis	Abilene 79602
Terrell	F4	1905	2	1880	Pecos	Brownfield 79316
* Terry	D4	1876	15		Bexar, attached to Martin from 1889 (Org. 1904)	

(Co Clk has b & d rec from 1941, m rec from 1904, pro, civ ct, Ind rec & marks & brands from 1904)

Throckmorton	D6	1858	2	1860-80	Fannin (1870 cen missing)	Throckmorton 76083

(Co Clk has b rec from 1903, m, d, div, pro rec from 1879, also civ ct & Ind rec)

* Titus	D10	1846	21	1850-80	Red River, Bowie	Mt. Pleasant 75455

(Co Clk has b, m, d, bur, pro, civ ct, Ind rec from 1895; Dis Clk has div rec from 1895)

Tom Green	E6	1874	85	1880	Bexar	San Angelo 76901

(Co Clk has b & d rec from 1903, m, pro, civ ct rec, deeds & mtgs from 1875)

* Travis	F8	1840	417	1850-80	Bastrop	Austin 78767

(Co Clk has b & d rec from 1903, m, pro, civ ct & Ind rec from 1840)

* Trinity	E10	1850	9	1860-80	Houston	Groveton 75845

(Courthouse burned 1876, some deeds refiled. Co Clk has b rec from 1911, d rec from 1919, m, Ind rec from 1876, div rec from 1920, pro, civ ct rec, County Judge has school rec)

Tyler	F10	1846	15	1850-80	Liberty	Woodville 75979

(Co Clk has b rec from 1838, m rec from 1849, d, bur rec from 1903, pro rec from 1845, Ind rec from 1846; Dis Clk has div, civ ct rec)

* Upshur	D10	1846	28	1850-80	Harrison, Nacogdoches	Gilmer 75644

(Co Clk has b & m rec from 1873, d rec from 1903, pro rec from 1853, civ ct rec from 1876 & Ind rec from 1845; Dis Clk has div rec)

Upton	E5	1867	5		Tom Green (Org. 1910)	Rankin 79778

(Co Clk has b, m, d, div & civ ct rec from 1910, pro rec from 1910)

*§ Uvalde	G6	1850	22	1860-80	Bexar	Uvalde 78801

(Co Clk has b & d rec from 1903, m rec 1856, pro rec 1857 & civ ct rec 1876)

Val Verde	G5	1885	36		Crockett, Kinney, Pecos	Del Rio 78840

(Co Clk has b, d rec from 1903, pro, civ ct, Ind rec from 1885, m rec; Dis Clk has div rec)

* Van Zandt	D9	1848	31	1850-80	Henderson	Canton 75103

(Co Clk has b, d rec from 1903, m, pro, Ind rec from 1848; Dis Clk has div rec)

* Victoria	G8	1836	69	1850-80	Old Mexican Municipality	Victoria 77903

(Co Clk has b, d rec from 1903, m, pro, Ind rec from 1838, civ ct rec from 1867; Dis Clk has div rec)

Walker	F9	1846	42	1850-80	Montgomery	Huntsville 77340

(Co Clk has b rec from 1881, m, pro, commissioner's ct rec from 1846, d red from 1900, civ ct rec from 1860's, Ind rec from 1831; Dis Clk has div rec)

Waller	F9	1873	19	1880	Austin, Grimes	Hempstead 77445

(Co Clk has b, d rec from 1903, m, pro, civ ct, Ind rec from 1873)

Name	Map Index	Date Created	Pop. By M 1980	U.S. Cen Reports Available	Parent County or Territory From Which Organized	County Seat
Ward	E4	1887	14		Tom Green	Monahans 79756

(Co Clk has b, d, m, pro, civ ct, Ind rec from 1892; Dis Clk has div rec; City funeral homes have bur rec)

| Washington | F9 | 1836 | 22 | 1850-80 | Texas Municipality | Brenham 77833 |

(Co Clk has b, d rec from 1903, m rec from 1837, pro, Ind rec; Dis Clk has div rec)

| Webb | H7 | 1848 | 99 | 1850-80 | Bexar | Laredo 78040 |

(Co Clk has b & d rec from 1856, m rec from 1850 & pro rec from 1870)

| * Wharton | G9 | 1846 | 40 | 1850-80 | Matagorda, Jackson | Wharton 77488 |

(Co Clk has b & d rec from 1903, m rec from 1857, pro rec from 1849 & Ind rec from 1846)

| * Wheeler | B6 | 1876 | 7 | 1880 | Bexar, Young | Wheeler 79096 |

(Co Clk has b & d rec from 1906, m, pro, civ ct & Ind rec from 1879; Dis Clk has div rec)

| * Wichita | C7 | 1858 | 120 | 1880 | Youngland District | Wichita Falls 76301 |

(Co Clk has limited b rec from 1890, limited d rec from 1900, m, pro & Ind rec from 1882; Dis Clk has div & civ ct rec)

| * Wilbarger | C7 | 1858 | 16 | 1880 | Bexar (Org. 1881) | Vernon 76384 |

(Co Clk has b, m, d, civ ct & pro rec from 1887; City Sec has bur rec; Dis Clk has div rec)

| Willacy | I8 | 1911 | 17 | | Hidalgo, Cameron (Org. 1921) | Raymondville 78580 |

(Co Clk has b, m, d, pro, civ ct rec from 1921, Ind rec from 1891)

| * Williamson | F8 | 1848 | 76 | 1850-80 | Milam | Georgetown 78626 |

(Co Clk has b & d rec from 1903, m, pro, civ ct & Ind rec from 1848; Dis Clk has div rec)

| § Wilson | G7 | 1860 | 17 | 1870-80 | Bexar, Karnes | Floresville 78114 |

(Co Clk has b & d rec from 1903, m rec from 1860, pro rec from 1862 & co ct rec from 1876)

| * Winkler | E4 | 1887 | 10 | | Tom Green (Org. 1910) | Kermit 79745 |

(Co Clk has b rec from 1919, d, pro rec from 1912, m, co ct rec from 1911, Ind rec from 1887; Dis Clk has div, civ ct rec)

| * Wise | D8 | 1856 | 26 | 1860-80 | Cooke | Decatur 76234 |

(Co Clk has b, d rec from 1903, m rec from 1881, pro rec from 1882, Ind rec from 1852, civ ct rec)

| Wood | D9 | 1850 | 25 | 1860-80 | Van Zandt | Quitman 75783 |

(Co Clk has b, d rec from 1903, m, pro, Ind rec from 1879, civ ct rec; Dis Clk has div rec)

| Yoakum | D4 | 1876 | 8 | | Bexar (attached to Martin from 1904 to 1907) | Plains 79355 |

(Co Clk has b rec from 1878, m & d rec from 1908, pro rec from 1907, civ ct rec from 1930 & Ind rec from 1898; Dis Clk has div rec)

| * Young | D7 | 1856 | 19 | 1860-80 | Bosque, Fannin | Graham 76046 |

(Co Clk has b & d rec from 1903, m, pro, civ ct, deeds, comm ct min & old brands from 1856; Dis Clk has div rec)

| * Zapata | I7 | 1858 | 7 | 1860-80 | Starr, Webb | Zapata 78076 |
| Zavala | G6 | 1858 | 12 | 1860-80 | Uvalde, Maverick (Org. 1884) | Crystal City 78839 |

(Co Clk has b, m, d, pro & civ ct rec from 1884, Ind rec; Dis Clk has div rec, also some copied rec from parent cos)

* - At least one county history has been published about this county.

§ - Inventory of county archives was made by the Historical Records Survey. (see introduction)

UTAH

CAPITAL, SALT LAKE CITY - TERRITORY 1850 - STATE 1896 - (45TH)

As the Puritans, the Pilgrims, the Quakers, the Huguenots, and many other religious devotees came to American shores for the opportunity to worship Almighty God according to their conscience, so the members of the Church of Jesus Christ of Latter-day Saints, or the so-called "Mormons," came to the then arid, forbidding valleys of Utah. When they came the land was barren and desolate, nothing but the bluish gray of the sagebrush and greasewood covered the land. Not a sign of human life, except a few Indian wigwams that were scattered along the shores of a small lake or the banks of a tiny mountain stream. Not even the hoofprints of the horses that carried Father Escalante and Father Dominguez on a hurried journey through part of the state seventy-one years earlier were anywhere to be found.

It was on 24 July 1847 that the colonization of the Great Salt Lake Basin began with the arrival on the site of the present Salt Lake City of the first Pioneer group 148 - 143 men, three women, and two boys. New groups arrived several times each month. After three years, in 1850, there were 11,380.

Most of the early settlers of Utah came from New England, Ohio, Illinois, Missouri, and Canada, and since then from almost every state in the Union. Most of the Europeans who have come, in order of their numerical strength, are English, Germans, Danes, Swedes, Norwegians, Swiss, Hollanders, Welsh, and Scottish, with a sprinkling of Piedmont Italians, and a few Czechs. Many Austrians, Greeks, Mexicans and Italians, not affected by church affiliation, have come to work in the mining and smelting operations of the state.

The Bureau of Health Statistics, State Department of Health, 150 West North Temple Street, P.O. Box 2500, Salt Lake City, Utah 84110 has records of births and deaths since 1905. Marriage records are at the offices of the County Clerks.

The Genealogical Society of Utah is one of the most active genealogical organizations in the world. The main library is located at 50 East North Temple Street, Salt Lake City, Utah 84150. Although this genealogical society was founded to assist the members of the Church of Jesus Christ of Latter-day Saints (Mormons) in compiling genealogies of their own families, the general public is welcome to use its facilities. The library does not have the personnel to do research for individuals, however, private researchers are accredited by the Genealogical Society of Utah to provide professional help. A list of these accredited researchers may be obtained upon request by stating the locality of the research problem.

The library is open on Mondays from 7:30 a.m. to 6:00 p.m.; Tuesdays through Fridays from 7:30 a.m. to 10:00 p.m.; Saturdays from 8:00 a.m. to 5:00 p.m.

This library's holdings include thousands and thousands of books. But, in addition, they also have over 1,000,000 rolls of microfilm which have been accumulated through the society's world-wide microfilming program. The negative rolls of microfilm are stored in the great Granite Mountain Records Vault, which was constructed for processing, distributing, and storing a tremendous volume of microfilms under conditions which insure permanent safe keeping of these valuable records. The positive copies are made available to patrons of the society in their main library in Salt Lake City, Utah and also to their many branch libraries located throughout the country. Please write to the Genealogical Society at their Salt Lake City address for a list of branch libraries in your area.

Genealogical Archives, Libraries, Societies, and Publications

Brigham Carnegie Library, 26 E. Forest, Brigham City, UT 84302.

Brigham Young University, Harold B. Lee Library, Provo, UT 84602.

Cedar City Public Library, Cedar City, UT 84720.

Dixie Genealogical Library, St. George, UT 84770.

Genealogical Society of the Church of Jesus Christ of Latter-day Saints, 50 East North Temple St., Salt Lake City, UT 84150.

LDS Church Historical Library, 50 East North Temple, Salt Lake City, UT 84150.

Ogden Public Library, Ogden, UT 84402.

Public Library, Manti, UT 84642.

Public Library, Springville, UT 84663.

St. George Genealogy Club, P.O. Box 184, St. George, UT 84770.

Temple Area Genealogical Library, Manti, UT 84642.

University of Utah, Marriott Library, Salt Lake City, UT 84112.

Utah County Genealogical and Historical Society, 110 South 300 West, Provo, UT 84601.

Utah Genealogical Association, P.O. Box 1144, Salt Lake City, UT 84110.

Utah Historical Society Library, 300 South Rio Grande, Salt Lake City, UT 84101.

Utah State Archives, 2333 South 2300 West, Salt Lake City, UT 84104.

Utah State University Library, Logan, UT 84321.

Genealogical Journal, Utah Genealogical Association, P.O. Box 1144, Salt Lake City, UT 84110.

Printed Census Records and Mortality Schedules

Indexes (Territory): 1850, 1860, 1870, 1851

Printed Census Records (Counties)   Davis-1850, 1851   Salt Lake-1851   Utah-1850
                                     Iron-1870; 1851   Tooele-1850   Weber-1850

Kearl, J.R., Clayne L. Pope and Larry T. Wimmer. *Index to the 1850, 1860, 1870 Census of Utah, Heads of Households.*

Zabriskie, George Olin. *Green River Precinct, 1850 Census* (Typewritten copy)

Mortality Schedules (Printed): 1850, 1860, 1870, 1880

Valuable Printed Sources

Atlases, Gazetteers

Gannett, Henry. *Gazetteer of Utah.* Washington D.C. Government Printing Office, 1900.

Miller, David E. *Utah History Atlas.* David E. Miller, 1964, 1977.

Place Names

Leigh, Rufus Wood. *Five Hundred Utah Place Names, Their Origin and Significance.* Salt Lake City: Deseret News Press, 1961.

Utah Writer's Project. *Origins of Utah Place Names.* Salt Lake City, 1940.

Guides To Genealogical Research

Cunningham, Ronald and Evan Evans. *A Handy Guide to The Genealogical Library and Church Historical Department,* Revised edition. Logan, Utah: The Everton Publishers, 1980.

Guide to Official Records of Genealogical Value in the State of Utah. State of Utah, Department of Finance, Utah State Archives and Records Service, 1980.

Jaussi, Laureen R. and Gloria D. Chaston. *Genealogical Records of Utah.* Salt Lake City: Deseret Book Company, 1974.

Histories

Jenson, Andrew. *Encyclopedic History of the Church.* Salt Lake City: Deseret News Publishing Company, 1941. Index, 1975.

Whitney, Orson F. *History of Utah.* George Q. Cannon and Sons, 1892.

Genealogical Sources

Brown, Mary J. *Handy Index to the Holdings of the Genealogical Society of Utah.* Logan: The Everton Publishers, 1971.

Esshan, Frank. *Pioneers and Prominent Men of Utah.* Salt Lake City: Utah Pioneers Book Publishing Company, 1913.

Guide to Obituary and Death Records in Salt Lake City (Deseret News, Salt Lake Tribune, etc.). Salt Lake City; Genealogical Society Reference, 1979.

Jaussi, Laureen R. and Gloria D. Chaston comp. *Register of L.D.S. Church Records.* Salt Lake City: Deseret Book Company, 1968.

Special Collections Department Merrill Library. *Name Index to the Library of Congress Collection of Mormon Diaries.* Logan: Utah State University Press, 1971.

Sperry, Kip. *A Guide to Indexes to Mormon Works, Mormon Collections and Utah Collections.* Salt Lake City, Utah: Historical Department of The Church of Jesus Christ of Latter-day Saints, 1974.

Bibliography

Dean, Elva, comp. *A Representative List of Genealogical Materials Held in the University of Utah Libraries, Western Americana Collection.* Salt Lake City: University of Utah Libraries, 1969.

Flake, Chad J. *A Mormon Bibliography 1830-1930.* Salt Lake City: University of Utah Press, 1978.

UTAH COUNTY HISTORIES
(Population figures to nearest thousand - 1980 U.S. Census)

Name	Map Index	Date Created	Pop. By M 1980	U.S. Cen Reports Available	Parent County or Territory From Which Organized	County Seat
* Beaver	E1	1856	4	1860-80	Iron, Millard	Beaver 84713

(Co Clk has b rec from 1897 to 1905, m rec from 1887, d rec from 1900 to 1905, div rec from 1871, pro rec from 1872, civ ct rec from 1856; Beaver City Office has bur rec)

*§ Box Elder	A1	1856	33	1860-80	Unorganized Territory	Brigham City 84302

(Co Clk has b & d rec from 1898 to 1905, m rec from 1887, div, pro, civ ct & Ind rec from 1856)

* Cache	A2	1856	57	1860-80	Unorg. Terr.	Logan 84321

(Co Clk has b, d rec from 1898 to 1905, m rec from 1888, div, civ ct rec from 1896, pro rec from 1884; Co Rcdr has Ind rec)

*§ Carbon	C3	1894	22		Emery	Price 84501

(Co Clk has b rec from 1898 to 1899, m, div, pro, civ ct rec from 1894 & naturalization rec from 1896; Co Rcdr has Ind rec from 1894)

*§ Daggett	B4	1917	1		Uintah	Manila 84046

(Co Clk has m, bur, div, pro, civ ct & Ind rec from 1918)

* Davis	B2	1850	146	1850-80	Salt Lake	Farmington 84025

(Co Clk has b, d rec from 1898 to 1905, m rec from 1887, pro rec from 1896, div, civ ct rec)

* Duchesne	C3	1913	13		Wasatch	Duchesne 84021

(Co Clk has m, div, pro & civ ct rec from 1915; Co Rcdr has Ind rec from 1915)

*§ Emery	D3	1880	11	1880	Sanpete, Sevier	Castle Dale 84513

(Co Clk has div rec from 1900 & civ ct rec from 1890)

* Garfield	F3	1864	4		Iron, Sevier, Kane	Panguitch 84759

(Co Clk has m rec from 1887, div, pro & civ ct rec from 1888) (Garfield Co boundaries were set up in 1864 but there were no co officials and they did not function as a co until Mar 1882)

§ Grand	D4	1890	8		Emery, Uintah	Moab 84532

(Co Clk has m & pro rec from 1890, div & civ ct rec 1896)

* Iron	F1	1852	17	1850-80	Unorg. Terr.	Parowan 84761

(Co Clk has m, div, pro, civ ct rec from 1887; Co Rcdr has Ind rec)

* Juab	C1	1852	6	1860-80	Original county	Nephi 84648
* Kane	F2	1864	4	1870-80	Washington, Unorg. Terr.	Kanab 84741

(Co Clk has m, div, pro & civ ct rec)

* Millard	D1	1851	9	1860-80	Juab	Fillmore 84631

(Co Clk has m rec from 1887, div, pro & civ ct rec; Co Rcdr has Ind rec)

*§ Morgan	B2	1862	5	1870-80	Davis, Summit	Morgan 84050

(Co Clk has m rec from 1888, div & civ ct rec from 1896, pro rec from 1869 & Ind rec from 1860)

Piute	E2	1866	1	1870-80	Sevier	Junction 84740

(Co Clk has b & d rec from 1898, m rec from 1887, div, pro & civ ct rec from 1872)

* Rich	A3	1864	2	1870-80	Formerly Richland	Randolph 84064

(Co Clk has partial b & d rec from 1898 to 1905, m rec from 1888, div, pro, civ ct & Ind rec from 1872)

* Salt Lake	B2	1849	618	1850-80	Orig. Co. (Great S.L.)	Salt Lake City 84110

(Co Clk has m rec from 1887, div & civ ct rec from 1896, pro rec from 1852; Co Rcdr has Ind rec)

* San Juan	F4	1880	12	1880	Kane	Monticello 84535

(Co Clk has m rec from Nov 1888, div rec from 1891, pro rec from 1888 & civ ct rec from 1891)

*§ Sanpete	D3	1852	15	1850-80	Original county	Manti 84642

(Co Clk has b rec from 1897 to 1905, d rec from 1898 to 1905, m rec from 1888, div, pro & civ ct rec from 1878 & Ind rec from 1870)

* Sevier	D2	1864	15	1870-80	Sanpete	Richfield 84701

(Co Clk has limited b, d rec from 1898 to 1906, m, Ind rec from 1888, div rec from 1889, pro, civ ct rec from 1896, Ind rec from 1888; Utah State Division of Health, Salt Lake City, has b, d rec aft 1906)

* Summit	B3	1854	10	1860-80	Salt Lake	Coalville 84017

(Co Clk has b rec from 1898 to 1905, d rec from 1898 to 1901, m rec from 1888, div, pro & civ ct rec from 1896; Co Rcdr has Ind rec)

*§ Tooele	B1	1852	26	1850-80	Original county	Tooele 84074

(Co Clk has b, d rec from 1897 to 1905, m rec from 1887, div rec from 1874, pro rec from 1859, civ ct rec from 1896; Co Rcdr has Ind rec)

*§ Uintah	C4	1880	20	1880	Wasatch	Vernal 84078

(Co Clk has m, div, pro & civ ct rec; Co Rcdr has Ind rec)

*§ Utah	C2	1852	217	1850-80	Original county	Provo 84601

(Co Clk has m rec from 1887, div & pro rec from 1859, civ ct rec from 1885; Co Rcdr has Ind rec)

*§ Wasatch	B3	1862	9	1870-80	Summit	Heber 84032

(Co Clk has b & d rec from 1897 to 1905, m rec from 1862, div, pro & civ ct rec from 1897)

* Washington	F1	1852	26	1860-80	Unorg. Terr.	St. George 84770

(Co Clk has m rec from 1887, div rec from 1878, pro & civ ct rec from 1874; Co Rcdr has Ind rec)

COUNTY MAP FOR THE STATE OF UTAH

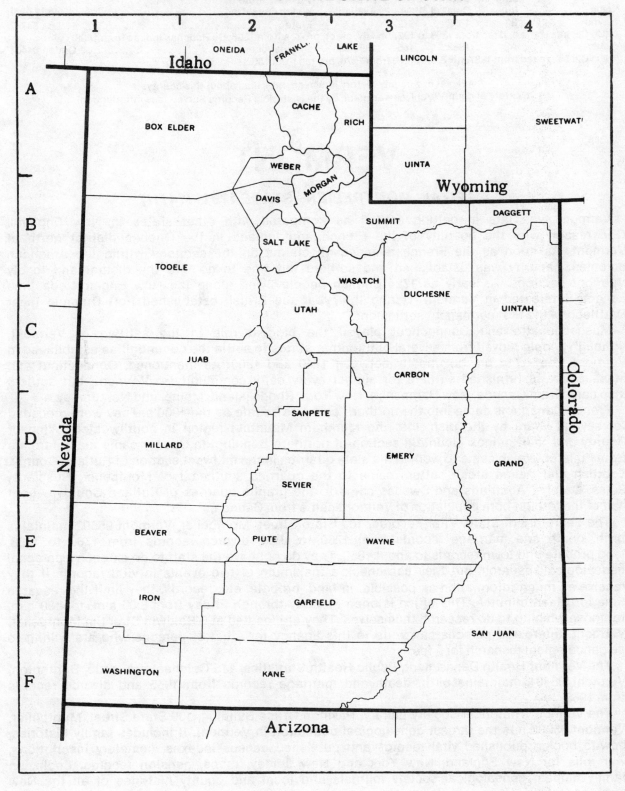

Name	Map Index	Date Created	Pop. By M 1980	U.S. Cen Reports Available	Parent County or Territory From Which Organized	County Seat
* Wayne	E3	1892	2		Piute	Loa 84747

(Co Clk has some b, d rec from 1898 to 1927, m, div, civ ct, pro rec from 1898; Co Rcdr has lnd rec from 1898)

| *§ Weber | A2 | 1852 | 145 | 1850-80 | Original county . . . . | Ogden 84401 |

(Co Clk has m rec from 1887, div & civ ct rec from 1878, pro rec from 1902)

* - At least one county history has been published about this county.
§ - Inventory of county archives was made by the Historical Records Survey. (see introduction)

VERMONT

CAPITAL, MONTPELIER - STATE 1791 - (14TH)

Vermont was late in getting settled as compared with other states in New England. One reason was the hostility of the French and Indians in the Quebec district north of Vermont. As soon as the French released all claims on the sections within the American colonies, security was established and settlers felt free to go into the distant and lonely Vermont sections. As early as 1724 English people living along the New England coastline became interested in Vermont. During that year the British established Fort Dummer (near Brattleboro) the first permanent settlement.

Massachusetts and Connecticut played the biggest role in the settling of Vermont, although people moved from several of the other states to settle the communities established in Vermont from 1714 on, but mostly between 1740 and 1800. As mentioned, Connecticut and Massachusetts furnished settlers for almost every early community in Vermont, but settlers also came from Canada, New Hampshire, New York, Rhode Island, Maine, and New Jersey.

French Canadians came into the northern counties as late as the 1900's. They were preceded for several years by the Irish. Into the Markham Mountain region in southwestern Windsor County and the Equinox Mountain section of northern Bennington County came many farmers from Finland. Welsh came to work in the slate quarries in the midwest section of Rutland County. Scottish and Italian stone cutters came to the quarries southeast of Montpelier; Russians, Poles, Czechs, Austrians and Swedes came to the granite quarries of Rutland County. About half of the foreign-born population of Vermont came from Canada.

The Secretary of State, Vital Records, 109 State Street, Montpelier, Vermont 05602 maintains birth, death and marriage records from 1760 to 1955, divorce records from 1760 to 1968, land probate and town records to about 1850. They do not have the staff to do extensive personal genealogical research, but they can check a maximum of two events in vital records if they receive as much information as possible. In land, probate, etc. records, they limit the research time to fifteen minutes. This office is open Monday through Friday from 8:00 a.m. to 4:00 p.m. for those wishing to do research themselves. They are located at 6 Baldwin Street in Montpelier, Vermont. Interested persons can write to this agency for a list of persons who are willing to do genealogical research for a fee.

The Vermont Health Department, Public Health Statistics, 115 Colchester Avenue, Burlington, Vermont 05401 maintains birth, death and marriage records from 1955 and divorce records from 1968.

The Vermont Historical Society Library, Pavilion Office Building, 109 State Street, Montpelier, Vermont 05602 has the largest genealogical collection in Vermont. It includes family histories, how-to books, published vital records and published census indexes, cemetery inscriptions, war rolls for New England, New York and New Jersey, maps, pension records, books on family names, genealogical society journals and local and county histories of all the New England states.

The Law and Document Unit, Department of Libraries, 111 State Street, Montpelier, Vermont 05602 has a list of genealogical research materials.

The Division of Public Records, 6 Baldwin Street, Montpelier, Vermont (mailing address: c/o State Administration Building, 133 State Street, Montpelier, Vermont 05602) has microfilm copies of early town records, probate records, vital records through 1908, cemetery records and land records.

All liens, mortgages, deeds and similar documents are recorded in the office of the Town Clerk of the town wherein the parties reside or the property is located. All land records are maintained by town clerks except old records for Rutland County, 1779-1826. These are filed in the County Clerk's Office, County Courthouse, Rutland, Vermont.

Divorce matters and civil court records, old land records, 1779-1826, are recorded in the offices of the various county clerks.

VERMONT TOWNS ORGANIZED BEFORE 1800

ADDISON, organized 1785. Addison, 1783; Bridport, 1786; Cornwall, 1774; Ferrisburgh, 1769; Leicester, 1774; Lincoln, 1790; Middlebury, 1766; Monkton, 1774; New Haven, 1769; Orwell, 1775; Panton, 1764; Ripton, 1781; Salisbury, 1774; Shoreham, 1766; Starksborough, 1788; Vergennes, 1764; Waltham, S. bef. Rev.; Weybridge, 1775; Whiting, 1773.

BENNINGTON, organized 1779. Arlington, 1763; Bennington, 1761; Dorset, 1768; Glastenbury, 1661; Landgrove, 1761; Manchester, 1764; Peru abt. 1773; Pownal, 1762; Rupert, 1767; Sandgate, 1771; Shaftsbury, 1763; Sunderland, 1766; Winhall, 1761.

CALEDONIA, organized 1796. Barnet, 1770; Burke, 1790; Cabot, 1785; Danville, 1785; Groton, 1787; Hardwick, 1790; Kirby, 1799; Lyndon, 1788; Peacham, 1775; Ryegate, 1774; Sheffield, 1792; St. Johnsbury, 1786; Sutton, 1791; Walden, 1789; Waterford, 1797; Wheelock, 1785.

CHITTENDEN, organized 1787. Bolton, 1763; Burlington, 1773; Charlotte, 1776; Colchester, 1772; Essex, 1783; Hinesburg, 1774; Huntington, 1786; Jericho, 1774; Milton, 1783; Richmond, 1775; Shelburne, 1768; St. George, 1784; Underhill, 1786; Willistown, 1774.

ESSEX, organized 1797. Bloomfield, 1762; Brunswick, 1780; Canaan, 1791; Concord, 1783; Guildhall, 1764; Lunenburg, 1770; Maidstone, 1772; Victory, 1781.

FRANKLIN, organized 1796. Bakersfield, 1799; Berkshire, 1780; Enosburgh, 1797; Fairfax, 1783; Fairfield, 1788; Fletcher, 1781; Franklin, 1789; Georgia, 1784-5; Highgate, 1763; Montgomery, 1780; Richford, 1797; Sheldon, 1790; Swantown, 1787; St. Albans, 1775.

GRAND ISLE, organized 1802. Alburgh, 1782; Grand Isle, 1783; Isle La Motte, 1785; North Hero, 1783; South Hero, 1779.

LAMOILLE, organized 1835. Cambridge, 1783; Elmore, 1790; Hyde Park, 1787; Johnson, 1784; Morristown, 1790; Sterling, 1799; Stowe, 1793; Waterville, 1789; Wolcott, 1781.

ORANGE, organized 1781. Bradford, S. 1765; Braintree, S. 1783; Brookfield, S. 1771; Chelsea, S. 1784; Corinth, O. 1777; Fairlee, S. 1766; Newbury, S. 1763; Orange, O. 1793; Randolph, O. 1781; Stratford, S. 1768; Thetford, S. 1764; Topsham, S. 1781; Turnbridge, S. 1776; Vershire, O. 1780; Washington, O. 1785; W. Fairlee, 1761; Williamtown, 1784.

ORLEANS, organized 1797. Barton, 1789; Craftsbury, 1788; Derby, 1795; Glover, 1797; Greensborough, 1789; Holland, 1800; Jay, S. bef. Rev.; Salem, 1798; Westfield, 1790.

RUTLAND, organized 1781. Benson, 1783; Brandon, 1772; Castleton, 1767; Chittenden aft. Rev.; Clarendon, 1768; Danby, 1765; Fairhaven, 1779; Hubbardton, 1775; Ira, 1779; Mendon, 1781; Middletown, 1774; Mt. Holly, 1787; Mt. Tabor, 1761; Pawlet, 1761; Pittsford, 1767; Poultney, 1777; Rutland, 1769; Sherburn, 1785; Shrewsbury, 1763; Sudbury, bef. Rev.; Tinsmith, 1770; Wallingsford, 1773; Wells, 1768; West Haven, 1770.

WASHINGTON, organized 1810. Barre, 1780; Berlin, 1785; Calais, 1787; Duxbury, 1786; Payston, 1798; Marshfield, 1782; Middlesex, 1787; Montpelier, 1786; Moretown, 1790; Northfield, 1785; Plainsfield, 1794; Roxbury, 1789; Waitsfield, 1789; Warren, 1797; Waterbury, 1784; Worcester, 1797.

WINDHAM, 1781. Athens, 1780; Brattleboro, 1724; Brookline, 1777; Dover, 1780; Fullam, 1760; Grafton, 1768; Guilford, 1761; Halifax, 1761; Jamacia, 1780; Londonderry, 1773; Marlborough, 1763; Newfane, 1766; Putney, 1744; Rockingham, 1753; Townsend, 1761; Woodborough, 1780; Westminister, 1741; Whitington, 1771; Wilmington S. bef. Rev.; Windham, 1773.

WINDSOR, organized before Statehood. Andover, 1776; Baltimore, 1794; Barnard, 1774; Bethel, 1779; Bridgewater, 1779; Cavendish, 1769; Chester, 1764; Hartford, 1763; Hartland, 1763; Ludlow, 1714; Norwich, 1762; Plymouth, 1777; Pomfret, 1770; Reading, 1772; Royalton, 1771; Sharon, 1764; Springfield, 1761; Stockbridge, 1784; Weathersfield, 1761; Weston, 1790; Windsor, 1764; Woodstock, 1768.

Genealogical Archives, Libraries, Societies, and Publications

Brooks Memorial Library, 224 Main St., Brattle-boro, VT 05301.

Billings Library, Burlington, VT 05401.

Fletcher Free Library, 246 Main St., Burlington, VT 05401.

Genealogical Library, Bennington Museum, Bennington, VT 05201.

Genealogical Society of Vermont, Westminster West RFD 3, Putney, VT 05346.

Public Library, Court St., Rutland, VT 05701.

University of Vermont Library, Burlington, VT 05401.

Vermont Department of Libraries, Law and Documents Unit, 111 State Street, Montpelier, VT 05602.

Vermont Historical Society, Pavilion Office Building, 109 State Street, Montpelier, VT 05602.

Vermont Historical Society Library, State Administration Bldg., Montpelier, VT 05602.

Branches and Twigs, Genealogical Society of Vermont, Westminster West, RFD 3, Putney, VT 05346.

Printed Census Records and Mortality Schedules

State Indexes: 1790, 1800, 1810, 1820, 1830, 1840, 1850; 1857; Partial Index 1880

Printed Census Records (Counties):

Addison-1850
Bennington-1810
Windham-1830

Mortality Schedules: (Printed)

State-1850, 1860

Valuable Printed Sources

Atlas and Gazetteer

DeLorme, David and Company, comp. *The Vermont Atlas and Gazetteer.* Yarmouth: Maine, 1978.

Place Names

Swift, Esther Munroe. *Vermont Place Names.* Brattleboro, Vermont: Stephen Greene Press, 1977.

Guides To Genealogical Research

New England Library Association. *Genealogist's Handbook for New England Research.* Lynnfield, Massachusetts: Bibliography Committee, 1980.

Hanson, Edward W. "Vermont Genealogy: A Study in Migration," *New England Historical and Genealogical Register,* Vol. 133 (1979), pages 3-19.

Rubicam, Milton, ed. *Genealogical Research Methods and Sources* Vol. I. Washington D.C.: American Society of Genealogists, 1972. "Vermont" by Jean Stephenson, pages 105 to 112.

Histories

Barden, Merritt Clarke. *Vermont Once No Man's Land.* Rutland Vermont: Tuttle Company, 1928.

Hemenway, Abby M. *Vermont Historical Gazetteer,* 5 Vols. Burlington, Vermont: author 1869-1891.

Genealogical Sources

Clark, Byron N, ed. *A List of Pensioners of the War of 1812.* Baltimore: Genealogical Publishing Company, reprint. 1969.

D.A.R. collection*

Dewey, William T. and Byron N. Clark, comp. *Vermont Marriages - Montpelier, Burlington, and Berlin.* Baltimore: Genealogical Publishing Company, 1967, reprint.

Genealogical Society of Vermont, *Some Vermont Ancestors: The Bicentennial Project of the Genealogical Society of Vermont.* Brattleboro, VT 05301.

Goodrich, John E. *Rolls of Soldiers in the Revolutionary War, 1775-1783.* Rutland, Vermont, Tuttle Company, 1904.

Vital Statistics in Town and Proprietors Records, 1770-1870, with general index.*

Walton, Eliakim Persons. *Records of the Council of Safety and Governor and Council of the State of Vermont, 1775-1836.* 8 Vols.

Bibliography

Gilman, Marcus Davis. *The Bibliography of Vermont.* Burlington: Free Press Association, 1897.

*Microfilm - Genealogical Society of The Church of Jesus Christ of Latter-day Saints, Salt Lake City, Utah.

COUNTY MAP FOR THE STATE OF VERMONT

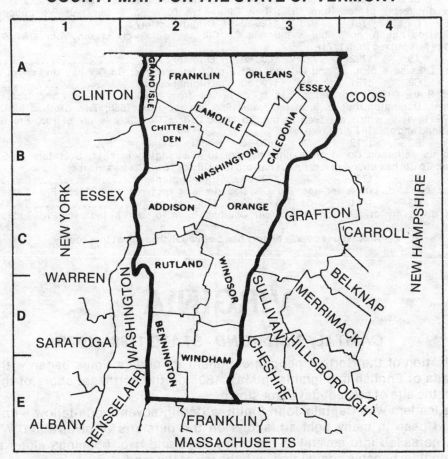

VERMONT COUNTY HISTORIES
(Population figures to nearest thousand - 1980 U. S. Census)

Name	Map Index	Date Created	Pop. By M 1980	U.S. Cen Reports Available	Parent County or Territory From Which Organized	County Seat
* Addison	C2	1785	29	1790-80	Rutland	Middlebury 05753

(Twn Clk has b, m, d & bur rec; Co Clk has div & civ ct rec from 1797; Pro Judge has pro rec)

* Bennington	D2	1779	33	1790-80	Original county	Bennington 05201

(Bennington Twn Clk has b, m, d & bur rec; Co Clk has div rec from 1899, civ ct rec from 1861; Pro Judge has pro rec; Twn Clk, Glastenbury has b rec from 1868 to 1928, d rec from 1883 to 1895, m rec from 1869 to 1927 & Ind rec from 1833 - Glastenbury is an unorg twn or gore, while all rec should be here, some may be found in Shaftsbury Twn Clk office)

* Caledonia	B3	1792	26	1800-80	Newly Organized Terr.	St. Johnsbury 05819

(Twn Clk has b, m, d, bur & Ind rec; Co Clk has div & civ ct rec from 1797; Pro Judge has pro rec)

* Chittenden	B2	1787	116	1790-80	Original county	Burlington 05401

(Twn Clk has b, m, d, bur, pro & Ind rec; Co Clk has div rec from 1829 & civ ct rec from 1798)

Name	Map Index	Date Created	Pop. By M 1980	U.S. Cen Reports Available	Parent County or Territory From Which Organized	County Seat
* Essex	A3	1792	6	1800-80	Unorg. Terr.	Guildhall 05905

(Co Clk has b & d rec from 1884, m rec & bur rec very few, div, co ct rec from 1800, Ind rec from 1762; Pro Judge has pro rec from 1800; Unorg twns & gores of Essex Co consists of: Averill, Avery's Gore, Ferdinand, Lewis, Warren's Gore, Warner's Grant)

Name	Map Index	Date Created	Pop. By M 1980	U.S. Cen Reports Available	Parent County or Territory From Which Organized	County Seat
* Franklin	A2	1792	35	1800-80	Chittenden	St. Albans 05478

(Co Clk has d & civ ct rec from 1900; Twn Clk has b, m, d, bur & Ind rec; Pro Judge has pro rec)

Name	Map Index	Date Created	Pop. By M 1980	U.S. Cen Reports Available	Parent County or Territory From Which Organized	County Seat
Grand Isle	A2	1802	5	1810-80	Franklin	North Hero 05474
* Lamoille	B2	1835	17	1840-80	Chittenden, Orleans, Franklin	Hyde Park 05655

(Co Clk has div & civ ct rec from 1837; Twn Clks have b, m, d & bur rec; Pro Judge has pro rec)

Name	Map Index	Date Created	Pop. By M 1980	U.S. Cen Reports Available	Parent County or Territory From Which Organized	County Seat
* Orange	C3	1781	23	1790-80	Original county	Chelsea 05038

(Twn Clk, Chelsea has b, m, d, bur & Ind rec; Co Clk has div & civ ct rec from 1781 & Ind rec from 1771; Pro Judge has pro rec from 1771)

Name	Map Index	Date Created	Pop. By M 1980	U.S. Cen Reports Available	Parent County or Territory From Which Organized	County Seat
* Orleans	A3	1792	23	1800-80	Original county	Newport 05855

(Town or City Clks have b, m, d, and Ind rec. Dist Pro Ct has pro rec; Co Clk has div, civ ct rec from 1800)

Name	Map Index	Date Created	Pop. By M 1980	U.S. Cen Reports Available	Parent County or Territory From Which Organized	County Seat
* Rutland	C2	1781	58	1790-80	Original county	Rutland 05701

(Secretary of State Office, Montpelier, has b, d, m rec from 1760 to 1955, div rec from 1760 to 1968; Vt Health Dept, Burlington, has b, d, m rec from 1955, div rec from 1968; Twn Clk has Ind rec except old rec from 1779 to 1826 which are filed in the Co Clk's Office; Co Clk has civ ct rec; Pro Ct has pro rec located in Rutland and also in Fair Haven, Vt.)

Name	Map Index	Date Created	Pop. By M 1980	U.S. Cen Reports Available	Parent County or Territory From Which Organized	County Seat
* Washington	B2	1810	52	1820-80	Addison, Orange	Montpelier 05602

(Incorporated as Jefferson Co in 1810, nm changed to Washington in 1814; Secretary of State, Montpelier, has b, d, m rec; Co Clk has div, civ ct rec; Pro Ct has pro rec; City or Town Clk has Ind rec)

Name	Map Index	Date Created	Pop. By M 1980	U.S. Cen Reports Available	Parent County or Territory From Which Organized	County Seat
* Windham	E2	1781	37	1790-80	Bennington	Newfane 05345

(Twn Clk has b, m, d, bur & Ind rec; Co Clk has div & civ ct rec from 1825; Pro Judge has pro rec)

Name	Map Index	Date Created	Pop. By M 1980	U.S. Cen Reports Available	Parent County or Territory From Which Organized	County Seat
* Windsor	C3	1781	51	1790-80	Original county	Woodstock 05091

(Co Clk has div & civ ct rec from 1782; Twn Clk has b, m, d, bur & Ind rec; Pro Judge has pro rec)

* - At least one county history has been published about this county.

VIRGINIA

CAPITAL, RICHMOND - STATE 1788 - (10TH)

The colonization of the North American continent in modern times began with the arrival of three boatloads of English immigrants in May, 1607 on the northeast shore of the James River in Virginia, on the site of present-day Jamestown.

One of the leaders was Captain John Smith, a daring adventurous fellow with an inquisitive mind who had been in many tight situations on the outskirts of civilization. With a score of companions, he sailed into several of the many bays and river openings along the zigzagging east coast, and thus became acquainted with the lay of the land.

Having done nothing to provide food for the winter, more than half of the colony succumbed from illness and lack of nourishing food.

The summer of 1608 brought them new supplies from England and 120 more immigrants.

In the fall of 1608 the colony of 130 or 140 persons was augmented by the arrival of seventy more immigrants in the third expedition to Virginia.

At the beginning of the winter of 1609 the colony consisted of 490 persons. When the spring of 1610 arrived there were only 60 persons left in the colony.

Determined to return to England, the group embarked. The ship was coming out of the mouth of the James River when Virginia bound ships under the command of Lord Delaware came in sight. Against their own judgment, the disgruntled colonists were persuaded to return to their abandoned homes.

Early in 1610 more food and additional colonists arrived from England.

Virginia became a royal colony in 1624. From then until 1776 when it announced its independence it was in almost constant trouble with the Crown or its representatives. Mainly, the colonists objected to the arbitrary action of the colony officials and their ruthless demands.

Every month in the year, with the exception of the winter months, saw boatloads of new immigrants arriving. More and more settlements were established, some as far north as the Potomac River. By 1700 there were more than 80,000 persons living in the Tidewater region of Virginia. Twenty thousand more had come by 1717. During the next 37 years, the population increased by almost two hundred percent, reaching 284,000 by 1754.

Even before that time the settlers scattered over the coastal plain, the Piedmont plateau, and had crossed over the Blue Ridge highlands and settled in the Valley of Virginia, with the Appalachian Plateau at their backs. There they settled along the rivers, hundreds of miles from the coastline.

As early as 1730 there was a heavy immigration from Pennsylvania into Virginia of Scotch-Irish, Welsh, and Germans, most of whom settled in the upper valleys. Naturally, therefore, the Welsh Baptist Church, the English Quakers, and the Scotch Presbyterians flourished in that section. Methodist churches were established about 1800.

Virginia was well settled by 1775. By 1800 it had upwards of 90 counties and a population of nearly a million.

Nine other states preceded Virginia into the Union when she entered in June 1788. In the first three U.S. Census reports, 1790, 1800 and 1810, Virginia registered the highest population in the nation. In 1820 she was second to New York. In 1830 she was surpassed by New York and Pennsylvania.

Foreign born residents predominate in the following order in Virginia: Russians, English, Germans, Italians, Greeks, Polish, Czechs, Irish, Austrians and Hungarians.

Until 1786, the Anglican Church was the State Church of Virginia. Following English custom and law, as an agency of the government, the Church was responsible for maintaining a system of Parish Registers recording vital statistics. Very few such registers have survived. Photocopies of most of those that exist are in the Virginia State Library. All but one has been transcribed and published.

The Quit Rent list is used as a census report or schedule. In 1704 all Virginia landowners, except those in Lancaster, Northumberland, Westmoreland, Richmond and Stafford Counties, had to pay the King a Quit Rent of one shilling for each fifty acres bought.

Since the 1790 U.S. Census records were destroyed in a fire, Fothergill and Naugle in "Taxpayers of Virginia" have tried to augment similar lists gathered from other counties by the government.

In the 1790 to 1860 Federal Census schedules for Virginia will be found 50 counties now in West Virginia. These counties withdrew from Virginia in 1861 and in 1863 became our thirty-fifth state.

The Archives Division, Virginia State Library, Richmond, Virginia 23219, has copies of all existing Virginia birth, death, and marriage records prior to 1896. These records are available on microfilm for use by the public and there is no charge for viewing the records.

Generally for most areas of the State, records are available for the period 1853-1896. Any "Marriage Bonds" prior to 1853 that are still in existence would also be in the Virginia State Library, as would war records prior to and including the Civil War, deeds, wills, and other court records.

Events that occurred in the portion of Virginia that is now West Virginia are recorded in the Department of Archives and History, Capitol Building, Charleston, West Virginia 25300.

With the exception of the years 1896 to 1912, the Bureau of Vital Records and Health Statistics has records of births, deaths, and marriages since 1853. There are no records prior to 1853, and there was no law for the registration of births and deaths between 1896 and June 14, 1912.

The Virginia Bureau of Vital Records and Health Statistics is not equipped to do genealogical research; any such research should be done in the Archives Division of the Virginia State

Library as indicated above. Copies of records which are known to be on file by a review of the Archives Division microfilm may be obtained from the Bureau of Vital Records and Health Statistics upon application and payment of the fee. Applications for copies of records must include full names and date and place of the event.

Virginia's independent cities are Alexandria, Bristol, Buena Vista, Charlottesville, Chesapeake, Clifton Forge, Colonial Heights, Covington, Danville, Fairfax, Falls Church, Fort Monroe, Franklin, Fredericksburg, Galax, Hampton, Harrisonburg, Hopewell, Lynchburg, Martinsville, Newport News, Norfolk, Norton, Petersburg, Portsmouth, Radford, Richmond, Roanoke, South Boston, Staunton, Suffolk, Virginia Beach, Waynesboro, Williamsburg, and Winchester.

Genealogical Archives, Libraries, Societies, and Publications

Albemarle County Historical Society, University of Virginia, Alderman Library, Charlottesville, VA 22903.

Alderman Library, University of Virginia, Charlottesville, VA 22903.

Alexandria Library, 717 Queen St., Alexandria, VA 22314.

Augusta County Virginia Historical Society, P.O. Box 686, Staunton, VA 24401.

Blue Ridge Regional Library, 310 E. Church St., Martinsville, VA 24112.

Bristol Public Library, 701 Goode St., Bristol, VA 24201.

Clark County Historical Association, Berryville, VA 22611.

College of William and Mary Library, Williamsburg, VA 23185.

Commonwealth of Virginia, Virginia State Library, 1101 Capitol, Richmond, VA 23219.

Culpeper Town and County Library, Main and Mason Sts., Culpeper, VA 22701.

Danville Public Library, 511 Patton St., Danville, VA 24541.

E. Lee Trinkle Library, University of Virginia, Mary Washington College, Fredericksburg, VA 22402.

Ft. Eustis Historical and Archaeological Assn., P.O. Box 4408, Ft. Eustis, VA 23604.

Fairfax County Public Library, Virginia Room, 3915 Chain Bridge Road, Fairfax, VA 22030.

Fairfax Historical Society, P.O. Box 415, Fairfax, VA 22030.

Genealogical Society of Tidewater, Virginia, Thomas Nelson Community College, P.O. Box 9407, Hampton, VA 23670.

Greene County Historical Society, P.O. Box 185, Stanardsville, VA 22973.

Hampton Public Library, 4205 Victoria Blvd., Hampton, VA 23669.

Harrisonburg-Rockingham Historical Society, P.O. Box 541, Harrisonburg, VA 22801.

Jones Memorial Library, 434 Rivermont Ave., Lynchburg, VA 24504.

King and Queen Historical Society, Newtown, VA 23126.

Kirn Norfolk Public Library, The, 301 E. City Hall Ave., Norfolk, VA 23510.

Norfolk Historical Society, Room 708, Professional Arts Bldg., Norfolk, VA 23510.

Northern Neck Historical Society, Westmoreland County, Montross, VA 22520.

Petersburg Public Library, 137 S. Sycamore St., Petersburg, VA 23803.

Radford Public Library, Recreation Building, Radford, VA 24141.

Roanoke Valley Historical Society, P.O. Box 1904, Roanoke, VA 24008.

Rockingham County Historical Society, Box 1141, Harrisonburg, VA 22801.

Rockingham Public Library, 45 Newman Ave., Harrisonburg, VA 22801.

Southwest Virginia Historical Society, Wise, VA 24293.

Virginia Genealogical Society, P.O. Box 1397, Richmond, VA 23211.

Virginia Historical Society Library, P.O. Box 7311, Richmond, VA 23211.

VA-NC Piedmont Genealogical Society, P.O. Box 2272, Danville, VA 24541.

Virginia State Library, 1101 Capitol, Richmond, VA 23219.

Waynesboro Public Library, 600 South Waynes Avenue, Waynesboro, VA 22980.

Southwest Virginian, The, Journal of Genealogy and History Covering Virginia this Side of the Blue Ridge, 1046 Spruce Street, Norton, VA 24273.

Virginia Appalachian Notes, published by the Southwestern Virginia Genealogical Society, 2609 Hillcrest Avenue, N.W., Roanoke, VA 24012.

Virginia Genealogists, The, Box 4883, Washington, DC 20008.

Virginia Tidewater Genealogy, Genealogical Society of Tidewater, Virginia, 131 Wilderness Road, Hampton, VA 23669.

Printed Census Records and Mortality Schedules

State Indexes:1790, 1810, 1820, 1830, 1840, 1850, 1860

Printed Census Records (Counties):

Accomack-1800, 1810
Albemarle-1810
Amelia-1810
Amherst-1810
Augusta-1810
Bath-1810
Bedford-1810
Berkeley-1810, 1820; 1774-1810 (Reconstructed Census)
Boone-1860
Botetourt-1810, 1820, 1850; 1785
Brooke-1810
Brunswick-1810, 1830
Buckingham-1810
Campbell-1810
Caroline-1810
Charles City-1800, 1810
Charlotte-1810, 1820
Chesterfield-1810
Clay-1850
Craig-1870
Culpeper-1810
Cumberland - 1810
Dinwiddie-1810
Doddridge-1850
Elizabeth City-1810
Essex-1810
Fairfax-1810, 1820
Faquier-1810, 1820
Fluvanna-1810
Franklin-1810, 1820
Frederick-1810, 1820
Giles-1810
Gilmer-1850
Gloucester-1810, 1820
Goochland-1810, 1820, 1830
Greenbrier-1850

Greensville-1810
Hampshire-1810, 1820
Hancock-1810, 1820, 1850
Hanover-1810, 1820, 1850
Hardy-1840
Harrison-1810, 1820
Henrico-1810, 1850
Henry-1820, 1830
Highland-1850
Isle of Wight-1810
Jackson-1860
Jefferson-1810
Kanawah-1810
King and Queen-1810
King George-1810
King William-1810, 1820
Lancaster-1810, 1820, 1850
Lee-1820, 1830, 1850
Logan-1830, 1850, 1860
Loudoun-1810
Lunenburg-1810, 1850
Madison-1810
Marion-1850
Mason-1810, 1820
Mathews-1810
Mecklenburg-1810, 1820, 1830, 1850
Mercer-1840, 1850
Middlesex-1810
Montgomery-1810
Monongalia-1810, 1820, 1850
Monroe-1810, 1850
Morgan-1850
Nansemond-1850
Nelson-1810
New Kent-1810, 1850
Nicholas-1850
Norfolk-1810

Northumberland-1810, 1850
Nottoway-1810, 1850
Orange-1782
Patrick-1850
Pendleton-1810
Ohio-1810
Powhatan-1810
Prince Edward-1810
Prince George-1810
Prince William-1810
Princess Anne-1810
Randolph - 1810, 1820, 1830, 1850, 1860
Rappahannock-1850
Richmond-1810, 1850
Ritchie-1850
Rockbridge-1810
Rockingham-1810
Russell-1810, 1850, 1870
Scott-1850
Shenandoah-1810, 1820
Southampton-1810
Spotsylvania-1810
Stafford-1810
Surry-1810
Sussex-1810
Tazewell-1820, 1830
Tyler-1850
Warwick-1810, 1820, 1850
Washington-1810
Webster-1850
Westmoreland-1810
Wetzel-1850
Wood-1810, 1820
Wyoming-1850
Wythe-1810
York-1810

1850 Census Richmond City

Other Printed Census Records

Norfolk-1810
Petersburg-1810
Richmond City-1850

Louisa County, Virginia, Tithable and Census 1743-1785

1779 A Short Census of Virginia (National Genealogical Society Quarterly 1958, Vol. 46 No. 4 (Dec. 1958)

Valuable Printed Sources

Gazetteers

Gannett, Henry. *A Gazetteer of Virginia.* Washington D.C.: Government Print Office (1904)

Gannett, Henry. *A Gazetteer of Virginia and West Virginia.* Baltimore: Genealogical Publishing Company (1975).

Martin, Joseph. *A New and Comprehensive Gazetteer of Virginia and the District of Columbia.* Charlottesville: J. Marin (1835).

Maps

Sames, James W. III, comp. *Index of Kentucky and Virginia Maps 1562 to 1900.* Frankfort: Kentucky Historical Society (1976).

Sanchez-Saavedra's, Eugene Michael. *A Description of the Country: Virginia's Cartographers and Their Maps 1607-1881.* Richmond: Virginia State Library, 1975.

Place Names

Hanson, Raus McDill. *Virginia Place Names; Derivations, Historical Uses.* Verona, Virginia: McClure Press (1969).

Hiden, Matha W. *How Justice Grew: Virginia Counties.* Williamsburg, Virginia: Jamestown 350th Anniversary Corp., 1957.

Hummel, Ray O. Listing of Places Included in 19th Century Virginia Directories Richmond: Virginia State Library.

Guides To Genealogical Research

Clay, Robert Young. *Virginia Genealogical Resources.* Detroit: Detroit Society for Genealogical Research, 1980.

McCay, Betty L., comp. *Sources for Genealogical Searching in Virginia and West Virginia.* Indianapolis, Indiana: Privately published (1971).

Stone, Kathryn Crossley, comp. *Research Aids for the Colonial Period: Emphasis Virginia: Dictionary Encyclopedia for Genealogical Research.* Boulder, Colorado. Empire Printing (1976).

Histories

Andrews, Matthew Page. *Virginia the Old Dominion.* Richmond: Dietz Press, 1949.

Boogher, William Fletcher. *Gleanings of Virginia History.* Baltimore: Genealogical Publishing Company (1965 reprinted).

Bruce, Philip Alexander. *Virginia: Rebirth of the Old Dominion.* New York: Lewis Publishing Company.

Genealogical Sources

College of William and Mary (Swem Library): Virginia history and manuscripts.

Daughters of the American Revolution Collection*

Genealogies of Virginia Families: A Consolidation of Family History Articles from The Virginia Magazine of History and Biography. Baltimore: Genealogical Publishing Company, 1981, 5 Vols.

University of Virginia (Alderman Library): Virginia local history, newspapers, and manuscripts.

Virginia Historical Society: Manuscripts about Virginia History and some family histories.

Virginia State Library: Archives Section - State records, county records, church records and Bible records. Reference Section - Printed local and county histories, family histories and Virginia newspapers.

Bibliographies and Indexes

Brown, Stuart E. *Virginia Genealogies, A Trial List of Printed Books and Pamphlets.* Berryville, Virginia: Virginia Book Company (1967).

Critz, Lalla Campbell, comp. *Magazine of Bibliographies: Featuring Shenandoah Valley.* Fort Worth, Texas: The Magazine of Bibliographies (1972).

Stewart, Robert Armistead. *Index to Printed Virginia Genealogies Including Key and Bibliography (1970 reprinted) Baltimore: Genealogical Publishing Company.*

Swem, Earl Gregg, comp. *Virginia Historical Index.* Gloucester, Massachusetts: Peter Smith (1965).

Boundary Changes

Byrd, William. *History of the Dividing Line Betwixt Virgina and North Carolina,* various editions.

Crumrine, Boyd. *The Boundary Controversy between Pennsylvania and Virginia 1748-1785.* Pittsburgh: 1902.

Sames, James Waller. *Four Steps West: A Documentary Concerning The First dividing line in America, and its three extensions between Virginia and North Carolina, Kentucky and Tennessee.* Versailles, Kentucky, 1971.

VIRGINIA COUNTY HISTORIES
(Population figures to nearest thousand - 1980 U.S. Census)

Name	Map Index	Date Created	Pop. By M 1980	U.S. Cen Reports Available	Parent County or Territory From Which Organized	County Seat
Accawmack (was Northampton prior to 1642)						
* Accomack	A2	1634	31	1810-80	Northampton	Accomac 23301
* Albemarle	C2	1744	56	1810-80	Goochland, Louisa	Charlottesville 22902
(Clk Cir Ct has m rec from 1780, Ind rec from 1748, div, pro & civ ct rec)						
* Alexandria (Ind City)		1801		1850-80	Fairfax, became part of District of Columbia	Alexandria 22314
(See Dis of Columbia for cen rec of 1800-40; 1920 changed to Arlington) (Alex. Health Center has b, d & bur rec; Clk Cir Ct has m & div rec from 1870, pro, civ ct & Ind rec from 1783)						
* Alleghany	D2	1822	14	1830-80	Bath, Botetourt, Monroe	Covington 24426
(Clk Cir Ct has m rec from 1845, div, pro, civ ct & Ind rec from 1822)						
§ Amelia	C2	1734	8	1810-80	Brunswick, Prince George	Amelia C.H. 23002
(Clk Cir Ct has m, div, pro, civ ct & Ind rec from 1734)						
* Amhurst	D2	1761	29	1810-80	Albemarle	Amhurst 24521
(Clk Cir Ct has m, div, pro, civ ct & Ind rec from 1761)						
Appomattox	D2	1845	12	1850-80	Buckingham, Campbell, Charlotte, Prince Edward	Appomattox 24522
(Clk Cir Ct has m, div, pro & civ ct rec from 1892)						
* Arlington	B1	1847	152		Fairfax	Arlington 22210
* Augusta	D2	1738-45	54	1810-80	Orange	Staunton 24401
(Clk Cir Ct has b & d rec from 1853 to 1896, m rec from 1785, pro rec, deeds, original survey bks from 1745, personal prop tax rec from 1800 to 1851, Ind tax rec from 1786 & ct of claims rec from 1782 to 1785)						
* Bath	D2	1790-1	6	1810-80	Augusta, Botetourt, Greenbrier	Warm Springs 24484
(Clk Cir Ct has b rec from 1854 to 1880, d rec from 1854 to 1870, div, pro, law & chan rec from 1791)						
Barbour				1850-60	See W. Va.	
* Bedford	D2	1753	35	1810-80	Albemarle, Lunenburg	Bedford 24523
(Clk Cir Ct has b & d rec from 1854 to 1897, m, div, pro, civ ct & deeds from 1754)						
Berkeley				1810-60	See W. Va.	
* Bland	E3	1861	6	1870-80	Giles, Taxewell, Wythe	Bland 24315
(Clk Cir Ct has m, pro & Ind rec from 1861, div rec from 1900)						
Boone				1850-60	See W. Va.	
* Botetourt	D2	1769	23	1810-80	Augusta	Fincastle 24090
(Clk Cir Ct has b & d rec from 1853 to 1870, m, div, pro & civ ct rec from 1770)						
Braxton				1840-60	See W. Va.	
Bristol					Ind. City	Bristol 24201
(Clk Co Ct has m, div, pro, civ ct & Ind rec from 1890)						
Brooke				1810-60	See W. Va.	
*§ Brunswick	C3	1720	16	1810-80	Prince George, Isle of Wight, Surry	Lawrenceville 23868
(Clk Cir Ct has m, div, pro rec from 1732, Ind rec from 1900)						
Buchanan	F3	1858	37	1860-80	Russell, Tazewell	Grundy 24614
(Clk Cir Ct has m, div, pro, civ ct & Ind rec from 1885; Courthouse burned 1885)						
Buena Vista					Ind. City	Buena Vista 24416
(Clk Cir Ct has m, div, pro, civ ct, Ind, service discharge, and company charters rec from 1892)						
* Buckingham	C2	1758	12	1810-80	Albemarle, Appomattox	Buckingham 23921
(Clk Cir Ct has b & d rec from 1869 to 1896, m, div & pro rec from 1869)						
Cabell				1820-60	See W. Va.	
Calhoun				1860	See W. Va.	
* Campbell	D3	1781-2	45	1810-80	Bedford	Rustburg 24588
(Clk Cir Ct has b & d rec from 1912 to 1918, m, div, pro & deeds from 1782, civ ct & Ind rec, deeds of conveyances from 1782)						
* Caroline	C2	1727-8	18	1810-80	Essex, King and Queen, King William	Bowling Green 22427
(Clk Cir Ct has m rec from 1787 to 1853, Ind rec from 1836, also div, pro & civ ct rec)						
Carroll	E3	1842	27	1850-80	Grayson, Patrick	Hillsville 24343
(Clk Cir Ct has b rec from 1842 to 1896, m, div, pro, Ind rec from 1842)						
Charles City	B2	1634	7	1810-80	Original Shire	Charles City 23030
Charles River (see York)					(changed to York 1642)	

Name	Map Index	Date Created	Pop. By M 1980	U.S. Cen Reports Available	Parent County or Territory From Which Organized	County Seat
* Charlotte	C3	1764-5	12	1810-80	Lunenburg	Charlotte Court House 23923

(Co Clk has b, d rec from 1853 to 1870, m, pro, civ ct, Ind rec from 1765, and div rec)

| Chesapeake (Ind. City) | | | 114 | | 1810-80 (Norfolk (q.v.) & City of So. Norfolk, both discontinued | Chesapeake 23320 |

(Clk Cir Ct, P.O. Box 15205, has b rec from 1853 to 1920, m rec from 1600 to 1962, d rec from 1853 to 1870, div & Ind rec from 1637, pro rec from 1775 - all rec of Norfolk Co)

| *§ Chesterfield | C2 | 1749 | 141 | 1810-80 | Henrico | Chesterfield 23832 |

(Clk Cir Ct has m rec from 1771, Ind rec from 1749, also div, pro & civ ct rec)

| * Clarke | C1 | 1836 | 10 | 1840-80 | Frederick | Berryville 22611 |

(Clk Cir Ct has m, div, pro, civ ct & Ind rec from 1836)

| Clay | | | | 1860 | See W. Va. | |
| Clifton Forge | | | | | Ind. City | Clifton Forge 24422 |

(City Clk has m, div, Ind rec from 1906, also pro rec)

| Colonial Heights | | | | | Ind. City | Colonial Heights 23834 |

(Clk Cir Ct has m, div, pro, civ ct, Ind rec from 1961; Clk Cir Ct., Chesterfield Co, has div, pro, civ ct, land rec prior to 1961)

| Craig | E2 | 1851 | 4 | 1860-80 | Botetourt, Giles, Roanoke, Monroe, Alleghany, Montgomery | New Castle 24127 |

(Clk Cir Ct has b rec from 1864 to 1896, m, div, pro, civ ct rec & deeds from 1851)

| * Culpeper | C1 | 1748 | 22 | 1810-80 | Orange | Culpeper 22701 |

(Clk Cir Ct has Ind, pro rec from 1749, m rec from 1781, b rec from 1864 to 1896 and from 1912 to 1917, d rec from 1864 to 1896, Chancery and Civ Ct rec from 1831; Town Clk has bur rec)

| * Cumberland | C2 | 1748-9 | 8 | 1810-80 | Goochland | Cumberland 23040 |

(Clk Cir Ct has m, div, pro & civ ct rec from 1749, b & d rec from 1853 to 1870)

| * Dickenson | F3 | 1880 | 20 | | Buchanan, Russell, Wise | Clintwood 24228 |

(Co Health has b, d & bur rec; Clk Cir Ct has m, div, civ ct & Ind rec from 1880, also wills & mil dis)

| *§ Dinwiddie | C3 | 1752 | 22 | 1810-80 | Prince George | Dinwiddie 23841 |

(Clk Cir Ct has b, d rec from 1865 to 1896, m, pro, civ ct, Ind rec from 1833, div rec from 1870)

Doddridge				1850-60	See W. Va.	
Dunmore (see Shenandoah)						
* Essex	B2	1692	9	1810-80	Old Rappahannock	Tappahannock 22560

(Clk Cir Ct has m rec from 1814, div & Ind rec from 1865, pro rec from 1656 & civ ct rec from 1692)

| * Fairfax | C1 | 1742 | 596 | 1810-80 | Prince William, Loudoun | Fairfax 22030 |

(Clk Cir Ct has b rec from 1853 to 1912, m rec from 1853, div rec from 1850, pro, civ ct & Ind rec from 1742)

| Falls Church | | | | | Ind. City | Falls Church 22046 |

(City Clk has civ ct rec; Fairfax Co Clk Cir Ct has b, m, div, pro, civ ct & Ind rec)

| * Fauquier | C1 | 1759 | 36 | 1810-80 | Prince William | Warrenton 22186 |

(Clk Cir Ct has b, d rec from 1853 to 1896 and from 1912 to 1917, m pro, Ind rec from 1759, div rec from 1925, civ ct rec from 1937)

Fayette				1840-60	See W. Va.	
Fincastle		1772			Botetourt (discontinued 1777)	
Floyd	E3	1831	12	1840-80	Montgomery, Franklin	Floyd 24091

(Clk Cir Ct has b & d rec from 1852 to 1872, m, div, pro, civ ct & Ind rec from 1831)

| Fluvanna | C2 | 1777 | 10 | 1810-80 | Albemarle | Palmyra 22963 |

(Clk Cir Ct has b, d rec from 1853 to 1896, m, div, pro, civ ct, Ind rec from 1777, some bur rec)

| Fort Monroe | | | | | Ind. City | Fort Monroe 23351 |

(City Clk has m, div, pro rec & deeds from 1865)

| Franklin | D3 | 1785 | 36 | 1810-80 | Bedford, Henry, Patrick | Rocky Mount 24151 |
| Franklin | | | | | Ind. City | Franklin 23851 |

(Southampton Co Clk Cir Ct has div, pro, civ ct & Ind rec)

| * Frederick | C1 | 1738-43 | 34 | 1810-80 | Orange, Augusta | Winchester 22601 |

(Nine square miles of Frederick County annexed to city of Winchester) (Clk Cir Ct has b rec from 1853 to 1912, m rec from 1782, d rec from 1853 to 1896, div rec from 1870, pro, Ind rec from 1743)

| Galax | | | | | Ind. City | Galax 24333 |

(Galax, Va 24333 is on the line between Grayson & Carroll Cos, contact both cos for their rec of Galax)

| * Giles | E3 | 1806 | 18 | 1810-80 | Montgomery, Monroe, Tazewell, Craig, Mercer, Wythe | Pearisburg 24134 |

(Clk Cir Ct has m rec from 1806, b & d rec from 1858 to 1896, div, pro, civ ct & Ind rec)

| Gilmer | | | | 1850-60 | See W. Va. | |
| * Goucester | B2 | 1651 | 20 | 1810-80 | York | Gloucester 23061 |

(Clk Cir Ct has b rec from 1863 to 1890 and from 1912 to 1916, m rec from 1853, d rec from 1865 to 1890, div, pro, civ ct, land rec from 1865)

| * Goochland | C2 | 1727 | 12 | 1810-80 | Henrico | Goochland 23063 |

(Clk Cir Ct has m, pro, civ ct, Ind rec from 1728, div rec from 1800)

COUNTY MAP FOR THE STATE OF VIRGINIA

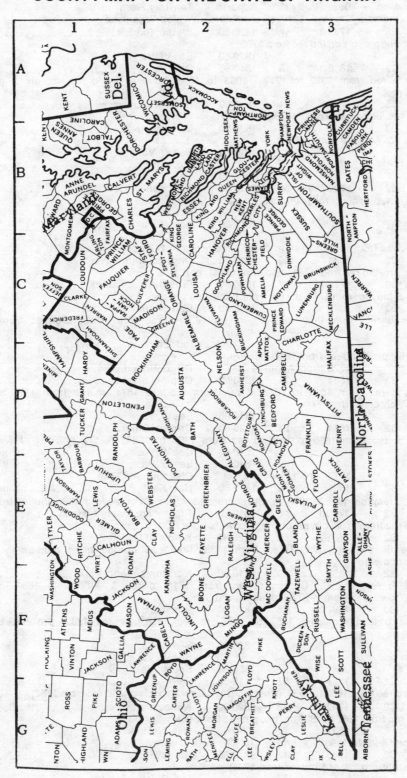

Name	Map Index	Date Created	Pop. By M 1980	U.S Cen Reports Available	Parent County or Territory From Which Organized	County Seat
* Grayson	E3	1792-3	16	1820-80	Wythe, Patrick	Independence 24348

(Clk Cir Ct has m, div, pro, civ ct, Ind rec from 1793)

Greenbrier				1820-60	See W. Va.	
Greene	C2	1838	8	1840-80	Orange	Stanardsville 22973

(Clk Cir Ct has b rec from 1912 to 1919 - 1853 to 1896, have a few d rec, m, div & pro rec from 1838, some civ ct & Ind rec)

* Greensville	C3	1781	11	1810-80	Brunswick, Sussex	Emporia 23847

(Clk Cir Ct has m rec, div, pro, civ ct & Ind rec from 1781)

* Halifax	D3	1752	30	1820-80	Lunenburg	Halifax 24558

(Clk Cir Ct has m, pro & deeds from 1752)

Hampshire				1810-60	See W. Va.	
Hampton					Ind. City	Hampton 23369
Hancock				1850-60	See W. Va.	
* Hanover	C2	1720	50	1810-80	New Kent	Hanover 23069

(Clk Cir Ct has m, div, pro, civ ct rec from 1865)

Hardy				1820-60	See W. Va.	
Harrison				1810-60	See W. Va.	
Harrisonburg					Ind. City	Harrisonburg 22801

(City Clk has b & d rec from 1862 to 1894, m, civ ct & Ind rec from 1778, pro rec from 1803)

* Henrico	C2	1634	180	1810-80	Original Shire	Richmond 23261

(Clk Cir Ct has m, pro, Ind rec from 1781, also div & civ ct rec)

* Henry	D3	1776-7	57	1820-80	Pittsylvania, Patrick	Martinsville 24112

(Clk Cir Ct has m & Ind rec from 1777, div rec from 1909, also pro rec)

* Highland	D2	1847	3	1850-80	Bath, Pendleton	Monterey 24465

(Clk Cir Ct has b rec from 1850 to 1898, m, div & Ind rec from 1850, pro rec from 1860, civ ct rec from 1937)

Hopewell					Ind. City	Hopewell 23860

(City Clk has m, div, pro & Ind rec from 1916)

Illinois		1778	(from Augusta Co)		Discontinued 1784	
§ Isle of Wight	B3	1634	21	1810-80	Original Shire	Isle of Wight 23397

(Clk Cir Ct has b rec from 1853 to 1876, d rec from 1853 to 1874, m rec from 1772, div rec from 1853, pro rec from 1647, civ ct rec from 1746)

Jackson				1840-60	See W. Va.	
James City	B2	1634	23	1820-80	Original Shire	Williamsburg 23185

(Clk Cir Ct has b rec from 1865 to 1883, d rec from 1864 to 1884, m, div, pro, civ ct & Ind rec from 1865)

Jefferson				1810-60	See W. Va.	
Kanawah				1810-60	See W. Va.	
Kentucky		1777	(from Fincastle Co)		Discontinued 1780	
* King and Queen	B2	1691	6	1810-80	New Kent	King & Queen C. H. 23085

(Clk Cir Ct has b, d rec from 1865 to 1898, m div rec from 1864, pro, civ ct rec from 1865, Ind rec from 1782)

King George	B2	1720-1	10	1810-80	Richmond, Westmoreland	King George 22485

(Clk Cir Ct has m rec from 1786, div, civ ct, Ind, pro, wills from 1721)

* King William	B2	1701-2	9	1820-80	King and Queen	King William 23086

(Clk Cir Ct has m, div, pro, civ ct rec from 1885; fire 1855 burned most rec; some rec back to 1702 have been photo copied)

* Lancaster	B2	1651	10	1810-80	Northumberland, York	Lancaster 22503

(Co Health has b rec; Clk Cir Ct has m rec from 1715, d rec & wills from 1652, div rec from 1800, pro rec from 1700, civ ct rec from 1910 & Ind rec from 1652)

* Lee	G3	1792-3	26	1810-80	Russell, Scott	Jonesville 24263

(Clk Cir Ct has b & d rec from 1853 to 1877, m rec 1830, div rec 1832, pro rec 1800, civ ct rec & deeds from 1793)

Lewis				1820-60	See W. Va.	
Lincoln					See W. Va.	
Logan				1830-60	See W. Va.	
* Loudoun	C1	1757	57	1810-80	Fairfax	Leesburg 22075

(Clk Cir Ct has b, d rec from 1853 to 1859, m rec from 1793, div, pro, civ ct, Ind rec from 1757)

* Louisa	C2	1742	18	1820-80	Hanover	Louisa 23093

(Clk Cir Ct has b rec from 1867 to 1896, m, div, pro rec from 1742)

Lower Norfolk		1637			New Norfolk	

(See Princess Anne and Norfolk)

* Lunenburg	C3	1746	12	1810-80	Brunswick	Lunenburg 23952

(Clk Cir Ct has m, div, pro, civ ct & Ind rec from 1746)

Lynchburg				67	Ind. City	Lynchburg 24505

(Clk Cir Ct has b, d rec from 1853 to 1868, m, div, pro, civ ct, Ind rec from 1805, slave register, mil discharge rec from WW1, mil rec from CW, criminal rec, business charters from 1805)

Name	Map Index	Date Created	Pop. By M 1980	U.S. Cen Reports Available	Parent County or Territory From Which Organized	County Seat
* Madison	C2	1792-3	10	1810-80	Culpeper	Madison 22727

(Clk Cir Ct has m rec also div, pro, civ ct & Ind rec from 1793)

Name	Map Index	Date Created	Pop. By M 1980	U.S. Cen Reports Available	Parent County or Territory From Which Organized	County Seat
Marion				1850-60	See W. Va.	
Marshall				1840-60	See W. Va.	
Martinsville					Ind. City	Martinsville 24112

(Clk Cir Ct has m, div, pro, civ ct & Ind rec from 1942)

Name	Map Index	Date Created	Pop. By M 1980	U.S. Cen Reports Available	Parent County or Territory From Which Organized	County Seat
Mason				1810-60	See W. Va.	
Mathews	B2	1790-1	8	1810-80	Gloucester	Mathews 23109

(Clk Cir Ct has m, div, pro, civ ct & Ind rec from 1865)

Name	Map Index	Date Created	Pop. By M 1980	U.S. Cen Reports Available	Parent County or Territory From Which Organized	County Seat
McDowell		1858		1860	See W. Va.	
* Mecklenburg	C3	1764-5	29	1820-80	Lunenburg	Boydton 23917
Mercer				1840-60	See W. Va.	
*§ Middlesex	B2	1673	8	1820-80	Lancaster	Saluda 23149

(Clk Cir Ct has b rec from 1840, m rec from 1840, pro, civ ct, Ind rec from 1673)

Name	Map Index	Date Created	Pop. By M 1980	U.S. Cen Reports Available	Parent County or Territory From Which Organized	County Seat
* Montgomery	E3	1776-7	64	1810-80	Fincastle, Botetourt, Pulaski	Christiansburg 24073

(Clk Cir Ct has b, d rec from 1853 to 1871, m, div, pro, civ ct, Ind rec from 1773)

Name	Map Index	Date Created	Pop. By M 1980	U.S. Cen Reports Available	Parent County or Territory From Which Organized	County Seat
Monongalia				1810-60	See W. Va.	
Monroe				1810-60	See W. Va.	
Monroe				1810-60	See W. Va.	
Morgan				1830-60	See W. Va.	
* Nansemond	B3	1637	35	1820-80	Upper Norfolk	Suffolk 23434

(Nansemond County and Suffolk City merged January 1, 1974. Clk Cir Ct has m, pro, civ ct, Ind rec from 1866)

Name	Map Index	Date Created	Pop. By M 1980	U.S. Cen Reports Available	Parent County or Territory From Which Organized	County Seat
* Nelson	D2	1807-8	12	1810-80	Amherst	Lovingston 22949

(Clk Cir Ct has m, div, pro, civ ct & Ind rec from 1808)

Name	Map Index	Date Created	Pop. By M 1980	U.S. Cen Reports Available	Parent County or Territory From Which Organized	County Seat
New Kent	B2	1654	9	1810-80	York (Pt. James City)	New Kent 23124

(Clk Cir Ct has b, d rec from 1865 to 1888, m, div, pro, civ ct, Ind rec from 1865)

Name	Map Index	Date Created	Pop. By M 1980	U.S. Cen Reports Available	Parent County or Territory From Which Organized	County Seat
New Norfolk		1636			Elizabeth City	
Nicholas				1820-60	See W. Va.	
* Norfolk	B3	1636		1810-80	Lower Norfolk (changed to Chesapeak City 1963)	
Northampton	A2	1634	15	1820-80	Original Shire (prior to 1642 was called Accawmack)	Eastville 23347

(Clk Cir Ct has m rec from 1706 & pro rec from 1632)

Name	Map Index	Date Created	Pop. By M 1980	U.S. Cen Reports Available	Parent County or Territory From Which Organized	County Seat
Northumberland	B2	1648	10	1810-80	Indian Dist. of Chickacoan	Heathsville 22473

(Clk Cir Ct has m, div, pro, civ ct (Ind rec)

Name	Map Index	Date Created	Pop. By M 1980	U.S. Cen Reports Available	Parent County or Territory From Which Organized	County Seat
Norton					Ind. City	Norton 24273

(all rec with Wise Co)

Name	Map Index	Date Created	Pop. By M 1980	U.S. Cen Reports Available	Parent County or Territory From Which Organized	County Seat
* Nottoway	C3	1788-9	15	1810-80	Amelia	Nottoway 23955

(Clk Cir Ct has m, div rec from 1865, pro, civ ct, Ind rec from 1789)

Name	Map Index	Date Created	Pop. By M 1980	U.S. Cen Reports Available	Parent County or Territory From Which Organized	County Seat
* Orange	C2	1734	18	1820-80	Spotsylvania	Orange 22960

(Clk Cir Ct has b rec from 1860 to 1895, m rec 1757, pro, civ ct & deeds from 1734)

Name	Map Index	Date Created	Pop. By M 1980	U.S. Cen Reports Available	Parent County or Territory From Which Organized	County Seat
Page	C1	1831	19	1840-80	Rockingham, Shenandoah	Luray 22835

(Clk Cir Ct has m, div, pro, civ ct & Ind rec from 1831)

Name	Map Index	Date Created	Pop. By M 1980	U.S. Cen Reports Available	Parent County or Territory From Which Organized	County Seat
* Patrick	E3	1790-1	17	1820-80	Henry	Stuart 24171

(Clk Cir Ct has b rec from 1853 to 1896, m, div, Ind rec from 1791)

Name	Map Index	Date Created	Pop. By M 1980	U.S. Cen Reports Available	Parent County or Territory From Which Organized	County Seat
Pendleton				1810-60	See W. Va.	
Ohio				1810-60	See W. Va.	
Petersburg					Ind. City	Petersburg 23803

(City Clk has b rec from 1853 to 1896, d rec from 1853, m, div, pro & Ind rec from 1784)

Name	Map Index	Date Created	Pop. By M 1980	U.S. Cen Reports Available	Parent County or Territory From Which Organized	County Seat
* Pittsylvania	D3	1766-7	66		Halifax	Chatham 24531

(Clk Cir Ct has m, div, pro, civ ct, accounts current & inventories of estates from 1767)

Name	Map Index	Date Created	Pop. By M 1980	U.S. Cen Reports Available	Parent County or Territory From Which Organized	County Seat
Pleasants		1851		1860-80	See W. Va.	
Pocahontas				1830-60	See W. Va.	
Portsmouth	B3				Ind. City	Portsmouth 23705

(Clk Cir Ct has b, d rec from 1858 to 1896, m, div, pro, civ ct, Ind rec from 1848; Portsmouth Pub Health Dept., P.O. Box 250, Portsmouth, Va 23705 has b, d, bur rec. Territory taken from Norfolk County and annexed to Portsmouth County in 1848, 1960 and 1968)

Name	Map Index	Date Created	Pop. By M 1980	U.S. Cen Reports Available	Parent County or Territory From Which Organized	County Seat
*§ Powhatan	C2	1777	13	1810-80	Cumberland, Chesterfield	Powhatan 23139

(Clk Cir Ct has m, div, pro, civ ct & Ind rec from 1777)

Name	Map Index	Date Created	Pop. By M 1980	U.S. Cen Reports Available	Parent County or Territory From Which Organized	County Seat
Preston				1820-60	See W. Va.	
* Prince Edward	C3	1753-4	16	1810-80	Amelia	Farmville 23901

(Clk Cir Ct has b rec from 1853 to 1896, d rec from 1853 to 1869, m, div, pro, civ ct & deeds rec also guardian bk from 1754)

Name	Map Index	Date Created	Pop. By M 1980	U.S. Cen Reports Available	Parent County or Territory From Which Organized	County Seat
*§ Prince George	B3	1702-3	26	1810-80	Charles City	Prince George 23875

(Clk Cir Ct has partial b rec from 1865 to 1896, m, div, pro rec from 1865 & civ ct rec from 1945)

Name	Map Index	Date Created	Pop. By M 1980	U.S. Cen Reports Available	Parent County or Territory From Which Organized	County Seat
* Prince William	C1	1730-1	144	1810-80	King George, Stafford	Manassas 22110

(Clk Cir Ct has m rec from 1859, div rec, pro rec from 1734 & Ind rec from 1732)

Name	Map Index	Date Created	Pop. By M 1980	U.S. Cen Reports Available	Parent County or Territory From Which Organized	County Seat
Pulaski	E3	1839	35	1840-80	Montgomery, Wythe	Pulaski 24301

(Clk Cir Ct has m rec from 1882, div, pro, civ ct rec from 1839)

Putnam				1850-60	See W. Va.	
Radford					Ind. City	Radford 24141

(Clk Cir Ct has m, div, pro, civ ct & Ind rec from 1892)

Raleigh				1850-60	See W. Va.	
Randolph				1810-60	See W. Va.	
Rappahannock	C1	1833	6	1840-80	Culpeper	Washington 22747

(Clk Cir Ct has m, div, pro & civ ct rec from 1833, Ind rec from 1836 & some personal property rec from 1834)

Rappahannock, Old					Abolished 1692	Lancaster 22503
Richmond					Ind. City	Richmond 23219

(Dept of Health, Bureau of Vit Rec Madison Building, Richmond, Va 23219 has div rec from 1870 to 1954; Chan Ct for the City of Richmond, City Hall, Richmond, Va 23219 has pro rec; Civ Ct for the City of Richmond City Hall, Richmond, Va 23219 has civ ct rec; Clk Cir Ct has Ind rec for New Kent Co from 1863 to 1865; Chan Ct has Ind rec for the City of Richmond, City Hall, Richmond Va 23219)

Richmond	B2	1692	7	1810-80	Rappahannock (old)	Warsaw 22572

(Clk Cir Ct has b & d rec from 1853 to 1895, m rec from 1853, div, pro, deeds & wills from 1693)

Ritchie				1850-60	See W. Va.	
Roane				1860	See W. Va.	
Roanoke	E2	1838	73	1840-80	Botetourt Montgomery	Salem 24153

(Clk Cir Ct has m, div, pro, civ ct & Ind rec from 1838)

* Roanoke			100		Ind. City	Roanoke 241010

(Clk Cts has b rec from 1884 to 1896, m, div, pro, civ ct & Ind rec from 1884; P.O. Box 2610, Roanoke, Va 24010)

* Rockbridge	D2	1778	18	1810-80	Augusta, Botetourt	Lexington 24450

(Clk Cir Ct has b rec from 1853 to 1896, d rec from 1853 to 1870, m, div, pro, civ ct, Ind rec from 1778)

* Rockingham	D1	1778	57	1810-80	Augusta	Harrisonburg 22801

(Clk Cir Ct has b rec from 1862 to 1894, d rec from 1890 to 1894, m, pro, civ ct, Ind rec from 1778, div rec from 1833. Some rec burned in 1864)

Russell	F3	1785	31	1820-80	Washington	Lebanon 24266

(Clk Cir Ct has m rec from 1853, div & civ ct rec from 1786, pro rec from 1803 & Ind rec from 1787)

* Scott	F3	1814	25	1820-80	Lee, Russell, Washington	Gate City 24251

(Clk Cir Ct has b & d rec from 1857 to 1870, m, div, pro, Ind, chan & law rec from 1815)

* Shenandoah	D1	1772	27	1810-80	Frederick (Dunmore 'til 1778)	Woodstock 22664

(Clk Cir Ct has m, div, pro, civ ct & Ind rec from 1772)

* Smyth	F3	1832	33	1840-80	Washington, Wythe	Marion 24354

(Clk Cir Ct has m, div, pro & civ ct rec from 1832)

*§ Southampton	B3	1749	19	1810-80	Isle of Wight, Nansemond	Courtland 23837
Spotsylvania	C2	1720-1	34	1810-80	Essex, King and Queen, King William	Spotsylvania 22553

(Clk Cir Ct has m rec from 1795, div & Ind rec from 1875, pro & other rec of int to genealogists from 1722; Co Ct has civ ct rec)

Stafford	C1	1664	40	1810-80	Westmoreland	Stafford 22554

(Clk Cir Ct has m rec from 1854, div & civ ct rec 1664, pro & deeds 1699)

Staunton					Ind. City	Staunton 24401

(Clk Cir Ct has b rec from 1853 to 1896, d rec from 1853 to 1892, m, div, pro, civ ct, Ind rec from 1802)

Suffolk			47		Ind. City	Suffolk 23434

(City Ct has m, div, pro, Ind rec from 1866. (See Nansemond County)

* Surry	B3	1652	6	1810-80	James City	Surry 23883

(Clk Cir Ct has b & d rec from 1853 to 1896, m rec from 1768, pro & Ind rec from 1652, civ ct rec from 1671, orph accounts intermittent from 1744, guardian accounts intermittent from 1865, fiduciary accounts from 1831 & div rec)

* Sussex	B3	1753-4	11	1810-80	Surry	Sussex 23884

(Clk Cir Ct has b, m, pro, civ ct & Ind rec from 1754)

Taylor				1850-60	See W. Va.	
* Tazewell	F3	1799	50	1820-80	Russell, Wythe	Tazewell 24651

(Clk Cir Ct has b, d rec from 1853 to 1870, m, pro, law, Ind rec from 1800, chancery rec from 1832)

Tucker				1860	See W. Va.	
Tyler				1820-60	See W. Va.	
Upper Norfolk		1637			New Norfolk (see Nansemond)	
Upshur				1860	See W. Va.	
Virginia Beach					Ind. City	Virginia Beach 23456

(City Clk has b rec from 1884 to 1895, div rec from 1936, m & pro rec)

Warren	C1	1836	21	1840-80	Frederick, Shenandoah	Front Royal 22630

(Clk Cir Ct has m, div, pro, civ ct & Ind rec from 1836)

Name	Map Index	Date Created	Pop. By M 1980	U.S. Cen Reports Available	Parent County or Territory From Which Organized	County Seat
Warrosquoyacke		1634			Changed to Isle of Wight 1637	
* Washington	F3	1776-7	46	1810-80	Fincastle, Montgomery	Abingdon 24210

(In 1974 nine square miles of Washington County was annexed to the city of Bristol, which is an independent city with its own Clk's office and rec. Clk Cir Ct has m, div, pro, civ ct, Ind rec from 1777)

Name	Map Index	Date Created	Pop. By M 1980	U.S. Cen Reports Available	Parent County or Territory From Which Organized	County Seat
Wayne				1850-60	See W. Va.	
Waynesboro					Ind. City	Waynesboro 22980

(Clk Cir Ct has m, div, pro, civ ct & Ind rec from 1948)

Name	Map Index	Date Created	Pop. By M 1980	U.S. Cen Reports Available	Parent County or Territory From Which Organized	County Seat
Webster				1860	See W. Va.	
* Westmoreland	B2	1653	14	1810-80	Northumberland	Montross 22520

(Clk Cir Ct has b & d rec from 1855 to 1895, m rec from 1786, div rec from 1850, pro, civ ct & Ind rec from 1653)

Name	Map Index	Date Created	Pop. By M 1980	U.S. Cen Reports Available	Parent County or Territory From Which Organized	County Seat
Wetzel				1850-60	See W. Va.	
Williamsburg					Ind. City	Williamsburg 23185

(Clk Cir Ct has m, div, pro, Ind rec from 1865, District Ct rec from 1953)

Name	Map Index	Date Created	Pop. By M 1980	U.S. Cen Reports Available	Parent County or Territory From Which Organized	County Seat
Wirt				1850-60	See W. Va.	
* Wise	F3	1856	42	1860-80	Lee, Russell, Scott	Wise 24293

(Clk Cir Ct has m & div rec from 1856)

Name	Map Index	Date Created	Pop. By M 1980	U.S. Cen Reports Available	Parent County or Territory From Which Organized	County Seat
Wood				1810-60	See W. Va.	
Wyoming				1850-60	See W. Va.	
* Wythe	E3	1789	25	1810-80	Montgomery (Pt. Grayson)	Wytheville 24382

(Clk Cir Ct has m, div, pro, civ ct & Ind rec from 1790)

Name	Map Index	Date Created	Pop. By M 1980	U.S. Cen Reports Available	Parent County or Territory From Which Organized	County Seat
Yohogania		1776 (from Augusta County)			Discontinued 1786	
* York	B2	1634	35	1810-80	Formerly Charles River	Yorktown 23490

(changed from Charles River)

* - At least one county history has been published about this county.

§ - Inventory of county archives was made by the Historical Records Survey. (see introduction)

WASHINGTON

CAPITAL, OLYMPIA - TERRITORY 1853 - STATE 1889 - (42ND)

Washington became a territory in 1853, after having been part of Oregon Territory since 1848. Included in that territorial domain was all of the present Idaho. It was reduced to its present dimensions in 1889 when Washington became the forty-second state to enter the Union.

During the years of its greatest growth, Washington received thousands of former residents of Wisconsin, Minnesota and other western states. Many Canadian farmers flocked there to secure good land at a low price. Most of the newcomers at that time were Canadians, Swedes, Norwegians, English, Germans, Finns, Italians, Russians, Danes, and Scots. The Scandinavian immigrants felt especially at home since the country and climate reminded them of the places they had previously inhabited.

Since 1907 the State Department of Health, Bureau of Vital Statistics, now located in the General Administration Building, Olympia, WA 98501, has had control of all birth and death records within the state. Records prior to that time are on file in the offices of the County Auditor of the respective counties. In the cities of Seattle, Spokane, Bellingham and Tacoma, they may be obtained at the city health departments.

Records of marriages are at the offices of the respective County Auditors. All land records are also filed in those offices.

The County Clerks have charge of the records of wills and all probate matters.

Genealogical Archives, Libraries, Societies, and Publications

Clallam County Historical Society, Genealogical Dept., P.O. Box 1045, Port Angeles, WA 98362.

Clark County Museum, 1511 Main, Vancouver, WA 98660.

Clark County Genealogical Society, 1511 Main Street, Vancouver, WA 98660.

Eastern Washington Genealogical Society, P.O. Box 1826, Spokane, WA 99210.

Ephrata Genealogical Society, c/o Mrs. R. E. Stevenson, 124 G. Street, S.W., Ephrata, WA 98823.

Everett Public Library, 2702 Hoyt Avenue, Everett, WA 98201.

Ft. Vancouver Historical Society, Box 1834, Vancouver, WA 98663.

Ft. Vancouver Regional Library, 1007 E. Mill Plain Blvd., Vancouver, WA 98660.

Grant County Genealogical Society, c/o Ephrata Public Library, 339 1st Avenue, SW, Ephrata, WA 98823.

Grays Harbor Genealogy Club, Aberdeen, WA 98520.

Lower Columbia Genealogical Society, P.O. Box 472, Longview, WA 98632.

Maple Valley Historical Society, P.O. Box 123, Maple Valley, WA 98038.

North Central Washington Genealogical Society, P.O. Box 613, Wenatchee, WA 98801.

Olympia Genealogical Society, c/o Olympia Public Library, 7th and Franklin, Olympia, WA 98502.

Public Library, P.O. Box 1197, Bellingham, WA 98225.

Public Library, 1120 So. Tacoma Ave., Tacoma, WA 98402.

Puget Sound Genealogical Society, 4430 Pine Avenue, NE, Bremerton, WA 98310.

Seattle Genealogical Society, P.O. Box 549, Seattle, WA 98111.

Seattle Public Library, 4th Ave. and Madison, Seattle, WA 98104.

Spokane Public Library, West 906 Main Ave., Spokane, WA 99201.

State Capitol Historical Association, 211 W. 21st Ave., Olympia, WA 98501.

Tacoma Genealogical Society, The, P.O. Box 1952, Tacoma, WA 98401.

Tri-City Genealogical Society, Route 1, Box 5006, Richland, WA 99352.

University of Washington Library, Seattle, WA 98105.

Walla Walla Valley Genealogical Society, P.O. Box 115, Walla Walla, WA 99362.

Washington State Historical Society Library, State Historical Bldg., 315 North Stadium Way, Tacoma, WA 98403.

Washington State Library, State Library Bldg., Olympia, WA 98501.

Whatcom Genealogical Society, P.O. Box 1493, Bellingham, WA 98225.

Yakima Valley Genealogical Society, P.O. Box 445, Yakima, WA 98907.

Yakima Valley Regional Library, 116 E, "A" St., Yakima, WA 98902.

Bulletin of the Seattle Genealogical Society, Inc., P.O. Box 549, Seattle, WA 98111.

Eastern Washington Genealogical Society Bulletin, P.O. Box 1826, Spokane, WA 99210.

Researcher, The, The Tacoma Genealogical Society, P.O. Box 1952, Tacoma, WA 98401.

Tacoma Researcher, P.O. Box 11232, Tacoma, WA 98411.

Printed Census Records and Mortality Schedules

Indexes (Territory):1860, 1870, 1880

Printed Census Records (Counties):

Franklin-1880	Mason-1880	Walla Walla-1880
Kittitas-1860, 1870, 1880	Spokane-1880	Whitman-1880
Lewis-1880	Stevens-1880	Yakima-1880

Valuable Printed Sources

Maps

Abbott, Newton Carl and Fred E. Carver; J. W. Helm, comp. *The Evolution of Washington Counties.* Yakima: Yakima Valley Genealogical Society and Klickitat County Historical Society (1978).

Place Names

Meany, Edmond S. *Origin of Washington Geographic Names.* Seattle: University of Washington Press (1923) republished Detroit: Gale Research Company (1968).

Phillips, James W. *Washington State Place Names.* Seattle: University of Washington Press (1971).

Guides To Genealogical Research

Washington (State) Division of Archives and Records Management. *Genealogical Sources in Washington State.* Olympia, Washington: n.d. (10 page pamphlet prepared by the State Archivist).

Histories

Hawthorne, Julian. *History of Washington.* New York: American Historical Publishing Company (1893).

Hines, Rev. H. K. *An Illustrated History of the State of Washington.* Chicago: The Lewis Publishing Company (1893).

Stewart, Edgar I. *Washington, Northwest Frontier.* New York: Lewis Historical Publishing Company, 1957. 4 Vols.

WASHINGTON COUNTY HISTORIES
(Population figures to nearest thousand - 1980 U. S. Census)

Name	Map Index	Date Created	Pop. By M 1980	U.S. Cen Reports Available	Parent County or Territory From Which Organized	County Seat
§ Adams	B4	1883	13		Whitman	Ritzville 99169
(Co Aud has b & d rec to 1907, also m rec; Co Clk has div & pro rec; Co Asr has Ind rec)						
*§ Asotin	C4	1883	17		Garfield	Asotin 99402
(Co Aud has b & m rec from 1891, d rec from 1891 to 1907; Co Clk has div & pro rec; Co Asr has Ind rec from 1891)						
§ Benton	C3	1905	109		Yakima, Klickitat	Prosser 99350
(Co Aud has b rec from 1905 to 1907, m rec from 1905; Co Clk has div, pro & civ ct rec; Co Asr has Ind rec)						
Chehalis				1860-80	Original Co. - now Grays Harbor, changed 1915	
§ Chelan	B3	1899	45		Kittitas, Okanogan	Wenatchee 98801
(Co Aud has b & d rec from 1900 to 1907, m rec from 1900; City Clk has bur rec; Chelan Co Clk has div, pro & civ ct rec)						
Clallam	A1	1854	51	1860-80	Jefferson	Port Angeles 98362
* Clark	C2	1844	192	1860-80	Original county (formerly Vancouver Co, changed 1849	Vancouver 98660
(Co Aud has b, d rec from 1890 to 1906, m rec from 1890, Ind rec from 1850; Co Clk has div, pro, civ rec from 1890)						
* Columbia	C4	1875	4	1880	Walla Walla	Dayton 99328
(Co Clk has b, d rec from 1891 to 1907, m rec from 1876, div, pro, civ ct rec from 1891, Ind rec from 1890)						
§ Cowlitz	C2	1854	79	1860-80	Lewis	Kelso 98626
(Co Aud has m rec from 1867, d rec from 1891 to 1907; Co Clk has div & civ ct rec from 1874, pro rec from 1889)						
* Douglas	B3	1883	22		Lincoln	Waterville 98858
(Co Aud has b rec to 1907, bur rec to 1909, Ind rec to 1925, m, d, div, pro & civ ct rec, also mining claims from 1890)						
* Ferry	A4	1899	6		Stevens	Republic 99166
(Co Clk has div, pro & civ ct rec from 1899)						
Franklin	C3	1883	35		Whitman	Pasco 99301
(Co Aud has b, d & bur rec from 1891 to 1910, m rec from 1891; Co Clk has div & pro rec from 1891)						
*§ Garfield	C4	1881	2		Columbia	Pomeroy 99347
(Co Aud has b & d rec from 1891 to 1907, m rec from 1891, bur rec from 1891 to 1918; Co Clk has div, pro & civ ct rec from 1882; Co Aud has Ind rec from 1891)						
Grant	B3	1909	48		Douglas	Ephrata 98823
(Co Aud has m & Ind rec from 1909; Co Clk has div, pro & civ ct rec)						
Gray's Harbor	B1	1854	66		Organized as Chehalis, q.v. changed 1915	Montesano 98563
(Co Aud has b, d rec from 1891 to 1907, m rec from 1891, Ind rec from 1855; Co Clk has div, pro, civ ct rec from 1860)						
Island	A2	1853	44	1860-80	Original county	Coupeville 98239
(Co Aud has b & d rec from 1870 to 1907, m rec from 1855 & Ind rec from 1853; Co Clk has div, pro & civ ct rec)						
Jefferson	B1	1852	16	1860-80	Original county	Port Townsend 98368
(Co Aud has b & d rec from 1891 to 1907, m rec from 1853; Co Clk has div rec from 1886 & pro rec from 1891)						
*§ King	B2	1852	1,265	1860-80	Original county	Seattle 98104
(Rec & Election Dept, Rec Div has b & d rec from 1891 to 1907 & Ind rec from 1852; License Dept, 401 Administration Bldg, Seattle, WA 98104 has m rec; Judicial Dept, Room 609 Court House, Seattle, Wash has div & pro rec)						
* Kitsap	B2	1857	146	1860-80	King	Port Orchard 98366
(Co Aud has b rec from 1891 to 1907, d rec from 1892 to 1907, also m rec from 1892; Co Clk has div & civ ct rec from 1888, pro & adoption rec from 1861 & Ind rec from 1857)						

COUNTY MAP FOR THE STATE OF WASHINGTON

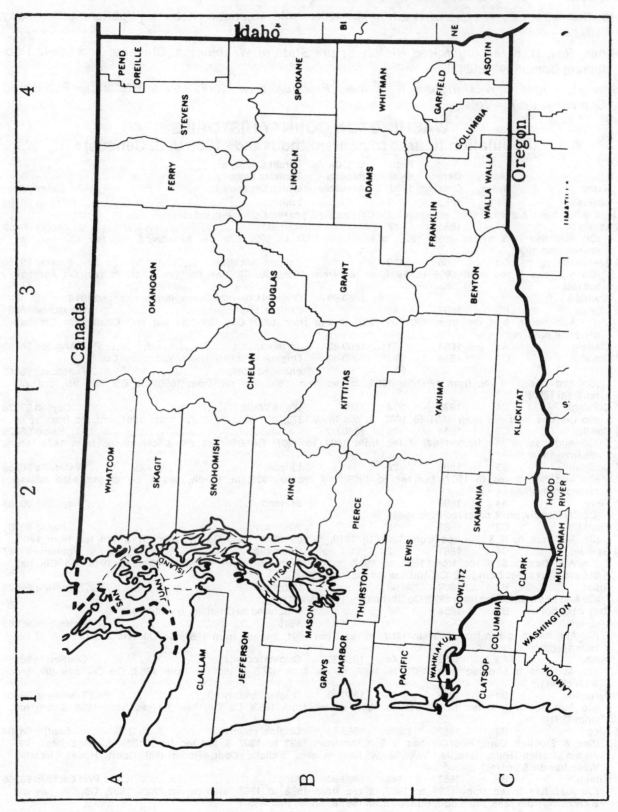

Name	Map Index	Date Created	Pop. By M 1980	U.S. Cen Reports Available	Parent County or Territory From Which Organized	County Seat
Kittitas	B3	1883	25		Yakima	Ellensburg 98926

(Co Aud has b, d rec from 1891 to 1907, m rec from 1884, Ind rec from 1882; Co Clk has div, pro, civ ct rec from 1890's)

| Klickitat | C2 | 1859 | 16 | 1860-80 | Walla Walla | Goldendale 98620 |

(Co Clk has div, pro, civ ct rec; Co Aud has m rec; Bureau of Vit Stat Olympia, has b & d rec)

| § Lewis | B2 | 1845 | 55 | 1860-80 | Original county | Chehalis 98532 |

(Co Aud has b & d rec from 1891 to 1907, m rec from 1850; Co Clk has div, pro & civ ct rec from ca 1870)

| § Lincoln | B4 | 1883 | 10 | | Spokane | Davenport 99122 |

(Co Aud has b, d rec from 1891 to 1907, m, Ind rec from 1891; Co Clk has div, pro, civ ct rec)

| Mason | B1 | 1854 | 31 | 1870-80 | Thurston | Shelton 98584 |

(Co Aud has b & d rec from 1891 to 1906, m rec from 1907; Co Clk has div rec from 1899, pro rec from 1858 & civ ct rec from 1889)

| Okanogan | A3 | 1888 | 31 | | Stevens | Okanogan 98840 |

(Co Aud has b, d rec from 1891 to 1908, m rec from 1891, Ind rec from 1891, patents from 1892 and mines from 1888; Co Clk has div, pro, civ ct rec from 1896)

| * Pacific | B1 | 1851 | 17 | 1860-80 | Original county | South Bend 98586 |

(Co Aud has b & d rec from 1891 to 1905, m rec from 1868; Co Clk has div, pro & civ ct rec; Co Asr has Ind rec)

| § Pend Oreille | A4 | 1911 | 9 | | Stevens | Newport 99156 |

(Co Aud has b & m rec from 1911; Co Clk has div, pro & civ ct rec)

| * Pierce | B2 | 1852 | 483 | 1860-80 | Original county | Tacoma 98402 |

(Co Aud has b rec from 1891 to 1907, m & Ind rec from 1860; Co Clk has div, pro & civ ct rec)

| San Juan | A1 | 1873 | 8 | 1870-80 | Whatcom | Friday Harbor 98250 |

(Co Clk - Aud has b rec from 1892 to 1907, d rec from 1890 to 1907, m rec from 1878, div, pro & civ ct rec from 1890)

| Sawamish | | | | 1860 | See Mason | |

| *§ Skagit | A2 | 1883 | 63 | | Whatcom | Mount Vernon 98273 |

(Co Aud has b, d rec from 1891 to 1907, Ind rec from 1872, m rec from 1884; Co Clk has div, pro, civ ct rec from 1883)

| Skamania | C2 | 1854 | 8 | 1860-80 | Clark | Stevenson 98648 |

(Co Aud has b rec from 1898, m rec from 1856, deeds, mining claims & U.S. patents from 1856; Co Clk has bur, div, pro & civ ct rec from 1856)

| *§ Snohomish | B2 | 1861 | 336 | 1870-80 | Island | Everett 98201 |

(Co Aud has b, d rec from 1891 to 1907, m rec from 1891; Co Clk has div, pro, civ ct rec)

| *§ Spokane | B4 | 1858 | 341 | 1860-80 | Walla Walla | Spokane 99201 |

(Spokane Co was organized in 1858 from Walla Walla, then disorganized & reorganized in 1879 from Stevens Co) (Co Aud has b & d rec from 1890 to 1907, m rec from 1890 & Ind rec; Co Clk has div, pro & civ ct rec)

| § Stevens | A4 | 1863 | 29 | 1870-80 | Walla Walla | Colville 99114 |

(Co Aud has b, d rec from 1891 to 1907, m rec from 1861, Ind rec (deeds) from 1883; Co Clk has div, pro, civ ct rec)

| * Thurston | B1 | 1852 | 124 | 1860-80 | Original county | Olympia 98501 |

(Co Aud has b & d rec from 1891 to 1907, m rec from 1891; Co Clk has div, pro & civ ct rec)

| Wahkiakum | C1 | 1854 | 4 | 1860-80 | Lewis | Cathlamet 98612 |

(Co Aud has b rec from 1891 to 1907, m rec from 1891; Co Clk has bur, div, pro, civ ct rec & Ind rec from 1868)

| * Walla Walla | C3 | 1854 | 47 | 1860-80 | Original county | Walla Walla 99362 |

(Co Clk has div, pro & civ ct rec from 1860)

| Whatcom | A2 | 1854 | 105 | 1860-80 | Original county | Bellingham 98225 |

(Co Aud has b, d rec from 1891 to 1907, m rec from 1869, Ind rec; Co Clk has div, pro, civ ct rec)

| Whitman | B4 | 1871 | 40 | 1880 | Stevens | Colfax 99111 |

(Co Aud has b & d rec from 1891 to 1907, m & Ind rec from 1873; Co Clk has div & civ ct rec from 1864 & pro rec from 1870)

| *§ Yakima | C2 | 1865 | 171 | 1870-80 | Walla Walla | Yakima 98901 |

(Co Aud has b & d rec from 1891 to 1907, m rec from 1880 & Ind rec; Co Clk has div, pro & civ ct rec from 1890)

* - At least one county history has been published about this county.

§ - Inventory of county archives was made by the Historical Records Survey. (see introduction)

WEST VIRGINIA

CAPITAL, CHARLESTON - STATE 1863 - (35TH)

West Virginia came into existence as a direct result of the Civil War. That section had always been part of Virginia, even though the two sections never had much in common.

One of the main reasons for this, no doubt, is the rugged Allegheny mountain range separating the two sections which made traveling between them rather difficult. When Virginia cast its lot with the Confederacy, the settlers west of the Alleghenies began to murmur. The complaint eventually became so loud and demanding that a separate government for the western section was organized in 1861 under the name of Kanawha. Two years later West Virginia was admitted into the Union as the thirty-fifth state with a total of 50 counties. Since then five counties have been added.

The physical features of the section make West Virginia more accessible from Pennsylvania than from Virginia. At least, it was so in the early days. In those days the Indian trails served as roads and much of the travel was in the direction from Pennsylvania to West Virginia. Germans, Welsh, and Irish came as early as 1670. The English in 1671, and various nationalities came in 1715 and 1725. Some of the early settlers merely crossed over from Maryland and made their homes in the present Berkely and Jefferson Counties.

Among different nationalities who have come to West Virginia to man various factories are Italians, Poles, Hungarians, Austrians, English, Germans, Greeks, Russians, and Czechs.

Most of the counties in West Virginia were settled years before they were organized. Here are figures showing the years the respective counties were settled:

Brooke, 1744; Pendleton, 1747; Randolph, 1753; Monroe, 1760; Monongalia, 1767; Greenbrier and Ohio, 1769; Harrison, Marion, and Preston, 1772; Kanawha, 1773; Mason and Tucker, 1774; Cabell and Mercer, 1775; Hancock, 1776; Marshall, 1777; Barbour and Wetzel, 1780; Jackson and Wirt, 1796; Wood, 1797; Boone, 1798; Lincoln, 1799; Putnam and Roan, 1800.

The Division of Vital Statistics, State Health Department, Charleston, West Virginia 25305, has the records of births and deaths from 1917 to the present. For earlier records write to Clerk of County Court in county where event occurred. This office has marriage indexes only from 1921 through 1963, and individual records from 1964 to present. For copies of records prior to 1964 write to Clerk of County Court in county where license was issued. Divorce records: index only from 1968 to present. For copies write to Clerk of Circuit Court in county where decree was granted. There is a fee for searching the records (each three year period searched) which includes a copy if recorded in this office.

Genealogical Archives, Libraries, Societies, and Publications

Boone County West Virginia Genealogical Society, Box 10 Hewett, WV 25108.

Cabell County Public Library, 900-5th Ave., Huntington, WV 25701.

Division of Archives and History, Cultural Center, Capitol Complex, Charleston, WV 25305.

Hamilton National Genealogical Society, Inc., P.O. Box 6386, Charleston, WV 25302.

Huntington Public Library, Huntington, WV 25701.

Kanawha Valley Genealogical Society, P.O. Box 8765, South Charleston, WV 25303.

Lincoln County Genealogical Society, P.O. Box 92, Griffithsville, WV 25521.

Logan County Genealogical Society, P.O. Box 783, Logan, WV 25601.

KYOWVA Genealogical Society, P.O. Box 1254, Huntington, WV 25715.

Marion County Genealogy Club, Helen White, President, Fairview, WV 26570.

Morgantown Public Library, 373 Spruce St., Morgantown, WV 26505.

Ritchie County Historical Society, 200 S. Church St., Harrisville, WV 26362.

West Augusta Historical and Genealogical Society, 118 - 11th St., Parkersburg, WV 26101.

West Virginia and Regional History Collection, Colson Hall, West Virginia University Library, Morgantown, WV 26506.

West Virginia Historical Society, Cultural Center, Capitol Complex, Charleston, WV 25305.

Wetzel County (West Virginia) Genealogical Society, P.O. Box 464, New Martinsville, WV 26155.

Wheeling Area Genealogical Society, 2237 Marshall Ave., Wheeling, WV 26003.

Wheeling Public Library, 52 16th Street, Wheeling, WV 26003.

KYOWVA Genealogical Society Newsletter, published by the KYOWVA Genealogical Society, P.O. Box 1254, Huntington, WV 25715.

Wetzel County Genealogical Society Newsletter, P.O. Box 464, New Martinsville, WV 26155.

Printed Census Records and Mortality Schedules

West Virginia (see Virginia for records prior to 1863)

Printed Census Records (Counties):

Barbour-1850, 1880	Kanawha-1810	Pendleton-1810
Boone-1860	Lewis-1850, 1870, 1880	Preston-1880
Calhoun-1860	Logan-1830, 1840, 1850	Randolph-1810
Clay-1850	Marion-1860	Ritchie-1850
Doddridge-1850	Mason-1810, 1820	Taylor-1850, 1880
Gilmer-1850	Mercer-1840, 1850	Tyler-1850
Hampshire-1782, 1784	Monongalia-1810	Upshur-1860, 1880
Hardy-1840	Monroe-1850	Webster-1850
Harrison-1810, 1820, 1840, 1850	Morgan-1850	Wetzel-1850
Jefferson-1810		

Mortality Schedules (Printed): 1850, 1860, 1870, 1880

Valuable Printed Sources

Atlas and Gazetteer

Gannett, Henry. *A Gazetteer of Virginia and West Virginia.* Baltimore: Genealogical Publishing Company (1975).

New Descriptive Atlas of West Virginia. Clarksburg, West Virginia: Clarksburg: Clarksburg Publishing Company (1933).

Place Names

Kenny, Hamill. *West Virginia Place Names.* Piedmont, West Virginia: Place Name Press (1945).

Guides To Genealogical Research

McCay, Betty L. *Genealogical Searching in Virginia and West Virginia.* Indianapolis: Ye Olde Genealogy Shoppee (1971).

South Charlestown, West Virginia: Kanawha Valley Genealogical Society (1981).

Stinson, Helen S. *The Handbook for Genealogical Research in West Virginia.*

Histories

Callahan, James Morton. *History of West Virginia Old and New.* Chicago and New York: The American Historical Society, Inc. (1923).

Sims, Edgar Barr. *Making a State.* Charlestown: State of West Virginia (1956).

Genealogical Sources

Cabell County Public Library - Huntington, West Virginia.

Crozier, William Armstrong. *A Key to Southern Pedigrees.* Baltimore: Genealogical Publishing Company, 1953.

James E. Morrow Library, Special Collections, Marshall University - Huntington, West Virginia.

Johnston, Ross B. *West Virginia Estate Settlements 1753-1850.* Fort Worth, Texas: American Reference Publishers, 1969 (Reprint from West Virginia Quarterly).

Johnston, Ross B. *West Virginians in the American Revolution.* Parkersburg, West Virginia: West Augusta Historical and Genealogical Society, 1959.

Lewis, Virgil A. *The Soldiery of West Virginia.* Baltimore: Genealogical Publishing Company, 1967 reprinted.

Reddy, Anne Waller. *West Virginia Revolutionary Ancestors.* Baltimore: Genealogical Publishing Company, 1963 reprinted.

Sims, Edgar Barr. *Index to Land Grants in West Virginia.* Charlestown, West Virginia: Auditor's Office, 1952.

West Virginia State Archives - Charleston, West Virginia.

West Virginia University - Colson Hall Library, Morgantown, West Virginia.

Bibliographies and Guides to Collections

Forbes, Harold M. *West Virginia Genealogy, A Bibliography and Guide to Research.* Morgantown, West Virginia: West Virginia University Press.

Hess, James W. Comp. *Guide to Manuscripts and Archives in the West Virginia Collection.* Morgantown: West Virginia University Library (1974).

Mertins, Barbara. *Newspapers in the University of West Virginia Library,* Morgantown: West Virginia University Library, 1973.

Shetler, Charles. *Guide to the Study of West Virginia History.* Morgantown: West Virginia University Library (1960).

Stewart, Robert Armistead. *Index to Printed Virginia Genealogies.* Baltimore: Genealogical Publishing Company, reprinted 1970.

Swem, Earl Gregg, comp. *Virginia Historical Index.* Gloucester, Massachusetts: Peter Smith, 1965.

WEST VIRGINIA COUNTY HISTORIES
(Population figures to nearest thousand - 1980 U. S. Census)

Name	Map Index	Date Created	Pop. By M 1980	U.S. Census Reports Available	Parent County or Territory From Which Organized	County Seat
* Barbour	B3	1843	17	1850-80	Harrison, Lewis, Randolph	Philippi 26416
(Co Clk has b & d rec from 1853, m rec from 1843 & Ind rec from 1845; Clk Cir Ct has div, pro & civ ct rec)						
* Berkeley	C4	1772	47	1810-80	Frederick	Martinsburg 25401
(Co Clk has b & d rec from 1865, m rec from 1781, pro rec from 1772 & Ind rec from 1880; Clk Cir Ct has div rec)						
Boone	B1	1847	30	1850-80	Kanawha, Cabell, Logan	Madison 25130
(Co Clk has b, m, d, pro, Ind rec from 1865; Cir Clk has div, civ ct rec)						
* Braxton	B2	1836	14	1840-80	Kanawha, Lewis, Nicholas	Sutton 26601
Brooke	A3	1796	30	1810-80	Ohio	Wellsburg 26070
(Co Clk has b, d rec from 1853, m, Ind rec from 1797; Cir Clk has div, pro, civ ct rec)						
* Cabell	A1	1809	106	1820-80	Kanawha	Huntington 25701
(Co Clk has b & d rec from 1853, m rec from 1809 & Ind rec from 1808; Clk Cir Ct has div & civ ct rec from 1809)						
Calhoun	B2	1856	8	1860-80	Gilmer	Grantsville 26147
(Co Clk has b, m, d, pro, Ind rec from 1856)						
Clay	B2	1858	11	1860-80	Braxton, Nicholas	Clay 25043
(Co Clk has b, m, d & pro rec from 1858)						
Doddridge	B3	1845	7	1850-80	Harrison, Tyler, Ritchie, Lewis	W. Union 26456
(Co Clk has b rec from 1853, m rec from 1850 & d rec from 1862)						
* Fayette	B2	1831	57	1840-80	Kanawha, Greenbrier, Logan	Fayetteville 25840
(Co Clk has b, d rec from 1866, m, pro, Ind rec from 1831; Cir Clk has div, civ ct rec)						
§ Gilmer	B2	1845	8	1850-80	Lewis, Kanawha	Glenville 26351
(Co Clk has b, d & civ ct rec from 1853, m, pro & Ind rec from 1845)						
*§ Grant	B3	1866	10	1870-80	Hardy	Petersburg 26847
(Co Clk has b, m, d, div, pro, civ ct & Ind rec from 1866)						
* Greenbrier	B2	1777	37	1820-80	Montgomery	Lewisburg 24901
(Co Clk has b, d rec from 1853, m rec from 1781, pro, Ind rec from 1780, Court Order rec)						
* Hampshire	B4	1753	15	1810-80	Frederick	Romney 26757
(Co Clk has b, m, d rec from 1865, pro rec from 1780 inc, chan rec from 1831 & Ind rec)						
Hancock	A4	1848	41	1850-80	Brooke	New Cumberland 26047
(Co Clk has b, m, d, pro & Ind rec from 1848; Clk Cir Ct has div rec)						
* Hardy	C3	1785	10	1820-80	Hampshire	Moorefield 26836
(Co Clk has b, m, d & bur rec from 1853, pro & Ind rec from 1786, civ ct rec from 1960 & div rec)						
Harrison	B3	1784	77	1810-80	Monongalia	Clarksburg 26301
(Co Clk has b & d rec from 1853, m & survey rec from 1784, pro rec from 1788 & Ind rec from 1786)						
Jackson	A2	1831	26	1840-80	Kanawha, Mason, Wood	Ripley 25271
(Co Clk has b, d, pro rec from 1853, m, Ind rec from 1831; Cir Clk has div rec, civ ct rec from 1831)						
* Jefferson	C4	1801	30	1810-80	Berkeley	Charles Town 25414
(Co Clk has b, d rec from 1853 (except CW years), m, pro, wills, Ind rec from 1801)						

COUNTY MAP FOR THE STATE OF WEST VIRGINIA

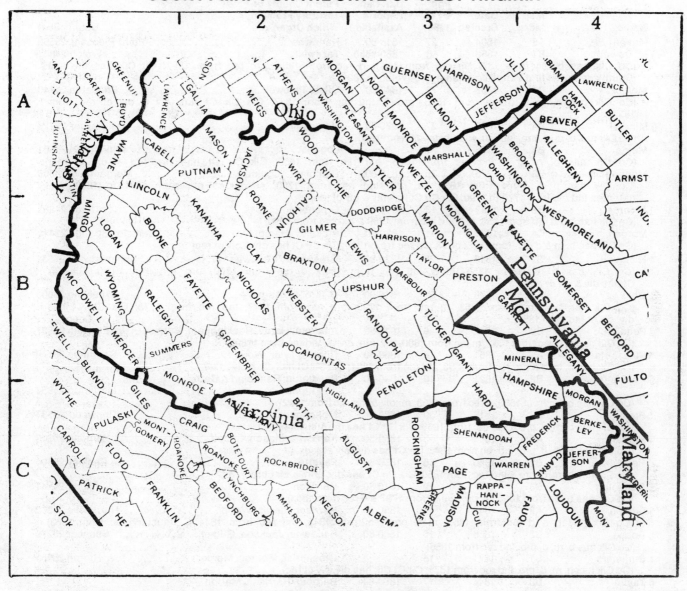

Name	Map Index	Date Created	Pop. By M 1980	U.S. Cen Reports Available	Parent County or Territory From Which Organized	County Seat
* Kanawha	B2	1788	224	1810-80	Greenbrier, Montgomery	Charleston 25301
(Co Clk has b, d rec from 1853, m rec from 1824, pro rec from 1831, Ind rec from 1790)						
* Lewis	B3	1816	19	1820-80	Harrison	Weston 26452
(Co Clk has b, d rec from 1853, m, pro, Ind rec from 1816, sale bills, appr. wills; Clk Cir Ct has div rec)						
*§ Lincoln	A1	1867	23	1870-80	Boone, Cabell, Kanawha	Hamlin 25523
(Co Clk has b, m, d, pro & Ind rec from 1909)						
* Logan	B1	1824	51	1830-80	Kanawha, Cabell, Giles	Logan 25601
(Co Clk has b, m & d rec from 1872)						
*§ Marion	B3	1842	66	1850-80	Harrison, Monongalia	Fairmont 26554
(Co Clk has b & d rec from 1854, m & Ind rec from 1842 & pro rec)						
* Marshall	A3	1835	41	1840-80	Ohio	Moundsville 26041
(Co Clk has b & d rec from 1853, m & deeds rec from 1835, pro rec from 1850; Cir Clk has div & civ ct rec)						

Name	Map Index	Date Created	Pop. By M 1980	U.S. Cen Reports Available	Parent County or Territory From Which Organized	County Seat
Mason	A2	1804	27	1810-80	Kanawha	Point Pleasant 25550
* McDowell	B1	1858	50	1860-1880	Tazewell	Welch 24801

(Co Clk has b rec from 1872, m rec from 1861, d rec from 1894, pro rec from 1897; Cir Clk has div rec)
(County seat was first Perryville, changed to Welch in 1892)

| * Mercer | B1 | 1837 | 73 | 1840-80 | Giles, Tazewell | Princeton 24740 |

(Co Clk has b, m & d rec from 1853, pro & Ind rec from 1837; Clk Cir Ct has div & civ ct rec from 1837)

| *§ Mineral | B4 | 1866 | 27 | 1870-80 | Hampshire | Keyser 26726 |

(Co Clk has b, m, d, pro, Ind rec, wills & deeds from 1866)

| Mingo | B1 | 1895 | 37 | | Logan | Williamson 25661 |

(Co Clk has b, m, d & Ind rec from 1895, bur rec from 1959; Clk Cir Ct has div, pro & civ ct rec)

| * Monongalia | B3 | 1776 | 75 | 1810-80 | Dist of W. Augusta | Morgantown 26505 |

(Co Clk has b & d rec from 1853, m, pro, Ind rec from 1790, surveyor's rec from 1781 to 1862, unpatented Ind rec from 1779 to 1790; Clk Cir Ct has div & civ ct rec)

| * Monroe | B2 | 1799 | 13 | 1810-80 | Greenbrier | Union 24983 |

(Co Clk has b & d rec from 1853, m & Ind rec from 1799 & bur rec from 1890)

| Morgan | C4 | 1820 | 11 | 1830-80 | Berkeley, Hampshire | Berkeley Springs 25411 |

(Co Clk has b, m & d rec from 1865, pro & Ind rec from 1820; Clk Cir Ct has div & civ ct rec)

| * Nicholas | B2 | 1818 | 28 | 1820-80 | Greenbrier, Kanawha | Summersville 26651 |

(Co Clk has b rec from 1855, m & Ind rec from 1812, d rec from 1890, pro rec from 1880; Clk Cir Ct has div & civ ct rec)

| * Ohio | A3 | 1776 | 61 | 1810-80 | Dist. of W. Augusta | Wheeling 26003 |

(Co Clk has b, d rec from 1853, m rec from 1793, pro rec from 1777, Ind rec from 1778; Clk Cir Ct has div, civ ct rec from 1884)

| *§ Pendleton | C3 | 1787 | 8 | 1810-80 | Augusta, Hardy, Rockingham, Bath | Franklin 26807 |

(Co Clk has b, d rec from 1853, m rec from 1800, div, pro, civ ct, Ind rec from 1789)

| * Pleasants | A3 | 1851 | 8 | 1860-80 | Ritchie, Tyler, Wood | St. Marys 26170 |

(Co Clk has b, m, d & pro rec from 1853, Ind rec from 1851; Clk Cir Ct has div & civ ct rec)

| *§ Pocahontas | B2 | 1821 | 10 | 1830-80 | Pendleton, Randolph & Bath, all Virginia | Marlinton 24954 |

(Co Clk has b rec from 1852, d rec from 1853, m, div & Ind rec from 1822)

| * Preston | B3 | 1818 | 30 | 1880 | Monongalia | Kingwood 26537 |

(Co Clk has b, m, d, pro & Ind rec from 1869; Clk Cir Ct has div & civ ct rec)

| § Putnam | A2 | 1848 | 37 | 1850-80 | Kanawha, Mason, Cabell | Winfield 25213 |

(Co Clk has b, m, d, pro, Ind rec from 1848; Cir Ct has div, civ ct rec)

| Raleigh | B1 | 1850 | 86 | 1850-80 | Fayette | Beckley 25801 |

(Co Clk has b, m, d, pro & Ind rec from 1850; Clk Cir Ct has div, crim & cir ct rec)

| *§ Randolph | B3 | 1787 | 29 | 1810-80 | Harrison | Elkins 26241 |

(Co Clk has b rec from 1856, m, pro, wills from 1787 & d rec from 1853)

| *§ Ritchie | A2 | 1843 | 11 | 1850-80 | Harrison, Lewis, Wood | Harrisville 26362 |

(Co Clk has b & d rec from 1853, m & pro rec from 1843, Ind rec from 1844 & fiduciary rec from 1863)

| *§ Roane | B2 | 1856 | 16 | 1860-80 | Kanawha, Jackson, Gilmer | Spencer 25276 |

(Co Clk has b, m, d, pro, Ind rec from 1856)

| * Summers | B1 | 1871 | 15 | | Greenbrier, Monroe, Mercer | Hinton 25951 |

(Co Clk has b, m, d, pro, Ind rec from 1871; Cir Ct Clk has div, civ ct rec)

| § Taylor | B3 | 1844 | 17 | 1850-80 | Barbour, Harrison, Marion & Preston | Grafton 26354 |

(Co Clk has b, m, d, pro, Ind rec from 1853, Cir Ct Clk has div, civ ct rec)

| * Tucker | B3 | 1856 | 9 | 1860-80 | Randolph | Parsons 26287 |

(Co Clk has b, m, d, pro, Ind rec, deeds & agreements; Clk Cir Ct has div & civ ct rec)

| Tyler | A3 | 1814 | 11 | 1820-80 | Ohio | Middlebourne 26149 |

(Co Clk has b, m & d rec from 1853, Ind rec from 1815; Clk Cir Ct has div, pro & civ ct rec)

| * Upshur | B3 | 1851 | 24 | 1860-80 | Randolph, Barbour, Lewis | Buckhannon 26201 |

(Co Clk has b, m, d, Ind rec from 1853; Cir Ct Clk has div, pro, civ ct rec)

| Wayne | A1 | 1842 | 45 | 1850-80 | Cabell | Wayne 25570 |

(Co Clk has b & d rec from 1853 & m rec from 1854)

| * Webster | B2 | 1860 | 12 | 1860-80 | Braxton, Nicholas | Webster Springs 26288 |

(Co Clk has b, m, d, bur, pro & Ind rec from 1887)

| * Wetzel | A3 | 1846 | 22 | 1850-80 | Tyler | New Martinsville 26155 |

(Co Clk has b, m & d rec from 1854, pro rec from 1847 & Ind rec from 1846; Clk Cir Ct has div rec)

| Wirt | A2 | 1848 | 5 | 1850-80 | Wood, Jackson | Elizabeth 26143 |

(Co Clk has b & d rec from 1870, m rec from 1854, pro & Ind rec from 1848; Clk Cir Ct has div rec)

| * Wood | A2 | 1798 | 92 | 1810-80 | Harrison | Parkersburg 26101 |

(Co Clk has b, d rec from 1853, m, pro rec from 1800, Ind rec from 1798; Cir Ct Clk has div, civ ct rec)

Name	Map Index	Date Created	Pop. By M 1980	U.S. Cen Reports Available	Parent County or Territory From Which Organized	County Seat
Wyoming	B1	1850	36	1850-80	Logan	Pineville 24874

(Co Clk has b, m, d, pro, Ind, bond bk, co court order bks, fiduciary rec from 1850; Clk Cir Ct has div, civ ct rec)

* - At least one county history has been published about this county.

§ - Inventory of county archives was made by the Historical Records Survey. (see introduction)

WISCONSIN

CAPITAL, MADISON - TERRITORY 1836 - STATE 1848 - (30TH)

Settlers established themselves in the Wisconsin area as early as 1766. In 1840, according to the first U.S. Census taken, the population was 130,945. The real influx of people came about 1848 when tens of thousands of people, mainly from the northern European countries came into the territory. The 1850 Census registered a population of 305,391 and the 1860 Census 775,881.

By far the largest number of these immigrants were Germans.

About 1840 nearly all of the counties facing Lake Michigan had received thousands of settlers. The Rock River Valley in Rock County also had many settlers at that time and earlier.

Wisconsin became a territory in its own name in 1836. Previously it had been part of several territories, including Indiana from 1800 to 1809; Illinois, 1809 to 1818; Michigan, 1818 to 1836. In 1848 it became the thirtieth state in the Union.

The leading nationalities represented in Wisconsin, in their numerical order are German (nearly three to one), Polish, Norwegian, Russian, Austrian, Swedish, Czech, Italian, Danish, Hungarian, English, Finnish, Greek, Irish and French.

The Bureau of Vital Statistics, P.O. Box 309, Madison, Wisconsin 53701, has birth and death records from 1860 to date.

Wills, deeds, land grants, taxpayers lists - all of these records are available in the various county courthouses. Address inquiries to the County Clerk.

War Service Records - Adjutant General's Office, State Capital, Madison.

Cemetery Records - a few have been transferred to the various county clerks, but the practice is not at all general. Contact the local sexton.

Guardianship and Orphan Court Proceedings are held by the issuing court and by the Public Welfare Department, State Capital.

Genealogical Archives, Libraries, Societies, and Publications

Brown County Library, Local History and Genealogy Dept., 515 Pine Street, Green Bay, WI 54301.

Fond du Lac County Historical Society, P.O. Box 131, Fond du Lac, WI 54935.

Fond du Lac Public Library, 32 Sheboygan Street, Fond du Lac, WI 54935.

Heart O'Wisconsin Genealogical Society, 5340 Townline Road, Wisconsin Rapids, WI 54495.

LaCrosse Area Genealogical Society, P.O. Box 1782, LaCrosse, WI 54601.

Manitowoc County Genealogical Society, P.O. Box 342, Manitowoc, WI 54220.

Milwaukee County Genealogical Society, The, 916 E. Lyon St., Milwaukee, WI 53202.

Milwaukee Public Library, 814 West Wisconsin Ave., Milwaukee, WI 53202.

Oshkosh Public Library, 106 Washington Ave., Oshkosh, WI 54901.

Public Library, Wausau, WI 54401.

State Historical Society of Wisconsin, University of Wisconsin, 816 State St., Madison, WI 53706.

Stevens Point Area Genealogical Society, 5569 Hwy 10, Stevens Point, WI 54481.

University of Wisconsin, The Milwaukee Library, P.O. Box 604, Milwaukee WI 53211.

Village of North Fond du Lac Public Library, 719 Wisconsin Ave., North Fond du Lac, WI 54935.

White Pine Genealogical Society, P.O. Box 512, Marinette, WI 54143.

Wisconsin State Old Cemetery Society, 4319 North 70th St., Milwaukee, WI 53216.

La Crosse Area Genealogical Quarterly, P.O. Box 1782, LaCrosse, WI 54601.

Wisconsin State Genealogical Society Newsletter, 5049 LaCrosse Lane, Madison, WI 53705.

Wisconsin Then and Now, State Historical Society of Wisconsin, 816 State St., Madison, WI 53706.

Printed Census Records and Mortality Schedules

Indexes (State and Territory): 1820, 1830, 1840, 1850, 1880

Indexes to the Territorial Census are available on microfilm for the following years: 1836, 1838, 1842, 1846, 1847, 1905.

Printed Census Records (Counties):

Brown-1830
Calumet-1905
Dane-1905
Florence-1905
Jefferson-1905
Portage-1850; 1905
St. Croix-1850

Valuable Printed Sources

Atlases, Gazetteers, Maps

Collins, Charles W., comp. *An Atlas of Wisconsin.* Madison, 1968.

Fox, Michael J., comp. *Maps and Atlases Showing Land Ownership in Wisconsin.* Madison: State Historical Society of Wisconsin, 1978.

Hunt, John Warren. *Wisconsin Gazetteer.* Madison: B. Brown, 1853.

Robinson, Arthur Howard. *The Atlas of Wisconsin: General Maps and Gazetteer.* Madison: University of Wisconsin Press, 1974.

Place Names

Gard, Robert E. *The Romance of Wisconsin Place Names.* New York: October House, 1968.

Peck, George Wilbur, ed. *Wisconsin; Comprising Sketches of Counties, Towns, Events, Institutions and Persons Arranged in Cyclopedic Form.* Madison: Western Historical Association 1906.

Guides to Genealogical Research

Gleason, Margaret. *Printed Resources for Genealogical Searching in Wisconsin: A Selective Bibliography.* Detroit: Detroit Society for Genealogical Research, 1964.

Ryan, Carol Ward. *Searching for Your Wisconsin Ancestors in the Wisconsin Libraries.* Green Bay, Wisconsin; Privately Published, 1979.

Swift, Betty Owens. *"Genealogical Research in Wisconsin" National Genealogical Society Quarterly,* Vol. 68, pages 270 - 285, Dec. 1980 #4. (Mrs. Swift is an instructor of genealogy courses at the college level. This paper is based on a presentation made to the National Genealogical Society on 5 May 1979).

Wilson, Mrs. Victoria. *Wisconsin Genealogical Addresses.* Milwaukee: Privately published, 1978.

Wilson, Victoria. "Researching in Wisconsin," *Journal of Genealogy.* March 1978.

Histories

Collections of the State Historical Society of Wisconsin, 1855-1917, 24 Vols. Madison: State Historical Society.

Nesbit, Robert Carrington, *Wisconsin: A History.* Madison: University of Wisconsin Press, 1973.

Usher, Ellis Baker. *Wisconsin Its Story and Biography, 1848-1913.* 8 Vols. Chicago: Lewis Publishing Company, 1914.

Genealogical Sources

D.A.R. Collection*

Draper, Lyman Copeland, comp. *Draper Manuscript Collection.* Chicago: University of Chicago Library. Collection is housed in the State Historical Society of Wisconsin.*

Milwaukee Central Public Library, Local History Room (houses the Wisconsin Marine Historical Collection).

State Historical Society of Wisconsin Collection. Madison.

Bibliographies and Indexes

Oehlerts, Donald E. comp. *Guide to Wisconsin Newspapers 1833-1957.* Madison: State Historical Society of Wisconsin, 1958.

Patterson, Betty, ed. *Some Pioneer Families of Wisconsin: An Index.* Madison: State Genealogical Society, 1977.

Schlinkert, Leroy, comp. *Subject Bibliography of Wisconsin History.* Madison: State Historical Society of Wisconsin, 1947.

WISCONSIN COUNTY HISTORIES
(Population figures to nearest thousand - 1980 U.S. Census)

Name	Map Index	Date Created	Pop. By M 1980	U.S. Cen Reports Available	Parent County or Territory From Which Organized	County Seat
Adams	D3	1848	13	1850-80	Portage	Friendship 53934

(Reg Deeds has b, m rec from 1876, d rec from 1873; Twp Dexton has bur rec; Clk Ct has div, civ ct rec; Reg in Pro has pro rec from 1873, Reg of Deeds has Ind rec from 1852)

* Ashland	A2	1860	17	1860-80	Unorg. Terr.	Ashland 54806

(Reg Deeds has b rec from 1863, m rec from 1879, d rec from 1877; Clk Cir Ct has div & civ ct rec from 1873; Reg in Pro has pro rec from 1890; Reg Deeds has Ind rec from 1860)

Bad Ax				1860	See Vernon	
*§ Barron	B1	1859	39	1870-80	Formerly Dallas (changed 1869) & Polk	Barron 54812
Bayfield	A2	1845	14	1870-80	Ashland, Orig. La Pointe (changed 1866)	Washburn 54891

(Reg Deeds has b, m, d rec, also Ind rec from 1850; Clk Cir Ct has div rec from 1889, pro rec from 1870 & civ ct rec from 1888)

* Brown	C4	1818	175	1840-80	Territorial county	Green Bay 54301

(Reg Deeds has b rec from 1846, m rec from 1821 & d rec from 1834; Clk Cir Ct has div & civ ct rec 1825; Reg Pro has pro rec 1828; see Mich. for 1820-30 cen)

*§ Buffalo	C1	1853	14	1860-80	Trempealeau	Alma 54610

(Reg Deeds has b, m, d & bur rec; Clk Cir Ct has div & civ ct rec; Reg in Pro has pro rec)

* Burnett	B1	1856	12	1860-80	Polk	Grantsburg 54840

(Reg Deeds has b, m, d rec from 1861, Ind rec from 1856, service discharge rec from 1919, school rec from 1912; Clk Ct has div rec, civ ct rec from 1856; Reg Pro has pro rec from 1856)

Calumet	D4	1836	29	1840-80	Territorial county	Chilton 53014

(Reg Deeds has b rec from 1851, m rec from 1846 & d rec from 1866; Clk Cir Ct has div rec from 1880 & civ ct rec from 1877; Reg in Pro has pro rec from 1868; Reg Deeds has Ind rec from 1840)

*§ Chippewa	C2	1845	52	1850-80	Crawford	Chippewa Falls 54729

(Reg Deeds has b rec from 1858, m rec from 1855 & d rec from 1867; Clk Cir Ct has div & civ ct rec from 1850; Reg in Pro has pro rec from 1856)

*§ Clark	C2	1853	33	1905	Crawford	Neillsville 54456

(Co Clk has b & m rec from 1880, d rec from 1885, div, civ ct rec, naturalization & crim rec from 1875, pro rec from 1870)

* Columbia	D3	1846	43	1850-80	Portage	Portage 53901

(Reg Deeds has Ind, b, m, d & bur rec; Clk Cir Ct has div & civ ct rec; Reg in Pro has pro rec)

* Crawford	E2	1818	16	1840-80	Territorial county	Prairie du Chien 53821

(Co Clk has b rec from 1866, m rec 1820, d & bur rec 1880, div & civ ct rec 1848, pro rec 1819; see Mich. for 1820-30 cen)

Dallas		1859	319	1860	Changed to Barron	
* Dane	E2	1836	319	1840-80	Territorial county	Madison 53701

(Reg Deeds has b, m, d rec from 1904; Clk Ct has div, civ ct rec from 1848, pro rec from 1935)

* Dodge	D3	1836	75	1840-80	Territorial county	Juneau 53039

(Reg of Deeds has b, m, d, div & pro rec from 1887)

* Door	C4	1851	25	1860-80	Brown	Sturgeon Bay 54235

(Reg Deeds has b, m, d, Ind rec from 1850; Clk Ct has div, civ ct rec from 1850; Reg Pro has pro rec from 1850)

*§ Douglas	A1	1854	44	1860-80	Unorg. Terr.	Superior 54880

(Reg Deeds has b, m & d rec from 1878; Clk Cts has div & civ ct rec from 1878; Co Clk has pro rec from 1878; Co Treas has prop owners rec from 1854)

Name	Map Index	Date Created	Pop. By M 1980	U.S. Cen Reports Available	Parent County or Territory From Which Organized	County Seat
*§ Dunn	C1	1854	34	1860-80	Chippewa............................	Menomonie 54751

(Reg Deeds has b, m & d rec from ca 1860)

| *§ Eau Claire | C2 | 1856 | 78 | 1860-80 | Chippewa............................ | Eau Claire 54701 |

(Reg Deeds has b, m, d, Ind rec from 1856; Clk Ct has div rec from 1856, civ ct rec from 1929)

| * Florence | B3 | 1882 | 4 | | Marienette, Oconto.................... | Florence 54121 |

(Reg Deeds has b, m, d & Ind rec; Clk Cir Ct has div, pro & civ ct rec)

| * Fond du Lac | D3 | 1836 | 89 | 1840-80 | Territorial county.................... | Fond du Lac 54935 |

(Reg Deeds has b rec from 1847, m rec from 1849 & d rec from 1868)

| Forest | B3 | 1885 | 9 | | Langlade, Oconto........................ | Crandon 54520 |

(Reg Deeds has b & Ind rec from 1886, m & d rec from 1887; Clk Cir Ct has div rec from 1890 & civ ct rec from 1885)

| Gates (see Rusk) | | | | | | |
| *§ Grant | E2 | 1836 | 51 | 1840-80 | Territorial county.................... | Lancaster 53813 |

(Reg Deeds has b, m, d & Ind rec; Clk Cir Ct has div & civ ct rec; Reg in Pro has pro rec)

| * Green | E2 | 1836 | 30 | 1880-1905 | Territorial county.................... | Monroe 53566 |

(Reg of Deeds has b rec from 1907, m rec from 1846, d rec from 1878; Clk Cir Ct has div & civ ct rec; Co Judge has pro rec)

| Green Lake | D3 | 1858 | 18 | 1860-80 | Marquette District.................... | Green Lake 54941 |

(Reg Deeds has b, d rec from 1876, m rec from 1852, Ind rec from 1845; Cir Ct Clk has div, civ ct rec; Reg Pro has pro rec)

| * Iowa | E2 | 1829 | 20 | 1840-80 | Territorial county.................... | Dodgeville 53533 |

(Reg Deeds has b, m & d rec from 1866, Ind rec from 1835; Clk Cir Ct has div rec from 1860 & civ ct rec from 1809; Reg in Pro has pro rec from 1890; see Mich for 1830 cen)

| Iron | A2 | 1893 | 7 | | Ashland, Oneida.......................... | Hurley 54534 |

(Reg Deeds has b, m, d & Ind rec)

| § Jackson | C2 | 1853 | 17 | 1860-80 | LaCrosse..................... | Black River Falls 54615 |

(Reg Deeds has b, m, d, bur, Ind rec; Clk Ct has div, civ ct rec; Pro Clk has pro rec)

| * Jefferson | E3 | 1837 | 66 | 1840-80 | Milwaukee............................. | Jefferson 53549 |

(Reg Deeds has b & m rec from 1850, d rec from 1840 & Ind rec from 1838; Clk Cir Ct has div rec from 1851 & civ ct rec from 1843; Reg in Pro has pro rec from 1840)

| * Juneau | D2 | 1856 | 21 | 1860-80 | Adams................................. | Mauston 53948 |

(Reg Deeds has b, m, d & Ind rec; Clk Cir Ct has div & civ ct rec; Co Judge has pro rec)

| * Kenosha | E4 | 1850 | 123 | 1850-80 | Racine................................. | Kenosha 53140 |

(Co Clk has m rec from 1900)

| * Kewaunee | C4 | 1852 | 20 | 1860-80 | Manitowoc............................. | Kewaunee 54216 |

(Reg Deeds has b & Ind rec from 1873, m & d rec from 1874; Reg in Pro has pro rec from 1867)

| *§ La Crosse | D2 | 1851 | 90 | 1860-80 | Unorg. Terr............................. | La Crosse 54601 |

(Reg Deeds has b, m, d & Ind rec from 1851; Clk Cir Ct has div & civ ct rec; Reg in Pro has pro rec from 1851)

| * Lafayette | E2 | 1846 | 17 | 1850-80 | Iowa.................................... | Darlington 53530 |

(Reg Deeds has b rec from 1890, m rec from 1850, d rec from 1877, Ind rec from 1840; Clk Ct has div, civ ct rec; Reg Pro has pro rec)

| La Pointe | | 1845 | | 1850-60 | See Bayfield | |
| * Langlade | B3 | 1880 | 20 | 1880 | Lincoln, Oconto (formerly New, changed 1880)............................. | Antigo 54409 |

(Reg Deeds has b & d rec; Co Clk has m rec from 1918; Clk Cir Ct has div & civ ct rec; Reg in Pro has pro rec; Co Asr has Ind rec)

| * Lincoln | B3 | 1874 | 27 | 1880 | Marathon.............................. | Merrill 54452 |
| * Manitowoc | D4 | 1836 | 83 | 1840-80 | Territorial county.................... | Manitowoc 54220 |

(Reg Deeds has b, m, d & bur rec; Clk Cir Ct has div, pro & civ ct rec)

| *§ Marathon | C3 | 1850 | 109 | 1850-80 | Portage................................. | Wausau 54401 |

(Reg Deeds has b, m & d rec from 1900, Ind rec from 1850; Clk Cir Ct has div & civ ct rec from 1900; Co Ct has pro rec from 1900)

| * Marinette | B4 | 1879 | 39 | 1880 | Oconto................................. | Marinette 54143 |

(Reg Deeds has b, m, d & Ind rec from 1879; Clk Cir Ct has div & civ ct rec from 1879; Reg in Pro has pro rec from 1879)

| Marquette | D3 | 1836 | 12 | 1840-80 | Marquette District........................ | Montello 53949 |

(Reg Deeds has b rec from 1876, m, d rec from 1869, Ind rec; Clk Cir Ct has div, civ ct rec from 1878, naturalization rec from 1868 to 1936; Reg Pro has pro rec from 1890)

| Menominee | | 1961 | 3 | | Menominee Indian Reservation........... | Keshena 54135 |

(Co Clk has b, m, d & Ind rec)

| * Milwaukee | E4 | 1834 | 962 | 1840-80 | Territorial county.................... | Milwaukee 53233 |

(Co Clk has m rec from 1834)

COUNTY MAP FOR THE STATE OF WISCONSIN

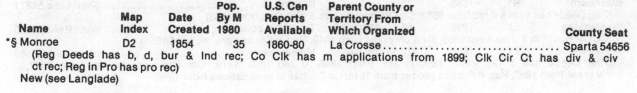

Name	Map Index	Date Created	Pop. By M 1980	U.S. Cen Reports Available	Parent County or Territory From Which Organized	County Seat
*§ Monroe	D2	1854	35	1860-80	La Crosse	Sparta 54656

(Reg Deeds has b, d, bur & Ind rec; Co Clk has m applications from 1899; Clk Cir Ct has div & civ ct rec; Reg in Pro has pro rec)

New (see Langlade)

Name	Map Index	Date Created	Pop. By M 1980	U.S. Cen Reports Available	Parent County or Territory From Which Organized	County Seat
Oconto	C4	1851	29	1860-80	Unorg. Terr.	Oconto 54153

(Reg Deeds has b, m, d & bur rec; Clk Cts has div & civ ct rec; Reg in Pro has pro rec; Oconto Hist Soc has hist rec)

*§ Oneida	B3	1885	30		Lincoln	Rhinelander 54501

(Reg Deeds has b, m, d & Ind rec; Clk Cir Ct has div & civ ct rec; Reg in Pro has pro rec)

* Outagamie	C3	1851	129	1860-80	Brown	Appleton 54911

(Reg Deeds has b, m & d rec from 1852; Clk Cts has div & civ ct rec from 1855; Reg in Pro has pro rec from 1855)

* Ozaukee	E4	1853	66	1860-80	Milwaukee	Port Washington 53074

(Reg Deeds has b, d & bur rec from 1853, m rec from 1845 & Ind rec from 1835; Clk Cts has div & civ ct rec from 1846; Co Treas has tax rolls from 1851)

§ Pepin	C1	1858	7	1860-80	Dunn	Durand 54736

(Reg Deeds has b, m, d & Ind rec; Clk Cir Ct has div & civ ct rec; Reg in Pro has pro rec)

* Pierce	C1	1853	31	1880-1905	St. Croix	Ellsworth 54011

(Co Clk has b & d rec from 1876, m rec from 1855, div rec from 1875, pro rec from 1878 & civ ct rec from 1869)

§ Polk	B1	1853	32	1860-80	St. Croix	Balsam Lake 54810

(Reg Deeds has b rec from 1862, m rec from 1861, d rec from 1866, Ind rec; Clk Cir Ct has div rec; Co Judge has pro rec)

* Portage	C3	1836	57	1840-80	Territorial county	Stevens Point 54481

(Reg Deeds has b rec from 1863, m rec from 1772, d rec from 1856; Clk Cir Ct has div, civ ct rec from 1844; Co Judge has pro rec from 1890)

Price	B2	1879	16	1880	Chippewa, Lincoln	Phillips 54555

(Reg Deeds has b & m rec from 1880, d rec from 1884, Ind rec from 1867; Clk Cir Ct has div & civ ct rec from 1882; Reg in Pro has pro rec from 1879; Co Clk has m applications)

* Racine	E4	1836	172	1840-80	Territorial county	Racine 53403

(Reg Deeds has b rec from 1876, m rec from 1837, d rec from 1853, Ind rec from early 1800's; Fam Ct has div rec; Pro Ct has pro rec; Clk Cts has civ ct rec)

* Richland	D2	1842	17	1850-80	Iowa	Richland Center 53581

(Reg Deeds has b, d rec from 1870, m, Ind rec from 1850; Clk Ct has div, civ ct rec from 1860; Reg Pro has pro rec from 1851; City Clks have bur rec)

* Rock	E3	1836	136	1840-80	Territorial county	Janesville 53545

(Reg Deeds has b, m & d rec from 1849, Ind rec from 1839)

*§ Rusk	B2	1901	16		Chippewa (name changed from Gates 1905	Ladysmith 54848

(Reg Deeds has b, m, d rec from 1863, Ind rec; Co Ct has div, pro, civ ct rec)

*§ St. Croix	C1	1840	43	1840-80	Territorial county	Hudson 54016

(Reg Deeds has b, m, d & Ind rec; Clk Cir Ct has div & civ ct rec; Reg in Pro has pro rec)

* Sauk	D2	1840	43	1840-80	Territorial county	Baraboo 53913

(Reg Deeds has b rec from 1860, m rec from 1850, d rec from 1870; Clk Cir Ct has div rec; Reg in Pro has pro rec)

* Sawyer	B2	1883	13		Ashland, Chippewa	Hayward 54843

(Reg Deeds has b, m, d, bur, div, pro & civ ct rec)

*§ Shawano	C3	1853	36	1860-80	Oconto	Shawano 54166
*§ Sheboygan	D4	1836	101	1840-80	Territorial county	Sheboygan 53081

(Reg Deeds has b, m, d, bur, div, pro & civ ct rec, they are inc up to 1910)

*§ Taylor	B2	1875	19	1905	Clark, Lincoln, Marathon, Chippewa	Medford 54451

(Reg Deeds has b, m, d, Ind rec from 1875; Clk Ct has div, civ ct rec from 1875; Judge's Office has pro rec)

*§ Trempealeau	C2	1854	26	1860-80	Crawford, LaCrosse	Whitehall 54773

(Reg Deeds has b, m, d & bur rec; Clk Cir Ct has div & civ ct rec; Reg in Pro has pro rec)

*§ Vernon	D2	1851	25	1870-80	Richland, Crawford (formerly Bad Ax changed 1862)	Viroqua 54665

(Reg Deeds has b, m, d & Ind rec; Clk Cir Ct has div & civ ct rec; Reg in Pro has pro rec)

* Vilas	B3	1893	17		Oneida	Eagle River 54521
* Walworth	E3	1836	71	1840-80	Territorial county	Elkhorn 53121

(Reg Deeds has b, rec from 1845, m, Ind rec from 1839, d rec from 1872, bur rec from 1969, div, civ ct rec from 1850, pro rec from 1800's.

Washburn	B1	1883	13		Burnett	Shell Lake 54871

(Reg Deeds has b, m & d rec from 1883; Clk Cts has div, pro & civ ct rec from 1883)

* Washington	E4	1836	85	1840-80	Territorial county	West Bend 53095

(Co Clk has b, m & d rec from 1850, div & civ ct rec from 1849; Reg in Pro has pro rec from 1851)

* Waukesha	E4	1846	279	1850-80	Milwaukee	Waukesha 53186

(Reg Deeds has b rec from 1860, m rec from 1846, d rec from 1879; Clk Cts has div rec from 1847, civ ct rec from 1962; Reg in Pro has pro rec from 1846; Co Clk has m applications from 1899)

Name	Map Index	Date Created	Pop. By M 1980	U.S. Cen Reports Available	Parent County or Territory From Which Organized	County Seat
* Waupaca	C3	1851	43	1860-80	....	Waupaca 54981

(Reg Deeds has b, m, d, Ind rec from 1852; Clk Ct has div rec from 1907, civ ct rec from 1880; Cir Ct has pro rec from 1857)

| *§ Waushara | D3 | 1851 | 18 | 1860-80 | Marquette .... | Wautoma 54982 |

(Reg Deeds has b, d rec from 1876, m, Ind rec from 1852)

| * Winnebago | D3 | 1838 | 131 | 1840-80 | Territorial county .... | Oshkosh 54901 |

(Reg Deeds has b & Ind rec from 1861, m rec from 1870 & d rec)

| * Wood | C2 | 1856 | 72 | 1860-80 | Portage......................... | Wisconsin Rapids 54494 |

(Reg Deeds has b, m & d rec from 1875; Clk Cts has div & civ ct rec from 1875; Reg in Pro has pro rec from 1875)

* - At least one county history has been published about this county.
§ - Inventory of county archives was made by the Historical Records Survey. (see introduction)

WYOMING

CAPITAL, CHEYENNE - TERRITORY 1868 - STATE 1890 - (44TH)

When Wyoming was organized as a territory in 1868 it had only six or seven thousand white inhabitants. The middle west and the southern states provided most of the settlers who came into the state to take advantage of the opportunity to get into the cattle business. Hundreds of thousands of cattle roamed the western hills unherded. The eastern section had good agricultural soil.

In 1940 the foreign-born population of Wyoming ranked in this order in numbers: England, Germany, Sweden, Russia, Italy, Austria, Greece, Denmark, Norway, Ireland, Poland, Finland, Czechoslovakia, France and Hungary.

Birth and death records from 1909 to the present, and marriage records from 1 May 1941 are at the office of the Division of Vital Statistics, Cheyenne, WY 82001.

The County Clerk of each county is custodian of the birth and death records from the beginning of the county until 1909, the marriage records from the beginning of the county until 1 May 1941, the wills, probate matters, and all land records.

Genealogical Archives, Libraries, Societies, and Publications

Cheyenne Genealogical Society, Laramie County LIbrary, Central Ave., Cheyenne, WY 82001.

Goshen County Public Library, 2001 East A Street, Torrington, WY 82240.

Laramie County Public Library, Cheyenne, WY 82001.

Natrona County Genealogical Society, P.O. Box 9244, Casper, WY 82601.

Western History and Archives Dept., University of Wyoming, Laramie, WY 82070.

Wyoming State Archives and Historical Department, State Office Bldg., Cheyenne, WY 82001.

Wyoming State Library, Supreme Court Bldg., Cheyenne, WY 82001.

Bits and Pieces, Box 746, Newcastle, WY 82701. (Covers North Dakota, South Dakota, Wyoming and Montana).

Printed Census Records and Mortality Schedules
Indexes (Territory): 1870, 1880

Valuable Printed Sources

Place Names

Urbanek, Mae. *Wyoming Place Names.* Boulder, Colorado: Johnson Publishing Company (1967).

Guides To Genealogical Research

Homsher, Lola. *Guide to Wyoming Newspapers 1867-1967.* Cheyenne, Wyoming: Wyoming State Library (1971).

Histories

Chamblin, Thomas S. ed. *The Historical Encyclopedia of Wyoming.* Dallas, Texas: Taylor Publishing (1970).

Coutant, C.G. *The History of Wyoming.* Laramie: Chaplin, Spafford and Mathison (1899-

Larson, T. A. *History of Wyoming.* Lincoln: University of Nebraska Press, 1965.

Genealogical Sources

Beach, Cora M. *Women of Wyoming.* Casper: S.E. Boyer and Company, 1927.

Daughters of the American Revolution Collection*

Progressive Men of the State of Wyoming. Chicago: A. W. Bowen and Company, 1903.

Murray, Robert A. *Military Posts of Wyoming.* Fort Collins, Colorado: The Old Army Press (1974).

---

*Microfilm - Genealogical Society of The Church of Jesus Christ of Latter-day Saints, Salt Lake City, Utah.

WYOMING COUNTY HISTORIES
(Population figures to nearest thousand - 1980 U. S. Census)

Name	Map Index	Date Created	Pop. By M 1980	U.S. Cen Reports Available	Parent County or Territory From Which Organized	County Seat
* Albany	D4	1868	29	1860-80	Original county	Laramie 82070
(Co Clk has m rec from 1869, Ind rec from 1865)						
Big Horn	A3	1890	12		Fremont, Johnson	Basin 82410
(Clk Dis Ct has div, pro & civ ct rec; Co Clk has m & Ind rec from 1898)						
* Campbell	B4	1911	24		Crook, Weston	Gillette 82716
(Co Clk has m, Ind, election rec, automobile titles & chattels; Clk Dis Ct has div, pro & civ ct rec)						
Carbon	D3	1868	22	1860-80	Original county	Rawlins 82301
(Co Clk has m rec from 1876, Ind rec from 1880; for 1860 cen see Nebr)						
Carter (changed to Sweetwater 13 Dec 1869)						
Converse	B4	1888	14		Laramie, Albany	Douglas 82633
(Co Clk has m, Ind, mil discharge, tax rec from 1888, poll rec from 1930; Clk Ct has div, pro, civ ct rec)						
Crook	A5	1885	5	1880	Pease	Sundance 82729
(Co Clk has m, Ind rec from 1855; Clk Ct has div, pro, civ ct rec; Bur Vital Statistics, Cheyenne, Wyo has b, d rec)						
Fremont	B2	1884	39		Sweetwater	Lander 82520
§ Goshen	C5	1911	12		Platte, Laramie	Torrington 82240
(Co Clk has m & Ind rec; Clk Dis Ct has div, pro & civ ct rec)						
Hot Springs	B2	1911	6		Fremont	Thermopolis 82443
(Co Clk has m rec from 1913 & Ind rec; Clk Dis Ct has div, pro & civ ct rec) (Ind rec transcribed from Fremont Co)						
Johnson	B4	1875	7	1880	Pease	Buffalo 82834
(Co Clk has m & Ind rec; Clk Dis Ct has div, pro & civ ct rec)						
§ Laramie	D5	1867	69	1860-80	Original county	Cheyenne 82001
(Co Clk has m rec from 1868; for 1860 cen see Nebr)						
Lincoln	C1	1913	12		Uinta	Kemmerer 83101
(Co Clk has m rec from 1913 & Ind rec; Clk Dis Ct has div & pro rec from 1913 & civ ct rec)						
* Natrona	C3	1888	72		Carbon	Casper 82601
(Co Clk has m & Ind rec from 1888, soldier's discharge, power of attorneys, notary & commissions tax license-state & fed; Clk Dis Ct has div, pro & civ ct rec)						
Niobrara	B5	1911	3		Converse	Lusk 82225
(Co Clk has m & Ind rec from 1888; Clk Dis Ct has div, pro & civ ct rec)						
§ Park	A2	1909	22		Big Horn	Cody 82414
(Co Clk has m, Ind rec from 1911; Clk Ct has div, pro, civ ct rec; Bur Vital Statistics, Cheyenne, Wyo. has b, d rec)						
Pease (changed to Johnson 13 Dec, 1879)						
§ Platte	C5	1913	12		Laramie	Wheatland 82201
(Co Clk has m & Ind rec from 1890; Clk Dis Ct has div, pro & civ ct rec)						
* Sheridan	A3	1888	25		Johnson	Sheridan 82801
(Co Clk has m & Ind rec from 1888; Clk Dis Ct has div, pro & civ ct rec)						
Sublette	C2	1921	5		Fremont	Pinedale 82941
(Co Clk has m rec from 1923, Ind rec from 1900; Clk Dis Ct has div, pro & civ ct rec from 1923)						

Name	Map Index	Date Created	Pop. By M 1980	U.S. Cen Reports Available	Parent County or Territory From Which Organized	County Seat
§ Sweetwater	D2	1867	42	1860-80	Original county (formerly Carter changed 1869)	Green River 82935

(Co Clk has m rec from 1864 & Ind rec from 1876; Clk Dis Ct has div, pro & civ ct rec; for 1860 cen see Nebr)

Name	Map Index	Date Created	Pop. By M 1980	U.S. Cen Reports Available	Parent County or Territory From Which Organized	County Seat
Teton	B1	1921	9		Lincoln	Jackson 83001

(Co Clk has m, div, pro & civ ct rec)

Name	Map Index	Date Created	Pop. By M 1980	U.S. Cen Reports Available	Parent County or Territory From Which Organized	County Seat
* Uinta	D1	1869	13	1860-80	Original county	Evanston 82930

(for 1860 cen see Nebr) (Co Clk has m rec; Clk Dis Ct has div & pro rec)

Name	Map Index	Date Created	Pop. By M 1980	U.S. Cen Reports Available	Parent County or Territory From Which Organized	County Seat
Washakie	B3	1911	9		Big Horn, Johnson	Worland 82401

(Co Clk has m & Ind rec; Clk Dis Ct has div, pro & civ ct rec)

Name	Map Index	Date Created	Pop. By M 1980	U.S. Cen Reports Available	Parent County or Territory From Which Organized	County Seat
Weston	B5	1890	7		Crook	Newcastle 82701

(Co Clk has m from 1890, bur & Ind rec; Clk Dis Ct has pro, div & civ ct rec)

* - At least one county history has been published about this county.

§ - Inventory of county archives was made by the Historical Records Survey. (see introduction)

COUNTY MAP FOR THE STATE OF WYOMING

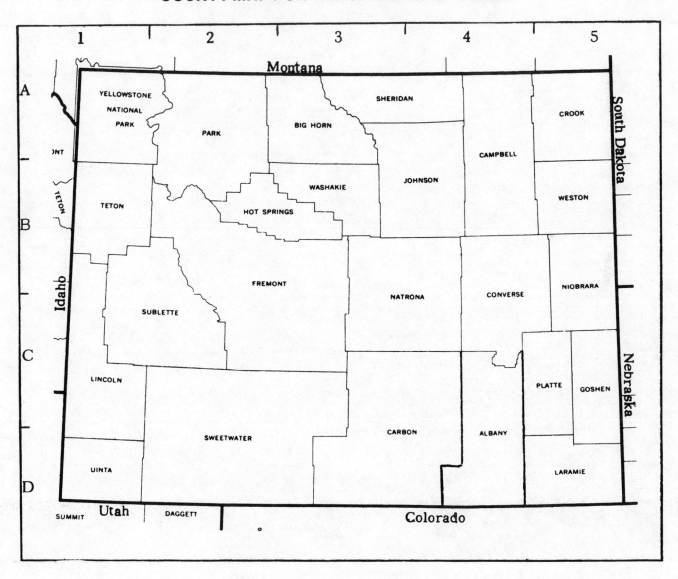

AUSTRALIA

Capital, Canberra - Settled 1788 - Commonwealth 1901

Under the command of Captain Arthur Phillip (first governor), eleven ships with approximately 1500 persons aboard, including nearly 800 prisoners, sailed from England 13 May 1787 and arrived at Botany Bay, Australia on 18 January 1788. Eight days later the colony was transferred to the site now occupied by Sydney. Other new settlements were started in 1803 which included Hobard and Tasmania. In 1824 Brisbane and Queensland were settled. Swan River, Western Austrailia 1829; Victoria, Melbourne, 1835; and Adelaide, South Australia 1836. It was not until the discovery of gold in 1851 in the Bathurst District and Victoria that there was any great influx of settlers to Australia.

Valuable Sources

Gazetteer

Gross, Alexander, *Gazetteer of Australia.* Melbourne, Australia: Geographia LTD. 1822 (On microfilm 952,648 at Genealogical Society Library of The Church of Jesus Christ of Latter-day Saints, Salt Lake City, Utah)

Place Names

Praite, R. and J. C. Tolley. *Place Names of South Australia.* Rigby Limited, 1970.

Reed, A. W. *Place Names of Australia.* Sidney: A. H. and A. W. Reed, 1974.

Guides To Genealogical Research

Blaze, B. R. ed., and Muriel E. Runting, comp. *Ancestors for Australians How to Trace Your Family Tree,* Melbourne: The Genealogical Society of Victoria, 1977.

Hansen, Niel T. *Guide to Genealogical Sources - Australia and New Zealand.* Victoria: Hall's Book Store Pty. LTD, 1963.

Harris, Tina. "Genealogical Interest is on the Increase in Australia" The *Genealogical Helper,* May 1975 issue, pages 281-283. Logan: Everton Publishers.

Major Genealogical Record Sources in Australia. Research Paper Series E, No. 2, Salt Lake City, Utah: Genealogical Society of The Church of Jesus Christ of Latter-day Saints, 1968.

Histories

Clark, Charles Manning Hope. *A History of Australia.* Melbourne, Australia: Melbourne University Press, 3 vols.

Bibliographies and Genealogical Sources

Census 1837, Western Australia. Perth: Library Board of Western Australia (G.S. call number 994.1 X2c or film 973,232)

Downs, Robert B. *Australian and New Zealand Library Resources.* Melbourne: D.W. Thorpe Pty. Ltd. 1979.

Ferguson, John Alexander. *Bibliography of Australia.* Canberra: National Library of Australia, 1976. 7 vols.

Guide to Collections of Manuscripts Relating to Australia. (G.S. call no. 994 A35n)

"Sources for Family History in Australia and New Zealand." Panel by G. Napoleon Trujillo, D. John Cross, and Edna M. Johnson. Salt Lake City: World Conference on Records, 1980. #813.

AUSTRIA
Capital, Vienna
Modern day Austria includes the following Provinces:

German	English	Capital City	Sq. mi
Burgenland	Burgenland	Eisenstadt	1,531
Kärnten	Carinthia	Klagenfurt	3,681
Niederösterreich	Lower Austria	Wien	7,402
Oberösterreich	Upper Austria	Linz	4,625
Salzburg	Salzburg	Salzburg	2,763
Steiermark	Styria	Graz	6,326
Tirol	Tyrol	Innsbruck	4,883
Vorarlberg	Vorarlberg	Bregenz	1,005
Wien	Vienna	Wien	160

Province Map of Austria

Valuable Sources

Gazetteer

Österreichischen Statistischen Zentralamt. Ortsverzeichnis von Österreich. Wien: Druck und Verlag der Osterreichischen Staatsdruckerei, 1965.

Guide To Genealogical Research

Blodgett, Steven W. "Great-Grandfather was in the Imperial Cavalry: Using Austrian Military Records as an Aid to Writing Family History." Salt Lake City: World Conference on Records Lecture Paper #504. 1980.

Senekovic, Dagmar. *Handy Guide to Austrian Genealogical Records.* Logan, Utah: Everton Publishers, 1979.

Senekovic, Dagmar. "How to Establish the Place of Birth in the Austro-Hungarian Empire and Where to Write for Further Information." Logan, Utah: Everton Publishers, 1979, Dec. issue page 9, and 10, Vol. 33, Number 6. *The Genealogical Helper.*

Genealogical Collections

Genealogical Society of The Church of Jesus Christ of Lattery-day Saints: The Vienna War Archives are being microfilmed; however, it will be several years before this extensive project is completed. These records cover the former Austro-Hungarian Empire.

Vital Records from Niederösterreich, Austria for the late 1500's to generally the 1800's have been microfilmed.

BELGIUM

Capital, Brussels

The history of Belgium dates from 1831 when the South Netherlands parted from Holland and became an independent kingdom.   (See page 351 for map)

PROVINCES OF BELGIUM

PROVINCE	MAP INDEX	CAPITAL
Antwerpen (Antwerp)	D3	Antwerpen (Antwerp)
Brabant	E3	Bruxelles (Brussels)
Hainaut	E2	Mons (Bergen)
Liege	E4	Liege (Luik)
Limbourg (Limburg)	D3	Hasselt
Luxembourg	F4	Aarlon (Arlon)
Namur	F3	Namur (Namen)
Oost Vlaanderen (East Flanders)	E2	Gent (Gand or Ghent)
West Vlaanderen (West Flanders)	E1	Brugge (Bruges)

Valuable Sources

Atlases, Gazetteers, Maps, Place Names

Belgium - Official Standard Names Approved by the United States Board on Geographic Names. Washington D.C.: Office of Geography, Department of Interior, 1963. (G.S. Ref. 949.3 E5u; or film 874,468)

De Seyn, Eugene. *Dictionnaire Historique et Geographique des Communes Belges.* 2 vols. Turnhout: Etablissements Brepols S.A. n.d. (G.S. 947.3 E2s)

Guides To Genealogical Sources

Major Genealogical Record Sources in Belgium. Salt Lake City: Genealogical Society, 1976. Series G. No. 3.

World Conference on Records and Genealogical Seminar. Salt Lake City: Genealogical Society, 1969. Series F Nos. 4 and 4b:
Mispelon, Michiel B. "Genealogical Research Sources in the French-Speaking Parts of Belgium, Part II, Emigration from Flanders in the XIXth Century."

Pardon, Jean-Michel. "Genealogical Research Sources in the French Speaking Parts of Belgium." (F-4)

Genealogical Sources

Leenaerts, Remy J. *General Genealogical and Heraldic Index of Southern-Netherlands.* 5 vols. Handzame, Belgium: Familia et Patria, 1969. (G.S. 949.3 A3L). (Volume 5 includes a good index to Belgium surnames).

Many important records from Belgium have been microfilmed by the Genealogical Society and are available for searching in the Genealogical Society Library Salt Lake City, Utah. Check the Dictionary Card Catalog (DCC) and the International Genealogical Library Catalog (IGLC).

CANADA

Capital, Ottawa

By virtue of discovery and settlement, France claimed possession of Canada as early as 1532. By 1642, Acadia, Quebec, and Montreal were founded. Following the French and Indian Wars extending over a 70-year period, the Treaty of Paris transferred Canada to British rule in 1763.

After Canada came under British control, many of the early American colonists, unwilling to sever their British citizenship rights, migrated to Canada where they established their homes. The French, who had come there earlier, remained and later became Canadian citizens, but they retained their French language and customs.

Canada is divided into ten provinces: Alberta, British Columbia, Manitoba, New Brunswick, Newfoundland, Nova Scotia, Ontario, Prince Edward Island, Quebec, and Saskatchewan. Canada also has two territories, Yukon created in 1898 and the Northwest Territories which Canada secured in 1870 from Britain and the Hudson Bay Company.

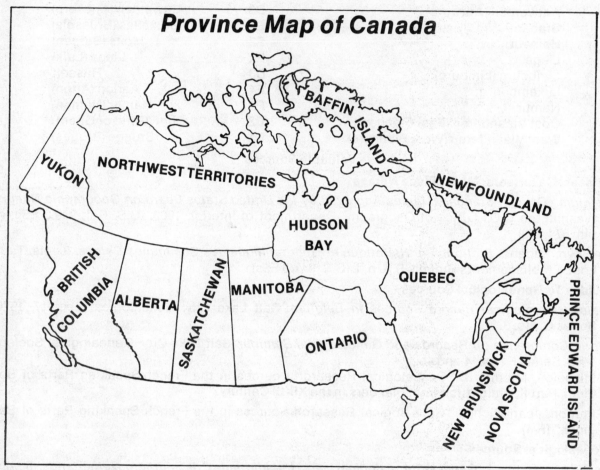

Province Map of Canada

Valuable Sources

Atlases, Gazetteers, Maps

Department of Energy, Mines and Resources. *Atlas and Gazetteer of Canada.* Ottawa: The Queen's Printer, 1969.

Department of Mines and Technical Surveys. *Gazetteer of Canada, Ontario.* Ottawa:, 1962.

Kerr, D. G. G. *Historical Atlas of Canada.* Don Mills, Ontario: Thomas Nelson and Sons, 1966. 2nd edition.

Répertoire Toponymique du Quebec. Commission de Toponymie Conseil Exécutif. Quebec, 1979.

Smith, Wm. H. *Smith's Canadian Gazetteer.* 1846. Reprint. Toronto: Coles, 1970.

Place Names

Bullinger's Postal and Shippers Guide for the United States and Canada. Westwood, New Jersey: Bullinger's Guides, Inc., 1897- annual.

Guides To Genealogical Research

Baxter, Angus. *In Search of Your Roots, A Guide for Canadians Seeking Their Ancestors.* Toronto: MacMillan of Canada, 1978.

Jonasson, Eric. *The Canadian Genealogical Handbook,* 2nd edition. Winnipeg, Manitoba, Wheatfield Press, 1978.

Keffer, Marion Christina. "Ontario Genealogical Resources. *National Genealogical Quarterly,* March 1979, pages 14-24.

Records of Genealogical Value for Canada. Salt Lake City: Genealogical Society of The Church of Jesus Christ of Latter-day Saints, 1976. Series B, No. 3.

Genealogical Sources

Canadian Almanac and Directory. Toronto: Copp Clark, 1848- Annual.

Census Records in Canada. Salt Lake City: U.S. (G.S. 971.3 X2a film 599,496) Canada Reference Staff, Genealogical Department Library, The Church of Jesus Christ of Latter-day Saints, 1980.

Check List of Ontario Census Returns 1842-1871. Public Archives of Canada Manuscript Division, 1963.

The Loiselle Marriage Index - An index to marriage records in Quebec; Madawska County, New Brunswick; and Manchester, Hillsboro, New Hampshire, 1642-1963.*

The Rivest Index - Marriage records located in the notarial districts of Joliette, Saint-Jerome, Mont-Laurien, and Sorell, Quebec, about 17th century - 1972.*

Union List of Canadian Newspapers Held by Canadian Libraries. Ottoawa: National Library of Canada, 1977.

Union List of Manuscripts in Canadian Repositories. Ottowa: Public Archives Canada, 1975.

Bibliographies

Morley, William F. E. *Canadian Local Histories to 1950, A Bibliography.* Toronto.

* Microfilm - Genealogical Society of The Church of Jesus Christ of Latter-day Saints, Salt Lake City,Utah.

CZECHOSLOVAKIA

Capital, Prague
Valuable Sources

Gazetteers

Administratives Gemeindelexikon der Čechoslovakischen Republik (Administrative Gazetteer of the Czechoslovak Republic). Prague: 1928 (G.S. Library Call number: Eur. Ref. 943.7 e5a. Microfilm call numbers 496,716 and 496,720)

Gazetteers of the old Austrian Provinces. Vienna: 1905. Vol. 9 Bohemia microfilm number 1,187,927; Vol. 10, Moravia, film no. 924,736; Vol. 11 Silesia, film no. 1,187,927.

Hungarian Gazetteer (for Slovakia)
Dvorzsak, Janos. *Magyar ország Helységnévtára.* G.S. Library call number: Eur. Ref. 943.9 E5d. Film no. 599,564 (index) and film no. 973,041

Place Names

Názvy Obcí na Slovensku za Ostatných dvesto rokov (Place names in Slovakia during last 200 years). Bratislava: 1972. (G.S. Library call number Eur. Ref. 943.73 e2m; Film no. 1,181,569)

Maps

Austro-Hungarion Empire. (G.S. Film no. 1,045,395)

Auto Atlas CSSR. G.S. Library call number 943.7 E3as.

Guides to Genealogical Research

Miller, Olga. *Genealogical Research for Czech and Slovak Americans.* Detroit: Gale Research-Company, 1978.

Schlyter, Daniel M. *A Handbook of Czechoslovak Genealogical Research.* Logan, Utah: The Everton Publishers, pending.

Wellauer, Maralyn A. *Tracing Your Czech and Slovak Roots.* Milwaukee: author, 1980.

Histories

Seton-Watson, R. W. *History of the Czechs and Slovaks.* Hamden, Connecticut: 1965. (G.S. Library Call number Eur. 943.7 H2s.)

Genealogical Collections

The Genealogical Society of The Church of Jesus Christ of Latter-day Saints has limited census material for some areas of Slovakia (formerly part of the Kingdom of Hungary). - 1869 census of Zemplen County.

No records have been microfilmed in Czechoslovakia. Records are well organized and preserved in Czechoslovak State and Regional Archives. Genealogical research in these records can be undertaken through the services of the Czechoslovak Embassy in Washington D.C. (Embassy of the Czechoslovak Socialist Republic, Consular Division, 3900 Linnean Ave. N.W. Washington, D.C. 20008.)

Political Subdivisions of Czechoslovakia

DENMARK
Capital, Copenhagen (Kobenhavn)
Valuable Sources

Atlases, Gazetteers, Maps

Geodaetisk Instituts Kort. Copenhagen: Geodaetisk Institut, lastest edition. Map scale 1:200,000. (G.S. Library Call No. Ref. 948.9 E3ge - 1976 edition)

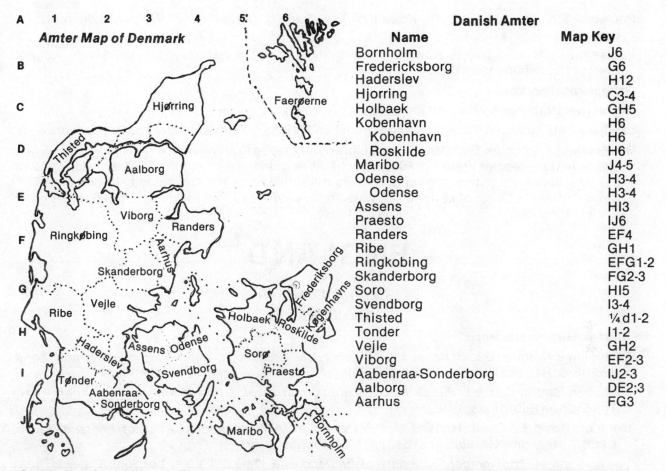

Amter Map of Denmark

Danish Amter

Name	Map Key
Bornholm	J6
Fredericksborg	G6
Haderslev	H12
Hjorring	C3-4
Holbaek	GH5
Kobenhavn	H6
Kobenhavn	H6
Roskilde	H6
Maribo	J4-5
Odense	H3-4
Odense	H3-4
Assens	HI3
Praesto	IJ6
Randers	EF4
Ribe	GH1
Ringkobing	EFG1-2
Skanderborg	FG2-3
Soro	HI5
Svendborg	I3-4
Thisted	¼d1-2
Tonder	I1-2
Vejle	GH2
Viborg	EF2-3
Aabenraa-Sonderborg	IJ2-3
Aalborg	DE2;3
Aarhus	FG3

Smith, Frank and Finn A. Thomsen. *Genealogical Guidebook and Atlas of Denmark* Salt Lake City: Bookcraft, 1969.

Trap, J.P. *Kongeriget Danmark.* 5 vols. Kjøbenhavn: G.E.C. Gad, 1898. (G.S. film 599,364-368).

Trap, J. P. *Danmark.* 5th edition. 31 vols. 1953-1972. Kφbenhaven: G.E.C. Gads.

Place Names

Post-og Telegraf Adressebog for Kongeriget Danmark. Kφbenhavn: Generaldirektoratet for Post-og Telegrafvaesenet, 1960. (G.S. Library Call No. Ref. 948.9 E8g; fiche 6030021-26) Postal Guide for Denmark - it lists farm names, villages and the parish and county to which each belongs. Many county names changed after 1970. The card file is based on pre-1970 names so it is best to use postal guides prior to 1970.

Guides To Genealogical Research

Fabritius, Albert and Harald Hatt. *Haandbog i Slaegtsforskning.* Kφbenhavn: J. H. Schultz Forlag, 1963. (Handbook for Family Research)

Genealogical Society of The Church of Jesus Christ of Latter-day Saints. Research Papers: *Major Genealogical Record Sources in Denmark,* series D no. 5 (fiche 6030005)

Church Records of Denmark, series D, no. 6 (fiche 6030006)

Census Records of Denmark, series D, no. 7 (fiche 6030007)

Military Levying Rolls of Denmark, series D, no. 8 (fiche 6030008)

Probate Records of Denmark, series D, No. 9 (fiche 6030009)

Danish-Norwegian Paleography, series D, no. 16 (fiche 6030017)

Poulsen, Elly M. and Gay P. Kowallis. *The Danish Genealogical Helper,* Logan, Utah: Everton Publishers, 1969.

Poulsen, Elly M. and Gay P. Kowallis. The Scandinavian Genealogical Helper, 3 vols. Logan: Everton Publishers, 1969-1972.

Genealogical Sources

Rigsarkivet (National Archives of Denmark)

Landsarkivet - Sjaelland (Copenhagen); Nørrejylland (Viborg); Fyen (Odense) and Sønderjydske

Det Kongelige Bibliotek (Denmark's Royal Library) located in Copenhagen.
   The important records from the Rigsarkivet and Regional Archives; the Military Archives and the Raastuearkiver (city archives) have been microfilmed by the Genealogical Society of The Church of Jesus Christ of Latter-day Saints and are available for searching in the Genealogical Society Libraries.

ENGLAND

Capital, London
Valuable Sources

Atlases, Gazetteers, Maps

Bartholomew, John. *Gazetteer of the British Isles.* Edinburgh: John Bartholomew and Sons. 1966 (G.S. Ref. 942 E5ba; microfilm 990234)

Humphery-Smith, C.R. ed. *Parish Maps of the Counties of England and Wales.* Logan, Utah: The Everton Publishers, 1982.

Gardner, David E., Derek Harland and Frank Smith. *A Genealogical Atlas of England.* Provo, Utah: Stevenson's Genealogical Center, 1960, reprint 1975.

Lewis, Samuel. *Topraphical Dictionary of England and Wales.* 4 Vols. London: S. Lewis, 1831 (G.S. Ref. 942 E5L, 1831; microfilm 413, 519-413,522; also on fiche).

Wilson, John Marius, ed. *The Imperial Gazetteer of England and Wales.* 6 vols. Edinburgh: A. Fullerton, n.d. (G.S. Ref. 942 E5i; microfilm 897,325,-26,-27. fiche 6020308-36)

Guides To Genealogical Research

Camp, Anthony J. *Everyone Has Roots, An Introduction to English Genealogy.* Baltimore: Genealogical Publishing Co., 1978.

Gardner, David E. and Frank Smith. *Genealogical Research in England and Wales,* 3 vols. Salt Lake City: Bookcraft, 1959.

Hamilton-Edwards, Gerald. *In Search of Ancestry.* London: Phillimore and Company, latest edition.

Research Papers for English Research. Salt Lake City: Genealogical Society of the Church of Jesus Christ of Latter-day Saints.

Histories

Smith, Frank. *The Lives and Times of Our English Ancestors.* 2 vols. Logan: Everton Publishers, 1969, 19

The Victoria History of the Counties of England. London: Institute of Historical Research, University of London, various dates. (Printed and film copies)*

Genealogical Sources

Burke, Arthur M. *Key to the Ancient Parish Registers of England and Wales.* Baltimore: Genealogical Publishing Co. Reprint.

Camp, Anthony J. *Wills and Their Whereabouts.* London, author, 1974.

Census Records 1841-1881.* Film numbers for the census records available at the Genealogical Society, (Salt Lake City, Utah) are listed in the Census Register: Ref. Q 942 X2pi or film 883,769.

Civil Registration from 1 July 1837 to present, copies of certificates available from: General Register Office, St. Catherine's House, 10 Kingsway, London WC2B 6JP England (Write for current price list)

Crockford's Clerical Directory. London: Oxford University Press, latest edition.

Gibson, J. S.W. *Wills and Where to Find Them.* Chichester, Phillimore, 1974.

Hall, Joseph. *The Genealogical Handbook for England and Wales.* Salt Lake City: Everton Publishers 1977.

Original Parish Registers in Record Offices and Libraries. Matlock, Derbyshire: Local Population Studies, Tawney House, 1974. Supplements, 1976, 1978, 1980.

Record Repositories in Great Britain. London: Her Majesty's Stationery Office, latest edition.

Steel, D. J. *National Index of Parish Registers.* Baltimore: Genealogical Publishing Company, 1967.

Steel, D. J. *Sources for Nonconformist Genealogy and Family History.* Chichester, England. Phillimore, 1973.

*Microfilm - Genealogical Society of The Church of Jesus Christ of Latter-day Saints, Salt Lake City, Utah.

Counties and/or Shires Of England

Name	County Town	Name	County Town
Bedfordshire	Bedford	Norfolk	Norwich
Berkshire	Reading	Northamptonshire	Northampton
Buckinghamshire	Aylesbury	Northumberland	Newcastle
Cambridgeshire	Cambridge	Nottinghamshire	Nottingham
Cheshire (Chester Co.)	Chester	Oxfordshire	Oxford
Cornwall	Truro	Rutlandshire	Oakham
Cumberland	Carlisle	Shropshire	Shrewsbury
Derbyshire	Derby	Somersetshire	Taunton
Devonshire	Exeter	Staffordshire	Stafford
Dorsetshire	Dorchester	Suffolk	
Durham	Durham	East Suffolk	Ipswich
Essex	Chelmsford	West Suffolk	St. Edmunds
Gloucestershire	Gloucester	Surrey	Kingston on Thames
Hampshire	Winchester		
Herefordshire	Hereford	Sussex	
Hertfordshire	Hertford	East Sussex	Lewes
Huntingdonshire	Huntingdon	West Sussex	Chichester
Isle of Ely (north half Cambs)	Marck	Warwickshire	Warwick
Isle of Wight	Newport	Westmorelandshire	Kendal
Kent	Maidstone	Wiltshire	Trowbridge
Lancashire (Lancaster Co.)	Preston	Worcestershire	Worcester
Leicestershire	Leicester	Yorkshire	
Lincolnshire	Lincoln	East Riding	Beverly
London	London	North Riding	Northallerton
Middlesex	London	West Riding	Wakefield
Monmouthshire	Newport		

ENGLAND
AND
WALES

FINLAND

Capital, Helsinki

Valuable Sources

Atlases, Gazetteers, Maps

Granlund, Ake, and Kurt Zilliacus, ed. comp. *Svenska Ortnamn i Finland.* Helsinki: Mercator, 1963 (G.S. call no. Ref. E2sv)

The Geographical Society of Finland. *Atlas of Finland 1925.* Helsinki: Otava, 1929. Issued in Finnish, Swedish and in English (G.S. Call no. Ref. Q 947.1 E3a pt. 4 English)

Maanmittaushallitus. *Fennia Suuri Suomi-kartasto.* Weilin - Göös, 1979. (G.S. Call no. Ref. 947.1 E7f) English and Finish.

Pauninkoski, P. *Suomen Paikkakuntahakemisto.* Kuopio, Kirjapaino: Osakeyhtiö Savo, 1949. (G.S. 947.1 E5p)

Tarmio, Hannu, ed. *Suomenmaa.* Porvoo: Werner Söderström Oy, 1967 (G.S. 947.1 E2s)

Place Names

Posti-ja Lennätinlaitoksen Osoitehakemisto. Helsinki: Valtion Painatuskeskus, 1968. (Postal guide for Finland - text in Swedish and Finnish G.S. call no. Ref. 947.1 E8)

Guides To Genealogical Research

Blomstedt, Yrjö. "Elements of Finnish Genealogy". *Genealogical Journal,* Dec. 1977, Vol. 6 no. 4 pages 175-180. Salt Lake City: Utah Genealogical Association.

Brenner, Alf. *Släktforskning - Praktisk Handbok for Finland.* Helsinki: Soderström and Co., 1947 (G.S. call no. 929.1471 B751s)

Huuskonen, Pirkko. *Sukututkimus - Jäljitä Juuresi.* Helsinki: Kansanvalistusseuran Kirjeopisto, 1979. (G.S. call no. 947.1 D27h). Written in Finnish.

Major Genealogical Record Sources in Finland, series D no. 4. Salt Lake City: Genealogical Society of The Church of Jesus Christ of Latter-day Saints, 1973 (G.S. call no. 929.148 G286gs).

Histories

Juva, Einar and Mikko Juva: *Suomen Kansan Historia,* 5 vols. Helsinki: Otava, 1966.

Genealogical Sources

Suomen Sukututkimusseura (Finnish Genealogical Society) established in 1917, served as a central organization for Finnish genealogy. Maintains a central library and publishes "Genos", Collection includes family histories, local histories, biographies, obituaries, school and University Lists.

University Library of Helsinki - Collection includes newspapers of Finland.

National Archives - Riksarkivet - Collection includes accounts, some military records, court records and central administration records.

Five Regional Archives - Vital statistics on a parish level, private inventories and other court records, local administration.

Many important records from Finland have been microfilmed by the Genealogical Society and are available for searching in the Genealogical Society Library in Salt Lake City, Utah. Check the Dictionary Card Catalog (DCC) and the International Genealogical Library Catalog (IGLC).

MAP OF FINLAND SHOWING COUNTY
BOUNDARIES AS OF 1831

1. Turku Pori - Åbo och Björneborg
2. Uusimaa (Undenmaa) - Nyland
3. Viipuri - Viborg
4. Häme - Tavastehus
5. Mikkeli - St. Mickels
6. Vaasa - Vasa
7. Kuopio - - - - -
8. Oulu - Uleåborg

LAANI - LAN COUNTY

I Ahvenanmaa - Åland	VII Vaasa - Vasa
II Turku Pori - Åbo och Björneborg	VIII Keski Suomi - Mellersta Finland
III Uusimaa (Undenmaa)- Nyland	IX Kuopia - -----
IV Kymi - Kymmene	X Pohjis Karjala - N. Karelen
V Häme - Tavastehus	XI Oulu - Uleåborg
VI Mikkeli - St Mickels	XII Lapi - Lappland

NAMES OF FINNISH PROVINCES

1. Ahvenanmaa - Åland
2. Varsinais - Egentliga
3. Uusimaa - Nyland
4. Satakunta - Satakundá
5. Hame - Tavastland
6. Savo - Savolaks
7. Karjala - Karelén
8. Pohjanmaa - Österbotten
9. Länispohja - Västerbotten
10. Lappi - Lappland

MAAKUNTA - PROVINCE (LANDSKAP)

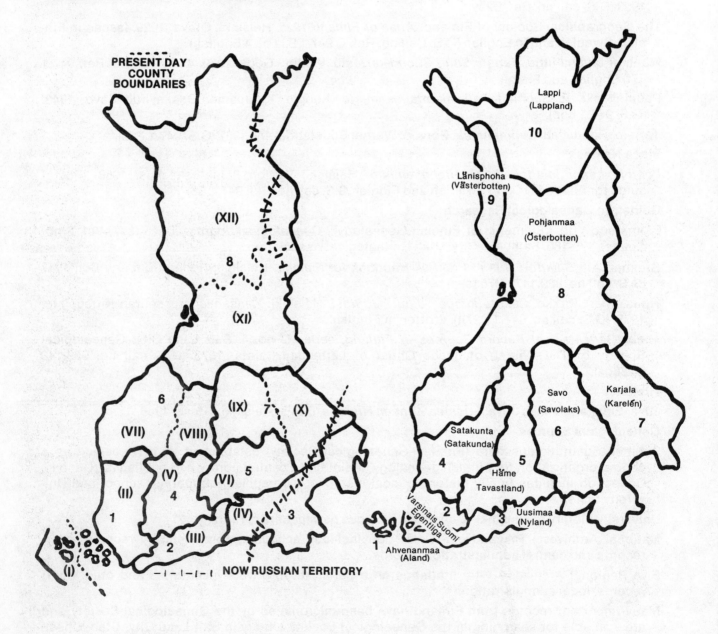

PRESENT DAY COUNTY BOUNDARIES

NOW RUSSIAN TERRITORY

FRANCE
Capital, Paris

In identifying ancestors, genealogical researchers need the answers to four key questions regarding record sources: 1. What types of records exist that will aid in identification of ancestors? 2. What periods of time do the existing records cover? 3. What genealogical information do they contain? 4. What is their availability for searching?

These questions are answered in the research paper, "Genealogical Record Sources of France" Series G, No. 1, published by the Genealogical Society of the Church of Jesus Christ of Latter-day Saints, 50 East North Temple Street, Salt Lake City, Utah 84150. This paper lists 36 types of records, the periods they cover, type of information given and availability.

According to the above paper, "The most important sources for France will be found in the Civil registration (état-civil) from 1792 to present: Parish registers 16th century to 1792; Notarial records 14th or 15th centuries or later to present. "Guide des Recherches Génealogigues aux Archives Nationales" (Paris: *Imprimerie Nationale,* 1956) and "Que saisje?" series No. 917, *La Genealogie* by Pierre Durye (Paris: Presses Universitaires de France, 1936) are excellent aids for those searching the records of France. An index to names of about 48,000 French sailors and soldiers who participated in the American Revolution can be found in *Les Combattants Francais de la Guerre Américaine, 1778-1783,* Genealogical Publishing Company, 1905.

The earliest parish registers of baptisms, marriages and burials were written about 400 years ago. These registers were kept by the parish priest who, beginning in about 1700, deposited copies of his registers with the Clerk of the Court. At the time of the revolution (1789) the task of recording births, marriages and deaths was transferred to the Mairies (town halls) where the parish priests were compelled by law to deposit all the registers in their possession. The new registers (since 1789) are known as Registres de l'Etat Civil. It is, therefore, to the town hall that one should write to consult the records of births, marriages and deaths either prior to or subsequent to the year 1789. Occasionally the Departmental Archivist has insisted on the transfer of the old parish registers to his archive when they have not been carefully preserved in the town halls.

The National Library and the National Archives together with the various departmental and town or city archives supply inexhaustable sources of information.

In these public archives are preserved millions of manuscript volumes extending into the middle ages where the researcher might spend many months and still continue to find new data.

DEPARTMENTS OF FRANCE
(Departement)

Departments are listed alphabetical with the map index in parenthesis and the department capital following.

Ain (C4) Bourg; Aisne (A3) Laon; Allier (C3) Moulins; Alpes-Maritimes (D4) Nice; Ardéche (C3) Privas; Ardennes (A3) Mézières; Ariège (D2) Foix; Aube (B3) Troyes; Aude (D3) Carcassonne; Aveyron (C3) Rodez.

Bas-Rhin (B4) Strasbourg; Basses-Alpes (D4) Digne; Basses-Pryénéss (D2) Pau; Territoire Belfort (B4) Belfort; Bouches-du-Rhône (D4) Marseille; Calvados (A2) Caen; Cantal (C3) Aurillac; Charente (C2) Angoulême; Charente-Maritime (C2) La Rochelle; Cher (B3) Bourges; Corrèze (C3) Tulle; Corse (an island SE of Var) Ajaccio; Côte-D'or (B3) Dijon; Cotês-du-Nord (B1) St. Brieuc; Creuse (C3) Gueret.

Deux-Sèyres (B2) Niort; Dordogne (C2) Périgueux; Doubs (B4) Besancon; Drôme (C4) Valence; Eure (A2) Évreux; Eure-et-Loir (B2) Chartres; Finistère (B1) Quimper; Gard (D3) Nimes; Gers (D2) Auch; Gironde (C2) Bordeaux; Haute-Garonne (D2) Toulouse; Haute-Loire (C3) Le Puy; Haute-Marne (B4) Chaumont; Hautes-Alpes (C4) Gap; Haute-Saône (B4) Vesoul; Haute-Savoie (C4) Annecy; Hautes-Pyrénées (D2) Tarbes; Haute-Vienne (C2) Limoges; Haut-Rhin (B4) Colmar; Hérault (D3) Montpellier.

Ille-et-Vilaine (B2) Rennes; Indre (B2) Châteauroux; Indre-et-Loire (B2) Tours; Isère (C4) Grenoble; Jura (B4) Lons-le-Saunier; Landes (D2) Mont-de-Marsan; Loire (C3) St. Étienne; Loire-Atlantique (B2) Nantes; Loiret (B3) Orleans; Loir-et-Cher (B2) Blois; Lot (C3) Cahors; Lot-et-Garonne (C2) Agen; Lozere (C3) Mende.

Maine-et-Loire (B2) Angers; Manche (A2) St. Lô; Marne (A3) Châlons-sur-Marne; Mayenne (B2) Laval; Meurthe-et-Moselle (B4) Nancy; Meuse (A4) Bar-le-Duc; Morbihan (B1) Vannes; Moselle (A4) Metz; Nievre (B3) Nevers; Nord (A3) Lille; Oise (A3) Beauvais; Orne (B2) Alencon; Pas-de-Calais (A3) Arras; Puy-de-Dôme (C3) Clermont-Ferrand; Pyrénées-Orientales (D3) Perpignan.

Rhône (C3) Lyon; Saône-et-Loire (B3) Macon; Sarthe (B2) Le Mans; Savoie (C4) Chambéry; Seine (B3) Paris; Seine-et-Marne (B3) Melun; Seine-et-Oise (B3) Versailles; Seine-Maritime (A2) Rouen; Somme (A3) Amiens; Tarn (D3) Albi; Tarn-et-Garonne (D2) Montauban; Var (D4) Draguignan; Vaucluse (D4) Avignon; Vendée (B2) La Roche sur-Yon; Vienne (C2) Poitiers; Vosges (B4) Epinal; Yonne (B3) Auxerre.

Map of Departments of France

FORMER PROVINCES
OF
FRANCE

FORMER PROVINCES OF FRANCE

1, Flanders; 2, Artois; 3, Picardy; 4, Normandy; 5, Ile de France; 6, Champagne; 7, Lorraine; 8, Alsace; 9, Brittany; 10, Maine; 11, Orleanais; 12, Burgundy; 13, Franche-Comte; 14, Anjou; 15, Touraine; 16, Berry; 17, Nivernais; 18, Poitou; 19, Marche; 20, Bourbonnais; 21, Aunis; 22, Saintonge; 23, Angoumois; 24, Limousin; 25, Auvergne; 25A, Lyonnais; 26, Dauphine; 27, Guyenne; 28, Gascony; 29, Bearn; 30, Foix; 31, Roussillion; 32, Languedoc; 33, Comtat; 34, Provence.

Valuable Sources

Atlases, Gazetteers, Maps

Denis-Papin, M., Martin, J.L., and Bonnard. *Dictionnaire National des Communes de France.* Paris: Editions Albin Michel. (G.S. Ref. 944 E5di).

Atlas Bottin, 2 vols. (G.S. Staff 944 E3b)

Place Names

Chevin, M. l'Abbe. *Dictionnaire Latin-Francais Des Noms Propres de Lieux.* Paris: 1897 (G.S. Film 1,070,223)

Guides To Genealogical Research

Law, Hugh T. "How to Trace Your French Ancestors" *The Genealogical Helper,* January-February issue 1978 pages 5-8.

Law, Hugh T. *How to do French Genealogical Research.* Salt Lake City: Genealogical Society, 1973. (G.S. film 908,366 item 5)

Law, Hugh T. *Tracing Huguenot Ancestors Back to France.* Salt Lake City: Genealogical Society, 1981.

Genealogical Society: *Major Genealogical Record Sources in France.* Series G No. 1 Salt Lake City, 1976.

Wolff, Christian. *Guide des recherches généalogiques en Alsace.* Strasbourg: Oberlin, 1975. (Guide to Genealogical Research in Alsase. G.S. 944.383 D2g)

World conference on Records - Lecture Papers (G.S. film 897,215 items 19-29)

Genealogical Sources

Arnaud, Etienne. *Répertoire de Généalogies Francaises Imprimées.* 2 vols. (G.S. Europe 944 D23A)

Boyenval, Abbe R., Berger, R. and Bougard, P. *Repertoire des Nons de Famille du Pas-de-Calais en 1820.* Arras: Archives du Pas-de-Calais, 1960.

Card index to emigration records of Europeans traveling through the Alsace Region of France. G.S. film numbers:

Surnames   A-C on film 1,125,002
                  D-G - 1,125,003
                  H-K - 1,125,004
                  L-P - 1,125,005
                  Q-S - 1,125,006
                  T-Z - 1,125,007

Genealogical Society of The Church of Jesus Christ of Latter-day Saints has microfilmed French Departmental Records Check the Dictionary Card Catalog (DCC) and the International Genealogical Library Catalog (IGLC).

Societe de l'Histoire du Protestantisme Francais. *Bulletin de la Societe . . . (Bulletin of the Society of History of French Protestantism)* Vols. 1 to 115 (1852 to 1969) on films 885,753 to 885,729. (G.S. 944 B2sp; index 944 B2sp Index or on film 1,045,348)

Histories

Guerard, Albert. *France, A Modern History.* New Edition. Revised and Enlarged by Paul A. Gagnon. Ann Arbor: The University of Michigan Press, 1959, 1969.

Roche, O. J. A. *The Days of the Upright, The Story of the Huguenots.* New York, 1965 (G.S. 944 K2ro)

GERMANY

The history of Germany has been a history of change. Dramatic changes in its boundaries and political structure have been a feature of Germany's history throughout the centuries. Kingdoms have been born, have grown to immense sizes by conquering other principalities, and then have either become extinct or diminished in size due to the conquest of others. Germany is actually many countries in one. It has been comprised of kingdoms, provinces, duchies, earldoms, etc., most of which have never remained constant in either size or in the ruling families that governed them. The boundaries of these principalities changed due to many causes; some through marriage, some through conquest and still others through inheritance when families died out and the next closest related ruling family added it to their own area. Other changes occurred due to the impact of the countries that surrounded Germany. Among these have been the French, the Scandinavians and the Slavs. Germany, as a country, has grown and diminshed in size by conquering and being conquered by these countries. When this has occurred it has usually caused a great impact on the German people and their records, because with the conquerors came also their laws, their records, and their customs.

Within Germany's kingdoms, provinces etc., existed still smaller independent states; their size and number also varying from time to time. By the mid-1600's there were approximately 300 of these states. By the time of the French Revolution in 1792 there were, interestingly enough, 1792 independent German states. Each of these, along with the kingdoms they belonged to, had the power to create records and establish laws that affected the people that belonged to them. The end result of this was the fact that there were no central repositories of records. There often was no consistency in the records as to what they contained, when they began, and who controlled them. For this reason it is critical that a researcher know the specific locality or parish in Germany their ancestors came from because it is in the local areas that the records were kept.

Many excellent records have been kept in Germany including the following: parish records, civil records, passenger lists, land, probate, guild, census, citizenship, and tax records. Before writing to Germany for information, the researcher should check the holdings of the Genealogical Society in Salt Lake City, Utah; as many records from Germany have been microfilmed by them. To determine what records are available, a researcher needs to check their two catalog files:

1. The *Dictionary Card Catalog* which was discontinued at the end of 1979. It is based on modern country boundaries which means that parts of what was Germany will now be filed under Poland, Russia, France, Denmark, Belgium, and Czechoslovakia; these were areas of Germany which were lost after World War II. (See Figure 2 which is a map of Germany showing modern boundaries).

2. *International Genealogical Library Catalog* (IGLC). Since the beginning of 1980 all material which has been acquired by the Genealogical Society has been entered into their computer and is cataloged and printed out on microfiche. Eventually, the information within the Dictionary Card Catalog will be entered into and become a part of the IGLC. This computer catalog is based on former boundaries of Germany as they existed prior to World War I. (See Figure 1)

Valuable Sources

Atlases, Gazetteers and Maps

Hall, Charles, *The Atlantic Bridge to Germany.* Logan, Utah: The Everton Publishers, 1974-1978. Vol. 1 - Baden-Württemberg; Vol. 2, Hessen and Rheinland-Pfalz; Vol. 3, Bavaria (Bayern); Vol. 4, Saarland, Alsace-Lorraine, Switzerland; Vol. 5, Bremen, Hamburg and Schleswig-Holstein.

Karte Des Deutschen Reiches. (Maps of the German Empire) (Film No. 068,814) General Maps of the former kingdoms, provinces and duchies of the Germany Empire are published in the *Meyers Konversations Lexikon.* Leipzig: Bibliographisches Institut, 1885-1892. (Film No. 1,181,575 - Item 1)

Kowallis, Otto K. and Vera. *Genealogical Guide and Atlas of Silesia.* Logan, Utah: Everton Publishers, 1976.

A detailed listing of special gazetteers for locating parishes and determining modern names are included in *A Genealogical Handbook of German Research* by Larry O. Jensen.

Mairs Geographical Verlag. *Der Grosse Shell Atlas Deutschland Und Europa.* Stuttgart: Mairs Geographischer Verlag, revised each year. Scale: 1:500,000

Müller, Fritz. *Müllers Grosses Deutsches Ortsbuch,* Wuppertal-Barmen: Post- und Ortsbuchverlag Postmeister A. D. Friedrich Muller, 1958.

Uetrecht, E. (comp.) *Meyers Orts-und Verkehrs - Lexikon Des Deutschen Reiches* Leipzig: Bibliographisches Institut, 1912 (Film No. 496,640 and 496,641)

Westermann Grosser Atlas Zur Weltgeschichte. Braunschweig: Georg Westermann Verlag, 1972.

MAP #1

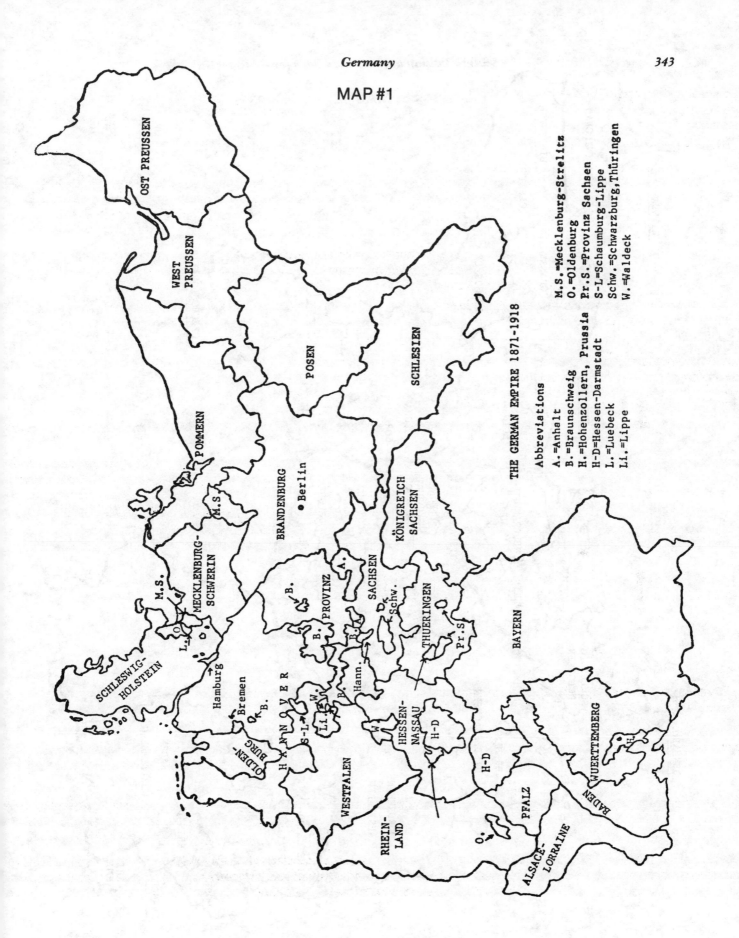

MAP #2

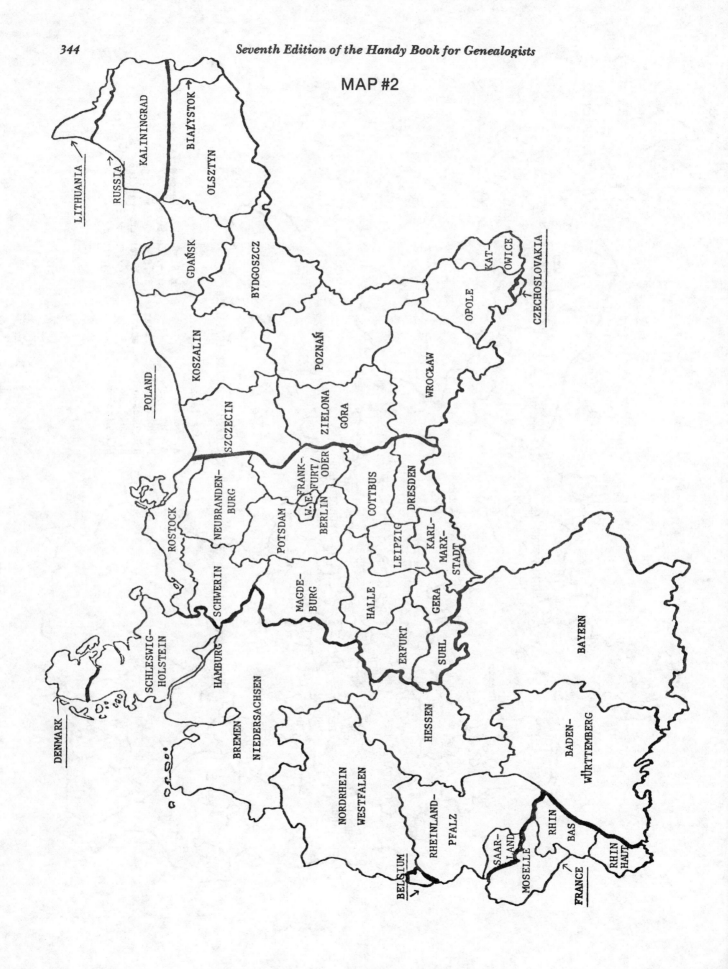

Guides To Genealogical Research

Jensen, Larry O. *A Genealogical Handbook of German Research,* rev. ed., P.O. Box 441, Pleasant Grove, Utah 84062.

Smith Clifford Neal. *Encyclopedia of German-American Genealogical Research,* New York and London: R. R. Bowker Co., 1976.

Thode, Ernest. *Address Book For Germanic Genealogy.* Marietta, Ohio: Thode Translations, 1977.

Histories

Barraclough, Geoffrey. *The Origins of Modern Germany.* New York: Capricorn Books, 1963.

Reinhard, Kurt F. *Germany: 2,000 Years.* 2 vols. New York: Frederick Unger Publishing Company, 1961.

Important Genealogical Sources

Auerbach, Inge and Otto Frohlick. *Hessische Truppen Im Amerika-Nischen Unabhängigkeitskrieg* (Hetrina Series - Hessian Troops in the American War of Independence). Marburg: 1974-1976. (Available from St. Louis Genealogical Society).

Brenner Collection

Deutsch Geschlecturbuch

The Hamburg Passenger Lists

HUNGARY
Capital, Budapest
Valuable Sources

Atlases, Gazetteers, Maps

Hungary. Official Standard Names Approved by the U.S. Board on Geographic Names. Washington, D.C.: Office of Geography, Department of Interior, 1961. (G.S. Ref. 943.9 E5u or Film 874,461)

Magyarország Helységnévtára. Budapest: Központi Statisztikai Hivatal, Statisztikai Kiado, 1962. (G.S. 943.9 E5k or Film 844,957)

Magyarország Geographiai Szótará. Pest: Nyomatott Kozma Vazulnál, 1851. (G.S. Film 844,956)

Guides To Genealogical Research

Suess, Jared H. *Handy Guide to Hungarian Genealogical Records.* Logan: Everton Publishers, 1980.

Suess, Jared H. "Using Hungarian Gazetteers." *The Genealogical Helper,* Jan.-Feb. 1979 issue, pages 5-8, Logan: Everton Publishers, 1979.

Genealogical Sources

The Genealogical Society of The Church of Jesus Christ of Latter-day Saints in Salt Lake City has microfilmed many records from Hungary. The following are some of the records available in the Genealogical Society Library:

Parish Register records of different faiths - early 18th century to 1895.

Muster rolls from the 19th century.

Nobility records from the 17th, 18th and 19th centuries.

Land registration records of 1828.

Census of 1828, parts of the 1848 census of the Jews and parts of the 1857 and 1869 enumerations.

Civil registration records (started in 1895) are kept at the Civil Registrar's offices in the Town halls. Duplicates are in the local county archives or in the National Center of Archives - address: Levéltárak Országos Központja, Budapest 1, Uri Utca 54-56.

HUNGARY

HUNGARY

IRELAND

Republic of Ireland — Capital, Dublin — Northern Ireland — Capital, Belfast

Valuable Sources

Atlases, Gazetteers, Maps

Lewis, Samuel. *A Topographical Dictionary of Ireland.* London: S. Lewis and Company, 1837. *(G.S. 941,5E5L; or film 599,557; also microfiche)

Parliamentary Gazetteer of Ireland. Dublin: A. Fullarton and Company 1844. 10 vols.* (G.S. 941,5 E5p; films 824,043 Localities A-C, 824,044 D-M, 824,045 N-Z; fiche 6020358 - 82 localities A-C, -83 D-M, -84 N-Z)

Parish County Maps Showing the Locations of Churches. Genealogical Research Papers, Series A, nos. 54-57. Salt Lake City: Genealogical Society, (Fiche 6020301-3 and 6020386)

Place Names

Alphabetical Index to the Townlands and Towns of Ireland. Dublin: Alexander Thom, 1877.* (G.S. Ref. 941.5 X2ci; film 476,999 item 2; or fiche 6020345 to -53)

Guides To Genealogical Research

Burdick, Carol. "Genealogical Research in Ireland." *The Genealogical Helper,* May-June 1975, pages 3-5.

Clare, Rev. Wallace. *A Simple Guide to Irish Genealogy.* London: Irish Genealogical Research Society, 1937. Revised 1966 Rosemary Folliott.

Falley, Margaret Dickson, *Irish and Scotch-Irish Ancestral Research.* 2 vols. 1962. Reprint. Baltimore: Genealogical Publishing Company, 1981.

Genealogical Society: *A Basic Genealogical Research Guide for Ireland.* Series A, No. 58. Salt Lake City: 1978. (Fiche 6020288)

Genealogical Sources

Researchers should check the holdings of the Genealogical Society of The Church of Jesus Christ of Latter-day Saints in Salt Lake City, Utah as it has microfilmed records from Ireland. Check the Dictionary Card Catalog (DCC) and the International Genealogical Library Catalog (IGLC).

---

*Microfilm - Genealogical Society of The Church of Jesus Christ of Latter-day Saints, Salt Lake City, Utah.

ITALY

Capital, Rome

Valuable Sources

Gazetteer

Nuovo Dizionario dei Comuni E Frazioni di Comune. Rome: Dizionario Voghera dei Comuni, 1954. (Italian gazetteer naming towns and hamlets with provinces in which they are located). (G.S. Call Number: Ref. 945 E5n, 1954)

Maps

Atlante Automobilistico. Milano: Touring Club Italiano, 1971. Vol. 1, Italia Settentrionale (Northern); Vol. 2, Italia Centrale e Sardegna (Central) Vol. 3, Italia Meridionalee Sicilia (Southern). (G.S. Europe Ref. 945 E7tou)

Place Names

Amico, Vito. *Dizionario Topografico, 1856*
Reprinted, Bologna, Italy: Arnaldo Forni Editore.

Map of Italy Showing Provinces, Regions, and Some Large Cities

VIII. EMILIA - ROMAGNA: 32 Bologna, 33 Ferrara, 34 Forli, 35 Modena, 36 Parma, 37 Piacenza, 38 Ravenna, 39 Reggio Emilia.

CENTRAL ITALY

IX. TOSCANA: 40 Massa Carrara (formerly Apuania), 41 Arezza, 42 Firenze, 43 Grosseto, 44 Livorno, 45 Lucca, 46 Pisa, 47 Pistoia, 48 Siena.

X. MARCHE: 49 Ancona, 50 Ascolia Piceno, 51 Macerata, 52 Pesaro-Urbino.

XI. UMBRIA: 53 Perugia, 54 Terni.

XII. LAZIO: 55 Frosinone, 56 Latina (formerly Littoria), 57 Rieti, 58 Roma, 59 Viterbo.

SOUTHERN ITALY

XIII. ABRUZZI e MOLISE: 60 Campobasso, 61 Chieti, 62 L'Aquila, 63 Pescara, 64 Teramo.

XIV. CAMPANIA: 65 Avellino, 66 Benevento, 67 Caserta, 68 Napoli, 69 Salerno.

XV. PUGLIE: 70 Bari, 71 Brindisi, 72 Foggia, 73 Lecce, 74 Taranto (formerly Ionio).

XVI. BASILICATA (formerly Lucania); 75 Matera, 76 Potenza.

XVII. CALABRIA: 77 Catanzaro, 78 Cosenza, 79 Reggio Calabria.

ISLAND PROVINCES

XVIII. SICILIA: 80 Agrigento, 81 Caltanisseta, 82 Catania, 83 Enna, 84 Messina, 85 Palermo, 86 Ragusa, 87 Siracusa, 88 Trapani.

XIX. SARDEGNA: 89 Cagliari, 90 Nuoro, 91 Sassari.

The above information on Italy record sources and history was taken from the Research Paper Series G, No. 2, "Major Genealogical Record Sources in Italy." It is published by The Genealogical Society of the Church of Jesus Christ of Latter-day Saints and may be purchased from the Church Distribution Center, 33 Richards St., Salt Lake City, Utah 84101.

NORTHERN ITALY

I. PIEDMONT: 1 Alessandria, 2 Asti, 3 Cuneo, 4 Novara, 5 Torino, 6 Vercelli.

II. VALLEY OF AOSTA: 7 Aosta.

III. LIGURIA: 8 Genova, 9 Imperia, 10 La Spezia, 11 Savona.

IV. LOMBARDIA: 12 Bergamo, 13 Brescia, 14 Como, 15 Cremona, 16 Mantova, 17 Milano, 18 Pavia, 19 Sondrio, 20 Varese.

V. TRENTION - ALTO ADIGE: 21 Bolzano, 22 Trento.

VI. VENETO: 23 Belluno, 24 Padova, 25 Rovigo, 26 Treviso, 27 Venezia, 28 Verona, 29 Vicenza.

VII. FRIULI - VENEZIA GIULIA: 30 Udine, 31 Gorizia.

Annuario delle diocesi d'Italia. Marietti: 1951. Diocese index and yearbook. (G.S. microfilm numbers 780,555 (for the yearbook) and 780,556 for the index, the index lists towns arranged alphabetically, names the parish in these towns, and indicates to which diocese they belong.

Codice di Avviamento Postale. Roma: Ministero delle Poste e Telecomunicazioni (Zip code book for Italy)

Silvio, Pieri. *Toponomastica della valle dell 'Arno.* Roma: Tipografia della R. Accademia dei Lincei, 1919. (Dictionary of geographic names and their origins in the Valley of the Arno River in the Tuscany region of Italy.

Guides to Research

Archivio Genealogico, Rivista semestrale di Studi Araldici e Genealogici storici legali archivistici diplomatici. Firenze: Organo Ufficiale della Societa Italiana de Studi Araldici e Genealogici, 1961. (G.S. Call No. 945 B2As, yr. 1 Nos. 1-2, film copy 908856)

Major Genealogical Record Sources in Italy, Series G, No. 2 Revised 1977 Salt Lake City: Genealogical Department of The Church of Jesus Christ of Latter-day Saints.

Genealogical Sources

Istitut Genealogico Italiano - Conte Cav. Guelfo Guelfi Camajani and his staff have made a card index based on surnames contained in their large library of Italian genealogical works. They will consult their index upon request (fee - at present $10.00). Address: Conte Cav. Guelfo Guelfi Camajani, Istituto Genealogico Italiano, Via Torta 14, Florence, Italy. For additional information regarding the Istituto Genealogico see *The Genealogical Helper,* Jan. 1973 issue, page 8.

Piedmont Project: family group sheets compiled from the microfilmed records in the Genealogical Society of the Church of Jesus Christ of Latter-day Saints, pertaining to 16 Protestant parishes in the Province of Torino, Italy. 43 rolls, handwritten.

Researchers should check the holdings of the Genealogical Society of The Church of Jesus Christ of Latter-day Saints in Salt Lake City, Utah as it has microfilmed some Italian records. Check the Dictionary Card Catalog and the International Genealogical Library Catalog (IGLC).

NETHERLANDS

Capital, Amsterdam
Valuable Sources

Atlas

Bos, P. R. - van Balen, C. L. *Kleine Schoolatlas der Gehele Aarde.* J. B. Wolters Groningen, 1965. (G.S. Europe Q Area 949.2 E3b)

Geographic Dictionary

van der Aa, A. J. *Aardrijkskundig Woordenboek der Nederlanden.* Gorinchem: Jacobus Noorduyn, 1839-1851. 13 vols. with supplement. (Ref. 949.2 E2a)

Maps

Kuyper, J. *Gemeente-Atlas Van Nederland.* Leeuwarden: Hugo Suringar, 1865-. 11 vols. (G.S. Europe Reg. Table 949.2 E3k or film 1,181,567)

Place Names

Wijnaendts van Resandt, W. *Repertorium DTB.* Centraal Bureau voor Genealogie, 1969. (Includes short descriptions of baptism, marriage and burial records with the names of towns and provinces). (G.S. 949.2 A5w or film 908,159)

Province Map of Netherlands and Belgium

The Netherlands is divided into eleven provinces. Each province controls its own archive.

Name	Map Index	Capital	Name	Map Index	Capital
Drenthe	B4	Assen	Noord (North) Holland	B2	Haarlem
Friesland	A3	Leeuwarden	Overijssel (Overyssel)	B4	Zwolle
Gelderland	C3	Arnhem	Utrecht	C3	Utrecht
Groningen	A4	Groningen	Zeeland	D2	Middleburg
Limburg	D4	Maastricht	Zuid (South) Holland	C2	Rotterdam
Noord (North) Brabant	D3's	Hertogenbosch			

Guides To Genealogical Research

Genealogical Society of The Church of Jesus Christ of Latter-day Saints. *Research Papers.* Salt Lake City: 1971-1977. Series C, Nos. 5-15 and 20-28.

Van Weezep, John. *Resources for Genealogical Research in the Netherlands.* Logan: Everton Publishers, pending.

Genealogical Sources

Van Beresteyn, Jhr. Mr. E. A. *Genealogisch Repertorium.* 2 vols. Centraal Bureau voor Genealogies den Haag, 1972. (Family history index) (G.S. Ref. 949.2 A3b)

Many important records from the Netherlands have been microfilmed by the Genealogical Society and are available for searching in the Genealogical Society Library in Salt Lake City, Utah. Check the Dictionary Card Catalog (DCC) and the International Genealogical Library Catalog (IGLC).

NORWAY

Capital, Oslo

Valuable Sources

Atlases, Gazetteers, Maps

Cappelen Bilkartbok. Oslo: J. W. Cappelen, latest edition. (Road atlas)

Norges Civile, Geistlige, Rettslige of Militaere Indeling. Oslo: H. Aschehoug and Company. (G.S. film 564,358 - Guide to determine parishes, clerical districts, civil districts, indicating the county - the film includes four editions, 1917, 1922, 1941, 1951; fiche 6030088-92)

Norge, Geografisk Leksikon Med Atlas. 4 vols. Oslo: J. W. Cappelen Publishers, 1963.

Place Names

Norsk Stedfortegnelse. Kristiania, 1901. (Norwegian Postal Guide). (G.S. film 123,205; fiche 6030038-49)

Rygh, O. *Norske Gaardnavne.* 18 vols. and a supplement. Kristiana: W. C. Fabritius and Sønner, 1897-1924 (Ref. 948.1 E2s; films 908,594-908,600, 924001)

Guides To Genealogical Research

Poulsen, Elly and Gay P. Kowallis. *The Scandinavian Genealogical Helper.* 3 vols. Logan: Everton Publishers, 1969-1972.

Research Papers. Salt Lake City: Genealogical Society
   Major Genealogical Record Sources in Norway, Series D no. 1
   Church Records of Norway, Series D no. 11
   Census Records of Norway, Series D no. 12
   Probate Records of Norway, Series D no. 13
   Danish-Norwegian Paleography, Series D no. 16
   Standards and Procedures for Genealogical Research in Norway, Series D no. 28.

Genealogical Sources

Many important records from Norway have been microfilmed by the Genealogical Society and are available for searching in the Genealogical Society Library in Salt Lake City, Utah. Check the Dictionary Card Catalog (DCC) and the International Genealogical Library Catalog (IGLC).

Ulvestad, Martin. *Normaendene i Amerika, deres historie og rekord.* 2 vols. Minneapolis: History Book Company, 1907-1913. (G.S. film 896,612, 896,613)

Old (Amt) Name	New (Fylke) Name
Akershus Amt	Akershus Fylke
Bratsberg Amt	Telemark Fylke
Buskerud Amt	Buskerud Fylke
Finnmark Amt	Finnmark Fylke
Hedemarken Amt	Hedmark Fylke
Jarlsberg and Larviks Amt	Vestfold Fylke
Kristians Amt	Oppland Fylke
Lister and Mandal Amt	Vest-Agder Fylke
Nedenes Amt	Aust-Agder Fylke
Nordland Amt	Nordland Fylke
Nordre Bergenhus Amt	Sogn and Fjordane Fylke
Nordre Trondhjem Amt	Nord-Trøndelag Fylke
Romsdal Amt	Møre and Romsdal Fylke
Smaalenene Amt	Østfold Fylke
Stavanger Amt	Rogaland Fylke
Søndre Bergenhus Amt	Hordaland Fylke
Søndre Trondhjem Amt	Sør-Trøndelag Fylke
Tromsø Amt	Troms Fylke

NORWAY IN 1905

Norway is divided into 20 counties (fylke), including the cities of Oslo and Bergen. Norway has nine bishoprics (bispedømme), 560 clerical districts (prestegjeld), and 1047 parishes (sogne). A prestegjeld consists of one or more sogn. The parish minister, or sognepriest, resides in the head parish (hovedsogn).

The use of farm names, or locality names, as the family surnames was a common practice in Norway. These names were usually derived from the place of residence and are frequently helpful in identifying persons.

The official central repositories in Norway are: The National Archives (Riksarkivet); the Regional State Archives (Statsarkivet) (1) Statsarkivet i Oslo, Kirkegaten 14-18, Olso, Norway, (2) Statsarkivet i Hamar, Strandgaten 71, Hamar, Norway, (3) Statsarkivet in Kristiansand, Vesterveien 4, Kristiansand, Norway, (4) Statsarkivet i Bergen Aarstadveien 32, Bergen, Norway, (5) Statsarkivet i Trondheim, Høgskole-veien 12, Trondheim, Norway, (6) Statsarkivkontoret i Tromsø, Petersborg gate 21-29, Tromsø, Norway, (7) Statsarkivkontoret i Stavanger, Domkirkeplassen, Stavanger, Norway.

POLAND

Capital, Warsaw
Valuable Sources

Atlases, Gazetteers

Samochodowy Atlas Polski (Modern Road Atlas). (G.S. call no. Europe Ref. 943.8 E3s).

Spis Miejscowosci Polskiej Rzeczypospolitej Ludowej. 2 vols. Warsaw: Wydawnictwa Komunikacji i Łacznosci, 1967. (Eur. Ref. 943.8 E5s) (Film 844,922).

Słownik Geograficzny Królestwa Polskiego, 15 vols. (Films 920,957-920,972) (943.8 E5c)

Maps

The following detailed maps are available at the Genealogical Society in Salt Lake City, Utah:

Atlas of the Kingdom of Poland, printed in 1907. This includes only that part of Poland formerly ruled by Imperial Russia. (Film 873,665, item 3).

Austro-Hungarian Empire (scale 1:75,000) (Film 1,045,395).

Former German Empire (scale 1:100,000) (Film 068,814)

Guides To Genealogical Research

Gnacinski, Len and Jan. *Polish and Proud, Tracing your Polish Ancestry.* West Allis, Wisconsin: Janlen Enterprises, 1979.

Ortell, Gerald A. *Polish Parish Records of the Roman Catholic Church, Their Use and Understanding in Genealogical Research.* Astoria, New York: author, 1979.

Genealogical Sources

The Genealogical Society in Salt Lake City, Utah has microfilmed many vital records from Poland including some from parts of Soviet Ukraine formerly in Galicia and Volhynia. A large part of the library's Polish collection comes from the Polish state archival system. These include:

Civil registration records which begin 1808 or later from the area of Napoleon's Duchy of Warsaw and later under Imperial Russian rule. These include many Jewish communities.

Civil / church registration records from the former Austrian province of Galicia. A few records from Russian Volhynia are included. Some records begin as early as 1784.

Parish registers (Catholic and Protestant) mainly from parishes in former German and Russian ruled areas. Some records begin as early as 1589 but the majority begin in the mid to late 1700's.

The Polish State Archives has records for many localities which have not been filmed at the present time. The researcher may write to the following address to determine the availability of records not in the Genealogical Society's collection: Naczelna Dyrekcja Archiwów Panstowych
Ul. Długa 6 s.p. 1005
00-950 Warszawa, Poland

Periodical

Polish Genealogical Society Newsletter
984 North Milwaukee Avenue
Chicago, Illinois 60622

SCOTLAND

Capital Edinburgh

County Map of Scotland

COUNTIES OF SCOTLAND

County	Map Index	County Seat
Aberdeen	C4	Aberdeen
Angus	D4	Forfar
Argyll	D2	Lochgilphead

Includes islands of Jura, Islay, Colonsay, Mull, Coll, Tiree, Scarba, Luing, Siel, Kerrera, Lismore, and Others.

County	Map Index	County Seat
Ayr	F3	Ayr
Banff	C4	Banff
Berwick	E4	Duns
Bute	E2	Rothesay

Includes islands of Bute, Arran, Gr. Cumbrae, Little Cumbrae, Holy Island, etc.

County	Map Index	County Seat
Caithness	B3	Wick
Clackmannan	E3	Clackmannan
Dunbarton	E2	Dumbarton
Dumfries	F3	Dumfries
East Lothian	E4	Haddington
Fife	D4	Cupar
Inverness	C3	Inverness

Includes islands of Skye, Raasay, Muck, Eigg, Rum, Canna, Sanday, Scalpay, Harris, Scalpa, Pabbay, Bernera, Boreray, North Uist, Benbecula, South Uist, Barra, and many little islands.

County	Map Index	County Seat
Kincardine	D4	Stonehaven
Kinross	E3	Kinross
Kirkcudbright	F3	Kirkcudbright
Lanark	E3	Lanark
Midlothian	E4	Edinburgh
Moray	C3	Elgin
Nairn	C3	Nairn
Orkney	A3	Kirkwall
Peebles	E4	Peebles
Perth	D3	Perth
Renfrew	E3	Paisley
Ross & Cromarty	C2	Dingwall

Includes Lewis Island

County	Map Index	County Seat
Roxburgh	F4	Jedburgh
Selkirk	E4	Selkirk
Shetland	B4	Lerwick

Also called Zetland Islands.

County	Map Index	County Seat
Stirling	E3	Stirling
Sutherland	B3	Dornoch
West Lothian	E3	Linlithgow
Wigtown	F3	Wigtown

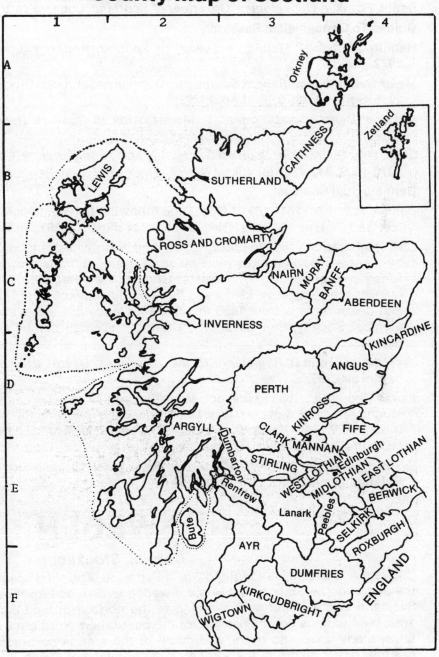

Valuable Sources

Atlases, Gazetteers, Maps

Groome, Francis H., ed. *Ordinance Gazetteer of Scotland: A Survey of Scottish Topography, Statistical, Biographical, and Historical.* 6 vols. Edinburgh: Thomas C. Jack, Grange Publishing Works, 1882-1885. (G.S. call no. Ref. 941 E5g; or films (874,305 and 874,306; or fiche 6020391-411)

Smith, Frank. *A Genealogical Gazetteer of Scotland.* Logan: Everton Publishers, 1971.

Guides To Genealogical Research

Hamilton-Edwards, Gerald. *In Search of Scottish Ancestry.* London: Phillimore and Company, 1972.

Major Genealogical Record Sources in Scotland. Salt Lake City: Genealogical Research Papers, 1975. Series A, no. 3. (Fiche 6020292)

McLeod, Dean L. and Norman L. Moyes. *Aids to Scottish Research.* Salt Lake City: authors, 1978.

Steel, D. J. *Sources for Scottish Genealogy and Family History.* London: Phillimore and Company, 1970. (G.S. 942 V26 ste, Vol. 12 *National Index of Parish Registers).*

Genealogical Sources

Census Records - 1841-1891.* Check the following for Genealogical Society Library call numbers: *Scotland Census 1841-1891* (Reg. 941 X2cr or film 990,269 or fiche 6020420)

Civil Registration - 1855 to present. Scotland was divided into registration districts presided over by a superintendant registrar. Copies of birth, marriage and death records are sent annually to the central depository - Register General, New Register House, Edinburgh, EH 1, 3YT. The records are compiled and indexed by year. The indexes from 1855 - 1955 and the birth, marriage and death records from 1855 to 1875, 1881 and 1891 are available on microfilm at the Genealogical Society, Salt Lake City, Utah. Library call numbers are recorded in the following register:

Workman, Beth B. *Register of Births, Marriages, Deaths of Scotland.* (Call number Reg. 941 v2 or film 599,269)

Parish Registers - 1558 to present. Microfilm copies of parish registers are available at the Genealogical Society, Salt Lake City, Utah. Check the following for Library Call numbers:
Bloxham, V. Ben. *Key to the Parochial Registers of Scotland From the Earliest Times Through 1854.* Provo, Utah: B.Y.U. Press, 1970.

Sasines, Services of Heirs and Deeds Register. Salt Lake City: Genealogical Society, British Reference, 1981. (G.S. call no. British Reg. Table 941 R2ss.)

SWEDEN

Capitol, Stockholm

Sweden is 978 miles long and 310 miles wide. The total area is 173,296 square miles, about the same as the State of California. Sweden is divided into three parts: Götaland in the south, Svealand in the center, and Norrland in the north. Norrland comprises 60 percent of the total area, but contains only 18 per cent of the population. Northern Sweden has snow covered mountains, many lakes and rivers, and much of the area is covered with forests. Southern Sweden has flat, fertile plains. In the southernmost province of Skåne 71.4 per cent of the total area consists of cultivated land.

For administrative purposes, Sweden is divided into divisions, known as län. The borders of the län have changed very little since they were established in 1635. The genealogical researcher in the United States, not understanding the administrative divisions in Sweden, often confuses the "län" with the "landskap". The "landskap" is not an administrative unit, but a geographical and historical concept. There may be more than one "län" in a "landskap". As an example, Småland contains three "län": Kronoberg, Jönköping and Kalmar.

Maps of Län and Landskap are shown on the opposite page.

Each "län" is sub-divided into smaller units, known as "härad". The "län" is also divided into smaller units known as parishes. A parish is valled "socken", but today known as forsamling. In 1952 many old parishes united under a new "kommun" (civil administration) name. Each parish consists of several villages (byar), farms (garder, hemman) and individual houses (hus).

Church records in Sweden include registers of births, marriages, and deaths; household examination records (husförhörslängder), removal from or arrival into the parish, and lists of confirmed members in the parish. The "husförhörslängder" records, called clerical survey records, or house examination rolls were records kept by the ministers of their visits to members of their parishes. The ministers were to examine every member of the household regarding their knowledge of the scriptures and their reading ability. The examinations took place once a year and records were kept of the information. The record books were usually used for a number of years (about a five year period) and included additions to the family record. There were no printed forms issued for the "husförhörslängd", however, some dioceses had their own printed forms. The records give information about all members of the household including husband, wife, children, servants, and other people living in the household such as aged parents. The earliest church records date from 1622, but it was not until 1686 that the Swedish law required the ministers to keep the records.

For statistical purposes, extracts of all births, marriages, and deaths from 1860 to 1947 have been made annually by the clergy, and sent to the Statistiska Centralbyrån for filing.

Valuable Sources

Atlases, Gazetteers, Maps

Bilatlas. Stockholm: Generalstabens Litografiska Anstalt, latest edition. (Road maps of Sweden - does not indicate parish boundaries).

Rosenberg, C. M. *Geografiskt-Statistiskt-Handlexikon öfver Sverige.* 2 vols in 5. Stockholm: A. V. Carlsons Forlag, 1882. (Ref. 948.5 E5r; film 873,678-679; fiche 6030050-74).

Sjögren, Otto. *Sverige - Geografisk Beskriving.* 5 vols. Stockholm: Wahlström and Widstrand, 1929.

Svensk Orter - Atlas över Sverige med Ortbeskrivning. Stockholm: Generalstabens Litografiska Anstalt, 1932. (Ref. 948.5 E5so; film 874,376-378).

Guides To Genealogical Research

Johansson, Carl-Erik. *Cradled in Sweden.* Logan: Everton Publishers, 1972. Revised 1981.

Poulsen, Elly M. and Gay P. Kowallis. *The Scandinavian Genealogical Helper,* 3 vols. Logan: Everton Publishers, 1969-1972.

Genealogical Sources

Olsson, Nils William. *Swedish Passenger Arrivals in New York 1820-1850.* Chicago: The Swedish Pioneer Historical Society, 1967.

Many important records from Sweden have been microfilmed by the Genealogical Society and are available for searching in the Genealogical Society Library in Salt Lake City, Utah. Check the Dictionary Card Catalog (DCC) and the International Genealogical Library Catalog (IGLC)

Bibliographies

Katalog For Genealogisk Forskning Vid Landsarkivet I Göteborg. Göteborg, 1976.

Vagledande Forteckning Over Genealogiskt Kallmaterial I Landsarkivet I Lund Malmöhus Län. Lund, 1977.

LANDSKAP

LÄN

Sweden

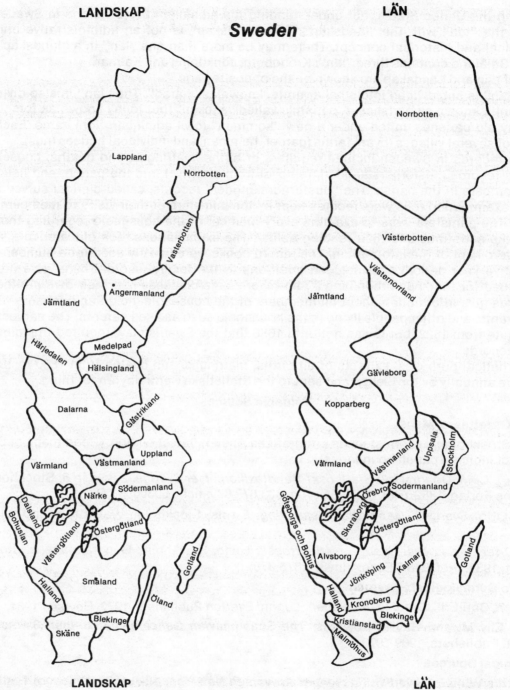

LANDSKAP

Blekinge	Närke
Bohuslän	Skåne
Dalarna	Småland
Dalsland	Södermanland
Gotland	Uppland
Gästrikland	Värmland
Halland	Västerbotten
Hälsingland	Västergötland
Härjedalen	Västmanland
Jämtland	Ångermanland
Lappland	Öland
Medelpad	Östergötland
Norrbotten	

LÄN

Blekinge	Norrbotten
Gotland	Skaraborg
Gävleborg	Stockholm
Göteborgs och Bohus	Södermanland
Halland	Uppsala
Jämtland	Värmland
Jönköping	Västerbotten
Kalmar	Vasternorrland
Kopparberg	Västmanland
Kristianstad	Älvsborg
Kronoberg	Örebro
Malmöhus	Östergötland

SWITZERLAND

Capital, Bern

Switzerland, anciently known as Helvetia, covers an area about half as large as South Carolina and into that little space is crowded a population twice that of South Carolina plus half a million. Switzerland is surrounded by France, Germany, Austria, and Italy, Languages represented are German, French, Italian and Romansch.

Switzerland consists of twenty-two states or cantons which form the Swiss Republic. For admiinistrative purposes three cantons, Appenzell, Basel, and Unterwalden, have been divided into two districts each.

Among the available genealogical sources are the church or parish registers, the baptismal, the confirmation, the marriage, and the death books. The confirmation books contain the names and records of the fifteen year old boys and girls who have prepared themselves in special study groups under the direction of the minister prior to their participation for the first time in the Lord's Supper. Among the non-church records are the Burger Rodel (Citizen Roll) in which is recorded the name of each citizen, together with his parent's and grandparent's names, and the Zivilstand-samt (civilian position) containing about the same information.

Valuable Sources

Atlases, Gazetteers, Maps

Geographisches Lexikon der Schweiz. (Geographical Encyclopedia of Switzerland). 6 vols. Neuenburg (Newchâtel): Verlag von Gebrüder Attinger, 1910. (G.S. Ref. 949.4 E5g; Film 599,323).

Jacot, Arthur. *Schweizerisches Ortslexikon.* Lucerne, Switzerland: C. J. Bucher, 1969.

Maps can be ordered from: Eidgenössische Landestopographie, CH - 3084 Wabern-Bern, Switzerland or Kümmerly änd Frey, Kartographischer Verlag, CH - 3001 Bern. Switzerland. (Ask for price list).

Place Names

Historisch-Biographisches Lexikon der Schweiz. (Historical-Biographical Encyclopedia of Switzerland). 7 vols. plus supplement. (G.S. Ref. 030.494 H629a; Films 1,181,541 - 543). This encyclopedia also lists families, histories of towns and some coats of arm.

Guides to Genealogical Research

Familiennamenbuch der Schweiz, Les noms de famille suisses, I nomi di famiglia svizzeri. (Swiss family surname book). Zürich: Polygraphischer Verlag, 1940. 2 vols (G.S. Ref. 949,4D4f; film 441,670.)

Suess, Jared H. *Handy Guide to Swiss Genealogical Records.* Logan, Utah: Everton Publishers, 1979.

Histories

Bonjour, E., Offler, H.S., Potter, G. R. *A Short History of Switzerland.* London: Oxford University Press, 1970.

Genealogical Sources

Thousand of Swiss family lines have been searched by Julius Billeter, a Swiss genealogist. Information regarding these records is found in the following article: Suess, Jared H. "Beginning Swiss Research". *The Genealogical Helper,* May-June 1978 issue, pages 16-18, 117, 118. Logan: Everton Publishers.

Many parish registers have been microfilmed by the Genealogical Society. Check the Dictionary Card Catalog and the International Genealogical Library Catalog.

Cantons of Switzerland

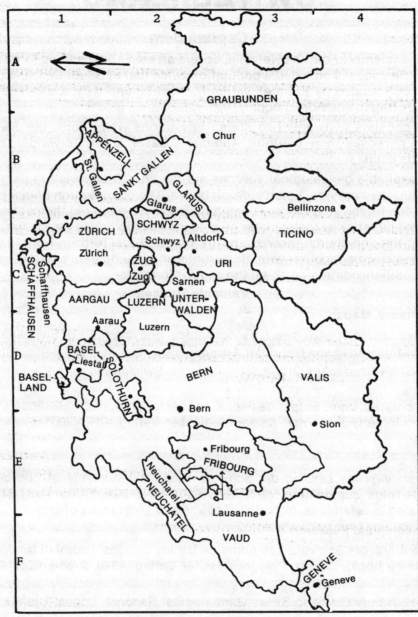

Cantons of Switzerland

Name	Capital	Map Index	Entry Date	Langage	Name	Capital	Map Index	Entry Date	Language
Aargau	Aarau	C1	1803	Ger.	Nidwalden	Stans	C2	1291	Ger.
Appenzell Inner Rhodes	Appenzell	B1	1513	Ger.	Obwalden	Sarnen	C2	1291	Ger.
Appenzell Outer Rhodes	Herisau	B1	1513	Ger.	Saint Gall	Saint Gall	B2	1803	Ger.
Basel-Land	Liestal	D1	1501	Ger.	Schaffhausen	Schaffhausen	C1	1501	Ger.
Basel-Stadt	Basel	D1	1501	Ger.	Schwyz	Schwyz	C2	1291	Ger.
Bern, Fr. Berne	Bern	D2	1353	Fr.; Ger.	Solothurn	Solothurn	D2	1481	Ger.
Fribourg, Ger. Freiburg	Fribourg	E2	1481	Fr.; Ger.	Thurgau	Frauenfeld	B1	1803	Ger.
Geneva, Fr. Geneve	Geneva	F3	1815	Fr.	Ticino	Bellinzona	C3	1803	Ital.
Glarus	Glarus	B2	1352	Ger.	Uri	Altdorf	C2	1291	Ger.
Graubunden, Fr. Grisons	Chur	B3	1803	Ger.; Rom.	Valais, Ger. Wallis	Sion	D4	1815	Fr.; Ger.
Lucerne, Ger. Luzern	Lucerne	D2	1332	Ger.	Vaud	Lausanne	F3	1803	Fr.
Neuchatel	Neuchatel	E2	1815	Fr.	Zug	Zug	C2	1352	Ger.
					Zurich, Ger. Zurich	Zurich	C1	1351	Ger.

WALES

For nearly five hundred years England and Wales have been one country. The Welsh government affairs have been conducted in London just as those of England. In everything else the two peoples are entirely different. The Welsh, or Cymry, have their own traditions, history, language, literature, and songs.

"English and Welsh records were compiled under the same conditions and laws," says David E. Gardner, a Utah student and teacher of genealogy. "This means that parish registers, probate court wills and administrations, and civil registering of vital statistics (since 1837), taxing, militia records, and overseeing of the poor and highways were practically the same."

Valuable Sources

Atlases, Gazetteers, Maps, Place Names

Davies, Elwyn. ed. *A Gazetteer of Welsh Place-Names.* Cardiff: University of Wales Press, 1967.

Davies, Margaret. *Wales in Maps.* Cardiff: University of Wales Press, 1958.

Hill, Ellen and Del Ora Guymon Cook. *A Gazetteer of Wales.* 5 vols. Salt Lake City: authors, 1953.

Rees, William. *An Historical Atlas of Wales From Early to Modern Times.* London: Faber and Faber, 1951, new edition 1972.

Guides To Genealogical Research (see England)

Evans, Evan. "The National Library of Wales and Its Genealogical Holdings" *Genealogical Journal,* March 1977, pages 43 to 45.

Genealogical Sources

Handlist of Manuscripts in the National Library of Wales. Aberystwyth: National Library of Wales, 1943-

Manuscripts of Genealogical Value in the National Library of Wales, Selected and Filmed by the Genealogical Society, 1950. Salt Lake City: Genealogical Society, 1968. (G.S. call no. Reg. 942.9 D2w)

Welsh Will Abstracting and Indexing Project. (The first set of indexes and abstracts is available on microfiche. Check the *Register of Microfiche Call Numbers)* Salt Lake City: Genealogical Society, 1978.

Bibliography

A Bibliography of the History of Wales, 2nd edition. Cardiff: University of Wales Press, 1962.

COUNTIES OF WALES

Name	Abbrev.	County Town
Anglesey	Ang.	Llangefini
Brecknockshire	Brec.	Brecknock or Brecon
Caernarvonshire (Carnarvon)	Caern.	Caernarvon
Cardiganshire	Card.	Aberystwyth
Carmarthenshire	Carm.	Carmarthen
Denbighshire	Denb.	Ruthin
Flintshire	Flint.	Mold
Glamorganshire	Glam.	Cardiff
Merionethshire	Meri.	Dolgelly
Montgomeryshire	Mont.	Welshpool
Pembrokeshire	Pemb.	Haverfordwest
Radnorshire	Rad.	Llandrindod Wells

A LIST OF GENEALOGICAL REFERENCE BOOKS

The following is a list of books that have been recommended by leading genealogists. All of the books are published by the **Genealogical Publishing Company,** 111 Water Street, Baltimore, Maryland 21202. Readers are encouraged to write the company for current prices or for catalogues of its publications.

GENERAL REFERENCE

Allan, Morton
MORTON ALLAN DIRECTORY OF EUROPEAN PASSENGER STEAMSHIP ARRIVALS, For the Years 1890 to 1930 at ... New York, and ... 1904 to 1926 at ... New York, Philadelphia, Boston and Baltimore. 268 pp. (1931). 1980.

American Council of Learned Societies
SURNAMES IN THE UNITED STATES CENSUS OF 1790. 339 pp. (1932). 1971.

Armstrong, Zella
NOTABLE SOUTHERN FAMILIES. 6 vols. in 3. 2,027 pp. (1918-1933). 1974.

Austin, John Osborne
ONE HUNDRED AND SIXTY ALLIED FAMILIES. xxi, 288 pp. (1893). 1977.

Baird, Charles W.
HISTORY OF THE HUGUENOT EMIGRATION TO AMERICA. 2 vols. in 1. 354 and 448 pp. (1885). 1973.

Banks, Charles Edward
THE ENGLISH ANCESTRY AND HOMES OF THE PILGRIM FATHERS Who Came to Plymouth ... in 1620 ... 1621 and ... 1623. 187 pp. (1929). 1980.

Banks, Charles Edward
TOPOGRAPHICAL DICTIONARY OF 2885 ENGLISH EMIGRANTS TO NEW ENGLAND, 1620-1650. xxxviii, 295 pp. (1937). 1981.

Banks, Charles Edward
THE WINTHROP FLEET OF 1630. An Account of the Vessels ... Passengers and Their English Homes. ix, 119 pp. (1930). 1980.

Bardsley, Charles Wareing
A DICTIONARY OF ENGLISH AND WELSH SURNAMES WITH SPECIAL AMERICAN INSTANCES. Rev. edn. xvi, 837 pp. (1901). 1980.

Bolton, Charles Knowles
MARRIAGE NOTICES, 1785-1794, for the Whole United States From the Massachusetts Centinel, and the Columbian Centinel. 139 pp. (1900). 1980.

Bolton, Charles Knowles
SCOTCH IRISH PIONEERS IN ULSTER AND AMERICA. 398 pp. (1910). 1981.

Bolton, Ethel Stanwood
IMMIGRANTS TO NEW ENGLAND, 1700-1775. 235 pp. (1931). 1979.

Bowman, George Ernest
THE MAYFLOWER READER. A Selection of Articles from The Mayflower Descendant. 537 pp. (1899-1905). 1978.

BURKE'S AMERICAN FAMILIES WITH BRITISH ANCESTRY. The Lineages of 1,600 Families ... Now Resident in the United States. 494, 48 pp. (1939). 1977.

Cameron, Viola Root
EMIGRANTS FROM SCOTLAND TO AMERICA, 1774-1775. 117 pp. (1930). 1980.

Clark, Murtie June
LOYALISTS IN THE SOUTHERN CAMPAIGN OF THE REVOLUTIONARY WAR. Official Rolls of Loyalists. 3 vols. Approx. 1,800 pp. 1981.

Clemens, William Montgomery
AMERICAN MARRIAGE RECORDS BEFORE 1699. Reprinted with a "Supplement" from Genealogy Mag. 259 pp. (1926, 1929-1930). 1979.

Crozier, William Armstrong.
A KEY TO SOUTHERN PEDIGREES. 80 pp. (1911). 1978.

Daughters of the American Revolution
INDEX OF THE ROLLS OF HONOR (ANCESTOR'S INDEX) IN THE LINEAGE BOOKS of the National Society of the Daughters of the American Revolution. 4 vols. in 2. 1,734 pp. (1916-1940). 1980.

Draper, Lyman C.
KING'S MOUNTAIN AND ITS HEROES: History of the Battle of King's Mountain, October 7th, 1780. 612 pp. (1881). 1978.

Eelking, Max von
THE GERMAN ALLIED TROOPS IN THE NORTH AMERICAN WAR OF INDEPENDENCE, 1776-1783. 360 pp. (1893). 1969.

Ellis, Eilish
EMIGRANTS FROM IRELAND, 1847-1852. State-Aided Emigration ... from Crown Estates. 68 pp. (1960). 1978.

Farmer, John
A GENEALOGICAL REGISTER OF THE FIRST SETTLERS OF NEW-ENGLAND [1620-1675]. 355 pp. (1829, 1847). 1979.

Faust, Albert B., and Gaius M. Brumbaugh
LISTS OF SWISS EMIGRANTS IN THE EIGHTEENTH CENTURY to the American Colonies. Reprinted with Leo Schelbert's "Notes on Swiss Immigrants." 2 vols. in 1. 122 and 255 pp. (1920, 1925, 1972). 1976.

Flagg, Ernest
GENEALOGICAL NOTES ON THE FOUNDING OF NEW ENGLAND. 440 pp. (1926). 1973.

Fontaine, Rev. James
MEMOIRS OF A HUGUENOT FAMILY. 512 pp. (1853). 1973.

Fothergill, Gerald
EMIGRANTS FROM ENGLAND, 1773-1776. 206 pp. (1913). 1976.

French, Elizabeth
LIST OF EMIGRANTS TO AMERICA FROM LIVERPOOL, 1697-1707. 55 pp. (1913). 1978.

Gannett, Henry
THE ORIGIN OF CERTAIN PLACE NAMES IN THE UNITED STATES. 2nd edn. 334 ppg. (1905). 1977.

Giuseppi, Montague Spencer
NATURALIZATIONS OF FOREIGN PROTESTANTS in the American and West Indian Colonies, etc. 196 pp. (1921). 1979.

Greenwood, Val D.
THE RESEARCHER'S GUIDE TO AMERICAN GENEALOGY. 535 pp. 1973.

Hanna, Charles A.
THE SCOTCH-IRISH or the Scot in North Britain, North Ireland, and North America. 2 vols. 623, 602 pp. (1902). 1968.

Hardy, Stella P.
COLONIAL FAMILIES OF THE SOUTHERN STATES OF AMERICA. 643 pp. (1958). 1981.

Genealogical Reference Books

Hargreaves-Mawdsley, R.
BRISTOL AND AMERICA ... the First Settlers in the Colonies of North America, 1654-1685. 182, xvi pp. (1929, 1931). 1978.

Heitman, Francis B.
HISTORICAL REGISTER OF OFFICERS OF THE CONTINENTAL ARMY DURING THE WAR OF THE REVOLUTION. Rev. edn. 698 pp. (1914, 1932). 1973.

Holmes, Frank R.
DIRECTORY OF THE ANCESTRAL HEADS OF NEW ENGLAND FAMILIES, 1620-1700. 274 pp. (1923). 1980.

Hotten, John Camden
THE ORIGINAL LISTS OF PERSONS OF QUALITY; Emigrants, Religious Exiles ... and Others Who Went From Great Britain to the American Plantations, 1600-1700. 580 pp. (1874). 1980.

Jacobus, Donald Lines
GENEALOGY AS PASTIME AND PROFESSION. 2nd edn. 120 pp. 1968.

Jacobus, Donald Lines
INDEX TO GENEALOGICAL PERIODICALS. 3 vols. in 1. 365 pp. in all. (1932, 1948, 1953). 1981.

Knittle, Walter Allen
EARLY EIGHTEENTH CENTURY PALATINE EMIGRATION. xxi, 320 pp. (1937). 1979.

Landis, John Tannehill
MAYFLOWER DESCENDANTS AND THEIR MARRIAGES FOR TWO GENERATIONS AFTER THE LANDING. 37 pp. (1922). 1981.

Lart, Charles Edmund
HUGUENOT PEDIGREES. 2 vols. in 1. xv, 113 and xii, 118 pp. (1924, 1928). 1973.

MacLean, John P.
AN HISTORICAL ACCOUNT OF THE SETTLEMENTS OF SCOTCH HIGHLANDERS IN AMERICA Prior to ... 1783. 455 pp. (1900). 1978.

Munsell's Sons, Joel
AMERICAN ANCESTRY: Giving the Name and Descent ... of Americans Whose Ancestors Settled in the U.S. Previous to ... 1776. 12 vols. 2,621 pp. (1887-1899). 1968.

Munsell's Sons, Joel
INDEX TO AMERICAN GENEALOGIES; And to ... Works Such as Town Histories, County Histories, etc. 5th edn. 2 vols. in 1. 352 and 107 pp. (1900, 1908). 1979.

New England Historic Genealogical Society
NEW ENGLAND HISTORICAL AND GENEALOGICAL REGISTER. (INDEXES: 1847-1896). 4 vols. 1,714 pp. (1906-1911). 1972.

O'Brien, Michael J.
IRISH SETTLERS IN AMERICA. A Consolidation of Articles from The Journal of the American Irish Historical Society. 2 vols. 664, 638 pp. 1979.

Pine, Leslie G.
AMERICAN ORIGINS. 357 pp. (1960). 1980.

Reaman, George Elmore
THE TRAIL OF THE HUGUENOTS IN EUROPE, THE UNITED STATES, SOUTH AFRICA AND CANADA. 318 pp. (1963). 1972.

Sabine, Lorenzo
BIOGRAPHICAL SKETCHES OF LOYALISTS OF THE AMERICAN REVOLUTION. 2 vols. 608, 600 pp. (1864). 1979.

Savage, James
A GENEALOGICAL DICTIONARY OF THE FIRST SETTLERS OF NEW ENGLAND. 4 vols. 2,541 pp. (1860-1862). 1981.

Schlegel, Donald M.
PASSENGERS FROM IRELAND. Lists of Passengers Arriving at American Ports Between 1811 and 1817. 158 pp. 1980.

Scott, Kenneth
BRITISH ALIENS IN THE UNITED STATES DURING THE WAR OF 1812. 420 pp. 1979.

Sherwood, George
AMERICAN COLONISTS IN ENGLISH RECORDS. 2 vols. in 1. 216 pp. (1932, 1933). 1978.

Stoddard, Francis R.
THE TRUTH ABOUT THE PILGRIMS. 206 pp. (1952). 1976.

Tepper, Michael
IMMIGRANTS TO THE MIDDLE COLONIES ... Ship Passenger Lists ... from The New York Genealogical and Biographical Record. 178 pp. (1879-1970). 1979.

Tepper, Michael
NEW WORLD IMMIGRANTS ... Ship Passenger Lists ... From Periodical Literature. 2 vols. 568, 602 pp. 1980.

Tepper, Michael
PASSENGERS TO AMERICA ... Ship Passenger Lists From The New England Historical And Genealogical Register. 554 pp. (1847-1961). 1980.

United States. Bureau of the Census
A CENTURY OF POPULATION GROWTH. From the First Census ... to the Twelfth, 1790-1900. 303 pp. (1909). 1970.

United States. House of Representatives
DIGESTED SUMMARY AND ALPHABETICAL LIST OF PRIVATE CLAIMS ... Presented to the House ... from the First to the Thirty-First Congress. 3 vols. (1853). 1970.

United States. Pension Bureau
LIST OF PENSIONERS ON THE ROLL, January 1, 1883. 5 vols. 3,952 pp. (1883). 1970.

United States. (War Department)
PIERCE'S REGISTER, Register of the Certificates Issued by John Pierce ... to Officers and Soldiers of the Continental Army. 566 pp. (1915). 1976.

Virkus, Frederick Adams
IMMIGRANT ANCESTORS. A List of 2,500 Immigrants ... Before 1750. 75 pp. (1942). 1980.

Waters, Henry F.
GENEALOGICAL GLEANINGS IN ENGLAND: Abstracts of Wills Relating to Early American Families. 2 vols. 1,760 pp. (1901, 1907). 1981.

Weis, Frederick Lewis
ANCESTRAL ROOTS OF SIXTY COLONISTS Who Came to New England Between 1623 and 1650. 5th edn. xxxvii, 186 pp. (1976). 1979.

Weis, Frederick Lewis, and Arthur Adams
THE MAGNA CHARTA SURETIES, 1215. The Barons Named in the Magna Charta, 1215, and Some of Their Descendants ... in America, 1607-1650. 3rd. edn. xiv, 125 pp. 1979.

ALABAMA

ALABAMA CENSUS RETURNS, 1820, And an Abstract of Federal Census of Alabama, 1830. 192 pp. (1944). 1980.

Alabama Society, DAR.
INDEX TO ALABAMA WILLS, 1808-1870. 180 pp. (1955). 1977.

Saunders, Col. James Edmonds
EARLY SETTLERS OF ALABAMA. 530, xxiv pp. (1899). 1969.

ARKANSAS

Shinn, Josiah H.
PIONEERS AND MAKERS OF ARKANSAS. 423 pp. (1908). 1967.

Genealogical Reference Books

CALIFORNIA

Bancroft, Hubert Howe
CALIFORNIA PIONEER REGISTER
AND INDEX, 1542-1848. 392 pp.
(1884-1890). 1964.

Bowman, Alan P.
INDEX TO THE 1850 CENSUS OF
THE STATE OF CALIFORNIA. xxi,
605 pp. 1972.

CONNECTICUT

Abbott, Susan W.
FAMILIES OF EARLY MILFORD,
CONNECTICUT. 875 pp. 1979.

Bailey, Frederic W.
EARLY CONNECTICUT MARRIAGES
... Prior to 1800. 7 books in 1. 994
pp. in all. (1896-1906). 1979.

Barbour, Lucius Barnes
FAMILIES OF EARLY HARTFORD,
CONNECTICUT. 736 pp. 1977.

Cothren, William
HISTORY OF ANCIENT WOODBURY,
CONNECTICUT. xi, 833, vii pp.
(1854). 1977.

Davis, Charles H. S.
EARLY FAMILIES OF WALLING-
FORD, CONNECTICUT. 363 pp.
(1870). 1979.

Goodwin, Nathaniel
GENEALOGICAL NOTES ... of Some
of The First Settlers of Connecticut
and Massachusetts. xx, 362 pp.
(1856). 1978.

Hinman, Royal R.
A CATALOGUE OF THE NAMES OF
THE FIRST PURITAN SETTLERS of
... Connecticut. 336 pp. (1846).
1968.

Jacobus, Donald Lines
ANCIENT FAMILIES OF NEW HAVEN.
9 vols. in 3. 2,067, 301 pp. (1922-
1932, 1939). 1981.

Jacobus, Donald Lines
HISTORY AND GENEALOGY OF THE
FAMILIES OF OLD FAIRFIELD. 2
vols. in 3. 2,051 pp. (1930-1932,
1943). 1976.

United States. Bureau of the Census
HEADS OF FAMILIES AT THE FIRST
CENSUS OF THE UNITED STATES
TAKEN IN THE YEAR 1790. CONNEC-
TICUT. 227 pp. (1908). 1980.

Wheeler, Richard A.
HISTORY OF THE TOWN OF STON-
INGTON, COUNTY OF NEW LON-
DON, CONNECTICUT. With a
Genealogical Register. 754 pp.
(1900). 1977.

DELAWARE

Colonial Dames of Delaware
A CALENDAR OF DELAWARE WILLS,
NEW CASTLE COUNTY, 1682-1800.
218 pp. (1911). 1977.

Maddux, Gerald, and Dorris O.
1800 CENSUS OF DELAWARE. 220
pp. (1964). 1976.

Olmsted, Virginia L.
INDEX TO THE 1850 CENSUS OF
DELAWARE. 370 pp. 1977.

GEORGIA

*Daughters of the American Revolu-
tion, Georgia. Joseph Habersham
Chapter*
HISTORICAL COLLECTIONS OF THE
JOSEPH HABERSHAM CHAPTER. 3
vols. 1,371 pp. (1902, 1910). 1967, 1968.

Georgia Historical Society
INDEX TO UNITED STATES CENSUS
OF GEORGIA FOR 1820. 2nd edn. 167
pp. 1969.

Knight, Lucian Lamar
GEORGIA'S ROSTER OF THE
REVOLUTION. 658 pp. (1920). 1967.

McCall, Mrs. Howard H.
ROSTER OF REVOLUTIONARY SOL-
DIERS IN GEORGIA. 3 vols. 972 pp.
1941-1969.

Register, Alvaretta K.
INDEX TO THE 1830 CENSUS OF
GEORGIA. 520 pp. 1974.

Smith, George Gillman
THE STORY OF GEORGIA AND THE
GEORGIA PEOPLE, 1732 to 1860. 2nd
edn. xx, 664 pp. (ca. 1901). 1968.

White, George
HISTORICAL COLLECTIONS OF
GEORGIA. 3rd edn. xvi, 688, 41, 58
pp. (1855, 1920). 1969.

ILLINOIS

Norton, Margaret Cross
ILLINOIS CENSUS RETURNS, 1810
[and] 1818. xxxii, 329 pp. (1935).
1969.

Norton, Margaret Cross
ILLINOIS CENSUS RETURNS, 1820.
466 pp. (1934). 1969.

INDIANA

Waters, Margaret R.
REVOLUTIONARY SOLDIERS BURIED
IN INDIANA. 2 vols. in 1. 42, 165 pp.
(1949, 1954). 1970.

KENTUCKY

Ardery, Mrs. William Breckenridge
KENTUCKY [COURT AND OTHER]
RECORDS. [Vol. I]. Early Wills and
Marriages, Old Bible Records and
Tombstone Inscriptions. 206 pp.
(1926). 1981.

Ardery, Mrs. William Breckenridge
KENTUCKY COURT AND OTHER
RECORDS. [Vol. II]. Wills, Deeds,
Orders, Suits, Church Minutes, Mar-
riages, Old Bibles and Tombstone In-
scriptions. 257 pp. (1932). 1979.

Clift, G. Glenn
KENTUCKY MARRIAGES, 1797-1865.
258 pp. (1938-1940). 1978.

Clift, G. Glenn
KENTUCKY OBITUARIES, 1787-1854.
254 pp. (1941-1943). 1979.

Clift, G. Glenn
"SECOND CENSUS" OF KENTUCKY,
1800. 333 pp. (1954). 1976.

Darnell, Ermina Jett
FORKS OF ELKHORN CHURCH, With
Genealogies of Early Members. xvii,
322 pp. (1946). 1980.

*Felldin, Jeanne Robey, and Gloria Kay
Vandiver Inman*
INDEX TO THE 1820 CENSUS OF
KENTUCKY. 318 pp. 1981.

Fowler, Ila Earle
KENTUCKY PIONEERS AND THEIR
DESCENDANTS. 460 pp. (ca. 1951).
1978.

GENEALOGIES OF KENTUCKY
FAMILIES From The Register of the
Kentucky Historical Society and The
Filson Club History Quarterly. 3 vols.
2,665 pp. 1981.

Heinemann, Charles Brunk
"FIRST CENSUS" OF KENTUCKY,
1790. 118 pp. (1940). 1981.

Jillson, Willard Rouse
THE KENTUCKY LAND GRANTS: A
Systematic Index to ... Land Grants
Recorded in the State Land Office ...
1782-1924. 1 vol. in 2. 1,844 pp.
(1925). 1971.

Jillson, Willard Rouse
OLD KENTUCKY ENTRIES AND
DEEDS. A Complete Index to ... the
Earliest Land Entries ... Deeds and
Wills of the Commonwealth. 571 pp.
(1926). 1978.

Kozee, William C.
EARLY FAMILIES OF EASTERN AND
SOUTHEASTERN KENTUCKY AND
THEIR DESCENDANTS. 886 pp.
(1961). 1979.

Genealogical Reference Books

Kozee, William C.
PIONEER FAMILIES OF EASTERN AND SOUTHEASTERN KENTUCKY. 272 pp. (1957). 1980.

McAdams, Mrs. Harry Kennett
KENTUCKY PIONEER AND COURT RECORDS. Abstracts of Early Wills, Deeds and Marriages. 381, [2] pp. (1929). 1981.

Wagstaff, Ann T.
INDEX TO THE 1810 CENSUS OF KENTUCKY. 230 pp. 1980.

LOUISIANA

Deiler, J. Hanno
THE SETTLEMENT OF THE GERMAN COAST OF LOUISIANA AND THE Creoles of German Descent. xvi, 154 pp. (1909). 1975.

Maduell, Charles R., Jr.
THE CENSUS TABLES FOR THE FRENCH COLONY OF LOUISIANA, From 1699 through 1732. 171 pp. 1972.

MAINE

THE MAINE HISTORICAL AND GENEALOGICAL RECORDER. 9 vols. in 3. 2,500 pp. (1884-1898). 1973.

Noyes, Sybil, Charles T. Libby and Walter G. Davis
GENEALOGICAL DICTIONARY OF MAINE AND NEW HAMPSHIRE. 5 parts in 1. 795 pp. (1928-1939). 1979.

Pope, Charles Henry
THE PIONEERS OF MAINE AND NEW HAMPSHIRE, 1623-1660. A Descriptive List, Drawn from . . . Contemporary Sources. 252 pp. (1908). 1973.

United States. Bureau of the Census
HEADS OF FAMILIES AT THE FIRST CENSUS OF THE UNITED STATES TAKEN IN THE YEAR 1790. MAINE. 105 pp. (1908). 1973.

MARYLAND

Barnes, Robert
MARYLAND MARRIAGES, 1634-1777. 233 pp. (1975). 1978.

Barnes, Robert
MARYLAND MARRIAGES, 1778-1880. 300 pp. 1979.

Brumbaugh, Gaius Marcus
MARYLAND RECORDS. Colonial, Revolutionary, County and Church. 2 vols. 513, 688 pp. (1915, 1928). 1975.

Magruder, James M., Jr.
INDEX OF MARYLAND COLONIAL WILLS, 1634-1777. 3 vols. in 1. 543 pp. (1933). 1975.

MARYLAND GENEALOGIES. A Consolidation of Articles from the Maryland Historical Magazine. 2 vols. 549, 548 pp. 1980.

Maryland Historical Society
MUSTER ROLLS AND OTHER RECORDS OF SERVICE OF MARYLAND TROOPS IN THE AMERICAN REVOLUTION, 1775-1783. 736 pp. (1900). 1972.

Nead, Daniel Wunderlich
THE PENNSYLVANIA-GERMAN in the Settlement of Maryland. 304 pp. (1914). 1980.

Newman, Harry Wright
MARYLAND REVOLUTIONARY RECORDS. Data Obtained from 3,050 Pension Claims and Bounty Land Applications. 155 pp. (1938). 1980.

Passano, Eleanor Phillips
AN INDEX TO THE SOURCE RECORDS OF MARYLAND: Genealogical, Biographical, Historical. 478 pp. (1940). 1974.

Scharf, John Thomas
HISTORY OF BALTIMORE CITY AND COUNTY. 1 volume bound in 2. 948 pp. (1881). 1971.

Skordas, Gust
THE EARLY SETTLERS OF MARYLAND. An Index of . . . Immigrants Compiled From . . . Land Patents, 1633-1680. 525 pp. (1968). 1979.

United States. Bureau of the Census
HEADS OF FAMILIES AT THE FIRST CENSUS OF THE UNITED STATES TAKEN IN THE YEAR 1790. MARYLAND. 189 pp. (1907). 1977.

Williams, Thomas J. C., and Folger McKinsey
HISTORY OF FREDERICK COUNTY, MARYLAND. 2 vols. 1,724 pp. (1910). 1979.

Wyand, Jeffrey A., and Florence L.
COLONIAL MARYLAND NATURALIZATIONS. 104 pp. 1975.

MASSACHUSETTS

Appleton, William S.
BOSTON BIRTHS, BAPTISMS, MARRIAGES, AND DEATHS, 1630-1699. [and] BOSTON BIRTHS, 1700-1800. 2 vols. in 1. 281 and 379 pp. (1883, 1894). 1978.

Bailey, Frederic W.
EARLY MASSACHUSETTS MARRIAGES PRIOR TO 1800. 3 vols in 1. [bound with] PLYMOUTH COUNTY MARRIAGES, 1692-1746. 661 pp. (1897, 1914). 1979.

Banks, Charles Edward
THE PLANTERS OF THE COMMONWEALTH . . . in Massachusetts, 1620-1640. xiii, 231 pp. (1930). 1979.

Bentley, Elizabeth Petty
INDEX TO THE 1800 CENSUS OF MASSACHUSETTS. 305 pp. 1978.

Bodge, George Madison
SOLDIERS IN KING PHILIP'S WAR. Official Lists of the Soldiers of Massachusetts Colony. 502 pp. (1906). 1976.

Davis, William T.
GENEALOGICAL REGISTER OF PLYMOUTH FAMILIES. 363 pp. (1899). 1977.

Hammatt, Abraham
THE HAMMATT PAPERS: Early Inhabitants of Ipswich, Massachusetts, 1633-1700. 448 pp. (1880-1899). 1980.

Hills, Leon Clark
HISTORY AND GENEALOGY OF THE MAYFLOWER PLANTERS. 2 vols. in 1. 177 and 284 pp. (1936, 1941). 1981.

McGlenen, Edward W.
BOSTON MARRIAGES FROM 1700 TO 1809. 2 vols. 468, 710 pp. (1898-1903). 1977.

Munroe, J. B.
A LIST OF ALIEN PASSENGERS, Bonded From January 1, 1847 to January 1, 1851 . . . in the Commonwealth. 99 pp. (1851). 1971.

PLYMOUTH CHURCH RECORDS, 1620-1859. 2 vols. lxii, 848 pp. (1920-1923). 1975.

Pope, Charles Henry
THE PIONEERS OF MASSACHUSETTS [1620-1650]. 550 pp. (1900). 1981.

Shurtleff, Nathaniel B.
RECORDS OF PLYMOUTH COLONY: Births, Marriages, Deaths, Burials, and Other Records, 1633-1689. 293 pp. (1857, 1911, 1913). 1979.

United States. Bureau of the Census
HEADS OF FAMILIES AT THE FIRST CENSUS OF THE UNITED STATES TAKEN IN THE YEAR 1790. MASSACHUSETTS. 363 pp. (1908). 1973.

Genealogical Reference Books

MICHIGAN

Flagg, Charles Alcott
AN INDEX OF PIONEERS FROM MASSACHUSETTS TO THE WEST, Especially ... Michigan. 86 pp. (1915). 1980.

MISSISSIPPI

McBee, May Wilson
THE NATCHEZ COURT RECORDS, 1767-1805. 635 pp. (1953). 1979.

MISSOURI

Bryan, William S., and Robert Rose
A HISTORY OF THE PIONEER FAMILIES OF MISSOURI. xvii, 569 pp. (1876, 1935). 1977.

NEW HAMPSHIRE

Potter, Chandler E.
THE MILITARY HISTORY OF THE STATE OF NEW HAMPSHIRE. From ... 1623 to ... 1861. 2 parts in 1. 879 pp. in all. (1866, 1868). 1972.

United States. Bureau of the Census
HEADS OF FAMILIES AT THE FIRST CENSUS OF THE UNITED STATES TAKEN IN THE YEAR 1790. NEW HAMPSHIRE. 146 pp. (1907). 1973.

NEW JERSEY

Chambers, Theodore Frelinghuysen
THE EARLY GERMANS OF NEW JERSEY: Their History, Churches and Genealogies. 667 pp. (1895). 1969.

Hinshaw, William Wade
ENCYCLOPEDIA OF AMERICAN QUAKER GENEALOGY. Vol. II (New Jersey and Pennsylvania Monthly Meetings.) 1,126 pp. (1938). 1969.

Littell, John
FAMILY RECORDS, OR GENEALOGIES OF THE FIRST SETTLERS OF PASSAIC VALLEY (AND VICINITY). 512 pp. (1852). 1981.

Nelson, William
NEW JERSEY BIOGRAPHICAL AND GENEALOGICAL NOTES. 222 pp. (1916). 1973.

Nelson, William
NEW JERSEY MARRIAGE RECORDS 1665-1800. cxxvi, 678 pp. (1900). 1973.

Nelson, William
PATENTS AND DEEDS AND OTHER EARLY RECORDS OF NEW JERSEY, 1664-1703. xii, 770 pp. (1899). 1976.

New Jersey. Department of State
INDEX OF WILLS, INVENTORIES ... Prior to 1901. 3 vols. 1,452 pp. (1912-1913). 1969.

Shourds, Thomas
HISTORY AND GENEALOGY OF FENWICK'S COLONY. 581 pp. (1876). 1976.

Stewart, Frank H.
NOTES ON OLD GLOUCESTER COUNTY, NEW JERSEY. 4 vols. in 2. 662, 947 pp. (1917-1964). 1977.

Stillwell, John Edwin
HISTORICAL AND GENEALOGICAL MISCELLANY. Vols. I and II: Data Relating to ... New York and New Jersey; Vols. III-V: Early Settlers of New Jersey. 5 vols. 2,582 pp. (1903-1932). 1970.

NEW YORK

Fernow, Berthold
[NEW YORK] CALENDAR OF WILLS ... 1626-1836. xv, 657 pp. (1896). 1967.

Fernow, Berthold
THE RECORDS OF NEW AMSTERDAM From 1653 to 1674. 7 vols. 2,743 pp. (1897). 1976.

Hinshaw, William Wade
ENCYCLOPEDIA OF AMERICAN QUAKER GENEALOGY. Vol. III: (New York Monthly Meetings). 540 pp. (1940). 1969.

Hoes, Roswell Randall
BAPTISMAL AND MARRIAGE REGISTERS OF THE OLD DUTCH CHURCH OF KINGSTON ... 1660-1809. 797 pp. (1891). 1980.

Holland Society of New York
RECORDS OF THE REFORMED DUTCH CHURCH OF ALBANY, NEW YORK, 1683-1809. 922 pp. (1904-1927). 1978.

MacWethy, Lou D.
THE BOOK OF NAMES. Especially Relating to the Early Palatines and the First Settlers in the Mohawk Valley. 209 pp. (1933). 1981.

New York (Colony)
NEW YORK MARRIAGES PREVIOUS TO 1784. 618 pp. (1860, 1898, 1915-1916, 1967). 1968.

O'Callaghan, Edmund B.
LISTS OF INHABITANTS OF COLONIAL NEW YORK. 351 pp. (1849-1851). 1979.

Pearson, Jonathan
CONTRIBUTIONS FOR THE GENEALOGIES OF THE FIRST SETTLERS OF THE ANCIENT COUNTY OF ALBANY, FROM 1630 TO 1800. 182 pp. (1872). 1978.

Scott, Kenneth
EARLY NEW YORK NATURALIZATIONS. Abstracts of Naturalization Records ... 1792-1840. 452 pp. 1981.

Scott, Kenneth, and Rosanne Conway
NEW YORK ALIEN RESIDENTS, 1825-1848. 122 pp. 1978.

Talcott, Sebastian V.
GENEALOGICAL NOTES OF NEW YORK AND NEW ENGLAND FAMILIES. 747, xxxix pp. (1883). 1973.

United States. Bureau of the Census
HEADS OF FAMILIES AT THE FIRST CENSUS OF THE UNITED STATES TAKEN IN THE YEAR 1790. NEW YORK. 308 pp. (1908). 1976.

NORTH CAROLINA

Bentley, Elizabeth P.
INDEX TO THE 1800 CENSUS OF NORTH CAROLINA. 270 pp. 1977.

Bentley, Elizabeth P.
INDEX TO THE 1810 CENSUS OF NORTH CAROLINA. 282 pp. 1978.

DeMond, Robert O.
THE LOYALISTS IN NORTH CAROLINA DURING THE REVOLUTION. 286 pp. (1940). 1979.

Grimes, J. Bryan
ABSTRACT OF NORTH CAROLINA WILLS. 670 pp. (1910). 1980.

Hathaway, James Robert Bent
NORTH CAROLINA HISTORICAL AND GENEALOGICAL REGISTER. Vol. I, no. 1- Vol. III, no. 3. 1,760 pp. (1900-1903). 1979.

Hinshaw, William Wade
ENCYCLOPEDIA OF AMERICAN QUAKER GENEALOGY. Vol. I: (North Carolina Yearly Meeting.) 1,185 and 12 pp. (1936, 1948). 1978.

McBee, May Wilson
ANSON COUNTY, NORTH CAROLINA: ABSTRACTS OF EARLY RECORDS. 180 pp. (1950). 1980.

North Carolina. Adjutant-General's Office
MUSTER ROLLS OF THE SOLDIERS OF THE WAR OF 1812 Detached from the Militia of North Carolina. 193 pp. (1851). 1980.

Genealogical Reference Books

North Carolina, Daughters of the American Revolution
ROSTER OF SOLDIERS FROM NORTH CAROLINA IN THE AMERICAN REVOLUTION. 709 pp. (1932). 1977.

Olds, Fred A.
AN ABSTRACT OF NORTH CAROLINA WILLS From About 1760 to About 1800. 330 pp. (1925). 1978.

Potter, Dorothy Williams
INDEX TO 1820 NORTH CAROLINA CENSUS. 509 pp. (1974). 1978.

Register, Alvaretta K.
STATE CENSUS OF NORTH CAROLINA, 1784-1787. 233 pp. (1971). 1978.

United States. Bureau of the Census
HEADS OF FAMILIES AT THE FIRST CENSUS OF THE UNITED STATES TAKEN IN THE YEAR 1790. NORTH CAROLINA. 292 pp. (1908). 1978.

OHIO

Dyer, Albion Morris
FIRST OWNERSHIP OF OHIO LANDS. 85 pp. (1911). 1978.

Hanna, Charles A.
HISTORICAL COLLECTIONS OF HARRISON COUNTY ... Ohio. 636 pp. (1900). 1975.

Hinshaw, William Wade
ENCYCLOPEDIA OF AMERICAN QUAKER GENEALOGY. Vol. IV: (Ohio). 1,424 pp. (1946). 1973.

Hinshaw, William Wade
ENCYCLOPEDIA OF AMERICAN QUAKER GENEALOGY. Vol. V: (Ohio). 1,060 pp. (1946). 1973.

Smith, Marjorie
OHIO MARRIAGES Extracted from The Old Northwest Genealogical Quarterly. 350 pp. (1977). 1980.

PENNSYLVANIA

Dunaway, Wayland F.
THE SCOTCH-IRISH OF COLONIAL PENNSYLVANIA. 273 pp. (1944). 1981.

Egle, William Henry
EARLY PENNSYLVANIA LAND RECORDS. Minutes of the Board of Property of ... Pennsylvania. 787 pp. (1893). 1976.

Egle, William Henry
NOTES AND QUERIES, Historical ... and Genealogical Relating Chiefly to Interior Pennsylvania. 12 vols. 4,546 pp. (1893-1901). 1970.

Egle, William Henry
PENNSYLVANIA GENEALOGIES, Chiefly Scotch-Irish and German. 798 pp. (1896). 1969.

Eshleman, H. Frank
HISTORIC BACKGROUND AND ANNALS OF THE SWISS AND GERMAN PIONEER SETTLERS of South-Eastern Pennsylvania. 386 pp. (1917). 1969.

Fulton, Eleanore J., and Barbara K. Mylin
AN INDEX TO THE WILL BOOKS AND INTESTATE RECORDS OF LANCASTER COUNTY, PENNSYLVANIA, 1729-1850. 136 pp. (1936). 1981.

GENEALOGIES OF PENNSYLVANIA FAMILIES From The Pennsylvania Magazine of History and Biography. xviii, 949 pp. 1981.

Hinshaw, William Wade
ENCYCLOPEDIA OF AMERICAN QUAKER GENEALOGY. Vol. II (New Jersey and Pennsylvania Monthly Meetings.) 1,126 pp. (1938). 1969.

Hocker, Edward W.
GENEALOGICAL DATA RELATING TO THE GERMAN SETTLERS OF PENNSYLVANIA ... From Advertisements in German Newspapers ... 1743-1800. 242 pp. 1981.

Jordan, John W.
COLONIAL AND REVOLUTIONARY FAMILIES OF PENNSYLVANIA. 3 vols. 1,706 pp. (1911). 1978.

Linn, John B. and William H. Egle
PENNSYLVANIA MARRIAGES PRIOR TO 1790 ... Marriage Licenses ... Issued in the Province ... Previous to 1790. 376 pp. (1890, 1908, 1915, 1960). 1979.

Linn, John B. and William H. Egle
RECORD OF PENNSYLVANIA MARRIAGES PRIOR TO 1810. 2 vols. 790, 601 pp. (1880). 1968.

Richards, Henry Melchior Muhlenberg
THE PENNSYLVANIA-GERMAN IN THE REVOLUTIONARY WAR, 1775-1783. 542 pp. (1908). 1978.

Rupp, Israel Daniel
A COLLECTION OF UPWARDS OF THIRTY THOUSAND NAMES OF GERMAN, SWISS, DUTCH, FRENCH AND OTHER IMMIGRANTS IN PENNSYLVANIA FROM 1727 TO 1776. 2nd edn. With Index from 3rd edn. 583 pp. (1876, 1931). 1980.

Strassburger, Ralph Beaver
PENNSYLVANIA GERMAN PIONEERS. ... Original Lists of Arrivals in the Port of Philadelphia from 1727 to 1808. 2 vols. 776, 709 pp. (1934). 1980.

Tepper, Michael
EMIGRANTS TO PENNSYLVANIA, 1641-1819 ... Ship Passenger Lists From The Pennsylvania Magazine of History and Biography. 292 pp. (1877-1934). 1979.

United States. Bureau of the Census
HEADS OF FAMILIES AT THE FIRST CENSUS OF THE UNITED STATES TAKEN IN THE YEAR 1790. PENNSYLVANIA. 426 pp. (1908). 1977.

Yoder, Don
PENNSYLVANIA GERMAN IMMIGRANTS, 1709-1786. Lists ... from Yearbooks of the Pennsylvania German Folklore Society. 394 pp. 1980.

Yoder, Don
RHINELAND EMIGRANTS. Lists of German Settlers in Colonial America. xii, 170 pp. 1981.

RHODE ISLAND

Austin, John Osborne
GENEALOGICAL DICTIONARY OF RHODE ISLAND; Comprising Three Generations of Settlers Who Came Before 1690. 496 pp. (1887). 1978.

United States. Bureau of the Census
HEADS OF FAMILIES AT THE FIRST CENSUS OF THE UNITED STATES TAKEN IN THE YEAR 1790. RHODE ISLAND. 71 pp. (1908). 1977.

SOUTH CAROLINA

Charleston Free Library
INDEX TO WILLS OF CHARLESTON COUNTY, SOUTH CAROLINA, 1671-1868. 324 pp. (1950). 1974.

Ervin, Sara Sullivan
SOUTH CAROLINIANS IN THE REVOLUTION. With Service Records and Miscellaneous Data; Also Abstracts of Wills, Laurens County (Ninety-Six District) 1775-1855. xiii, 217 pp. (1949). 1981.

Holcomb, Brent H.
INDEX TO THE 1800 CENSUS OF SOUTH CAROLINA. 264 pp. 1980.

Holcomb, Brent H.
SOUTH CAROLINA MARRIAGES, 1688-1799. 349 pp. 1980.

Holcomb, Brent H.
SOUTH CAROLINA MARRIAGES, 1800-1820. 171 pp. 1981.

Revill, Janie
A COMPILATION OF THE ORIGINAL LISTS OF PROTESTANT IMMIGRANTS TO SOUTH CAROLINA, 1763-1773. 163 pp. (1939). 1981.

Genealogical Reference Books

United States. Bureau of the Census
HEADS OF FAMILIES AT THE FIRST CENSUS OF THE UNITED STATES TAKEN IN THE YEAR 1790. SOUTH CAROLINA. 150 pp. (1908). 1978.

TENNESSEE

Acklen, Jeannette Tillotson, et al.
TENNESSEE RECORDS. Bible Records and Marriage Bonds. 521 pp. (1933). 1980.

Acklen, Jeannette Tillotson, et al.
TENNESSEE RECORDS. Tombstone Inscriptions and Manuscripts, Historical and Biographical. 517 pp. (1933). 1976.

Allen, Penelope Johnson
TENNESSEE SOLDIERS IN THE REVOLUTION, A Roster of Soldiers Living ... in the Counties of Washington and Sullivan. 71 pp. (1935). 1977.

Bentley, Elizabeth Petty
INDEX TO THE 1820 CENSUS OF TENNESSEE. 287 pp. 1981.

Moore, Mrs. John Trotwood
RECORD OF COMMISSIONS OF OF-FICERS IN THE TENNESSEE MILITIA, 1796-1815. 273 pp. (1942-1950, 1956). 1977.

Ray, Worth Stickley
TENNESSEE COUSINS: A History of Tennessee People. 811 pp. (1950). 1980.

Whitley, Edythe Rucker
RED RIVER SETTLERS ... Settlers of Northern Montgomery, Robertson, and Sumner Counties. 189 pp. 1980.

Whitley, Edythe Rucker
TENNESSEE GENEALOGICAL RECORDS: Records of Early Settlers from State and County Archives. 393 pp. 1981.

TEXAS

Mullins, Marion D.
REPUBLIC OF TEXAS: Poll Lists for 1846. 189 pp. 1974.

VERMONT

United States. Bureau of the Census
HEADS OF FAMILIES AT THE FIRST CENSUS OF THE UNITED STATES TAKEN IN THE YEAR 1790. VER-MONT. 95 pp. (1907). 1975.

Vermont
SECOND CENSUS OF THE U.S. (1800). 233 pp. (1938). 1972.

VIRGINIA

Bentley, Elizabeth P.
INDEX TO THE 1810 CENSUS OF VIRGINIA. 366 pp. 1980.

Brock, Robert Alonzo
HUGUENOT EMIGRATION TO VIR-GINIA. xx, 255 pp. (1886). 1979.

Chalkley, Lyman
CHRONICLES OF THE SCOTCH-IRISH SETTLEMENT IN VIRGINIA: Extracted from ... Court Records of Augusta County, 1745-1800. 3 vols. 1,988 pp. (1912). 1980.

Crumrine, Boyd
VIRGINIA COURT RECORDS IN SOUTHWESTERN PENNSYLVANIA. Records of ... West Augusta and Ohio and Yohogania Counties, Virginia, 1775-1780. 542 pp. (1902-1905). 1981.

des Cognets, Louis, Jr.
ENGLISH DUPLICATES OF LOST VIRGINIA RECORDS. 380 pp. (1958). 1981.

du Bellet, Louise Pecquet
SOME PROMINENT VIRGINIA FAMILIES. 4 vols. in 2. 1,715 pp. (1907). 1976.

Eckenrode, Hamilton J.
LIST OF THE COLONIAL SOLDIERS OF VIRGINIA. 91 pp. (1917). 1980.

Felldin, Jeanne Robey
INDEX TO THE 1820 CENSUS OF VIRGINIA. 486 pp. (1976). 1981.

GENEALOGIES OF VIRGINIA FAMILIES From Tyler's Quarterly Historical and Genealogical Maga-zine. 4 vols. Approx. 3,600 pp. 1981.

GENEALOGIES OF VIRGINIA FAMILIES From The Virginia Maga-zine of History and Biography. 5 vols. 4,827 pp. 1981.

GENEALOGIES OF VIRGINIA FAMILIES From the William and Mary College Quarterly Historical Magazine. 5 vols. Approx. 4,700 pp. 1981.

Greer, George Cabell
EARLY VIRGINIA IMMIGRANTS, 1623-1666. 376 pp. (1912). 1978.

Gwathmey, John H.
HISTORICAL REGISTER OF VIRGIN-IANS IN THE REVOLUTION. 872 pp. (1938). 1979.

Gwathmey, John H.
TWELVE VIRGINIA COUNTIES Where the Western Migration Began. 469 pp. (1937). 1981.

Hayden, Horace Edwin
VIRGINIA GENEALOGIES. A Geneal-ogy of the Glassell Family of Scotland ... and Others, of Virginia and Maryland. xviii, 759 pp. (1891). 1979.

Hinshaw, William Wade
ENCYCLOPEDIA OF AMERICAN QUAKER GENEALOGY. Vol. VI: (Virginia). 1,049 pp. (1950). 1973.

Meade, Bishop William
OLD CHURCHES, MINISTERS AND FAMILIES OF VIRGINIA. [with] DIGESTED INDEX AND GENEA-LOGICAL GUIDE. 2 vols. 490, 496, 144 pp. (1857, 1910). 1978.

Nugent, Nell Marion
CAVALIERS AND PIONEERS: Ab-stracts of Virginia Land Patents and Grants, 1623-1666. Vol. I. xxxv, 767 pp. (1934). 1979.

Stewart, Robert Armistead
INDEX TO PRINTED VIRGINIA GENEALOGIES. 265 pp. (1930). 1970.

Summers, Lewis Preston
ANNALS OF SOUTHWEST VIRGINIA, 1769-1800. 1 volume bound in 2. 1,757 pp. (1929). 1970.

Torrence, Clayton
THE EDWARD PLEASANTS VALEN-TINE PAPERS. 4 vols. 2,768 pp. (1927). 1979.

Torrence, Clayton
VIRGINIA WILLS AND ADMINISTRA-TIONS, 1632-1800. x, 483 pp. (1930). 1981.

United States. Bureau of the Census
HEADS OF FAMILIES AT THE FIRST CENSUS OF THE UNITED STATES TAKEN IN THE YEAR 1790. VIRGINIA. Records of the State Enumerations: 1782 to 1785. 189 pp. (1908). 1979.

Watson, Walter A.
NOTES ON SOUTHSIDE VIRGINIA. 346 pp. (1925). 1977.

Wayland, John W.
VIRGINIA VALLEY RECORDS. Gene-alogical ... Materials of Rockingham County. 491 pp. (1930). 1978.

Withington, Lothrop
VIRGINIA GLEANINGS IN ENGLAND. Abstracts of 17th and 18th-Century English Wills and Administrations. 745 pp. (1903-1929). 1980.

WEST VIRGINIA

Butcher, Bernard L.
GENEALOGICAL AND PERSONAL HISTORY OF THE UPPER MONON-GAHELA VALLEY, WEST VIRGINIA. 2 vols. Pp. 363-1,399. (1912). 1978.

Genealogical Reference Books

Johnston, Ross B.
WEST VIRGINIA ESTATE SETTLE-
MENTS: An Index to Wills . . . and
Surveys to 1850. 176 pp. (1955-
1963). 1978.

Johnston, Ross B.
WEST VIRGINIANS IN THE AMERI-
CAN REVOLUTION. 320 pp. (1939-
1947). 1977.

Lewis, Virgil A.
THE SOLDIERY OF WEST VIRGINIA
in the French and Indian War . . . to
. . . the Civil War. 227 pp. (1911).
1978.

CANADA

**United Empire Loyalist Centennial
Committee, Toronto**
THE OLD UNITED EMPIRE LOYAL-
ISTS LIST. 334 pp. (1885). 1976.

BRITAIN

Burke, Arthur Meredyth
KEY TO THE ANCIENT PARISH
REGISTERS OF ENGLAND AND
WALES. 163 pp. (1908). 1981.

Burke, Sir Bernard
A GENEALOGICAL HISTORY OF THE
DORMANT, ABEYANT, FORFEITED,
AND EXTINCT PEERAGES OF THE
BRITISH EMPIRE. 642 pp. (1883).
1978.

Burke, John
A GENEALOGICAL AND HERALDIC
HISTORY OF THE COMMONERS OF
GREAT BRITAIN AND IRELAND. 4
vols. 3,113 pp. (1834-1838, 1907).
1977.

Burke, John, and John Bernard Burke
A GENEALOGICAL AND HERALDIC
HISTORY OF THE EXTINCT AND
DORMANT BARONETCIES OF ENG-
LAND, IRELAND, AND SCOTLAND.
2nd edn. 644 pp. (1841). 1977.

Fairbairn, James
FAIRBAIRN'S BOOK OF CRESTS OF
THE FAMILIES OF GREAT BRITAIN
AND IRELAND. 2 vols. in 1. 773 and
314 pp. (1905). 1968.

Hamilton-Edwards, Gerald
IN SEARCH OF BRITISH ANCESTRY.
293 pp. 1974.

Pine, L. G.
THE NEW EXTINCT PEERAGE,
1884-1971. Containing Extinct,
Abeyant, Dormant & Suspended
Peerages. 313 pp. 1973.

Turton, Lt.-Col. W. H.
THE PLANTAGENET ANCESTRY . . .
Tables Showing Over 7,000 of the
Ancestors of Elizabeth. 274 pp.
(1928). 1975.

ENGLAND

Camp, Anthony B.
EVERYONE HAS ROOTS. An Introduction to English Genealogy. 189 pp.
1978.

Ellis, Henry
A GENERAL INTRODUCTION TO
DOMESDAY BOOK. 2 vols. 515, 545
pp. (1833). 1973.

Gibson, J. S. W.
WILLS AND WHERE TO FIND THEM
(in England). 210 pp. 1974.

Loyd, Lewis C.
THE ORIGINS OF SOME ANGLO-
NORMAN FAMILIES. xvi, 140 pp.
(1951). 1980.

Marshall, George W.
THE GENEALOGIST'S GUIDE. 4th
edn. xiii, 880 pp. (1903). 1980.

Shaw, William A.
THE KNIGHTS OF ENGLAND. A Complete Record . . . of the Knights of All
of the Orders of Chivalry in England,
Scotland and Ireland. 2 vols. 479, 420,
253 pp. (1906). 1971.

Sims, Richard
AN INDEX TO THE PEDIGREES AND
ARMS CONTAINED IN THE
HERALDS' VISITATIONS AND OTHER
GENEALOGICAL MANUSCRIPTS IN
THE BRITISH MUSEUM. 330 pp.
(1849). 1970.

Smith, Frank
A GENEALOGICAL GAZETTEER OF
ENGLAND. An Alphabetical Dictionary of Places . . . in England. xv,
599 pp. (1968). 1977.

IRELAND

Falley, Margaret D.
IRISH AND SCOTCH-IRISH ANCES-
TRAL RESEARCH. 2 vols. 813, 354
pp. (1962). 1981.

O'Hart, John
IRISH PEDIGREES; OR, THE ORIGIN
AND STEM OF THE IRISH NATION. 2
vols. xxxii, 896 and xxiii, 948 pp.
(1892). 1976.

**Phillimore, William P. W., and Gertrude
Thrift**
INDEXES TO IRISH WILLS. 5 vols. in
1. 827 pp. (1909-1920). 1970.

SCOTLAND

Adam, Frank
THE CLANS, SEPTS AND REGI-
MENTS OF THE SCOTTISH HIGH-
LANDS. 8th edn. 624, 112 pp. (1970).
1977.

Hamilton-Edwards, Gerald
IN SEARCH OF SCOTTISH ANCES-
TRY. 252 pp. (1972). 1980.

Innes of Learney, Sir Thomas
SCOTS HERALDRY. A Practical Handbook. 2nd edn. 258, 46 pp. (1956).
1971.

Stuart, Margaret
SCOTTISH FAMILY HISTORY. A
Guide to Works of Reference on the
. . . Genealogy of Scottish Families.
386 pp. (1930). 1979.

HERALDRY

Burke, Sir John Bernard
THE GENERAL ARMORY OF ENG-
LAND, SCOTLAND, IRELAND, AND
WALES, Comprising a Registry of Armorial Bearings from the Earliest to
the Present Time. cxxx, 1,185 pp.
(1884). 1976.

Morant, Alfred
GENERAL ARMORY TWO. Additions
and Corrections to Burke's General
Armory, ed. Cecil Humphery-Smith.
230 pp. 1974.

Child, Heather
HERALDIC DESIGN, A Handbook for
Students. 180, 32 pp. (1966). 1976.

**Lynch-Robinson, Sir Christopher, and
Adrian**
INTELLIGIBLE HERALDRY. 205 pp.
(1948). 1967.

Rietstap, Johannes Baptiste
ARMORIAL GENERAL. 2nd edn. 2
vols. 1,149, 1,316 pp. (1950). 1972.

Zieber, Eugene
HERALDRY IN AMERICA. 427 pp.
(1909). 1977.

Accelerated Indexing Systems, Inc.®

INTERNATIONAL HEADQUARTERS
70 East South Temple, Mezzanine Floor, Bank of Utah Building
Salt Lake City, Utah 84111
(801) 531-0098

#1001 1980

NEW · COMPUTER SEARCHES≈MICROFICHE ·

MICROFICHE (ACCELERATED INDEXING SYSTEMS-COMPUTER DATA BASE) which comprise the COMPUTER SEARCHES 1, 2, 3, 4, 5, 6, 7, and 7a are now available on microfiche. The microfiche (about 3,500) contain a total of more than 38,000,000 names entries. Search 7a is a total national alphabetical listing of all the names in searches 5, 6, and 7. Each computer search is a national alphabetical listing of names giving the following general information. Last name, first name, middle name or initial if given, title such as Dr.=Doctor, JP= Justice of the peace, Minister, if given, county or territory, state page number in the census or other documents if available, age date in many of the 1790, 1800, and 1810 censuses or township if given or a listing of No Township given, and finally the date of the document such as 1790, 1800 1810, or 1774 Rhode Island, 1607 Virginia, 1803 State Census of Ohio, or odd years 1804, 1805, 1806 for tax lists entries. Your will find double entries for names when more than one source was used. Searches cover the following time period:

Search 1	1607 thru 1819	*Search 5	1850 thru 1900 Southern States,
Search 2	1820 thru 1829	*Search 6	1850 thru 1900 New England & Northern States
Search 3	1830 thru 1839	*Search 7	1850 thru 1906 Mid-Western & Western
Search 4	1840 thru 1849	*Search 7a	1850 thru 1906 combined searches 5, 6 and 7

*Unless otherwise noted these searches are Heads of Household and any other surnames found within that household. For general content please send for listing. Send a SASE, MICROFICHE DATA BASE, A.I.S., P.O. Box 2127, Salt Lake City, Utah, 84111

COST. $3,800.00 plus $120.00 for insurance and postage. Price is extended thru August 31, 1983, After September 1, 1983 the cost will be $7,800.00 plus $120.00 postage and insurance. Merchandise is delivered by special currier. Price in 1984 to be determind. Update for the 1984 edition for those who by in 1983 will be about $600.00

FSM CATALOG

FSM Catalog $15.00 ← This is a detailed computerized publication of all known Federal, State, Colonial, and Continental Census records, along with slave schedules, and Mortality schedules. This publication lists by county and state the available census records and mortality schedules and the film catalog numbers in the National Archives and cross referenced to the film number in the Genealogy Society of Utah and it's 400 affiliates. Also included in this publication are many references to lost census records which are found and available & notes on missing and never taken censuses. Totally unique!!!!!

NEW RELEASES

RESEARCH AIDS		BRITISH RESEARCH AIDS		CENSUS RECORDS		MORTALITY SCHEDULES	
400 Ency of US Counties 1.	$25	5000 English Ancestry		711 Alabama 1810	$18	279 Florida 1850 MS	$16
416 Ency of US Censuses 2.	$35	by David Bethell MA,RG	$50	738 Ala 1811-1819	$30	280 Florida 1860 MS	$18
401 So.Carolina Land Grants	$38	5001 English Steps in the		739 Ala 1821-1829	$35	281 Florida 1870 MS	$20
405 Military Men of NJ	$35	Dark by David Bethel MA,RG	$35	740 Ala 1831-1839	$35	282 Florida 1880 MS	$28
1775-1815				741 Arkansas 1820	$24	283 Georgia 1860 MS	$35
417 NJ Wills 1689-1890	$100	The EARLY MORMON SERIES		259 Arizona 1867	$24	256 Kentucky 1860 MS	$30
404 Kentucky Wills to 1851	$32	By David L. Grundvig		261 Arizona 1869	$24	060 Pennsylvania 1850 MS	$50
028 County Records of Ky by		875 Salt Lake Wards V.1 1854-61	$30	543 New Mexico 1870		061 Pennsylvania 1860 MS	$65
Mrs. Beverly Hathaway	$20	877 Parowan,Iron Co.Ut V.2 1854	$16	Every Name	$60	062 Tennessee 1860 MS	$30
391 South Carolina Waterways		876 Salt Lake,Ut Tax Lists 1854-		272 Washington State		064 Texas 1860 MS	$25
by Miriam Cropper	$20	1861-Computer printout	$22	1857-1861	$28	065 Texas 1870 MS	$32
036 Ohio Biographical and		878 Parowan,Iron Co.Ut 1854 Cen.	$16	735 Washington 1850	$30	354 Missouri 1860 MS	$32
Portrait Index Vol.1	$35	888 Salt Lake City Census 1852	$20	727 Missouri 1820 Cen.	$22	889 Nevada 1860 MS	$15*
646 US Ency.Family Assoc.&		710 Utah 1857 Census	$45	734 Minnesota 1840 Cen	$16	890 Washington 1850 MS	$15*
manuscripts & publicat.	$40	The EARLY AMERICAN SERIES		732 Montana 1860 Cen.	$16	*These are small	
410 A Guide to Vital Stastics		883 North Carolina Vol. 6	$30	733 No.Dakota 1885 V.1	$18	Many more mortality schedules	
of the United States and		884 North Carolina Vol. 7	$35	731 Pambina,Dakota 1850	$18	are under preparation	
Where to write	$4	882 Early Maryland Vol. 2	$35	886 Mississippi 1810	$25		

ACCELERATED INDEXING SYSTEMS, INC.

The genealogies of the individuals listed below have been compiled because of either their importance in American History or their contributions to their profession.
We make no claim of having an exclusive claim to their genealogy and may differ in some circumstances with other published lineages.
Pricing is done with both the cost of materials and the amount of information. Many of the subjects have very limited ancestry. Understand that there are limits. We invited new information for the benefit of all.

PRESIDENTS OF THE U.S. AND THEIR WIFE	ORDER #	PRICE
JOHN JAY & SARAH LIVINGSTON		$25.00
GEORGE WASHINGTON & MARTHA DANDRIDGE	587	25.00
JOHN ADAMS & ABIGAIL SMITH	588	25.00
THOMAS JEFFERSON & MARTHA WAYLES	589	25.00
JAMES MADISON & DOLLEY PAYNE	590	20.00
JAMES MONROE & ELIZABETH KORTRIGHT	591	20.00
JOHN Q. ADAMS & LOUISA JOHNSON	592	25.00
ANDREW JACKSON & RACHEL DONELSON 2ND ED	593	25.00
MARTIN VAN BUREN & HANNAH HOES	594	20.00
WILLIAM H. HARRISON & ANNE SYMMES	595	20.00
JOHN TYLER & LETETINA CHRISTIAN	596	20.00
ZACHARY TAYLOR & MARGARET SMITH	598	20.00
MILLARD FILLMORE & ABIGAIL POWERS	599	20.00
FRANKLIN PIERCE & JANE APPLETON	600	20.00
JAMES BUCHANAN ------	601	20.00
ABRAHAM LINCOLN & MARY TODD	602	30.00
ANDREW JOHNSON AND ELIZA McCARDLE	603	20.00
ULYSSES GRANT & JULIA BOGGS	604	35.00
RUTHERFORD HAYES & LUCY WEBB	605	20.00
JAMES GARFIELD & LUCRETIA RUDOLPH	606	20.00
CHESTER ARTHUR & ELLEN HERNDON	607	20.00
GROVER CLEVELAND & FRANCES FOLSOM	608	30.00
BENJAMIN HARRISON & CAROLINE SCOTT	609	20.00
WILLIAM MCKINLEY & IDA SAXTON	610	20.00
THEODORE ROOSEVELT & ALICE LEE	611	35.00
JAMES POLK & SARAH CHILDRESS	597	20.00
WILLIAM TAFT & HELEN HERRON	612	20.00
WOODROW WILSON & ELLEN AXON	613	20.00
WOODROW WILSON & EDITH BOLLING	840	25.00
WARREN HARDING & FLORENCE KLING	614	20.00
CALVIN COOLIDGE & GRACE GOODHUE	615	50.00

HERBERT HOOVER & LOU HENRY	616	40.00
FRANKLIN ROOSEVELT & ELEANOR ROOSEVELT	617	60.00
HARRY TRUMAN & ELIZABETH WALLACE	618	20.00
DWIGHT EISENHOWER & MARY DOUD	619	20.00
RICHARD NIXON & THELMA RYAN	622	30.00
JOHN KENNEDY & JACQUELINE BOUVIER	620	20.00
LYNDON JOHNSON & CLAUDIA TAYLOR	621	20.00
JAMES CARTER & ROSALYNN SMITH	624	30.00
RONALD REAGAN & NANCY DAVIS	625	20.00

UNITED STATES VICE PRESIDENTS

AARON BURR & THEODOSIA BARTOW	841	25.00
GEORGE CLINTON & CORNELIA TAPPEN	842	20.00#
ELBRIDGE GERRY & ANN THOMPSON	843	20.00#
DANIEL D. TOMPKINS & HANNAH MINTHORN	844	20.00#
JOHN CALHOUN & FLORIDE CALHOUN	845	20.00
RICHARD MENTOR JOHNSON	846	20.00#
GEORGE DALLAS & SOPHIA NICKLIN	847	20.00#
WILLIAM RUFUS KING	848	20.00
JOHN C. BRECKINRIDGE & MARY BURCH	849	20.00#
HANNIBAL HAMLIN & SARAH EMERY	850	25.00
SCHUYLER COLFAX & EVELYN CLARK	851	20.00
HENRY WILSON & HARRIET HOWE	852	20.00#
WILLIAM WHEELER & MARY KING	853	20.00
THOMAS HENDRICKS & ELIZA MORGAN	854	20.00#
LEVI MORTON & LUCY KIMBALL	855	25.00
LEVI MORTON & ANNA STREET	856	20.00
ADLAI STEVENSON & LETITIA GREEN	857	20.00#
GARRET HOBART & ESTHER TUTTLE	858	20.00#
CHARLES FAIRBANKS & CORNELIA COLE	859	20.00#
JAMES SHERMAN & CARRIE BABCOCK	874	20.00#
THOMAS MARSHALL & LOIS KIMSEY	861	20.00#
CHARLES DAWES & CAROLINE BLYMER	862	30.00
CHARLES CURTIS & ANNE BAIRD	863	20.00#
JOHN GARNER & ELIZABETH RHEINER	864	20.00#
HENRY WALLACE & ILO BROWNE	865	20.00#
ALBEN BARKLEY & DOROTHY BROWER	866	20.00#
ALBEN BARKLEY & ELIZABETH RUCKER	867	20.00#
HUBERT HUMPHREY & MURIEL BUCK	868	20.00
SPIRO AGNEW & ELEANOR JUDEFIND	869	20.00#
NELSON ROCKEFELLER & MARGARETTA FITLER	870	35.00
WALTER MONDALE & JOAN ADAMS	871	20.00#
GEORGE BUSH & BARBARA PIERCE	872	20.00#
BETSEY ROSS BY POPULAR REQUEST	873	20.00#

#information is scarce

JOSEPH SMITH	553	$50.00
BRIGHAM YOUNG 2VLS.	554	250.00
JOHN TAYLOR	555	40.00
WILFORD WOODRUFF	556	50.00
LORENZO SNOW	557	50.00
JOSEPH F. SMITH	558	70.00
HEBER J. GRANT	559	100.00
GEORGE A. SMITH	560	70.00
DAVID O. McKAY	552	30.00
JOSEPH FIELDING SMITH	553	50.00
HAROLD B. LEE	550	50.00
SPENCER W. KIMBALL	549	50.00
SARAH ORNE JEWETT	875	35.00
ABBOTT LAWRENCE	876	30.00
ELISH CLARKE LEONARD	877	30.00
AMOS DEFOREST LOCKWOOD	878	30.00
HENRY W. LONGFELLOW	879	35.00
JAMES RUSSELL LOWELL	880	30.00
HORACE MANN	881	35.00
DONALD GRANT MITCHELL	882	30.00
MARIA MITCHELL	883	30.00
JOHN P. MORGAN	884	35.00
SAMUEL F.B. MORSE	885	30.00
JOHN L. MOTLEY	886	30.00
JOEL MUNSELL	887	30.00
JOHN G. PALFREY	888	30.00
THEODORE PARKER	889	30.00
FRANCIS PARKMAN	890	30.00
GEORGE PEABODY	891	30.00
ALICE PECKHAM	892	30.00
WENDELL PHILLIPS	893	30.00
EDGAR ALLAN POE	894	30.00
SARAH HELEN POWER	895	30.00
GEORGE D. PRENTICE	896	30.00
WILLIAM H. PRESCOTT	897	30.00
JOSIAH QUINCY	898	30.00
JAMES PIERCE ROOT	899	30.00
LEVERETT SALTONSTALL	901	30.00
NATHANIEL PARKER WILLIS	902	30.00
JOHN G. WHITTIER	903	30.00
HENRY WHEATON	904	30.00
NOAH WEBSTER	905	30.00
DANIEL WEBSTER	906	30.00
CHARLES DUDLEY WARNER	907	30.00
BENJAMIN SILLIMAN	908	30.00
CATHARINE MARIA SEDGWICK	909	30.00

BIBLIOGRAPHY - ACCELERATED INDEXING SYSTEMS, INC.
COMPLETED AND PROPOSED PROJECTS   DO NOT ORDER TBA PROJECTS !
SEND FOR CURRENT CATALOG FOR PRICES ! PRICES ARE SUBJECT TO CHANGE WITHOUT NOTICE !

#269 1820 Alabama State Census Index
Includes research aids. $22.00

#301 1830 Alabama Federal Census Index
Includes research aids. $26.00

#317 1840 Alabama Federal Census Index
Includes research aids. $39.00

#101 1850 Alabama Federal Census Index
Includes research aids. $54.00

#257 1855 Alabama State Census Index
Includes research aids.   TBA

#071 1860 Alabama Federal Census Index
Includes research aids.   TBA

#253 1870 Alabama Federal Census Index
Includes research aids.   TBA

#254 1880 Alabama Federal Census Index
Includes research aids.   TBA

#057 1850 Alabama Mortality Schedules
Vital records indexed.   TBA

#058 1860 Alabama Mortality Schedules
Vital records indexed.   TBA

#253 1870 Alabama Mortality Schedules
Vital records indexed.   TBA

#254 1880 Alabama Mortality Schedules
Vital records indexed.   TBA

#392 1870-1907 Alaska Census Records
Includes research aids.   TBA

1850 Arizona see New Mexico 1850
#092 1860 Arizona Federal Census Index
Includes research aids. $25.00

#190 1864 Arizona State Census Index
Includes research aids. $25.00

#258 1866 Arizona State Census Index
Includes research aids. $25.00

#259 1867 Arizona State Census Index
Includes research aids.   TBA

#261 1869 Arizona State Census Index
Includes research aids.   TBA

#091 1870 Arizona Federal Census Index
Includes research aids. $32.00

#473 1880 Arizona Federal Census Index
Includes research aids.

#501 1870 Arizona Mortality Schedules
Vital records indexed. $14.00

#502 1880 Arizona Mortality Schedules
Vital records indexed . $16.00

#049 1819-1829 Arkansas Tax Lists Index
Includes research aids. $25.00

#048 1823&1829 Arkansas Sheriff Censuses
Includes research aids. $25.00

#096 1830 Arkansas Federal Census Index
Includes research aids. $22.00

#498 1830-1839 Arkansas Tax Lists Index
Includes research aids. $38.00

#314 1840 Arkansas Federal Census Index
Includes research aids. $23.00

#102 1850 Arkansas Federal Census Index
Includes research aids. $31.00

#073 1860 Arkansas Federal Census Index
Includes research aids.   TBA

#074 1870 Arkansas Federal Census Index
Includes research aids.   TBA

#075 1880 Arkansas Federal Census Index
Includes research aids.   TBA

#450 1850 Arkansas Mortality Schedules
Vital records indexed. $16.00

#458 1860 Arkansas Mortality Schedules
Vital records indexed. $16.00

#462 1870 Arkansas Mortality Schedules
Vital records indexed. $16.00

#463 1880 Arkansas Mortality Schedules
Vital records indexed.   TBA

1790 California Census See Early
California Volume 1.
#708 1850 California Federal Census In-
dex.Includes research aids$35.00

#489 1836 California State Census Index
Los Angeles California
Includes research aids   TBA

#633 1844 California State Census Index
Los Angles California
Includes research aids.   TBA

#262 1852 California State Census Index
Includes research aids.   TBA

#076 1860 California Fed. Census Index
Includes research aids.   TBA

#077 1870 California Fed. Census Index
Includes research aids.   TBA

#078 1880 California Fed. Census Index
Includes research aids.   TBA

#634 1897 California State Census Index
Los Angeles California
Includes research aids.   TBA

#274 1850 California Mortality Sched.
Vital records indexed.   TBA

#275 1860 California Mortality Sched.
Vital records indexed.   TBA

#276 1870 California Mortality Sched
Vital records indexed.   TBA

#277 1880 California Mortality Sched.
Vital records indexed.   TBA

#184 1860 Colorado Federal Census Index
Includes research aids. $12.00

#041 1861 Colorado State Census Index
Includes research aids.   TBA

#331 1870 Colorado Federal Census Index
Includes research aids. $37.00

#466 1880 Colorado Federal Census Index
Includes research aids. $53.00

#266 1885 Colorado Federal Census Index
Includes research aids   TBA

#503 1870 Colorado Mortality Schedules
Vital records indexed. $13.00

#504 1880 Colorado Mortality Schedules
Vital records indexed. $16.00

#434 1885 Colorado Mortality Schedules
Vital records indexed   TBA

#025 1790 Connecticut Fed. Census Index
Includes research aids $27.00

#132 1800 Connecticut Fed. Census Index
Includes research aids $32.00

#321 1810 Connecticut Fed. Census Index
Includes research aids. $33.00

#201 1820 Connecticut Federal Census Index
Includes Research aids. $36.00

#332 1830 Connecticut Federal Census Index
Includes research aids. $41.00

#333 1840 Connecticut Federal Census Index
Includes research aids. $48.00

#334 1850 Connecticut Federal Census Index
Includes research aids. $64.00

#079 1860 Connecticut Federal Census Index
Includes research aids.   TBA

#080 1870 Connecticut Federal Census Index
Includes research aids   TBA

#081 1880 Connecticut Federal Census Index
Includes research aids.   TBA

#008 1850 Connecticut Mortality Schedules
Vital records indexed. $20.00

#009 1860 Connecticut Mortality Schedules
Vital records indexed. $22.00

#029 1870 Connecticut Mortality Schedules
Vital records indexed. $24.00

#278 1880 Connecticut Mortality Schedules
Vital records indexed.   TBA

#500 1860 Dakota Federal Census Index
Includes research aids. $21.00

#411 1870 Dakota Federal Census Index
Includes research aids. $23.00

#428 1880 Dakota Federal Census Index
Includes research aids. $56.00

#260 1665-1697 Delaware Census Index
Includes research aids. $21.00

#131 1800 Delaware Federal Census Index
Includes research aids. $21.00

#328 1810 Delaware Federal Census Index
Includes research aids. $21.00

#202 1820 Delaware Federal Census Index
Includes research aids. $22.00

#335 1830 Delaware Federal Census Index
Includes research aids. $25.00

#336 1840 Delaware Federal Census Index
Includes research aids. $27.00

#337 1850 Delaware Federal Census Index
Includes research aids. $33.00

#082 1860 Delaware Federal Census Index
Includes research aids.   TBA

#083 1870 Delaware Federal Census Index
Includes research aids.   TBA

#084 1880 Delaware Federal Census Index
Includes research aids.   TBA

#564 1850 Delaware Mortality Schedules
Vital records indexed. $12.00

#585 1860 Delaware Mortality Schedules
Vital records indexed. $14.00

#586 1870 Delaware Mortality Schedules
Vital records indexed. $16.00

#567 1880 Delaware Mortality Schedules
Vital records indexed. $18.00

BIBLIOGRAPHY - ACCELERATED INDEXING SYSTEMS, INC.
COMPLETED AND PROPOSED PROJECTS   DO NOT ORDER TBA PROJECTS !
SEND FOR CURRENT CATALOG FOR PRICES !   PRICES ARE SUBJECT TO CHANGE WITHOUT NOTICE !

#148 1800 D.C. Federal Census Index
Includes research aids. $13.00

#268 1810 D.C. Federal Census Index
Includes research aids. $15.00

#123 1820 D.C. Federal Census Index
Includes research aids. $17.00

#338 1830 D.C. Federal Census Index
Includes research aids $22.00

#339 1840 D.C. Federal Census Index
Includes research aids. $27.00

#337 1850 D.C. Federal Census Index
Includes research aids. $27.00

#526 1855 D.C. Federal Census Index
Includes research aids TBA

#562 1860 D.C. Federal Census Index
Includes research aids TBA

#527 1867 D.C. Federal Census Index
Includes research aids TBA

#563 1870 D.C. Federal Census Index
Includes research aids. TBA

#698 1880 D.C. Federal Census Index
Includes research aids TBA

#304 1830 Florida Federal Census Index
Includes research aids. $16.00

#303 1840 Florida Federal Census Index
Includes research aids. $18.00

#337 1850 Florida Federal Census Index
Includes research aids. $20.00

#088 1860 Florida Federal Census Index
Includes research aids. TBA

#089 1870 Florida Federal Census Index
Includes research aids TBA

#093 1880 Florida Federal Census Index
Includes research aids TBA

#638 1885 Florida Federal Census Index
Includes research aids TBA

#279 1850 Florida Mortality Schedules
Vital records indexed. TBA

#280 1860 Florida Mortality Schedules
Vital records indexed. TBA

#281 1870 Florida Mortality Schedules
Vital records indexed. TBA

#282 1880 Florida Mortality Schedules
Vital records indexed. TBA

#306 1820 Georgia Federal Census Ind.
Includes research aids. $30.00

#725 1821-1839 Georgia Census Records
Includes research aids TBA

#305 1830 Georgia Federal Census Ind.
Includes research aids $30.00

#341 1840 Georgia Federal Census Ind.
Includes research aids. $55.00

#639 1841-1849 Georgia Census Records
Includes research aids TBA

#103 1850 Georgia Federal Census Ind.
Includes research aids. $70.00

#641 1851-1859 Georgia Census Records
Includes research aids. TBA

#098 1860 Georgia Federal Census Index
Includes research aids. TBA

#099 1870 Georgia Federal Census Index
Includes research aids. TBA

#100 1880 Georgia Federal Census Index
Includes research aids. TBA

#451 1850 Georgia Mortality Schedules
Vital records indexed. $25.00

#039 1860 Georgia Mortality Schedules
Vital records indexed. TBA

#040 1870 Georgia Mortality Schedules
Vital records indexed. TBA

#282 1880 Georgia Mortality Schedules
Vital records indexed. TBA

1860 Idaho see Utah 1850
#412 1870 Idaho Federal Census Index
Includes researaids $24.00

#421 1880 Idaho Federal Census Index
Includes research aids. $30.00

1860 Idaho Mortality Schedules
See Utah 1850 Mort, Schedules
#506 1870 Idaho Mortality Schedules
Vital records indexed. $11.00

#465 1880 Idaho Mortality Schedules
Vital records indexed. $16.00

#203 1820 Illinois Federal Census Ind.
Includes research aids. $24.00

#642 1825 Illinois State Census Index
Includes research aids TBA

#419 1830 Illinois Federal Census Ind.
Includes research aids. $28.00

#643 1830 Illinois State Census Index
Includes research aids TBA

#646 1835 Illinois State Census Index
Includes research aids TBA

#342 1840 Illinois Federal Census Ind.
Includes research aids. $50.00

#645 1840 Illinois State Census Index
Includes research aids. TBA

#647 1845 Illinois State Census Index
Includes research aids. TBA

#343 1850 Illinois State Census Index
Includes research aids. TBA

#648 1855 Illinois State Census Index
Includes research aids. TBA

#106 1860 Illinois Federal Census Ind.
Includes research aids. TBA

#649 1865 Illinois State Census Index
Includes research aids. TBA

#111 1870 Illinois Federal Census Ind.
Includes research aids. TBA

#115 1880 Illinois Federal Census Ind.
Includes research aids TBA

#507 1850 Illinois Mortality Schedule
Vital records indexed. $25.00

#042 1860 Illinois Mortality Schedules
Vital records indexed. TBA

#043 1870 Illinois Mortality Schedules
Vital records indexed. TBA

#044 1880 Illinois Mortality Schedules
Vital records indexed. TBA

#319 1820 Indiana Federal Census Index
Includes research aids. $24.00

#318 1830 Indiana Federal Census Index
Includes research aids. $30.00

#344 1840 Indiana Federal Census Index
Includes research aids. $48.00

#343 1850 Indiana Federal Census Index
Includes research aids. $82.00

#140 1860 Indiana Federal Census Index
Includes research aids TBA

#141 1870 Indiana Federal Census Index
Includes research aids TBA

#142 1880 Indiana Federal Census Index
Includes research aids TBA

#452 1850 Indiana Mortality Schedules
Vital records indexed. $25.00

#045 1860 Indiana Mortality Schedules
Vital records indexed. TBA

#046 1870 Indiana Mortality Schedules
Vital Records indexed. TBA

#047 1880 Indiana Mortality Schedules
Vital Records indexed. TBA

#150 1836 Iowa State Census Index
Includes research aids. $16.00

#031 1838 Iowa State Census Index
Includes research aids. $20.00

#429 1840 Iowa Federal Census Index
Includes research aids $35.00

#426 1841-1849 Iowa Census Records V.1
Includes research aids. $25.00

#248 1841-1842 Iowa Census Records V.2
Includes research aids $25.00

#104 1850 Iowa Federal Census Index
Includes research aids. $35.00

$498 1851-1859 Iowa Census Records V.1
Includes research aids. $35.00

#143 1860 Iowa Federal Census Index
Includes research aids. TBA

#144 1870 Iowa Federal Census Index
Includes research aids. TBA

#147 1880 Iowa Federal Census Index
Includes research aids. TBA

#651 1885 Iowa Federal Census Index
Includes research aids TBA

#652 1895 Iowa Federal Census Index
Includes research aids TBA

#752 1905 Iowa State Census Record
Includes research aids TBA

#284 1850 Iowa Mortality Schedules
Vital records indexed. TBA

BIBLIOGRAPHY - ACCELERATED INDEXING SYSTEMS, INC.
COMPLETED AND PROPOSED PROJECTS   DO NOT ORDER TBA PROJECTS !
SEND FOR CURRENT CATALOG FOR PRICES ! PRICES ARE SUBJECT TO CHANGE WITHOUT NOTICE !

#285 1860 Iowa Mortality Schedules
Vital records indexed.   TBA

#286 1870 Iowa Mortality Schedules
Vital records indexed.   TBA

#287 1880 Iowa Mortality Schedules
Vital records indexed.   TBA

#653 1850-1859 Kansas Census Records
Includes research aids. TBA

#315 1855 Kansas State Census Index
Includes research aids. $25.00

#094 1860 Kansas Federal Census Index
Includes research aids. $31.00

#654 1865 Kansas State Census Index
Includes research aids. TBA

#160 1870 Kansas Federal Census Index
Includes research aids. TBA

#655 1875 Kansas State Census Index
Includes research aids. TBA

#161 1880 Kansas Federal Census Index
Includes research aids. TBA

#656 1885 Kansas Federal Census Index
Includes research aids. TBA

#657 1895 Kansas State Census Records
Includes research aids. TBA

#508 1860 Kansas Mortality Schedules
Vital records indexed. $16.00

#433 1870 Kansas Mortality Schedules
Vital records indexed. $16.00

#470 1880 Kansas Mortality Schedules
Vital records indexed. $22.00

#126 1810 Kentucky Federal Census Ind.
Includes research aids. $34.00

#308 1820 Kentucky Federal Census Ind
Includes research aids $38.00

#307 1830 Kentucky Federal Census Ind.
Includes research aids. $46.00

#346 1840 Kentucky Federal Census Ind.
Includes research aids $69.00

#105 1850 Kentucky Federal Census Ind.
Includes research aids. $72.00

#162 1860 Kentucky Federal Census Ind.
Includes research aids. TBA

#163 1870 Kentucky Federal Census Ind.
Includes research aids. TBA

#164 1880 Kentucky Federal Census Ind.
Includes Research aids. TBA

#453 1850 Kentucky Mortality Schedules
Vital records indexed. $22.00

#256 1860 Kentucky Mortality Schedules
Vital records indexed.   TBA

#288 1870 Kentucky Mortality Schedules
Vital records indexed.   TBA

#289 1880 Kentucky Mortality Schedules
Vital records indexed.   TBA

#127 1810 Louisiana Federal Census Ind.
Includes research aids. $20.00

#310 1820 Louisiana Federal Census Ind.
Includes research aids. $38.00

#309 1830 Louisiana Federal Census Ind.
Includes research aids. $46.00

#347 1840 Louisiana Federal Census Ind.
Includes research aids. $46.00

#479 1850 Louisiana Federal Census Ind.
Includes research aids. $46.00

#165 1860 Louisiana Federal Census Ind.
Includes research aids. TBA

#166 1870 Louisiana Federal Census Ind.
Includes research aids. TBA

#167 1880 Louisiana Federal Census Ind.
Includes research aids. TBA

#470 1850 Louisiana Mortality Schedules
Vital records indexed. $16.00

#049 1860 Louisiana Mortality Schedules
Vital records indexed.   TBA

#050 1870 Louisiana Mortality Schedules
Vital records indexed.   TBA

#051 1880 Louisiana Mortality Schedules
Vital records indexed.   TBA

#024 1790 Maine Federal Census Index
Includes research aids. $25.00

#133 1800 Maine Federal Census Index
Includes research aids. $27.00

#323 1810 Maine Federal Census Index
Includes research aids. $29.00

#322 1820 Maine Federal Census Index
Includes research aids. $33.00

#349 1830 Maine Federal Census Index
Includes research aids $48.00

#350 1840 Maine Federal Census Index
Includes research aids. $52.00

#351 1850 Maine Federal Census Index
Includes research aids. $65.00

#168 1860 Maine Federal Census Index
Includes research aids. TBA

#169 1870 Maine Federal Census Index
Includes research aids. TBA

#170 1880 Maine Federal Census Index
Includes research aids. TBA

#290 1850 Maine Mortality Schedules
Vital records indexed.   TBA

#291 1860 Maine Mortality Schedules
Vital records indexed.   TBA

#292 1870 Maine Mortality Schedules
Vital records indexed.   TBA

#293 1880 Maine Mortality Schedules
Vital records indexed.   TBA

#023 1790 Maryland Federal Census Index
Includes research aids. $21.00

146 1800 Maryland Federal Census Index
Includes research aids. $30.00

#101 1810 Maryland Federal Census Index
Includes research aids. $31.00

#131 1820 Maryland Federal Census Index
Includes research aids. $41.00

#349 1830 Maryland Federal Census Index
Includes research aids. $41.00

#362 1840 Maryland Federal Census Index
Includes research aids. $48.00

#363 1850 Maryland Federal Census Index
Includes research aids. $65.00

#171 1860 Maryland Federal Census Index
Includes research aids. TBA

#172 1870 Maryland Federal Census Index
Includes research aids. TBA

#173 1880 Maryland Federal Census Index
Includes research aids. TBA

#294 1850 Maryland Mortality Schedules
Vital records indexed.   TBA

#295 1860 Maryland Mortality Schedules
Vital records indexed.   TBA

#296 1870 Maryland Mortality Schedules
Vital records indexed.   TBA

#297 1880 Maryland Mortality Schedules
Vital records indexed.   TBA

#151 1790 Massachusetts Federal Census Index
Includes research aids. $30.00

#134 1800 Massachusetts Federal Census Index
Includes research aids. $45.00

#011 1810 Massachusetts Federal Census Index
Includes research aids $46.00

#014 1820 Massachusetts Federal Census Index
Includes research aids. $52.00

#129 1830 Massachusetts Federal Census Index
Includes research aids. $67.00

#355 1840 Massachusetts Federal Census Index
Includes research aids. $76.00

#356 1850 Massachusetts Federal Census Index
Includes research aids. $90.00

#660 1855 Massachusetts State Census Index
Includes research aids. TBA

#174 1860 Massachusetts Federal Census Index
Includes research aids. TBA

#661 1865 Massachusetts State Census Index
Includes research aids. TBA

#175 1870 Massachusetts Federal Census Index
Includes research aids. TBA

#176 1880 Massachusetts Federal Census Index
Includes research aids. TBA

#298 1850 Massachusetts Mortality Schedules
Vital records indexed.   TBA

#299 1860 Massachusetts Mortality Schedules
Vital Records indexed.   TBA

#300 1870 Massachusetts Mortality Schedules
Vital Records indexed.   TBA

#329 1880 Massachusetts Mortality Schedules
Vital records indexed.   TBA

#389 1799,1806,1827 Michigan Fed.Census Ind.
Includes research aids. $15.00

BIBLIOGRAPHY - ACCELERATED INDEXING SYSTEMS, INC.
COMPLETED AND PROPOSED PROJECTS   DO NOT ORDER TBA PROJECTS !
SEND FOR CURRENT CATALOG FOR PRICES !   PRICES ARE SUBJECT TO CHANGE WITHOUT NOTICE !

#871 1820 Michigan Federal Census Index
Includes research aids $20.00

#357 1830 Michigan Federal Census Index
Includes research aids $23.00

#662 1821-1839 Michigan Census Records
Includes research aids. TBA

#358 1840 Michigan Federal Census Index
Includes research aids. $33.00

#359 1850 Michigan Federal Census Index
Includes research aids. $68.00

#664 1851-1859 Michigan Census Records
Includes research aids TBA

#177 1860 Michigan Federal Census Index
Includes research aids TBA

#665 1861-1869 Michigan State Census
Includes research aids. TBA

#178 1870 Michigan Federal Census Index
Includes research aids. TBA

#666 1871-1879 Michigan State Census
Includes research aids. TBA

#179 1880 Michigan Federal Census Index
Includes research aids. TBA

#667 1884 Michigan Federal Census Index
Includes research aids. TBA

#668 1894 Michigan Federal Census Index
Includes research aids. TBA

#432 1850 Michigan Mortality Schedules
Vital records indexed. $16.00

#052 1860 Michigan Mortality Schedules
Vital records indexed.   TBA

#053 1870 Michigan Mortality Schedules
Vital records indexed.   TBA

#054 1880 Michigan Mortality Schedules
Vital records indexed.   TBA

#021 1849 Minnesota State Census Records
Includes research aids. $12.00

#112 1850 Minnesota Federal Census Ind.
Includes research aids. $40.00

#669 1857 Minnesota State Census Records
Includes research aids.   TBA

#471 1860 Minnesota Federal Census Ind.
Includes research aids. $57.00

#670 1865 Minnesota State Census Records
Includes research aids   TBA

#420 1870 Minnesota Federal Census Ind.
Includes research aids $78.00

#671 1875 Minnesota State Census Records
Includes research aids.   TBA

#180 1880 Minnesota Federal Census Ind.
Includes research aids.   TBA

#672 1885 Minnesota State Census Records
Includes research aids.   TBA

#673 1895 Minnesota State Census Records
Includes research aids.   TBA

#565 1850 Minnesota Mortality Schedules
Vital records indexed. $6.00

#437 1860 Minnesota Mortality Schedules
Vital records indexed. $16.00

#566 1870 Minnesota Mortality Schedules
Vital records indexed. $16.00

#463 1880 Minnesota Mortality Schedules
Vital records indexed. $16.00

#408 1820 Mississippi Federal Census Ind.
Includes research aids. $34.00

#311 1830 Mississippi Federal Census Ind.
Includes research aids. $27.00

#183 1840 Mississippi Federal Census Ind.
Includes research aids. $36.00

#360 1850 Mississippi Federal Census Ind.
Includes research aids. $58.00

#185 1860 Mississippi Federal Census Ind.
Includes research aids.   TBA

#186 1870 Mississippi Federal Census Ind.
Includes research aids.   TBA

#187 1880 Mississippi Federal Census Ind.
Includes research aids.   TBA

#454 1850 Mississippi Mortality Schedules
Vital records indexed. $16.00

#517 1860 Mississippi Mortality Schedules
Vital records indexed. $22.00

#056 1870 Mississippi Mortality Schedules
Vital records indexed. $24.00

#255 1880 Mississippi Mortality Schedules
Vital records indexed. $26.00

#316 1830 Missouri Federal Census Index
Includes research aids. $23.00

#407 1840 Missouri Federal Census Index
Includes research aids. $45.00

#361 1850 Missouri Federal Census Index
Includes research aids. $88.00

#185 1860 Missouri Federal Census Index
Includes research aids.   TBA

#186 1870 Missouri Federal Census Index
Includes research aids.   TBA

#674 1876 Missouri State Census Records
Includes research aids.   TBA

#187 1880 Missouri Federal Census Index
Includes research aids.   TBA

#348 1850 Missouri Mortality Schedules
Vital records indexed.   TBA

#354 1860 Missouri Mortality Schedules
Vital records indexed.   TBA

#387 1870 Missouri Mortality Schedules
Vital records indexed.   TBA

#393 1880 Missouri Mortality Schedules
Vital records indexed.   TBA

#413 1870 Montana Federal Census Index
Includes research aids. $25.00

#193 1880 Montana Federal Census Index
Includes research aids.   TBA

1850 Montana Mortality Schedules
See Oregon 1850
1860 Montana Mortality Schedules
See Oregon 1860

#006 1870 Montana Mortality Schedules
Vital records indexed. $10.00

#007 1880 Montana Mortality Schedules
Vital records indexed. $12.00

#709 1854,55,56 Nebraska State Census
Includes research aids. $32.00

#097 1860 Nebraska Federal Census Index
Includes research aids. $35.00

#144 1870 Nebraska Federal Census Index
Includes research aids. TBA

#195 1880 Nebraska Federal Census Index
Includes research aids. TBA

#675 1885 Nebraska Federal Census Index
Includes research aids. TBA

#701 1860 Nebraska Mortality Schedules
Vital records indexed. $15.00

#702 1870 Nebraska Mortality Schedules
Vital records indexed. $17.00

#703 1880 Nebraska Mortality Schedules
Includes research aids. $22.00

#192 1860 Nevada Federal Census Index
Includes research aids. $20.00

#414 1870 Nevada Federal Census Index
Includes research aids. $35.00

#422 1880 Nevada Federal Census Index
Includes research aids. $45.00

#509 1870 Nevada Mortality Schedules
Vital records indexed. $11.00

#152 1790 New Hampshire Federal Census
Includes research aids. $20.00

#135 1800 New Hampshire Federal Census
Includes research aids. $27.00

#324 1810 New Hampshire Federal Census
Includes research aids. $29.00

#016 1820 New Hampshire Federal Census
Includes research aids. $34.00

#362 1830 New Hampshire Federal Census
Includes research aids. $36.00

#363 1840 New Hampshire Federal Census
Includes research aids. $39.00

#364 1850 New Hampshire Federal Census
Includes research aids. $48.00

#196 1860 New Hampshire Federal Census
Includes research aids. TBA

#197 1870 New Hampshire Federal Census
Includes research aids. TBA

#198 1880 New Hampshire Federal Census
Includes research aids. TBA

#398 1850 New Hampshire Mortality Schedules
Vital records indexed.   TBA

#399 1860 New Hampshire Mortality Schedules
Vital records indexed.   TBA

BIBLIOGRAPHY - ACCELERATED INDEXING SYSTEMS, INC.
COMPLETED AND PROPOSED PROJECTS   DO NOT ORDER TBA PROJECTS !
SEND FOR CURRENT CATALOG FOR PRICES ! PRICES ARE SUBJECT TO CHANGE WITHOUT NOTICE !

#534 1870 New Hampshire Mortality Schedule
Vital records indexed.   TBA

#406 1880 New Hampshire Mortality Schedule
Vital records indexed.   TBA

#800 1772-1822 New Jersey Tax Lists
Includes research aids. $150.00

#365 1800 New Jersey(Cumberland Co.)Census
Includes research aids. $18.00

#519 1824-1832New Jersey Patterson,Census
Includes research aids. $20.00

#149 1830 New Jersey Federal Census Index
Includes research aids. $40.00

#366 1840 New Jersey Federal Census Index
Includes research aids. $50.00

#109 1850 New Jersey Federal Census Index
Includes research aids. $85.00

#199 1860 New Jersey Federal Census Index
Includes research aids.   TBA

#676 1865 New Jersey State Census Records
Includes research aids.   TBA

#200 1870 New Jersey Federal Census Index
Includes research aids.   TBA

#206 1880 New Jersey Federal Census Index
Includes research aids.   TBA

#677 1885 New Jersey State Census Records
Includes research aids.   TBA

#678 1895 New Jersey State Census Records
Includes research aids.   TBA

#409 1850 New Jersey Mortality Schedules
Vital records indexed.   TBA

#424 1860 New Jersey Mortality Schedules
Vital records indexed.   TBA

#425 1870 New Jersey Mortality Schedules
Vital records indexed.   TBA

#427 1880 New Jersey Mortality Schedules
Vital records indexed.   TBA

#366 1850 New Mexico Federal Census Index
Includes research aids. $35.00

#472 1860 New Mexico Federal Census Index
Includes research aids. $52.00

#207 1870 New Mexico Federal Census Index
Includes research aids.   TBA

#208 1880 New Mexico Federal Census Index
Includes research aids.   TBA

#679 1885 New Mexico Federal Census Index
Includes research aids.   TBA

#431 1850 New Mexico Mortality Schedules
Vital records indexed.   TBA

#435 1860 New Mexico Mortality Schedules
Vital records indexed.   TBA

#436 1870 New Mexico Mortality Schedules
Vital records indexed.   TBA

#438 1880 New Mexico Mortality Schedules
Vital records indexed.   TBA

#153 1790 New York Federal Census Index
Includes research aids. $40.00

#137 1800 New York Federal Census Index
Includes research aids. $45.00

#113 1810 New York Federal Census Index
Includes research aids. $50.00

#017 1820 New York Federal Census Index
Includes research aids. $70.00

#368 1830 New York Federal Census Index
Includes research aids. $105.00

#369 1840 New York Federal Census Index
Includes research aids. $126.00

#110 1850 New York City Federal Census
Includes research aids. $73.00

#204 1850 New York Federal Census Index
New York City in separate volume
Includes research aids. $190.00

#536 1825 New York State Census Records
Includes research aids. TBA

#537 1835 New York State Census Records
Includes research aids. TBA

#538 1840 New York State Census Records
Includes research aids. TBA

#680 1855 New York State Census Records
Includes research aids. TBA

#209 1860 New York Federal Census Index
Includes research aids. TBA

#210 1870 New York Federal Census Index
Includes research aids. TBA

#682 1875 New York State Census Records
Includes research aids. TBA

#211 1880 New York Federal Census Index
Includes research aids. TBA

#683 1892 New York State Census Records
Includes research aids. TBA

#723 1905 New York State Census Records
Includes research aids. TBA

#724 1925 New York State Census Records
Includes research aids. TBA

#439 1850 New York Mortality Schedules
Vital records indexed. TBA

#440 1860 New York Mortality Schedules
Vital records indexed. TBA

#441 1870 New York Mortality Schedules
Vital records indexed. TBA

#442 1880 New York Mortality Schedules
Vital records indexed. TBA

#154 1790 North Carolina Federal Census
Includes research aids. $30.00

#125 1800 North Carolina Federal Census
Includes research aids. $42.00

#312 1810 North Carolina Federal Census
Includes research aids. $46.00

#018 1820 North Carolina Federal Census
Includes research aids. $48.00

#108 1830 North Carolina Federal Census
Includes research aids. $53.00

#370 1840 North Carolina Federal Census
Includes research aids. $60.00

#101 1850 North Carolina Federal Census
Includes research aids. $72.00

#212 1860 North Carolina Federal Census
Includes research aids. TBA

#213 1870 North Carolina Federal Census
Includes research aids. TBA

#214 1880 North Carolina Federal Census
Includes research aids. TBA

#443 1850 North Carolina Mortality Sch.
Vital records indexed. TBA

#444 1860 North Carolina Mortality Sch.
Vital records indexed. TBA

#445 1870 North Carolina Mortality Sch.
Vital records indexed. TBA

#446 1880 North Carolina Mortality Sch.
Vital records indexed. TBA

#518 1798,99,1817 Cincinnati Ohio Census
Includes research aids. $18.00

#408 1800-1810 Ohio Tax Lists
Includes research aids. $45.00

#138 1800-1810 Ohio Census Records
Includes research aids. $20.00

#202 1820 Ohio Federal Census Index
Includes research aids. $60.00

#371 1830 Ohio Federal Census Index
Includes research aids. $81.00

#372 1840 Ohio Federal Census Index
Includes research aids. $100.00

#101 1850 Ohio Federal Census Index
Includes research aids. $140.00

#215 1860 Ohio Federal Census Index
Includes research aids. TBA

#216 1870 Ohio Federal Census Index
Includes research aids. TBA

#217 1880 Ohio Federal Census Index
Includes research aids. TBA

#455 1850 Ohio Mortality Schedules
Vital records indexed. $24.00

#470 1860 Ohio Mortality Schedules
Vital records indexed. TBA

#895 1870 Ohio Mortality Schedules
Vital records indexed. TBA

#474 1880 Ohio Mortality Schedules
Vital records indexed. TBA

#373 1850 Oregon Federal Census Index
Includes research aids. $26.00

#218 1860 Oregon Federal Census Index
Includes research aids. TBA

#219 1870 Oregon Federal Census Index
Includes research aids. TBA

#220 1880 Oregon Federal Census Index
Includes research aids. TBA

#704 1850 Oregon Mortality Schedules
Vital Records indexed. $6.00

#705 1860 Oregon Mortality Schedules
Vital records indexed. $18.00

BIBLIOGRAPHY - ACCELERATED INDEXING SYSTEMS, INC.
COMPLETED AND PROPOSED PROJECTS   DO NOT ORDER TBA PROJECTS !
SEND FOR CURRENT CATALOG FOR PRICES ! PRICES ARE SUBJECT TO CHANGE WITHOUT NOTICE !

#640 1870 Oregon Mortality Schedules
Vital records indexed. $16.00

#037 1880 Oregon Mortality Schedules
Vital records indexed. $20.00

#155 1790 Pennsylvania Federal Census
Includes research aids. $40.00

#145 1800 Pennsylvania Federal Census
Includes research aids. $49.00

#012 1810 Pennsylvania Federal Census
Includes research aids. $55.00

#015 1820 Pennsylvania Federal Census
Includes research aids. $72.00

#112 1830 Pennsylvania Federal Census
Includes research aids. $77.00

#375 1840 Pennsylvania Federal Census
Includes research aids. $115.00

#139 1850 Pennsylvania Federal Census
Includes research aids. $160.00

#221 1860 Pennsylvania Federal Census
Includes research aids. TBA

#222 1870 Pennsylvania Federal Census
Includes research aids. TBA

#223 1880 Pennsylvania Federal Census
Includes research aids. TBA

#059 1850 Pennsylvania Mortality Sched
Vital records indexed.   TBA

#060 1860 Pennsylvania Mortality Sched
Vital records indexed.   TBA

#430 1870 Pennsylvania Mortality Sched
Vital records indexed. $36.00

#061 1880 Pennsylvania Mortality Sched
Vital records indexed.   TBA

#156 1790 Rhode Island Federal Census
Includes research aids. $20.00

#124 1800 Rhode Island Federal Census
Includes research aids. $26.00

#313 1810 Rhode Island Federal Census
Includes research aids. $26.00

#118 1820 Rhode Island Federal Census
Includes research aids. $37.00

#338 1830 Rhode Island Federal Census
Includes research aids. $40.00

#377 1840 Rhode Island Federal Census
Includes research aids. $34.00

#114 1850 Rhode Island Federal Census
Includes research aids   TBA

#224 1860 Rhode Island Federal Census
Includes research aids. TBA

#225 1870 Rhode Island Federal Census
Includes research aids. TBA

#226 1880 Rhode Island Federal Census
Includes research aids. TBA

#861 1850 Rhode Island Mortality Sche
Vital records indexed.   TBA

#862 1860 Rhode Island Mortality Sche
Vital records indexed.   TBA

#475 Rhode Island Mortality Schedules
Vital records indexed.   TBA

#863 Rhode Island Mortality Schedules
Vital records indexed.   TBA

#689 1865 Rhode Island State Census
Includes research aids. TBA

#700 1875 Rhode Island State Census
Includes research aids. TBA

#708 1885 Rhode Island State Census
Includes research aids. TBA

#157 1790 South Carolina Federal Census
Includes research aids. $21.00

#124 1800 South Carolina Federal Census
Includes research aids. $30.00

#313 1810 South Carolina Federal Census
Includes research aids. $35.00

#118 1820 South Carolina Federal Census
Includes research aids. $37.00

#117 1830 South Carolina Federal Census
Includes research aids. $40.00

#377 1840 South Carolina Federal Census
Includes research aids. $45.00

#277 1850 South Carolina Federal Census
Includes research aids. $63.00

#117 1860 South Carolina Federal Census
Includes research aids. TBA

#228 1870 South Carolina Federal Census
Includes research aids. TBA

#229 1880 South Carolina Federal Census
Includes research aids. TBA

#391 1835 South Carolina Waterways,
Indes of all rivers or bodies of
water. By M. Cropper $15.00

#476 1850 South Carolina Mortality
Vital records indexed.   TBA

#477 1860 South Carolina Mortality
Vital records indexed   TBA

#478 1870 South Carolina Mortality
Vital records indexed   TBA

#480 1880 South Carolina Mortality
Vital records indexed   TBA

#230 1810 Tennessee Federal Census
Includes research aids. $13.00

#130 1820 Tennessee Federal Census
Includes research aids. $31.00

#378 1830 Tennessee Federal Census
Includes research aids. $48.00

#119 1840 Tennessee Federal Census
Includes research aids. $61.00

#379 1850 Tennessee Federal Census
Includes research aids. $82.00

#231 1860 Tennessee Federal Census
Includes research aids. Counties
Anderson-Knox,plus aids $85.00

#524 1860 Tennessee Federal Census
Lake-Wilson,plus aids. TBA

#232 1870 Tennessee Federal Census
Includes research aids. TBA

#233 1880 Tennessee Federal Census
Includes research aids. TBA

#456 1850 Tennessee Mortality Sched.
Vital records indexed. $22.00

#062 1860 Tennessee Mortality Sched.
Vital records indexed. TBA

#063 1870 Tennessee Mortality Sched.
Vital records indexed. TBA

#064 1880 Tennessee Mortality Sched.
Vital records indexed. TBA

#499 1820-1829 Texas Census Records
Includes research aids. $22.00

#514 1830-1839 Texas Census Records
Includes research aids. $35.00

#515 1840-1849 Texas Census Records
Includes research aids. $45.00

#320 1850 Texas Federal Census Index
Includes research aids. $35.00

#234 1860 Texas Federal Census Index
Includes research aids. TBA

#235 1870 Taxas Federal Census Index
Includes Research aids. TBA

#236 1880 Texas Federal Census Index
Includes research aids. TBA

#457 1850 Texas Mortality Schedules
Vital records indexed. $16.00

#460 1860 Texas Mortality Schedules
Vital records indexed. $16.00

#065 1870 Texas Mortality Schedules
Vital records indexed. TBA

#066 1880 Texas Mortality Schedules
Vital records indexed. TBA

#380 Utah Federal Census Inde
Includes research aids $35.00

#249 1856 Utah Federal Census Index

#380 1850 Utah Federal Census Index
Includes research aids. $35.00

#249 1856 Utah State Census Records
Includes research aids. TBA

#423 1860 Utah Federal Census Index
Includes research aids. $55.00

#237 1870 Utah Federal Census Index
Includes research aids. TBA

#238 1880 Utah Federal Census Index
Includes research aids. TBA

#510 1850 Utah Mortality Schedules
Vital records indexed. $13.00

#511 1860 Utah Mortality Schedules
Vital records indexed. $16.00

#512 1870 Utah Mortality Schedules
Vital records indexed. $16.00

#095 1880 Utah Mortality Schedules
Vital records indexed. $16.00

BIBLIOGRAPHY - ACCELERATED INDEXING SYSTEMS, INC.
COMPLETED AND PROPOSED PROJECTS   DO NOT ORDER TBA PROJECTS !
SEND FOR CURRENT CATALOG FOR PRICES ! PRICES ARE SUBJECT TO CHANGE WITHOUT NOTICE !

#158 1790 Vermont Federal Census Index
Includes research aids. $22.00

#517 1800 Vermont Federal Census Index
Includes research aids. $25.00

#327 1810 Vermont Federal Census Index
Includes research aids. $28.00

#019 1820 Vermont Federal Census Index
Includes research aids. $30.00

#381 1830 Vermont Federal Census Index
Includes research aids. $36.00

#382 1840 Vermont Federal Census Index
Includes research aids. $44.00

#383 1850 Vermont Federal Census Index
Includes research aids. $60.00

#239 1860 Vermont Federal Census Index
Includes research aids. TBA

#240 1870 Vermont Federal Census Index
Includes research aids. TBA

#244 1880 Vermont Federal Census Index
Includes research aids. TBA

#707 1850 Vermont Mortality Schedules
Vital records indexed. $22.00

#699 1860 Vermont Mortality Schedules
Vital records indexed. $25.00

#068 1870 Vermont Mortality Schedules
Vital records indexed. TBA

#069 1880 Vermont Mortality Schedules
Vital records indexed. TBA

#159 1790 Virginia(Mixed tax lists)
Includes research aids. $35.00

#122 1800 Accomac Co. Va. Federal Census
Includes research aids. $14.00

#128 1810 Virginia Federal Census Index
Includes research aids. $42.00

#020 1820 Virginia Federal Census Index
Includes research aids. $50.00

#121 1830 Virginia Federal Census Index
Includes research aids. $56.00

#348 1840 Virginia Federal Census Index
Includes research aids. $88.00

#120 1850 Virginia Federal Census Index
Includes research aids. $110.00

#242 1860 Virginia Federal Census Index
Includes research aids. TBA

#243 1870 Virginia Federal Census Index
Includes research aids. TBA

#244 1880 Virginia Federal Census Index
Includes research aids. TBA

#485 1850 Virginia Mortality Schedules
Vital records indexed. TBA

#486 1860 Virginia Mortality Schedules
Vital records indexed. TBA

#487 1870 Virginia Mortality Schedules
Vital records indexed. TBA

#491 1880 Virginia Mortality Schedules
Vital records indexed. TBA

#250 1850 Washington Clark Co. Census
Includes research aids. TBA

#728 1860 Washington Federal Census
Includes research aids. $25.00

#415 1870 Washington Federal Census
Includes research aids $35.00

#467 1880 Washington Federal Census
Includes research aids $38.00

#492 1860 Washington Mortality Sched.
Vital records indexed $10.00

#493 1870 Washington Mortality Sched.
Vital records indexed. $12.00

#494 1880 Washington Mortality Sched.
Vital records indexed. $18.00

#825 1870 West Virginia Federal Census
Includes research aids. TBA

#826 1880 West Virginia Federal Census
Includes research aids. TBA

#458 1850 West Virginia Mort. Sched.
Vital records indexed. $16.00

#461 1860 West Virginia Mort. Sched.
Vital records indexed. $16.00

#464 1870 West Virginia Mort. Sched.
Vital records indexed. $16.00

#706 1880 West Virginia Mort. Sched.
Vital records indexed. $25.00

#390 1836 Wisconsin State Census
Includes research aids. $15.00

#385 1840 Wisconsin Federal Census
Includes research aids. $30.00

#548 1841-1849 Wisconsin State Census
Includes research aids. TBA

#386 1850 Wisconsin Federal Census
Includes research aids $56.00

#630 1860 Wisconsin Federal Census
Includes research aids. TBA

#631 1870 Wisconsin Federal Census
Includes research aids. TBA

#632 1880 Wisconsin Federal Census
Includes research aids. TBA

#629 1885 Wisconsin Military Census
Includes research aids. TBA

#495 1850 Wisconsin Mortality Sched.
Vital records indexed. TBA

#496 1860 Wisconsin Mortality Sched.
Vital records indexed. TBA

#497 1870 Wisconsin Mortality Sched.
Vital records indexed. TBA

#067 1880 Wisconsin Mortality Sched.
Vital records indexed. TBA

#713 1855 Wisconsin State Census
Includes research aids TBA

#716 1875 Wisconsin State Census
Includes research aids. TBA

#717 1885 Wisconsin State Census
Includes research aids. TBA

#027 1870 Wyoming Federal Census Index
Includes research aids. $30.00

#468 1880 Wyoming Federal Census Index
Includes research aids. $45.00

#831 1870 Wyoming Mortality Schedules
Vital records indexed. TBA

#832 1880 Wyoming Mortality Schedules
Vital records indexed. TBA

EARLY AMERICAN(COLONIAL &PIONEER)SERIES

#575 Early Alabama Volume 1 $24.00
Early Alabama Volume 2 $22.00
Early California Vol.1 $15.00
#692 Early California Vol.2 $15.00
#574 Early Connecticut Vol.1 $20.00
#573 Early Delaware Vol.1 $25.00
#513 Early Florida Vol.1 $16.00
#690 Early Georgia Vol.1 $35.00
#572 Early Illinois Vol.1 $21.00
#584 Early Indiana Vol.1 $11.00
#697 Early Kentucky Vol.1 $35.00
#582 Early Louisiana Vol.1 $22.00
#697 Early Maine Vol.1 $22.00
#580 Early Maryland Vol.1 $26.00
#581 Early Massachusetts V.1 $24.00
#034 Early Michigan Vol.2 $15.00
#035 Early Michigan Vol.3 $25.00
#516 Early Michigan Vol.4 $30.00
#693 Early Mississippi Vol.1 $20.00
#579 Early Missouri Vol.1 $12.00
#571 Early New Hampshire V.1 $24.00
#576 Early New Jersey Vol.1 $26.00
#001 Early New Jersey Vol.2 $35.00
#577 Early New York Vol.1 $12.00
#570 Early North Carolina V.1 $33.00
#694 Early North Carolina V.2 $35.00
#002 Early North Carolina V.3 $30.00
#570 Early North Carolina V.4 $30.00
#521 Early North Carolina V.5 $30.00
#022 Early Ohio Vol.2 $15.00
#578 Early Pennsylvania V.1 $24.00
#695 Early Pennsylvania V.2 $35.00
#004 Early Pennsylvania V.3 $27.00
#005 Early Pennsylvania V.4 $38.00
#026 Early So. Carolina V.1 $22.00
#522 Early So. Carolina V.2 $22.00
#696 Early Tennessee Vol.1 $22.00
#568 Early Vermont Vol.1 $20.00
#569 Early Virginia Vol.1 $35.00
#523 Early Virginia Vol.2 $18.00

Marriage records are being prepared
on a state wide bases for 34 states

Wills and probates are being prepared
on a state wide bases for 34 states